GERMAN TRAGEDY
IN THE AGE
OF ENLIGHTENMENT

ROBERT R. HEITNER, Associate
Professor of German and Chairman of
the Department of Germanic Lan-
guages at the University of California,
Los Angeles, is a specialist in 17th and
18th century German literature. He
has contributed numerous articles to
scholarly publications.

GERMAN TRAGEDY
IN THE AGE
OF ENLIGHTENMENT

A Study in the Development of
Original Tragedies, 1724–1768

BY ROBERT R. HEITNER

UNIVERSITY OF CALIFORNIA PRESS

Berkeley and Los Angeles 1963

University of California Press
Berkeley and Los Angeles, California

Cambridge University Press
London, England

Library of Congress Catalog Card Number: 63-10461

Designed by Theo Jung

Printed in the United States of America

To
My Parents
Henry John Heitner
and
Anna Waltke Heitner

PREFACE

FOR THE SAKE of reading facility, I have translated all quotations used in the main text of this book from German into English; but should the reader wish to consult the German text, it may be obtained on microfilm from the Library at the University of California, Los Angeles. It is hoped that this arrangement will be welcomed even by readers perfectly conversant with German, for they too might well prefer a uniform text (either all in German or all in English) to one which would otherwise present a somewhat macaronic appearance. Titles, however, as well as quotations in the footnotes, have been left in their original form.

The decision to make translations formed a logical part of my effort and desire to write about a recondite scholarly subject in a manner that would render it both less formidable for the non-specialist and more agreeable for the specialist, without, to be sure, the sacrifice of depth or thoroughness. In this endeavor, as in many other matters, I owe my inspiration ultimately to my former professor, the late Dr. Fred O. Nolte of Washington University, St. Louis, who for many years was my friend and counsellor. It was he who first awakened and then nourished my interest in the eighteenth century, and who early taught me the importance of looking for the significant, though sometimes little, facts and details behind the broad generalities current in literary history. If a trace of the gracious, urbane spirit and healthy humane judgment that fill his own books is detectable in the pages of this one, then that would be its best ornament.

Furthermore, I am greatly indebted to my colleague at the University of California, Los Angeles, Dr. Victor A. Oswald, Jr., for his effective encouragement of my work from its inception to its conclusion, and for his invaluable, ungrudging service in reading manuscript and returning manifold constructive criticisms and suggestions. Warm thanks go also to my colleague Dr. Eli Sobel for his constant interest and assistance in the project, and to my colleague Dr. Carl W. Hagge for his willingness to confer at any time about the problems that arose. I am grateful to Mr. Edmond Mignon of the UCLA Library for his dedicated and unremitting efforts in acquiring through interlibrary loan the rare books needed for this study. Special thanks are due Mr. Dian I. Lindberg, Instructor of German at Pomona College, for his researches in various German libraries in my behalf. Finally, I wish to express my gratitude to the staff of the University of California Press, and especially to Mr. Robert Y. Zachary, Los Angeles Editor, for their friendly and expert assistance in all phases of publication.

CONTENTS

ix

INTRODUCTION

ALTHOUGH A modest number of good books are available on the subject of German comedy during the period between the end of Baroque and the beginning of Storm and Stress, the condition and development during the same period of its sister-genre, tragedy, have somehow been all but entirely neglected by modern scholars. There appears to be tacit agreement among specialists in German literature (who otherwise tend toward great tolerance in questions of intrinsic literary value) that the tragedies of the 1720's, 30's, 40's, 50's, and 60's are, with rare exceptions, the shallowest, most amateurish works imaginable, and that they therefore scarcely merit attention even from a purely historical point of view. As a result, these tragedies have remained virtually unread and unknown. But what is unread cannot be properly appreciated, or, for that matter, properly condemned.

It is to the credit of Fritz Brüggemann that he brought most of the tragedies of Christian Felix Weisse, as well as Gottsched's *Agis*, Johann Elias Schlegel's *Canut*, and several early bourgeois tragedies, to the attention of a wider reading public in the series *Deutsche Literatur*.[1] In addition to the texts themselves he provided, for the first time, some thought-provoking and appreciative critical introductions to these dramas. Tragedies by Gottsched, Cronegk, Brawe, and Weisse are also available in Kürschner's series *Deutsche National-Litteratur*,[2] and the *Haupt- und Staatsaktionen* of Josef Stranitzky have been printed in the *Schriften des literarischen Vereins in Wien*.[3] Most of the tragedies of the time, however, are to be found only in contemporary collections and individual volumes that are often quite difficult to obtain.

There would be little justification for bringing all these obscure works to light again in new printings, because it is true that in great part they deserve the oblivion into which they have been cast. On the other hand, it is regrettable that this body of tragedy has not been closely examined in regard to its role in building the foundation for the great works that were to arise in the last three decades of the eighteenth century. Moreover, little or nothing has been made of the opportunity which these early tragedies offer for arriving, through objective comparison, at a more accurate interpretation of their great successors. A modicum of attention has been given to the reflection of eighteenth-century thought and taste that is to be found in the early tragedies; but concerning this much more remains to be said, and in a less condescending manner. A few of the authors, notably J. E. Schlegel, C. F. Weisse, Brawe, and Cronegk, have been made the subject of individual studies,[4] and Gottsched's three tragedies (especially his *Sterbender Cato*) have received some critical attention.[5] Lessing's early attempts at tragedy, thanks to their author's prominence, have of course been extensively investigated; and, to a lesser degree, Wieland's and Klopstock's tragedies have also received the attention of scholars. Finally, two doctoral dissertations concerning Alexandrine tragedy have been published by Alexander Schum and Erich Kriessbach,[6] and there is a noteworthy unpublished dissertation by Charlotte von Wymetal which concentrates on the development of hero and antagonist in a representative selection of the tragedies of the epoch.[7] There has been, nevertheless, no comprehensive treatment of tragedy in Germany during the Age of Enlightenment, and it is to make up for this deficiency, at least in some measure, that the present study has been undertaken.

Although a large number of tragedies come under discussion here, this study is not intended to be a complete reference work for all the tragedies that appeared within the announced time span 1724 (the date of Stranitzky's manuscripts) to 1768 (Gerstenberg's *Ugolino*). All translations and close adaptations of foreign tragedies have been omitted, aside from Gottsched's *Cato*, which is in a category of unique importance. More than twenty *bona fide* original works have also, perforce, been omitted because all efforts to secure texts of them in both American and European libraries have so far proved unsuccessful.[8] Fortunately, in some cases the general style and contribution of the author can be adequately judged from another play (or plays) by him which *has* been examined and discussed. In other cases—indeed, in almost all—the missing works represent the obscurest of the obscure among the published tragedies of the period; some may well have vanished completely. The numerous so-called "tragedies" of Johann Jakob Bodmer (1698–1783), the industrious and eccentric literary critic of Zürich, have purposely been excluded because they are either clumsy parodies of other dramas or else mere hapless historical dialogues totally unrelated to the demands of the real theater.[9] There is no discussion of *Gafforio*, a tragedy submitted in the second prize contest announced by the journal, *Bibliothek der schönen Wissenschaften*, in 1758, inasmuch as it is so wretchedly bad that it was printed in the *Bibliothek* [10] only as an object of scorn. In spite of these omissions, both voluntary and involuntary, the present study still offers a reasonably exhaustive account of the tragedies of the designated epoch. This fact, however, is only incidental to its main purpose, which is to illustrate the tragic concepts of authors writing in an age whose outlook was essentially optimistic and untragic, and to demonstrate the line of development in the means used to arouse tragic emotions from the days of the *Haupt- und Staatsaktionen* to the advent of Storm and Stress. The fulfillment of this purpose, while it requires copious examples and attention to much apparent trivia, is not prevented by a lack of absolute completeness.

It is hoped that the matters discussed in this study will be useful not only to specialists in German literature, but also to everyone with an interest in the drama of the eighteenth century, or in the popular philosophical attitudes of that time.

If one wishes to reach an understanding and thereby a certain appreciation of the "Enlightened" tragedies, it is wise to begin by abandoning the usual search for accuracy and individuality of characterizations, for imaginative poetry of dialogue, and for gripping realism of events. The tragedies to be dealt with here seldom have any of these qualities. Many of them, however, do have one technical quality that deserves admiration. This is a workmanlike plot construction that aims at catching the spectator's attention immediately and directing it to one main issue that is quickly developed and concluded without tedious and confusing side-actions. In consequence, the majority of these tragedies are not boring to read, once one has set one's mind to the task. Even if the event treated is not in itself one that enlists very strongly the sympathies of the reader, there is still the pleasure of observing how the author has economically arranged the steps that lead to the climax and conclusion of the striking and unheard-of incident he has set out to dramatize. Nevertheless, a study of plot construction alone would never result in an understanding of the tragedies, and it must be admitted that excellence in this regard is often outweighed by an awkwardness in dialogue which occasionally becomes downright ludicrous. The really important thing about the tragedies is not their technique but their ethical content and purpose. Their authors were conscious of a solemn obligation owed to the audience: the obligation to instruct and to confirm the public in the prevailing practical philosophy of the day. Thus each tragedy is a treatise and an example dedicated to the proper conduct of man in his relationships to God, his family, and his fellowman. Each one is an object lesson showing both what is to be emulated and what is to be avoided. If the modern reader can interest himself in eighteenth-century answers to these universal problems, then he has the first key to an understanding and appreciation of these tragedies.

Lessing, for all the freedom from "narrow" moral purpose which is attributed to him, by no means broke away from the obligation to instruct and confirm either in practice, as his own tragedies show, or in theory. His well-known denunciation of Weisse's *Richard III* is based to a great extent on that drama's questionable philosophy, and his interpretation of *catharsis* is summed up in the revealing phrase, "the transformation of the passions into virtuous capabilities." [11] Certainly, the editors of the early large collections of German drama were eager to tell the public that the works being offered it were written for a predominantly educative purpose. In the preface to the fifth volume (1754) of *Die deutsche Schaubühne zu Wienn* [12] a strong defense is made for the publication of a drama collection "in these hard times of famine." The editor is not interested in diverting his readers, but in educating them, particularly those who have not yet learned to control their emotions and desires through the exercise of reason:

Above all one must seek to make human beings, and this is the business of the rational moral philosophy. All well-constructed dramas are based on this philosophy; according to its laws, the excellence of virtue and the ugliness of vice will be painted with living colors in all the plays in this collection. Those persons who are slaves of their passions and who never trouble their heads with any learned pursuit will declare that serious treatises on the duties of man and about what is called right and wrong, laudable and shameful, virtue and vice are foes of their pleasure and they will not deign to read them. Such self-indulgent natures may, however, be lovers of witty writings, even though their professions do not constrain them to read books; and there is no other way possible to bring them to a rational contemplation of their follies except through such ingenious fancies as these, which can act imperceptibly as a sugared medicine for the soul. The proper use of well-constructed dramas, such as this collection contains, can turn a rough and vicious brute into a rational, good, and virtuous human being.

A more outspoken statement of the moral goal of drama can hardly be imagined. Yet the fact that it appears in this preface—in a collection presumably designed for wide popular consumption—is a strong implication that this was the opinion of drama generally held by serious-minded persons, and not just the individual view of a few mossy theorizers.

In the "Vorbericht des Verlegers" or editorial preface of a second large play collection, the *Theater der Deutschen*,[13] one reads a similar declaration regarding the moral function of drama, which the writer treats as a foregone conclusion:

We do not find it necessary here to say anything more about the origin and usefulness of the stage, because the authors of dramas have, themselves, already spoken about this at sufficient length in many places. We believe, rather, that we may spare ourselves those often repeated words of praise, because every person above the plebeian level is already sufficiently convinced that the stage's actual goal is not to provide a ruinous pastime —as the vulgar, creeping man thinks—but to produce the improvement in morals which, especially in our midst, has come to be so necessary. It was precisely this wish, born of true love for mankind, which aroused the resolve in us . . . to make the present collection of original German dramas.

In the face of such round declarations of moral intent, which are fully borne out by the dramas, and especially the tragedies, contained in these collections, the isolated voices of more esthetically-minded critics do indeed seem to be crying in the wilderness—and not heard. Theoretically, Johann Elias Schlegel could state rebelliously about literature in general: ". . . the strictest moralists may look as sour as they please, but I must confess that pleasure takes precedence over instruction, and that a poet who pleases but does not instruct is to be more highly esteemed, as a poet, than one who instructs but does not please." [14] In practice, however, this same Schlegel was himself careful always to be a poet who both pleased *and* instructed, and his more mature tragedies have very strongly marked moral-philosophical teaching. Again, C. F. Nicolai, who in the first part of his *Abhandlung vom Trauerspiel* bravely raises a new banner inscribed ". . . the true, single purpose of tragedy [is] to arouse the emotions . . . ," soon thereafter backs down and admits that tragedy must not transgress moral laws. He goes on to say, "If then tragedy does not conflict with the laws of moral philosophy, if, rather, it frequently has occasion to present the consequences of these laws to us in living examples, thus it can serve to make the doctrine of virtue livelier in us. Thus at last our hearts, after having been repeatedly pleased with examples of virtue, and angered by vicious characters, will acquire the tendency to accept the commands of moral philosophy more easily." [15] In sum, there was really no one to be found who did not believe that tragedy, as a prominent part of literature in general, was charged with the serious responsibility of improving the character of the German public.

In a period whose leading philosopher, Leibnitz, along with his countless followers, interpreters, and popularizers, had evolved the profoundly optimistic concept of a rational universe, nothing else could logically be expected. Since the goal of civilization was the perfecting of the human race through the development of individual reason and virtue, no effort could be spared to achieve this goal, and certainly the powerful medium of tragedy was not to be wasted on anything less serious. The literary activity of the German Enlightenment may be compared to that of the Old High German period, when not a word was written (except surreptitiously on the backs of some manuscripts) which was not meant to further the conversion of the populace to Christianity. Rare indeed in the history of German literature is any time that matches the first two-thirds of the eighteenth century in uniformity of thought and intent shown by the writers. With the fervor of people who believe themselves to be in possession of ultimate truth, these authors never tired of presenting the same moral lessons, precepts, and conclusions. As though it were a new Gospel, their simple central doctrine could never be repeated too often: virtue equals proper reason, a pure heart, trust in Providence, resistance to despair, and—virtue is rewarded. Vice equals false reason, a cold heart, blind passions, despair, and—vice is punished. As applied to tragedy, this doctrine imposed an obligation on authors to seek out examples in history or legend which they might dramatize to demonstrate their thesis.

Corneille might well express doubt in his *Discours de la tragédie* about the true efficacy of the genre in purging spectators of their evil inclinations. He was referring, however, to specific sins committed by the personages of the drama and to the fear supposedly engendered in the spectator that he would suffer a similar punishment if he should commit a similar sin. The theater as a house of correction for actual or potential criminals is probably one of the less successful of such institutions. But the writers of tragedy in eighteenth-century Germany had something subtly different in mind. Their works were primarily designed, not to combat particular sins and crimes, but to establish the fact that this is a rational universe ruled by a benevolent Providence. These writers aimed at instilling a moral Weltanschauung, at teaching and persuading, rather than at warning and intimidating. Indeed, the prevailing assumption made in the tragedies seems to be the positive one that the audience *already believes* in the rational universal system, and that its members only need to be confirmed in their belief by the assurance that vice does not triumph and that misfortunes are not sent to virtuous people in order to beat them down, but at most to improve their virtue. It cannot be fairly said that in these tragedies a shallow "poetic justice" is employed to satisfy the crude demands of a Philistine public. It is more correct to see in the unfailing punishment of vice and rewarding of virtue a conscious effort to preserve and foster belief in the basic philosophy of the period. Thus one comes to an understanding of the peculiar function of tragedy at this time, a function that no other genre was so well suited to perform, that is, to apologize for the presence of evil in the best of all possible worlds.

To be sure, there are specific moral teachings contained in the tragedies, exhortations relating to parent-child relationships, to conduct in government and war, to the sin of deception, and the like. Nevertheless, it is not so much individual virtues, but Virtue itself —the way of life that results from a genuine understanding of God and the world—which is preached; and it is not so much individual vices, but Vice itself—the way of life that results from a twisted view of the world—which is condemned. Therefore Gottsched's famous rule, that the author should choose a particular moral precept and build his tragedy around it, as though tragedy were only a grander type of fable, was not consistently adhered to, even by Gottsched himself. Rather, it was always the great basic precept that was illustrated, namely, that one should trust in the rational world. The specific sins, of which there are of course examples in all the tragedies, can be seen emanating from a broader base of vice, which may consist either in an error of judgment or in the triumph of passion over reason. In either case, vice rests upon an incorrect attitude, whether permanent, protracted, or temporary, toward the organization of the universe as recognized by the reason.

Inasmuch as this one general viewpoint pervades all the tragedies, one can scarcely expect to find in them a great variety of strikingly original characterizations. Each personage represents a certain degree of moral perfection or imperfection rather than a recognizable human personality with individual quirks and notions, although it should not be categorically assumed that there are *no* memorable characterizations in the plays. Sometimes the situation in which the personage is placed is sufficient to render him memorable, as for instance Cato's situation as the last of the old-style Roman republicans, or Dido's situation as a forsaken lover, or Ugolino's desperate situation in the starvation tower. More frequently, the intensity of vice may make a character memorable, as in the case of Ulfo in Schlegel's *Canut*, or of Richard the Third in Weisse's tragedy, or of Marwood in *Miss Sara Sampson*. Quite rarely, toward the end of the period, there are occasional characterizations that include some moving individualistic traits. For the most part, however, instead of true characters one sees a severely limited series of set *roles:* the father, the mother, the son, the daughter, the brother, the lovers, the tyrant, the patriot, the rash youth, the traitor, the conspirator. This arrangement must have made things easier for the small theatrical troupes of not very versatile actors. Variation and novelty, then, were supplied not by characterization, but by choice of situation and locale. The authors evidently devoted much effort to the search for historical and legendary incidents that had not yet been made the subjects of tragedies. No era was too remote, no country too distant and unfamiliar, no king or hero too obscure to be haled pell-mell on to the German stage. The Near East was particularly fascinating to German writers, as to their French counterparts. The turn to bourgeois subjects in the 1750's can be explained partly as a result of this frantic search for novelty which was dictated by the paralyzing uniformity of theme and characterization.

In spite of this uniformity, however, it would be greatly erroneous to conclude that no progress or development took place in the writing of tragedy during the approximate half-century covered by this study. On the contrary, definite trends established themselves successively in choice of plot and character type, as well as in treatment of subject matter; and as the emphasis in philosophical outlook gradually shifted from reason to feeling, this change was also reflected in tragedy. Through constant change and experimentation the tragic genre, which at the outset of the period had been a hodgepodge of silly plots and clownish nonsense, grew into a rich, varied, tested medium for the service of authors of genius.

I

TRAGEDY IN CAP AND BELLS

IN THE FIRST thirty years of the eighteenth century, tragedy as a special genre was practically extinct in Germany. The Baroque tragedy of Gryphius, Lohenstein, Hallmann, Haugwitz, and Weise had already had its not very illustrious day, and its now old-fashioned style was preserved only in occasional epigonous efforts such as Johann Christian Günther's *Die von Theodosio bereute Eifersucht* (1715), Gottfried Schwarz's *Der durch Nebucadnezar geblendete Zedekias* (performed by school boys in 1715 but not published until 1728), and H. C. L. Stockhausen's *Zenobia* (1720) and *Uladislaus* (1721). The early decades of the century were dominated by the opera, particularly in Hamburg, Leipzig, Dresden, and Vienna, and by the remarkable serio-comic plays known as *Haupt- und Staatsaktionen*, which were to be seen in all the many towns where the wandering troupes set up their stages. Many operas dealt with subjects of a decidedly tragic nature, to be sure, but since music, singing, and spectacle were the opera's main attraction, for which the libretto served chiefly as a framework, it appears justifiable—as well as more practicable—to leave opera out of the discussion. While the *Haupt- und Staatsaktionen* in many cases were adapted from opera libretti,[1] their greater emphasis on the spoken word, that is, their status as drama rather than *Gesamtkunstwerk*, makes them a more appropriate point of departure for a study of the condition of tragedy during this period. Insofar as they set forth personages of high rank, sometimes dramatized historical events, and not infrequently showed suicides, murders, and executions, they may be said to constitute the closest approach to tragedy available to audiences of the time.

An exact judgment of the total value of the *Haupt- und Staatsaktionen* is difficult to make, because only a relatively few texts of them have survived. Truly, there is little enough in those which are still extant to suggest that Gottsched and Lessing, together with the other learned men of their respective generations, were excessively harsh in their condemnation of the *Haupt- und Staatsak-*

tionen. As a whole they must have represented drama on a very low and primitive level, one on which tragedy can scarcely exist at all. For the most part they were not even original, but crude and crass adaptations of the works of older authors, both domestic and foreign.[2] The reader of these curiously hybrid plays may easily receive the impression that they are uninhibited parodies of serious dramas. It is indeed true that in the period before Gottsched's reform poor Melpomene was customarily decked out in the cap and bells of a jester.

The fourteen plays in manuscript form which are attributed to the famous Viennese *Hanswurst* Josef Anton Stranitzky (1676– 1726) constitute the richest and most easily accessible supply of genuine textual material for a study of *Haupt- und Staatsaktionen* between 1700 and 1730.[3] The validity of these plays as models of the genre in general is limited by the fact that they are the work of but one author and that they were presented, presumably, in but one locality, namely Vienna. Nevertheless, the fame of Stranitzky, author, actor, and troupe-principal, was such that Christian Heinrich Schmid calls him the father of German *Hanswürste*.[4] And the most outstanding feature of his plays, that is, the integral role played by Hanswurst in all "serious" as well as purely comic proceedings, is apparently typical of the whole genre in Stranitzky's time.[5] Although the fourteen manuscripts are dated 1724, this is obviously a reference merely to the year in which they were copied down, and the actual dates of composition cannot be given. A thorough interpretation of this entire corpus of drama would exceed the bounds of this study, since Stranitzky's work is believed to be largely derivative and unoriginal.[6] In addition, one play is so much like the other in plot and intrigue that an intensive discussion of each one would prove to be unprofitably repetitious. Therefore it seems to serve the purposes of the present study best to discuss only two of the plays, *Der betrogene Ehemann* and *Die Enthaubtung des weltberühmten Wohlredners Ciceronis.* No definite sources have been found for either of these, so that they possess at least a technically possible claim to originality.[7] Both of them contain genuinely tragic problems that resolve themselves in catastrophes, and this combination is not found in any of the other dramas.[8]

Der betrogene Ehemann presents a practical moral lesson in the hard, unsentimental manner of a sixteenth-century *Schwank.* Its titular hero is an unreasonably jealous husband who keeps his beautiful wife locked up in a separate palace where she can see no one except him and her maid. This treatment injures the lady's sense of personal dignity, and her revenge, of course, is to deceive her husband in spite of his precautions and to run off with another man. When he perceives his loss, the husband commits suicide. It is plain that this plot could be used as the material for a real tragedy, since it is related in its broad outlines to the plot of Hebbel's *Herodes und Mariamne*.

Stranitzky, however, bypasses the tragic potentialities of his material through his failure to arouse sympathy for any of the characters. The husband, King Admetus, is regarded with as much coolness as the main figure in a fable or anecdote. One feels no more sympathy for him than for the Aesopian frog who blew himself up until he burst. Nor does the victimized wife, Queen Alcumene, awaken any kindly feelings. Her bitter complaints and fierce desire for revenge make her unworthy of pity, while her complete hypocrisy in showering the tenderest wifely affection on Admetus, whom she hates so deeply, is an offense to moral sentiments. Such a pair can arouse, at best, a sort of detached curiosity in the spectator. The Queen's lover, Osiride, with his selfish and ruthless desires, is no more attractive. He is determined to possess Alcumene even while he still believes her to be devoted to Admetus. After he has caused a tunnel to be built giving access to Alcumene's palace, he cold-bloodedly orders the murder of the builder so that the secret will be kept. He feels no compunction at refusing marriage with his fiancée, a princess named Philistone. But Philistone, too, wards off any sympathy inherent in her situation by continuing to plan revenge against Osiride, even though she has already fallen in love herself with Candace, a captive king. Candace, in spite of the fact that he has been befriended by Osiride, is not slow to agree to murder him because the vengeful Philistone so orders it.

There is, moreover, not a vestige of charm or tenderness in the illicit affair between Osiride and Alcumene. After forcing his way into the Queen's chamber through the secret tunnel, Osiride assaults her, dagger in hand, as she makes a show of resisting him. When their liaison is established, Alcumene twice deliberately maneuvers Osiride into a situation where it seems that Admetus will discover and kill him—merely because she delights in deceiving Admetus and in terrifying Osiride. When Osiride finally emerges safely from the second of these ticklish encounters, he remarks rather ruefully: "I extol your artfulness, but it is more like cruelty than love thus to terrify a lover's heart" (III. ii).

Indeed, love is only a matter of sexual gratification to the Fury-like Alcumene. Her real passion is to deceive Admetus, in fact, it would seem, to drive him insane. She decides that Osiride must accomplish the impossible-sounding task of presenting her to Admetus as his bride, and of winning Admetus' approval to this. She says to Osiride, who naturally balks at the plan, "Coward! Leave it up to me. Admetus must be tricked with his eyes open and in full possession of his reason" (III. ii). Soon this bold deception begins to develop: Alcumene comes before Admetus and introduces herself as Artenice of Thrace, a princess who is to marry Osiride. Admetus is perplexed by her exact resemblance to his own wife and hurries off to the palace to see if Alcumene is still there. In the meantime Alcumene makes use of the secret tunnel and arrives before Admetus. The king returns convinced and agrees to give the hand of "Artenice" to Osiride. He obligingly accompanies the couple to the harbor, where they sail off in a ship that has been awaiting them. Of course, no sooner is the ship away from shore than Admetus realizes he has been tricked. Mad with rage, he curses the lovers, challenges the gods and the Furies, and stabs himself to death. No tears are shed at his demise. Candace coolly remarks that credulity was his undoing. Philistone, however, pointing up the "moral" of the play, contradicts her lover: "Say, rather, his strictness; for excessive harshness towards a wife often produces unfaithfulness. Candace, let this be an example to you!" (III. xiii).

In spite of the practical truth in Philistone's conclusions, the actions of Alcumene and Osiride are obviously not moral, and the author's uncritical acceptance of these actions, his allowing them to be crowned with success, is evidence of his amoral, or at least careless viewpoint. Yet Stranitzky must have been aware of the sentimental value of acts of generosity, for he also included several instances of such acts in this and in other plays. In Act One he has Osiride befriend the conquered king Candace and also shows Admetus relieving Candace of his chains, after the latter has berated him for not knowing how to treat a distinguished captive. In Act Three, Osiride forgives Candace for having tried to murder him and excuses this attempted crime because it originated in love. His heart melted by such a display of humanity on the part of Osiride (otherwise a complete scoundrel), Candace freely admits his guilt before Admetus, proclaims his love for Philistone, and declares his willingness to suffer the cruelest death for his deed. Admetus, no less moved by the charm of noble generosity, pardons Candace and lets him marry Philistone. This scene (III. v) represents the high point of sentiment in a play chiefly devoted to raw passion, cruel cynicism, and clownishness.

The few references to the gods in the play have as little essential relationship to the action as do the instances of sentimental generosity, and are apparently included only because the author was not willing to relinquish any possible theatrical effect. While still in chains, Candace adds easy conventional pathos to his situation by accusing the gods of injustice: "O cruel Heaven! When, when will you tire of tormenting me? Must all your thunderbolts be directed at my head alone?" (I. i). But soon afterwards he tells himself optimistically, "Heaven, whom it has pleased to cast you down, will also be able to raise you up again" (I. ii). This transition from despair to faith will remain a standard feature in the tragedies written after Gottsched's reform. Equally typical of what is to be used time and again later on is Admetus' defiant rebellion against the gods just before his suicide: "Where are you, Jupiter? Come, I want to fight you" (III. xii).

So far, this *Haupt- und Staatsaktion* has been discussed as if there were no comedy elements in it, in order to show that at its core it is, or might be, a serious, even tragic drama. Actually Hanswurst, his sweetheart Florinde, and his rival Scapin take prominent part in the proceedings, and their affairs are an imitation on a lower level of the actions of the main plot. The burlesque antics of these clowns are naturally gravely detrimental to the establishment of any sort of sustained tragic mood. It is as if the rather disturbing "porter scene" in *Macbeth* (II. iii) were multiplied ten or twenty times. But Stranitzky's Hanswurst does not even confine his "*Lustbarkeiten*" and "*lazzi*" to the personages of his own milieu. It is difficult to take serious interest in a princess who, like Philistone, will so far forget her dignity as to slap Hanswurst's face when he brings her a letter containing Osiride's declaration that he does not love her. It is harder still to maintain respect for Osiride when *his* face is slapped by Hanswurst to show how Philistone rewards messengers.

That Hanswurst is a figure with social significance has, to be sure, been long recognized. It has been said that the audience of common folk derived satisfaction from seeing one as lowly as themselves associating so intimately with the famous and powerful of modern and ancient times.[9] Hanswurst has been regarded as the spokesman of popular common sense counterbalancing the passions of the highborn, and as the protesting voice of a people crushed by petty despotism.[10] His comic, mood-destroying antics have also been interpreted as a kind of necessary reassurance to naive audiences that what they were viewing was just a play after all.[11] Whatever the reason may have been, the public, which included persons of high as well as low degree,[12] was satisfied to come to the theater only to laugh and be amused. Perhaps they felt that they could weep enough at home. In Stranitzky's plays they saw every serious human failing turned into an object of ridicule, with Hanswurst the master of ceremonies over this gruesome carnival. Diderot's sultana in the *Bijoux indiscrets,* who was disposed to shriek with laughter when everyone else was weeping at a French classical tragedy, might have found cause to weep when everyone else was laughing at a Viennese *Haupt- und Staatsaktion,* if she perceived the lack of culture of minds that could not endure tragedy without laughter.

In *Die Enthaubtung des Weltberühmten Wohlredners Ciceronis* Stranitzky tried his hand at the writing of historical tragedy. As might be expected, he proves to be an atrocious mangler of facts and a reveler in anachronisms. The work is really two plays in one, with the first plot treating Cicero's personal tragedy and death and the second one treating the romantic problems of Cicero's daughter and her lover. Insofar as Cicero and his wife Terentia are concerned, Stranitzky for once makes what appears to be a sincere attempt to portray worthy and dignified characters. Cicero faces a dilemma which will be repeated in many guises by writers of tragedy throughout the eighteenth century: is he to act according to high moral principles and put his life in jeopardy, or is he to follow natural inclinations and be safe, though ignoble? This is the same dilemma that faced Gryphius' hero Aemilius Papinianus, but Cicero meets it with an optimism that suggests that the author was not unaware of the new philosophical attitude that his century had engendered. Terentia (in this respect comparable to Arete in Weisse's *Die Befreiung von Theben,* see p. 265) wants Cicero to compromise his principles, because she recognizes only personal family ties, not suprapersonal moral ideals. As a last resort she uses threats and anger in order to dissuade her husband from his dangerous practice of defending innocent persons in court and thereby incurring the wrath of their powerful enemies: "Then fight for justice, defend innocence, make your name immortal!—but first plunge me and your daughter into the cold grave, and when you have triumphed over us both, then follow after our pale shades like a guilty victor" (I. ix). Although shaken by this plea, Cicero remains steadfast, saying, "No, no! Let Cicero die, let Terentia and Tulia perish, but let justice flourish!" (I. ix). In spite of the ranting dialogue, this scene is reasonably touching; but its effect is allowed to stand only momentarily. Hanswurst enters and asks Cicero if he may see this wonderful "Justice" whom Cicero prefers to his wife and daughter. Cicero gives Hanswurst a book of philosophy, but Hanswurst is disappointed. He had thought "Justice" was the name of Cicero's mistress (I. x). The audience has been brought perilously close to a serious mood, and therefore Hanswurst has been sent in to turn the ideal of justice into a jest. The author was far more sure of pleasing his audience with laughter than with idealistic sentiment.

The death of Cicero, however, required another brush with seriousness, and here Stranitzky ventured to broach a problem that very soon was to become indispensable to German tragedy: will God protect a just man from danger and dishonor? Stranitzky's solution of this problem finally turns out to be the stoical one of the previous century, namely that the hero meets his unjustified death unflinchingly, satisfied to exchange earth for heaven and proudly confident of his righteousness. Before that final solution is shown, nevertheless, a touch of the new century's philosophical optimism makes itself felt, even though the unscholarly Hanswurst-author could hardly lay claim to being a disciple of Leibnitz and Wolff. For while it is still possible, Cicero clings to this world and to the rationalistic conviction that Providence defends the temporal interests of good men. Herein lies the subtle heresy, so prevalent in eighteenth-century thought, that virtue in man puts an obligation on God to provide him with a happy life on earth. Thus Cicero tries to save himself from his enemies by having himself borne away from Rome in a sedan-chair. In a forest some distance from the city he believes himself to be out of danger and says optimistically, "The gods, who provide for the welfare of mankind, will protect me. My innocence is known to them, and my holy zeal in promoting justice will deliver me from all danger" (I. xiii). Soon afterwards, alas, Marcus Antonius and other conspirators catch up with Cicero and it is clear that he will have to die at their hands. Without another word about the security of the virtuous, Cicero relinquishes optimism for stoicism and offers his head (very literally and on stage) to the assassins' swords. His last speech, which is couched in Alexandrine verse to emphasize the dignity of the moment, could quite as well have been written in the seventeenth century: "Heaven will seek revenge for my innocence/ And will extend my fame indeed after this death,/ Great Themis will curse not me, but the murderous deed/ And bring me at once into the house of the gods./ Proceed, I fear nothing, death cannot terrify me,/ Strike this grey head from my shoulders" (I. xiv).

So shocking an event as the murder of a totally virtuous person like Cicero would have been studiously avoided by a rationalistic author as an abrogation of his optimistic philosophy. Stranitzky, on the other hand, welcomed the shock like any other strong effect; but then, lest his audience really fall into a tragic mood (and walk out in disgust?), immediately called upon Hanswurst to swing the merry carrousel faster again. Accordingly Hanswurst picks up Cicero's severed head, pops it into a sack, and says he hopes he will get a generous tip from Terentia and Tulia for returning it. Before long, he and Scapin are fighting over the sack, because each one wants the tip, and finally Tulia has to snatch the sack from Hanswurst's grasp. She pulls out the bloody relic, and this is a moment of—what? It could have been one of unbearable tragic intensity, but actually what results is nothing more than grotesque and gruesome horseplay, thanks to the incredible irreverence of Hanswurst and the undignified behavior of Tulia. At first she says, with the usual tragic hyperbole, "If my progenitor is dead, then I do not want to live either" (II. ii); but then she boxes Hanswurst's ears because he has asked for a tip. The unfortunate head in a sack has ceased to be a symbol of noble Cicero and has become merely a pawn in a clownish game.

The second part of the *Enthaubtung Ciceronis*, which begins at this point, deals with the troubles of young Julius, son of the murderer Marcus Antonius, in convincing his sweetheart Tulia that he tried hard to prevent her father's death. Before she will believe in his innocence, she demands that he kill his own father to avenge Cicero's death. Faced with this critical dilemma, poor Julius nearly despairs. But along comes his friend Lucius Scipio, who offers what sounds like Enlightened advice, except that Providence is regarded as being rather more frivolous than rationally benevolent: "Ah, I understand what you want to say, but let despair find no place in your heart, for Heaven, whose custom often is to play with human beings, will eventually make everything turn out well for you" (II. iv). But Heaven enjoys playing with Julius for quite some time. Tulia goes so far in her obstinacy as to become engaged to Julius' arch-rival Cecina, whom she does not love. Like the female figures in *Der betrogene Ehemann* she is something of a *Machtweib*, hard, shrill, and capricious. To celebrate the wedding of Cecina and Tulia, the Emperor Augustus holds a wild animal fight that takes place directly on stage—how, one can only guess! Cecina inadvertently drops a small portrait of Tulia into the arena, whereupon she, like the cruel lady in Schiller's ballad, commands him to go down and retrieve it. When he refuses, preferring his life to his love, the gallant Julius rises up from the sidelines, crying, ". . . I shall be the one who prizes his life less highly than love" (III. ix). Down into the arena he plunges, and the unwilling Hanswurst is thrown down after him, by the Emperor's order, perhaps to keep the frightened audience from putting their hands over their eyes. Once the portrait has been successfully retrieved, the despicable Cecina demands that it be given to him, and he provokes a duel in which Julius mortally wounds him.

Julius' brave exploit does not deter the inexorable Tulia from upbraiding him for having killed Cecina. The latter, however, experiences a remarkable change of heart just before he expires, so that the audience may be treated to the sentimental delight of an angelic deathbed scene: "Beloved Tulia, I die and want no revenge, but forgive him quite willingly, because I myself am the cause of my death" (III. xi). Cecina's unexpected nobility now inspires Tulia to a soaring paean of eternal devotion which demonstrates that the idea of love consummated in heaven was used in German literature before Klopstock: "Farewell, my beloved, in the Elysian Fields our souls will be united, because this was not vouchsafed us here . . . I, too, have no desire to live any longer. Come, then, pleasant Death, and close my grieving eyes, so that we may remain in each other's company forever" (III. xi). The unaccountability of Tulia's emotion over a man she does not love (for she is still in love with Julius) is only one of several non-sequiturs and lost threads in the play. While this *Haupt- und Staatsaktion*, like others of its genre, has a definite plot that is carried through from beginning to end, the plot is not allowed to interfere with certain effects that the author wants to produce, whether these fit in logically or not. He wished to provide his spectators with the sentimental pleasure of witnessing a dying man's change of heart and of hearing a bereaved sweetheart's vows of fidelity. That the attainment of these effects would bring a serious inconsistency into the characterization of Tulia was not reason enough to forego them. Likewise, the author wanted to produce as many burlesque-comic effects as possible. No matter how inconsistent they may be with the seriousness of the plot and no matter how long they last, the action is held up for them and then proceeds on its way again. The inclusion of all these disparate effects does not necessarily indicate the author's contempt for the basic plot and characters; but it does indicate a naive desire to please, amuse, and astonish without a moment's pause.

The eventual happy dénouement of the lovers' difficulties is brought about by a *deus ex machina*, Cicero's ghost, who reveals to Tulia that Julius is innocent, as he has claimed. This apparition may be august and awe-inspiring, as is proper to a tragedy, but ghosts also can have their comical side, and Stranitzky cannot resist showing it. Before the momentous supernatural message is delivered to Tulia, the ghost sneaks up behind Hanswurst and grabs him by the hair, whereupon Hanswurst runs away in terror. Here again is this strange mixture of the serious and the absurd which made the young Gottsched recoil in disgust when he first saw a *Haupt- und Staatsaktion* in Leipzig in 1724. Whether Hanswurst or Harlequin, all clowns were anathema to Gottsched from that time on, and before 1740 he and his friends had succeeded in breaking their hold on German stage. The modern reader will be less prone to judge so harshly, but on the other hand may be too quick to conclude that any play in which the clown appears, as, for example, this one about Cicero, is wholly meant to be an outrageous farce. One needs to be capable of switching, as the early eighteenth-century audiences presumably were, abruptly and constantly from seriousness to hilarity.

Not all plays characterized as *Haupt- und Staatsaktionen*, however, were as much dominated by comic elements as those of Stranitzky. One entitled *Die glorreiche Marter Joannes von Nepomuck* demonstrates that when piety and religious zeal were among the motivations of the author the serious elements of the plot could possibly outweigh the mood-shattering antics of an interfering comical personage. In the frequent scenes from which the clown is entirely excluded, and even in some where he is present, this drama seems to be closer in spirit to old-fashioned Baroque tragedy and the Latin Jesuit dramas than to the *Haupt- und Staatsaktion* as purveyed by Stranitzky. The date and authorship of *Nepomukh* are unknown,[13] but the manuscript containing its text bears the same date (1724) as the Stranitzky manuscripts.[14] The comic personage is not called Hanswurst, but Dr. Babra, which would suggest that this author did not write under Stranitzky's influence. In later years, when *Haupt- und Staatsaktionen* were played no longer, this drama was adapted into an Alexandrine tragedy of five acts entitled *Johannes von Nepomuck* and published both in Innsbruck (1766) and in Linz (no date). The anonymous adapter, who tried to avoid every crudeness in the original, of course omitted the clown-figure entirely.

The plot is derived from the history (whether factual or legendary) of the patron saint of Bohemia, John of Nepomuck, who suffered martyrdom in 1393. Yet the rather awkward and naive handling of the successive events does not allow the titular hero to emerge clearly as the principal character. Interest is divided between the martyrdom of the saint and the equally sad fates of Queen Augusta and her innocent admirer Quido. All three of these figures, however, are subordinate in dramatic power to the villain, King Wenceslaus, who wants to get rid of his queen in order to marry the ravishing Ahalibama, a Serbian princess. Wenceslaus and his paramour are characterized with enough complexity and subtlety to raise them above the level of mere stock figures, while the same can hardly be said of the three sympathetic personages, whose virtue and steadfastness leave little room for individualistic traits. In Wenceslaus, on the other hand, one has a full-length portrait of an impressive and believable tyrant. He dominates the action from the opening scene, which is a stiff ceremonial pageant showing Wenceslaus as he receives the praise and gratitude of Prague for his many victories. The king is full of pride and self-confidence as he lauds his own greatness, and his cold cruelty is revealed as he gloats over the deaths which his wars have caused:

The Danube and the Raab are swollen with the bodies of rebels. The Bosporus receives more blood than water and increase of its waves. . . . The fields are sown with weapons and heaped up with wounded. Here a son dies in his father's arms, there with a bullet one robs the life of him from whom his own was received, only to free him of his pain. Here one sees a wife drenching the corpse of her husband with blood more than with tears, there a grief-stricken mother dying with her children hanging at her breasts. And all these spectacles are the fruits of our victories (I. i).[15]

But this is not all. In the interest of peace and justice (respectable goals!) he intends to start a reign of terror:

. . . let the scaffolds be adorned with bloody spectacles, let the stinking jails be filled with the guilty, let the obstinate be brought to torture, let there be cutting, chopping, burning, so that hereby the peace of our kingdom be made secure and the common welfare not be infected with infernal broods of vipers. It is proper to punish the wicked and to succor justice. We hope that this procedure will not blacken the gold of our crown with any mist of cruelty, but that we shall rather be lauded as an administrator of justice, *maneat justitia, ne pereat mundus* (I. i).

Such speeches, although naive in their unvarnished directness, give a clear insight into the personality of a tyrant whose justifiable desire for victories and domestic quiet is deeply contaminated by a pathological bloodthirstiness. With effective irony the author lets the fawning courtiers applaud Wenceslaus' wicked plans as if they were indeed virtuously motivated. The comical remarks of the clownish Dr. Babra do not destroy the lingering mood of horror. The fantastic lawyer Babra is tolerated as a sort of court jester, in which capacity his outspokenness detracts nothing from the somber majesty of the tyrant. Moreover, Babra is bitterly cynical rather than merrily prankish. Essentially there is no true humor in him, and he uses levity and eccentricity coldly and heartlessly as he goes about the dirty business of pandering to the king's desires. Thus he remains confined to his role like the other characters and does not become a master of ceremonies or mediator between stage and audience like Stranitzky's Hanswurst.

Wenceslaus shows another side of his repulsive but credible personality in his relationship to the beautiful Ahalibama. Here the weakness of a man who presumes to rule others without being able to rule himself comes to light. Ahalibama is not the *Machtweib* frequently found in Stranitzky's works—indeed, it is rather the virtuous Augusta who seems like one in her outraged attitude toward Wenceslaus. Although Ahalibama is a clinging, softly feminine creature,[16] she knows how to impose her will upon the king by gently refusing him her favors until she is made his legal wife. She is far too clever to demand the removal of Queen Augusta in a straightforward, drastic manner. With grace and subtlety she points out how only a wife can claim a man's affections, and she pretends respect, even fear in regard to Augusta. At the end of an interview during which she never loses control of the situation nor makes any overt attacks on Augusta, she has succeeded in bringing Wenceslaus to the fatal decision of disposing of his rightful queen.

The work of ruining Augusta is put into the hands of Dr. Babra and two other courtiers, who counterfeit a letter in Augusta's handwriting and give it to the cupbearer Quido. The latter is, as a matter of fact, in love with the queen, but has never dreamt of expressing his feelings. Now Babra persuades him to write her a tender answer, and this is brought immediately to Wenceslaus. The king is consequently able to play the role of the deceived husband with seeming justice, and both Quido and Augusta are imprisoned. Ahalibama preserves her modest and gentle demeanor and even pretends compassion when she hears that Augusta has been confined in a dog kennel. Her real thoughts are expressed in a quick aside: "Augusta unfaithful? O welcome news!" (II. i). The lovely princess, however, is not merely a clever adventuress. The fact that she is actually in love with Wenceslaus adds considerable depth to her character. She can see that she will be getting a very dangerous kind of husband when Wenceslaus flies into a rage against a cook who has served her an unroasted capon. For even her tender pleas cannot save the unfortunate cook from being dragged off and roasted alive on a spit. The king upsets the whole table and stalks away, while Ahalibama asks in fearful amazement, "Heavens, is the king out of his mind?" (II. ii). After this, the audience can no longer be in any doubt that Wenceslaus will be capable of killing a queen, and even a saint.

Although the saintly Nepomuck appears in Act One as the

spiritual comforter of Augusta, the action that really involves him begins only when Wenceslaus in the middle of Act Two tries to wrest from him the secrets of the confessional, in order that completely damning evidence of infidelity may be brought against the queen. As might be expected, Nepomuck refuses to divulge these secrets. This rigid uprightness, however, would have a firmer connection with the plot if Augusta had actually been an unfaithful wife and had confessed her transgressions to Nepomuck. Inasmuch as there is no indication that she has confessed anything, Nepomuck is doing her more harm than good by maintaining silence. This difficulty is ignored by the author, whose primary purpose was to glorify the virtue of the saint's stand on the privacy of the confessional—but without soiling the spotless innocence of the queen's character. Like Stranitzky, he was more concerned with immediate effects than with the consistent logic of his plot. Another example of his search for effects without regard for logic is the scene in which Augusta and Quido are brought on stage simultaneously in their separate prisons (hers a dog kennel), so that they can engage in a duet, with speeches in identical strophe-form, on the favorite Baroque subject of eternity versus earthly vanity (II. viii). This unrealistic juxtaposition of dog kennel and dungeon proves convenient also for two succeeding scenes (II. ix, x) in which Nepomuck exhorts both prisoners to patience and piety and Babra cruelly mocks them; but it must have seemed inconvenient for the scene in which Quido is beheaded by the order of Wenceslaus (II. xi), because in this one Augusta leaves the stage. How she can leave, and yet still remain in the kennel, is not explained. One must imagine that it has ample recesses.

The beheading of Quido provides a momentary shock to Nepomuck's confidence in God, for he cries, "Heaven, can you behold this?" before he recovers his pious composure with the words, "Still your judgments are just and we men—" (II. xii). In the next and last act [17] Nepomuck also finds himself incarcerated, and his prison cell is visited by "an angel in a machine" who strengthens him for his coming martyrdom. Augusta is forced to shift for herself without such supernatural comfort, and one sees her for the last time in her kennel dying of hunger because the "black dog's bread" does not afford her sufficient nourishment. She is fully convinced now that worldly splendor is but transitory, and she is ready to die: "Worthless throne on which my foot formerly stepped, your excellence turns into a dwelling-place of worms" (III. iii). Soon Wenceslaus, in part following the advice of the clever and feline Ahalibama, decides to forego a regular execution in the queen's case and instead orders her prison to be sealed up. Nevertheless, the steadfast silence of Nepomuck is proving more and more frustrating to him, since he is still looking for evidence against Augusta to save his own reputation. In a rage he commands that the saint be thrown from a bridge into the Moldau, but this death sentence holds no terrors for Nepomuck, who mounts the bridge in happy anticipation of thereby entering heaven's portals. As soon as he is cast into the river, five stars begin to gleam miraculously over the spot and a "pleasant music" is heard (III. vii).

The serenity of this saintly demise stands in sharp contrast to the subsequent overthrow and death of Wenceslaus, who now finds that he has overstepped the bounds of his power. When the people rebel because of Nepomuck's martyrdom, thus suddenly interfering with the king's plans to wed the beauteous Ahalibama, all that Wenceslaus can think of, characteristically, is more punishment for them: "Quickly take a thousand swords, a thousand wheels and gallows, make all the fields into funeral pyres, butcher, burn, consume all the rebellious dogs" (III. x). But since this proves to be no longer possible, he turns to self-pity, and finally, when he is felled by an apoplexy, to defiance of God: "O cursed disloyalty of Heaven, shall then Wenceslaus die, the hero of all heroes perish so miserably? No, I shall not die, my fist shall show that I can strive even against Heaven" (III. x). With his next, last breath, however, he gasps, "O woe, it burns, I am going—to Hell" (III. x). It is an exemplary death for an exponent of evil, including fear, self-pity, impenitence, defiance, and hell-fire. And much the same as it is found here in an unpretentious *Haupt- und Staatsaktion* it will be found again in many a later regular tragedy. In fact, the death of Wenceslaus is quite similar to that of Franz Moor in Schiller's *Räuber*.

The Nepomuck drama is not the only instance demonstrating that some feeling for the solemnity appropriate to tragic subject matter could develop even in the realm of *Haupt- und Staatsaktionen*. There is also a crudely written but surprisingly impressive play called *Der unglückseelige Todes-Fall Caroli XII*, which is contained in a manuscript dated 1724, like the other works discussed in this chapter. Possibly it was composed in the same year by the person who signed the manuscript, the actor Johann Joseph Kohlhard.[18] The death in 1718 of the popular king Charles XII of Sweden was hardly the kind of subject that offered free rein to the antics of a clown. The hero's dignity could not be exposed to any irreverence. A contemporary notice from Dresden, where the drama was presented by the Haacke troupe, clearly intimates that the function of the clown was to mitigate for the audience the all too gloomy mood that this work would otherwise have induced.[19] If the author had not feared an unfavorable reaction, he might have eliminated clownishness from his drama altogether, for his intent seems to have been a very serious one. He allowed neither Arlequin (as the clown is named here) nor his female partner Plapperliesgen to have the slightest connection with the plot. Their own sphere is kept wholly separate, and their scenes could be cut from the play without the slightest effort. Arlequin and Plapperliesgen carry on their own grotesque-comic plot concerning Arlequin's attempt to escape marriage with Plapperliesgen by joining the army, and they do not offer a single comment about the main action. This procedure is completely at variance with that of Stranitzky and suggests that the author regarded his clowns merely as unavoidable nuisances. As if to get revenge for having to include them at all, he lets them both be gruesomely executed on stage in the last act—Arlequin for trying to desert from the army, and Plapperliesgen for being found with him. If this scene (III. ix), carried out with the realistic effects beloved in the popular theater, was *only* meant to be funny, then surely the joke was being stretched very far.

As in *Die Enthaubtung Ciceronis*, the tragic hero of the play is an upright man who trusts in Providence, is disappointed in his hopes, and must lose his life for no good reason. But there is also a critical difference here in the fact that fate, instead of wicked men, is the hero's antagonist. Fate is malicious and inexorable, seemingly more powerful than God, and the mystery of it creates an atmosphere of dark pessimism in the drama, against which the resolute heroism of King Charles shines forth like a bright light. In spite of Aristotle's judgment that the misfortune of a completely good man will shock the spectators and prevent their enjoyment of the proper tragic emotions, this simple drama leaves one with a feeling of resignation and deep solemnity that is acceptably tragic. Unpolished as the work is, it nevertheless puts its audience face to face with the sight of a brave man pitting himself against a hostile universe, being inevitably defeated, and yet retaining the dignity of his humanity. The drama is pervaded from beginning to end with a sense of impending disaster, and one knows that Charles is doomed. One watches his efforts to recapture Sweden's glory by means of a daring march on the Danish stronghold of Friedrichshall, and one knows he is destined to failure. One hopes that somehow he will prove the facts of history to be wrong, and attain success, and yet on the other hand a happy ending would be actually a disappointment. This is perhaps a test for tragedy: if the spectators, aside from all surface hopefulness, are being persuaded all along to look for and to *want* a catastrophic ending, then the author has written a tragedy. If the spectators could genuinely be satisfied with a happy ending, then he has written a mere melodrama. The truest tragic hero is the personage who, like a great tree designated for removal, has his roots already cut and still strives to put forth leaves and fruit. German literature would have to wait many years until another tragic hero like Charles XII would appear in its course.

The author of the *Todes-Fall Caroli XII,* apparently less affected by the early Enlightenment than Stranitzky (or Stranitzky's sources), does not include in his play the speeches and situations that were to become commonplaces of eighteenth-century tragedy. It is true that the same problem is set as in *Die Enthaubtung Ciceronis:* is a virtuous man justified in his confidence that Providence will protect him from harm? But here the question is not begged (as it is also in the Nepomuck drama) by a quick exchange of heaven for earth. With complete forthrightness, the question is answered in the negative. Charles has known both victory and defeat in his time, but the vagaries of fortune, he assures his counsellors, cannot disturb his optimism: ". . . the Lord has rescued me from six afflictions, and He will not abandon me in the seventh" (I. ii).[20] This trustful optimism is not quite the same as that taught by the philosophers of the Enlightenment, because it is based on Charles' *experience* rather than on a priori reasoning, and it is stated in biblical terms. Charles' situation is not a practical illustration to Leibnitz' *Essais de théodicée* or to Wolff's *Vernünftige Gedanken von der Menschen Tun und Lassen;* however, it is akin to the situation of Job and still more to that of the warrior king David.

The action of the drama, as in a Greek or French tragedy, is concentrated on the short last period of the hero's life. Very little battle action is shown. Mostly, there are conversations and, it must be admitted, not very dramatic ones. The chief subject of the conversations is whether Charles' efforts to take Friedrichshall will meet with success—what superhuman forces are for him and what ones are against him. Charles always carefully hews to the line of integrity and honor. When it is suggested that he might save himself by negotiating a peace with the Danes, he replies dauntlessly, "A peace without honor is no peace, but the root of many following embitterments" (I. ii). In spite of the solid entrenchment of the enemy and the unusual hardships of a winter campaign, Charles counts on the loyalty of his Swedish forces and is ready to share all the discomforts of the common soldier. But the hopeful atmosphere produced by the decision to march is effectively clouded by a dream-apparition of fate, a suprapersonal force which presents an unconquerable and utterly irrational opposition to Charles' plans (I. viii). Fate does not offer any moral objections to the march against Friedrichshall and does not act as the avenger of any sin Charles has committed. It simply sets up its unfathomable will against Charles' rational and justifiable will, and warns him to desist.

There is nothing like Greek hybris in Charles' refusal to heed the voice of fate, for he is only piously putting his trust in God as a suprapersonal force different from and stronger than fate: "I trust Heaven and defy fate" (I. viii). The mundane action of the plot is transcended by a celestial struggle, tacit and remote, between God and fate, and Charles counts on the former: "Thus Norway shall not make a corpse of me,/ I will commend my affairs to Heaven's grace,/ My war is just and therefore I am not afraid,/ Because my Creator Himself will smooth my path to victory" (I. viii). But underlying Charles' confidence there lurks the uneasy feeling that men can never know definitely what God has in mind for them. Thus, as he exhorts his soldiers, the thought inadvertently creeps in that victory does depend on fortune, or fate, after all: "Come, my brothers, come, and arm yourselves to fight,/ I know the hand of Heaven protects the just,/ Where Charles the Twelfth is, you will also remain,/ Fortune herself opens the door of victory to us./ But no, not Fortune, Heaven must lead me,/ Yes, yes! thus let it be, therefore I will march" (I. ix). There is an effective note of doom and helplessness in these words. Charles' situation mirrors that of all ordinary men who seek for some assurance of the future without really finding any. Moreover, all of Charles' piety does not obscure the pagan worldliness of his interests. He is thinking about his fame and his kingdom, not about salvation and the world to come.

The initial success of Charles' campaign against the Danes in Norway seems to justify his confidence in God, and it is to God that he ascribes this success, like all his previous ones: "Who was I at that time when with a handful of men I brought ruin to the Muscovite army of 100,000 troops at Narva? A boy of sixteen years. However, it was not I, but a stronger hand which made of me a second Gideon" (II. i). Another apparition comes to Charles. This time it is Bellona, goddess of battle, who is friendly and encouraging but quite ignorant of future happenings. Bellona applauds Charles' trust in God, and when he says that fate hates him, she rejoins, "It is the attribute of heroes that fortune must serve them against its will" (II. ii). Like Schiller's Wallenstein, Charles is tempted to consult the stars: "Do tell me, all-ruling stars! what have I to hope for in Norway?" (II. ii). In a second apparition, however, Bellona is less encouraging. When Charles asks why she did not help him in former defeats, she replies that her hands were tied "With the chains of an irresistible fate" (II. vi). Then Charles breaks out in a lament which includes, besides fate and the stars, an "unmerciful Heaven." Charles is here coming to the realization that his confidence in God may be misplaced after all. He is left with his own human resources, which may not be sufficient for victory, but are enough to preserve his status as a man and a hero in the face of a hostile universe. Now the tragic strength of the drama is beginning to unfold.

In a formal parley between Charles' representatives and the defenders of Friedrichshall an important word is quietly spoken by the Danish commander which underlines the uselessness of entrusting the success of a venture to God's benevolence, no matter how convinced one may be of the venture's justice. Charles' representative boasts, "We are relying on the support of Heaven," and the Dane answers, "This very thing is the protection of our resistance" (II. x). Thereby a deeply ironical *finis* is written to Charles' confidence, and the situation is left wholly in the lap of unfathomable fate. Such is the pessimistic viewpoint of this drama; only through such pessimism, however, can the tragic dignity of man as man be highlighted.

Act Three opens with the good news that Swedish peace negotiations with Russia are proceeding well. Technically considered, this is a well-placed final ascending action before the catastrophe. All the forces under control of human power are being well handled, and according to human calculations Charles ought to succeed in wresting Norway from Danish control. But what are men's plans and forces in comparison to irresistible fate? Even divine assistance is shown to be a delusion and surely good actions and a just character are no defense against fate's juggernaut. Indeed, Charles' punctilious fairness is the indirect cause of his death and failure. Out of respect for the strict rules of war, he orders that the stronghold of Friedrichshall be formally challenged and given the chance to surrender without bloodshed. This procedure, however, only gives the Danes a respite in which to reassemble their defensive forces. The hero's death occurs with shocking suddenness as he is busy directing the bombardment (III. x). He does not have time to utter one word, so that the death scene is altogether unsentimental. The siege of Friedrichshall immediately collapses and the tragedy is over. An epilogue that follows presents the body of the king dressed in white and lying in state against a black background. At intervals, three salvos are fired while the allegorical figures of Fama, Bellona, and Mars sing and speak a solemn dirge. The lines assigned to Mars are the most interesting, for they contain an indictment of fate:

Cruel fate! must, through your thunderclaps,/ Then Sweden's cedar and Bashan's oak fall this day?/ Do you not spare the purple, do you attack crowns?/ What a marvel, that the world can still endure you! . . . When in future someone asks for Charles the Twelfth,/ Then all Sweden will say with a thousand tears:/ My king is gone! His body has grown pale,/ Why? Because destiny hated the second Mars.

The only consolation offered is that Charles' fame will live forever.

Like the essentially pagan *Nibelungenlied*, which appeared in the solidly Christian thirteenth century, so also the *Todes-Fall Caroli XII* in the programmatically optimistic eighteenth century seems to give expression to a submerged popular Weltanschauung which looks at life sternly, factually, and fatalistically, whatever the church and the philosophers may say comfortingly about it. And just as the *Nibelungenlied* stands isolated in its time, so the *Todes-Fall Caroli XII* is without predecessors or successors, at least insofar as can be judged on the basis of the few manuscripts from that period which have survived. As soon as tragedy became a medium practiced by the learned elite, it was kept under the strict surveillance of religion and philosophy. The history of the development of tragedy in the eighteenth century, with the coming of Gottsched, abruptly leaves the realm of *Haupt- und Staatsaktionen* almost completely.

II

THE FIRST ORIGINAL
"REGULAR" TRAGEDIES

THE REPUTATION of Johann Christoph Gottsched as a literary artist has never been salvaged from the ignominy to which it was consigned during his own later lifetime. Nevertheless, no knowledgeable student of eighteenth-century German theater will any longer be disposed to agree with Lessing's ruthless statement in the seventeenth *Literaturbrief:* "It would have been better if Mr. Gottsched had never at all meddled with the theater." [1] Someone, after all, had to make a clean break with the unliterary crudeness and frequent vulgarity of the popular stage and restore the writing of drama to the hands of cultured and educated authors. Gottsched with his strong personality, determination, and talent for organizing people was eminently suited for such a task. A genius, if there had been one present during those early years when Gottsched was gaining recognition in Leipzig, would certainly have written better dramas and better theoretical essays than Gottsched—but would he also have launched a successful campaign to banish the tasteless *Haupt-und Staatsaktionen* and the fatuously extravagant operas? As Schiller's poem "Pegasus im Joche" points out, a winged steed is poorly suited for field work. A sturdier, more obstinate, less sensitive creature is needed for making a clearing in the wilderness.

Although Gottsched's earnest respect for clarity of thought and expression and his rationalistic assumption that artistic phenomena can be reduced to easily understandable rules and regulations led him into the pitfall of oversimplification, still his discussion of tragedy in the *Versuch einer critischen Dichtkunst* (1730) had definite practical merits. His handy set of rules for the writing of tragedy was workable and usable, as is demonstrated by the fact that he himself and a number of other educated men of little talent, by following these rules, were able to turn out some acceptably expert tragedies. Such external technical matters as the Unities of Time and Place, the exclusion of subplots, the liaison of scenes, the equal length of acts, and the avoidance of violent and bloody action on stage could be mastered by anyone who set his mind to the task. The

Alexandrine verse, coupled with a certain selective dignity of diction, was an elegant and convenient cloak for poverty of thought and lack of ability to write natural and characteristic dialogue. The strict elimination of complicated crowd and processional scenes was a boon for authors unfamiliar with the techniques of stagecraft. And not least, the elimination of Hanswurst and all humorousness meant that minds of a sober and unwitty bent need not strain after comic effects. The apprenticeship which Gottsched recommended, that of translating French tragedies before trying one's hand at original work, was eminently practical. Such translation was the best and quickest way of familiarizing novice authors with the details of the neoclassical tragic technique. Finally—however pedestrian and unesthetic it may now seem—the idea that the first step in writing a tragedy is to choose a definite moral principle and then to search around in history and mythology for a story illustrating that principle was altogether made to order for uninspired authors since it let them substitute busy work for the all too elusive divine spark. The process was made still easier inasmuch as the authors generally did not concern themselves about selecting one specific moral principle. What they did was to look through the pages of history books for unusual and striking events.

Gottsched found the German theater in the hands of professionals. True, student performances were still given in the preparatory schools before audiences no doubt composed mainly of parents; but the expense of elaborate costumings and properties, the skill in manipulating complicated stage-settings and special effects, the training and talent necessary especially for extemporized clown scenes, all these things made the real theater a monopoly of professional troupes whose directors were more interested in making money than in raising the German cultural *niveau*. Opportunities for enjoying the theater were restricted to those towns at which the troupes stopped and to the times of year when they stopped. Although Gottsched made use of the advantages that the Neuber troupe afforded him, his new drama was not strictly dependent on professional skills but could be played with fair success by amateurs at any place and time. *Der sterbende Cato*, to cite the most outstanding example, was presented everywhere, not only in larger towns but also in the smaller, remote places.[2] Moreover, Gottsched broke the influence of the professional directors and actor-authors by proving that they had been wrong after all: German audiences *were* able to enjoy tragedies in which the melancholy events were not interrupted and mitigated by Hanswurst's buffoonery. They could tolerate one single, simple stage setting from beginning to end and did not have to be diverted by elaborate costumings, realistic horrors, and astounding stage effects.

The victory of the new "regular" tragedy was, of course, neither immediate nor complete; otherwise the Neuber troupe, which acted as the practicing herald and apostle of Gottsched's reform, would have enjoyed more financial success. It is clear from the letters sent to Gottsched by the Neubers that it was sometimes difficult to attract the less educated people into the new theater.[3] More important than financial gain, however, was the *succès d'estime* won for Gottsched by the Neubers, because many of the people who came to see and to applaud the regular tragedies were persons of the class that determines the taste of a nation. From Hanover in September, 1730, Johann Neuber reported, "The beginning was made by the privy councillors appointed to the local Land-government, and because they were pleased, the other nobility and all the upperclass people soon followed after, and now everyone declares that he has never seen anything to match them (i.e., the new regular dramas)." [4] Before long, the regular neoclassical tragedy as taught by Gottsched gained recognition everywhere in Germany, and for at least twenty-five years it was regarded as the *only* proper type of tragedy.

There is some question about which of the earliest works still extant should be considered the first original neoclassical tragedy. *Der sterbende Cato,* written in 1730 and first presented in January, 1731, has been generally called the first one, and there is no doubt whatever that it was by far the most influential and widely known. But this play was, of course, essentially an amalgamation, adaptation, and translation of two foreign tragedies, so that its claim to originality is a very tenuous one. Behrmann's *Timoleon,* which was played for the first time in 1735 in Hamburg, was published with a preface that proclaimed it to be the first German original, while *Cato,* by clear inference, was included among the "many well-done translations and imitations." [5] In rebuttal to the claim made for *Timoleon,* Gottsched himself called attention to another play, Ludwig's *Ulysses,* which, according to Gottsched's rather vague dating, must have been written at the same time or even before *Cato.*[6] Unfortunately, *Ulysses* did not appear in print until 1752 anonymously in the third volume of *Die deutsche Schaubühne zu Wienn,* so that one cannot be very sure that the text that has survived is an unaltered one.[7] Nevertheless, this text proffers a drama that shows little or no influence of the serious ethical concept of tragedy preached by Gottsched and exemplified by him in *Cato.* Indeed, it makes the impression of being a *Haupt- und Staatsaktion* written in accord with external neoclassical rules. Therefore it appears feasible to discuss this *Ulysses* before *Cato,* and to regard it as a transitional work. It is written entirely in rhymed Alexandrines, with five acts and formal scene division whenever a personage leaves or enters on stage. The Unities are observed, and there is no comic person. If the play was indeed composed and performed, as Gott-sched indicated, in 1729 or 1730, then it antedates the author's departure on a botanical expedition to North Africa (1730–1733). On his return from this trip he continued his medical studies at Leipzig, where he eventually became professor of medicine. Christian Gott-lieb Ludwig lived from 1709 until 1773.[8] Of his other attempts at drama nothing has survived.[9]

The dialogue of *Ulysses, oder der für todt gehaltene aber endlich glücklich wieder gefundene Ehe-Gemahl* is liberally salted with moral sentiments that show that its youthful author was conversant with the ethical teachings of the Enlightenment. The plot itself, however, presents nothing more profound than a suspenseful adventure story in which the main effect rests upon the hero's having disguised himself as Phaon, a native of Crete. This latter feature, and the easy, shallow excitement which it could provide for those in the audience clever enough to penetrate Ulysses' disguise, are more appropriate to a *Haupt- und Staatsaktion,* opera, or comedy than to a genuine tragedy. The happy ending of the drama was, to be sure, not out of harmony with the tragic concept of the epoch, and, philosophically considered, it upholds an optimistic view of the world order. On the other hand, the actions of the sympathetic characters are not always such as would entitle them to the particular protection of Providence—at any rate, these characters do not seem to be as much concerned about the virtue of their actions as about the effectiveness thereof. Especially striking, in contrast to most later tragedies, is the fact that Ulysses feels no compunction about the deception that he carries out. Yet deceitfulness in any form was regarded as one of the worst breaches of the moral code in Enlightened tragedies, and sometimes even the vicious characters would express their deep distaste for it.

At the beginning of the play the two chief counsellors of faithful Penelope are discovered in an argument about the best means of ridding Ithaca of the burdensome suitors who have taken virtual possession of the land. Philetas is in favor of taking up arms against them, while Mentor advises complete passivity and confidence in the gods: "The kindly gods will direct everything wisely./ Let us wait patiently: this is the best counsel" (I. i). Mentor is a strict rationalist who objects to Penelope's lamentations and interprets noble-mindedness (*Großmuth*) as stoicism: "Banish your sorrow.

How can tears help?" (I. ii). Penelope's confidante Eurinome also
advocates patient passivity, saying, ". . . in abundance of trouble/
One must trust the gods, and always be patient:/ For this alone can
conquer misfortune" (I. iii). But Penelope is unimpressed by the
arguments of idealistic passive virtue as well as by those of hot-
blooded emotion. She has little of the cool nobility of Homer's heroine. Like a scheme-spinning *Machtweib* in a *Haupt- und Staatsaktion*
she commands Eurimone to sow the seeds of discord between her
two most pressing suitors, Antinous and Eurimach: "I want you to
deceive them today by means of a trick" (I. iii). Eurinome, without
a moment's reflection on the strict ideal of honesty, quickly accomplishes the wish of her mistress by telling both of the suitors
separately that Penelope has made her choice between them. In
consequence, they fall out with each other.

In the second act Penelope's son Telemachus is won over to the
ideas of the counsellor Philetas, who wants to use force against
the suitors: "And though a cowardly heart may bear its grief in
silence,/ Yet I am ready to venture any extreme/ Rather than bear
a burdensome yoke until death" (II. i). Telemachus is able to comfort
his mother—who is growing impatient with the gods and adjures
them, "You are called just, therefore help us out of distress!" (II. ii)
—by telling her he has had word "by post" that Ulysses is still alive.
Penelope urges Telemachus to be intelligently cunning like his father:
"Your father in his time experienced many a distress./ This instils
wisdom! This clarifies the understanding!/ How did Ulysses gain
victory at Troy?/ Was it the brave Greek army? Oh, no! His clever
counsel,/ This supported them in all their heroic deeds" (II. vi).
She is, however, very much opposed to Telemachus' plan for attacking the suitors with the help of Philetas. The emotional character of
the project is out of harmony with her peculiar concept of "noble-
mindedness": "Whither is error leading you? Do you still not real-
ize/ That rashness is a departure from noble-mindedness?" (II. vi).
Far more pleasing to Penelope is Telemachus' later and more rational
decision to stop acting like a typically headstrong youth: "Now I
shall forcibly stem the violence of youth,/ Now I shall not venture
into a lively strife./ The gods themselves may supply me the means./
Most certainly I shall raise myself through their strength" (IV. iii).
Youthful heroes in the emotional 1760's would evince far less restraint than this. But Telemachus is not the passive hero of the 1740's
and 1750's, either. His words do not signify inaction. They mean
that he is going to bide his time cleverly and await his opportunity.
If this drama has any message at all, it is the practical, not very ideal-

istic one that craftiness and cunning constitute the most rational and God-pleasing method of procedure.

The drama's titular hero, under the name "Phaon," does not appear until the third act. Craftiness is the mainspring of his character —at least of the small amount of character drawn for him—and his true identity is not revealed until the very end of the play. His first move is to tell the suitors that Ulysses is alive and approaching Ithaca. Then, at the command of the suitors and perhaps also to test his wife's faithfulness, he tells Penelope that Ulysses is dead. Next he tells Philetas that Ulysses is *not* dead, and that he has been sent ahead by Ulysses to spy out the situation in Ithaca. It is hard to decide whether the author really intended this disguise to be a mystery to the audience, so that they would be pleasantly startled and surprised at the end, or whether he was counting on the majority of spectators to possess enough knowledge of Homer that they would recognize "Phaon" at once or before very long. In any case, the initial interview between "Phaon" and Penelope would have gained in dramatic interest if the author had made it clear that a husband and wife separated for many years were here seeing each other again for the first time, without the wife's knowledge. Moreover, the alternating news of Ulysses' death and survival would not be a rather exasperating complication, but an understandable stratagem, while "Phaon" would no longer run the risk of seeming to be just a tiresome episodic character. The play would still not be a profound tragedy, of course, but at any rate the superficial suspense that it is capable of generating would not be hampered by obscurity. Here is a case that proves the correctness of Lessing's recommendation that the author keep no secrets from the audience.[10]

Only once in the play is there a hint that the author realized that deception was an offense against the Enlightened moral code. At the end of Act Four "Phaon" finds it expedient to reverse his earlier sad report to Penelope and to inform her that Ulysses is still alive, so that she will be encouraged to hold off the suitors a while longer. In order to assure her that he is on her side, and is not really an ally of the suitors as she fears, he makes a brief apology for his duplicity: "Though I dissemble now,/ Yet I am forced to do so, to conduct everything well" (IV. iv). To be sure, this is less an apology for questionably moral behavior than a necessary maneuver to win back Penelope's confidence. Ulysses-Phaon, with his suspicious-looking actions and his pleas for trust, is an early prototype of Schiller's Marquis Posa. Schiller, however, indicates that Posa oversteps the bounds of propriety, while Ludwig grants his Ulysses-Phaon full approval. In the last and weakest act the well-known archery contest between the suitors takes place off-stage (either as a concession to decorum or because of the technical difficulties involved) while the author struggles to keep up interest in the embarrassing lack of action on-stage by having still another false report of Ulysses' death brought to Penelope and subsequently an eyewitness account of the archery contest and the fight that follows it. Finally "Phaon" enters with Telemachus and Philetas, to announce their victory over the suitors, and now "Phaon" reveals that he is actually Ulysses. The last speech belongs to Philetas, and it puts the stamp of divine approval on deceitful craftiness: "The gods are favorably inclined. Ulysses' cunning has won" (V. vi). Such sentiments may be close to the theology and ethics of Homer's *Odyssey*, but they are in contradiction to the strict idealistic philosophy of the German Enlightenment. Technically inept as the play is, Ludwig did a better job of accommodating Homer's story to the neoclassical external dramatic rules than he did of making Ulysses and Penelope into paragons of eighteenth-century virtue.

To turn from Ludwig's *Ulysses* to Gottsched's *Der sterbende Cato* is to turn from a shallow melodrama veneered with rationalistic phraseology to a deeply serious and thought-provoking tragedy which, in spite of the stiffness of its dialogue and wooden characterizations, does deserve a little more respect than is generally given to it.[11] Since, as Gottsched freely admitted in the preface to the first edition, this drama is mainly an amalgamation of two plays by Addison and François Deschamps, with only a little more than a tenth of the verses counting as original composition,[12] *Der sterbende Cato* has scant claim to being a genuine original. It might be argued that in putting two different dramas together Gottsched in effect created a third new drama, especially since it was necessary to eliminate features of both older plays which would not logically fit together and also to add new features of his own invention in order to construct a unified whole. The play as it stands conforms to Gottsched's own *ideas*, even if he has made use of the work of others to put forth these ideas. Naturally that does not constitute so worthy an achievement as does a completely original work; on the other hand, however, this *Cato* was such a remarkable success both on stage and in print that its popularity and influence can be said to make up in great measure for its "illegitimate" origin. Without any doubt this was the most important play to appear in Germany before Lessing's *Miss Sara Sampson*. One might go so far as to say, before *Minna von Barnhelm*. It became, and still is, the symbol of Gottsched's reform of the theater.

The problem of the drama is that very basic one already touched upon in some *Haupt- und Staatsaktionen:* why does a virtuous man come to grief? Cato, the elderly Roman patriot, sets virtue and republican ideals above every other consideration. Although evidently a great warrior and statesman, Cato is called a hero not for those qualities, but because he has clung firmly to virtue in spite of many misfortunes. The Parthian princess Arsene says of him, "Admire the hero! There is none like him./ With many strokes of misfortune have the gods/ Heretofore tried him in vain. He still stands fast,/ Because his fortitude does not let him waver even once" (I. i).[18] He knows absolutely no compromise with evil: "My destiny ever leads me to combat evil,/ And though I should prepare a grave for myself thereby" (I. ii). The similarity of his attitude to Cicero's in Stranitzky's play is obvious, but Gottsched develops it with much more seriousness and profundity. Faithful to his ideal of strict republicanism, Cato regards Caesar, against whose forces he is making a last-ditch stand in Utica, as nothing more than a tyrant and dictator. A tempting possibility of much-needed military aid is opened up to Cato when he discovers that the Parthian princess staying with him is none other than his long-lost daughter Porcia. As heiress to the Parthian throne she could order the military forces of that country to support him; but this advantage is outweighed by a critical disadvantage: "How can Porcia please me in crown regalia!/ My blood does not permit it, and Rome forbids it to all!" (I. iv).

As in the dramas concerning Cicero and Charles XII, and in many others still to follow, the touchy point is brought up about the virtuous man's security in time of trouble. Cato is quite confident: "Virtue is well able to rescue us from danger" (I. iv). It is interesting to observe how Gottsched endeavors to keep this statement from being meaningless. In the first place, the most villainous character in the play, Pharnaces, is shown to be powerless against virtue. He wants desperately to marry Arsene-Porcia, who hates him, among other reasons, because he has killed the youth she thinks is her brother (until she discovers she is the daughter of Cato). When Cato refuses Pharnaces as a son-in-law because he is a king, and consequently loses him also as a military ally, the villain turns to Caesar and offers to murder Cato for him. Caesar, who himself loves Arsene-Porcia, rejects the proposal. Finally Pharnaces takes matters into his own hands, attacks Utica in order to steal Arsene-Porcia, but is killed in the attempt. He represents one danger against which the virtuous Cato is protected.

Another, subtler danger lies in the attraction Caesar holds for Cato's children. While Pharnaces is obviously and repulsively evil,

Caesar has mostly good qualities and a pleasant personality. He can truthfully say of himself, "My heart is sincere and free of dissimulation," and, "I myself never took pleasure in shedding blood,/ A tender heart beats in my paternal breast" (III. i). Cato's son Porcius only feels kindly disposed toward Caesar; but Arsene-Porcia is deeply in love with him. Apparent advantages (Wolff's *Scheingüter*) would accrue to Cato if he countenanced his children's feelings and shared them: an honorable cessation of hostilities, a brilliant marriage for Arsene-Porcia, and preservation of his own civic prestige, for Caesar is willing to divide the "mayorship" of Rome with him. But these apparent advantages are really a serious threat to the genuine good, which is the preservation of Cato's republican ideals. Cato's virtue proves equal to the temptation. In a parley he points out to Caesar that, for all his good qualities, he is worse than Pharnaces, because he has robbed Rome of its liberty. Knowing that Caesar is capable of real virtue, however, Cato makes a strong appeal to him: "But the time is passing away. Will you stand by your ideas,/ And not let yourself be won over by reason and virtue?" (III. iii). Unfortunately, Caesar is neither wise nor strong enough to grasp the genuine good. Like Schiller's King Philip, he is attracted by pure humaneness but cannot adopt it himself: "Oh, what a noble heart! Were I not who I am,/ I would wish nothing more for myself than Cato's free mind,/ Which wants no king" (III. iii). Although unable to convert Caesar, Cato successfully preserves the virtue of his children. Porcius is easily persuaded to swear his undying hate for Caesar, while Arsene-Porcia is more stubborn. When Cato commands her to stop loving Caesar, she speaks out for the rights of human feeling and human nature: "Say, must then a Roman, in order to seem true to Rome,/ Deny the very humanity in his soul/ And be insensitive?" (IV. ii). This is a powerful argument, but the author of the play is not a sentimentalist—he is a Wolffian rationalist, to whom natural feelings must be completely subservient to the dictates of reason. Thus in a little while Arsene-Porcia gains mastery over her blind feelings, and virtue is victorious over love. Cato is pleased: "Now I call you my child. By such tests of virtue/ I recognize my blood-line" (IV. ii). Indeed, the girl's love for Caesar is so absolutely extinguished by rational insight into what is genuinely good that it apparently has been transformed into hate. When Caesar leaves Cato's presence, declaring war on him, Arsene-Porcia shouts in rage, "Go, monster! Go, tyrant! You are a bloodthirsty villain!" (IV. iv).

At the end of the fourth act, then, Cato stands victorious, and his confidence in virtue is so far justified. Pharnaces is dead, Caesar is unmasked, and his children are secured in their virtue. Cato's second son Marcus, to be sure, has been treacherously killed by Pharnaces, but this sad event is counterbalanced by the glory surrounding a heroic death and mitigated for the audience by the fact that Marcus has not been previously seen alive on stage. Cato says over the dead body, "How beautiful it is to die,/ When we obtain our death and grave through virtues!" (IV. v). Marcus will find in the other world that his death has not been in vain. But it cannot be denied that the greatest danger of all, the imminent battle with the forces of Caesar, still threatens. In fact, the attacking army is so far superior in numbers that Cato advises against resistance. This decision, however, is the prelude to his departure from virtue.

The dramas concerning Cicero and Charles XII pessimistically allowed their perfect heroes to go down in defeat, without explanation, before the forces of evil and of fate. Gottsched, the Enlightened optimist, was not ready to let Cato's death and defeat upset the doctrine of a rational universe in any such manner. Therefore he answers the question: why does a virtuous man come to grief? with this explanation: the virtuous man may fall into error, and consequently be himself responsible for his misfortune. The tragedy *Cato* does not bring the spectator to awe-inspiring contemplation of the cruel reality of man's helplessness against a hostile universe. It is not stern and sobering, but edifying and schoolmasterish. Virtue, even in the best of men, is a matter of constant vigilance!

In the first scene of Act Five, Cato is found all alone, reading Plato's *Phaedo* and ruminating on the question of whether virtue is rewarded or not: "If there is a highest Being,/ —Yet Nature and World offer a thousand proofs/ And shout: There is a God—then it doubtless follows/ That God is always graciously inclined to virtue./ He to whom God is gracious must also become happy./ But when does this happen? and where? Surely not here on earth./ That falls to the lot of Caesar and is made for him./ Where then? —that I do not know, as much as I have pondered." Evidently Cato has reached the point of despair, a great contrast to his mood in the first four acts. The tests sent by Providence to prove his virtue have finally become too much for him, and he is about to resort to suicide. Naturally, the act of suicide was completely out of harmony with the philosophy of German Enlightenment, because it was the most overt admission possible that one did not believe in a benevolent Providence ruling over a rational universe, and that one's emotions had run away with reason. In order that no one might draw the false conclusion that he condoned suicide under some circumstances, Gottsched pointed out in his preface to the first edition (1732)

that "we never intend to excuse suicide, let alone praise it." [14]
Cato thinks because he has done no wrong in his life that he need
not fear death: "He who is plagued by conscience, has his slumber
disturbed by fear./ Cato knows nothing of that, no vice grieves me./
Therefore sleep and death are all the same to me;/ For both re-
fresh me and put an end to sorrow" (V. i). This would be a fine
attitude toward an inevitable death, but not toward suicide. Cato
is evidently not using his reason here with utmost precision. How
can this be in such a rational person? Wolff had supplied an answer
for that question in the first chapter of his treatise on ethics, *Vernünftige Gedanken von der Menschen Tun und Lassen:* ". . . No
human being (least of all through his natural powers) is capable of
complete bliss and happiness, for the very reason that he does not
completely attain virtue, but on the contrary, even when he has torn
himself altogether loose from vices, he is still subject to human
weaknesses." [15] These unavoidable human weaknesses, according to
Wolff, can often bring about worse results than actual vices: "Therefore it is necessary to combat the human weaknesses as well as the
vices and with all diligence to watch out for them." [16] Quite in
harmony with Wolff's remarks is Gottsched's explanation in the
preface: "But just in this way Cato has become a proper hero for
a tragedy, in that he has been very virtuous, but nevertheless in
the customary manner of human beings, namely that they still always have certain errors in them, which can make them unhappy.
This is how Aristotle wants the chief personages in tragedy to be
formed." [17] Gottsched, then, conceives of tragic guilt (so to speak)
as a practically unavoidable imperfection in the exercise of human
reason. Although nearly unavoidable, it is by no means excusable;
consequently the benevolence—and justice—of Providence and the
wisdom of being virtuous are preserved as unalterable principles.

Yet Providence does seem rather remote and legalistic in its
refusal to recognize Cato's human weakness and give him spiritual
strength when he needs it. Arsene-Porcia, fearing the worst, appeals
to the gods: "Remember how much good he has done,/ And show
us mortals that you love virtue" (V. iii). This challenge to Providence, which faintly calls to mind the stirring address of Goethe's
Iphigenia, is not answered, although Arsene-Porcia has complete
faith, saying, "Heaven itself can watch for our good fortune,/ On
that I rely" (V. iv). The proof that Providence indeed loves and
protects virtue comes in another way, after Cato has already given
himself the mortal thrust. First, word is brought that Caesar still
wants a peaceable settlement, and then, far better, Porcius announces
the news that Pompey's son in Spain has offered to help Cato against

Caesar. Accordingly, if Cato had had just a little more patience and trust, the cause of virtue might well have triumphed over evil. Unfortunately, Cato's love of freedom, in itself a great virtue, has gradually become less of a rational conclusion and more of an emotional resolution never to bear the outward signs of servitude, the chains of a captive. Gottsched explains in his preface, "But he carries his love of freedom too far, so that it is transformed into obstinacy." [18] When the moribund Cato is carried on to the scene, his words are, "I die without chains" (V. iii). This minor and, to a certain degree, foolish goal has been achieved, but at a grievous cost to his character.

On the other hand, Cato is not permitted to die in despair, for he is given time to recognize and repent of his error: "You gods, if I have here/ Perhaps done too much, ah! then forgive me./ You know our hearts, after all, and test our thoughts./ The best man can so easily depart from the path of virtue" (V. viii). This speech provides a conciliatory ending for the tragedy, so that the spectators' reaction might be one of unalloyed trust in Providence, which not only rewards virtue, but also understands human weakness and makes certain provisions for it. A feeling of melancholy is aroused by the realization that even a Cato is not proof against emotional conduct and grave errors of judgment, but this does not lead to hopelessness. Man in this tragedy is viewed, not as a lone being achieving a sad greatness in his defiance of the hostile universe, but as an honestly striving, somewhat handicapped pupil, trying to emulate his supreme, perfect Teacher, failing a little through weakness, but forgiven and rewarded in the life to come. Life is a trial or period of testing which is followed by an existence of greater perfection in the other world. This is the doctrine of salvation through reason and virtue. It is a secularized Christianity applicable to people of all times and of all religions—or no specific one. In the neat and orderly universe of this play, the same general rule of reason and virtue is held up to every action, so that all regrettable occurrences can be explained as the result of failure to observe the rule, and can be used as a positive stimulus for better future observation of it. The final line of the play thus places the ultimate blame for Cato's tragedy on the unvirtuous actions of the Roman people, whose lack of civic peace destroys their best citizens: "O Rome! this is the fruit of your civil wars!" (V. viii). This remark is no mere elegiac sigh; it is a schoolmasterish rebuke and admonition.

In addition to Gottsched's *Cato* and Ludwig's *Ulysses* the earliest repertory of the Neuber troupe included two never-printed "originals" by the actor Heinrich Georg Koch, *Titus Manlius* and *Der Tod des Cäsar*.[19] The texts of these dramas are altogether unknown. To judge from a remark of J. E. Schlegel's, the former may have been less a tragedy than a pastoral play with comic overtones,[20] while the latter, as the title suggests, was possibly an adaption of Marie Anne Barbier's *Mort de Jules César*.[21] In 1733, a year after the publication of *Cato*, Madame Neuber presented with considerable success a new tragedy entitled *Die Horazier*. Composed by a Hamburg patrician named Friedrich Georg Behrmann (1704–1756), this drama, although an adaptation of Corneille's *Horace*, probably had as much claim to the title of "original" as Gottsched's *Cato*. Behrmann did not have it printed, however, until 1751, and the version that was then published, according to the statement of the author himself, was an almost completely different one from the first.[22] Fortunately, Behrmann's second and more significant work, *Timoleon, der Bürgerfreund*, presented on stage for the first time in 1735, has not been lost. It was published in 1741—presumably unchanged —with an interesting preface by Johann Matthias Dreyer,[23] who made the assertion that *Timoleon* was the first original German tragedy (i.e., in the new "regular" style).

Although Dreyer's assertion tacitly attacks the prestige of *Der sterbende Cato*, nevertheless the preface gives due credit to Gottsched as the reformer of the German theater, and there is no doubt that Behrmann was inspired and encouraged by Gottsched's teachings and example. At one point the author of the preface (no doubt echoing the opinions of Behrmann himself) goes beyond the *Critische Dichtkunst*, wherein Gottsched took a very liberal view of historical accuracy in tragedy, by remarking with obvious pride, "The plot for this tragedy has been taken from the most reliable writers of history." On the other hand, historicity is not proclaimed as a *sine qua non*: "Who does not know that in a drama the touching probability is better than the purest truth which we must listen to without emotion." Even in this period of strictest rationalism the basically emotional appeal of tragedy could not be forgotten. Gottsched, too, was pleased to report that his Cato had "squeezed out tears" from all kinds of spectators, and he based the success of his poetic endeavor on the emotion aroused.[24]

Unlike *Cato*, Behrmann's "first German tragedy" does not present a hero with a tragic fault, but a perfect hero with an insoluble dilemma. If Timoleon follows the commands of reason and virtue, he will do violence to his natural and sacred feelings as a brother, and yet if he allows these feelings to prevail he will incur guilt.

Timoleon's act of fratricide, so Dreyer's preface states, "was admired by rational persons." But while it redounds to the good of the state of Corinth, it carries no personal reward for the perpetrator, indeed, quite the opposite. Timoleon emerges as a martyr to his own virtue, and this is a tragic concept that does not reflect the optimism of the period very well. The hero is worthy of pity for his mental suffering and worthy of admiration for his steadfastness; but the emptiness of his triumph tends to raise doubts about whether the world order is truly rational and just. Because of this uneasy, unsatisfactory ending, Behrmann's play is more genuinely tragic than its author may have intended it to be.

The villain is Timoleon's brother Timophanes, who wishes to rule Corinth as a tyrant, in spite of this city-state's republican tradition. He has achieved absolute control with the aid of mercenary troops, and his furious determination to rule despotically makes him dangerous even to the members of his own family. He has put his father-in-law into prison under sentence of death for refusing to acknowledge his authority, and his anger will next descend upon Timoleon and his wife's brother, Aeschylus. Timoleon at first advises gentleness as the best method of bringing Timophanes back to his senses: "Through anger you gain nothing, keep trying with kindness" (I. i). That is to say, one man's irrational passion is not to be countered with another man's equally irrational passion. It is wiser to maintain calmness, sweet reasonableness, for "Who knows, whether his rage will not finally succumb to gentleness" (I. ii). If this method does not succeed, Timoleon recommends passivity, by leaving matters up to Providence: "Then the wrath of the gods will burn upon him" (I. i). He warns the more excitable Aeschylus against any rash action: "Friend, you are far too bold in your undertakings,/ One must accommodate one's self to patience and to time" (I. ii). Sentimental appeals, like his wife's tears and pleas, seem to have no effect on Timophanes. Timoleon, however, hopes that the temperate voice of reason will have a beneficial influence: "He has raged enough, now he must combat himself,/ Through gentleness I still hope to quell the fury in him" (I. iii). Timoleon explains that tyranny is something new for the Corinthians: "We are not born to slavery, no, to freedom./ We know no master, except duty and fatherland,/ Except council and citizenry, except wisdom and understanding,/ Except law and propriety, except loyalty and honesty" (I. iii). That is to say, Corinth is a Utopia peopled with mature, rational, virtuous citizens—quite unlike the Rome referred to in Gottsched's *Cato*, where the sins of the populace brought down deserved punishment on its head. Timophanes is not a scourge sent from God, to be endured with pious passivity. To dethrone him is not rebellion, but plain duty.

As a villain, Timophanes is easily understood. He is simply an erring individual who has allowed his blind passions to run away with his reason. He is a glaring example of how this foolish procedure can utterly ruin all moral character. Moreover, he is the first of a line of tyrants in German tragedy (a line which culminates in Schiller's Philip of Spain) who have no respect for the ability of human beings to govern themselves: "Citizens are never fit for sovereignty./ They have no wit and are barren of insight./ One thing will be discussed twenty times by them,/ And they still will have come to no decision./ . . . The state must rest on princes, and not on citizens" (I. vi). In view of Timoleon's earlier description of the excellence of the Corinthians, the tyrant's attitude is a false one, and the author could expect his first audience, the citizens of free Hamburg, to be suitably enraged against the villain by these words. Timophanes further demonstrates his incorrect thinking by deriding the value of honesty: "How can an honest heart profit a clever statesman?/ Dissimulation is a far better protection than loyalty and faith" (II. ii). What Ludwig allowed to stand as an admirable trait in his Ulysses is here exposed as the characteristic of a degenerate soul. This man's "wisdom" is a mere unscrupulousness which appears the very opposite of true wisdom to the Enlightened rationalist. Machiavellianism found virtually no admirers among the literary spokesmen of eighteenth-century Germany.

There is optimism in the play, insofar as justice does win out over tyranny. Aeschylus reports, for instance, that his father—the father-in-law of Timophanes—is confident that Providence will not abandon him although he has been condemned to execution: "The citizenry and I shall some day obtain justice./ Innocence does not have to look for human aid,/ The gods must protect it for virtue's sake." Even execution, however, would not be a proof that virtue goes unrewarded: "He who dies innocently is raised even by death,/ And though it were by dagger and poison, still it is beautiful" (II. i). Such a steadfast attitude appears to differ little from the Christian stoicism of Gryphius' seventeenth-century tragedies, except for the fact that death is looked upon as a circumstance that would not alter the proposition that virtue always is rewarded, rather than as the natural fate of a virtuous person in a pessimistically regarded, depraved world. And, as a matter of fact, the old father is eventually saved from execution. In another instance, a character named Orthagoras expresses optimism combined with outspoken passivity. He points out the transitoriness and falseness of the apparent happiness of the tyrant's life: "They are punished enough already, their life is accursed,/ Often their fall is already at hand, before one seeks it." To the impatient Aeschylus he emphasizes the folly of taking revenge into one's own hands: "One must not interfere with the providence of the gods,/ Who knows what end it serves, when fear and distress are heaped up./ . . . Ah, who indeed recognizes the secrets of the gods?/ Often one thinks one sees them, and is nevertheless misled./ Therefore control yourself, my friend, do not interfere in their council,/ One does not see their work, until the deed is accomplished" (III. i).

In view of such sentiments as these, it is surprising to hear that force is going to be employed against Timophanes after all. Orthagoras himself makes the first important decision in this direction: "We must oppose ourselves to violence with might" (III. v). Timoleon is still eager to try entreaties, and goes so far as to offer his own exile or death as a price for Corinth's freedom. When Timophanes merely continues to breathe out threats and fury, and orders the death of his father-in-law, Timoleon at last becomes convinced that the assassination of the tyrant is inevitable. He furnishes Orthagoras and Aeschylus with daggers, for it is they, and not he himself, who will do the actual killing. So great is Timoleon's natural revulsion against fratricide that even as the two assassins are leaving to perform their task he is still ineffectually begging them not to do it! One would expect some sort of theoretical explanation for the shift from patient passivity to independent initiative, but none is forthcoming in the play. One can only surmise that the author wishes his audience to understand that when every opportunity has been given Providence to act in its own mysterious way, and still nothing happens, then the virtuous man may assume that *he* himself is nothing less than the chosen instrument of Providence, and may accordingly take action into his own hands. That this is actually what Behrmann had in mind is suggested by the speech of Orthagoras after the assassination has been accomplished: "This work in Corinth did not take place through men,/ Surely the gods themselves took part therein,/ And aroused Timoleon to the act of rescue" (V. iv). A similar sanction of independent initiative, when all other means have been exhausted, is to be observed in Lessing's *Henzi,* and also in *Emilia Galotti* Odoardo is shown to recognize that God intends some action on his part when he cries, "He wants my hand, he wants it." [25] In *Timoleon* the principle of rational calm and pious confidence in Providence has not yet reached the point of completely supine passivity, as it was to do under increased sentimental and Pietistic influence.

The reaction of the two female characters in *Timoleon* to the death of Timophanes is irrational to an extreme. Because they are women, Behrmann represents them as subject to a separate code of behavior which it is their duty to follow in spite of the fact that they have reason enough to understand the behavior of the men. This is most strikingly demonstrated in the case of Acradina. She is heartily opposed to the crimes of her husband Timophanes, but she will not hear her brother and Timoleon call him a tyrant: "Silence, he is my husband" (I. ii). Her loyalty as a wife takes precedence over her filial piety, although she does beg Timophanes to take her life in exchange for that of her father. Furthermore, her loyalty does not depend on the faithfulness of her spouse. He may be an adulterer, yet, "I know to what duty and marriage compels us women" (III. iii). If the monster should die, her grief would be eternal, for "He is after all my husband" (IV. i). When Timophanes has been killed, Acradina turns against the gods, without apology, and censures them for permitting what was in the eyes of the rest of Corinth a benevolent act: "You stern gods, you, you have denied us,/ I accuse you, you are the origin of our torment" (V. i). Although she agrees that Timoleon's decision has helped Corinth and has saved the life of her father, still she says she will kill Timoleon in revenge. Evidently Behrmann wished to add pathos to his drama by depicting a remarkably faithful wife, and for the sake of this purpose he was willing to let her exhibit a kind of virtue that can scarcely be called rational.

The case of Demaristia, the mother of Timoleon and Timophanes, is somewhat different. During most of the play she acts rationally, siding with and encouraging her virtuous son Timoleon, and reprimanding the wicked Timophanes with the utmost severity. She goes so far as to curse the hour of his birth (II. ii). When he is dead, however, she makes a complete about-face and treats Timoleon like a murderer. She instructs the populace that Timoleon must die for his crime: "Away, you must shed his blood!" (V. i).[26] She turns a deaf ear to rational arguments, such as Aeschylus' question, "When one aids freedom, is that still a crime?" (V. iii). As she once cursed Timophanes, so now she curses Timoleon: "May the ghost which you sent to Hell frighten you,/ May you feel grief and fear as often as you see it,/ May you be tormented day and night by persecution, horror, troubles,/ Hatred, enmity—" (V. iv). She neither forgives Timoleon, nor consents to see him again. But if her behavior is inconsistent with rational thought, the author does not seem to blame her. Apparently he feels that a woman's highest duty consists in marital loyalty and maternal affection—although, to be sure, it is odd that Demaristia is unable to extend that affection to Timoleon. Dramatically, the emotional outbursts of Demaristia are both more effective and more credible than a calmly rational acceptance of the deed would have been. Her maternal lament is easily the truest and most affecting statement in the drama: "O difficult motherhood, how great your burden is!/ One wishes for a son, brings him with fear into the world,/ Rears him with sorrow, and when he comes to years,/ Then cares grow larger too" (V. iv).

Timoleon's own spiritual state after the assassination is divided equally between rational satisfaction and emotional despair: "No, the tyrant's death gives me no pain whatever,/ That he was my brother, only that penetrates to my heart." He would perform the deed again, without blushing. On the other hand, "A murder is still a murder, it must ever condemn me" (V. vi). His friends must forcibly prevent him from committing suicide, and he at last agrees to go on living only so that he may torture himself daily with the knowledge of his crime. He has broken the old law of nature in order to obey the higher law of patriotism, and while his reason congratulates him for his conquest of natural feelings, his heart condemns him for the fratricide. In a manner still more grievous than physical death he has sacrificed his existence for the welfare of his country. By showing his hero to be incapable of cold rational rejection of natural feelings Behrmann has succeeded in creating a genuinely tragic situation. No other author of this period was again willing to depict the service of reason and virtue as being quite so unrewarding. Steadfast virtue might occasionally result in an unmerited death—and this in itself was difficult enough to reconcile with optimism—but never in a bad conscience. A tragedy like Behrmann's *Timoleon* and a tragedy like Ludwig's *Ulysses* were to be expected at the beginning, before the moral goal had become set and clarified in all its particulars.

III

THE ORIGINAL TRAGEDIES
IN GOTTSCHED'S *SCHAUBÜHNE* [1]

IT WAS THE POLICY of the wandering theatrical troupes to guard their repertory of dramas jealously from their rivals, and never to allow the texts to appear in print. In complete contrast to this, Gottsched was most eager, especially after the departure of the Neuber troupe on its tour to Russia, to bring the texts of the new "regular" dramas to the attention of the reading public at large. His goal, of course, was not financial gain; rather, he was bent on forming and improving the theatrical taste of his countrymen and, with patriotic fervor, he wanted to demonstrate that Germans, too, were capable of writing correct dramas. To serve this dual purpose he undertook the publication of an extensive drama collection and gave it the impressive, somewhat pretentious title, *Die deutsche Schaubühne nach den Regeln und Exempeln der Alten* (or, also, *nach den Regeln der alten Griechen und Römer eingerichtet*). There had been no such collection—i.e., containing the dramas of more than one author—in Germany since the seventeenth century, and never before a collection of such scope, influence, and prestige. The six volumes of the *Schaubühne* were published in Leipzig between 1740 and 1745, with the second and third volumes preceding the first, which was delayed because the contents planned for it were too slowly prepared and then eventually changed. [2] In addition to *Cato*, the first three volumes offered only one original tragedy, *Darius*, and Gottsched's pastoral play *Atalanta*. Everything else was translation. The last three volumes, however, contained nothing but original works by German authors working under Gottsched's aegis. A collection like this one of printed plays, to be read and studied by persons of at least some culture, in all parts of Germany, might well be expected to have had a considerably greater effect in establishing the success of Gottsched's theater reform than the heroic efforts of the Neuber troupe. [3] That the *Schaubühne*, in spite of all its shortcomings (for which it was roundly condemned by the next generation), [4] indeed performed the apostolic function of carrying Gottsched's reform far and wide is indicated by the fact that a second edition followed directly on the heels of the first, and that other similar collections were soon published in imitation.[5]

The earliest original tragedy in the *Schaubühne* (except for *Cato*) was the *Darius* of Theodor Leberecht Pitschel (1717–1745),[6] one of Gottsched's most faithful adherents in his literary quarrel with Bodmer and Breitinger. According to the preface to Volume III (1741), in which the tragedy appeared, *Darius* was written in 1738 while Pitschel was still a student.[7] The author followed the example of his master in portraying a virtuous hero with a single fault which brings about the catastrophe. On the other hand, the defeat of the Persian nation by Alexander, which is connected with the downfall of Darius, is not attributed to any guilt incurred by the Persians themselves—as was the case in *Cato*, where the Romans are criticized for their civil strife—but to the treachery of two false leaders. This is made clear by Darius in his dying speech: "Inasmuch as Persia is now dying on account of traitors,/ And not through fault of its own" (V. vi). Although the character of the hero is composed of nine parts virtue and one part fault, Darius is a completely different personality from Cato. Whereas Cato's virtue makes him a pillar of strength, Darius possesses the kind of virtue that tends toward weakness. At a time that calls for resoluteness and action, when Alexander's army is threatening his empire, Darius is only kind, soft, and peace loving. He has a staunch admirer in the person of Patron, a Greek ally of the Persians, who says of him, presumably with the author's approval, "The sovereign is sweet and gentle,/ Gracious, loving, wise, the image of virtue,/ Not a cruel tyrant" (I. ii). One cannot help sympathizing, however, with the rebellious satrap Bessus and his co-conspirator General Nabarzanes when they complain of Darius' effeminate rule, his failure to enter bravely into battle, and his constant cowardly retreating and surrendering of territory after territory. Nabarzanes says, "Darius loves pleasure, jests, and repose more/ Than armor, helmet, and sword" (I. i), and even though this judgment is perhaps too harsh, it is nowhere in the play shown to be really false. The situation is somewhat like that depicted by Schiller at the court of the French dauphin in *Die Jungfrau von Orleans*, except that the passivity of the sovereign is evidently supposed to be regarded as laudable. In his brief introduction to the play, Gottsched wrote that he believed the tragedy would have a "touching" effect,[8] and it would seem that Pitschel, whether or not he was conscious of it, had a concept of tragedy which dictated that pity be the most important emotion aroused.

Actually, the character of Darius gives rise to a feeling that is more akin to contempt than to pity. It is easy to understand why Bessus and Nabarzanes have plotted against his ineffectual regime; but it is difficult to understand why Patron is loyal and admiring, or why his fiancée Thamiris loves him. It is surprising—and perhaps this is a prelude to his tragic error—to find that Darius does not have complete confidence in the gods, at any rate insofar as the fortunes of war are concerned: "But the gods do not regard just combat" (I. iv). He seems more inclined to put his trust in his generals' skill than in any divine intervention: "The gods can make me happy only through you" (I. iv). In command of a large army, his position is far less desperate than that of Cato; yet he is supinely ready to accept defeat. He does, however—like Cato—prefer an honorable death to the chains of servitude under a tyrant.

It would be hard to pick out one definite, restricted moral principle that this tragedy illustrates, although it may be confidently assumed that Pitschel had studied Gottsched's *Critische Dichtkunst* and was trying to follow the rules and procedure outlined in the chapter on tragedy. As in the case of Gottsched's own first tragedy, the only basic moral principle in *Darius* is the general one that Providence and the rational world-order are to be trusted, and that virtue is always rewarded, unless it breaks down through error or vice. Darius' error, and break with virtue, occurs when he believes the accusation that is brought by his enemies against his friend.

Although he has been given ample proof that Bessus and Nabarzanes are trying to depose him from his throne, still Darius is simple-minded enough to believe these rascals when they produce a bogus letter supposedly written by Alexander to Patron, in answer to Patron's alleged proposal to assassinate Darius. The king at once accepts this clumsy fraud, and releases Bessus and Narbazanes from the chains in which they have been placed as a result of Patron's report concerning their treasonable actions. Only when it is too late, and these conspirators are again in full command of the troops, does Darius listen to reason and have the soldier who "found" the incriminating letter interrogated. The soldier then confesses that the letter was given him by Nabarzanes. Darius is thunderstruck, realizing that he has prepared his own downfall and that he deserves his punishment: "Oh! Heaven! kill me! I am to blame,/ That I am now being deposed; that I of realm and life/ Am being robbed by murderous hands. I am my own enemy./ I release traitors, and my truest friend/ I condemn without his fault" (IV. v). The king's remorse is made still more painful when he receives assurance that Patron and Thamiris (who is Patron's sister) do not hold any resentment toward him for his lack of faith. Theirs is an ideal generosity and loyalty forming an edifying contrast to Darius' lack of steadfastness. Whatever happens to Darius now cannot be blamed on an unjust or aloof Providence. This is stated quite explicitly by Darius when he hears that the traitors are coming to murder him: "Heaven is punishing me/ For my inconstancy. Therefore must now openly/ Rebel against me this bold swarm of murderers,/ And death which is so near must teach me my mistake" (IV. vi).

It is noteworthy that in this play, even more than in Gottsched's *Cato,* the tragic fault is not construed as a deep-rooted moral defect or as a consuming passion. Darius has only made a mistake of a momentary and involuntary kind, the result of bad judgment rather than of bad nature. This is something altogether different from the tragic fault of a Macbeth or a Hamlet, or even of Othello, although some parallel might be drawn with the tragically bad judgment of King Lear. It is not like the tragic fault of Racine's Phèdre, which lies in the heroine's abandonment of herself to an uncontrollable passion. Rather, it is close to the Greek concept of *hamartia,* a misstep or mistake that connects the hero causally with his downfall. Gottsched's Cato developed a fault which was more morally reprehensible, for he allowed his love of liberty to obscure the faith he should have had in Providence, and the rational confusion that led to his suicide was conditioned by emotion. Not so Darius. His personality is not condemned, but his action *is* condemned.

In prescribing the procedure for composing a tragedy, Gottsched emphasized the primary importance of working out the plot, or "fable," and the secondary position of character.[9] Pitschel followed this procedure to the letter. His plot concerns a king who is treacherously conspired against, and who at the crucial juncture believes the conspirators instead of his supporters. The next step was to fit a character to this action, a character which above all would be consistent throughout. Accordingly, Pitschel made of Darius a weak and easily persuaded personality, always glad to take the line of least resistance, but virtuous and kindly withal. With these traits established, it was possible to make the conspiracy of Bessus and Nabarzanes understandable, and also to show Darius believing their lies about Patron. This characterization now forms, fairly skillfully, the background for Darius' misstep; but it is not in itself the tragic fault that justifies the catastrophe. The case can be compared to the *Oedipus* of Sophocles, where the rash and impatient nature of Oedipus forms the background for his killing of Laius at the crossroads, but this nature is not Oedipus' *hamartia* (as Gottsched believed).[10] The actual *hamartia* was Oedipus' failure to recognize Laius as his father, and this was an excusable error in judgment, not a deep-rooted moral failing. In the ancient Greek drama the innocence of Oedipus' misstep added to the main impression aimed at by the author, that man is utterly helpless in the face of overwhelming fate. But in Pitschel's eighteenth-century play, such an impression was to be avoided at all costs. Therefore Darius' misstep is not regarded as being free of moral turpitude. In a rational universe the root of all evil behavior is the faulty use of reason (just as under Christianity all evil behavior stems from lack of love for God), and accordingly in the final analysis a mistake is a sin—and vice versa.

The disintegration of personality which afflicts some of Shakespeare's heroes, as well as some of Racine's (e.g., Mithridate, Agamemnon, Phèdre, Athalie), and that temporarily threatens Gottsched's Cato has no place whatever in the tragedy at hand. Pitschel does not let his hero become desperate and take his own life. After recognizing and rueing his misstep, Darius swiftly regains his rational equilibrium and spurns the temptation to despair: "But no. What? shall a blade of steel end this wretched life?/ Only a fool commits suicide. Therefore from strangers' hands alone/ I desire my death, and not through guilt of my own./ Come, murderers, into my tent! There I wait with patience" (IV. vii). With these words of the king near the end of the fourth act, the tragic problem of the play is solved, and nothing is left to the fifth act except the presentation of the actual death scene.

The paucity of integral action in the last act leaves room for a gaudy coloratura display of grief on the part of Thamiris, the king's fiancée, whose passionate ravings against Providence for its "injustice" would come perilously close to destroying the whole dialectic of the drama, if it were not so obvious that her scene is brought in deliberately for its emotional and histrionic pyrotechnics, and for no more serious reason. Words that would be blasphemous temerity in the mouth of a man are merely the expected thing from a woman mad with grief and love: "You, Heaven, flee from my pleas!/ You yourself have attacked the king with cruelty!/ You love the band of murderers! You are the king's enemy!/ You yourself suppress his best friend,/ And help traitors to succeed" (V. i). Like Goethe's Iphigenia she wants Providence to live up to its reputation for rewarding virtue and punishing vice, but she expresses this thought very hysterically: "Do help support innocence!/ You yourself help defend my king from the traitors!/ You have indeed enough might for that. Up! plunge them into ruin!/ You yourself in wrath destroy this shocking alliance!/ Up! thunder, hail, lightning, and all flames of fire!/ Engulf this band of bloodthirsty villains!" (V. i). When her frantic appeals are not answered, and instead Darius comes in dying, Thamiris accepts the inevitable and does not break out in further resentment against Heaven.

The conspirators, naturally, must pay for their crimes. They have not been excused from guilt just because Darius is in a measure responsible for his own demise. Thus Nabarzanes is killed and Bessus, when captured, is turned over to Alexander, who will punish him because he does not like traitors, on whatever side they may be. Incidentally, this view of Alexander as a just ruler softens the fate of the Persian empire and prevents one from feeling that now millions of innocent people will be suffering harshly. The captive scoundrel Bessus does not show any remorse for his crimes, but continues spitting out defiance to the end. In this he is like Pharnaces in *Der sterbende Cato;* but whereas Pharnaces was a villain without dignity, acting more out of pique than purpose, and scorned by all as a small soul, Bessus has a dynamic will and self-confidence that raises his villainy to a dark eminence. Although reviled in the most scathing terms by Thamiris and Patron, he is able to answer with such brazen self-justification and scorn for their "virtue" that they both pale in comparison to him—in spite of the fact that the author puts them in the right and him in the wrong. Bessus is a new addition to the cast of characters in German eighteenth-century tragedy, and one full of promise. He foreshadows the type of ruthless, fascinating villain who soon was to become almost indispensable and even a kind of perverted hero. Presumably the spectacle of an unregenerate will to evil, an active principle maintaining itself with Satanic power against all the seductive but passive appeals of virtue and sweet submission to Providence, was peculiarly titillating to audiences (and authors) trained to believe that they were really charmed by nothing but spectacles of good and rational behavior. The shocked horror that the speeches of Bessus were meant to arouse probably included a goodly portion of secret delight.

Despite the relationship between Darius and Thamiris, this is not a tragedy of love (the "French" theme looked upon with great distaste by Gottsched, Schlegel, Nicolai, and even Gellert [11]), but a tragedy with a masculine, weighty subject, the death of a great king that brings with it the end of a great empire. No safer theme could be chosen by an author whose concept of a tragic action coincided with the old tradition of Renaissance criticism, and this tradition was the one to which conservative taste continued to subscribe throughout most of the century. Thus one may still read in the second edition (1794) of Johann Georg Sulzer's *Allgemeine Theorie der schönen Künste,* in the article "Tragisch," the follow-

ing definition: "Those events and undertakings are particularly to
be called tragic in which it is a question of the saving or the downfall of whole societies, of whole states. Such subjects as these possess
the true tragic greatness, by means of which the spectators are irresistibly carried away or shaken." [12] The prevalence of this concept of a tragic action helps one to understand the sarcasm in
Lessing's remark concerning his *Emilia Galotti*, that he considered
its subject quite tragic enough, and capable of stirring the whole
soul, "even though no overturning of the whole constitution of
the state should result." [13] Pitschel, however, is very dependent on
the impressiveness of the historical setting for his play's effect. The
unforceful character of Darius and his gullibility would be merely
silly and contemptible if he were not a great king whose action
seals the fate of an empire.

A more enthusiastic concept of virtue than is to be found either
in *Darius* or *Cato* makes its appearance in a tragedy by another
member of Gottsched's faithful young cohort, Theodor Johann
Quistorp (born 1722). This work, entitled *Aurelius, oder Denkmaal
der Zärtlichkeit*, was written in 1742 [14] and published the next year
in the fourth volume of the *Deutsche Schaubühne*.[15] *Aurelius* is
distinctly different from *Cato* and *Darius* in that its author has failed
to assign any tragic fault to the hero. The disappearance of the
tragic fault opened a delightful vista to the dramatists of the 1740's.
Now the battle could be fought out between closed ranks of the
good and the evil, without the embarrassing complication of a hero
partially responsible for his troubles. The kind of tragedy produced
by the inclusion of a tragic fault could not satisfy quite all the demands of a generation that was feeling more and more the influence
of Pietistic sentiment. Granted that *Cato* and *Darius* preserved the
rationalistic world-order by relieving Providence (one might say,
through a legalistic loophole) of responsibility for the sad ending;
still, these works stressed the sternness of God rather than His benevolence. Much more sentimentally appealing than a Cato fallen
from virtue is a hero like Aurelius, whose virtue is proof against all
temptation and tribulation and does not involve him, as was the
case with Timoleon, in a lifetime of remorse and regret. An Aurelius
could be inspirational to those weaker than he (almost everybody)
because he is not morally defeated by his sufferings. It is, however, important to add that his story does *not* have a fatal ending.
At the conclusion he is physically as well as morally triumphant,
and Providence is tangibly proved to have been benevolent, even
when it seemed not to be.

Since the tragic fault's main purpose was to excuse a fatal conclusion, it is not surprising that the disappearance of the fault was accompanied by the disappearance of a final catastrophe. This was easily possible at a time when a tragedy could be defined (in Schlegel's *Gedanken zur Aufnahme des dänischen Theaters*) simply as "an action involving high personages which arouses the passions." [16] Aristotle himself had not insisted on catastrophic endings. So long as the emotions were strongly stirred (at least in the hopeful author's estimation), the choice of a happy or sad ending could not affect the play's standing as a tragedy. Nevertheless, tragedy tends to be an anthropophagous genre, and where this sustenance is denied it, an anemic condition soon becomes apparent. The Aurelius material [17] no doubt attracted Quistorp because its perfect hero suffers and then is rewarded for his virtue. But when a drama stirs up insistent hopes for the saving of the hero—hopes so insistent that his death would arouse a feeling of outrage—instead of preparing the audience gradually for his inevitable death by arousing within the spectators a regretful but inexorable sense of justice, then one may rightly wonder whether this drama is not something less than a tragedy.

There is much talk of death in the drama, and the titular hero Aurelius is very ready and willing to die. He declares that he is "dead already in spirit" and adds, "I hasten with all delight to the dwelling of those heroes" (V. iii). He tells the emperor Trajan, who wants to save him as much as the audience does, "In me you are only raising a bent reed: / Better to break it off entirely! Yes, Emperor, let me die!" (V. iii). Such words would be commendable in the mouth of a hero with a tragic fault; indeed, the description of himself as a "bent reed" would be a very apt one for a tragic hero whose actions have destroyed his connection with life, so that physical death would come as a *coup de grâce*. Aurelius, however, has done nothing wrong. At the beginning of the play, in a sensational opening scene that takes great liberties with the neoclassical rule of decorum, Aurelius has slain his dear friend Valerius—but only to prevent Valerius from carrying out a vile conspiracy against Trajan. For all its violence, this was a just act, and Aurelius says it was.

The political opinions expressed in this first scene run directly counter to those in *Der sterbende Cato* and in *Timoleon*. In Quistorp's drama the monarchist is the just man, and the lover of freedom is portrayed as an unvirtuous conspirator. Valerius *seems* to have worthy principles when he asserts, "Thereby I want to give the people a laudable example, / That a citizen does not value his life more than his freedom" (I. i). But this desire for freedom is not a virtue, because Trajan is no tyrant. As Aurelius states, "He governs without haughtiness, compels us just with kindness:/ He has a citizen's heart, an imperial character:/ Is a master only over vices; a subject to virtue" (I. i). Insistence on freedom under such an ideal regime can only be wicked rebelliousness, and, it might be said, is tantamount to rebellion against God Himself. As in *Darius*, conspiracy is here treated with the utmost abhorrence, even though in both plays the conspirators give persuasive reasons for their dissatisfaction with the ruler. When Valerius makes it clear that he is going to kill Trajan at once, Aurelius strikes him down, not in passion, but only to protect the life of the emperor. The trouble with Valerius is that his emotions have not been tamed by his reason. As Aurelius says, he was not an evil person: "His heart was great and strong; only unfortunately! his youth/ Too impudent, too untamed; and not yet firm in virtue" (I. iii). Obviously the time had not arrived for a glorification and indulgence of youth. The first half of the eighteenth century belonged to the mature and settled man.

The killing of Valerius, although it puts an end to his conspiracy, is only the beginning of the play's action. It opens up a situation in which extreme refinement of feeling will provide almost the entire action, and thereby Aurelius becomes the most complicated and spiritual character yet to be seen in a German drama. He is, as it were, the great-grandfather of Iphigenia, Tasso, and Max Piccolomini. The transition from the view of virtue as a stern rule to that of virtue as a state of soul involving the most sensitive and delicate of feelings may be seen in this play; and this makes the play interesting, even if it is by no means a masterpiece and is particularly clumsy and absurd in its handling of the Unity of Place.[18] Aurelius, who has performed his bloody deed at a moment when it was clearly and cleanly dictated by necessity, finds immediately afterwards that other people are not going to recognize the purity of his motivation. His friend Maximinus urges him to hide the corpse and pretend that Valerius committed suicide, because the Roman populace loved Valerius and will demand revenge for his murder. This practical advice is rejected by Aurelius, for his tender conscience will not permit him to conceal what he has done. Maximinus, a "stoic," ridicules such fine feeling as effeminacy. Evidently, the suffering of Aurelius has now begun. It is meant to be a touching spectacle: virtue suffering, misunderstood, but maintaining itself intact.

Aurelius faces a harder trial when the slain man's mother, Fulvia, appears on the scene. He admits bravely to the distracted woman that he is the murderer. There is not only bravery and honesty in his admission, however. He is impelled by the desire to have the virtuousness of his action publicly vindicated, threshed out in open court, and officially judged. Only then will he feel able to regain his place in the world of men. Unlike Timoleon, he refuses to allow a disparity to exist between the demands of virtue and the demands of natural relationships. What he has done is either absolutely correct, and he may live happily, or it is absolutely wrong, and he will be punished. Pardon is not enough, for that would not remove the implication of guilt: "Very well! then I myself will go voluntarily before the court:/ Condemn myself unaccused, and demand my chains:/ Even though Trajan and the council would have pardoned me./ I want to be rid of the blood guilt, Rome shall be no murderers' den;/ Because I am a Roman" (I. v). Thus speaks the heroic martyr to virtue, spurning the clever and expedient ways of avoiding his difficulty. There must not be the slightest chance of murder's being condoned. The special justification for this one case of murder must come to light, or it is better that he die.

In view of his high principles, it is a little odd that in the second act Aurelius does not confess his deed to Trajan, but instead goes off to join the army that is setting out on a campaign against the Parthians. Before long, however, he returns to Trajan of his own accord. The gods have indicated to him that running away was not the proper procedure: the auguries for the campaign have been unfavorable, because an evildoer was present in the army. As soon as he leaves, the auguries become favorable again. This matter of auguries has a most unfortunate effect on Aurelius, who now believes that the gods themselves have failed to sanction the murder of Valerius. Far from rebelling against the authority of the gods, however, and of accusing them of injustice, Aurelius meekly submits to what he supposes is their verdict and prepares to die. This is the ultimate in virtue, to trust in Providence even when it seems that Providence has turned against one for no conceivable fault of one's own. Aurelius' lips are now sealed. He will not say a word in his own defense, because the gods wish his death. Since it is their will, he accepts the prospect of death, not only obediently, but eagerly: "My spirit grows more cheerful; my will is becoming purified:/ My glance discovers from afar the beam of eternity:/ In short, I feel repose, delight, and resigned composure" (III. i). In addition, he comforts himself with the thought that he is dying for a good cause, the preservation of Roman law and Trajan's honor.

The already very attenuated situation is rendered still more so in the fourth act, when Trajan gets clear proof of Aurelius' innocence through a tablet which bears the plans for Valerius' rebellion and also the names of all the rebels. This tablet is so strong a testimony for the justice of Aurelius' act that even Fulvia, the murdered man's mother, now hates her son and loves his killer. She is considerably more rational in this decision than the mother Demaristia in Behrmann's *Timoleon*—but perhaps less human. Trajan, however, realizes that something more is involved in this matter than just the facts surrounding a homicide. The real issue is Aurelius' refusal to defend himself. Therefore Trajan rashly destroys the tablet, so that the fate of Aurelius will depend solely on whether or not he will speak up for himself. It is the culmination of Aurelius' suffering when Trajan, the man for whose honor he is sacrificing himself, interprets this stubborn silence as sinful pride, as if Aurelius will not lower himself to plead his case before his master and expects to be set free without asking for it. To goad him into speaking, Trajan pretends that there is nothing Aurelius *could* say in his own defense. When this maneuver also fails to break Aurelius' silence, Trajan angrily tells him he can die, then, if he is determined to do so.

Left alone, forsaken, and misunderstood, Aurelius is suddenly assailed by doubts concerning the justice of the gods. He thinks of the Christian martyrs he has seen die and wishes he could be like them, accepting their unmerited punishment with rejoicing: "Oh! if I only knew the God,/ Who makes them so brave, whom they in all distress,/ When our butchers roast, saw, and cut them to pieces,/ Always worship as the Crucified One" (IV. iv). This is one of the few instances in eighteenth-century tragedy where a line is drawn between "the gods" and the Christian God. Usually "the gods" of whatever heathen variety are treated as valid representations of Providence, with the same attributes and responsibilities toward virtue that are expected of the supremely rational Being who controls the rational universe. In this play also, it is true, the Roman gods of Aurelius eventually prove themselves to be worthy of confidence. Presumably the author brings in Christianity here in an effort to show that this religion is a better, but not essentially different avenue to the proper appreciation of Providence. Although there is no possibility for Aurelius to find out more about Christianity, the very thought of it calms him, and he is again ready to face death uncomplainingly. Thus, as Wolff had said, religion comes to the rescue when reason grows weak, and helps to set a man back on the path of virtue.[19]

In the fifth act, Trajan repents of his anger and wishes he had not destroyed the tablet. The gods alone can repair the damage he has done: "Do not, great gods! do not concede to this injustice!/

Preserve Aurelius! grant me peace of conscience!" (V. i). Certainly it is fitting that matters should be left up to the gods, for they bear the responsibility, with the auguries they directed, of putting Aurelius in a position where he thinks he cannot speak in his own defense. Some sort of miracle is called for, because, as Maximinus says, "There is no possibility that the gods can forsake him!" (V. i). In this very optimistic tragedy virtue's reward must be enjoyed right here on earth. A *deus ex machina* is here not just a dramatic emergency measure, but a dialectical necessity required by the play's philosophical proposition: Providence rewards virtue. Therefore in the nick of time an augur enters with the report that a new augury has taken place which definitely shows that the gods are pleased with Aurelius: "The gods love him; and his good cause" (V. iv). Aurelius is completely astonished by the news and, in accord with Gottsched's preference for realistic dialogue in moments of great stress, can only stutter, "Eh?—what?" (V. iv). To make the happiness complete, Aurelius officially becomes Fulvia's son in place of the dead Valerius. The bright rays of a benevolent Providence warm everyone. The tenderness of Aurelius' conscience is now recognized as an ideal, not scorned as effeminacy. Trajan asks, "Has such delicacy ever been heard of in Rome?" and a representative of the citizenry answers, "No, Emperor! Such a work is worthy of a monument" (V. v).

The theme of the gentle ruler which is found first in *Darius* is more highly developed in *Aurelius*. An analysis of Trajan's exemplary government runs throughout the play and is second in importance only to the main theme of Aurelius' conscience. Trajan is a man of peace, and he has more respect for statesmen than for warriors. He tells Maximinus that he needs him more at Rome than in the field against the Parthians: "One day, and one battle can build hero-halls;/ And consign the laurel even to the lowest man:/ But no single day can produce a courtier./ He is not the work of a day; a long life builds him:/ What am I saying? Nature puts in many a century,/ Before she produces a masterpiece in this line" (II. i). Trajan believes in giving ear to the poor; in living simply; in protecting orphans; in being serious, but never angry; in being strict, but mild; in punishing vice only, and that quickly. He is that extremely rare ruler—in eighteenth-century German literature—who does not consider the business of ruling a burden: "Only let your conscience be free of any reproach;/ Then this burden will of necessity become very sweet to you./ This solace belongs alone to ruling" (III. i). His aim is to educate the Romans to good government through kindness and justice. When a mob gathers demanding revenge for Valerius' death, he bids a captain to quiet them, but not harshly: "Only combine gentleness with duty" (III. iv). The Romans are an obstinate people, ever ready to remember their lost freedom with bitterness, but "Lenience and kindness/ Will certainly constrain and shame the animal nature/ Which our masses harbor" (III. v). However, the most striking evidence of gentleness, indeed, of soft sentimentality in Trajan's rule is his decision not to punish the co-conspirators of Valerius. The second motive for his destruction of the tablet was that he did not want to know the names of these men. Maximinus tells him, "I handed you the document for this purpose,/ So that your grief should find the reason why I was comforted./ You, however, looked upon it as a judgment,/ Which had already put the death-sentence over many heads:/ And, as is your custom, you did not want to sign it./ Vengeance ought to be left only to the stern gods./ Therefore you consigned it to oblivion" (V. i). This very modern sounding sentimental humaneness stands out in glaring contrast to the cruel carelessness of Lessing's Prince Hettore Gonzaga, who would have signed a death sentence "right willingly."

The casual reader of Quistorp's *Aurelius* (providing such a person could be found nowadays) would probably consider it an absurdly inferior piece of work. Nevertheless, the modest merits that it does have can be established by a comparison with a later tragedy on the same subject, *Aurelius, oder Wettstreit der Großmuth* (1767) [20] by the Austrian playwright, Kornelius von Ayrenhoff (1733–1819). The difference is between an author of meager talent who sincerely tried to adapt his material to the Enlightened philosophy that filled his intellectual environment, and an author of slightly greater talent who was interested chiefly in writing a drama that would offer an audience as much cheap excitement as possible. The Austrian work was a product of the last, decadent period of Alexandrine tragedy. Ayrenhoff no longer understood Aurelius' tender conscience. His method of sealing Aurelius' lips was to introduce a love theme, something entirely absent in Quistorp's play. As Lessing would have said, scornfully, "Nothing . . . is graver than the anger of lovely eyes." [21] Aurelius in this later version is in love with Flavia, who is the sister of Valerius. If the truth about Valerius is told, then Flavia and her father will be banished from Rome. Aurelius' first way out of this dilemma is suicide, which Quistorp's Aurelius was too high-minded to consider for an instant. He is held back from this forcibly by his friend Susa. Aurelius is ready to admit that he killed Valerius, because he feels too desperate and bitter to conceal his deed. He tells Flavia that he did it "Because Hell and Heaven have conspired to my downfall;/ Because the hatred of the gods has chosen me for this atrocity;/ Perhaps, because their wrath begrudges me the good fortune/ Of being loved by you" (II. iii). Flavia defends the gods from Aurelius' blasphemy, but turns at once from pious thoughts to a bitter vengefulness befitting the heroine of a *Haupt- und Staatsaktion* as she swears to her brother's spirit that she regrets having pitied Aurelius for a moment: "I will rue my transgression unto my very grave;/ And consecrate my last breath to your revenge" (II. iv). For the careful analysis of Aurelius' state of mind and soul which Quistorp supplies, Ayrenhoff substitutes an intrigue of the judges who are to try the case. These judges are actually co-conspirators of the dead Valerius, and therefore they want to condemn Aurelius. The latter continues to think the worst of the gods. When Trajan is angered that Aurelius refuses to defend himself, Aurelius answers: "The gods, who hate me,/ They are compelling me to make the resolve which grieves you" (III. v). But by "compelling" he does not mean a moral judgment on the part of the gods; he means only that his situation is such that he cannot talk without endangering Flavia, and that the gods are cruel in this regard. The play revels in impieties of this kind. If Aurelius berates the gods, Flavia denigrates virtue. She deplores the fact that her father has pleaded for mercy for Aurelius: "Oh, what mortal will love virtue any more,/ If it itself misleads us to forbidden impulses?/ My father follows it—and it perverts him!" (IV. ii).

The intrigue of the false judges is successful. Trajan believes in the guilt of Aurelius and signs his death warrant, although with sorrow, because Aurelius has been his friend. This Trajan, no exception to the rule like Quistorp's, bewails the business of kingship: "Know the lauded greatness!/ Know the envied fortune of the rulers of this world!" (IV. vii). Valerius' father learns that his dead son was a traitor to Trajan and, in a further complication of the plot, tries to persuade Aurelius to save himself (and yet not make trouble for Flavia) by accusing his victim of a lesser crime than treason. Aurelius does not agree to this plan, for it still will not win him the favor of Flavia. He persists in his pessimism and tells Trajan, "How often does it not happen, that through the decree of fate/ The strictest virtue itself must suffer guiltlessly?" (V. iii). This speech is meant to excite pity, but its bald assumption that virtue often goes unrewarded is disquieting. Even though Aurelius is saved at last, his attitude throughout the play is one of bitterness and despair; and surely the sweet-natured submission of Quistorp's Aurelius was more exemplary. The written plans of the conspiracy

and the names of the conspirators, the destruction of which in
Quistorp's drama served to put the conflict out of the realm of
facts into the realm of spirit, here are used to bring about the dénouement itself. The father of Valerius brings the incriminating document to Trajan when it is obvious that nothing less than this can
save Aurelius. Of course Trajan frees Aurelius at once, and the
problem is solved—but in a rather unsubtle way, and on a low level
of human accomplishment. From the exalted *"Zärtlichkeit"* of the
first Aurelius there is a descent to the less astonishing *"Großmuth"*
of Valerius' father, who would have had to be a wicked person indeed if he had let Aurelius die when he knew that his own son deserved to be killed. In this play, too, Trajan destroys the document
with the names of the other conspirators, but only because he wants
to emulate the magnanimity of the old father. In any case, the conspirators meet their deaths, some through mob violence and others
by suicide. The happy ending clears the gods of the charge of injustice made against them by Aurelius, but only by implication,
whereas the flagrancy and frequency of the charges made would
seem to call for a more careful and explicit refutation. This second
Aurelius, with its complicated plot and love situation, bears the
stamp of the influence of inferior French tragedies. It is at once
theatrically more effective and artistically and philosophically less
impressive than Quistorp's drama. It uses the tried and true clichés
of French tragedy plots and fails to meet the special demands and
conditions put upon tragedy by the German Enlightenment.

The most exotic and colorful of the tragedies composed by Gottsched's immediate associates is the *Banise* of Friedrich Melchior
Grimm (1723–1807). Better known by his later title, Baron von
Grimm, this son of a Lutheran pastor at Regensburg was to have
a brilliant literary and social career in France between 1749 and
1792 which so far exceeded the worldly accomplishments of the
other members of the Leipzig coterie that it seems incredible he
started out humbly as one of their number.[22] *Banise*, although published in the fourth volume of the *Schaubühne* along with *Aurelius*,
was written a little earlier, in 1741,[23] while Grimm was still a student
in the Gymnasium at Regensburg. In the preface to the fourth
volume, Gottsched evidences a little embarrassment about having
accepted this play, because its plot was taken from Ziegler's Baroque
novel, *Die asiatische Banise* (1689),[24] and because there was a *Haupt-
und Staatsaktion* with the same title and subject matter. But he is
willing to brave the mockery and criticism that the name "Banise"
will arouse, for he maintains that basically there is something tragic
in the novel-plot "which is sufficiently qualified to touch even the

hardest natures." [25] In Gottsched's opinion, the young author has succeeded in producing the emotions that are peculiar to tragedy, namely, "pity and terror." [26] And, if nothing else, at least this new regular *Banise* will probably in time rid Germany of the old "irregular" *Banise*.[27] One gets the impression that Gottsched, in accepting this doubtful production, was somewhat hard-pressed to find enough original plays to fill his *Schaubühne*.

In spite of the actual historical background [28] on which the Baroque novel and consequently this drama are based, the exotic names and the totally unfamiliar old-Burmese locale give the tragedy a chilling aura of unreality. The land of Pegu, the god Karkovita, the tyrant Chaumigrem, the Rolim (a kind of priest): these names lack all connection with anything familiar and credible, although a generation brought up on Ziegler's novel [29] no doubt found them less strange than a modern reader does. The situation, which concerns the impending sacrifice of Princess Banise to the heathen god Karkovita, likewise promises to be macabre and horrible, without the human interest and old tradition that makes the comparable sacrifice of Iphigenia at Aulis more tolerable. It soon turns out, however, that the personages bearing these weird names and participating in this lurid situation are in themselves not at all strange or fantastic. The nobility of virtue, trust in Providence, calm resignation in the face of death, and, on the other hand, self-interest, tyranny, hypocrisy: these are the strengths and the weaknesses of the forces opposing each other in the play, and there is nothing exotic about them. Although love plays a large role in *Banise*, it is not "*la belle passion*" of French tragedy. The tyrant Chaumigrem loves Banise, not tenderly, but with a ferocity that demands that she either become his wife or submit to execution. Her refusal of this love is uncompromising. She is actually in love with Balazin, leader of the forces besieging Pegu, but there is not a single scene in which the two lovers exchange tender speeches. Balazin scarcely appears at all, and when he does, he is disguised as a priest. It is surely not the theme of love that sets *Banise* apart from the other tragedies in the *Schaubühne*.

What is different about *Banise*, making it seem more akin to modern cinematic melodrama than to the other tragedies, is its dependence on external circumstances for its effect. Suspense is aroused and maintained by the most unsubtle means; that is, the spectators' interest is courted by nothing more profound than the question: will the beautiful princess be saved in time from a cruel death? As in any cheap adventure story, one needs only to be told at the beginning who is "good" and who is "bad," and from then on there is no necessity of troubling oneself about character. One can just excitedly follow the actions which *must* in the end result in the vanquishment of the "bad" people. The happy ending of such a plot does not produce a feeling of inspiration (as in Quistorp's *Aurelius*) but merely a feeling of satisfaction; and an unhappy ending would be monstrous and meaningless. Grimm did make valiant efforts to put characterization into his play, and to raise some ethical questions, but these are superfluous additions because they do not genuinely affect the plot. All that really matters about Banise is that she is a beautiful princess in distress.

Grimm, however, makes his heroine a paragon of rational virtue. Her confidante Fylane reports that Banise is undergoing a spiritual conflict, the purpose of which is to learn to face death with composure: "She calls upon the gods to destroy faint-heartedness,/ And not to increase the torment of her afflicted breast./ She struggles. Her body, to be sure, grows weak from constant fainting:/ Her spirit is more and more strengthened; it knows no fatigue!" (I. ii). By the time Banise appears on the scene (not until Act Two), she is actually looking forward to death joyfully: "Welcome, dearest day, you end of my torment!/ . . . Through you I will receive a permanent good fortune,/ . . . Where virtue is not persecuted and oppressed;/ Where no tyranny stifles human feeling" (II. i). It is a bit disconcerting, when one considers that the whole plot depends on the horror of the execution and the necessity of a hairbreadth escape, to find the threatened heroine so reconciled, indeed so eager for death. It almost seems a pity that she is not going to be allowed to cross the threshold into the joyous afterlife. Such resigned composure (*Gelassenheit*), however, is to be construed as a defense against the ultimate misfortune of death rather than as a sincere desire for death. The greatest *Gelassenheit* does not preclude a tacit hope for a change of fortune that will restore one to life and happier circumstances. Moreover, this readiness to die, being regarded as the highest kind of virtue because it indicates the most perfect trust in Providence, is calculated to add the quality of touching sentiment, which must be present in the play no matter how much it might conflict with the primary effect. Accordingly, the author arranges matters so that one not only wishes for the deliverance of the princess in distress, but is also touched because she represents suffering virtue.

The evil people who are responsible for Banise's troubles interpret her composure as obstinacy and lack of sensitivity. The Rolim says to her, "No dying frightens you, for you are unfeeling" (II. ii), and Chaumigrem taunts her angrily: "Yes, do not tremble with fear—confront/ The altar with the composure which you boast of!" (II. iv). Again, the Rolim says, "She calls herself virtuous,/ But it is only obstinacy which lends her courage and strength" (II. v). This crass misunderstanding of Banise's virtue adds to her sufferings and makes her a more touching figure; at the same time, however, it illustrates the depravity of the Rolim and especially of Chaumigrem, who cannot comprehend the rational order of the universe. Far from having confidence in the gods (which produces composure), Chaumigrem calls the doctrine of their benevolence and support a delusion and sees this doctrine as a real detriment to the dignity and accomplishments of man. For even if he were victorious against the siege that Balazin has brought against Pegu, the people would not grant him adulation and fame, but would give their thanks to the god Karkovita: "No, this I do not want: I myself, I want to conquer:/ Then I, too, must alone receive the fame of the victory" (II. v). There is more petulance and irrational lack of comprehension in Chaumigrem than genuine evil dynamism (as detected in the character of Bessus in *Darius*). His nefarious desires keep meeting with frustration from the beginning. For one thing, he is having great trouble with the siege that threatens Pegu. For another, he is humiliated by his failure to overawe Banise: "Is it possible? Can I not coerce a weak woman?" (II. iv). Lastly, unlike most evil personages, who show remorse (if at all) only after their downfall, Chaumigrem is tormented from the outset by a bad conscience. He is nearly driven mad with ghostly visions of the king he slew, Xemindo, the father of Banise; and he also reveals that his ambition and striving have not brought him happiness: "All Pegu calls me great. Alas! if I had only never known/ What it is to rule. I could lead a peaceful life" (II. ix). One is almost tempted to pity this evil person because of the rudiments of a good heart still left to him. It is unlikely, however, that the author was trying to arouse any pity for Chaumigrem. In good rational fashion he was pointing out that unbridled passions and misdirected will do not bring happiness, however splendid the outward appearance of the unvirtuous person's life may be. Young Grimm was not to be the one who would allow the power of evil to exert any perverse attraction.

Conversely, the attraction of virtuousness is not compromised by the generation of doubts concerning the justice of the world-order. Banise, in all her trials, is notably clear about the reasons behind them, and this clarity shows that her trust in Providence is based on rational understanding rather than on blind faith: "I was born to pure distress, to constant torment:/ Therefore I am indeed also worthy of redemption./ The gods might perhaps have given me much good fortune,/ If they had not well seen that this would weaken virtue./ Where good fortune and prosperity bloom, there one does not find many just persons:/ And the charm of many good things soon makes virtue feeble" (III. iii). This is not pessimism, but an optimistic method of transforming troubles into benefits. Yet the testing of Banise would be incomplete if she were not brought to the very brink of despair—without crossing over into it. Her personal fate cannot force the noble-minded heroine to this extremity, but the fate of her beloved brother Xemin can, for dangers involving a loved one are always harder for a personage like Banise to bear. Xemin has been disguised as a priest in an effort to rescue Banise, but he is unmasked. He himself is of course not afraid to die; but she is horrified by his impending doom and turns to address the gods almost resentfully: "You gods! alas! how violently I struggle,/ So that my offended heart will not pronounce you guilty./ You are almost too hard on us! What crime have we committed?—/ However, you are just" (IV. v). Xemin indeed has to die, although he succeeds in killing himself before he has to submit to having his heart torn out on Chaumigrem's orders. It is possible that this act of suicide (which, in defiance of decorum, is performed on stage) is to be interpreted as a breach of rational composure (*Gelassenheit*), like the suicide of Cato, and that it absolves Providence of responsibility for the death of an innocent person. But Banise does not consider this technicality. Her brother's unmerited death is the ultimate test of her steadfast virtue just because it cannot be understood. If Xemin were the main character, then of course his death would call the philosophical stand of the play into question; but he is of minor importance, and his fate is to be considered only in connection with Banise's own state of mind.

Banise sits for a while with her face covered—the sign of deepest grief—and ponders the justice of the situation. She must admit that Xemin's fate does *look* like an open contradiction of the doctrine that the gods reward virtue. She questions the gods in amazement: "Do you so openly and freely/ Offend the impulse of virtue! Alas, gods! What crime/ Compels you to take vengeance so cruelly by means of so much torment./ How much farther do you intend to go? Who is unjust here,/ You, or Chaumigrem? How miserable, how poor/ The reward of virtue is, after all!" (IV. vi). At this point she can either make the decision that the doctrine of virtue is false and conclude like Chaumigrem that everything said about the gods is a lie; or she can loyally renew her trust and submit sweetly to the will of Providence and to her own reason. The possibilities of tragedy which lay in the first choice were never explored at this time. If Banise had made the first decision, this would have meant that the gods had made their testing of her altogether too rigorous, and the objective of their testing would not have been benevolent, but hostile and destructive. Such a thing would have been a base betrayal of the Enlightened philosophy. Consequently it is no surprise to find Banise making the second decision and dismissing her grievous doubts as "erring thoughts." Before long the gods will reveal to her their true (and good) purpose behind this seeming victory for the forces of evil: "Shall you teach me ere long the true purpose,/ Why deception and fury here oppress virtue?/ Why vice is elevated and esteemed?" (IV. vi). This "ere long" means the afterlife, for she is not so bold as to demand full understanding in this life. The prospect of acquiring this knowledge is an added reason for accepting death with equanimity.

At the end of the fourth act, however, Banise still makes an attempt to evade death by fleeing with Abaxar, a colonel of the army who has remained faithful to her. The flight is Abaxar's plan, not Banise's, and she agrees to it with reluctance, for she believes it is quite useless. That she attempts flight at all is proof of her great scrupulousness, for, as she says to Chaumigrem after being recaptured, "Flight was the only thing left for me to try./ I did it; but in vain. Now I die with composure" (V. ii). Without the attempt at flight she could not have been absolutely sure that her acceptance of death was not a suicidal tendency instead of God-pleasing rational composure. Chaumigrem, operating on a wholly irrational and selfish principle, regards both her flight and her composure as crimes: "Ha! vile vicious beast! you deck out/ The coarsest misdeeds with virtues" (V. ii). It will be observed that the language of this drama is not free of vulgarities reminiscent of the *Haupt- und Staatsaktionen*.

The elaborate and scenically impressive ending of *Banise* is unique among the tragedies printed in the *Schaubühne* and is at variance with the sober spirit that presides over this collection. The back part of the stage suddenly opens up to reveal a fantastic, barbaric spectacle. There is an idol representing Karkovita (whose relationship to the "gods" is never clarified), a sacrificial stone, a rope and a knife, and there are heathen priests bowing before the idol or swinging incense pots. The opera, pronounced dead by Gottsched,[30] seems to have come back to life, of all places, in his own *Schaubühne!* There is even a musical accompaniment, "a brief funeral march." Then Banise is ushered in by the soldiers. She is robed in white and wears a wreath on her brow. Chaumigrem turns his face away and covers it, as though Banise were Iphigenia and he were Agamemnon. In all of this, it should be noted, there is no trespass against the letter of Gottsched's laws. There is no breach with verisimilitude, and the suddenly widened stage is a gentle compromise with the Unity of Place, not a disregarding of that rule. Still, the color, the properties, the costumes, the large number of persons on stage, the ritualistic actions are things that speak to the senses rather than to the understanding or to the heart, and they are not related to any moral purpose. They open the door to a kind of theatrical pleasure that Gottsched had done everything to put behind lock and bolt.

Banise's formal speech of farewell, however, turns attention back to the word. It is a long recapitulation of the ethical implications of the situation and a final sermon in praise of virtue, a reminder that the "happiness" of vicious persons consists only of apparent good and is not equal even to the misfortune suffered by virtuous people. Banise's words, like her white costume, recall the close of Schiller's *Maria Stuart*. Like Mary, she feels that her death is liberation: "Step forward, freed spirit, this sacrificial stone/ Makes you completely free: now you know no more coercion" (V. ix). And at the end she says, "Farewell! nothing holds me back," which is similar to Mary's "Farewell!—Now I have nothing more on earth!"

Notwithstanding these exemplary words, Banise is saved from the knife by her lover Balazin, who, casting off his priestly disguise, puts Chaumigrem to death in the nick of time. As often in eighteenth-century plays, once the proper spiritual attitude toward misfortune has been attained, then the misfortune is suddenly removed and a material benefit is bestowed on the tested person. Banise is rescued and Pegu is restored to its rightful ruler. Thus it is proved that happiness is also possible on earth. Despite the heroine's fine philosophy, the melodramatic plot had urged the spectators all along to await a happy ending. Besides, the audiences of the time were often loath to accept a death unless there was a definite error in the actions of the hero which clearly deserved punishment. As late as 1776 the troupe-director Friedrich Ludwig Schröder had to provide *Romeo and Juliet*, *Othello*, and *Lear* with happy endings,[31] presumably because the chief characters in these plays—at any rate, the heroines—were guiltless. It is reported that Schröder's first, unaltered Shakespeare productions caused tumult and furious outrage among the spectators, along with fainting, convulsive weeping, and even premature labor in pregnant women.[32]

The only tragedy with a Moslem–Near Eastern setting among the original works in the *Schaubühne* (a very popular setting thereafter) is *Mahommed IV* by Ephraim Benjamin Krüger (c. 1724–1789), which was written in 1744 and appeared the same year in the fifth volume of the collection. Krüger, in later life a physician in Danzig,[33] was another of Gottsched's protégés while studying in Leipzig and Wittenberg, and his literary activities were confined to that early period of his life.[34] The young Danzig author's drama achieved a certain dubious kind of fame, for otherwise it would scarcely have prompted the mocking jingle, "A hanging, if it is well put on,/ Touches more than Krüger's *Mahommed* can." [35] The sharp jibe indicates that Krüger had failed to arouse sympathy for the personage chiefly affected by the end-catastrophe; that is, the ambitious woman who is punished in the end so richly deserves her fate that she is no more worthy of pity than any common criminal who is executed. For an ordinary villain this lack of sympathy would have been the normal expectation, but in this case the wicked personage is, in many respects, the principal character of the drama. Krüger had chosen a subject for his tragedy which exceeded his modest talents. He was attracted to the story of Mahommed IV evidently because he equated tragedy with sensationalism, and what could be more sensational than an old grandmother who plots against her grandson's life and throne, only to be executed at the end by his order? It was a difficult task, however, to turn this incredible story into a believable drama with characters capable of enlisting the sympathy of an audience. In his introduction, Gottsched asserted that Krüger had "followed history very exactly," [36] but either his source was not a very trustworthy one, or else "the few small circumstances . . . which he had to invent to accommodate to the theatrical rules" [37] were neither few nor small.

The kind of tragedy which featured a villain of fascinating, demoniacal evil, although heralded by Pitschel's *Darius*, had not yet made its appearance. The problem of the grandmother's character might have been solved by making her the heroine of such a tragedy, but this was not Krüger's way. He elected to relate his material principally to the question of patriotism versus blood relationship, as in Behrmann's *Timoleon*. Thus the main interest of Krüger's drama is not directed to the grandmother's unexampled wickedness but to Mahommed's soul conflict in the decision to have her executed. While this sounds like a legitimate way to handle the material, it proved to be inadequate because the conflict is lost in a maze of complicated off-stage intrigues, and, still worse, the grandmother changes her character by repenting of her misdeeds. The effect of this unexpected change is to remove the emphasis from the grandson's conflict to the grandmother's change of heart and final gallantry. One no longer knows who the hero is supposed to be or whom one should pity. The tragic emotions do not thrive in an atmosphere of such confusion.

When she first appears, Kiosem, the ambitious beldame, seems to be the ruthless embodiment of evil, equal to a Richard III. Having already, years earlier, put her own son Ibrahim to death, she does not scruple about killing her grandson Mahommed now too, if that will put her on the Turkish throne: "Let him die! if only I see us thereby come to power!" (I. i). The chief obstacle to her plan is the Grand Vizier Selim, who possesses the kind of moral nobility (*Großmuth*) which neither gifts, flattery, nor threats can affect. Among her co-conspirators, one is a eunuch who prefers to use deceit and cunning, and another is a militant Janissary, Bektas, who boasts to Kiosem that he has the good qualities of bravery and forthrightness: "A noble masculine heart combines courage and strength:/ You, however, love deceit, the trait of women" (I. ii). Nevertheless, Bektas himself is engaged in deceiving old Kiosem. Although not of royal blood, he secretly wants the throne for himself, and indeed, his ambition is a kind of disease of the passions which allows no room for rational thought: "I wish death for myself, if I cannot raise myself,/ And if I cannot, crowned, rule over a nation" (I. iii). Symptomatic of his uncontrolled passions is his love for Roxellane, the mother of Mahommed, a love which is presumptuous because of their different stations in life. He is what was called in the tragic parlance of that day a "tiger," that is, a person whose wicked passions are immune both to the control of reason and to the appeal of virtue.

It is part of the conspirators' plot to make Roxellane and Mahommed doubt the loyalty of their virtuous Grand Vizier Selim. But Selim has a stout defender in his confidant Murat, who vouches for his sincerity: "A hero does not dissemble, in him word and deeds/ Are always one and the same" (II. iii). Roxellane bewails the fact that not everyone is so honest and faithful as Selim, but he comforts her with the usual assurances about virtue's reward: "Virtue can never succumb to misfortune;/ And even though it is oppressed it must nevertheless conquer./ Him it crowns, whom it has found faithful and great" (II. v). When further proofs of the conspirators' machinations come to light, Roxellane challenges Providence (under the name of the Prophet) to keep its promises to good people; "Will you not restrain high treason with your power?/ Do you still have patience with such monsters?/ Oh, help, if you are just, oh, do protect my child!" (II. vi). This prayer, or rather, challenge, appears to receive an immediate answer in the news that

Kiosem has been taken captive; but Roxellane and Selim are still deeply concerned about Bektas, who can set the horde of Janissaries against them. For all her dislike of duplicity, Roxellane resolves to lure Bektas into their power by writing a letter to him which intimates that she returns his love. In this move of the plot the author regresses to the morally questionable standpoint of Ludwig's *Ulysses*. The "good" Selim advises the crafty maneuver, the "good" Roxellane accepts it without reluctance, and Heaven is asked to grant success to the deception! The spirit of craftiness, however, does not dominate this play as it does *Ulysses*.

The young ruler and titular hero does not actually appear on stage until the third act, and with his entrance commences the first dramatic conflict that goes deeper than mere surface action. Mahommed is characterized as a gentle prince who wins the loyalty of his subjects through kindness. One of his retainers says, "Your gentle rule makes all hearts yours;/ Therefore your great praise will increase even among posterity./ Where sweet mercy rules, there one serves with pleasure,/ And dies for one's lord" (III. i). In this respect Mahommed resembles Darius and Trajan, but he is not kind to the point of weakness. When he hears that a man he has trusted is one of the conspirators, he grows angry and orders the man's death: "Is that the reward of kindness? Very well! you shall feel,/ My wrath can be enkindled to avenge myself./ Go, Murat, bring me the head of my false friend" (III. i). Where his grandmother Kiosem is concerned, however, Mahommed finds it impossible to take the revenge to which he is entitled. The voice of natural affection drowns out the sterner tones of pure reason, whereas in Behrmann's *Timoleon* it was the other way round. However much Selim may emphasize the fact that the welfare of the state is to be placed above family feelings, Mahommed continues to regard filial piety as an unbreakable law and an elementary rule of virtue. Virtue here seems to depend more on an irrational feeling than on rational choice and decision—an indication that sentimentalism had begun to temper the rationalism of the 1740's. "A child must stand in fear of his parents out of love and respect,/ Even if they hate him. This is demanded by Nature:/ And whoever follows this impulse, follows the path of virtue also./ You, Selim, have yourself led me on this way:/ Since my desire does not conflict with virtue,/ Why do you then reject my loyal tenderness?" (III. iv). At most he will agree to banishing her from his sight forever. Nevertheless, he finally says, with the greatest hesitancy, that if the council or "Divan" sentences her to death he will not countermand their decision.

Rather unexpectedly, Kiosem finds an ally in Roxellane, and another in the high priest or Mufti. The latter is a staunch believer in mercy: "Mercy often is more effective than anger and law and sternness" (IV. i). He denies that revenge is ever justified: "Revenge, which inflames our spirit, is good for nothing./ Virtue hates it. Its impulse is an unjust one;/ Because it weakens the impulse towards good in our breast" (IV. v). Obviously the Mufti considers the heart as co-equal with, if not superior to the reason as the originator of virtuous actions. Moreover, he powerfully defends the principle, which is surely more sentimental than rational, that kindliness and mercy exert an irresistible influence on the most unregenerate persons: "No one who has chosen this method has ever regretted it./ The cruelest barbarian is conquered by tenderness./ The overly severe law tends to become unjust./ Gentleness is not encumbered with cruelty:/ Therefore one should choose clemency" (IV. v). Roxellane, who gratefully remembers that Kiosem once did her a good turn, joins in these pleas. When one considers the early date of this play, one must accord its author the distinction of being one of the pioneers of sensibility (*Empfindsamkeit*), or at least of that phase of sensibility that stressed the seductive attraction of mild, gentle virtue.

Selim, on the other hand, although his motives are unquestionably honorable, belongs to an older and less sentimental school of thought. Being rigorously rational, he believes that vice is kept in its place by merited punishment, just as virtue is promoted by deserved reward. While not unaware of the attraction of virtue (at one point he asks Bektas, "What? Tiger, are you not touched by the emperor's virtue?" [I. iv]), he does not share the opinion that gentle treatment will convert a criminal from vice to virtue: "Wickedness is only the more strengthened by such clemency,/ And the number of your enemies increases without your knowing it. . . . He who does not punish criminals is at the end altogether despised:/ The prince who does not make himself feared is mocked at./ Behold, Sire, that is how damaging the effect of your love is./ It robs you of your throne; therefore resist the impulse!" (IV. v). His attitude is shown still more clearly when he reprimands Mahommed for shedding tears over the fate of Kiosem. His extreme rationalism rebels against this external token of a badly disciplined heart: "A wise man suppresses even the strongest emotion./ Monarch, what shall I say about your tears?/ Nobility of mind, indeed, cannot tolerate a moist eye" (IV. vi). But the author, in spite of his evident admiration for Selim, is of the opinion that rationalism can go too far. The human heart cannot and should not be ruthlessly put down.

Therefore he has Mahommed answer, "It [nobility of mind] demands far too much. Is one not to be human?/ Friend, he is worthy of punishment who does not feel the greatest pain/ In his breast at the downfall of his mother" (IV. vi).

At this juncture Krüger has set up an interesting and important problem. Two philosophical attitudes, an older and a newer, are here placed in juxtaposition, and although the superficial dramatic suspense is directed toward the fate of Kiosem, a more refined suspense is aroused in connection with the philosophical problem. The appearance of Kiosem before her grandson-judge brings the situation to a head. She is the test case on which the two theories will be tried. She has already heard about her condemnation, and this severity (Selim's method) has not succeeded in making a better person of her. She proudly refuses to repent of her deeds: "I should make excuses? No./ Perfidy has caused my downfall. I have been tricked" (IV. vii). When Mahommed wavers, Selim reminds him, "Now you have no choice but to avenge the wrongdoing:/ Whoever is an emperor cannot evade this duty" (IV. vii). Kiosem in her way is just as rigidly disciplined and controlled as Selim. She, too, speaks of "nobility of mind" (*Großmuth*) in terms of a refusal to give in to emotions, and thinks she possesses this quality: "No noble spirit can ever altogether forget nobility of mind,/ And fear is never able to squeeze tears from him./ Only he who has done something evil begs and pleads;/ And I am free of that; therefore my courage never falters" (IV. viii). Is the author, as a herald of sensibility, trying to state that the quality of noble-mindedness has been overrated and overemphasized? That it lends itself with equal ease to characters ruled by evil passions and to characters ruled by cold rationalism? That noble-mindedness demands the same thing of both virtuous and nonvirtuous persons, namely the suppression of human feelings? That a better course of action would be to give less emphasis to noble-mindedness, and to promote cultivation of the good heart, which resides somewhere in even the worst of men and whose voice always speaks for virtue? The balance of the drama seems to bear out this impression.

In the case of Bektas, the author shows how noble-mindedness in an evil man can lead to inevitable destruction without hope of salvation. On account of his overweening pride he is easily tricked by Roxellane's letter into returning to the palace, and when the guards capture him his defiance only increases: "Nevertheless death will relieve me from this disgrace,/ So that I do not have to go on living in a realm/ Where a despicable slave has the highest sovereignty;/ And where one senses that the master has a slavish heart"

(V. iii). Like Bessus in Pitschel's *Darius*, Bektas rises to a pitch of evilness which is quite dynamic and impressive. Yet he retains enough conventional rationalism in his make-up so that he pins the blame for his downfall on a "passion"—his love for Roxellane: "Cursed passion! you have caused my fall" (V. iv). The sight of a captive Bektas drives the first wedge into Kiosem's armor of "noble-mindedness." It was his advice that led her to plot against the life of her grandson, but now he proves to have been a deceiver who wanted the throne for himself. However, it is the virtuous sympathy of Roxellane which really succeeds in awakening the heart of Kiosem. Roxellane's pleas have finally overcome Selim's influence over Mahommed, and he has agreed to free her. Unfortunately, the populace is insisting on her death, and Mahommed is forced to reverse his decision, or she would only become the victim of mob violence. This bad news affects Roxellane so much that she swears, absurdly enough, to avenge the death of her mother-in-law. The result of Roxellane's sentimentality is that now Kiosem suddenly becomes a good person. The point has been proved by demonstration: virtuous mercy and gentleness can accomplish what severe justice is unable to do.

The last scene of the play consists of a long monologue by the newly regenerate Kiosem in which she describes how Roxellane's virtue has affected her: "O great integrity! O virtue without parellel!/ Since you show me love and mercy, when I have shown you hate./ Your rare impulse of virtue excites my conscience!" She repents completely of all her sins: "Cursed be all my actions! Cursed be my undertaking!/ Cursed be this impulse which in my vain senses/ Was planted by the lust to rule!" However, she does not hope to escape the just punishment for her crime by her repentance: "I am too vicious, I must be punished./ . . . the very greatest torment/ Is scarcely sufficient for me." Without defiance and without whimpering, she can now practice a "noble-mindedness' based on the proper, passive acceptance of the comprehended, just will of God: "Kiosem, compose yourself, do not forsake noble-mindedness,/ Await the death which the Divan pronounces over you,/ With altogether patient mind" (V. vii). As the curtain falls, the hangmen come in and throw a noose around her neck; but she dies a better person than she has lived, thanks to the gentle power of sentiment. Krüger's tragedy not only strengthens faith in Providence, but shows also that mercy occupies an important place in the rational world-order.

Perhaps the weakest of the original tragedies in the *Schaubühne* is the *Panthea* of Luise Adelgunde Victorie Gottsched (née Kulmus), printed in the fifth volume the same year in which it was written (1744). Madame Gottsched was the first authoress to publish a tragedy in German,[38] but it can hardly be said that this work goes very far to prove that women have equal aptitude for the genre with men. Although Madame Gottsched had a remarkable flair for the writing of comedy, in tragedy she grew extremely wooden and stilted. Her husband, to be sure, found reasons for praising *Panthea* very highly.[39] He proudly assured the reading public that this tragedy was a literal dramatization of an episode in the *Cyropaedia* of Xenophon: "All the circumstances and personages of this tragedy are so exactly reproduced from this historian that, except for a few servants and the death of Araspes, not the slightest thing has been invented. . . . The characters of Cyrus, as well as of Panthea and Abradates, likewise correspond perfectly to history; indeed many speeches of the first-mentioned are even practically translated from Xenophon." [40] This assertion, which was calculated to forestall any possible criticism of the incredible virtuousness of the sympathetic characters in the play, is, however, not very accurate. Madame Gottsched actually allowed her imagination free play with the story of Panthea as told in the *Cyropaedia*.[41] In the second place, Gottsched hailed his wife's work for introducing a proper and suitable kind of love motif into German tragedy, that is, lawful conjugal love. He omitted to mention that Johann Elias Schlegel had already done this, albeit with less concentration, in his *Herrmann*. Gottsched was unalterably opposed, as were most German critics and authors, to the trite, frivolous eroticism of French tragedy; but his wife had chosen to dramatize a love story. Accordingly he stated in his introduction to *Panthea* that the depiction of virtuous married love might well be a profitable endeavor for German tragic poets, who could look to *Panthea* for a successful start in this direction: "Here, too, there is love . . . indeed, even a violent, ardent love: but it is at the same time a virtuous and chaste love, which conforms to the laws and to religion itself." [42] More conscientiously than anyone else, Madame Gottsched followed the procedure outlined in the *Versuch einer critischen Dichtkunst* of selecting a specific moral principle to illustrate through the medium of tragedy. Possibly for very good reasons of her own she decided to present the virtue of marital fidelity. Certainly, in her devotion and obedience to her taskmaster spouse, she was herself a latter-day Panthea.

The perfectly virtuous figure of Cyrus dominates this play almost as much as does the titular heroine. As a model ruler, serene and untouched in his complacent virtue, Cyrus anticipates by two years his closest counterpart in German tragedy, the titular hero of Schlegel's *Canut* (1746). In his *Gedanken zur Aufnahme des dänischen Theaters* Schlegel derisively quoted several banal moral "sentences" from *Panthea*, without indicating the drama by name;[43] nevertheless his own hero Canut seems to owe something to Madame Gottsched's Cyrus. According to the Persian general Hystaspes, all of Asia hopes Cyrus will defeat Croesus in the coming battle, because "It is tired of princes who, full of base delight,/ Have known nothing of the art of ruling except riotous living:/ Therefore it must now long for you as a prince/ Who through his example can accustom it to virtue" (I. i). Cyrus soon demonstrates how virtuous he is by giving orders that a captive queen, Panthea, be returned to her husband Abradates, now an ally of the Persians. He gives this order although strongly attracted to her himself, for, as Hystaspes says, "She is, to be sure, divinely beautiful,/ Yet her external charms are less than her inner virtue;/ In wisdom she is almost comparable to Cyrus himself" (I. i). But she is married, and Cyrus is also married. Hystaspes suggests that Abradates could be assigned a battle position where he would surely be killed, and then Panthea would be free. This vicious plan might appeal to a king like David, but Cyrus is far more virtuous than any mere Old Testament figure. He calls Hystaspes a villain and avers, "I tremble, even to have heard such a crime," and also warns, "But this I tell you, Hystaspes, mark it well!/ That one is to speak to me of nothing but virtue" (I. i). Panthea thanks Cyrus for returning her to her husband, and includes a remark surely directed against eighteenth-century European rulers: "How few princes there are on earth like you,/ Who protect marriages instead of disturbing them!" (I. vi). She is grateful that Cyrus has also shielded her from the advances of one of his officers, Araspes, and to this the king answers, "Virtue bade me do that. In every deed it is/ My sole aim" (I. vi). He grants her leave to speak about love with her newly restored husband, even though Abradates is a manly warrior without frivolous notions (as love might well appear to be): "Now speak about your love;/ It does not disgrace any hero, if virtue and understanding/ Are the basis of it" (I. vi). Panthea is confident that no harm will come to Abradates in the battle against Croesus, because God protects the virtuous: "And since Heaven's arm never forsakes virtue;/ Therefore in all other matters it will certainly/ Watch for Abradates' welfare and for his victory./ I have trusted the high protection of the gods all my life" (I. vii). For the same reasons, Hystaspes is sure that Cyrus will conquer Croesus: ". . . he is a son of virtue;/ And such are always protected by Heaven's high arm" (II. i).

Trouble starts, however, when Araspes, the rejected lover, determines to possess Panthea in spite of Abradates. Evil as he is, Araspes is enough of a rationalist (like Bektas in *Mahommed IV*) to be disdainful of blind impulses, as opposed to rational decisions, and it is as the former that he characterizes Panthea's affection for Abradates: "The impulse of blind love, which she consecrates to her spouse,/ Shuts up her breast with insensitivity" (II. i). It is interesting to note that in this instance the authoress equates or harmonizes sensitivity of heart with *virtuous* emotion guided by reason, while blind emotions unguided by reason result in lack of sensitivity. Of course, Araspes is quite wrong in supposing Panthea's love to be irrational—his own love is the irrational one; but nevertheless his words illuminate the process by which virtuous sentiment could be distinguished at that time from unvirtuous passion. Sensitivity of heart (*Empfindlichkeit*) was associated with a rational attitude, and conversely, vicious, blind emotion was associated with an irrational attitude. Thus the new sentimentality was able to slip in and assert a place for itself beside strict rationalism.

Cyrus offers Araspes a most eligible bride in the person of a maiden named Nikothris, but Araspes still wants Panthea. His motto is, ". . . to love freely, or to die" (II. v). He, who is motivated by wicked passion, now wins an accomplice motivated by equally wicked jealousy. This is Hystaspes, who is the first figure in eighteenth-century tragedy (in German) to be jealous of another person's *virtue*. Abradates is the object of this peculiar jealousy: "They esteem him far too highly, since that began, I have been hostile to him," and "The uncommon merit/ Which Cyrus sees in him has offended me too much./ It seems that no one thinks about older servants here anymore" (II. v). While this sounds very much like ordinary jealousy between the old and the new favorites of a ruler, and therefore not worthy of special attention, the point to be kept in mind is that Abradates has found favor because of his virtue, and Hystaspes has lost some favor *only* because he has shown a lack of virtue. Hystaspes is jealous because his character is not so virtuous as Abradates', and he has no reason to accuse Cyrus of unfair favoritism. The jealousy exhibited by vice was to become a popular theme in the next decade, and the jealous person's project could even become the spiritual destruction of his rival. Here, however, Hystaspes and Araspes are satisfied with arranging only Abradates' physical death in battle.

The authoress is tireless in pointing out the good qualities and rational thoughts of Cyrus, however little these may contribute to the progress of her plot. She makes it clear that Cyrus considers good or bad fortune less important than steadfastness of mind. It is reported that he has said, "He is the greatest hero, whether victorious or conquered,/ Who can bear what destiny arranges with nobility of mind" (III. i). The stoicism of this remark is apparent. More typical of eighteenth-century humanitarian thought is another reported statement: "In the worst conflict remember that you are fighting with human beings,/ Therefore do not let the humanity in yourselves be smothered" (III. i). Cyrus and his men are fighting for a just cause in a just manner: "I see with much delight/ A courageous heart in every Persian's breast;/ Which strives for honor more than it lusts for murder,/ Which fights for the sake of the right, and does not madly slaughter men" (III. ii). These are sentiments similar to those of Lessing's Major von Tellheim when he reprimands Werner for thinking like a butcher. Also more appropriate to the period are Cyrus' words concerning submission to God: "If now the Persian army is to experience its first disgrace;/ (Ah, Mithra, fend this off!), then it is the decision of Heaven,/ Which one must follow with respect, hard as it is" (III. iv).

It may be that Madame Gottsched wished to show that a legitimate marital love can equal in intensity the illicit love of a heroine like Schlegel's Dido. This may be the explanation for Panthea's ranting and raving, which otherwise seems to be out of place in the conduct of so rational a person. When Abradates sets off for battle, she upbraids him in a manner that would be understandable in a faithlessly forsaken Dido but seems merely witless in Panthea, especially since she has previously shown no opposition whatever to Abradates' participation in the war: "Alas! my afflicted heart does not hope for your return!/ Cruel one! does my torment no longer touch you at all?/ And do you only hasten from me, in order to know in the battle/ That I, from grief over you, must end my life?" (III. vi). To be sure, it was a commonplace of French tragedy that females would cast the word "cruel!" into the teeth of their lovers, using this expression as some sort of inverse means of showing the depth of their love. So Panthea also is trying to impress the audience with her affection for Abradates, which is supposed to be blotting out her better judgment, at least momentarily. Indeed, she goes so far as to start running into the fray after her husband, certainly a transgression against rational composure: "Whoever no longer knows what to do, and no longer can help,/ Let *him* exercise patience, that indolent excuse" (III. vii). When dissuaded from this plan, she laments that there is such a thing as love, and advises Nikothris to avoid it: "Defend your breast from all tenderness:/ Even when it is lawful, it bears nothing but sorrow" (IV. i).

Presumably none of these remarks are to be taken at face value. Their purpose is only to prove the depth of Panthea's feelings, and to arouse pity for her. She, however, has no pity for Araspes, who is tortured by his illicit passion for her. To him she speaks like Schlegel's heroine Thusnelda, saying, "My heart can have no pity for craven cowards:/ Go, fight, die in the battle! then I will lament for you" (IV. ii).

The news of Abradates' death brings great sorrow to both Panthea and Cyrus. The latter feels so strongly about it that he twice reproaches the gods for permitting it, and twice scuttles meekly away from his own boldness: "Ah, Mithra! have you not watched over Abradates?/ . . . Do you command gratitude, and punish the signs thereof?/ . . . Pardon! if my grief merits punishments because of these questions" (V. i) and: "O Heaven! were you not the author of this marriage?/ How can your grace be associated with so much bitter woe?/ . . . You, who never proclaim the reason for your actions,/ You gods! do not grow angry if my doubts are sinful" (V. iii). Panthea's grief drives her still farther away from passivity and trust in Providence. She does not stop to complain about the unsearchable decisions of the gods, but very actively states that she can help herself: "Yet, why should my grief accuse the decree of the gods,/ Since, if I am steadfast, I can help myself?" (IV. vii). Then, in the fifth act, she goes off the stage and commits suicide, as do three of her faithful slaves.

If Panthea's act were deplored as unvirtuous by the other characters, then one could say that Madame Gottsched had presented a heroine whose tragic fault was that her love was stronger than her ethical convictions. She would be a counterpart to Cato, whose love of freedom was so strong that it became a fault and drove him to suicide. But nothing of the sort. Nikothris comes in with a report of the suicide and says, "Oh, if I knew of an equal model of virtue!" (V. iv). The authoress evidently sees no fault in her heroine, makes no effort to set Providence in a better light, and lets suicide stand as a virtuous act. The only poetic justice at the end is that the guilty Araspes rues his crime and stabs himself. But even this satisfaction is weakened by the fact that the equally guilty Hystaspes escapes punishment completely. The authoress has written in many a speech about virtue and has injected an astonishing number of moral sentiments; but it does appear to have been beyond her powers to adapt an ancient story in such a way as to make it support the doctrine of rational optimism. She could take comfort later, however, in a remarkable academic lecture presented by her husband in 1751 on the question, "Must one, in theatrical poems, always present virtue as rewarded, and vice as punished?" Gottsched's noteworthy conclusion was that life itself does not always show forth the immediate results of vicious and virtuous behavior, and that a tragedy, which is limited by the Unity of Time to a brief period, cannot always indicate the ultimate rewards and punishments that will eventually come: "Virtues and vices are, to be sure, the seed of good fortune and misfortune of men; which however are harvested therefrom only after the passage of some time." [44] Nevertheless, he felt sure that the misfortune and death of good personages would not inspire pessimism, for, as in the case of Socrates: ". . . there is no one present who would not prefer to die innocently and noble-mindedly with him than to live in shame and disgrace with his unjust judges. So great, so invincible is the power of virtue! Even in misfortune, even in misery and death it wins approval and esteem for itself. But I am not putting it strongly enough! Very often misfortune itself has won for virtue far more adherents than good fortune has: just as, on the other hand, vice often becomes only the more hideous in men's eyes, the more a blind fortune heaps all temporal advantages upon it." [45] The opinions expressed in this lecture indicate a distinct change in Gottsched's tragic viewpoint and they give sanction to the martyr tragedy.

When Gottsched tried his own hand again at the composition of tragedy, he apparently already had these ideas of 1751 in mind. In addition, his attitude toward the role of history in tragedy had perceptibly changed since 1730. Now, instead of granting the tragic poet virtual freedom in the handling of historical facts (as in the *Versuch einer critischen Dichtkunst*), he makes a great point of emphasizing the historical accuracy of the events shown in his two new dramas. To the one, entitled *Die parisische Bluthochzeit König Heinrichs von Navarra*, he appended numerous quotations from his source work, an eyewitness account of the St. Bartholomew Massacre by Jacques Auguste de Thou,[46] "so that no one to whom the story itself might not be well known might think that the poet had put a much worse light on the affair than is warranted by the facts themselves." [47] He stated also, "Moreover, time and place and the characters of the persons coincide with truth and history. Nothing in it is invented, except that the old Admiral Coligny has himself brought to the king's court: while history says, rather, that the king, as well as Queen Catherine, visited him in his house with a large retinue. The rules of the theater prevented the retention of this circumstance." [48] In the introduction to the other tragedy, *Agis, König zu Sparta*, he asserted that everything had been taken literally from Plutarch's *Lives:* "Not a single personage is invented, not an event, not a character formed otherwise than he described it. Only the time has been shortened according to the rules of the theater, and that left out which could not be brought into the narrow space of a tragedy." [49]

The significance of this changed attitude toward history is, of course, to be found mainly in the relationship of tragedy to moral philosophy. No longer is Gottsched constrained to alter a particular historical event in the interest of promulgating moral-philosophical tenets. His choice of subject can now be guided solely by the dramatic or frightful qualities of an event, which will be reproduced almost exactly as it took place, regardless of whether the outcome supports the position of rational optimism or not. It is enough if violent emotions are aroused in the spectators, and they will be edified simply by observing the terrible lengths to which vice can go.[50] The impression made by the uniqueness or horror of the events depicted is heightened by the author's assurances that this is the way they really happened; therefore history is being enlisted to aid in producing terror, pity, and admiration. In adopting this somewhat dangerous procedure, Gottsched was turning his back on the contemporary tendency (still strongly defended by Lessing) to present an ideal world in tragedy, with pat answers and assurances for the audience's ever-present doubts. If he had been a more gifted poet, one might say that his insistence on historical factuality meant the beginning of a sterner, more awesomely impressive, realistic, and evocative kind of German tragedy. But Gottsched was a poet only by virtue of industry, as even his apologist Eugen Reichel admits.[51] Consequently, his new attitude, on the one hand, only provided a sanction for the martyr tragedy, in which a perfectly good hero does not receive virtue's reward on earth. On the other hand, it opened the way for an author like Christian Felix Weisse, who combed the history books for tales of terror and horror and made moral philosophy a secondary matter.

Die parisische Bluthochzeit, written in 1744 [52] and published the next year in the sixth and last volume of the *Schaubühne,* is glaringly at variance with the prevailing tragedy type of that day. With complete disregard for the preservation of optimism, it places the spectator directly into the lurid atmosphere of the St. Bartholomew Massacre, one of the horrors of history least calculated to inspire confidence in a benevolent Providence or in the reward of virtue. Those in the play who suffer, suffer innocently while the wicked prosper. Nor is the suffering of the virtuous conspicuously minimized by the prospect of a heavenly reward, for Gottsched does not dwell on this at all. Reichel termed this play the first "religious-political" tragedy in German and saw allusions in it to conditions in eighteenth-century Saxony.[53] One of the prominent causes promoted by the Enlightenment in all of western Europe was the prevention of religious wars and bloodthirsty fanaticism, and it is probable that Gottsched was interested in serving this particular progressive cause. Certainly the *Bluthochzeit* constitutes a strong protest against the irrational use of religion as an excuse for cruelty and bloodshed. But Gottsched declined (or was unable) to combine this protest with the comforting reassurance that there is after all a benevolent Providence regulating human affairs. The accomplishment of this task was left to Lessing and his *Nathan*.

The historical material with which Gottsched worked was too large and complicated for him and for the "rules" by which he abided. There were too many characters to be assimilated, so that not one of them succeeds in becoming really central. The manifold political issues involved are only sketchily indicated, and the ending is reached before any genuine climax is achieved. What characterization exists is based, as usual, on the degree of rationality possessed by an individual. Queen Catherine of Medici is the chief villainess simply because she has the most confused concept of moral virtue and mistakes the evil wishes of her heart for morally justified purposes. She is not, like later villains, a conscious adversary of God and virtue. Her faulty reasoning is remarkably demonstrated when she justifies the plan of a general massacre of the Huguenots on the grounds that God has shown He wills it by having frustrated their recent attempt to assassinate only the Huguenot leader, Coligny: ". . . because God did not permit/ That this brood be robbed of its head by a secret bullet:/ Therefore we are without guilt if our avenging sword/ Now turns upon all the members, instead of the head" (I. ii). Her son, Charles IX, is a person of strangely unstable rationality. At one time he opens his mind to the clear voice of reason and virtue, and at another he is completely deaf to it and acts by the dictates of the lowest animal desires. His swaying from unreason to reason and back again provides some of the drama's main action.

When all preparations for the massacre have been made, Charles suddenly has doubts about it: "Who, indeed, has ever heard of such a thing, that a king's power/ Has miserably killed the citizens of his state?/ Is that being a father, is that loving one's children?/ Tyrants, to be sure, have often annihilated nations:/ But good princes have not" (IV. i). That this is not mere caprice on his part is shown by his statement, "I have now given ear to reason" (IV. ii). In support of his decision he brings forward practical considerations which recall to mind the arguments used by Schiller's Marquis Posa [54]: "Fear counsels thousands to undertake quick flight,/ . . . In brief, the flower of France will be the booty of foreigners./ For artists, whom we here torment for the sake of religion,/ Will carry their wit and industry to foreign lands,/ And all of Europe will see, to our detriment,/ How great was the folly practiced by us here" (IV. ii). Furthermore, he realizes that his mother does not merit obedience: "The duty of children grows cold, when parents do not hesitate/ To desecrate the most sacred thing in the world through crime" (IV. iii). Like a model ruler he decides that the way to deal with opposing factions is to practice gentleness to all; "Therefore leniency now takes the place of raging:/ I do not want to be the crowned executioner of my people!" (IV. iv). After this apparently complete conversion to reason and virtue it is surprising, to say the least, to witness his abrupt change to unreason when he hears that Catherine has already given the signal for the start of the massacre. He cries, ". . . therefore Paris alone is/ Not to be a city of refuge for the Huguenot swarm, either./ Come, do give the signal! the brood of heretics shall die!" (IV. v). Still worse, one hears, in the fifth act, that Charles himself is shooting from the palace windows at people trying to save themselves by jumping into the Seine. Although Charles' character has been established from the start as changeable, such a complete reversal as this one is hard to accept, and the character becomes inconsistent. Yet Gottsched had written, "A self-contradicting character is a monster, and does not easily occur in nature." [55] It was poor policy to put the play's most notable speeches regarding virtuous government in the mouth of such a personage.

Potentially stronger and more interesting than Charles, although given only a minor role, is the Duke of Guise. He is bloodthirsty and cruel, like the Queen, but he does at least have the virtue of forthrightness. Catherine may boast of the trickery that she learned from her family's political methods in Florence; Guise, however, professes to detest all treachery: "A Guise fights freely; whereas sly deceit/ And perfidy and assassination are the strong point of his opponents" (II. iv). This combination of noble-mindedness and fanaticism make Guise akin to Bektas in *Mahommed IV*.

The virtuous characters in the drama are all Huguenots, except Catherine's daughter Margaret, and her loyalty to Catholicism is wavering. Her marriage to the Huguenot King Henry of Navarre is just being celebrated—hence the title of the play. A dutiful child, she is tormented because her concern for her new husband's safety conflicts with the carrying out of her mother's wishes. As in *Der sterbende Cato,* here again Gottsched contrasts the two approximately equal impulses of love and filial piety, but with a realignment toward virtue, for now it is the lover rather than the parent who stands for the right thing. King Henry offers Margaret a simple rational solution that relieves the situation of its dramatic tension: "A higher Being reigns in Heaven and on earth,/ To whom all fear of men must be subordinated./ If the parental command does not agree with His word,/ Then the latter takes precedence and must be fulfilled" (III. ii). Margaret is not excessively passive in her reaction to danger, for she urges flight from Paris. Henry does not agree to this, however, because he refuses to forsake his comrades. Reason tells Margaret that fanatical Catholicism cannot be in the right: "If God desired that the person who does not blindly honor Rome/ Should not draw breath, because he disturbs the church:/ Then, indeed, His arm is not lacking in lightning and thunderbolts/ To deal out punishments to the throng who think thus" (III. vi). To her belongs the most pessimistic statement in the play, "Oh, that integrity so rarely in the world/ Acquires its deserved happiness and receives its reward" (V. i). It is in line with Gottsched's new realistic view of tragedy that no one speaks up to refute this denial of optimism.

King Henry comes closer to the virtuous ideal than the doubtful and melancholy Margaret. He passively resists the suggestion that action be taken against the threatening danger. When his associate Clermont cries, "Are we then only lambs which one leads to the slaughter?" Henry answers that reason (*Klugheit*) advises against doing anything to sully their innocence, and then adds, "Then, however, one must also trust in the protection of Heaven!/ And not so impudently build on human reason alone./ Virtue protects itself, and if it succumbs;/ Still everyone will be on its side" (III. iii). At the end, when the massacre is already well under way and Henry is under strong pressure from King Charles to renounce Protestantism, the most optimistic thing that Henry can find to say is, "Nevertheless, at the right time noble-mindedness will display itself./ The day will still come in which truth will conquer,/ When, through Heaven's protection, error will be defeated!" (V. ix). Gottsched admitted being glad that the Unity of Time prevented him from depicting Henry's subsequent action, which was to forsake Protestantism for the sake of gaining the French crown. On the other hand, since the fate of Henry and his closest associates is left hanging in the air, the Unity of Time also forces an inconclusive and unsatisfactory ending on the play, without doing very much to enhance its moral and philosophical message.

The drama's most attractive characterization is that of the aged Admiral Coligny, who exhibits the sweet quality of rational composure (*Gelassenheit*) better than any other figure in German tragedy up to this point. He may therefore be said to inaugurate this type of sweetly passive personage, which was to be developed later particularly by Cronegk and Wieland. On account of his age, he looks forward to death and does not resent the first attempt made on his life: "I do not fear death . . . / . . . However, God's command and decree did not ordain/ That a perfidious bullet should rob me of my life:/ I accept this gratefully, of course: yet, as aged as I am,/ I could go to my fathers with a happy heart" (II. ii). He wants no revenge for himself, only tolerance for the Huguenots, and he is touchingly trustful of the King's good intentions. This does not speak very highly for his shrewdness, but the thing emphasized in his character is his good heart, rather than his reason. Gottsched seems to have fashioned him after a generally Pietistic ideal, but without the emotionality and tears of the really sentimental personage. His death, however, causes other characters to shed tears, tears that are less the result of grief than a reaction to the virtuous manner in which Coligny meets his murderers. That is to say, the spectacle of meekly suffering virtue produces here, for the first time, those special sentimental tears that are the visible outward sign and proof of a good and feeling heart. Coligny's speeches, as reported by another character, show that he has faced his death with perfect propriety: "They seek my death: I have never shrunk from it!/ Now also I die gladly. How fortunate I am today/ That I, in possession of my reason and with a composed soul,/ Can commend myself to the faithful mercy-hand of the Most High" (V. iii). Unlike Cato, who committed suicide when things went awry, the perfect Coligny tries with his last breath, but without loss of dignity, to preserve his life. He appeals to his murderer, ". . . but young man, if you have/ Felt a human heart, then spare these gray hairs!/ But then do what you will; the bier will carry me/ Out of the world in a brief time anyway" (V. iii). After such words, the cruelty of his death and the atrocities practiced on the corpse appear all the more heartless and barbaric, so that there can be no doubt that the Catholic side stands for evil, while the Protestant side stands for virtue. No play before Lessing's *Emilia Galotti* contained so high a degree of partisan tendentiousness as the *Bluthochzeit*. This tendentious purpose, directed against a Catholic influence in Saxony,[56] may well have contributed to Gottsched's decision to ignore the demands of optimism and justice in this tragedy.

One last remarkable feature of the *Bluthochzeit* is the attention given in it to the imagined locale beyond the visible stage setting. There are frequent references not only to happenings off-stage (which would not be unusual), but also to visual aspects of the city of Paris outside the Louvre, with the result that one receives a strong impression of realism otherwise absent in Alexandrine tragedies. This impression is also heightened, naturally, because the events are taking place in a city well-known to all either through hearsay or experience, and not in some remote or ancient locality. The same impression of realism does not come through at all, however, in Lessing's *Henzi*, which has the city of Berne, Switzerland, as its setting. Lines like the following help to lend actuality to the sinister preparations going on outside the palace for the coming massacre: "As many as there are windows to be counted in every house,/ That is how many lights there are; so that they are lacking nowhere./ Now the streets are bright, and the squares all flooded with light" (III. iv). Also, a certain theatrical thrill is provided when the turbulence outside finally penetrates into the relatively calm precincts of the stage itself in the person of murderers armed with swords and pistols who come to drag away Clermont, an associate of King Henry. One further small but noteworthy detail in the play is the speech by another associate, Condé, in which the important principle is introduced that the inner soul of man remains free of all physical compulsion. Thus Condé says to King Charles: "My head and life, sire, are truly in your hands;/ But not my conscience!" (V. viii).

It is not known whether Gottsched composed his *Agis, König zu Sparta* before or after the *Bluthochzeit*,[57] but it, too, was published in 1745 in the sixth volume of the *Schaubühne*. Since Gottsched later spoke of *Agis* and the *Bluthochzeit* as "a pair of hastily composed plays" that he had not had time to polish,[58] it appears likely that the two were written close together. In his introduction to *Agis*, the author stresses the fact that this story stirred his emotions: "If I moreover have expressed the character of Agis so well that it touches readers and spectators as much in my tragedy as it touched me in Plutarch: then I am certain there will be no lack of pity and terror in it."[59] Unfortunately, although *Agis* has much better construction and dialogue than either *Cato* or the *Bluthochzeit*, it is even less able to reach the emotions. Partly this is because the setting in ancient Sparta lacks all realism and familiarity; but more particularly it is because the hero is fighting for an extreme economic reform with which few persons, and in all probability not the author himself, can sincerely sympathize. The atmosphere of the play is exceedingly frigid. Gottsched explains that the hero makes a tragic error in trusting the advice of a false friend, "and so one pities him as a great man who, however, through a small misstep, and therefore not without his own fault, becomes unfortunate, indeed plunges his whole family into misfortune." [60] From this it is at once clear that *Agis* is closer in type to *Cato* than to the *Bluthochzeit*, where no poetic justice was operative. But Agis' error is without the emotional coloring of Cato's and is as specifically rational as that of Pitschel's *Darius*, to which it bears great similarity. To be sure, Darius' character was shown to be somewhat pusillanimous throughout, while Agis has no personality defect whatever beyond a slight lack of maturity. The poetic justice of Agis' downfall is only very technically preserved. His error exonerates Providence in a legalistic sense, but one is left with the impression that divine justice operates very harshly. As in the *Bluthochzeit*, the audience is expected to be attracted to virtue in spite of its misfortunes, rather than on account of its rewards.

Agis' economic reform consists in the proposal that rich people should cancel all debts owed to them and divide their possessions equally among all the citizens of Sparta. This is only one step removed from the ideal community described in the Utopian novel, *Insel Felsenburg* (1731–1743), wherein all possessions were communally enjoyed, as in the state of nature. In presenting such a reform as a virtuous ideal Gottsched was giving a very extreme expression to the widespread feeling among philosophically-minded persons of the time that riches, combined with luxurious living and indolence, were detrimental to virtue and out of harmony with rational simplicity of life—so extreme an expression, indeed, that he could not have taken it seriously. Inasmuch as the reform was an integral part of his material, Gottsched had no choice about including it, but doubtless he regarded it as an unattainable ideal which, when drastically watered down by the realities of life, would still leave a precipitate of nonmaterialistic feeling in the hearts of men. In this negative reaction to material goods, present also in Haller's poem *Die Alpen*, there is at least a beginning of the general pessimistic attitude toward culture popularized some years later by Rousseau.

Agis states the proposition at the beginning when he deplores the effects of the introduction of a monetary economy into Sparta: "Since gold and silver first came into our city,/ Riotous living has increased, while virtue has diminished" (I. i). Although a king, Agis lives and dresses like a simple citizen—an early precursor, one might say, of France's Louis-Philippe. His ambition is to put into practice again the laws of Lycurgus, not because he is a reactionary, but because reason dictates this: "As soon as reason opened my eyes,/ I looked upon Lycurgus' fame as my guiding principle" (I. i). The laws of Lycurgus will put an end to injustices: "I will . . . / Do away with the need and misery of the poor citizens,/ Curb the rich man, who oppresses all/ Who are poor and miserable" (I. i). To set a good example, Agis decides to divide up his own fortune among the poor, and he persuades his mother and grandmother to do like-wise. He expects more of a following among the young citizens than the old: "Stinginess makes the old men blind to the welfare of the state,/ Who have already grown grey and childish in vices" (I. ii). This represents a reversal of the usual Enlightened assump-tion that the old, being the most mature in reason, are also the most virtuous persons. More in conformity to one's expectations is the judgment passed on Agis at the end, that his mistakes were due to his *youthfulness*. Nevertheless, it is a noteworthy circumstance that the portrayals of benevolent, exemplary old men with wicked chil-dren are more numerous in tragedies written after 1755; whereas Alexandrine tragedies written before 1755 typically (though, of course, not exclusively) portray wicked parents with good chil-dren.

Counterpoised to Agis is his co-ruler Leonidas, the product of a luxurious (i.e., nonrational) upbringing and prone to vice: "He was reared in Asia according to a foreign style:/ From youth on-wards he imbibed voluptuousness,/ Which ruins blood and mind" (I. i). In the council meeting he speaks against Agis' reform, and carries the vote to his side. As Agesistrata, the mother of Agis, says, "Where avarice and voluptuousness bloom,/ There reason usually does not enter much into the deliberations" (II. i). But Agis is not averse to fighting with all legal means at his command for what he thinks is right. Leonidas has broken an old Spartan law by being married to a foreigner, and in consequence Agis succeeds in having him deposed from the throne in favor of his son-in-law Kleombrotus. The downfall of Leonidas provides a situation in which Chelonis, his daughter, plays a prominent role. Like Margaret in the *Blut-hochzeit*, Chelonis is torn between loyalty to her father and loy-alty to her husband; but no one solves her problem by saying that a guilty parent deserves no obedience. Agis' mother Agesistrata and his wife Agiatis recognize her sad plight, however, and sympathize with her. All three of these women, especially the two younger ones, are inclined toward heart, feeling, and tears. Indeed, tears are twice spoken of as means to move the heart of another person to sympathy and kindliness; they will serve to temper justice with mercy. Kleombrotus takes over his father-in-law's throne without covetousness: "His misfortune affects me very much, and the value of this crown/ Seems only half so great to me, because his downfall takes away its honor:/ But I have had to obey the republic" (III. iv). He has learned to put principle before filial piety. But Chelonis puts filial piety before principle and before marital loyalty, for she now accompanies Leonidas into exile.

Agis' most trusted adviser is his uncle Agesilaus. This wily hypocrite goes along with the plans for reform because through them he will be rid of his heavy debts. On the other hand, when it comes to dividing up real estate among the populace, he counsels Agis to move slowly, and not to try to accomplish everything at once. Naturally, this is because he does not want to forfeit his own holdings. The guileless Agis heeds his words, although his mother warns him not to do so: "The art of treachery is to pretend to be very loyal:/ But whoever notices it in time, he is not easy to fell./ Youth often makes the mistake of trusting perfidy;/ While the eye of experience sees through its innermost part" (II. iv). Since Agis does not listen to his wiser mother, he becomes personally responsible for his later downfall, even though his motives remain the purest. His "guilt" is simply a case of faulty reasoning power. What results is that the poor people of Sparta turn against Agis as a man who does not keep his promises. When this becomes clear, Agis is unhappy, but still expects divine protection: "Virtue never trembles!/ Let him who rules as a tyrant be terrified of rebellion;/ Because of my deed, the grace of Heaven must shield me" (IV. iii). His wife Agiatis, like Margaret in the *Bluthochzeit*, has a more pessimistic view: "Oh, if the world were always grateful for well-doing!" (IV. iii). It is true that Agesilaus does not reap the benefit of his trickery, for the populace, enraged by his attempt to assassinate Leonidas, drives him out of Sparta. But this event does not help Agis. Leonidas is coming back to the city with more power than ever, and Agis is doomed. Kleombrotus is now sent into exile by Leonidas, as his first move, and this gives Chelonis a second heartbreaking conflict. This time she turns against her father and accompanies her husband out of the city—twice exiled in one day! It is not clear whether she has made a moral decision, or whether she merely always sides with the loser.

As the tide moves against him, Agis meets failure and misfortune without complaint. Quite dispassionately, not making a great point of the matter, he does implicate the gods in his downfall: "The gods surely know it: my first purpose was good:/ Only they did not give me the unabated courage,/ Also prudently to despise the advice of false friends/ And to strive for the chosen goal with zeal" (V. iv). He seems to accept this fatalistically, as well as with a sense of guilt. Less calm is Agiatis, who pleads with Leonidas to spare Agis until her voice is choked by floods of tears, in the most flamboyant show of emotion in all three Gottsched tragedies. She calls on the gods to hinder and punish Leonidas, all in vain. The only bit of comfort is in Agis' words before his execution: "My death will be more glorious than the life of those/ Who are now murdering me so unjustly and cruelly" (V. ix). Cold as this comfort is, it is chilled still more by the report that not only Agis (who has committed an error), but also his mother and grandmother (who have committed none) have been ruthlessly executed. To make things complete, Agiatis resolves to die also. Such a depressing conclusion is not very conducive to an optimistic view of the world. It has been said that *Agis* in its tragic viewpoint corresponds more to Baroque tragedy than to Enlightened tragedy.[61] Because of the tragic fault, this judgment is less valid in respect to *Agis* than it would be in respect to the *Bluthochzeit*. Like the typical Baroque tragedy, however, both of these plays put more emphasis on the steadfastness of a moral character in the face of danger than on the justice and rationality of the world-order. Nevertheless, they both also so strongly advocate the eighteenth-century ideals of reason and virtue, and are so well larded with sententious statements drawn from the ethical doctrine of the time that they are unmistakable products of the German Enlightenment.

Whatever may be urged against the original tragedies in the *Schaubühne* as to lack of inspiration, of beauty, of interest, and of genius, they did at any rate carve out a solid niche for tragedy in an essentially untragic age. From the time of their appearance onward, more and more original tragedies were written in Germany. Authors of talent and finally of genius applied themselves to the genre. The first German writer of genuine talent who turned his attention to tragedy began his work, as a matter of fact, directly under Gottsched's aegis, and two of his tragedies were published for the first time in the *Schaubühne*. This was Johann Elias Schlegel.

IV

JOHANN ELIAS SCHLEGEL:
THE PYRRHIC VICTORY OF VIRTUE

GOTTSCHED'S sweeping reform of the theater had a particular attraction for very young authors, and it awakened ambitions not only in Leipzig itself, but also behind the cloisterlike walls of the preparatory schools. At Schulpforta, where he studied from 1733 until 1739, Johann Elias Schlegel (born 1718) was in the midst of receiving a rigorous training in the Greek and Latin classics when Gottsched's *Dichtkunst* and *Cato* came before his eyes, and he was forthwith inspired to try his own hand at something new and challenging: the writing of a German tragedy.[1] At first, to be sure, it was only the form of the new tragedy which the young Schlegel assimilated, while his concept of the tragic remained conditioned by his study of Sophocles and Euripides. In time, however, he learned to base his tragedies on the tragic concepts of his own time, and to turn from virtue betrayed and annihilated to virtue serene and triumphant. In so doing he not only diverged from his original mentor, Gottsched, who was tending away from poetic justice, but also, paradoxically, made the tragic stage a brilliant showplace for the activities of vice.

Schlegel's earliest drama, *Die Trojanerinnen* (originally entitled *Hekuba*), written in 1736, competently combines and integrates the plots of Euripides' *Hecuba* and the *Trojan Women* with some features of Seneca's *Trojan Women;*[2] it also breathes the hopelessness and cheerlessness of these ancient tragedies. The play in its first form has not been preserved. Nevertheless the extensive revisions of 1742 and 1745[3] must have extended primarily to versification alone, for the play as eventually published in 1747[4] is so pessimistic and somber in tone that it does not seem to have profited in the least from the author's philosophical development subsequent to 1736. In spite of all revision, then, there is little doubt that in *Die Trojanerinnen* we still possess Schlegel's tragic concept in its first stage. The play—naively—makes a mockery of the doctrine of benevolent Providence. This fact would have been less apparent if Schlegel had created a drama-world detached from cosmic considerations, one in which nothing counted except man's inhumanity to man, or if he had viewed the Greek gods as false and nonexistent instead of making them the customary valid substitutes for the Providence of rationalism. Actually, failing to weigh the sinister implications, Schlegel makes of his Hecuba a virtuous eighteenth-century character who recognizes and clings to a just, benevolent Providence, only to be cruelly deceived at the end when her unfaltering virtue is not rewarded. She has no defect whatever in her character. She does not so much as commit an error of judgment which might connect her sufferings with her actions. Moreover, her daughter Polyxena and her grandson Astyanax are totally innocent victims of the Greek lust for blood. What conclusion can be drawn except that God is not just, and that virtue is a delusion?

Early in the play Hecuba is brought the news that she is to become the slave of Ulysses, and that Troy's most beautiful woman must be a human sacrifice to bring the Greeks favorable winds for their voyage home. Hecuba assumes, of course, that Helen, the cause of the war, will be this sacrifice; but she is informed instead that Helen will be reinstated as Menelaus' queen. She correctly suspects that the sacrificial victim will be her own innocent daughter, Polyxena. Hereupon Hecuba breaks out in a vehement denunciation of the gods: "Now let no one tell me any more that never-sleeping gods/ Look upon our ways, and reward and punish./ . . . And instead of conscientiously assessing the reward for our deeds,/ Heaven takes pleasure in elevating wickedness." In the next moment, however, she catches herself. Reason returns, and she concludes her blasphemous outburst with a reaffirmation of faith: "Forgive, Justice, that I, in cursing the world,/ Have sought to invoke you with such blasphemy" (I. iii). From this time onward, Hecuba keeps her emotions well in hand, and her trust in Providence is unshakable. When Polyxena desperately rejoices that death is soon going to put an end to her woes, Hecuba quickly rebukes her: "That which is to befall us is not in our hands;/ Only Heaven knows it, and it is unknown to us./ We must not wish for death nor bring it on ourselves" (I. iv). These lines contain a pious criticism of the very mistakes that Gottsched's Cato made.

The meticulous correctness of Hecuba's attitude is given sharper outlines by being contrasted to the attitude of her other daughter, Cassandra, who rejoices in thoughts of revenge. She believes that Agamemnon's affection for her will be the means of her revenge, and she calls on the gods to curse the homeward journey of the Greeks. Hecuba, on the other hand, reproves herself when for a moment she feels joy that the Greeks are fighting one another over the question of sacrificing Polyxena: "Be silent, ignoble impulse! If only my cause finds support,/ If only my daughter lives; I demand no revenge" (V. i). Surely it is altogether unlikely that Schlegel put these exemplary words in Hecuba's mouth in order to show up her principles as foolish and the gods as wicked. Still, at the end of the play, far from receiving the just rewards of her virtue, Hecuba must hear that both her daughter and her grandson have been put to death. At this news she cannot speak either against or for the justice of the gods. Gottsched's rule about the natural lack of presence of mind in such situations [5] serves Schlegel well in this instance, and Hecuba says only, "I am dazed with grief, so that I cannot feel" (V. viii). It is Andromache, the mother of Astyanax, who in the final couplet of the play, finds a very feeble way out of this situation in which Providence looks so blamable. She does this by complaining, not that the gods have brought this terrible event to pass, but that they have allowed their names and authority to be used falsely by the bloodthirsty Greek priests: "O Heaven, will you always, when enemies hate us,/ Allow them to use your holy command as an excuse?" (V. viii). Accordingly the whole question of the responsibility of Providence is begged, and the only reproach left is the relatively light one that the gods did not prevent the Greeks from masking their wickedness in a cloak of religion. All the wickedness is the fault of human beings, the Greeks, while presumably innocence must not always expect protection and virtue is not always rewarded, at least not on earth. The important thing is to remain true to the rational concept of the world order, as Schlegel's Hecuba rather stoically manages to do. This Hecuba with eighteenth-century morals does not run amok with vengeance, like Euripides' heroine. Perhaps a sober philosopher, some thoroughgoing disciple of Leibnitz and Wolff, could have defended the conclusion of *Die Trojanerinnen* logically and could have proved with many a "Vernunftwahrheit" that these tragic happenings were not at variance with the unfathomable plan of a benevolent Providence; but for the audience the effect of the catastrophe must have been quite unsettling and disquieting.

Although this attempt to graft a weak branch of rational optimism onto a grim and battered old oak of Greek pessimism and despair was unsuccessful, there was something else in Schlegel's first tragedy that promised a sturdier growth. This was the characterization of Agamemnon, whose struggle with personal conviction and external necessity gives him a central position in the play, sometimes overshadowing that of Hecuba herself. His character is far more interesting in its mobility and development than that of the set and resolute Hecuba, and his fate could be called tragic, without reservations, if it were not eclipsed by the piteous deaths of Polyxena and especially of Astyanax. For the other characters in the play, both good and evil, there is no mental torment caused by a conflict of convictions and loyalties; but Agamemnon is plagued by doubts and inner problems, and thus he becomes the first truly introspective character in German drama, in this respect far outstripping Gottsched's Cato and Behrmann's Timoleon. Alone among the Greeks he has an Enlightened view of the gods, or, rather, he is working toward this Enlightened view: "It is impossible that the gods are always meditating on murder/ . . . The priest who leads us hears, instead of the voice of the gods,/ In himself perhaps the cry of his own anger" (II. i). He, or his reason, is the arbiter of religious truth, and he refuses to bow to authority when this does not coincide with his conception of the gods: "The oracle is hard, and therefore I rejected it,/ Because that which reveals only fury seemed unworthy of the gods" (II. i). Obviously, Schlegel is here already operating in the sphere of Goethe's *Iphigenie*.

Agamemnon's ideal conviction, however, must test its strength against the very real pressures brought to bear by Ulysses and by Pyrrhus, the son of dead Achilles. Agamemnon thereupon raises the usual lament of rulers: "Only believe, no man is free,/ Even princes are often bound in hidden slavery" (II. i). Growing in stature as the drama continues, Agamemnon tells Pyrrhus (and this, too, recalls Goethe's *Iphigenie*) that his dead father does not seek the vengeance that Pyrrhus thinks is essential. Agamemnon paints a word picture of the other world in which the soul of the dead hero cries out for mercy, not revenge: "Do you think that vengeance gives peace to the pale shades?/ Our condition in those times depends only on ourselves./ No person on earth can win repose for the dead./ The judge before whom Hell trembles does not ask/ Whether we are avenged; he asks how we have lived" (III. i). This difference of opinion between the chieftains leads to unrest in the army. Then Ulysses, with a multitude of practical arguments, seems to prevail over Agamemnon, who for a while, uneasily, chooses the path of expediency. One could call Agamemnon indecisive, but the author regards indecisiveness with favor. Agamemnon says, "An irresolute spirit, whom nothing can sway too quickly,/ Shows that he carefully reflects about his duty,/ And if he indeed finally chooses the false path,/ Then at least he has not erred without a struggle" (IV. iv). When he at last makes up his mind to defy his comrades and to protect Polyxena from death, it is a triumph of rational and virtuous will power which should be crowned with success. Instead, it proves to be an attempt doomed to defeat, and Agamemnon is forced to bow to the superior forces of Pyrrhus. Evidently Agamemnon also disgraces himself with cowardice in the struggle, for Pyrrhus mentions "the commander's craven fear . . ." (V. vii). Agamemnon wavers between good and evil; and although he wants the good, he is not strong enough to carry it out: surely a character with tragic potentiality.[6]

Schlegel's second tragedy, *Orest und Pylades,* was also written in Schulpforta and is also essentially a reworking of ancient tragedy, in this case Euripides' *Iphigenia in Tauris.* Completed in its first form in 1737 and originally entitled *Die Geschwister in Taurien,* it was given an amateur production by Schlegel's fellow students in 1738 and then presented on the professional stage in Leipzig in 1739. In 1742 Schlegel revised his work extensively and gave it the new title under which it was finally published in 1761.[7] The new title reflects Schlegel's turning away from Greek influence, for it emphasizes the contemporary Pietistic idea of sentimental friendship rather than the old themes of fate and consanguinity. But the play itself, despite revisions, remains quite Greek. While the unselfish devotion of Pylades for Orestes now provides the emotional high point of the play—the fifth scene of Act Five—still the friendship remains just an elaborate development that fails to affect the plot in any integral way.

The young author's attempt to make his ancient story palatable to an eighteenth-century audience and especially to the literary dictator in Leipzig can be seen in the "natural" explanation given for Iphigenia's escape from the sacrificial altar in Aulis.[8] She was not saved by the goddess, but by Achilles, and why? Because he was in love with her—the same motivation, surely borrowed from French tragedy, given by Gottsched to Julius Caesar for the latter's unhistorical appearance in Utica in *Der sterbende Cato.*[9] Unlike Goethe's heroine, Schlegel's Iphigenia does not live in ignorance of the bloody happenings in Mycenae. A "Thracian" has told her that Orestes has slain their mother Clytemnestra in revenge for the murder of Agamemnon, and she is only in doubt whether or not he has been punished for the deed. She admits that he deserves punishment, but at the same time she feels he ought to be excused because he meant well. In other words, she enunciates the doctrine that the end justifies the means, which most eighteenth-century writers rejected and deplored: "An anger whose excitement is based on loyalty and love,/ A zeal whose glow is ignited by virtue itself,/ Is to be excused; and even if it goes too far,/ Still the propriety of its final purpose always speaks for it" (I. i). It is clear that Schlegel was to have trouble from the outset in trying to accommodate the facts of this grim old story to the Enlightened moral views of his own century. According to these views, there really could be no excuse for Orestes' crime. Yet he had to be presented as a sympathetic figure. Therefore as little as possible is said about the cause of Orestes' subjugation to the Furies. The emphasis is laid instead upon the pitiable sight of one hounded by those creatures and, moreover, upon the importance of doing away with the barbarous religious practices of the Taurians. Consequently a more positive and optimistic theme carries the dramatic action. Nevertheless, Orestes' plight involves him in some highly questionable deceptions, and idealistic morality suffers many compromises. It is true that the benevolence of Providence is not called into question by this drama; but the idea that the end justifies the means does dominate it, as in Euripides' ancient drama. Schlegel is scarcely more successful in rising above the practical-minded amorality of his source than Ludwig was in his *Ulysses* some years before. Goethe's *Iphigenie*, with its insistence on strict, uncompromising morality of action, is a far better representative of Enlightened thinking.

Both Iphigenia and Orestes share a pessimistic attitude conditioned by their separate misfortunes. Iphigenia would like to die if she cannot escape from Tauris, and Orestes wishes with equal desperation to rid himself of the Furies. Pylades is at first optimistic, saying to Orestes, "Do you think that you will be fulfilling the word of Heaven thus,/ If you intend to conclude your madness by dying?" (I. iii). But he, too, when the death of Orestes seems imminent, wishes to die rather than to go on living without his dear friend: "This heart, which can die, and does not tremble before death,/ Shall now grow cold with the one for whom it has faithfully lived" (III. iv). Iphigenia, perhaps forgetting her own death wishes, answers to this, "No wise man wishes for death. He lives as long as he can" (III. iv), and later she adds, "I praise your loyalty, which gives birth to this grief:/ But I censure a grief which leads to the point of dying" (IV. i). Evidently the wish for death is used in this drama either to arouse pity—by showing the depth of melancholy and suffering endured by Iphigenia and especially Orestes— or to arouse admiration, by showing the exemplary loyalty of Pylades. In each case, however, the wish is regarded as being wrong in itself.

Since Orestes and Pylades have a single-minded purpose, which is to seize the statue of Diana from the temple and return to Greece with it, their characters are less interesting than Iphigenia's. Either they will succeed or fail in their endeavor, and the difficulties that they face are primarily of a physical nature. Even Orestes' recurring madness, brought on by the Furies which pursue him (presumably only in his imagination), is more a physical than a spiritual problem, for he does not worry about what he has done, only about what he is now suffering. Thus he addresses his dead mother without contrition: "How long will you torment me? When will your vengeance be satiated?" (II. i). Likewise, he says to Iphigenia, "My madness, my torment, is not the reward of wickedness" (II. ii). Iphigenia, on the other hand, does have mental conflicts and is unsure of her purposes. To be sure, she is remarkably unshaken by her gruesome task of slaying Greeks on the altar of Diana. This is distasteful, of course, but all blame is laid on King Thoas and his high priest, who order the sacrifices: "Indeed! my breast remains unspotted by the tyrant's murdering:/ Even if my hand has often been imbrued with blood" (III. iii). Her first real conflict comes when Orestes and Pylades, whom she believes to be Trojans, are condemned to die because a Greek inscription has been found in their possession. Iphigenia is the person who has really written the inscription and if she admits this, King Thoas will learn that she is a Greek and therefore worthy of death. She asks herself, "But would I then still be innocent of blood,/ If I with my own hand killed the heroes/ Who are guilty of death only through my silence?" (III. i). She resolves to tell Thoas the truth about the inscription, because: "My duty demands that I save innocent persons;/ and even if I myself were today put in their chains" (III. i). Her frankness and honesty is rewarded, insofar as Thoas decides to spare her life because she is a priestess. But she soon faces new problems. In a fit of his madness Orestes has wounded a shepherd boy without any provocation, and as a result of this King Thoas cruelly orders his execution, even though he is not a Greek. Now Iphigenia can no longer reproach herself with having had any part in his death, and yet she feels a new loathing for her office as official executioner. Reason, as shown above, may have exonerated her from guilt in her office; but now her heart refuses to be quiet any longer. She feels that Heaven has chosen her for an employment unsuited to her personality: "Wherefore would you have given me such a heart,/ Which is touched by the misery of others and afflicted by their sorrow;/ Which, when the timorous hand tremblingly slays them,/ Is tormented with their pain more than the dying persons themselves?" (III. v). When Pylades reveals that the man she is going to have to slay is actually her brother, she is horrified: "Alas, could it be possible? O Heaven, I am terrified!/ Do you want me to stain my hand with brother's blood?" (IV. i). She determines to die herself before she will commit this dreadful deed. However, the author does not intimate that it is actually God's will that Iphigenia should kill her brother. One of the main points made both in this play and in *Die Trojanerinnen* is that God never demands blood. Pylades states this at the beginning: ". . . for cruelty and rage/ Never pleases the gods. They are not refreshed with human blood" (I. iii). Accordingly, Iphigenia is not acting against God's will when she rebels at the thought of sacrificing her brother. Moreover, her determination to flee the country is not a breach of propriety, but a reasonable and virtuous decision. Schlegel still allows virtue to express itself in action.

Nevertheless, Iphigenia's next conflict is connected with the preparations for flight. Orestes wants to pave the way by killing King Thoas, but Iphigenia's conscience will not let her agree to this: "May Heaven prevent that we should murder the very one/ Who by right of arms has become my lord and king" (IV. iii). Thus far, but not farther, she insists on strict moral action. The next plan is a compromise, a use of questionable means toward a good goal. That is to say, Iphigenia resolves to deceive the king. In part, she is motivated by pride and revenge: "The king, who otherwise has often laughed at my helplessness,/ Shall see that this woman can finally get the better of him!" (IV. iv). This angry flare-up of wounded dignity is rather surprising in a supposedly virtuous character. It heralds the author's subsequent characterization of Dido. Then Iphigenia explains how she can reconcile herself to the use of deception: it is permissible when practiced on an enemy. She says: "I hate cunning and deceit, when used against friends./ But the common enemy, who afflicts the land of Greece,/ And who, because of his cruelty, is unworthy of the goddess;/ If someone deceives him; then I praise deceit and cunning" (IV. iv). She adds, however, that stealing the image of the goddess and rescuing Orestes will in the final analysis be of benefit to the person who is being deceived: "Force brings danger to you; cunning will more surely make you free,/ And will tear the king himself away from his fury and barbarism" (IV. iv).

Like Goethe's Iphigenia, Schlegel's heroine also addresses a solemn prayer to Diana for aid. She, too, puts divinity on its mettle and practically demands assistance as proof that the gods are as rational and benevolent as she believes them to be: "If you have not taken pleasure in the blood shed here,/ And the gods, do they indeed ever take pleasure in murder?/ Then hear me, then stand by me!" (IV. v). In Goethe's play, Iphigenia, through her absolute refusal to use deception, puts the whole responsibility on the gods and offers them no reward except her continued faith—and this is sublime and profoundly moving. But Schlegel's Iphigenia counts a great deal on human cleverness, asks the gods to take part in a deception, and offers the reward of animal sacrifice and rational worship: "O goddess, bring me happily back to Greece!/ . . . There some fat wild game will be your sweet sacrifice;/ There the hands of the Greeks will strew pure incense before you;/ And your priestess will in the midst of them,/ Indeed be devoted to you, but serve you rationally" (IV. v). One can see here that Schlegel has made an attempt to give his heroine Enlightened ideas, but he has not succeeded in making her over entirely into the image of the eighteenth-century ideal.

The plan is carried out: the statue of Diana is brought to the beach, Orestes is freed from his chains, and Pylades has taken both him and Iphigenia into a ship. While in pursuit of them, King Thoas has been mortally wounded. These events cause a sudden change of mind on the part of the Taurian high priest Hierarchus. It occurs to him now that Diana did not like the human sacrifices: "What is a divine service that is not protected by reason?/ An edifice which crashes down upon us, because nothing supports it" (V. iii). Thoas, on the other hand, is embittered toward the gods: "You idols are only stone; more powerless than we./ If not, then they themselves, who reward us from heaven, are/ More ungrateful than those who dwell upon the earth" (V. iv). As if the gods were unable to bear such reproaches without an answer, the fleeing Greeks are now unexpectedly brought back as prisoners before the dying Thoas. Their deception has not been crowned with success after all. Thoas again condemns Orestes to death, and this gives Pylades another opportunity to display his great friendship by offering to die in his place, while Iphigenia also tries to have the punishment put on herself alone. Such unselfishness, although understandable and admirable under the circumstances, grows a bit absurd and wearisome, so that one scarcely blames Thoas for condemning all three of them to death. At this juncture, instead of Euripides' *dea ex machina* (which would have been distasteful to Gottsched) [10] the high priest turns up a book of oracles in which he reads that Diana has predicted she is going to a better land where there are no more human sacrifices. Thoas hereupon dies, still shouting for revenge; but the high priest allows the three Greeks to go home in peace, saying, "If no oracle had snatched you from approaching death,/ Then your faithfulness and virtue would surely have saved you" (V. v).[11]

This final speech is obviously Schlegel's attempt to put a better face on the proceedings. He would like to have it appear that the virtues of Iphigenia, Orestes and Pylades have brought them their reward when in point of fact, outside of being eager to die for one another, they have done nothing very virtuous. The last scene might have been profitably employed to show that deception, even for a good cause, is never the proper method of solving difficulties. But Schlegel allows the deception to stand for what it is worth, and the return of the escapees is merely a device, anticlimactic at best (even though adapted from Euripides), to show the sympathetic persons in one last desperate situation. The author was not yet able to subordinate plot material to a consistent moral idea.

The third tragedy, *Dido*, represents a significant step forward in the process of philosophical mastery of subject matter. It, too, was written at Schulpforta, but in the last year of the author's residence there (1739). With a few revisions undertaken in Leipzig,[12] this drama was first published in the fifth volume of Gottsched's *Schaubühne* (1744). This time the maturing poet had no classical tragedy to use as his model. There was only Virgil's account of the story in the *Aeneid*, which could be treated with the same originality and freedom as any other historical or legendary source. Schlegel decided to make the story exemplify the dangers of the passion of love, and he carried this idea through consistently from beginning to end. By so doing, he was obeying more specifically than most authors Gottsched's dictum about the illustration of one particular moral principle. Perhaps the theme was not quite in accord with his own conviction that love, the preoccupation of the French theater, was unworthy to be a tragic subject.[13] The slave of love, however, is not the man Aeneas but the woman Dido; and her love is regarded as a pitiable fault, not a heroic virtue. Gottsched, who had been the first to raise objections to the love motif in French tragedy, did not consider the treatment of love in *Dido* as a blemish. On the contrary, in his introduction to the play Gottsched surprisingly enough praises *Dido* above Schlegel's *Herrmann* "because it has in itself more tender and strong passions, a more natural expression, and fewer didactic maxims . . . Here the heart speaks more . . ."[14] Gottsched calls Dido an excellent tragic heroine precisely because she has a tragic fault and is more pitiable than admirable: "The tragedy has as its chief purpose, by means of the excitation of terror and pity, to purify the emotions of the spectators and readers; or to edify them. The means to this is the verisimilar presentation, or poetic imitation, of an eminent and unfortunate person. Whoever wants to portray him in such a way that the goal will be attained must present him not only as worthy of admiration, but also chiefly as unfortunate and miserable; and indeed in such a way that he to a certain extent is to blame for this."[15] *Dido* is the only tragedy by Schlegel which has such a guilty protagonist. Hecuba

and Iphigenia are innocent of any wrong, and Orestes' guilt is played
down. Herrmann and Canut are paragons of virtue. But when he
wrote *Dido* Schlegel was more aware of the demands of Enlightened
rationalism, with its benevolent Providence and ideal of justice, than
he was in his first two tragedies; therefore, if his heroine was to
suffer and end badly, it was necessary to equip her with defects that
would justify this. At her side, as a contrast, is Aeneas, whose virtue
is not marred by defects. After *Dido*, it would again be the perfect
person who would be the main hero.

   At the very beginning Aeneas proves that he is a man of reason
with emotions under perfect control. The gods have commanded
him to leave Carthage at once. This is virtue, duty, honor, and takes
precedence over all emotion: "Honor beckons: very well! Aeneas
loves no more" (I. i).[16] The suddenness and completeness of such a
change of heart is neither absurd nor disgraceful, so long as one keeps
in mind the rationalistic basis for it. Once an emotion is shown to
be falsely directed, the sovereign reason is capable of snapping it off
abruptly. It is thus with Arsene-Porcia's love for Caesar in *Cato*,
and with Lottchen's love for Siegmund in Gellert's comedy *Die
zärtlichen Schwestern*. If love is a rational love in the first place, it
can be stopped or diverted as soon as the reason for it is removed.
The question of faithlessness toward Dido is not altogether ignored
by Aeneas, who admits, "I am not without fault, and am breaking
faith" (I. i). But Heaven has prior rights on him, and it was in
fact a careless disregard of his duty ever to have tarried in Carthage
at all. The parting will cause him pain, to be sure, but it will preserve
him from impiety: "Sooner let me be tormented by parting, than
by shame and remorse:/ Rather than be punished by Heaven, let
me be killed by grief" (I. i). Aeneas recognizes love, even rational
love, as a feeling of unparalleled attractive power. He laments to
his confidant, "Achates, alas! if I had only conquered the first impulse!/ . . . Is it not very hard to avoid loving a noble heart?/
Noble-mindedness attracts us and captivates our souls:/ And he who
will not love must at least be tormented" (I. iii). From these words
it is clear that Aeneas has not succumbed to any unworthy passion
aroused by a pretty face! It is noteworthy that Aeneas is also much
more concerned about deception than Iphigenia and Orestes were.
He is dissatisfied with himself for having secretly prepared his fleet
for departure: "Achates, he who is honest must feel disgust and
vexation/ As often as he is obliged to act and talk any other way;/
And hates in his heart the customs of this earth,/ Where one has
to become a liar in order to be considered clever" (I. iii). To make
matters worse, Dido's kingdom is in danger of attack by the Libyans,

whose leader Iarbas wants either to marry Dido or to conquer her.
This circumstance would make Aeneas' departure doubly faithless,
except for the fact that he determines to fight Iarbas before leaving:
"No! Heaven's resolve commands me indeed to be unfaithful;/ If
I am ungrateful, that will only be my own fault" (II. v).

Dido is characterized as being great and virtuous in every respect,
except where her love for Aeneas is concerned. She has been able to
endure the hostility of her brother Pygmalion without once losing
her sisterly feeling toward him: "Thus sorrow and grief have never
once elicited an 'alas' from me/ That would have desired his death"
(II. i). She is not intimidated by Iarbas and his Libyans. But when
it comes to Aeneas, she both thinks of killing him (and herself) and
is afraid of his departure. Moreover, her love gives her a guilty
conscience, because she swore an oath at the grave of her first husband, Sychaeus, that she would remain chaste for the rest of her
life. Accordingly, the passion she feels for Aeneas is truly a guilty
one, and virtue would demand that she stifle it. Knowledge of this
fact makes one judge Aeneas less harshly. He is acting rationally
and dutifully, and she ought to do likewise. The gods of Virgil were
arbitrary and could command Aeneas to act against morality and
conscience; but the Providence of Schlegel only requires that a man
master the improper desires of his heart.

Dido's sister Anna has heretical notions about the validity of
vows. She is an early spokesman for a concept of love that would
achieve prominence in tragedy some twenty years later, namely that
it is an emotion exempt from the control of reason. Vows of chastity
sworn under influence of grief are not binding: "Your oath? which
escaped you in grief and indiscretion?/ In vain a person thinks he
can abjure the impulses/ Which Nature ignites and our senses feed"
(II. iii). Temporarily, at least, Anna is able to reassure Dido of the
justice of her position, so that Dido can reject Aeneas' argument that
he is only obeying the will of the gods. She attributes his decision
to a coldness of heart and claims that the gods are not involved:
"What cares your stony heart about the tears of a woman?/ You
laugh when I have to speak your name with sighs./ Heart, that feels
no pity! intractable tiger-whelp!/ . . . Your defense, your Jupiter,
is more disgraced than I,/ Let him punish where he will, and avenge
himself and me" (II. iv). Something floridly Baroque enters Dido's
speeches when she contemplates killing Aeneas and then herself:
"How joyfully would then my sad eye see/ How your spirit would
flee from you, when you received your just deserts!/ Oh, what a
sight! if then with the streams of my blood/ The streams of your
blood would come to be mingled" (II. iv). The overheatedness of

words like these is not in harmony with the rational ideal of calm and decorum, and here is another indication that Dido has strayed from the path of virtue. Before long it becomes the fashion to let every *Machtweib* and deserted woman in tragedy utter such a passionate speech. Lessing, for example, has his Marwood and his Orsina talk in this way.

Dido's passion leads her next into deceit. She pretends to agree to the departure of Aeneas, merely to gain time in which to burn his ships. Of course, this trick is distasteful to her: "The gods know with what difficulty I compel myself to lie" (III. ii). The maneuver fails, however, and Aeneas, who now calls Dido a traitress, is more resolved than ever to go away. Thereupon Anna suddenly changes tack and reproaches Dido with a lack of reasonableness: "You follow altogether too much the impulse of your soul,/ And let your heart torment you after its own will" (IV. ii). Nevertheless, Dido goes on insisting that the gods are not in favor of Aeneas' departure. Clearly, her passion is obscuring her reason. When her general excuses himself for failing to burn the ships because Heaven was protecting them, she retorts, "Only your own cowardice is the divinity which protects them" (IV. iii). The qualms of conscience which she begins to feel only lead her farther into error. Thus her vision of the ghost of her dead husband, instead of making her give up her love for Aeneas, fills her with guilty despair and thoughts of suicide. And even in death her spirit will haunt and plague Aeneas. She no longer cares whether or not her purpose is rational and virtuous: "Let prevail what will in my dazed senses;/ Whether the influence of Heaven is here leading my spirit;/ Or whether it is the impulse of Hell which is pulling me away,/ Or the command of the Furies, who are beckoning to my shade;/ Or whether I am being bidden to sink into their abyss by a resolve/ Which reason has considered and my heart has grasped;/ Nevertheless my intention stands firm" (IV. vi). In the fifth act she confirms the fears of those around her and does indeed perform a suicidal act—off stage—and then comes in dying. The final words of Anna sum up Dido's character fault and contain the moral of the play: "The great heart is cold, which never struggled with fear:/ By its inclinations alone it was conquered" (V. iv). The intimation is: beware of unbridled passions, for they can destroy the noblest of souls.

It would be a misunderstanding of this tragedy to suppose that Dido is a pitiable figure primarily because she is forsaken by Aeneas. The author does everything possible to present Aeneas as an admirable character, worthy of all sympathy. Indeed, the major revision he made of the first version, according to his brother Johann

Heinrich, was to add the part about Aeneas' conquest of Iarbas before setting sail, so Aeneas cannot be accused of leaving his Cartha-
ginian friends in the lurch.[17] Dido is pitiable simply because she is
unable to control her emotions through the exercise of reason. As
a tragic heroine she is comparable to Cato and Darius, except that
in her case there is less intellectual error and more straightforward
passion involved. For this, his third effort, Schlegel has come around
to employing the original solution given by eighteenth-century
writers in Germany to the problem of fitting tragedy to the requirements of a rational and optimistic *Weltanschauung*. That is to
say, all will go well with a person so long as reason is uppermost in
the conduct of his affairs. Tragedy ensues, however, and is perfectly
justified, as soon as emotion or error of judgment is allowed to take
over. The spectator is supposed to feel pity for the hero because he
is mostly virtuous. As it happened, this solution did not remain the
only one for long. The course of German tragedy began to widen,
so that next to the hero with a fault more and more room was left
for the hero of perfect virtue, at whose side was then placed the
villain of absolute evil. The beginnings of this trend are already apparent in the *Schaubühne* tragedies *Aurelius, Banise, Mahommed,*
and *Panthea*. But it was Johann Elias Schlegel himself who contributed most to this development in his two last and most famous
tragic works.

It is interesting to note that two minor characters in *Dido* introduce motifs which were to be repeated time and again in subsequent tragedies. Ascanius, the son of Aeneas, is the first youth who
states that an older person has taught him to despise the so-called
glories of kingship: "My father taught me long ago to scorn the
crowns/ Which would make me mighty through the pain and sighs
of other men:/ And his kind of happiness gives me far more pleasure
than any throne" (III. i). Iarbas, the Libyan, is the first personage
to assert that virtue is more likely to be found among rude folk
than among the highly civilized. "But what you call barbarism in
our manners/ Is really solid courage, which knows no voluptous-
ness./ No treasure awakens envy in us. We use our weapons/ Only
to procure wild game for our food, and justice in a quarrel" (III. iv).
This represents quite a change from Schlegel's attitude toward the
barbarian Thoas, and is a preparation for his favorable attitude
toward the "barbarous" Germans in *Herrmann*.

In 1740 Schlegel broke entirely with classical models and materials and turned his attention to the dim past of his own people.
In his desire, which was that of a genuine dramatist, to find a way of
really moving the hearts of his audience, he came to the conclusion

"that those tragedies are more interesting and have a stronger effect on the emotions, whose materials are contained in the history of the nation for whom one is writing." [18] The next step, which, to be sure, Schlegel did not make, was to take one's materials from the contemporary life of the social class for which one was writing, and to compose bourgeois tragedies. Before he finished his new Germanic tragedy, however, Schlegel temporarily returned to the ancient classical world to work on a *Lucretia*. Evidently he was not moved to begin this endeavor by any true inspiration, but simply wished to disprove Gottsched's contention that the Lucretia story was unfit for dramatic treatment.[19] That his real interests lay elsewhere at the time is demonstrated by the fact that this *Lucretia* was not developed beyond its primary draft in prose. Only its first scene was ever put into Alexandrines. Even from the prose version, however, it can be seen that Schlegel was minded to portray a perfect heroine and a complete villain.

Schlegel's *Herrmann* was finished in 1741 and published originally in the fourth volume of Gottsched's *Schaubühne* (1743). He worked on it longer and more industriously than on any other tragedy, and it was his favorite among his own works,[20] although in Gottsched's opinion it was too much dominated by "wit." [21] The old Teutonic period had already been offered to the Baroque theater in Christoph Adam Negelein's opera, *Arminius, der Deutschen Erz-Held* (Nürnberg, 1697); but now for the first time it was brought, with long-lasting results, to the reformed German stage. Utilization of the Arminius material enforced the assumption (which was not made any less preposterous by the prevailing courtly theatrical costuming of the day—wigs, silk and velvet clothes) that the crude Germanic chieftain and his still cruder followers, roaming in the wild northern forests, were persons of a nobility and refinement suitable to tragedy and able to arouse the "noble emotions and passions" which for Schlegel were the goal of the tragic genre.[22] It might be argued that Roman civilization had had a polishing effect upon these barbarians; but this would conflict with the play's further assumption that everything Roman was effete and degenerate. At any rate, there was a precedent for Schlegel in the *Arminius* (1689) of Campistron. This older French tragedy, however, gave no precedent for Schlegel's originality in using tragedy to glorify the past of a modern nation, that is to say, in using the genre patriotically and nationalistically.[23] There was encouragement for this procedure in the circumstance that no other ancient people had had its solid moral character propagandized so thoroughly as the old Germans. Taking their lead from Tacitus, German historians and satirists were uniformly unable to view these fearsomely barbarous tribes with objectivity. Even today their sturdy natural morality and plain customs are frequently held up in comparison to the softness and degeneracy of more civilized peoples. It may not have been Schlegel's specific intention to glorify the Germanic past, for he was no Klopstock and no romanticist; but the kind of tragedy he wrote, with its emphasis on admirable, grandiosely virtuous characters, could not fail to do just that. Thus he inaugurated one of the most popular subjects in eighteenth-century German literature.

The theme of *Herrmann* is liberty, the same theme that had been treated in Gottsched's *Cato*, where the loss of freedom was mourned, and that had been touched upon in Quistorp's *Aurelius*, where, however, freedom was viewed in a bad light. In *Herrmann* liberty is virtuous and victorious. The state of the Germanic tribes before the coming of the Romans is represented as a golden age, when virtue was practiced for its own sake and no laws were necessary, when innocence and simplicity were honored. This happy time was presided over by the gods Thuiskon and Mannus, who were not cruel and bloodthirsty deities, but similar to the benevolent Providence of the eighteenth century. Sigmar, the father of Herrmann, counsels his son to remain true to these gods: "Through them came noble-mindedness, faithfulness, and fame to us./ The impulse which flees falseness and does not love soft manners,/ Knows nothing of laws, and yet practices virtue;/ The ambition to be free and never to live in bondage/ Was given into our breast by them" (I. i).[24] To take a stand against the Romans and to fight for freedom is to be on the side of virtue; and Herrmann, the newly elected chief of the Cheruscans, is very firmly on the side of virtue. There is never the slightest question about his integrity. Since he does not have to resist any temptation, and does not suffer, and always seems calmly self-possessed, he really does not enter into the central dramatic conflict of the play. For him virtue is truly a complete armor.

The conflict revolves, instead, around his brother Flavius. Like Agamemnon in *Die Trojanerinnen*, Flavius is a man torn between his duty or conviction and the demands of his associates. Having been educated by the Romans, Flavius is bound to them by ties of affection and gratitude. He sees only their advanced culture, which he prefers to the rude simplicity of Germanic life, and he believes he can escape being tainted by the vices which accompany this higher culture. In the delineation of Flavius' situation Schlegel brought something new, true, and universal into German drama. It is a domestic problem suitable for bourgeois plays and produces two scenes that spring the stiff shackles of the Alexandrine verse to become warm and alive. The first of the scenes is a dialogue between Flavius and his father Sigmar, in which Flavius, with the enthusiasm of a college student returned home to the backward village, defends the advanced skills and the better life of the Romans, while Sigmar, the rustic patriarch, condemns these things with stern moral asceticism. Sigmar thunders, "Cursed be art and wit, when they support vices!" and Flavius rejoins, "Then is the German always to live in rude huts?" To this Sigmar answers, "To be free here means more to me than to be a slave in palaces" (I. ii). The other scene shows Flavius meeting Marcus, a young Roman whom he has not seen for some time. Flavius' greeting to Marcus is the heartfelt expression of someone who has spent youthful years in a stimulating environment and is now sighing under the duller responsibilities of home and maturity: "The sight of you evokes all Rome in me,/ And all its pleasure, which I lost with grief" (I. iv). As a result of these two scenes Flavius becomes the most sympathetic character in the play. He stands between two worlds, and would like to hold on to that of Rome without becoming unfaithful to that of Germany. This is, however, a dangerous position, and the fact that Flavius is in love with Thusnelda, Herrmann's betrothed, adds another peril.

The family group Sigmar-Herrmann-Flavius, in which loyalty to Germany outweighs friendship to Rome, is contrasted to the family group Segestes-Thusnelda-Siegmund. In the latter, Thusnelda is the only one completely loyal to Germany and therefore a feminine counterpart of Herrmann and fit mate for him. Siegmund, her brother, has been consecrated as a Roman priest, but in spite of that, he leans strongly toward the German side and thus corresponds to Flavius in inverse proportion. Siegmund cannot stomach the self-deification of the emperor Augustus, principally because the gods are supposed to be just and benevolent, while Augustus is not: "No, he is not a god, who came to injure us,/ Who shed the blood of Germans and took away our freedom./ You, you immortals! I recognize in other works,/ And only good actions are the sign of true divinity" (II. i). The father Segestes is the element in this group which tips its balance away from loyalty, for he is an unprincipled realist whose only rule of conduct is his own material advantage. Although he is shrewd, he cannot properly be called a rationalist, because he seeks after "apparent goods" (Wolff's *Scheingüter*) exclusively. Segestes utters horrifying blasphemies when he tries to persuade Siegmund to remain a Roman priest: "Your fatherland is there, where you can hope for advantages,/ When this one promises nothing more, then another one stands open for you./ . . . Your god is anyone who can bring you profit and who can injure you./

A powerful man on earth can arouse greater fear/ Than gods above, who frighten only from a distance" (II. iii). Completely abusing the authority of a father, Segestes tells Siegmund it is his duty to obey unquestioningly—he must not think about any other virtue. Segestes' evil designs are not redeemed in the slightest degree by bravery or desire for greatness. He is small and utterly selfish, and portrays a cold and dispassionate kind of viciousness. Yet in his sophistical, pseudo-rationalistic denial of virtue and Providence, Segestes represents an important step on the way to Schlegel's ultimate conception of the villain in his last tragedy.

It must have cost Schlegel some concern that the historical defeat of Varus by the Germans was accomplished through cunning and under cover of night, for deceitfulness was the opposite of virtue and noble-mindedness. Nevertheless, he did not change the time of attack from night to day and in military affairs allowed the end to justify the means. In council the prince of the Chaucians advises, "Look for help in cunning, in darkness and night;/ In everything, so long as it makes our victory a certainty" (II. vi). All blame for deceitfulness is put on Segestes, who intends to reveal this plan to Varus. And Segestes, having forced his own children into submission (or so he believes), now goes to work on the weakest of the Sigmar family group, the unhappy Flavius. Like another, less polished Wallenstein, Segestes uses shrewd, practical arguments to bring Flavius over to his side, and, as an especially strong inducement, he offers Flavius the hand of Thusnelda as a reward—a step farther than Schiller's Wallenstein was prepared to go. Flavius, like Agamemnon, finds himself unable to make a decisive choice between good and evil, and the words he uses to describe his state of mind are like Agamemnon's, but also recall the sentiments of Schiller's Max Piccolomini: "My uncertain heart wavers between both sides./ It collects itself; it resolves: yet every moment/ A new flood of terror beats it back./ . . . Alas! Rome and Germany have equal rights to its gratitude./ And love for both struggles in me, and neither wins" (III. ii). Like Max Piccolomini, Flavius wants to make the woman he loves the arbiter over his course of action: "Princess, you put an end to my heart's long torment,/ What I shall resolve, I make your choice." But alas! Thusnelda is no Thekla, and besides, she does not return the love of Flavius: "Do not ask me for advice. I would properly be ashamed of myself,/ If I had more influence over you than your duty has" (III. ii). As if this cold rejoinder were not enough, the author has Thusnelda express herself still more explicitly in the next scene on the unsuitability of love as a motive for virtuous actions: "That is a lazy sort of hero, whom only love impels./ . . . It is a self-interest, which quickens slavish senses,/ And not a divine impulse, which touches heroic souls,/ When one does good only to obtain love,/ And shows oneself great only to carry off a heart" (III. iii). At this point Schlegel was performing less as a writer of German tragedy than as a critic of the lovelorn heroes of French tragedy, especially those of Campistron's *Arminius,* which he doubtless read before composing his own *Herrmann.*[25] As an example of a proper hero there is Herrmann himself, for whom love and duty belong in entirely separate compartments. Even when Thusnelda was a hostage in Varus' camp, Herrmann would have attacked if the time had been right: "Ah, believe, the danger in which I set you/ Truly moved my blood, but did not frighten me off" (III. iv). And he declares further, "Let them say, when they some day speak of my deeds:/ He loved Thusnelda very much: but his duty still more" (III. iv). Such manly integrity charms the equally heroic Thusnelda: "You, Herrmann, have chosen, as great hearts choose,/ And you love, more than yourself, the freedom of German souls" (III. iv). To these perfectly controlled characters, love is secondary and a selfish impulse. It does not have the educative and perfective relation to duty which is so inspiringly shown in Schiller's handling of the same theme in *Wallenstein's Tod.* Nor does it have the irresistible power shown in Schlegel's own *Dido.* In *Herrmann* the author has reached the peak of his rationalism.

The unfortunate Flavius gives in to the arguments of Segestes and does not join his countrymen in fighting against Varus. His heart is still torn, however, and he regrets that the Germans are getting the worst of the battle. To his great shame, Thusnelda and his own mother Adelheid, mere women, show themselves to be braver than he by resolving to die at the side of their men, whereas Flavius, corrupted by Segestes' materialism, feels that in joining the battle at this time he would be sacrificing himself to a hopeless cause. At last, however, when Segestes will not exert himself even to save his own daughter's life, Flavius becomes disgusted. He realizes that the possession of Thusnelda, which Segestes has promised him, is only an apparent good after all, and that he has forfeited his honor for nothing: "Cruel man, what profit do I have,/ That I am cowardly and lazy and disobedient?/ That the later world will still call me traitor?" (V. i). Now Flavius is ready to plunge into the battle; but it is too late, for the Germans have already conquered the Romans without him. This surprise victory has been won chiefly by Siegmund, who has torn off his priestly vestments to lead against the Romans those troops that Segestes had turned over to the

Romans. Thus one disobedient son has acted virtuously, and the other unvirtuously, in this logically balanced plot.

The returning German forces now surround Segestes and Flavius in order to punish their disloyalty. Segestes, ever the practical realist, pretends that he is happy the Romans are defeated and claims that he has been a loyal German all the while: "You have done with might, what I tried to do with flattery" (V. iii). But Flavius is too honorable to want to save himself in this manner. He exposes Segestes as a hypocrite, confesses his own part in the treason, and invites death. Hereby he redeems his character at last. Nevertheless, the drama ends in forgiveness, not punishment. Herrmann pardons his remorseful brother and also Segestes, who finally has the grace to regret his errors. Thusnelda, who has grasped a sword and fought in the battle like a man, returns alive, although presumed dead. The ending would be completely happy, if it were not for the fact that Sigmar, the father of Herrmann and Flavius, has been killed in battle. Poetic justice would seem to demand the death of Segestes rather than of Sigmar, but the author was more interested in moving his audience with Herrmann's magnanimity toward his enemies, and in showing how all the Germans, even the disloyal ones, are united after the defeat of Varus. Here sentiment and patriotism outweigh the demands of legality and justice.

In the person of Herrmann, Schlegel introduces the perfect and unsuffering hero, self-possessed throughout the drama and triumphant at the end, who can inspire admiration but certainly not pity. Such a character may be interesting, not in himself of course, but through the magnitude and complexity of the task that he successfully accomplishes. It is quite possible that the risks he undertakes will arouse fear and suspense in the spectators. One will also sympathize whole-heartedly with his project, and with him, as an excellent and dedicated person. It is difficult to see, however, in what sense he can be called tragic. It would almost seem that in *Herrmann*, the author, who had naively stepped off into the abyss of pessimism in *Die Trojanerinnen*, is making amends for past errors by removing in the later play all that was philosophically objectionable in the earlier one. That is to say, he retains a perfect character as titular hero (Hecuba was also perfect), but removes the suffering and the defeat. This adequately takes care of the treacherous pessimism. Then the tragic weight is shifted to the more suitable shoulders of a secondary, imperfect character, who does not have the full approval of the spectators and needs to be taught a severe lesson. To mitigate this severe lesson and punishment with generous forgiveness and to have it followed by definite moral improvement in the imperfect character is, from the viewpoint of the Enlightened philosophy underlying the play, a real master stroke—and one soon imitated by Krüger in his *Mahommed IV*. Here, then, is a "tragedy" that (supposedly) arouses strong emotions, and gives a positive model of virtue to be emulated, one pitiable and one execrable negative example of vice to be avoided, and a tableaulike finale of touching magnanimity. No Enlightened person could ask for more!

Beyond this high-water mark it was scarcely possible to go, even for Schlegel himself. Tragedy, in any case, refuses to remain tamed and civilized for long and tends to return ever again to its destructive primal appetites. Accordingly, in his last finished tragedy Schlegel was moved to create the character and fate of the demoniac Ulfo. Perhaps he only meant to give tragedy a somewhat longer leash; actually he opened its cage. It was five years after the completion of *Herrmann* when, in 1746, Schlegel wrote and published his *Canut* in Copenhagen. In the meantime he had busied himself mainly with comedies and critical essays, but when he turned to tragedy again it was to continue directly with the developments in his earlier works, and more than that, it was to produce his most popularly successful and influential drama.[26]

In this second attempt to treat an old Germanic subject [27] Schlegel was probably first attracted to the perfectly virtuous character of Canut, king of Denmark, who is, if it can be imagined, even more admirable and serene in his good qualities than Herrmann. Herrmann is a young man, still fighting battles. Canut has his victories comfortably behind him and possesses the wisdom that only age can bring. He sits on his throne like Providence in heaven, dispensing mercy and forgiveness, and he is secure and strong enough to grant freedom and favors to his avowed enemy. Suffering cannot reach Canut, as it cannot reach God. When Canut's semi-divine presence holds the stage, no one can believe for a moment that his enemy Ulfo's machinations will have the slightest success, and therefore fear for Canut is virtually ruled out. One does not really feel admiration for the old king; veneration would be an apter term for the feeling he inspires (unless "boredom" might be considered still more appropriate). Lessing recognized the godlike quality of Canut, saying with disapproval, "The hero or the best person must not, like a god, calmly and undisturbedly survey his virtues." [28] Nicolai suggested that Canut's kindliness itself could have been made into a fault, an error in judgment involving his bestowal of a troop command on the obviously hostile Ulfo,[29] and Lessing concurred with this, speaking of "the error of his not allowing his kindness to be ruled by intelligence." [30] But the author himself had no intention of suggesting that Canut may have had the slightest fault. He is the model of morality who must not suffer, who provides inspiration for positive emulation. Again, so to speak, Schlegel is doing penance for his unfortunate mistake with Hecuba. Though he said boldly enough in his *Abhandlung von der Nachahmung* that "pleasure takes precedence over instruction," [31] he was by no means ready in his own works to ignore the didactic, and much less to weaken morality by inviting the spectators to reflect pessimistically about virtue.

Nicolai felt that Canut was not actually the hero of the tragedy, the title notwithstanding: "If we now consider the tragedy *Canut*, we can come to no other conclusion but that Ulfo is the chief character and at the same time the main personage . . ." [32] Schlegel would hardly have agreed with this judgment; nevertheless, it is quite true that by exempting Canut from suffering and catastrophe he did place the tragic weight on Ulfo, who both suffers and dies— and richly deserves his punishment. Consequently the titular hero is reduced to a static position on the sidelines, while the main action and interest is reserved for the imperfect character, formerly secondary, now primary in importance. Simply because of the inertia inherent in perfection, the bad personage moves to the center of the stage. The development that originated in Pitschel's *Darius*, with the character Bessus, now has received a powerful forward impulse, and vice is allowed to become more interesting than virtue.

In the characterization of Ulfo, vice for the first time assumes the quality of greatness. Evil is no longer imperfect virtue, or even total lack of virtue, i.e., something negative, but an elemental principle of action rising up assertively in unappeasable hostility against the virtuous principle. The idea of evil versus good is not confined to any particular circumstance, as when a virtuous person seeks one goal and is hindered or bothered by an evil person who opposes the same goal; but, instead, evil and good combat each other as principles. Such a strife goes beyond the rational philosophy of the time, for Leibnitz' *Théodicée* did not provide for a dynamic concept of evil, and this was not to be found in the writings of Wolff or Shaftesbury either. It was a return to the ancient concepts of Christianity and Judaism.

Ulfo, it is true, does not consider himself evil. In fact, the question of good and evil does not interest him at all, and he hates and furiously combats the mental attitude that concerns itself with this question. He is the last spokesman of a past and discredited age, a barbaric age which possessed its own set of "moral" ideals, utterly different from and directly in contrast to those of the Enlightened persons who have taken over his world.[33] There could easily be something pathetic about the solitariness of a barbaric Ulfo lost in an environment that no longer has any sympathy left for his ideals —if Schlegel had permitted or wanted this to be so. There could have been something nobly tragic about his stubborn insistence on the maintenance of these outmoded ideals, even to the point of death. There could have been an awe-inspiring, although perverse grandeur in the way he grows angry at God and curses fate while dying, because both have failed him. The author, however, brands Ulfo's resistance not as unfortunate and pitiable, but as evil. Ulfo's powerful attempt to live life as he understands it is regarded as something altogether abhorrent. Yet, the author's skill in delineating Ulfo's motivation partially defeats his evident purpose, because it provides an understanding of Ulfo, and—"tout comprendre, c'est tout pardonner"—with that understanding there inevitably comes along a certain sympathy. One need not be a modern reader of the play to feel this sympathy. Nicolai, Schlegel's contemporary, recognized it, too. He said that certain scoundrels in drama can arouse a degree of pity in the spectators if the author gives them an "appearance of virtue" or a "false system of virtue." In the case of Ulfo, Nicolai speaks of "the false system of honor, the appearance of heroism which shines forth from all his words." [34]

It is doubtful, however, that Schlegel consciously put in the elements that made Nicolai feel a grudging pity for Ulfo. The obvious aim of the drama, after all, is to win the spectators' hearts for Canut and to arouse their admiration for his marvelous virtue. Any sympathy which goes out to Ulfo must necessarily be at the expense of one's feeling for Canut, since the person who is attracted to Ulfo's "heroism" cannot but be impatient of Canut's imperturbable virtue. And surely such a result was not the author's intention. What one learns of Ulfo's actions is uniformly bad, even atrocious. He has treacherously drowned a whole army of Canut's men. He has married Canut's sister Estrithe under false pretenses: by means of reporting that her true love Godewin acted in a cowardly fashion in a battle and by forging a letter stating that Canut had chosen Ulfo for her husband. He has deceived Estrithe into thinking that he has returned to the Danish capital to beg forgiveness of Canut, when he has come only to hatch new schemes against him. He accepts Canut's kindly proposal that he take charge of any army that will help the Slavic prince Godschalk to gain possession of his hereditary throne in Poland; but he does this only so that he can turn the army against Canut. He attempts to interest Godschalk in a treacherous plan to overthrow Canut. He persuades Canut to come to address the army, and when Godschalk warns Canut against this, Ulfo defiantly admits that he did indeed plan to overpower and kill Canut when he came. Ulfo is depicted throughout as merciless, treacherous, ruthless, and unrepentant. Only in one instance is he given a generous and honorable trait: in a duel with Godewin he disarms his opponent but does not kill him, saying, "No unarmed man has ever yet met death through me" (III. iii).[35] This generous impulse seems incongruous, however; it is either an inconsistency necessitated by the author's wish to keep Godewin alive, or it is not really something generous after all. Perhaps Ulfo's overweening pride would not be sufficiently fed by an easy victory.

In all of his evil actions, however, Ulfo is great. The sheer demoniac power of his selfish ambition prevents one from scorning him as Canut scorns him when he says at the end, ". . . the desire for fame, the noblest of impulses,/ Is nothing but madness, if it is not tamed by love of mankind" (V. v). Ulfo has shaken the foundations of passive virtue so strongly with his defiant speeches that this virtue begins to look pale and sickly and unmanly. In a scene reminiscent of the opening scene between Aurelius and Valerius in Quistorp's *Aurelius,* but far more vigorous and effective, Ulfo gives eloquent voice to the barbaric philosophy to which he is devoted, and he berates the virtuous Godewin for being passive:

What has become of the years, when the only pleasure was combat,/ When everyone thought only himself to be worthy of the crown,/ . . . When a spirit proved its nobility by defiance and restlessness,/ And it was not called a crime to be intractable?/ The field, when they had not yet learned to plough it, was/ Sown only with corpses, and the only harvest from it was fame./ Now everyone thinks he is fortunate to be a subject./ The kindness of Canut has stifled all courage./ The proud already love the gentle bonds of the ruler,/ And a coward considers ambition almost to be a disgrace./ . . . Obedience is a kind of fame— but only for inferior souls;/ For great spirits, honor is to give commands (II. iv).

After this glowing tirade it must have been difficult for the spectators of the time, especially if they were young men, to applaud the pious rejoinder of Godewin: "I demand no fame which grows out of wrong,/ Which nourishes itself from misfortune, and which deserves only curses" (II. iv). A moment's sober consideration, to be sure, would have convinced them that the right was on the side of Godewin.

Ulfo's indomitable attitude is less attractive in the later argument with Godschalk, the young Slavic prince, because it is not very agreeable to see Ulfo dangling the false promise of the Danish crown before Godschalk's eyes as a reward for joining in with Ulfo's treachery. On the other hand, it gives one pleasure to see Godschalk, out of gratitude to Canut, who has befriended him, resolutely reveal Ulfo's wicked plan. Ulfo seems less majestic than simply stubborn and unreasonable when he says, "I offered the foolish fellow both crown and scepter,/ And he does not have even the courage to keep silent./ . . . What good does it do, that a heart is stirred by the impulse of honor,/ When others are craven. . . ." (IV. iv). At times, Ulfo's character evinces a stoicism that enhances its heroic qualities. He is wounded in the duel with Godewin, and Canut, the soul of kindness, shows concern and tells him he should have the injury cared for; but Ulfo answers: "You know that I learned long ago to scorn my blood" (III. iii). This, of course, is heroism of a barbaric kind. With total disregard for the newer sentimental approval of tears as the noble outward sign of a sensitive and virtuous heart, Ulfo tells Estrithe, "Beloved, stand up, and be ashamed that you have wept" (V. ii). In general, Ulfo epitomizes perfectly what Lessing described in *Laokoon* as the barbarian: "Among the barbarians heroism was a bright, consuming flame which was always raging and which destroyed every other good quality in him, or at least blackened it." [36] On the other hand, Schlegel's concept of the desirable human personality constitutes the most complete contrast to Ulfo. It is a combination of rationality and sentiment typical of the mid-eighteenth century, and it is briefly stated in Canut's words about his sister Estrithe: "A spirit which *thinks* and *feels* can err only for a short time" (II. i, italics added). On such a well-balanced personage the attraction of virtue is not wasted. But Canut's attempt to convert Ulfo with kindness ("Believe me, I will, to tame the defiance of Ulfo,/ Put him to shame with kindliness, instead of sternness" [III. ii]) fails, because Ulfo, lacking any glimmer of humaneness, interprets this merely as weakness. He is therefore much worse than Kiosem in Krüger's *Mahommed*. And finally, since there is an end even to divine patience, Canut grows angry and orders the villain's execution: "He must, with his blood, give a lesson to the world:/ He who will not be humane is also not worthy to live" (V. iii).

The battle between good and evil, then, is won by the forces of good. Virtue remains secure and serene, while vice goes down to defeat and death. But in this last tragedy of Schlegel's the victory won by virtue is a Pyrrhic one; for the evil and vicious personage has become by far the most interesting figure, and has been allowed to acquire a morally dangerous attractiveness. In many tragedies to follow, vice, not virtue, will be the actual subject, and tragedy becomes a dramatic form in which forbidden strong emotions can be given an outlet.

V

THE HIGH TIDE
OF ALEXANDRINE TRAGEDY: 1746–1754

THE YEARS that passed between the appearance of Schlegel's *Canut* and the epoch-making debut of Lessing's *Miss Sara Sampson* were by no means such barren ones for the tragic genre as is generally assumed. True, more than the simple magnifying glass of the usual literary history is necessary for the discovery of the minute, yet opulent growth of tragedies in this period: the microscope of special investigation is needed to bring it to light. Then, however, the fact is revealed that this obscure decade saw the publication of as many original tragedies as the first fifteen years of Gottsched's reform, and these tragedies came into being, for the most part, without the disenthroned Master's direct prompting and outside his aegis. Nevertheless they were all written in the style and under the influence of the tragedies in the *Schaubühne* and thus are a convincing proof that Gottsched's word and model held sway—indeed, attained the summit of their prestige—long after the man himself had been "defeated" by his implacable Swiss adversaries. In these years it was not Schlegel's *Canut* with its revolutionary evil hero which set the pace for German authors. That important development was not exploited until middle-class tragedy began to be written. Since the main endeavor of these mid-century years was a conservative harvesting of the gains won by Gottsched, it is not surprising to find an element of torpid complacency in the tragedies. The patterns were set, it seemed, once and for all. Nothing more was necessary except to color in the empty spaces, one by one. Yet the authors of this period were not exclusively second- and third-rate talents. Among them were also Lessing and Justus Möser.

The first work to come under consideration here is *Vitichab und Dankwart, die Allemanischen Brüder*, by Krüger, the author of *Mahommed IV*. Written too late to be included in the *Schaubühne*, this play enjoyed the privilege of a separate publication in 1746 and, more remarkably, it won the distinction of being the first regular tragedy to appear on the stage in Vienna (1747). In spite of its exceedingly small intrinsic merit, *Vitichab und Dankwart* was given the enthusiastic approval of the Viennese audience, indeed to such an extent that the court theater director, Sellier, planned to make his stage "regular" from that time on.[1] This is a greater victory than one would expect to be gained by a rather fumbling and ineffective pair of "Alemannic brothers"; and, in point of fact, the "regular" German Alexandrine tragedy did not win a secure foothold on the Viennese stage until the 1760's, after it was already going out of fashion in Germany proper. Yet the temporary success of Krüger's drama in the city where Stranitzky had reigned supreme, and where his successors Prehauser and Kurz-Bernardon were presently reigning, is a noteworthy indication of the prestige of Gottsched's reform of the theater. Apparently any work that represented this reform with a fair amount of technical competence was able to attract the approving attention of persons dissatisfied with unliterary drama.

Krüger proclaimed to the world his allegiance to Gottsched by prefacing his play with a long poem in fulsome praise of Madame Gottsched's *Panthea* and with a letter addressed to the Master himself. In the letter, with careful obedience to the rules set down in the *Versuch einer critischen Dichtkunst*, Krüger formulates the specific moral lesson that his drama is supposed to illustrate, namely "that overhasty actions result in the greatest misfortune and cause nothing but confusion." [2] Evidently being motivated by an anxious desire to please Gottsched, this statement need not be taken too seriously, as though *Vitichab und Dankwart* were really a drama inspired by and based on one moral abstraction, and thus an exception to the general practice of tragic poets at that time. In fact, the unalerted reader of the play would scarcely guess that the mistake of overhastiness was being castigated in it, and the author must have had some difficulty himself in extracting this one "*Moralsatz*" from the action as presented. Krüger, no egotist, freely admits and describes the shortcomings of his play, as he sees them, and emphasizes the school-exercise quality of his work by humbly beseeching his Master to give him an expert opinion on it. Small wonder that Krüger asserted elsewhere that it had not originally been his idea to have this letter published, but that Gottsched had demanded it.[3] Nevertheless, Krüger was probably sincerely humble in his awareness that his tragedy was not a finished product, but only a modest contribution toward a greater goal, that is, the providing of Germany with a respectable body of regular dramas. Thus he replied in self-defense against a malicious criticism of the tragedy made by Christlob Mylius and M. Kästner: [4] "If it could be accomplished with empty wishes, then our fatherland would long ago have excelled the French. This, however, is not enough; one must also make attempts.

They themselves [Mylius and Kästner] are not able to venture anything, and therefore it vexes them when others do." [5]

In keeping with the strict rules, *Vitichab und Dankwart* has but one simple setting, before the tent of Vitichab, and its time is held to the passage of a few hours: "The story begins in the late afternoon, and lasts until the following morning." The Unity of Action, on the other hand, is not very skillfully maintained, as will be seen. Furthermore, the ideal of historical accuracy which Gottsched nurtured more and more appears to have been taken lightly, or understood with great latitude by Krüger. Existing documents [6] attest to the existence of an Alemannic king named Vithikab who was assassinated on the order of the Roman emperor Valentinian in the fourth century A.D.,[7] but the circumstances and characters represented in the drama are otherwise wholly fictional.

Vitichab is established at the outset (like Herrmann) as a representative of old-Germanic patriotic virtue standing steadfastly against the blandishments of the Romans: "The happiness of the fatherland, that is my only happiness" (I. i). He rejects the offer of Tiberius, who says that the Emperor Valentinian will make him ruler over all the Germans, not just the Alemannic tribe, if he will agree to sign a peace treaty with the Romans. The wily Tiberius has somewhat better success with Siegmar, an Alemannic prince, who also turns down the offer to be made ruler of all the Germans, but does allow certain suspicions about Vitichab's honesty to be aroused in him. Vitichab has delayed his marriage to Fredegund, the daughter of Siegmar, and now this strange delay awakes doubts in Siegmar's mind. These are strengthened by a conversation with Adelheid, the mother of Vitichab, who insists that there be no marriage until after the coming battle with the Romans. Adelheid is a woman of iron character who will condone no such happy occurrence as a marriage until the Alemannic tribe is free of Roman domination. Far from being convinced by her argument, Siegmar flies into an insensate rage and commands his son Radogast to slay Vitichab. If the reader expects this first-act conflict to be the main subject of the play, then he is soon disappointed—to the serious detriment of the Unity of Action. Siegmar's anger, which promises so much, actually serves only to produce a scene in which both his son Radogast and his daughter Fredegund show their great virtue by preserving an attitude of supreme filial piety and at the same time pleading for the life of innocent Vitichab. Radogast reminds his father that revenge is not a virtuous impulse: "And if he has committed some crime, let the gods avenge it" (I. vii). Siegmar is further enraged by their hesitancy to obey him and threatens to kill them as well as Vitichab; but Radogast and Fredegund re-establish their obedience by offering to die gladly at his hand. To make the situation still more touching, Fredegund begs him to take her life only, and to spare Radogast's. The effect of so much virtue and *Großmuth* is that Siegmar's heart is softened, at least a little.

In the second act a new element of the plot is introduced with Fredegund's report of a rebellion that is being fomented among the chieftains and soldiers against Vitichab. Contrary to expectations, it is not the embittered Siegmar who is at the bottom of this, but another German and a captured Roman who have been bribed to circulate a story showing that Vitichab is a traitor. Undismayed, Vitichab trusts in the safety afforded to innocence: "Banish this fear, for innocence will be victorious." Fredegund reminds him, "But, is not virtue often obliged to accept defeat?" To this Vitichab's sturdy answer is, "Not if one remains steadfast" (II. i). His confidence is shown to be justified when, a short time later, he is quickly able to vindicate himself before the assembled chieftains. The latter, now remorseful, beg him to continue as their leader. Thus the second plot possibility is terminated, and the main action has still not begun. With the battle against the Romans in the offing, Vitichab charges all the chieftains to be brave, and he underscores his words by swearing death to any man, of whatever rank, who retreats in the face of the enemy. Although it is not yet evident, this is the beginning of the main action. The result of Vitichab's oath will not become clear until the fourth act.

The somewhat confused reader is confronted with still another possible action when Vitichab commands Radogast to stay behind and guard the camp while the others go to battle. But Radogast, after some objections, simply acquiesces and that finishes the matter. There is a long farewell scene between Vitichab, his mother, and his sweetheart, which gives more than ample opportunity for the expression of heroic and virtuous sentiments. Fredegund is the spokeswoman for softer feelings: "Perhaps I am now seeing you for the last time, beloved Prince! / Therefore your bride cannot refrain from tears!" She is particularly distressed because she has learned of an oracle that prophesies the death of Vitichab at the hand of his brother—a brother of whose existence, however, he and everyone else are unaware. Adelheid, in contrast to Fredegund, is a Spartan mother who disapproves strongly of mixing love and patriotism: "Tenderness suffocates the courage in our breast,/ It only thinks of pleasure, and not of revenge and blood." Yet she has Enlightened concepts concerning the waging of war: "One does not hear heroes praised for the blood they have shed./ Wisdom makes them great, and not audaciousness,/ The one produces madness only, the other, bravery./ Therefore conquer yourself first. Spare the lives of your citizens./ . . . Thus hate victory and fame, for the welfare of your citizens./ Magnanimity, not the thirst for blood, should direct your sword./ Even in the hardest fray let yourself be stirred to pity." And finally she does shed some tears after all. Vitichab must cheer her and himself with some rather banal words of comfort: "And even though I die in the fray for my fatherland,/ Yet my fame will not die, it is impossible for that to die./ I died in order to win freedom for the German people" (II. vi).

The battle is fought during the third act, off-stage of course. Meanwhile, a number of distracting events take place back in the camp. Adelheid is arming herself morally for any eventuality. She believes that Vitichab's virtue, which he has practiced unceasingly from childhood on, will preserve his life. News of his death, however, would not shake her optimistic philosophy, since death is no real punishment for virtuous people: ". . . and even should he have to grow cold,/ Still through death he will receive the reward of virtue./ A virtuous man seeks his highest good in this,/ That he is satisfied, and with composure/ Tolerates good fortune and overcomes bad fortune;/ And bases his whole trust on the grace of the gods;/ And considers that to be best which they have sent to him,/ And faces it courageously, even if it be death itself" (III. i). This is a very neat summation of the rationalistic-virtuous attitude toward life. But Fredegund is still worried about Siegmar's hatred of Vitichab, which she now reveals to Adelheid. This issue is revitalized for no other reason than to furnish another scene in which Fredegund can demonstrate her really remarkable filial piety. For word now comes to her that Siegmar wants her to repair to "Hertha's woods" where she is to devote herself henceforth to celibate service of the goddess. This is the first instance in German tragedy of the nunnery theme that was to attain great popularity later on. Although this means eternal separation from Vitichab, Fredegund unhesitatingly resolves on obedience. Adelheid sheds tears at this, even though she is rationalistically opposed to a display of emotion: "I am moved! Who can refrain from tears?/ Though they disgrace me" (III. ii). Fredegund's ideal of obedience is so great that she rejects Adelheid's sensible suggestion that she should wait until the battle is over. But Adelheid, always dedicated to the principle of reason over inclination, does admit that Fredegund is acting virtuously: "Do not let love interfere with obedience./ Flee disobedience, avoid it to the grave./ The gods hate it, and the laws of nature/ Curse the person who practices it. Recognize these traps/ Which vice sets for you, in order to win you over./ If you love virtue, then you must flee in haste" (III. iii). This situation presents perhaps the most eccentric example of filial piety in all eighteenth-century tragedy. To appreciate fully the difference between the moral-rational attitude of the first half of the century and the sentimental-subjective attitude that arose so strongly after 1750, one need only compare Fredegund with C. F. Weisse's Julie in *Romeo und Julie* (1766).

Fortunately, Fredegund is prevented from becoming a celibate by Radogast. He is not a disobedient son, but he does have orders from a higher authority than his father, namely Vitichab, to allow no one to leave the camp: "Not I, the law of war offends my duty" (III. iii). Then suddenly Siegmar returns alone from the battlefield. It is not, as one might expect, to see whether Fredegund has obeyed his order or because he is still angry at Vitichab. Those matters are all forgotten, as though they had never existed. Instead, Siegmar tells how he saved the leader's life in a particularly bad moment of battle and then retreated, as he says, "only to withdraw the duke from danger" (III. iv). Unfortunately, the whole German army imitated his retreat. At this, Adelheid becomes enraged and declares she would prefer her son's death to his retreat. In the next instant, however, another warrior announces that Vitichab did not retreat after all, but returned to battle and defeated the Romans. Siegmar now stands there as a coward—and to make matters worse, Vitichab is believed to have been killed. True to her earlier sentiments, Adelheid takes the sad news with composure: "You gods! accept the thanks of a mother/ Whom your anger grieves, and your grace delights!/ Who mourns her son, and who is refreshed by his victory!/ You know that I rejoice in nothing else but Germany's welfare!" (III. v).

After this it is something of a surprise to find Vitichab, alive and well, opening the fourth act. He has been rescued from death by a German chieftain, and the day was a complete success. One wonders what has become of the tragedy? But then Siegmar confronts Vitichab. At long last, the true main action is beginning. Again without a word about the feeling of hostility so strongly emphasized in the first act, Siegmar now, with utmost respect, requests Vitichab to punish him for having left the field of battle. He acknowledges his guilt, denies all extenuating circumstances, and urges Vitichab to have him executed. Vitichab matches Siegmar's rational control by agreeing that the execution must take place at once: "You, father of my bride, how violently you wound me!/ You wish to be sentenced? Yes, I condemn you!/ As sovereign I must choose law, and not mercy./ Ah! friend, if you realized the pain which torments

me,/ . . . Then, O friend, you would pity me more than yourself!" (IV. ii). In this situation the two men present an ostensibly
inspiring and touching picture of strict virtue overcoming natural
inclinations. Fredegund's objections to the execution sway neither
father nor lover. Vitichab is no weak, un-German hero, for he does
not let his actions be dictated by his feelings for a woman: "I love
you more than myself, yet the law still more./ I am a sovereign, and
free, yet the slave of the laws" (IV. iii). The sternness of the punishment is mitigated only slightly by the fact that Vitichab decides to
have Siegmar fight a duel with Tiberius, the captured Roman, in
lieu of an outright execution.

If one compares the situation here with the quite similar conflict
between law and family ties in Krüger's earlier tragedy, *Mahommed
IV*, where a strong argument is made in favor of tempering justice
with mercy, then one might conclude that the author is here de-
ploring Vitichab's rational severity. Nevertheless, Vitichab is furnished with one impeccably noble speech after the other, and nothing
is said by any disinterested personage which would imply that the
author considers Vitichab to be in the wrong. His only tragic fault—
as was indicated in the prefatory letter to Gottsched—is his unre-
flective haste in sentencing Siegmar without first submitting the case
to the council of chieftains. And truly, this seems to be less a matter
of simple hastiness than of his concept of his own position: "Did
not the whole nation accept me as its duke?/ Just as their vote gave
the sovereignty to me,/ Thus also their oath gave me power over
life and death./ . . . It is the virtue of princes, that justice/ Rules
the world through them" (IV. iii). If this statement contains the
kernel of Vitichab's tragic error, then the author must have wished
to express some objection to the principle of absolutism. But he
should certainly have made his point clearer with prior explanations in the dialogue and some hints in the previous characterization
of Vitichab. Whatever the precise nature of the tragic fault may be,
it is at least definite that it is not rooted in passion, for all Vitichab's
emotion is working against the execution of a man who not only
was about to become his father-in-law, but has saved his life in battle:
"Although gratitude inclines me to clemency and grace,/ Still the
stern duties of a prince resist it" (IV. iv).

The duel with Tiberius, not unexpectedly, results in Siegmar's
death. The sorrowful Fredegund, when she hereupon questions the
justice of Providence, is treated to a moral sermon by Adelheid:
"Whoever consecrates himself to virtue,/ And willingly follows
destiny, him virtue cannot forsake./ When virtue oppresses such
persons, it only seems to hate them./ By this means it is only quelling

pride and testing their hearts,/ To see if they are steadfast. For we are by nature/ Inclined to vice, and lazy and slow toward virtue./ Its arm, by grace, often leads us through hidden ways,/ Though misfortune, through danger, to true happiness" (V. i). An interesting detail of this speech is the idea, very rarely encountered in the literature of this period, that human beings are given to vice "by nature." This is, however, the orthodox religious concept. Although Fredegund does not contradict Adelheid's arguments, she does nevertheless insist on her right as a bereaved person to indulge her feelings: "I much prefer to seem weak than insensitive." If the gods are displeased by this, then "Why did not their grace afford me a stronger heart?" (V. i).[8] Here the dawning Age of Sensibility sheds its mild rays over this otherwise sternly rationalistic tragedy.

If Vitichab's error remains somewhat doubtful, there is at least no question about Radogast's error—it is passion and overhastiness. Grief-stricken at his father's death, Radogast lends all too credulous an ear to Tiberius' false accusation that Vitichab ordered the fatal duel merely to rid himself of Siegmar's objections to his tyrannical rule. Maddened by this, Radogast feels justified in murdering Vitichab, and does so very dishonorably by stabbing Vitichab in the back. Although dying, Vitichab is still enough alive to be brought back on stage for some long speeches in which he awkwardly tries to establish the justice of his death. With the usual magnanimity of the dying tragic personage, he forgives Radogast, whose remorse is made all the sharper by the unexpected discovery that he is not the son of Siegmar after all, but a lost son of Adelheid—with the actual name of Dankwart—and consequently the brother of the man he has slain. The enormity of his crime stimulates Radogast-Dankwart to utter a long and frenzied speech full of the stereotyped ranting that passed at that time for tragic passion. At its conclusion he rushes out and kills himself in despair, thus suffering an even harder fate than Vitichab, who, it is reported, dies with a smile on his lips. Both brothers technically have no quarrel with Providence, since their tragic errors have been established, more or less artificially. The virtuous Adelheid, on the other hand, who now has lost two sons through no fault of her own, would appear to have good grounds for questioning the rationality of the world-order. Indeed, Krüger's second and last attempt at tragedy is considerably weaker than his first one. The Alexandrine dialogue is smooth and flowing, and there are a large number of interesting moralistic passages; but the faults of construction are so glaring and the characters so wooden and unconvincing that these good qualities are more than outweighed.

Next in line of appearance [9] was a tragedy entitled *Orest und*

Pylades, oder das Denkmaal der Freundschaft, which was published individually in Liegnitz in 1747.[10] The author was Christoph Friedrich von Derschau (1714–1799), a native of Königsberg and a court assessor in Glogau, who was to have a long career as a high governmental official in Cleves and Aurich. His personal contacts with Gottsched were made in the early 1740's [11] while he was an officer in the Prussian army. Since he was no student and already well past his thirtieth birthday when his *Orest und Pylades* was published, Derschau can scarcely be considered as one of Gottsched's circle of protégés. Yet there can be no doubt that he felt the Master's influence, and indeed Gottsched thoroughly approved of his tragedy. Ten years later, Gottsched went so far as to recommend Derschau's works to Fredrick II in a personal interview with the king in Leipzig.[12] When the king, however, came to write his notorious essay *De la littérature allemande* (1780), he must have forgotten Gottsched's recommendation, for he made no mention of Derschau in it. The royal critic's vague complimentary reference to a German poem, however, is thought to pertain to a work by Derschau.

Since Schlegel's version of the Iphigenia material had been presented on stage but not yet published, there is little reason to suspect that Derschau wrote his *Orest und Pylades* in a spirit of rivalry. One cannot say, however, that his drama is any worse, or any better than Schlegel's. In an extract from a letter published together with the drama he calls attention to Euripides' *Iphigenia in Tauris* and also to the *Oreste et Pylade* (1697) of Lagrange-Chancel, which latter work he justly claims is quite different from his own.[13] Derschau freely admits that he has changed the original story extensively, and feels no qualms about this, because it takes place "in very old times, and perhaps belongs completely to the realm of fiction." [14] His main alterations consist of a relegation of Iphigenia to a relatively minor role in the proceedings and the addition of a typically French love motif in the person of the princess Tomire, a complete newcomer to the traditional story. The name of this princess, however, and probably the idea of making her the rightful heir to the throne of Tauris, were suggested by the French tragedy of Lagrange-Chancel. Another feature which may well have come from Lagrange-Chancel, for it is to be found in the French play, too, is that Orestes and Pylades are separated by a storm and do not arrive in Tauris together.

Tomire is the daughter of the King of Tauris, Thoas.[15] She is in love with Pylades, a Greek stranger who has won the king's favor. But love has not brought her happiness: "How gently I used to pass my pleasant days/ In unworried peace when I was still without feeling!" (I. i). To be sure, if Thoas grants her permission to marry Pylades, her sorrow will be over. Into this situation, which is so ludicrously foreign to the traditional story, wanders Orestes, who is tormented by the sad result of his loyalty to his father, i.e., the disloyal murder of his mother. The Furies who pursue him are explained as figments of the imagination: "Every moment punishes the loyalty I offended,/ By day my reason, by night my phantasy" (I. ii). Pylades greets his refound friend joyously, and rationalistically tries to dissuade him from putting too much confidence in the oracle that has sent him to Tauris: "There rules a god in our breast, whom we must hear;/ His will can be made known to us, it is true, through the sybil's mouth,/ But much more clearly through the light of rational deductions" (I. iii). Orestes, however, apparently affected by the new Age of Sensibility, recognizes only too well the limits of human reason: "O sad reason, how dark is your light!/ Powerless weapon in the hands of weak human beings,/ Too feeble to turn aside the force of vice;/ You are, since you succumb to the fury of the passions,/ Only strong when you can point out the weight of crimes already done!" To Pylades, the grief of Orestes is only a sickness of the mind which reason and trust in the benevolence of the gods can cure. It is at first difficult to say whether it is Pylades or Orestes who speaks for the views of the author himself.

The villain of the drama, Thoas, is clearly in the wrong, of course. His concept of right and wrong is based on harsh and selfish realism, and therefore distinctly nonrational and un-Enlightened: "Whoever wishes to reign happily must lose no time,/ Nor dream of ideal magnanimity, that foolish illusion./ . . . Orestes' death is useful to me, and this makes it just" (I. v). The king has no prejudice against the Greeks as such. Evidently such a motive for having Orestes sacrificed seemed inadmissible and incredible to the author, and besides it would have been awkward to explain how Thoas could have accepted Pylades, also a Greek, and yet have summarily condemned Orestes. Therefore a much more "plausible" motive is invented, however trite, forced, and tasteless it may be: namely, Thoas is the brother of Aegisthus, the lover of Clytemnestra, whom Orestes has slain along with his mother. Revenge, then, is substituted for the weird and chilling barbarism of the original story. Thoas becomes just another king, and is no longer the somber chieftain of a remote Scythian realm.

Iphigenia's relationship to Thoas is quite cool and businesslike, and she seems to have no objections to sacrificing an enemy of the realm to Diana: "May this blood wipe out the troubles which threaten,/ Diana, accept it, and may it bring you pleasure!" (II. ii).

Very little is made of the reunion of brother and sister. She discovers that her intended victim is Orestes, and then reveals to him that she is his lost sister, and that she was miraculously brought to this place. To be sure, she does not allow the moment to pass without a conventional complaint to the gods: "Is such cruelty a pastime for you, a pleasure?" (II. iii). Pylades regards Iphigenia as a hardened butcher, and is somewhat surprised when his remonstrances concerning her misguided idea about serving the gods with bloody sacrifice make an impression on her. If even a heart like hers is not altogether immune to pity, "Then Providence will also break down the king's desire for revenge" (II. v).

The downgrading of Iphigenia, accomplished as described above, leaves room to devote the main action to the friendship of Orestes and Pylades. This friendship is stronger than Pylades' love for Tomire; based on virtue, it is even stronger than the gods themselves: "The sacred bond of virtue has united us so firmly,/ That the gods themselves lack the power to part us" (II. vi). Somewhat later Pylades declares that death itself cannot separate him from Orestes: "I know that even Pluto, as cruel as we may call him,/ Will not part two such friends in the underworld" (IV. v). Although the gods remain unperturbed by assertions of this kind, Tomire feels half depressed and half offended by it. She is too much a woman of feeling to be able to obey her father's command to stop loving Pylades. Nevertheless, she is disappointed in a lover who puts loyalty to a friend first and then excuses himself by saying, "When I swore allegiance to him, I did not yet know you" (III. v). Her lack of comprehension puts an added burden of care on Pylades, who embarks upon a very long, three-page soliloquy in which love and friendship are compared. As might be expected, friendship wins out—duty over inclination—and Pylades hopes that Orestes will forgive him for having wavered even an instant. Once the decision has been made, Pylades is able to combine enthusiasm with resolution. This is good rationalistic practice.

Pylades' first plan is to trick Thoas by asserting that he is actually Orestes; but the genuine Orestes promptly denies this before the king. In the midst of this confusion Pylades, trying to explain to Thoas why he has not revealed his "true identity" before this, gives voice to a rather ill-timed conventional denunciation of the cardinal sin of deception: ". . . the hateful constraint/ By means of which till now this pretense has almost killed me,/ A vice which makes Orestes himself [i.e., Pylades] blush" (IV. iii). The author could not neglect this opportunity to inveigh against deception, even though Pylades is at that moment involved in a deception of which one is supposed to approve. This is, of course, a very minor point against Pylades, if one takes it as such, in consideration of the next, higher development of his character. Thoas, not knowing which of the two men is Orestes, angrily decides to have both of them sacrificed. This decision readies the ground for a further refinement of Pylades' already exemplary virtue. Although his death now will no longer save the life of his friend, he refuses to accept Tomire's subsequent offer to help him to escape. He will accompany his friend to the altar, and bid farewell to the love of Tomire, just for the sake of mingling his ashes with those of Orestes in a common funeral urn. Lest this resolve appear all too incredible and really unfair to Tomire, the remark is made that the escape route offered by Tomire—a ship back to Greece—would separate Pylades from her anyway, and he would rather die than live without her. The evident torment of Pylades in this scene with Tomire adds an element of poignancy and humanity to his character. He cries out, "Where is the stony heart which would not be moved/ When a beloved eye is full of tears?/ The magical force of such power-filled weeping!" (V. ii). The special might of the love-sentiment is certainly given particular attention in this drama, but it is still subordinated to the claims of duty. Pylades in the end is not swayed by the tears of Tomire, and she herself is finally forced to admire his steadfastness and to wonder if she is worthy of such a man.

Although ideal friendship is the obvious theme of Derschau's play, there is also a remarkably strong note of stoicism present. It is not precisely the same as the apparent stoicism found here and there in the earlier dramas, where lack of feeling or abrupt changes in feeling are governed strictly by rational decisions that brand a given feeling as erroneous or evil. In *Orest und Pylades* stoicism becomes an end in itself, a weapon of defiance or, better, a wall of defense against a wicked and unjust world. It can be observed first in Pylades' long soliloquy, wherein the unhappy youth comes to the conclusion that life is hardly worth the living: "Therefore death never puts too soon an end to the stages of life/ And is never to be called more fortunate than when it is not expected" (III. vi). The attitude is revealed in a more pronounced way in Orestes and Iphigenia. They might well have increased the sentimentality of the play by a show of family affection. Instead they steel themselves for the coming ordeal of the sacrifice by eschewing all feeling, and Orestes instructs her: "Sister! Let us two most miserable people on earth/ Be similar to Fate in our insensibility./ Bore through my breast courageously and undauntedly,/ So that no flood of tears may show you are my sister" (IV. v). Iphigenia agrees to this, but her answer indicates that a stoical exterior should not be mistaken for mere callousness: "Tears can accompany only ordinary griefs" (IV. v). It is strange to find weeping relegated to this low position in a period when sentiment in its most extravagant forms was moving swiftly into dominance. On the other hand, the power of tears is referred to when Pylades and Tomire speak to each other. It would appear that the author was ever loath to omit any feature that might momentarily enhance the effect of a given situation. Stoicism is evident again in the bearing of Orestes and Pylades when they at last approach the altar. It is related of them that "No word of complaint was heard from their lips,/ No quiet sigh did honor to the king's wrath" (V. iv).

The happy conclusion of the play is brought about in a highly contrived manner which, although it keeps the action down to an earthly plane, is really no improvement over the *deus ex machina* of Greek drama. An old man—so we are told, for he does not so much as appear on stage—suddenly arrives in Tauris and announces to the people assembled for the sacrifice that Thoas is not the rightful king at all, and that Tomire is not his daughter, but the daughter of the virtuous king whom Thoas murdered. One wonders why Thoas should have gone to the trouble of raising Tomire so tenderly. However that may be, Orestes takes this opportunity to slay Thoas with the sacrificial knife, and now everyone is happy. Unfortunately, the author does not see fit to present any of this exciting action on the stage, but lets Pylades relate it all after its conclusion. This is one of the more flagrant examples—like the last act of the early play *Ulysses*—of the stifling effect exercised by the Unity of Place and the rule of *bienséance*. What might have been a fairly memorable dramatic spectacle is reduced to a pallid recitation spoken to two women standing on an otherwise bare stage. Quite possibly, however, it would have been beyond Derschau's modest talent to do justice to the omitted scene. For some, the classical rules acted as a welcome cloak of invisibility hiding incompetence. Since the most climactic action has been thus compromised, the high point of the play becomes the conciliatory ending, in which all the sympathetic characters smilingly face a bright future. Tomire becomes the queen and can marry Pylades after all. It is interesting to note in passing that she sighs briefly at the news of Thoas' death and mentions that he was always a good father to her. It would, of course, have been irrational to waste further sympathy on such a wretch! Orestes now discovers that the Furies are no longer assailing him. Presumably, as Pylades had tried to tell him from the beginning, the gods hold no grudge against him for the murder of his guilty mother. The voice of reason is rather to be trusted than the voice of despair, and

Orestes ends the play with an apostrophe to the benevolent rule of the gods: "O day! which has given all the world a great example/ How the council of the gods alone controls the outcome of deeds:/ For, without coming down to us on earth in person,/ How could they have shown their power more convincingly?" (V. vi). These lines would fit equally well—and perhaps better—at the end of *Nathan der Weise.*

In the next year (1748) appeared the first German tragedy since *Cato* to take for its subject an actual episode from Roman history. This was the *Octavia* [16] of Johann Friedrich Camerer (1720–1792), a native of the Riesgau who was in Danish governmental service.[17] The extreme weakness of this drama's plot structure, the absurdity of its characterizations, and the frequent downright obscurity of its clumsy dialogue indicate that Camerer was the most negligible talent as yet inspired to action by Gottsched's reform. Nevertheless, Gottsched, by this time grateful for any sympathizer who would fight with him against the detested Swiss critics, got in touch with Camerer in Braunschweig and spurred him on to polemical efforts.[18] *Octavia* is a martyr tragedy insofar as the whole play is devoted to a display of perfectly virtuous conduct in the face of adversity, and the heroine dies in the end. Only the element of Christianity is missing. The plot situation is similar to that of the *Haupt- und Staatsaktion* about St. Nepomuck. There is a sweet-mannered queen, Octavia, who is being rejected by her madly tyrannical husband, Nero, in favor of a wily temptress, Poppaea. The queen has an elderly spiritual adviser— Seneca—a young admirer, and a hypocritical enemy at court. These characters correspond so well to the figures of Augusta, Wenceslaus, Ahalibama, Nepomuck, Quido, and Dr. Babra (without the comedy of the latter) in the older play, that one could imagine that Camerer had taken *Nepomuck* for his model. Octavia is an extremely passive heroine for whom virtue means the maintenance of personal integrity, meek acceptance of humiliation, and complete dependence on Providence. She follows the teachings of Seneca, who, with the stoicism one expects from him, counsels rigid steadfastness and imperviousness to suffering and fear. As in Derschau's *Orest und Pylades,* the stoical attitude is recommended here as the best defense against an unjust and corrupt world. Both Derschau and Camerer allow their sympathetic characters to describe the world in pessimistic terms; but at least Derschau showed that in the end things were not so black as they seemed. Virtue was rewarded with happiness at last. Camerer, by providing no happy conclusion, makes the fate of his Roman empress akin to that of the saintly Admiral Coligny in Gottsched's *Parisische Bluthochzeit.* But at the same time he counteracts the pessimistic atmosphere with his contagious enthusiasm for the doomed heroine's virtue. He succeeds in expressing this enthusiasm far more emphatically than Gottsched. Obviously, for Camerer the concept of virtue has become an end and a religion in itself, free of all ties to practical results. Virtue, with or without Christianity, can lead to a martyrdom from which all bitterness and sense of defeat is removed. The heightened pathos of such a concept of virtue also proved attractive to other authors; the Enlightened martyr tragedy was a popular genre in the succeeding two decades. Some dramatists, however, arranged matters so that even the martyr-hero "earned" his death through some slight fault.

Octavia's confidante Epicharis paints a dreary, Gryphius-like picture of society, saying, "What is the world? A place of ever active torments,/ Full of illusion and nonsense. About which wise men lament,/ Where many a man lives godlessly, is full of great wickedness,/ And judges virtue only according to his own ideas and deeds." But Epicharis softens this pessimistic view with the further argument that troubles from the outside are without significance so long as one's soul remains free of guilt: "The black source of torments gushes from our hearts,/ An unsatisfied spirit is its own Hell, there is no other./ Nothing, nothing robs us of our worth, except what we ourselves do" (I. iii). This philosophical speech has the effect of giving Octavia courage and cheer, and makes her give up all thought of taking revenge on Nero for his faithlessness. She needs, it is true, the help of God to overcome her outraged feelings: "Providence! Ah! do not forsake my weakness,/ Since vengefulness is fighting against virtue in my breast" (I. iii). Much of the play's action is devoted to showing how Octavia refuses all temptation to take revenge and how she progressively gives up all chances to save herself physically in the interest of the higher goal of maintaining herself spiritually. Not even the welfare of Rome is of enough importance to persuade her to transgress against or compromise her ideas. Her admirer Tyridates, the exiled king of Parthia, urges her, as the descendant of Augustus, to stand up for her rights against Nero and not leave the city which needs her as protection against the tyrant. Octavia, however, will not hear of anything so undutiful and, as far as Rome is concerned, God must see to that. But stoicism has not weakened her confidence in the power of virtuous emotion. She still has a fund of what she believes to be effective tears and these, she hopes, will soften Nero's "wild heart" (I. iv). Whatever the outcome, she says, stoically again, "If my obedience cannot bend my dissolute husband,/ Then in dying I shall still display the noble-mindedness of innocence" (I. iv). Octavia is more deeply touched and disturbed when Tyridates next offers her his love and a life of peace as his queen in Parthia, which Nero has promised to restore to him. Since she is being sent away, i.e., divorced, by Nero, it would seem that she could legitimately accept Tyridates' suggestion, and indeed the temptation is strong. Epicharis sums up the situation for her: "Here husband struggles with friend, here duty struggles with youth./ Oh! far too difficult a position for a virtue which is being tested" (I. viii). Nevertheless, Octavia manages to gather strength and refuse Tyridates.

Nero is portrayed as an entirely selfish and arbitrary man, who recognizes no authority over himself except the beauty of Poppaea, to whom he has become a slave. He does not listen to the reproaches of Seneca, but gives ear to the flattering Paris, who confirms him in his madness: "Are sovereigns under the law? The people are subject./ For that is why a prince rules, so that he can give orders" (II. iii). To this Seneca retorts in good Enlightened manner, "You were born for the people, not they for you" (II. iii). Bad as Nero is, however, his wickedness stems from weakness of character rather than from elemental evil. Infatuation with Poppaea has dulled his reason, and bad counsel from Paris does the rest, so that one is again reminded of the important part that wicked advisers play in the making of a tyrant. The glimmerings of conscience which still stir in Nero's heart are allayed by Paris' lies: according to him, Octavia is guilty of infidelities with Tyridates, and Seneca is a hypocrite who lives in luxury and thirsts for the imperial power himself. Further pressure is put on Nero by Poppaea, who threatens to withhold her favors unless Octavia is done to death. Consequently Octavia's sentimentally worded appeal to Nero, on which she had put all her hopes, falls short of success. Too much the slave of his own passions, he answers, "My heart speaks for her, but love says no" (III. iii).

At this juncture Octavia is again tempted to use force in her own defense and to accept the offer of the imperial guard, which is ready to rebel against Nero in her behalf. But Seneca points out the fallacy of this temptation, and she answers, "I am happy/ That your wise voice leads me back to my duties/ And touches my inflamed heart with new humanity" (IV. ii). As a result of this, Octavia renews her appeal to Nero, and shows again that her stoicism is combined with a large dose of sentimentality: "Ah! give in to your tears, consider your [good] impulses" (IV. iii). To this Seneca adds his strong admonitions about the danger of surrendering to lustful desires. The dual assault on heart and on reason softens Nero somewhat, but then Paris comes in and Nero, forgetful of all else, goes off with him to look after Poppaea. Octavia realizes now that she is inevitably doomed. Nevertheless, she unhesitatingly refuses Tyridates' renewed invitation to flee with him, and she again resists the urging of the imperial guard. The people of Rome are up in arms to defend her, but Octavia persists in holding to her own notion of virtuous behavior. For steadfastness in this she has Seneca's promise that her spirit will never perish.[19] Her death, as reported by Epicharis, is a model one. Not only is she not afraid to die, but she prays for Nero's life and for his happiness with Poppaea. There is triumph instead of defeat in this demise, because Octavia has lived up to Seneca's teachings, which are designed to release the virtuous individual from all compulsion and depression. These teachings are summed up in Seneca's last speech to Nero: "No steel can wound the man who feels no wounds,/ Who in his steadfastness makes sport of pain and wounds./ No enemy frightens me, no injustice can attack me,/ Because no power nor misfortune can injure a wise man" (V. ii).

Octavia's moral victory is not put in jeopardy by anything so cynical as a depiction of the subsequent happiness and success of her wicked adversaries. On the contrary, Nero's bubble of happiness is pricked as soon as he hears of Octavia's execution, and he is seized with remorse. There is no more talk of lustful delights with Poppaea, who now unaccountably drops out of sight. Nero recognizes the perfidy of Paris and sees himself deserted by all whom he considered to be his friends. His conscience is torn by the memory of all the deaths he has caused and he begins to fear the horrors of Hades which are in store for him. In the end, according to the stage directions, he "runs off stage raging." His situation is comparable to that of Schiller's Queen Elizabeth in the last scene of *Maria Stuart*, with this difference, that he suffers regret in addition to defeat. It constitutes the usual and most satisfactory conclusion for a martyr tragedy.

In this period of imitations and meager talents it is no cause for wonder that the only tragic production that has conspicuously escaped oblivion should be an unfinished play, a torso. For the torso was the work of the young Lessing, and that is reason enough, at mid-century, to name *Henzi*, even in its unfinished state, the most important tragedy of its day. Although *Henzi* was published for the first time in 1753, in Lessing's *Briefe* (Nos. 22 and 23),[20] it was composed in 1749, not long after *Octavia*. In 1749 Lessing was still engaged in competition with the disciples of Gottsched to produce *better* comedies and tragedies, but of the same general type as had been presented to the public in the *Deutsche Schaubühne*. *Henzi*, too, as far as it goes, is a quite regular Alexandrine tragedy showing perfect obedience to the Unities and to all conventions, except that it has an all-male cast of characters—a situation that might well have been changed if the play had been completed. Its one great innovation is that the historical event selected for dramatization was an immediately contemporary news story. The other pupils of Gottsched had left such plot material quite alone; but the authors of *Haupt- und Staatsaktionen* had sometimes dramatized modern incidents, with a preference, it is true, for more illustrious heroes than Samuel Henzi. Lessing's choice of a citizen-hero instead of a king or a high noble was not a daring move, and emphatically does not mean that he wrote a bourgeois tragedy. There was sufficient precedent for his choice: Henzi's position in republican Berne is not essentially different from Timoleon's position in republican Corinth or even from Cato's in republican Rome. Criticism of the time was not directed against the choice of hero in this play, but against Lessing's characterization of him, which some felt to be out of harmony with the actual facts.[21] Such politically-grounded criticisms may well have helped to fashion Lessing's later opinions, in the *Hamburgische Dramaturgie*, regarding the unimportance of historical accuracy in the tragedy. From this experience Lessing could learn how the demand for historical accuracy, so often voiced by Gottsched in his prefaces to tragedies, might expose a work of art to the prejudiced judgment of political opinion.

Henzi, like the other tragedies at mid-century, shows no influence of J. E. Schlegel's *Canut*, with its new element of diabolical evil. It is a work conceived wholly in the early rationalistic spirit, and it follows Gottsched's original precept better than most tragedies of this period in being dedicated to the discussion of one definite moral problem, namely, the difference between justified and unjustified revolution. In doing so, however, it adopts a leisurely pace which, with long speeches and little action, greatly hampers the development of any dramatic vitality. As far as the fragment goes, the hero is represented as perfect, without a tragic fault. It is possible, even logically probable, that Lessing may have intended to introduce a tragic error into his behavior before the catastrophe, as Gottsched did with his Cato. The emphasis on passivity which was observed in *Octavia* and which characterizes many later tragedies is lacking in *Henzi*. As in *Der sterbende Cato*, in *Timoleon*, and in the tragedies found in Gottsched's *Schaubühne*, active resistance to the forces of evil is not regarded as contrary to virtue. The titular hero is a thoroughgoing rationalist who permits himself no emotions except those that reason sanctions: his patriotism and his friendship. The political situation in Berne causes him anger and grief, it is true, but not to the point that they affect the clarity of his thinking. Thus he counsels his rash friend Wernier: "Go! and let wisdom overcome your anger" (I. i). A degree of sentimentality is noticeable in the manner adopted by Wernier to persuade Henzi to explain his concern and grief: "Have I deserved this, that he is so cruel/ And closes off to me the sweet path to similar grief?" (I. i). This emotional attitude does not altogether meet with Henzi's approval, for he would rather overcome his sorrow than seek any comfort in sharing it: "What does it profit me to have my friend join me kindly in weeping?/ Nothing, except that I seem twice as miserable to myself in him" (I. i). But Wernier persists in his morbid desire to "enjoy" a melancholy feeling: "How blessed it is, Henzi, to grieve oneself for one's fatherland" (I. i).

The absolute justice of Henzi's decision to rebel against the town council of Berne is underlined at length. To begin with, Henzi states that he is not motivated by private grievances, even though he does have some. What troubles him enough to provoke action is that the whole council is composed of unvirtuous tyrants who are depriving all the citizens of liberty. He lists a series of the vices which characterize the council: selfishness, tyranny, nepotism, graft, punishment of those who speak up for liberty. These offenses cannot be accepted with indifference by any honest man: "Freedom! when nothing remains to us of you, you seed of all virtue,/ You antidote to all vice, nothing except your name,/ And then if my decadent heart is deaf to just anger:/ Then I am not worthy of my blood—not worthy of the day" (I. i). Next, he unequivocally states that the aim of the revolutionaries is not to seize power, to substitute one tyranny for the other: "May the thrice powerful God punish us and our children/ If His all-seeing eye finds us to be self-seeking;/ If we want to take revenge on tyranny only/ So that our brothers should exchange it for ours" (I. i). Thirdly, although Henzi stands ready to use armed force, he will do this only as a last resort: "But we will do everything before we venture this extreme measure./ No sword can honorably bear the blot of a fellow citizen's blood" (I. i).

Unfortunately, Henzi's immaculate program for revolution is endangered by the presence of a rival leader, a professional troublemaker named Dücret. This individual is not motivated by idealism, but by coarse passions of revenge, cruelty, and blood lust. As Wernier says, if freedom must be won with the help of such as Dücret, it would be better to accept continued slavery. Wernier is passionate enough himself, however, to wish to kill Dücret and thus get rid of him in the most expeditious manner. As mentioned before, the rational Henzi tells Wernier to curb his anger. In a scene between

Henzi and Dücret, their different characters are clearly highlighted. Henzi reflects at length before he acts, while Dücret is thoughtless and rash. Therefore Henzi rebukes him, saying, "A spirit like yours always rejects precautions./ What do you know besides foolhardy audacity?/ I am not lacking in courage. But you are lacking in circumspection" (I. ii). In other words, bravery must be combined with reason before it can qualify as a virtue—as Thomasius had taught.[22] Dücret's villainy stems from his total lack of rationality, his self-abandonment to blind passions. His fury knows no moderation, and he contemplates the cruelest deeds with relish: "Terrify, murder, burn, wipe out child and house,/ And with fire and sword erase Berne's shame and slavery!" (I. ii). He does not share Henzi's confidence in God, either as the primary agent of vengeance or as the guardian of virtuous human causes, for he declares, "He does not look down from His high seat on anything so small./ Free from cares, He, for the punishment of tyrants,/ Has created feelings and rage and steel and fists" (I. ii). For such deistic cynicism and all too active impatience, Henzi calls Dücret a blasphemer. He points out that Dücret, whether he knows it or not, is actually a slave: "Do you not serve, when you serve vice?" (I. ii). But Dücret refuses to listen, and propounds the opportunistic theory that "Need sanctions everything. It cancels out vice,/ And soon turns it into virtue, if only good fortune and victory are the result" (I. ii). His argument is similar to one used by the villain Pharnaces in *Cato;*[23] but it is also very like that of Gräfin Terzky in *Wallensteins Tod.*[24] In the savagery of his intentions Dücret seems to be related to Schlegel's Ulfo, but nevertheless he is still an old-fashioned villain, the product of insufficient rational control. He can rationalize to justify his wrong actions, but he is not able, like Ulfo and his literary progeny, to use reason perversely in the service of a diabolical, anti-virtuous code. Furthermore, Dücret is made to seem childish and rather foolish in comparison to Henzi. He has acquired none of Ulfo's hellish grandeur.

Dücret's most effective argument is that pure virtue, minus action, will never achieve a successful revolution. The rational attitude results in impotence: "For you can do nothing more than take counsel, doubt, arrive at conclusions,/ As virtuous as you are, as eager as you are for honor;/ And a heroic deed requires something more. . . . Bravery in the breast must be accompanied by steel in the hands/. . . . O effeminately brave time!" (II. i). The council of Berne neither will listen to honest pleas nor does it deserve any consideration: "Of what use are rights and pleadings in dealing with a tyrant/ Who has to support his vices with new vices?" (II. i).

With such words he convinces some of the conspirators that patience is pointless, and one of them says, "Let this night show/ Whether virtue only makes cowardly citizens of us,/ Whether it never takes the sword of vengeance into its pious hands" (II. i). This same speaker is also very eager to outdo, it would appear, even Timoleon in his fanatical patriotism: "But blood and happiness belong first of all to the state./ Its beckoning, its welfare shall be to us the holiest of duties,/ And though our fists and steel be directed against a father" (II. i).

Henzi is obliged to use all his eloquence to counteract the force of Dücret's persuasion. He tells the conspirators that they are not worthy of liberty, because they do not understand either virtue or duty. In their misguided zeal, they have been about to conduct themselves as tyrannically as the members of the council. He asks, "Has then bloodthirstiness also become a virtue?/ And is it civil duty to murder the citizens?" (II. ii). Then he reveals that Dücret has made a list of council members who are to be slaughtered, and high on the list stands a man whom they all admire. The conspirators, now realizing that Dücret has been leading them down paths of vice, turn against him. Henzi reminds them that they are to be "Indeed the enemies of vice, but always humane enemies" (II. ii). This in one sentence sums up the moral of the play—action must be taken against oppression, but action need not necessarily be understood in terms of bloodshed. Is it a more refined moral than that of Behrmann's *Timoleon*, which did in the final analysis give consent to bloodshed, even to fratricide, in the name of liberty? It is to be remembered that the tyrant killed in *Timoleon* had been given every chance to reform and would not, and that the assassination was carried out with the utmost reluctance and repugnance. On the other hand, Henzi himself has stated that he would agree to the use of arms if everything else failed. In both works, the feeling is that liberty may be defended with forceful physical action, if need be, but that the action must be virtuous and preceded by careful reflection. Lessing's *Henzi* contains no new development in political-rational thought. Furthermore, it contributes nothing new to the development of tragedy. This fragment of a drama, however, has the aspect of a quite well-completed philosophical dialogue, and the leisurely, undramatic form of the work lends support to this view of its essential character.

In the same year that Lessing was writing *Henzi*, the somewhat older Justus Möser (1720–1794), whose name is associated more with Storm and Stress than with Enlightenment, published his one tragedy, *Arminius*.[25] Like *Henzi*, Möser's tragedy is an intensely serious, very thoughtful work which seems to be less dedicated to entertainment than to philosophical discussion of a political theory. The question that Möser raises on stage is whether monarchy as a form of government is preferable to democracy or oligarchy. The author decides for monarchy. Following the suggestions of the *Critische Dichtkunst*, Möser adapted the meager historical facts surrounding the death of Arminius to serve as a vehicle for an idea of his own which he wished to illustrate. Instead, however, of choosing a universal moral precept, as Gottsched had directed, he took a debatable political theory. To be sure, he bolstered the theory of monarchy with moral and virtuous principles, but the theory itself still stands aside from general morality and remains subject to debate. Consequently the effect of the tragedy is ambiguous and depends on the spectator's personal views. This is not the case in other tragedies of the time in which political questions arise. For example, the effect of *Cato*, *Timoleon*, or *Aurelius* does not depend on whether one personally favors monarchy or democracy, for in these plays one has only to be on the side of moral virtue and against error and depravity in order to comply with the authors' intentions. In Möser's *Arminius*, however, the hero will appear either sympathetic or unsympathetic in direct relationship to one's individual feelings about monarchy. His opponent is not vicious or even deluded, but simply a virtuous man with a different political opinion. It is true that there is also a villain on the opposing side, but his evil actions are not sufficient to obscure the political issues at stake.

The chief characters are Arminius, who wants to be king of all the German tribes; his father-in-law, Sigestes, who opposes these ambitions out of selfish reasons; and Sigismund, son of Sigestes and brother-in-law of Arminius, who is opposed to monarchy on idealistic grounds. Thusnelda and some German princes play subsidiary roles. From the beginning, Sigestes reveals himself to have an irrational, passionate, self-seeking nature. Suspecting Arminius' ambition, he immediately seizes upon murder as the only way to combat it—not for patriotic reasons, but because he fears that Arminius as king will ruin him personally. His son Sigismund vainly reminds him that it is irrational to expect the worst, ". . . since reason teaches us to hope for the best" (I. i). Sigestes is disinclined to let reason influence his emotions: "Reflection weakens just anger" (I. i). At once Sigismund is caught between his father, who demands unquestioning filial obedience, and his friend Arminius, who is bent on having an office to which Sigismund feels no one has a right. Sigismund is completely rational, but Arminius is no less so. The two have equally cogent

arguments to support their differing opinions. One might say they
have moved on to free ground, where debate is possible—a rare
thing in eighteenth-century German tragedy. Arminius, however,
is less passive than Sigismund. While Sigismund is against further
war with the Romans, inasmuch as the Germans are now independent, Arminius judges that continued attacks are necessary to wipe
out the danger completely: "For whoever loves the fatherland with
rational zeal,/ He knows that false quietness hides treacherous cunning,/ That the only fruit of peace is a worse war" (I. ii). Without
shame Arminius confesses that he wants to be king. He believes
that the people will take away his temporary power as leader as
soon as they no longer need him for war. He dislikes this ingratitude,
but he is also worried lest disunity result among the tribes when they
have no single leader. The liberty of which Sigismund speaks he terms
a "false freedom" (I. iv), because it will lead to civil strife worse
than Roman domination. This attitude stiffens Sigismund's opposition to Arminius, although he does not forget his friend's good
points: "My heart, removed from hate, removed from flattery,/
Admires your merit, curses your actions" (I. iv).

There is fanaticism on Arminius' side, as well as on Sigismund's.
Arminius' associate Adelbert advises fast action, the slaughter of the
princes before they have a chance to confuse the common people
with their talk of freedom. Arminius is not prepared to do this: "I
feel humanity aroused in my breast" (I. v). In reply, Adelbert produces arguments in favor of expediency, like Pylades in Goethe's
Iphigenie: "Necessity, carrying a scepter of hard diamond,/ Ruling
undisputed even over the might of destiny,/ Must here, according
to your wish, settle the strife of outraged duties/ In favor of the
death of your enemies and your welfare" (I. v). Adelbert speaks
also, like Selim in Krüger's *Mahommed*, against showing mercy to
one's enemies: "An enemy whom one pardons believes that one fears
him./ Severity alone can cultivate patient slaves./ God Himself is
not honored unless He sends avenging thunderbolts/ Which punish
those who scorn Him as well as protect the innocent" (I. v). But
Möser, influenced by the increasing sentimentality of the day, has
Arminius emphasize the mercy of God rather than His justice:
"Cursed be he who borrows only the thunder from God/ And who
does not, like Him, grant pardon to the weaker enemy" (I. v).
Arminius believes that virtuous kindness will be enough to win
over the rebellious princes: "If my noble-mindedness can touch their
free hearts,/ Then their hatred will turn to shame and depart against
its will,/ And their contrite hearts will kneel before me in humility"
(I. v).

Through the actions of Sigestes the author demonstrates that the love of freedom may lead to vicious exaggerations, just as monarchy may spawn tyranny and harshness. In urging defiance of Arminius, Sigestes declares that not even God could make him abandon his liberty. Sigismund loves freedom too; but he is no more willing to preserve it through a vicious deed (the killing of Arminius) than Arminius is willing to become king through murder of the princes. Yet Sigismund is tormented because he owes filial obedience to Sigestes, and Sigestes has commanded him to kill Arminius. Duty here runs exactly counter to virtuous feeling, and Sigismund exclaims, "I am being cast into the stream; I obey against my will,/ Dehumanizing my feeling in order to answer the call of freedom" (II. iii). When Arminius gets wind of the plot against him he cannot imagine that his friend Sigismund, whose life he once saved, would seriously consider assassinating him. Adelbert, however, points out to Arminius that reason, falsely employed, may succeed in stifling the humane feelings of the heart (just as it is able, correctly employed, to stifle wicked passions): "He who thinks he is right/ And then combines a hard heart with his delusion,/ He becomes blind, proud, and wild for the sake of imagined duties,/ And will annihilate the whole world as a sacrifice to his delusion" (III. ii).

Adelbert is given the task of persuading Sigismund of the advantages of monarchy. In attempting to do this, Adelbert paints a picture of an Enlightened, benevolent king: "Fortunate is the country which is ruled by only one prince,/ Who wields the scepter of divinity only in order to do good;/ To whom the most sacred law is the welfare of his people,/ And whose inexhaustible treasure is their willingness./ Such a one, believe me, is Arminius" (III. iii). He assures Sigismund that monarchy does not mean the end of personal liberty: "You err: freedom stands unharmed next to the throne./ The prince is made the servant of the people by nature" (III. iii). In spite of these liberal statements, Sigismund retains his doubts. When he asks Arminius the searching question whether he, Arminius, would like to lose his freedom, Arminius is unable to answer (III. vi). Nevertheless, Sigismund cannot bring himself to kill Arminius, saying, "I am paralyzed; a god holds me back" (III. vii). In addition, he stops Sigestes from drawing his sword against Arminius.

Sigestes thereupon goes from bad to worse, and does not hesitate to add deceitfulness to his list of crimes. He pretends to Thusnelda that he has decided to accept Arminius as king, but does this only to throw Arminius off guard and to preserve his own life. The love for liberty excuses everything for Sigestes and makes of him a fire-breathing fanatic like Dücret in Lessing's *Henzi:* "For where the fatherland's hereditary freedom is concerned,/ There I do not know any feeling, and do not hear Heaven./ There I have no friend, no happiness, no children./ In relation to this sacred duty everything else grows incomparably small" (IV. vi). It is obvious that in such a speech the author is trying to discredit the concept of freedom, which can so easily develop into a mania. He is, however, fair-minded enough to demonstrate in the character of Sigismund that not every stubborn liberty-lover is such a maniac. Still, Sigismund chooses an alternative to submission which can hardly be termed strictly virtuous. This alternative is suicide, which is as great an error in Sigismund's conduct as it was in Cato's, although Sigismund is indeed caught in a well-nigh insoluble dilemma. Whichever way he turns, he is offending some duty, giving up some principle. Tragically, he does not even have a sure belief in a happy afterlife to comfort him; but nonexistence seems more tolerable to him than his present position: "O unbroken night!/ If it is true that a man never awakens from your rest,/ Then take my spirit now into your dark valleys" (IV. vii). The fate of Sigismund seems unduly harsh for so estimable a person, and one might well see in it a departure from the optimism of the Enlightenment, were it not for the fact that Sigismund is Möser's object-lesson for the doctrine that monarchy is the best form of government and that freedom (democracy or oligarchy?) is a snare even for the virtuous.

Arminius, meanwhile, has not been deceived by Sigestes' apparent change of heart. Indeed, rational persons in these tragedies are frequently shown to be proof against deception, while irrational ones often are not. Arminius has also retreated somewhat from his earlier forgiving attitude. Possibly, Möser wished to make it clear that Arminius was not a counterpart to Schlegel's Canut, whose boundless gentleness and forbearance, being carried out almost to the end, gave the appearance of weakness. Now Arminius is determined to punish Sigestes: "It is kingly to pardon. But never to punish,/ Out of indolent kindness always to close one's eyes to all crime,/ Does not befit any prince. He encourages evil/ And weakens virtue's spirit, who can always pardon" (IV. viii). Certainly Sigestes has not been softened by Arminius' kindness, and the death of Sigismund has only served to infuriate him still more: "I recognize no son who stabs himself out of fear,/ Who can deny me, the fatherland, and himself" (V. i). He defies God, crying out, "What do I care for thunderbolts? The fatherland/ Is more than all power—" (V. i). In all of this raving there is not a jot of grandeur, for he is simply a confused man blinded by his own passions. He is shown up in his stupidity by a German soldier who leads him to prison. When this good man says he does not have sufficient rank to judge a quarrel between such high personages as Arminius and Sigestes, Sigestes upbraids him for his slavish attitude: "Too little? Are you already using the language of venal slaves?/ Does not freedom give us all equal rights?" (V. iii). But the simple, yet straight-thinking German replies, "We are free and act so, but according to reason and law./ If this is being slavish, then I too am a slave" (V. iii).

This speech by a contented subject of the new monarch would have been a fitting ending to the drama insofar as its political message is concerned. But Möser could not very well pretend that Arminius lived and reigned happily ever after when it was a matter of record that his hero had been treacherously murdered. Consequently, the play ends with the death of Arminius at the hands of Sigestes, who breaks away from his guards just as Arminius is giving orders that Sigestes should be treated kindly in prison. In deference to decorum, Möser lets this violence occur off stage. What justification is there for Arminius' unhappy end? Sigestes, to be sure, is adequately punished by being torn to pieces on the spot by the people. But Arminius dies guiltless, unless his kindness to Sigestes can be construed as a tragic error; for Adelbert says, "Noble-mindedness was his death" (V. viii). On the other hand, anyone who remains unconvinced by the author's arguments in favor of monarchy may feel that Arminius' desire to become king constitutes his tragic fault, and that his death is completely justified. In Vienna, where the tragedy was performed in 1751, sympathy probably went out to Arminius. In a free city the audience might have chosen Sigismund as the hero. In any case, Möser's drama is one of the best-written Alexandrine tragedies, with excellent dialogue and careful construction. The ambiguity of its effect is a result of the author's honest effort to present both sides of a question fairly, and is not the mark of mere ineptitude. The modern reader, being less concerned with the philosophical justice of a tragic hero's death, can enjoy the play as the tragedy of two well-intentioned men who are victims of their own unalterable idealism. It would be to Möser's credit if one could imagine that he intended the play to be understood in this way. In the middle of the eighteenth century, however, pure virtue could not be treated with such irony.

Möser was not the only historian who, at this period, tried his hand at tragedy. Another was Johann Gottfried Bernhold (1720–1766), who in 1752 published two dramas entitled *Irene oder die von der Herrschsucht erstickte Mutter-Liebe* and *Johanna die Heldin von Orleans*.[26] Bernhold, the son of a prominent theologian, was a professor of history at the University of Altdorf and also "Inspector" of resident students and university management.[27] Although he was over thirty years of age when his two dramas were, in the same year, presented to the reading public, there seems to be considerable justification for assuming that *Irene* was written by a less mature author than *Johanna*. *Irene* is an overly complicated, poorly constructed hodgepodge of themes borrowed from other tragedies of the Gottsched school, notably from Krüger's *Mahommed*. *Johanna*, while far from a brilliant play, is clearly and solidly constructed. The choice of plot is original and shows self-confidence. Indeed, in *Johanna* the author is sufficiently independent of Gottsched's authority to venture a change of scene in the last act. *Irene* makes the impression of being, like most other Alexandrine tragedies, a sensational exploitation of a historical event, while *Johanna* is perhaps the first German drama to strive for the honest delineation of an interesting historical character.

The tragedy *Irene* is a prime example of the perverse talent of dramatists influenced by Gottsched for making history seem like stupid and hackneyed fiction. The sad story of Constantine VI of Byzantium (ruled 770–797 A.D.) and his ruthless but fascinating mother Irene is excellent material for tragedy, but in Bernhold's hands it furnishes only a dull and confusing picture of palace intrigue, lacking pathos and suspense. Constantine is a conventionally benevolent ruler who includes among his other virtues a very persistent filial piety. It is obvious from the beginning that this will be another of those tiresome cases where a rather inactive and myopic king is assailed alternately by the rantings of virtuous and evil advisers, while ill-defined plots and counterplots swirl about in the background. Yet this play has its remarkable features: it is the first German tragedy since Gottsched's reform to be named after its villain instead of its hero, and this villain (i.e., villainess) possesses an important new characteristic.

Irene's personality is not impressive enough to dominate the drama and she does not exert the perverse attraction of a diabolically evil personage like Ulfo in *Canut*. Basically she is still a tedious old-fashioned villain, but there is one difference: Irene, aside from her one ruling passion of ambition, cultivates a surprisingly rational control over her emotions and takes pride in the power of her intellect. This is clearly shown in her scornful remarks concerning Alexis, a faithful friend of Constantine, who is easily hoodwinked into taking an action very harmful to Constantine because he is more impulsively courageous than he is wise: "That is what bravery does, which without reflection/ Operates in accord with its enthusiasm. Its wit resides only in its sword,/ Which a clever head can put to use at will./ If a hot-headed hero performs a task of any consequence,/ Then this has most often been thought out by others,/ And he only fights to obtain that which clever heads have achieved" (I. viii). Now it is quite true that Alexis has allowed his feelings to substitute for his rational faculty; and Thomasius, Leibnitz, and Wolff, all three, would have judged him just as Irene does. But it sounds very strange to hear such words from a wicked person! Irene has borrowed one of the cardinal principles of rationalism—control of the emotions—but this principle has not made a better person of her. She represents therefore, although still in a mild and undeveloped form, the evil or perverted rationalist. Such a person uses reason only to quell the softer emotions and those that might tend to obscure the cool calculation necessary for putting a plan into action. His reason has no control whatever over the evil ruling passion, and is, indeed, completely subservient to it. In Irene, as stated before, evil rationality only makes a hesitant start. When it is combined with the dynamic power and conscious amorality seen in Schlegel's Ulfo, then the true evil rationalist is created. This is the new villainous type who will thrive in the sentimental age, because his actions prove, consolingly, that the reason may be less efficacious in producing virtue than is a simple warm heart. Reason's control may extend only over the good emotions, while the strong and vicious ones, unmitigated by the former, will run riot.

The relationship of Constantine to his mother and his reluctance to take severe measures against her are parallel to the situation in *Mahommed IV*. This play, one may assume, was Bernhold's chief model, despite the fact that history itself also provided the parallel between the two sovereigns. The tragic fault of Constantine, however, could well have been suggested to Bernhold by a reading of Pitschel's *Darius*. Like Darius, Constantine permits himself to be persuaded to distrust his truest friend (Probus) and thus brings about the catastrophe indirectly through his own actions. But one difference illustrates the fact that Bernhold wrote in a more sentimental time than Pitschel. Constantine's fault is not represented as a rational error, but rather as surrender to a humane and natural sentiment, his love for his mother. It is unfortunate that this love is not more convincingly portrayed.

In an opening monologue, Constantine naively tells the audience what a good ruler he is. His conscience is clear, he has taken the best Roman emperors for his ideals, and he is not out for fame and conquest. But his crown rests insecurely on his head, and he opines that not even virtue is protection enough for a king: "If only I had been born to a lowly position in the world!/ I know: the protection afforded by innocence would not be lost to me" (I. i). Constantine can get little consolation from his advisers, for one of them, Leo, paints a falsely reassuring picture of conditions, and the other one, with the significant name Probus, honestly tells him that the only thing to do is to arrest his mother, who is leading a rebellion. Constantine does not believe Leo and he cannot bring himself to follow Probus' hard, practical advice. Probus regards the problem of filial duty in a purely rational manner, assuming that a mother is a mother only so long as she acts like one: "Oh! Her crime releases you from all duties" (I. iii). In Constantine's absence Probus and Leo fall to arguing, then to dueling with each other, and when Irene and her aide Bonifacius observe this, they join in the fray on the side of Leo. Then Alexis comes on the scene, and it is all too easy for Irene to persuade him that Probus has made an attempt on her life. Alexis thereupon goes off to accuse Probus before Constantine.

Constantine, however, is not so easily made a fool of as Alexis. At first he does not believe Irene's tale about Probus and the attempted murder, even when Alexis corroborates it as an eyewitness. Constantine tells Irene that she should depart from the court and stay away until she is bidden. It is this mild severity that plays into Irene's hands. She puts on a great show of being offended, and in drastic terms demands to know how she as a mother could ever betray him. Her tirade awakens Constantine's feelings as a son and, somewhat incredibly, he is now completely won over to her and to her friends. Natural feelings, moreover, now prevail over Constantine's feeling of friendship for Probus, whom he harshly orders to be imprisoned and executed. This sudden change in fortune does not disturb Probus, who is stoically virtuous and very noble-minded: "I can stand before God's throne, encouraged by innocence./ Just men are not afraid of any judge,/ Because justice pleads their case." And he adds, "O lovely martyrdom! to die for one's duty!" (II. iv).

Just when Constantine by his own fault loses a strong ally in Probus, Irene gains one in the person of Prince Nicephorus, who puts his army at her service. To make the situation still more complicated, Nicephorus himself is also ambitious to possess the throne, although he naturally hides this from Irene. Here again is a parallel to *Mahommed IV*, where Kiosem's strongest supporter, Bektas, is actually her rival for the throne. Nicephorus has an un-Enlightened view of the function of kings, as well as of God, for in his opinion both are within their rights when they act arbitrarily: "Laws and courts are only for subjects;/ . . . A regent is supposed to bear the name of divinity;/ He is an image of the Most High, who made/

The world and preserves it in His essence, as He wishes./ There-fore no prince may insult his Original through lowness,/ And may submit to no law, even that of conscience" (III. v). With such "principles" Nicephorus feels quite justified in deceiving both Irene and Constantine. The latter, however, has begun to have many mis-givings about the sentence passed on Probus, and has put off his execution. It is again a matter of sentiment: "An inward impulse enforces the delay/ And causes my heart to be divided between anger and pity" (III. x). It infuriates Constantine when a mob which has gathered outside the palace begins to demand the head of Probus. Then his righteous fury departs and he gives in to the mob after all. This ignoble weakness is described by Alexis in an elaborate Homeric simile—a rhetorical feature for which the author has great fondness, but little talent: "Just as the sea's flood with quick and hurrying waves/ Customarily swells up the shallow banks in a brief time/ And on the other hand through the ebb loses itself in itself,/ So that one notices the retreat, but does not feel the running:/ So it was with the Emperor's wrath" (IV. i).

Only when it is too late does Constantine realize that Probus was loyal and that Irene was defaming him. His wife Theodora urges Constantine to flee from the palace. Too great passivity in the face of danger seems wrong to her: "He who will not save him-self, turns himself over to death/ And will put upon himself the guilt of suicide" (IV. viii). But Constantine is not ready for flight. Instead, he turns on Irene furiously, and has her arrested—but then immediately feels sorry for treating his mother so harshly. She does not remain in arrest long, for the mob overpowers her captors. Now Constantine's rage is directed a second time against the people. He rejects Bonifacius' hypocritical theory that the voice of the people is the voice of God and rebukes the mob for not having appreciated his gentle rule: "You will lose much in me, but I nothing in you./ My yoke was too light for you, my scepter too gentle;/ I was too slow in punishing you, and too quick in rewarding" (IV. xv). He is not criticizing himself. Clearly, the fault lies with the unregenerate people.

In her moment of triumph Irene finds that she is not so unfeeling as she had believed. The essential humanity of her nature is aroused, quite unexpectedly, through her maternal instinct, and she tells herself, "Forsake the path of ambition,/ And finally cease whoring after your idol!/ For once listen to nature!" (V. i). It is not reason, but *heart* that here nearly succeeds in restoring this wicked woman to virtue. And it is through Bonifacius' appeal to her noble-minded-ness (here as in *Mahommed IV* interpreted as a stoical indifference to normal human emotions for the sake of some "higher" goal) and to her *reason*, with the argument that it is the people who are her children, that Irene's good heart is subdued. It is truly perverse rationalism when Irene cries, "The realm is now my son! the citizens my friends!/ The miserable Constantine is the foremost of my enemies!" (V. i). Later she boasts about the supremacy of her rational self-control; "Certainly! my high mind, enraptured by crown and realm,/ Knows how to raise itself courageously above nature,/ And how to kill off soft emotions with nobility" (V. v). It is nevertheless due to these very weak "soft emotions" that Irene graciously decides to have Constantine blinded instead of executed outright. When the operation proves fatal anyway, her "mother-heart" once more makes itself felt, but again she is able to master herself and enjoy the idea of being a ruler.

Before he dies, Constantine reveals what is presumably the author's own view of this character's tragic guilt. Constantine feels that his punishment is justified because he gave in to the mob's demand for Probus' head. But behind this rash act was a more consistent fault, his reluctance to face the facts concerning Irene. As previously stated, however, this "fault" is more laudable than deplorable, and consequently Constantine's situation is equivocal. Some way out has to be discovered, to uphold the justice of Providence and the value of sentiment, and this is it: Constantine's love will be punished on earth, and it will be rewarded in heaven. He says, "I sinned through mercy, because I did not want to punish./ To err through exaggerated love and filial duty/ Can be punishable; but this cannot hide all fame, either./ I shall be punished only here. But yonder comes my reward" (V. v).[28] Although Constantine's deeds are thus carefully weighed and disposed of, his wicked mother is outrageously permitted to go free and enjoy the fruits of her inhuman actions. As a sop to the audience's sense of justice, and their philosophy, the author has Nicephorus remark at the end, "Just go on, you proud woman! You shall fall by my hand!" (V. viii); but nothing is said about the historical fact that Nicephorus would not depose Irene for five more years. And, of course, there is no mention that Irene was subsequently made a saint of the Greek Orthodox church! [29]

Bernhold's *Johanna* presents no such tricky questions of guilt and sentiment, and turns abruptly away from the rather scandalous practice of making a villainess the chief personage. The titular and actual heroine of the second play is well-nigh a saint, and the work is plainly a martyr tragedy. The long preface that Bernhold published with this drama provides evidence of his serious purpose and his strong sense of personal involvement with the presentation of this particular historical figure. Never before had any author of German tragedy regarded his dramatic character with so much respect and affection, with the thought uppermost in mind that this had been a real person who must now be dramatically interpreted —not exploited. Bernhold describes Joan of Arc in glowing terms as "this excellent maid" and he speaks of "her splendid deeds." [30] He defends her, in good rational manner, both against those superstitious people who say she talked with angels and against those who falsely charged her with witchcraft. Nor will he permit her to be passed off as a fanatic with a crazy imagination: "Certainly! a mere fanaticism, which has its origin *in intellectu corrupto*, has seldom done great things; at any rate, it has never carried them to conclusion." She was not a crafty deceiver working under a religious guise like Mohammed, Cromwell, or Zinzendorf (!), but someone motivated by "secret divine impulses . . . which a human being cannot ignore without sinning." She was not a kind of bugaboo invented by the nobles around the French king; and furthermore she was a chaste girl, not the mistress of Dunois or anyone else. Her deeds are proof that God Himself was acting through her, and that she was His means of stabilizing the throne of France. Bernhold remarks in conclusion that God is still working in this manner— for has He not recently sent Eugene of Savoy to save the House of Austria? The whole preface is devoted to a defense and eulogy of Joan, and not a word is said about the tragedy and the problems of writing one. Obviously Bernhold considered Joan a thoroughly suitable tragic heroine, and the only purpose of his preface was to underline the intent of his play, that is, to do homage to a remarkable personage who interested him. This respectful treatment of the Joan of Arc theme was no novelty in literature. Shakespeare's denigration of the heroine's character was an isolated exception based on nationalistic prejudice, for the numerous poems and dramas written about Joan in France were uniformly laudatory and adoring.[31] Yet these works all belonged to earlier centuries than the eighteenth, and the reputation of Joan in the period of Enlightenment was a subject of controversy, the various sides of which Bernhold indicates in his preface. Voltaire in his *Pucelle* (1755) made himself the leader of those anti-clerical rationalists who saw in Joan nothing but an invention of the medieval church, a common wench dressed up as a saint and miracle-worker. Bernhold, who was also an Enlightened rationalist, but representative of that German branch of rationalism which was not hostile to God, religion, and church, found a way out of the controversy, so that Joan's mission and character could still be appreciated without recourse to belief in matters contrary to reason. Unlike Schiller, Bernhold did not employ Joan as a symbol for a philosophical ideal, and retain supernatural elements and religious language and concepts merely for the sake of effect, or as part of the panoply of a bygone historical period. He presented a Joan of Arc in every way acceptable to a common-sense epoch. If he changed the manner of her death, that was only because burning at the stake seemed too repugnantly barbaric a spectacle—even though it would have been treated as an off-stage occurrence—for his Enlightened taste and too ignominious an end for his noble heroine. Of course, Bernhold's modest literary talents were not nearly able to defend his version of the Joan of Arc story against the witty, outrageous mock epic of Voltaire, and it was Voltaire's *Pucelle* that overwhelmingly dominated popular opinion.

In order to include Joan's death in his drama and yet not break with the Unity of Time, Bernhold found it necessary to restrict the action to the very last part of her career with the French army. This concentration on the final phase was, naturally, in accord with the practice of neoclassical tragedy. It meant that Bernhold had to leave out all the colorful events which led up to the Dauphin's coronation at Rheims, events which constitute so great a part of the charm and interest of Schiller's *Jungfrau von Orleans*. Bernhold's drama deals only with Joan's betrayal to the English, admittedly the most tragic episode in her history, to which he, however, assigned a rather trite and quite unhistorical motivation: the revenge of a rejected lover. According to the prefatory stage directions, the action of the play covers some twenty hours, and although this is longer than was usual for an Alexandrian tragedy, still it was by no means long enough to provide time for a regular trial scene. Joan's death follows almost immediately upon her capture. The main conflict is not in the English camp; rather it is within the French bastion of Compiègne. The conflict has no political significance, for Bernhold was not concerned with analyzing the historical situation that led to Joan's downfall. He wanted only to glorify his heroine.

It goes without saying that Bernhold was forced to bring in a great deal of direct exposition concerning Joan's prior adventures. Since he knew no better means of doing this than through long, dull recitals of names and events, complete with explanatory footnotes, the dramatic movement of the first two acts is severely hampered, and this is the play's most obvious and irritating weakness. The very first scene almost bogs down completely under the weight of a prosy chronicle of the history of the One Hundred Years War delivered by Joan's brother Louis. Joan's account of her own entry

into the war is a little more interesting, even though it is most unrealistic that she should tell all this to her own brother, who presumably is already well acquainted with the story. She describes her
awakening to her mission as the answer to an inward call, remarkable,
perhaps, but not supernatural: "I, who remote from instruction, the
school of wisdom,/ Dwelled among peasants and my herd, and
learned only as much/ As pertains to handling the shepherd's staff,
not swords,/ I felt within me a capacity and desire for war;/ I knew
what I never had been told before;/ I dared more than the boldest
warrior ever dared,/ And was always supported by good fortune/
Which Heaven gave me and which profits our king" (I. i). Divine
intervention, to judge from these words, restricts itself to two unusual but not unheard-of matters: the gift of an unfeminine talent,
nay, genius for things military, and the granting of good fortune
in all her enterprises. Thus God shows His power and His will very
definitely, but without stepping over into the realm of miracle and
heavenly visions. Moreover, Joan's rare talent has not transformed
her into an unnatural or specially hallowed individual, however
much popular opinion may ascribe saintly qualities to her. She
admits freely that she is in love with Count Dunois, and when her
friend Olon expresses surprise at this, she answers, "You err; human
emotions stir in my heart;/ And if Count Dunois is not with me, ah,
then I feel pain" (I. ii). To a noble and rational person like Joan,
love has nothing to do with lust and sensuality. She has been attracted
to Dunois solely on account of his virtue: "How did Count Dunois
penetrate to my faithful heart?/ With his bravery, not with insipid
jesting;/ With his sublime actions, and not with flattery;/ No impudent appeal to carnality has induced me to love!" (I. ii). Dunois'
affection for Joan is sufficient to make him address her with a very
involved and rather absurd gallantry, a typical example of the author's
"style" when he attempts to be picturesque: "How gently your
sweet mouth blows into the candles/ Which I have set up to you
in my enkindled heart" (I. iii). Both being reasonable and self-
controlled, they agree that there can be no marriage for them until
the war is over.

There is no suggestion that the French have lost faith in Joan,
or that she has political enemies. King Charles will not even suffer
her to kneel in his presence, because he regards her as an angel from
heaven. The French have been beating the British back from Compiègne ever since Joan's arrival, and the king orders that her commands shall be obeyed just like his own. It is true that the governor
of Compiègne, Guillaume de Flavy (called "Flaui" by the author)
begins to feel jealous of the deference paid this woman while he, the

"old servant," is neglected. But this thought is soon swallowed up in the passionate love that has been aroused in Flavy by his first sight of the heroine's beauty of body—and soul. The development of this action, the central one of the play, is delayed now until the third act, while the second act is devoted to the return of Joan's father. Jacques d'Arc comes before the king dressed in ragged clothes, saying that he has been imprisoned by the Burgundians for the last eight years. Now he is looking for his lost daughter who, he has been told, is at the king's court. Like the father in Schiller's *Jungfrau von Orleans,* this Jacques d'Arc is opposed to court life, and wants to take his daughter away from it and back to the countryside where she belongs. He is not pleased to see his daughter dressed in splendid clothes, and tells her, "If I could see you once again in shepherd's dress,/ Then there would be no sorrow in my heart and senses" (II. iv). Again, like the father in Schiller's play, Bernhold's character bases his dismay on a dream that he has had about his daughter. But whereas Schiller speaks of a dream in which Joan appears in power and prestige, and her father misinterprets this, Bernhold has his Jacques d'Arc describe a dream in which Joan is betrayed, captured, and executed. When Joan hears this, she loses courage for a while: "But now I myself feel that I have perhaps done enough./ My woman's heart is almost giving way to fearfulness" (II. iv). It may be that Heaven is sending her a warning not to go on. But then King Charles refuses to dismiss her, and since God would surely not want her to disobey the king, she takes heart again and feels sure of her mission. It occurs to her that God means that she should give up her life to crown her other achievements, and she regards this as an honor and a glory: "How splendid will be my grave amidst the heaped-up corpses/ Of the enemies of France! I must attain this good fortune!" (II. iv). This heroic attitude in his daughter effects a startling change in Jacques d'Arc. Now he is eager to fight and die for his country, and he calls for a helmet and armor. Although Jacques' transformation is slightly ludicrous, the episode serves the author's evident purpose of depicting the contagiousness of Joan's patriotism and heroic spirit, so that one may better understand how she, without being either witch or angel, was able to inspire the amazing confidence and enthusiasm that history has recorded. Schiller also depicted Joan's power in this respect, but one is left with the impression that she derives it from her supernatural guidance, not from human resources.

In Act Three the governor of Compiègne, Flavy, gathers up courage to confess his love to Joan. Her initial defense is to plead lack of feeling and to pretend to be as hard as flint: "I am not made for tenderness and voluptuousness" (III. ii). When he persists, however, she has no recourse but to tell him the plain truth—that she is already in love with Dunois. Flavy is astonished and offended and, with his reason clouded by emotion and bitterness, he determines on villainous revenge. When Joan outlines a very dangerous plan for attacking the English, Flavy gladly gives his approval, because he sees in it a way of destroying her. At this juncture it is notable that Joan's relationship to God takes on a more personal aspect, one which does not jibe so easily with a rational, non-miraculous presentation of her personality, such as this drama is meant to make. Dunois ventures to dispute the wisdom of her battle plan, and she flatly contradicts him, saying, "I am glad to defer to you; but nevertheless,/ Where essential things are concerned, I keep my will free;/ Then Heaven directs it for me; and only in secondary matters,/ Brave hero, can you aid me with advice and support" (III. v). It is possible that in this instance Joan is again, as at first with Flavy, taking advantage of her supernatural reputation in order to avoid difficulties and opposition. In the preface the author speaks of Joan's "permissible deception" and "better cunning." [32] More probably, however, this passage is meant to be a pious-rational explanation of Joan's superior military intelligence. That is, she is not a miraculous female with a monstrously unfeminine talent for war, but a normal, muscular peasant woman whose will (or choice between various courses of action) is dictated by God rather than exclusively by human reason. If God really directs human affairs, and yet is rationalistically denied any miraculous procedures, then how can He be expected to perform His function except through this means? Bernhold saw no objection to the idea that God might influence the human will.

Joan's battle plan, for all its daring, is successful until spoiled by Flavy's treachery. On the return from the English camp to the walls of Compiègne, Flavy hurries his troops into the town and then closes the gates in Joan's face. The result, of course, is that she is captured by the enemy. King Charles wonders whether perhaps some hidden sin has turned Heaven from Joan, but this solution to the problem of a virtuous person's misfortune is rejected. As La Hire says, "God's purpose cannot so easily be fathomed,/ Why Joan must feel the weight of chains" (IV. iii). To be sure, Flavy's well-deserved punishment comes swiftly at the hands of Dunois and Joan's brother Louis; but with consummate sentimentality his death is turned into a supposedly edifying spectacle of forgiveness. Charles very readily agrees to forgive Flavy, but Louis, who mourns not only his sister's captivity but also his father's death in battle, is less quickly mollified.

Hereupon both Flavy and King Charles begin to treat Louis as a recalcitrant and proceed to catechize him. It sounds presumptuous when Flavy cries out to Louis, "O more than heathenish heart!" (IV. v). And it seems hardly necessary that Flavy should forgive Dunois for the latter's part in giving him a fatal wound. Indeed, the repentant Flavy draws his last breath very much in the manner of a saint. The irresistible desire to portray a beautiful death has led the author to expend his sympathy on the villain, to the detriment of those genuinely aggrieved by his actions.

It was necessary to break boldly with the Unity of Place in order to show Joan's last moments and death in the English camp. The author tried to render the scene change more acceptable by pointing out in the initial stage direction that the English camp, the tent of the Duke of Bedford, was merely behind the second curtain, on the inner stage. Obviously, whatever the stricter critics might say, he could not forego his most dramatic scene and substitute a narrative monologue for it. At the opening of the fifth act, the English leader Bedford is arguing with the Dukes of Luxemburg and Burgundy about how to dispose of Joan, and Burgundy is against burning her, because that would be barbaric. When Joan is brought in, loaded with chains, Bedford mocks her and bids her free herself through her magic arts. Knowing she must soon die, Joan accepts death as a token of the benevolence of God, not as a misfortune: "Heaven loves me still in my heavy chains,/ From which it could, indeed, yet easily rescue,/ If that were beneficial to me" (V. iii). The news that the English bishop has condemned her to the stake temporarily disturbs her calm and, as is conventional in such situations, she asks Heaven why no thunderbolts are cast at the evildoers. But in a little while she regains her composure and takes comfort in the thought that her death will so enflame the French that soon the English will be utterly defeated. She regards her martyrdom as the ultimate honor of an already remarkable career. In the face of such patriotism and bravery the usual question of whether she is getting the reward her virtue deserves loses its significance. The martyr-hero, whether religious or patriotic, transforms death into a thing to be desired. But the arrival of a French army, with Dunois at its head, at least saves Joan from burning. Bedford quickly stabs her to the heart, and her anxious lover finds her dying. As soon as her eyes are shut, she sees a marvelous vision: "O highest of all delight! I see heaven open!/ Now I already have everything that other people are only still hoping for!" (V. vii).

One cannot read this quaint drama without wondering if perhaps Schiller may not have known and used it for his own *Jungfrau von*

Orleans. Since Bernhold was a member of the Latin Society at Jena, it is possible that Schiller, as a professor in Jena, might have heard of him and his work, and it is not hard to imagine that a copy of this play might have come into Schiller's hands. Of course, it would have seemed absurdly stiff and old-fashioned to him, so great were the advances made by the intervening generation; but certain features of Bernhold's play do distinctly anticipate Schiller's own treatment of the theme. First of all, there is the friendly treatment of the heroine; but there are also the appearance of Joan's father, his objection to her military activity and role in state affairs, his dream about her, and the manner of her death. The entrance of the father in Schiller's *Jungfrau* could just as well have been prompted by Shakespeare's Joan of Arc play, *Henry VI*. But Joan's defiance in the English camp, the unhistorical changing of her execution, and her virtual entry into an opening heaven in the fifth act of Bernhold's drama are so reminiscent of the fifth act of the *Jungfrau* that it seems quite conceivable the older work was an influence thereon. It would not have been the only instance where Schiller found the work of a far less talented dramatist useful in his own composition.[33]

The year 1754 saw the publication of six new and original tragedies, as well as an anonymous tragedy *Urlogese* (an original?), which has been lost, and two awkward attempts by Bodmer, *Der erkannte Joseph* and *Der keusche Joseph*. This was the richest annual harvest since the beginning of the Gottschedian reform. At last German literature could begin to compare its output with that of French drama, numerically speaking. But this year of outstanding achievement for the Alexandrine tragedy was also the year before the advent of the prose middle-class tragedy. In the apparent strength there was actually great weakness. The six works gave all-too-plain evidence that a new form and new subject matter were urgently needed.

One of the six tragedies treated the stoic theme already brought forward in Camerer's *Octavia*. This was the *Seneca* [34] by the Hessian nobleman and statesman Friedrich Casimir von Creutz (1724–1770), who also published didactic poetry and a work on psychology entitled *Versuch über die Seele* (1753). To forestall the adverse criticism that so many authors of tragedy feared and expected, Creutz declared in the preface, with baronial arrogance and from the heights of his official position, that *Seneca* was but the trivial product of leisure hours spent away from his really important business. It is clear that he feels contempt for anyone, even a Racine, who would devote a long time to the perfecting of a drama: "Anyone like me, whose profession puts him into a position to perform more useful services for the public in one day than a poet who squanders two sad years on a tragedy, will truly be able to bear it with equanimity if he is not granted a place among the tragic poets." [35] Furthermore he let it be known that the other German tragedies he had read were not so good that he need be embarrassed about presenting his own effort in the genre. However, in an essay which he appended to the play, Creutz showed considerably more respect for what he was doing. This little work, entitled simply *Einige Gedanken von dem Trauerspiel*, reproduces almost word for word the procedure for writing a tragedy outlined by Gottsched in the *Versuch einer critischen Dichtkunst:* "Thus the poet's first purpose is a moral teaching, which he wants to impart to others in a way which will make a sudden impression. He clothes it in a fable which to him seems the most suitable for this. He mingles this fable with a true story, and thereby gives it more verisimilitude." [36] The chief effect to be aroused by a tragedy is a "profound meditation" (*ein tiefsinniges Nachdenken*), although astonishment and pity also are granted a place. To awaken the "passions" is the easiest and least admirable of the tragic poet's functions, for this is done also in operas, which lead to one's ruination.[37]

In view of such stern concepts about tragedy, it is not surprising to find that *Seneca* is a highly serious, highly moral, and rather unexciting play. There are emotions aplenty in the minor characters, but the hero himself is the epitome of stoical self-control, and he makes the violent emotions of the others seem childish—an easy victory, because those emotions are so superficially and tritely portrayed. The moral teaching that Creutz desired to embody in his "fable" and then to combine with the history of Seneca is evidently that absence of passion and a totally passive acceptance of fate are the height of virtue and wisdom. This is, of course, a fairly broad kind of moral and might be more aptly described as a general philosophy of life (stoicism), one not perfectly in accord with the philosophy taught by most German tragedies of that day, namely, that virtue is rewarded by a benevolent Providence that likes to see man happy here on earth. In *Seneca*, the world is viewed without apology as an unhappy place, and virtue is rewarded only in heaven, toward which the soul is justified in hastening even by means of suicide, if need be. Thus *Seneca* as altogether different in meaning from Gottsched's *Cato*, however great the superficial similarity of the two plays—their depiction of the last hours and death of a venerable Roman—may be.

The unseen villain of the drama is the emperor Nero, whose downfall and death are being plotted by almost everyone in the cast of characters except Seneca and his wife Pauline. Aurelia, a friend of Pauline, is motivated by two passions which are beyond her control: revenge and love. She wants revenge on Nero because he has killed her brother. Pauline regards this vengefulness as an interference with Heaven's plans, but fails to convince Aurelia, who is further tormented by her rash promise to marry the man who avenges her. If this does not turn out to be Piso, whom she loves, she will be terribly distressed. Love, to her, makes life more intolerable than outright physical slavery: "I feel, yes, I feel it, how very different is/ The torment which is suffered by the dull body alone,/ Which is ended by a faint; oh, what a short course!/ Quite another thing, however, is your feeling, O soul!" (I. i). The young men, Annäus, Piso, and Lucius, are motivated by the patriotic desire to dispose of Nero and reinstate freedom in Rome, but two of them, Piso and Lucius, are afflicted also with love and jealousy because of Aurelia. Seneca stands aloof from these emotional struggles, and, although he strongly disapproves of Nero, he will not lift a finger to depose or to assassinate him. Rome's destiny is not a happy one, and that is irrevocable. Still, if Nero is not overthrown, Seneca will have to die because of Nero's suspicions and Poppaea's hatred. The only way he can avoid death is to accept the crown offered him by the revolutionaries. This would give the Romans hope for a future of just government and provide the proper impetus for the success of the revolt. For a while Seneca is tempted, but he leaves the decision to the gods: "What shall I do? am I to choose death or the crown?/ Ye gods, choose for me; a mortal man can err" (I. v). And the decision of the gods, as Seneca interprets it, fatalistically and pessimistically enough, is that Rome's last chance for freedom died with Brutus. He, Seneca, is not so strong that he can resist the will of the gods. This kind of meek subjection makes the emotional and headstrong Lucius rave. He cannot understand gods who would put up with the wickedness of a Nero: "I would myself consign the gods to the realm of nothing,/ If Nero is to live, if his tyranny/ Is well pleasing to the gods—" (II. iv). But Seneca regards such rebelliousness as folly, declaring, "He who does not follow willingly will nevertheless follow under compulsion:/ No good fortune has ever come to anger, and no wish has been granted to grief./ He who comes close to Heaven itself in his constancy/ Is happy!" (II. v). Even when news comes that Nero has given orders to poison him, Seneca remains unshaken in his resolve not to take action: "Yes, I will gladly die, because the gods want it,/ And because we ought to follow their command without complaint./ That Nero is on the throne and is almost all-powerful/ Does not seem strange to me, because a God has decided on it/ Who conducts all things and loves even when He punishes us;/ Who gives everything its beginning and also its end./ If Nero should perish today, or should I;/ Just let Heaven command; I am agreeable to either" (II. vi). When he is told that a crowd of Romans has gathered outside to see him, he goes to teach them that "The image of the gods is to be honored even in tyrants" (II. vii).

Besides stoicism, strong overtones of eighteenth-century optimism and trust in Providence and a rational world-order are obvious in Seneca's utterances. His willingness to accept Nero "because a God has decided on it" bears a close resemblance to the willingness of Lessing's Nathan to accept the loss of his family because "That too was God's decree." [38] In Nathan's case, however, it was a question of coming to terms with the past so that the future might be faced hopefully and vigorously. In the case of Seneca, it is a question of interpreting the future, and of guessing at God's will, in a way that endorses total passivity. It was this supine and paralyzed "virtue" that Lessing, who advocated just revolution in *Henzi*, exposed and criticized so bitterly in *Emilia Galotti*. Creutz, on the other hand, undoubtedly regards Seneca's refusal to act as the ultimate in desirable behavior. A man's ability to bear wrongs and hardships without a murmur—and without a gesture of self-defense or retaliation—is the measure of his worth. Thus Seneca says to the impatient Piso, "A great heart will first venture to conquer itself:/ Then, Piso, it also learns to endure even tyrants,/ And never is it void of comfort, never of hope,/ However great the distress be, however hard the misfortune" (III. iii).

A man like Seneca will never accuse God of cruelty, as does the emotional Aurelia, whose dilemma regarding which of two men is going to avenge and consequently marry her, provokes her to one of those (usually female) outbursts without which a tragedy of this period could scarcely be considered complete: "You gods, can you put me into so much confusion?/ Can a divine eye take its pleasure in our torment?" (III. ii). As a thoroughgoing rationalist, Seneca knows that God's purposes must ever be good. He scolds Aurelia for her emotional vengefulness and her wilfullness, but she is too far gone in emotion, although dimly aware of the correctness of the advice, to profit from his words: "What help to us in grief are the stern doctrines of wisdom?" (III. vi). Emotions certainly do not help Aurelia's lovers to win their battle against Nero. Instead, their jealousy makes them kill each other off, and Nero comes out the victor.

At this news Seneca remains calm, even declining to flee Rome or his house. But still all is not lost. A nod from Seneca, and the captain of the imperial guard would dethrone Nero in his favor. Seneca, however, simply decides to die. Under the circumstances suicide seems a justifiable way out to a better life, for Nero will put him to death anyway: "Yes, a voluntary death is a true honor!/ Wisdom gave it to me, this divinely serious teaching!" (IV. vii). When one remembers that it was his own perfectly conscious decision that put him into this desperate situation, Seneca's resolve to die appears more like a genuine suicide and less like a mere escape from execution. No other construction, surely, can be placed on his wife Pauline's plan to die with him. At first Seneca seeks to dissuade her, admonishing her to wisdom and impassivity regarding his loss; but then he more or less acquiesces in her decision, and the two of them speak about meeting again on the far shore.

The opening scene of Act Five is an imitation of the corresponding scene in Gottsched's *Cato*. As in the earlier play, the hero is found all alone contemplating death and eternity with some doubt and trepidation. But he soon conquers his fears: "What a chasm before me! alas, are my hopes in vain?/ Is, or is there not, a God? Is there? shall I perish? No!/ He is, and because He is, I must also be eternal!" (V. i). He conceives of God as an omnipotent being with supremely stoical calmness, a rather chilling portrait which is relieved only by the assurance that God does at least punish every evil deed: "There is a God of the world,/ A Being Who puts limits to the heavens themselves!/ An eternal Being Who, hidden from our eyes,/ Observes with equal calm the quiet grief of the wise/ And the loud cares of fools, and for every crime,/ Even before it happens, has stipulated the reward" (V. i). In the final scenes, both Seneca and Pauline are carried on stage in chairs since, having opened their veins, they are too weak to walk. To the mind's eye this presents an almost ludicrous, certainly a grotesque and repulsive spectacle. Yet the effect is plainly meant to be touching and uplifting, and to be in edifying contrast to the loud despair of Aurelia, who, oddly and significantly, cannot bring herself to commit suicide although she holds her dagger to her breast. In this play, suicide is reserved for the virtuous. There is some question whether Pauline herself actually dies, or only faints, because mention is made that her wounds have been bandaged. Seneca, however, does definitely depart this life, and his last words are addressed to a pantheistically described deity of indeterminate attributes: "O Being, Whom we admire but do not know,/ And sometimes name in Jupiter with all the gods:/ And sometimes call Nature, and sometimes the all-purest Spirit!/ Thee I worship dying! be Thou what Thou mayest!/ . . .

Thou roarest in the sea, and shinest in the lightning,/ There a star is Thy throne, and here a grain of dust is Thy seat" (V. vii). With this speech the curious philosophy of this very static, poorly plotted drama is complete. One may wonder whether the author Creutz was trying to reproduce objectively the outlines of ancient stoical thought, or whether he himself was sincerely advocating the ideas expressed by Seneca in the play. From the remarks in his essay on tragedy, the second conclusion appears to be the more warranted one, for in the essay he speaks earnestly about imparting a moral lesson to the spectators. But Creutz's study of Seneca has led him beyond the reigning moral philosophy of his own day.

A most glaring contrast to the sober monochromatic tragedy of Creutz was another product of the year 1754, the tragedy *Araxane* published in the fifth volume of *Die deutsche Schaubühne zu Wienn*. This drama, which according to the title page was played in the *Theater am Kärntnertor*, is loosely accredited in the *Schaubühne* to one "Herr B. von Trenck," a "soldier." In the *Biographisches Lexikon des Kaiserthums Oesterreich*,[39] however, the author is identified more accurately as the Freiherr Friedrich von Trenck (1726–1794), one of the most colorful public figures of the eighteenth century, the lover of Frederick the Great's sister, the victim of years of unjust imprisonment, adventurer, journalist, author, and military hero, who was eventually guillotined in Paris during the latter days of the French Revolution. His *Araxane*, written in Vienna when von Trenck was twenty-eight years of age and shortly before he was imprisoned a second time by the relentless king of Prussia, is of such poor quality in construction, characterization, and dialogue that it borders on the ridiculous.[40] Nevertheless there are a few interesting and noteworthy features about the play. One is that von Trenck, in the midst of a development of tragedy that concentrated more and more on historical accuracy, ventured to write a tragedy that was wholly and admittedly fictional. The fact is proclaimed openly in the title: *Araxane, a fictional Tragedy (ein erdichtetes Trauerspiel)*. The first sentence of the play's short introduction is a travesty of the introductions Gottsched was wont to give to tragedies published under his aegis: "All the names in this work are fictional, and cannot be found in any real history . . ." Unfortunately, the author's original imagination was not so rich and varied as the circumstances of his actual life, and was capable only of inventing a far-fetched plot with endless tasteless complications. Instead of seeming original, the play gives the impression of being a potpourri of motifs drawn from other tragedies and from novels as well.

The theme of *Araxane*, insofar as it possesses any, is that love is a stronger and more valid emotion than the passion of revenge, and even than filial feeling. The novelty of this theme represents another of the play's interesting features. Along with the fictional plot, the supremacy of love is a herald of future developments in German tragedy. The titular heroine is a Persian princess who throughout most of the action is torn between her love of Osimann, prince of the Turks, and a desire to kill him because he has slain her brother. Such a conflict is no doubt a suitable tragic subject (which the author may have borrowed from Corneille's *Le Cid*), but in this drama it is made ludicrously superficial and exaggerated. Feelings of revenge precede feelings of love in Araxane's heart, so that it may be demonstrated strikingly how the one emotion can prevail over the other. At the beginning Araxane's brother Selim is carried in dying of a wound administered by Osimann in a battle between the Persians and the Turks. Selim demands more of Araxane than mere tears of grief: "I demand blood of you, and Osimann must die" (I. iii). Soon after, Osimann dashes into the presence of Araxane, who greets him with words of great violence. However, both she and Osimann fall in love at first sight. Araxane admits in an aside, "I feel an impulse . . ." (I. iv); but she considers her tender feelings to be unvirtuous; and Osimann likewise resists his love for her on the grounds that she is affianced already to his comrade-in-arms, the Moor Jarbas. Osimann has never been in love before and is surprised that he is not proof against it: "Friendship and reason put fear into my breast,/ Love, this burden, of which I knew nothing,/ Can affect even the heart of a hero, no matter how hard it is" (I. iv). There is no defense against love, it would seem, and no possibility of controlling the emotion. Such a concept of love is not to be found in any of the tragedies composed under Gottsched's influence. The lovers here make efforts to retain their integrity, but all in vain. Sentiment, in an advancing age of sentiment, proves to be stronger than reason. It is true that Schlegel's Dido was also unable to control her love, but she was regarded as a sad and terrible example to rational people. The author of Araxane, on the contrary, approves of his characters' love.

A third remarkable feature of the play is its extravagant number of scene changes, eleven in all. In the sixth scene of Act One the locale is transferred to a temple with weird and elaborate appointments. Completely unconcerned about accuracy of detail, the author directs that one shall see "the statue of Mohammed with a fiery altar" and many "Persian idol-priests." This is the same egregious ignorance about Mohammedanism for which Lessing was to castigate Cronegk in the first article of the *Hamburgische Dramaturgie*. In the temple, Shah Mulay, the father of Araxane and Selim, is also swearing revenge on Osimann. His rantings show the kind of absurdity to which the search for rhyme and meter could lead an unskilled writer: "May Osimann die! and you, just revenge,/ Grant that I soon sit, cooled and laughing, at your table" (I. vi). Mulay's advisor, Parsinor, suggests that Mulay can take revenge easily by making a human sacrifice of the captive Fatime, who is Osimann's sister. The idea appeals to Mulay until Fatime strides in and with fine defiance tells him to do his worst: "Plunge, executioner, your steel into these snowy breasts" (I. viii). Hereupon love takes possession of Mulay, too, in demonstration of the fact that this emotion has power over even the old and feeble, and of course Fatime escapes being sacrificed. She, however, is loved in turn by Achmet, another son of Mulay, and Achmet is not strong enough to keep love from overruling duty: "Alas, brother! ah, pardon!/ You demand revenge, but love says/ That its feeling often destroys the duties of virtue" (I. viii). Meanwhile Araxane finds her struggle made more difficult by Osimann's faultlessly generous behavior. Not only does he protect Araxane from Jarbas when he finds that the latter's attentions are unwelcome to her, but he also offers to let her satisfy the demands of revenge by killing him, Osimann. This Araxane cannot bring herself to do. A little later, while wandering sadly through the forest, Osimann is set upon by old Mulay and his soldiers, but Achmet, on account of his love for Fatime, prevents his father from doing harm to Osimann. This is startling proof that Achmet puts love before duty and filial piety, and Mulay upbraids him bitterly.

That love is a better and more virtuous emotion than revenge is clearly indicated when old Mulay betrays the fact that the motivation for his vengefulness springs from the realm of evil: "It is the will of Hell, and this I shall fulfill,/ Let it cost what it may" (II. i). Araxane has a more and more difficult struggle to keep up with her father's anger. Osimann gives her a second opportunity to kill him, and she does actually pick up a dagger to do it, but is glad when Parsinor interferes, saying this deed should be left to him. She does not allow Parsinor to commit the deed, but instead arranges for Osimann to be put into prison, unharmed. But before long she admits to herself that it is no use to try to deceive herself any longer: "I love an enemy who displays nothing but noble-mindedness,/ And although my honor keeps silence at my project,/ Yet I shall still with courage fulfill my resolve,/ No prejudice shall stifle the longing within me" (II, xiii). Revenge, then—but also obedience to a father's wishes!—is a prejudice, a hasty judgment, which must give way, not to better reason, but to a feeling. Accordingly, Araxane frees Osimann and says she will be his as soon as destiny permits. In Osimann love has overcome the rights of friendship, while in Araxane it has overcome the rights of a father and a slain brother. This victory is made more palatable by the circumstance that Osimann's friend Jarbas was not a true friend, and that Araxane's father is a wicked and tyrannical man. The rights of the slain brother, however, still await some satisfaction.

In Act Three Shah Mulay plunges to the nadir of viciousness by condemning both Achmet and Araxane to death for their insubordination. For good measure, Fatime is also included in the death sentence because she has spurned Mulay's advances. Mulay is strengthened in his resolve by the example of Parsinor, who wants his son Harbi condemned for helping Araxane to free Osimann. At this point all the young and sympathetic characters seem about to be slaughtered—a highly tragic situation, indeed! But before this can happen, Mulay is diverted by an opportunity to kill Osimann, who is again in the forest. This plan necessitates a final scene change, perhaps the most elaborate of all, for the stage direction reads, "In front is shown a forest; in back one can see the whole Turkish camp." It develops that the plan to kill Osimann in the forest was really just a clever deception on the part of Parsinor and Jarbas. These two are only conspiring to get Mulay and his soldiers out of the palace, so that Jarbas may enter and carry off Araxane. Now Mulay is informed about the kidnapping of Araxane by Achmet, who escapes from his prison during the melee. Mulay thinks that Osimann must be the kidnapper and gives Achmet an order that lacks polish but not directness: "My son, take my guard, and hurry as fast as you can,/ Look for this villain, and stick him through the belly" (III. vii). This command comes to naught when Parsinor treacherously has his soldiers seize both Mulay and Achmet. Parsinor and Jarbas are now masters of the situation. Jarbas leads the captive Araxane on the scene, and Fatime and Harbi soon appear as well.

Matters are always darkest, however, just before the dawn. Accompanied by his Turkish soldiers, Osimann now dashes on to the stage and a battle starts right before one's eyes in which Jarbas is quickly dispatched by Osimann and Parsinor is taken prisoner. Mulay hereupon utters a question which has long existed in the mind of the reader: "Ah, Heaven! what is this spectacle still going to come to?" (III. x). Gratitude to Osimann for having saved him from the conspirators, nevertheless, does not prevent Mulay from insisting on revenge for his son Selim. The happy ending could not even now take place, except for the confession, an impassioned, hyperbolical speech worthy of Lohenstein, which now unexpectedly issues from the lips of Parsinor. He reveals that Selim was not the son of Mulay after all, but his own child, whom he substituted for the real prince, and the real prince is the one thought to be his son Harbi. Parsinor's motive was ambition: he wanted his child to be the heir of Mulay. Thus, technically at least, there is no longer any reason for Mulay to feel vengeful; and the result is that he suddenly undergoes a complete change of heart. The curtain comes down on two happy pairs, Osimann and Araxane, Achmet and Fatime. Mulay is now the benevolent father, and even Parsinor is forgiven, not out of principle, but simply to avoid spoiling the universally happy mood. Mulay makes a suitably banal comment when he says, "I myself am half drowned in this sea of joy" (III. x).

From this brief résumé of the action, which by no means includes all the multifarious plot complications, one detects forthwith that von Trenck's drama is in great part grounded in the tradition of *Haupt- und Staatsaktion* as practised by Stranitzky. This impression is strengthened by the three-act division of the play, its many spectacular scene-changes, and the series of two-line curtain speeches delivered by the surviving characters. Except for the consistent use of Alexandrines and the total absence, not only of a Hanswurst, but also of any hint that the author does not take his story seriously, *Araxane* indeed comes quite close to being a latter-day *Haupt- und Staatsaktion*. Every year since 1747 a few "regular" German tragedies, either originals or translations from the French, had appeared at the *Theater am Kärntnertor* and then usually were printed in the series *Die deutsche Schaubühne zu Wienn*. In 1751, a banner year, six such plays, including *Agis, Darius, Mahommed IV, Panthea,* and *Ulysses*, had been staged.[41] But for all these efforts inspired by persons of Enlightened tastes, Vienna still remained the last stronghold of the old uninhibited, fantastic and absurd, pre-Gottschedian theater. In the very year in which *Araxane* was published (it had already been played in the 1752–1753 season)[42] the Harlequin Joseph Kurz-Bernardon was entering upon the second successful phase of his activity as actor and playwright,[43] and shortly thereafter produced his hilarious parody of the "regular" tragedy, *Prinzessin Pumphia* (1755 or 1756). The short preface to *Araxane* frankly states, ". . . the circumstances and complications [of the plot] . . . are arranged insofar as possible to suit the taste of the public here . . ." From this it is clear that the author's intent was to convert the Viennese to "regular" tragedy obliquely—by a compromise with local traditions.

Although the implicit moral of *Araxane*—love before all else—
is lax in comparison with the stern rationalistic morals of the tragedies written in Germany proper, it is still a humane and even
forward-looking moral that would soon be adopted by other sentimental dramatists. The play is free of the cynicism and fatalism
associated with *Haupt- und Staatsaktionen*. The frequent use in
the dialogue of the terms "reason" and "virtue" and the pious remarks continually assigned to Osimann, who rightly believes that
virtue is rewarded, indicate that von Trenck was genuinely interested in edifying the spectators. It is understandable that this, the
first Alexandrine tragedy written in Austria (though still not *by* a
native Austrian), should be less regular and less sober than a normal
product of the Gottsched school. With all its singularities of form
and content, it should be regarded not as a step backward but as
another victory (a minor one) for the Gottschedian reform.

The most prolific author of tragedies at mid-century was Gottsched's much-despised protégé, Freiherr Christoph Otto von Schönaich (1725–1807). In 1754 he published four tragedies in one convenient volume, along with short introductions of a strikingly casual
nature. This opus was entitled, with the self-conscious humility
typical of Gottsched's disciples, merely *Versuch in der tragischen
Dichtkunst*.[44] The actual dates and the order of composition are not
stated, but it seems likely that all four were already in existence in
1752, although perhaps not in final form, for in his speech at the
coronation of Schönaich as poet laureate of Germany (July 18,
1752) Gottsched spoke of "several excellent tragedies" which the
honoree had written.[45] Since Schönaich was first stimulated to literary
activity after his release from military service in 1747,[46] it appears
likely that the four dramas were composed in relatively quick succession between 1748 and 1752, and then polished up for publication
in 1754. None was ever again printed individually [47] or included
in any drama collections. The neat original volume in which they
appeared probably fell into the hands of a considerable reading
public, although the young critic of the *Berlinische privilegirte
Zeitung*, Lessing, did not encourage sales by writing: "When we
say that Baron von Schönaich, the scribbler of *Hermann*, is the
author of these attempts, then it is to be hoped that we have with
one blow passed the most complete judgment on them that can be
passed." [48] It is hardly to be expected that Lessing would have
dignified any production of Schönaich with a word of praise. The
solemn nonsense of Schönaich's coronation (*in absentia*) as poet
laureate by Gottsched in Leipzig, the critical attacks against Lessing
in Schönaich's *Aesthetik in einer Nuß* (1754) and in numerous

satires, and, in short, the entire feud between the Gottsched camp
and the rest of literary Germany precluded any possibility of an
unbiased judgment. To be sure, even the unbiased reader of Schönaich's dramas must be offended by the poor quality and frequent
downright obscurity of their Alexandrine verse. Nevertheless, at
least three of the plays have relatively fresh subject matter and include some motifs and concepts which are not without importance
for later and better works; indeed, perhaps also for one or more
plays by the scornful Lessing himself.

The first tragedy in the volume is *Zayde, oder die Afrikanerin.*
Surprisingly enough, although the author was as faithful a disciple as
Gottsched ever had, in this drama he has departed from the norm
set up by the man he calls his "Aristarch" and has chosen a fictitious
rather than an historical subject. It is still not an independently invented one, however. Quite candidly, Schönaich states in his preface
that the source of his tragedy is "a French novel"; but in the next
breath he apologizes for this, saying, "and I have thereby had the
opportunity to note well the difference between a true and an
imaginary hero." [49] With this remark he was deferring to Gottsched's adverse criticism of the character called Sanscho, whose so-
called virtue is neither convincing nor consistent. On the other hand,
the central personage of the play is the titular heroine Zayde, and
she is no less satisfactory than the historical characters treated in
German tragedy prior to that time. A Moslem princess, daughter
of the Bey of Tunis, her rational and tolerant views of religion
equal those of Sittah in Lessing's *Nathan der Weise*, even if they
are not quite so advanced as those of Nathan himself. Like Cato
and Darius, Zayde is perfect and virtuous until she is faced with a
struggle too complicated for her mentality, so that she takes a false
step which leads to her destruction. Her conflict is one between
love and duty, and when she follows the call of her heart this move
is regarded rationalistically as a definite mistake—in contrast to the
viewpoint shown in von Trenck's *Araxane*. But inasmuch as Zayde's
false step in the direction of love is not accompanied by the slightest
hardening of her nature nor cheapening of her virtue (in contrast
to Schlegel's Dido), it may be said that she in a measure anticipates
Lessing's Miss Sara.

The conflict between filial duty and sexual love (or, at any rate,
love between the sexes) which besets Zayde had already been depicted by Gottsched in his *Bluthochzeit* in the figure of Queen
Margaret and by Möser in *Arminius* in the figure of Thusnelda. But
in both these cases the parent to whom duty was owed was unvirtuous, whereas the love was conjugal. Zayde's father, however,

is a parent good to the point of sentimentality, like Sir William Sampson, while her lover, Don Sanscho, is not her husband, but someone else's. Thus the plot comes perilously close to losing itself in that ever suspect *"belle passion"* which was the hallmark of French tragedy. But during most of the play Schönaich successfully avoids this pitfall by supplying his heroine with a sober mental problem, the question of religion. As the play opens, Zayde is introduced as the innocent dupe of two enslaved Christians, Don Sanscho and Elvire. The latter have concealed the fact that they are a married couple and, with very dubious morality, have encouraged poor Zayde to fall in love with Don Sanscho, so that she will help them to escape back to Spain. Zayde rebels against the thought of hurting her father by accompanying the Christians to their homeland, and would prefer to keep Sanscho with her in Tunis. The father, Murath, shows both rationality and affection by sanctioning her marriage to this slave, but he makes one unalterable stipulation: Sanscho must adopt the Moslem religion. The Spaniard, who is, of course, already married, refuses the condition, pleading that he was born a Christian: "Every mortal, after all, considers his own sect to be true,/ The one in whose womb and sanctity he was born" (I. v). It is here noteworthy that Sanscho does not emphasize the single correctness of his religion, but only loyalty, as one is loyal to one's native land. Zayde is much more Enlightened in her view of religion: "Is not the God Whom you honor also the God of the Moors?/ . . . No! no! it is all the same to Him, however humans worship Him;/ It is vice alone that injures one's service to Him" (I. v). These unorthodox sentiments are quite the same as the ones later expressed in *Nathan der Weise*. In the face of such arguments there is nothing for Don Sanscho to do except to admit that he cannot marry Zayde in any case, since Elvire is already his wife. He is ashamed of having deceived the virtuous Zayde, but this confession does not do very much to redeem his character.

With surpassing generosity, Zayde now resolves to help the Christians escape anyway, telling them, "Learn that the merit of virtue also charms Moors" (II. ii). But even this virtuous resolve is fraught with moral difficulties, because Zayde will have to deceive her father in order to help Sanscho and Elvire. She wishes that she were a *Christian* so that she could learn how to lie: "Elvire's God! ah, teach me how to lie too!" But actually she is too rational to hold such a concept of God: "But no! You do not teach that; otherwise You would not be God!/ It is only that humans make a mockery of Your teaching" (II. iv). In this speech, with its bitter commentary on "Christian" practices, one feels again on common ground with Lessing's *Nathan*. This impression is strengthened by Murath's speech concerning the false beliefs of Christians: "Their folly even teaches that God is honored with blood:/ God, whose thunders only go against the wicked" (II. v). He repeats that he does not consider Don Sanscho an unworthy son-in-law: "I am not angry because a slave esteems you;/ For if a slave is a just man, then he is as worthy as a hero" (ii. v). It seems inconsistent with Murath's rationality in other matters that he should insist on a change of religion for Sanscho. Nevertheless, on this point he is adamant.

Meanwhile the escape of the Christians is under way—with poor success, however. Elvire is fatally shot and Sanscho is taken prisoner. At first Murath thinks of revenge, for kindness has its limits: "Through too much kindliness virtue itself is dishonored" (III. i). Then this momentary severity is vanquished by tender feelings, for he cannot resist his daughter's tears: "I detest that pride of domestic tyrants/ Who banish the voice of the heart from their hard breasts" (III. i). Twenty years earlier Gottsched's Cato had had a much different view of a father's authority and a daughter's obedience. Murath sees the love of Zayde for Sanscho as an act of God ("*eine Fügung*" [III. ii]), something over which the reason has no control. At this point the wounded Elvire conveniently dies, but without regret, for (like Sara Sampson) she regards long life as a danger to virtue. This thought is put rather clumsily: "A long life after all only makes virtue blush" (III. vi). In general, Elvire's death scene is rich in philosophical maxims. She reprimands Sanscho for using the word "destiny": "Not destiny! what a delusion! It is God Who rules!/ Yes, Who directs the path of the pious even over thorns./ Whither? whither He wishes! Where are we? in the hands/ Which also send forth lightning and thunder according to wise conclusions." She freely recognizes that she is being punished for deceiving Zayde: "He is punishing me; and justly! One should not prepare/ The ground for good paths with treason, deceit, and ingratitude./ To Him, evil is not made into good by the results;/ God hates even the good that is done by a villain." To this confession of faith in absolute morality she adds a weak statement of religious tolerance: "We did not think that God could also love Moors./ . . . Is virtue esteemed even in the desert?/ Here, I thought, God was only worshipped with vice" (III. vi). In conclusion she rises to the heights of nobility by urging Sanscho to marry Zayde after her death. Zayde, however, is not happy about Elvire's death and has grave doubts about the nature of her love—what is it? a mere emotional impulse or something divine in origin? She asks God, "Oh! why do You not extinguish the blind impulse in me?/ And if it is not Your command: then why do I love him?" (III. viii). Here, surely, are the beginnings of a new and nonrationalistic concept of love.

Once again Zayde is besieged by the conflict between father and lover. Don Sanscho tries to persuade her to turn Christian and flee with him. With Zayde's broadmindedness, naturally this conversion is not repugnant to her: "The name is not a sin! Ah! so long as I love God:/ I am not condemned by the way in which I exercise myself therein" (IV. i). But she is too soft-hearted in regard to her father to be able simply to leave with Sanscho, and in despair she grasps a dagger to commit suicide. Seeing this action, Murath grows very angry and accuses Sanscho of having perverted Zayde's virtue, since of course suicide is an unvirtuous act. Poor Zayde stands a victim between two men whose only irrational feature is their respective insistence on the name of a certain religion. In the end, however, it is the Christian who performs the meaner actions. To gain time, Sanscho pretends to be inclined toward Mohammedanism and then admits in a soliloquy, "Thus the first step of my flight has been accomplished" (IV. v). Apparently having learned nothing from his earlier deception, he calls this one just, although he dislikes the necessity for it. With a very bad conscience, Zayde finally agrees to accompany him. Love has finally won out over filial duty, but, lest this be interpreted by the audience as something excusable or even laudable, Zayde turns and says to them: "You, however, who are in love; ah! impress this on your memory:/ What seems a virtue to you can easily be a vice" (IV. viii).

The flight of Zayde is so painful to Murath that he breaks out in lamentations against Providence: "You are described as being so kind, but You are so hard!" (V. v). Where his daughter is concerned, however, he neither feels anger nor casts blame: "Oh! such a misstep deserves only lamentation;/ Virtue itself derives honor from such an error./ My vengeance shall strike the Spaniard alone!" (V. v). This paternal forebearance had no earlier model in German tragedy; but it was soon to be equaled (and perhaps imitated) by Sir William Sampson in Lessing's middle-class drama. Murath is completely the doting father-figure. When it is suggested that he would have a right to be angry, he cries out, "Eh? what? my anger just? From what sort of impudent fellow/ Does a father ever learn to rage at his children?" (V. v). But he is different from Lessing's Sir William in that he thirsts for revenge on his daughter's abductor. It is this desire for revenge which brings on the catastrophe. He rushes at the recaptured Don Sanscho with a dagger, and Zayde, who quickly interposes herself between her father and her lover, receives the fatal blow instead. Seeing this, Murath now turns his dagger on himself, but not without making a moral statement about the folly of revenge: ". . . that the sword of vengeance/ Always falls back with woe on the one who grasps it" (V. viii). The death of Zayde is a punishment for her rather sympathetic misstep. She dies with exactly the same combination of guilt and virtue as Miss Sara Sampson. The death of Murath is a suicide conditioned by sinful impulses toward revenge—and Providence cannot be blamed for that. Don Sanscho, however, is left alive at the end. He alone goes unpunished for his shortcomings, which were worse than those of the two Moslems. He does feel a certain embarrassment at being the only survivor, but his religion prohibits suicide. According to the preface, Schönaich intended Sanscho's survival as a kind of sop to orthodox opinion: "That Zayde dies is a misfortune; that Don Sanscho stays alive is required by religion." [50] As such, it comes far too late to preserve the dignity of Christianity, which has been so severely attacked in this play. Indeed, the effect of Sanscho's decision is to cast one more slur against Christians, i.e., that they will use their religion as an excuse to prolong their wretched lives.

The second tragedy in the collection is *Mariamne und Herodes*, and it is a most unskillful treatment of the same material that was to inspire Hebbel approximately a century later and that Voltaire had already used in 1724. In the preface to this play Schönaich imitates his Master by pointing out the historical authenticity of his plot and characters, both having been taken from Josephus. Unlike Gottsched, Schönaich feels a certain trepidity about claiming historical authenticity as a merit for his tragedy, and modestly declares that it is only regarded a merit by a timid poet like himself, who does not have enough self-confidence to substitute other agreeable features to make up for a deficiency in history. His modesty is more than justified in respect to this tragedy, which is surely the weakest of the four, in spite of the excellent material chosen. The character of Mariamne, her special kind of pride, was simply alien to the German Weltanschauung of the eighteenth century, especially since Schönaich wished to keep her an admirable figure. As a *Machtweib* ruled by unvirtuous passions, as a Dido ruined by resentment and love, she would have submitted with ease to the treatment a Schönaich was equipped to give her story. But as a virtuous, admirable heroine with Enlightened, rational ideas she is quite impossible. In the struggle to combine the facts of this barbaric story with the usual moral sentiments of his own time Schönaich succeeded only in having his characters utter one absurdity after the other, in making them contradict themselves fatuously, and in robbing them of all consistency. In addition, the dialogue is extremely weak, and in many instances unpardonably obscure.

The author really does not know what to make of Mariamne's melancholy frame of mind. At first he points out that her husband Herodes is guilty of the blood of her father, brother, and uncle. Accordingly she bears resentment toward him and fears for her own life. Yet, when her guardian Sohem announces that Herodes is coming home safely, Mariamne demands to drink the poison prepared for her in case he had not come home. She wants Sohem to tell Herodes a lie, that a false report of his death had arrived in Jerusalem, and that she had in consequence been forced to take the poison. In view of this plan, it is a little disconcerting to hear Mariamne in the next scene giving voice to the customary virtuous abhorrence of deceit merely because her confidante Elise urges her to indulge in the harmless pretense of acting joyful when Herodes returns: "Pretending is a poison that threatens our virtue,/ And my brow hitherto has blushed at vices./ I hate the arts of wily courtesans" (I. iii). Evidently Mariamne makes a distinction between outright lying and the false pretense of a sentiment one does not feel. This is the first time that falseness of facial expression has been specifically alluded to and described as an accomplishment peculiar to harlots. Lessing also makes use of this idea in his characterization of Marwood in *Miss Sara*, but it is generally supposed that he took it from Lillo's *London Merchant,* wherein the harlot Millwood also carefully arranges her facial expressions. The notion of connecting such artfulness, however, with the more abstract concept of deceit, the cardinal vice of the German Enlightenment, may have been suggested to Lessing by his reading of Schönaich. In any case, it is easier to understand Mariamne's reluctance to receive Herodes joyfully than it is to see why she is so stubbornly determined to die. Her confidante Elise speaks of this resolve as sinful pride: "For do you perhaps think that your pride pleases Him,/ Him who holds the scales of life in His hand?" (I. iii). Sohem adds to this his advice that she should keep her emotions under control, and Elise says that she should employ her reason rather than her heart. These arguments then seem to have a temporarily calming effect on Mariamne.

Herodes himself appears on stage in the second act. This figure presented Schönaich with an excellent opportunity to portray a diabolical titan who might have been a worthy descendant of Ulfo or a predecessor of Weisse's Richard. Instead, Schönaich proceeded to make of him an old-fashioned villain of passion and imperfect reasoning, with just a touch of folklore nonsense about him, that is, his hand literally itches for blood. He has enough rationality to regret his lack of control over his emotions, but he seeks to blame Providence for this rather than himself: "It itches; I feel it already; it itches for fresh blood:/ If only Heaven would desist from making me angry!" (II. iii). Moreover, Herodes is conscious of the fact that the emotion of love has been too little under his control, and the voice of conscience is not entirely silent within him: "For the worst bloodthirsty tyrant is not so blinded:/ That he does not secretly pass judgment upon himself" (II. iii). But Mariamne's coolness to him makes Herodes suspect that she has been unfaithful to him with her guardian Sohem, and this suspicion offends Mariamne so much that all her determination to die, which had been allayed, now returns. If he will not execute her, then she will kill herself. Torn between love and jealousy, Herodes laments the ultimate impotence of his reasoning power: "One sees the better choice; one sees it; one even approves of it;/ One goes so far as to praise it: and nevertheless follows after evil" (II. vi). Here is a case where human weakness, as Wolff described it, renders reason ineffective; but a little less obstinacy on Mariamne's part might well have assisted reason and resulted in an improvement of Herodes' character. Unfortunately, this "admirable" heroine remains stubborn and unreasonable. It is strange that she possesses no passivity (*Gelassenheit*) whatever, and that this lack is not consistently regarded as a character fault by the author. To designate her as an early forerunner of the active Storm and Stress titan, however, would be thoroughly misrepresentative. Rather, she is a lost character in search of a more modern author. Perhaps her most ludicrous speech is that in which she begs Heaven for death, for the end of a life "Which You, after all, have only given me out of hatred and fury" (IV. viii). It is safe to say that no other supposedly sympathetic character in the tragedy of the time ever hurled a more tasteless charge at Providence than this.

In the last act, which belongs entirely to Herodes, the tyrant believes he has won some sort of rational victory over his emotions, at any rate over the emotion of love, for he has ordered the execution of Mariamne to be carried out: "Very well! thus I am then rid of silly love!/ . . . I have won many a victory by my arm:/ Just one was still lacking: I have conquered myself!" (V. ii). Here Herodes does indeed come close to the character of the evil rationalist, the dynamic embodiment of evil which was soon to emerge as a prominent element of tragedy. Like this figure, he uses reason for an evil, rather than for a good purpose, and he conquers an emotion that could have led him to virtue. But the similarity is more apparent than real. Whereas the genuine evil rationalist is conscious of his actions and their meaning, Herodes is merely confused, and naively believes that he is doing the right and accepted thing in using self-control to subdue any and all emotions. One could call him a misguided rather than an evil rationalist. All his joy in his victory over himself is spoiled when definite news is brought to him that Mariamne was not guilty of infidelity after all. He has been the victim of a vicious lie told him—unaccountably—by some woman who never appears on stage at all and about whom one does not hear one word until the final scene. This is an incredibly amateurish piece of plot construction. At the news, Herodes of course wants to commit suicide. But it does not matter what he does. Neither he nor the author can possibly redeem this wretched play.

Somewhat better, in spite of serious faults of construction, is the third tragedy, *Thusnelde und Hermann*. It was probably inevitable that Schönaich, the author of the much ridiculed epic *Hermann*, should also write a drama about this hero. Was he not thereby following the practice of the Greek tragedians who dramatized episodes from Homer? To be sure, the effort to be Homer and Sophocles at once was considerably beyond the talents of Gottsched's protégé. Moreover, it was unfortunate that he chose an episode so static that the situation at the end of the tragedy is precisely the same as it was at the beginning. An additional misfortune was that the sacrosanct Unity of Place caused him insuperable difficulties, because the subject matter required that not only the Germanic state of affairs, but also the Roman side had to be presented. A single scene location had not proved embarrassing to the writers of German tragedy in general, and so long as one was able to accept the convention that one room in a palace, or one tent, or one outdoor spot could be for no apparent reason favored by all the members of the cast, then one's credulity was not overtaxed. As J. E. Schlegel said, most tragedies were "so arranged that they could have taken place just as well in a barn as in a room; so little thought is given to the theater in them." [51] As soon as greater attention was paid to the stage picture, however, the convention of this Unity began to work an occasional hardship on the author. Schönaich, to judge from the comparative elaborateness of the stage directions found at the beginning of his works, was clearly interested in some degree of stage realism. The scene here is a sacred grove decorated with statues of Germanic heroes, a sight calculated to make a definite sense impression on the spectators. And yet, in this grove there appear alternately Hermann and his Germans and, with very thin excuse, also Germanicus and his Romans, although a war is being waged between them. One can easily agree with Lessing, who wrote that Schönaich paid attention to all the mechanical rules and still composed works of no value.[52]

As usual, Hermann is represented as the perfect hero, prizing liberty and virtue above all material possessions. With ringing words he refuses a Roman offer of gold: "To be just and free: those, those are our laws!/ . . . A yoke, even one of gold, oppresses!" (I. i). The Roman leader Germanicus possesses, however, something even more tempting than gold. Through the treachery of Segestes, Hermann's father-in-law, Hermann's wife Thusnelda and their child are in the Roman camp. If Hermann will agree to leave off fighting the Romans, he will get his family back, but otherwise he will not. Less peremptory in his virtue than Schlegel's Herrmann, Schönaich's hero cannot decide so quickly to live only for idealism: "Alas! it is far too hard to be a hero and a human being!/ Must then a heroic spirit avoid the tests of human beings?" (I. iii). The emotion of love is not easily controlled: "I have fought, and yet not subdued myself" (I. iii). His friend Inguiomar reminds him that the fatherland is more important than love, and that Thusnelda herself would rebuke Hermann for any weakness in her behalf. Then Hermann, saying that people would blush if they knew how many weaknesses heroes can be afflicted with, reëstablishes control over himself: "I am ashamed of myself. Very well! You have promised!/ Help me to be myself! Then the torment is over,/ and Hermann is great again!" (I. iii). This little exchange is of interest because it demonstrates how the sternly rational attitude of early Alexandrine tragedy has now given way to an increased sentimentalism. Furthermore, Hermann is not long required to choose between love and duty. It develops that Germanicus is in love with Thusnelda and wants to marry her after Segestes divorces her from Hermann. Under these circumstances there would no longer be any point in holding off an attack. Now he can fight the Romans and save Thusnelda at the same time.

In the second act, oddly enough, Thusnelda and her father appear in the sacred grove. Rather lamely, Segestes explains that the Germans have had to forsake these precincts. In his conversation with Thusnelda, Segestes comes close to being a villain of the new mold, for his villainy is strikingly rational in character. He uses his intellect to get rid of all "prejudices," even those retained by virtuous rationalists, and he is an outright enemy of all religion and virtue. Thus he tries to convince Thusnelda that her marriage vows are not inviolable: "The oath, like the gods, is a bond only to the lower classes./ It holds the people in check but does not tie our hands./ The lightning bolts which zigzag from the dark clouds/ Oftentimes shatter the pious as well as the impudent./ . . . The gods are not what our lower classes think them to be" (II. i). Such cynicism clearly foreshadows that of Schiller's Franz Moor, Präsident von Walter, and Wurm. Segestes has the same relationship to the future evil rationalist as did Bernhold's Irene. Like her, he lacks volcanic dynamism, and the author has not conceived of him as a part of the elemental force of evil. It is not wickedness but rather a faulty, superficial understanding of God's wise Providence which prompts him to say, "Indeed the might of the gods supports fortunate vices!" (II. i). But he does have in common with the evil rationalists what Schiller called a "faithless sophistical wisdom"; [53] and Thusnelda attributes his errors not to a lack of reason but, sentimentally, to a lack of heart: "Here in the breast is something which teaches me my duties:/ You have one, too, a breast; and you have not heard it!" (II. iii).

Germanicus, in love with Thusnelda, is depicted in a sympathetic way. Again the author shows that he has been touched by sentimentalism, for it is indicated that the good element in Germanicus is his morally sensitive heart which has, however, exposed him to the immoral desire to marry the already married Thusnelda. He scorns an older adviser who recommends rational self-control: "How wisely speaks a graybeard of flames which have fled him!/ His heart is choked by frost; therefore Stertin can triumph" (II. iv). To be sure, what attracts Germanicus to Thusnelda is not mere lust, but the rational attributes of her virtue as compared to the loose morals of Roman women. He also has a high opinion of Hermann and wants him to know "That Rome honors virtue even in its enemies" (II. vi).

The third act advances the action of the play scarcely at all, since it consists mainly of scenes in which the loyal Germans, standing together with their adversaries in the sacred grove, which is now being used as a parley ground, castigate the disloyal ones and flatly turn down the Roman peace offers. In Act Four Hermann informs the assembled German princes (in the grove!) that the Romans have offered peace. Their decision again is to refuse. Germanicus, marching in on this decision, is generous enough to admire the Germans for their pride and virtue. Indeed, he makes invidious comparisons between them and his own countrymen. He will not, however, hear of surrendering Thusnelda. Meanwhile, Inguiomar has revealed at the beginning of Act Four that he has arranged by bribery for Thusnelda to be brought to the grove, where Hermann can rescue her. By the end of Act Four this plan appears to have been altered, for now we find Inguiomar telling Hermann that he knows the way to Thusnelda's tent and is going there himself. Then in Act Five one learns that some disguised Germans were sent in flight from Thusnelda's tent. They have dropped a letter, written by Thusnelda, in which she tells Hermann that she plans to meet him in the grove. This letter is then read by Germanicus. The whole point of this absurd and baffling complication, it would seem, is to show how Germanicus is apprised of the escape plan. Only a Schönaich, one is tempted to say, could be guilty of such abominably amateurish plot construction as this.

Since he is already in the grove when he reads the letter, nothing is easier for Germanicus than to set a trap for Thusnelda there. As she enters with her confidante, he hides. Thusnelda is lamenting that God allows such wicked things to happen as have happened to her. Immediately the confidante returns a stereotyped answer to this stereotyped complaint: "Do not injure the gods." They have afforded her good times, and even bad times are to be regarded as profitable trials: "The gods immerse us in cruel troubles/ In order that we, through resistance, may be purified./ Virtue grows out of distress, courage out of torment:/ Wherein only vice and cowardice were lost" (V. iii). These wise arguments might have had an effect, except that just then Germanicus steps forth from his hiding place. Thusnelda seems won over (like her father) to the idea that the gods do not support the righteous cause. Like Mariamne, she wants to provoke Germanicus to kill her. But quickly she takes a more rational course: "One must not, through mockery, increase the rage of one's enemies;/ Virtue, even in anger, must remain sacred to us" (V. iv).

Although the Germans soon afterwards storm the sacred grove, Germanicus succeeds in having Thusnelda dragged away by his men. Hermann closes the play by uttering a threat of revenge. His words are rather curious: "Then, then will appear the day, when we show the nations:/ That for the sake of the fatherland nature and love are silent" (V. vii). The import of this statement is far from clear. Does Hermann imply that his wish to rescue Thusnelda has restrained him from more decisive action against the Romans? But the Romans have accomplished nothing more than the repeated abduction of Thusnelda, and indeed, it was her captivity which throughout most of the play impelled Hermann to action against them. But it hardly seems worth the trouble to examine what Schönaich's intention may have been. At the end of the drama the situation is exactly what it was at the beginning. Nothing has been resolved, and no character has been developed or altered. Again, this play was one that should have been omitted from the collection.

Schönaich's foremost worry, to judge from his preface, was that he would be criticized for showing "so serious a gentleman as Germanicus" as a lover.[54] His real concern ought to have been that he wrote a play in which absolutely nothing happens.

The last of the four tragedies, *Zarine und Stryangäus*, is evidently based on some fabulous account [55] of a little-known Asian tribe, the Sakas (Sacae), which ancient writers generally associated with the Scythians. The quasi-historical flavor of the plot brings to mind the typical fantastic Baroque novel, and Schönaich acknowledges this fact rather apologetically in the preface, where he compares the plot to that of Buchholtz' novel *Herkuladiskus und Herkuladisla* [56] or to that of the Tancred-Clorinde episode in *Gerusalemme liberata*. The characters have the exotic names and live in the exotic regions so frequently characteristic of Baroque courtly literature, and the main feminine character is an Amazon type—this again being a feature of Baroque romance. Baroque fantasy, however, is only a veneer on this drama, which has an ethical content that is wholly rationalistic and of the eighteenth century. Zarine is an Enlightened ruler over her barbaric subjects, and her ambition is to educate them to virtue and humanity. She is a perfect character, a model heroine, as exemplary in her way as Schlegel's Herrmann or Canut. Her effect on her country is comparable to the effect of Goethe's Iphigenia on the realm of Tauris. The internal action, which is not wholly despicable in this drama, involves Zarine's spiritual conquest of the members of her court, as well as her conquest of herself when she is strongly tempted to act dishonorably. The second titular hero, Stryangäus, represents Zarine's temptation, and in his comparative spiritual weakness provides a foil for her moral strength. For once, at least, Schönaich was able to create a tragedy with a fairly logical construction and with unambiguous characters. Unhappily he was unable to keep it free of long empty speeches and occasional absurdities of action.

In her attempts to bring rational rule to her subjects, Zarine is opposed by her sister Tomire, who believes in war and revenge and the old barbaric "virtues." Whereas Zarine wants peace with the Medes, Tomire is in favor of continued war against them, because their former king treacherously poisoned the sisters' father at a banquet. Zarine thinks there has been enough vengeance for that deed: "Just revenge must not become raging fury" (I. i). But Tomire ascribes Zarine's mildness to something less noble than rationalism. According to her, Zarine has fallen in love with Stryangäus, the general of the Medes who, although he unhorsed her in battle, spared her life and, indeed, kissed her hand. Zarine denies the accusation and maintains that virtue, not love, is the guide of her actions: "Virtue, which leads me, has long ago bidden me/ To tear prejudices even out of my breast" (I. i). She wishes to use peace for constructive purposes, while Tomire sees in peacetime only a temptation to idle vices; her resistance to Enlightened culture has a tinge of Rousseauism about it: "A brook gave us our drink; the fortune of the bow our food:/ Yet the Scythian looked back with pleasure at his hut and his horse" (I. i). Serenely undeterred by Tomire's objections, Zarine is glad to receive Stryangäus when he desires audience with her. This is certain proof to Tomire that her sister is deceiving herself about admiring only the good qualities of Stryangäus. Underneath lurks passion and this will lead Zarine into the crime of loving an enemy: "For the force of habit combats the horror of vice,/ And a crime often looks like a virtue" (I. iii). Tomire's views are supported by the old counsellor Nomades, who is thunderstruck when Zarine forbids him to attack Stryangäus and his retinue of Medes. Now Tomire and he put their heads together and decide to disobey Zarine for her own good. They will prepare a banquet at which Stryangäus shall be poisoned. Although well-intentioned, these two plotters choose bad methods to achieve their ends, and they are not content to leave the outcome of events to Providence, a grievous mistake. Thus Tomire says: "Heaven itself often hinders virtuous deeds./ For good fortune it is not enough to be merely virtuous!" (II. ii). Yet they are incautious enough— an absurdity in view of their previous intention to serve Zarine without her knowledge—to betray their plan to the queen. Oddly, Zarine fails to give express orders that the plan should be abandoned. She only acts shocked.

For his part, Stryangäus is openly in love with Zarine, despite the fact that he is already married. He speaks as though he had never loved before, and like many a hero in these Alexandrine tragedies, is proud of it. Rationalists tended to regard love either as surrender to an ignoble passion or as an act of submission to another person; but Stryangäus consoles himself with the thought that Zarine is a person far above the common mold. He rejects the idea of concealing his feelings from her. Although actually such concealment would accord well with virtuous self-control, he argues that all concealment is deception and therefore bad: "Falseness is the fruit of the very poorest art:/ It is the wit of foolishness; for high minds, vapor" (II. vi). But before he can declare himself to Zarine, he is treacherously attacked by Nomades and his men, who follow the old man's mistaken advice that "Those things are not vices which virtue teaches us to do" (III. i). For some obscure reason—another of Schönaich's absurdities—Nomades has not waited for the poisoned banquet, but attacks with sword and arrows.

Stryangäus mortally wounds Nomades just as Zarine appears on the scene. She has no sympathy for her old counsellor's fate, but instead castigates him for lacking the wisdom that is supposed to come with age: "There he now lies, the graybeard who stained his honor/ And covered his snowy hair with disgrace!" (III. vi). She is not softened by sentimentalism as she sentences his henchmen: "The gods are pleased with the sight of just punishment" (III. vi). However, it is consistent with Stryangäus' tendency to let feelings be his guide (as in love) that he suggests a more sentimental treatment of the culprits: "It is I who have been injured by them: therefore it is mine to pardon./ Put them in my hand! their remorse shall be my revenge" (III. vii). Zarine enthralls Stryangäus when she speaks like a paragon of Enlightenment about her plans for rational rule. She will not be greedy: "I do not want to increase the tears of the nations with treasures;/ Nor to dismantle palaces in order to adorn my country with them." She will not be led into war over trifles: "Trow, the gods must laugh at our victories,/ When for a grain of sand we desolate the earth." And all of these good precepts, she confesses, were taught to her by the noble Stryangäus. Nevertheless, she maintains that she has no emotional interest in him and will not disturb his marriage: "Rhetäa may have your heart: I want to possess your spirit:/ Thus your pleasure will profit her, and your virtue, me" (III. vii). It is interesting to note here that a really rational love can exist altogether apart from emotional, to say nothing of physical, involvements. In his own way, Schönaich has found a *modus vivendi* for unfulfilled love; to be sure, it is not so enthusiastic and elegiacally attractive as the spiritual love of Klopstock's ode "To Fanny." But the relationship is there, nevertheless.

Undaunted by the death of Nomades, sister Tomire continues to hatch treacherous plans against Stryangäus. She salves her conscience with the idea that a good end justifies bad means: "Virtue itself often makes men criminal:/ Is that to be considered vice which punishes our enemies?" (IV. ii). Thus she tries to convince Stryangäus that Zarine is only pretending friendship for him, and that his best course of action would be to flee. He is too much in love, however, to leave. Instead, he makes another proposal to Zarine, who again coolly reminds him that he is already married and should control himself, as she has done. He is allowing a blind animal impulse to spoil the greatness of his soul: "Do not desire of me an indecent life,/ And pleasures which can also be given by courtesans,/ And which even an animal enjoys!" (IV. viii). Her rational words,

which would have had the full approval of Thomasius and Wolff,
fly straight to their goal, his reason: "My mind is touched by the
mind which speaks through her" (IV. ix). Nevertheless, his passion
is much too violent to be controlled. This is his tragic fault, and it
speedily leads to a catastrophe. In a curious scene that combines the
most interminable, artificial speeches with an unusual, perhaps ac-
cidental realism, Stryangäus is discovered (by the raising of a middle
curtain) at the back of the stage, getting up from a bed. Talking
bemusedly more to himself than to his confidant, he expresses disgust
with himself. In his grief over Zarine's coldness and his own disloyalty to his wife he feels, in his impulsive way, that the only
solution of the problem is to kill himself. His subsequent actions
are not stagey, but believably similar to those of an actual distraught
suicide. Still talking, he sits down at a table and almost casually
sticks a dagger into his heart, and immediately expires. The middle
curtain now descends on this rather effective tableau. Zarine's reaction to the death of Stryangäus is at first passionately irrational,
as she blames herself for not having loved him. But a moment later
she regains her equilibrium, saying that virtue enjoined her course
of action on her. She intends to erect a monument as a warning
to others that tenderness of heart, although generally (and certainly
in the 1750's) recognized as a good quality, can be a danger to the
preservation of virtue: "You and I show the kings of the earth/
That tenderness itself may become terrible to virtue" (V. iv). The
moral of this tragedy is not essentially different from that of Schlegel's *Dido* and it is quite old-fashioned for 1754. Schönaich, to
judge from his preface, seems to have been a little embarrassed himself by the stern rationalism of his heroine. Thus he comments, with
uneasy irony, "Zarine is a female philosopher; but do not all beauties
philosophize a little, before they become human?" [57]

Nothing could show more plainly than Schönaich's four plays
that the state of tragedy at mid-century, between the appearance
of Schlegel's *Canut* and Lessing's *Miss Sara Sampson*, was indeed
one of discouraging sterility. The dramas that were presented to
the public had some interesting aspects, but they contained no in-
novations of any consequence beyond a few barely discernible
moves in the direction of the evil rationalist. Whether produced by
the best of minds (Lessing and Möser) or by the most pedestrian,
these tragedies all stayed within the bounds laid out in the *Deutsche
Schaubühne*, with the exception of von Trenck's *Araxane*, and its di-
vergences belonged not to a new, but to an old and discredited form.
They testify to the relative rapidity with which the Alexandrine
tragedy had been able to establish itself—in scarcely more than

twenty years—as the single possible form of German tragedy; but, on the other hand, they show that for nine long years the German tragedy was merely marking time. After such a dull period, the theater was ripe for a bold and brilliant experiment, and that came with the prose middle-class tragedy. This vigorous new sub-genre, however, by no means signified the immediate end of the older type. After an initial pause, the Alexandrine tragedy reawakened to a few more years of life. Partly, perhaps, because of the competition offered by the prose works, these years saw the composition of some Alexandrine tragedies considerably superior to the ones written at mid-century.

VI

THE FIRST MIDDLE-CLASS TRAGEDIES

THE SAME YEAR that marked the highest tide of the Alexandrine tragedy in Germany, 1754, also witnessed the production of two imported dramas which were suddenly to provide the German tragedy with a startlingly new and different appearance. These were the famous middle-class tragedies from England, Lillo's *The London Merchant* (1731), produced by Schoenemann in Hamburg,[1] and Moore's *Gamester* (1753), produced by Ackermann in Breslau [2] as well as by Schoenemann in Hamburg.[3] The success of these English plays and, in addition, the universal popularity at the same time of Richardson's novels quickly encouraged young German dramatists to write German tragedies in which English names were used, in which the characters had become bourgeois, the dialogue prose, the time the present, and the plot wholly fictional, but close to reality. Nevertheless, in spite of this eye-catching and thrilling new dress, German tragedy did not surrender its old identity, but continued to evolve in a regular way on the basis of its previous self. The new appearance and the new subjects, however, gave its development the greatest impetus, by far, since the inception of Gottsched's reform.

In the first spate of middle-class tragedies published between 1755 and 1759—but concentratedly between 1755 and 1757—the *Rhynsolt und Sapphira* [4] of Christian Leberecht Martini (1728–1801) stands out as unique and independent, and therefore merits discussion even before *Miss Sara Sampson*, although the latter probably antedates *Rhynsolt und Sapphira* in the year 1755 by a few months.[5] The tradition of calling *Rhynsolt und Sapphira* an imitation of *Miss Sara* evidently begins with Schmid's *Chronologie des deutschen Theaters* (1775),[6] and it has been perpetuated by the entry in Goedeke's *Grundriß;* [7] but it is a false assumption. Nor does the influence of *The London Merchant* seem very strong, even if it is logical to believe that Martini, as an actor-author with the Schoenemann troupe in Hamburg, was encouraged by the example of *The London Merchant* to attempt a tragedy in prose with bourgeois characters.

Whereas Lillo's work was based on a contemporary English criminal case (which in Germany would have the same value as pure fiction), Martini's drama has an old historical subject [8] and presents a heroic historical figure, Charles the Bold of Burgundy. The locale is not eighteenth-century England, but medieval Zealand. In general, the play's unclassical and unexotic history, its three acts instead of five, the awkward handling of its plot, and even its prose dialogue suggest the old *Haupt- und Staatsaktionen* rather than the new English fashion. The author, who was not a scholarly theoretician but a man of the theater in the most literal sense, must have looked upon the *Haupt- und Staatsaktionen* with more tolerant eyes than the university-trained writers. Perhaps the simple fact that the English plays were in prose led him to regard them, in essence, as nothing more than *Haupt- und Staatsaktionen*, which might now be revived on the German stage. Such a superficial judgment is not incredible, if one keeps in mind the similar superficiality of much journalistic drama criticism of the day. To be sure, Martini was well aware of the changes wrought by Gottsched's reform, and his new "*Haupt- und Staatsaktion*" is not permitted to sink into barbarism. The Unities are conscientiously obeyed,[9] the Hanswurst has been banned from the proceedings, and there is an air of deep seriousness over the whole action, with plenty of emphasis on virtue.

The heroine of the play is a woman of the people. The historical incident on which the drama is based provided this circumstance, and it is a moot question whether Martini selected this subject specifically for that reason or whether he accepted it for its dramatic value in spite of the bourgeois element. The latter may be the more logical conclusion, when one considers the total lack of middle-class atmosphere in the work. The only scene is a room in a palace—a rather forbidding palace with a dungeon and execution chamber; and one of the leading roles is that of the reigning duke of the country, a figure equivalent to a king. Unlike Emilia Galotti, the bourgeois Sapphira is not surrounded by her family (her husband appears on stage only once, briefly), nor is she shown in her domestic milieu, nor is her unfortunate situation viewed as the result of political inequality. Consequently, one tends to regard her simply as a mistreated woman and not as a mistreated woman belonging to an unjustly oppressed social class. The play, therefore, has little or no social significance.

Its most important inner development, as differentiated from the important external innovation of prose dialogue, is the presence and crucial prominence of the character Rhynsolt, who may be termed the first genuine successor in German tragedy to Schlegel's Ulfo.

As in *Canut*, so also in Martini's play there is a virtuous sovereign, a virtuous woman, a virtuous man whom she loves (her husband), and opposed to these three a creature of dynamic wickedness. Rhynsolt, a general and the governor of the capital city of Zealand, is not weak or embittered; he is not in error regarding the integrity of Providence; nor is he a believer in the doctrine that the end justifies the means. Instead, he is coldly and programmatically nonvirtuous. To his secretary he says, "What do you mean by 'pangs of conscience'? The foolish prejudices, the fairy tales taught us by stupid people to whom our early years were entrusted?" (I. i). Scorn for virtuous behavior was to be observed, of course, in many of the earlier tragedies; but here, and with unmistakable emphasis, the terminology and system of rationalism are employed inversely, i.e., to subvert the very goal of rationalism, which was virtue. Rhynsolt, the evil genius, relegates the voice of conscience to the status of one of those irrational things taught defenseless children in the nursery. How shocked Thomasius would have been had he lived to see his argument on prejudices in the *Einleitung zur Vernunftlehre* misapplied in this way. Like Ulfo, Rhynsolt is possessed of a demonic intensity that increases his dramatic stature far above the somewhat dull villains of other tragedies. Ulfo's attack on virtue was naive and almost pitiful in that he tried vainly to set up an emotional and irrational ideology belonging to a bygone age. Rhynsolt, with much greater sophistication, seeks to upset virtue by attacking it internally through its very roots: reason. *Vernunft* becomes from now on a word in dramatic dialogue which can no longer be completely trusted. Villains, as well as good and wise people, may now use it to their own divergent advantage. The rational villain had appeared tentatively before, notably in Bernhold's *Irene* and Schönaich's *Hermann;* but now that Ulfo's seething violence has been added to give him mobility, drive, and dominance, it may be said that in Rhynsolt the true evil rationalist has been born. In this, to be sure, there is less evidence of Martini's inventiveness than of the general philosophical attitude of the new sentimental epoch. For in the weakening of reason's position there is an obvious victory for the heart as a better foundation for virtue. Martini, by making his villain a rationalist and his heroine a sentimentalist, demonstrates that he was in tune with his times, as a practical man of the theater should be.

Rhynsolt displays the typical paradox of the evil rationalist. Although cold, calculating, and able to control his feelings, he is the slave of a single passion, his illicit desire for Sapphira. To obtain possession of her, he has had her husband Danfeld thrown into a dungeon on false charges of treason. With diabolical rationality he essays to prove to Sapphira that she ought to give in to his passion: "Sapphira, forsake the ridiculous concept of virtue . . . you are destined for the highest sensual delights . . ." (I. v). When she remains adamant, he threatens to make Duke Charles sign Danfeld's death warrant. Sapphira's desperate plight calls forth the usual nearly blasphemous reproach against God: ". . . does it add to Your glory when Your creatures are tormented?" (I. vi). This statement is not countered by the customary reassurance that God is indeed good. The husband, Danfeld, takes a fatalistic and stoical view of the matter, saying, "Sapphira, let us be steadfast! No mortal can deflect the eternal decisions of the Most Unchangeable One from their course" (I. vii). Danfeld refuses to have his life saved by the sacrifice of Sapphira's honor, and the upshot is that he dies at Rhynsolt's command. This is undoubtedly a poor reward for a life of loyalty and virtue, and Rhynsolt's cynical philosophy seems to be the correct one: "The virtues, these chimeras, are not rewarded. False witness gets the reward, and nothing is left for the virtue of loyalty except despair and scorn" (II. ii). Rhynsolt preaches the doctrine of the emancipation of the flesh. What the true rationalists regarded as unworthy animalistic impulses and sensations, this evil rationalist with his "superior intellect" regards as an inevitable part of human life to be accepted and enjoyed. The desires of the senses neither can nor should be controlled: "Our days go past in the slavery of the senses, and our chains are sensual pleasures and delights" (II. ii). It is unreasonable not to face this, and evidently the faculty of reason should be used to serve our desires.

Evil thoughts like these can hardly be passed off as mere errors in judgment and human weakness. They are, rather, a demonstration that the eradication of ignorance and superstitious prejudice was not going to result in the general amelioration of human character, as the earlier generation had thought. The very sharpening of the rational faculty could just as easily result in the creation of a super-villain, more unregenerate and devastating than any before, because he understood the arguments for virtue and could refute them logically. Thus a double task has now been set before the virtuous character: not only does he have to reconcile himself (as always) to the unaccountable suffering imposed on him by a supposedly benevolent Providence, but he has to fend off the subtle and convincing reasoning of a human fiend who tells him that he is living under a delusion. It has now become more incumbent than ever on the author to produce a satisfactory vindication of Providence. If he does not, then his tragedy can have a seriously immoral effect.

Martini solved the problem by pointing up the inadequacy of

Rhynsolt's shrewd plotting. In spite of his cleverness, the truth about his victim's innocence comes to light, and Duke Charles has him punished. Therefore, treachery is *not* rewarded, as he believes; and virtue *does* receive recognition and reward. Sapphira gets Rhynsolt's whole estate as indemnification for the loss of her husband, and Danfeld himself gets a monument, while Rhynsolt must pay with his own blood for the innocent blood which he caused to be shed. The fact that evil has been severely punished must be taken for proof that the world-order is after all rational and just. If no punishment of his murderer will restore Danfeld to life, at any rate death has been sweetened for him by the prospect of bliss beyond the grave. The execution of Rhynsolt, on the other hand, has delivered this villain over to damnation. As a captain reports, "With teeth-grinding rage Rhynsolt cursed the days of his life and his fate" (III. v). Justice is clear, stern, and legalistic in this drama. Sapphira may still weep for Danfeld, but she has received compensation in cash and in honor for her loss.

Although the figure of Duke Charles is completely virtuous, it succeeds in being more human than the Canut of Schlegel's play, principally because Charles is neither omniscient nor serene. He is deceived by Rhynsolt, and when he realizes the mistake he has made about this trusted man's character he is bitterly remorseful: "Did the most honest prince, by means of his benevolent deeds, have to beget the greatest scoundrel?—You princes! When will there be an end to the unhappiest of your fates, that you so often warm in your bosom nothing but Lernaean monsters, nothing but four-headed serpents?" (III. ii). In this speech one hears the only pronouncement of any political significance in the play, and it can hardly be stated that the play itself is an intended illustration of the principle that princes should be careful about choosing their deputies. Instead, here is an early example of that proposition so often put forth by dramatists of the second half of the eighteenth century, namely, that princes ought not to be blamed for bad government, as it is usually the fault of their underlings. Traces of this pious convention are still to be found in Schiller's *Kabale und Liebe*, where the duke, although spoken of in bitterly critical terms, is nevertheless kept in the background while the active evil is performed by his minister. It is worthy of note that Lessing, at the end of his *Emilia Galotti*, let the Prince of Guastalla utter much the same complaint as Duke Charles': "Is it not sufficient for the misfortune of so many, that princes are human beings? Must devils disguise themselves as their friends, besides?" (V. viii). Morally, however, Duke Charles is far superior to Lessing's weak and lascivious prince. Unfortunately, his virtue has not brought him happiness, because, like many of the kings of Alexandrine tragedies, he cannot find the golden mean between too severe and too lenient government: "How wretched princes are after all! If they instill fear, then they become terrible and are hated; and if kindness is their objective, then they are misled into injustice or they grow despicable!" (III. v).

Making its first appearance in this drama is a theme destined to experience much repetition in subsequent German tragedy. It is that of the unwilling and conscience-stricken accomplice to evil. Siegmund, Rhynsolt's secretary, is very much bothered by the false "proofs" he has prepared in order to show Danfeld's treason. He wishes he could undo his part in the affair, but he is forced to keep abetting the nefarious schemes of his employer. Characteristic of his plight is the statement, "To how many new vices one is driven, once vain ambition has seduced us into accepting the first!" (I. i). Again, this sentiment finds an echo in *Emilia Galotti*, when the servant Pirro regrets that he cannot get free of his former criminal associates: "Ha! Let the devil grasp you by one single hair, and you are his forever!" (II. iii). Unlike Pirro and most of his other descendants, Siegmund manages to withdraw his foot from the devil's snare by making a full confession. Such a mundane figure as a secretary had never been permitted in an Alexandrine tragedy. His presence already provides us with a glimpse of the historically realistic atmosphere of a play like Goethe's *Egmont*.

Rhynsolt und Sapphira, insofar as it operates without the principle of *hamartia*, is in line with the more sentimental of the preceding Alexandrine tragedies. But whereas the latter tended to grow paler and paler, and duller and duller, the melodramatic enhancement of the evil character in Martini's drama brought a renewal of nerve and life to tragedy which had been missing since *Canut* in 1746. There was, nevertheless, a danger in this emphasis on the villain, which would become apparent very quickly and reach a climactic point in Weisse's works. That is to say, a personage as evil as Rhynsolt is a freak of nature or, better, the product of an overheated imagination. He dashes about the stage breathing fire and fascinating the spectators, providing a fine theatrical thrill, but little more. Thanks to him the German tragedy would become more and more a purveyor of horror and thrills, and the assumption of bourgeois costume would at first do nothing to mitigate that condition. Comedy, on the other hand, was growing ever gentler and more appealing to the heart. It was left to Lessing, an essentially nontragic writer, to offer an alternative by combining tragedy with sentimental comedy in his *Miss Sara Sampson*. When *Miss Sara* was imitated, however, this most basic ingredient of its composition was overlooked, and the search for thrills and horror went on apace. Thus, although *Rhynsolt und Sapphira* stands aside from other middle-class tragedies as described above, still, on account of its dominant villain and its sensationalism, it is more typical of the early development of the genre in Germany than is the universally hailed model, *Miss Sara Sampson.*

Lessing worked against the Schlegel-Martini current by maintaining virtue in its old position of dominant interest. The virtuous character of Sara is not overshadowed by the evil adversary Marwood because Sara's suffering is kept interesting throughout. Lessing fulfilled here in practice what he later stated theoretically in his letter to Nicolai of November, 1756: "I only demand that the persons who captivate me most should be the most unhappy ones during the play." [10] Lack of suffering on the part of Canut took interest away from that virtuous character, as Lessing saw it; therefore he let his Sara suffer spiritually as few had done before. But he was also careful to preserve the principle of *hamartia.* Sara's suffering is the result of a misstep: she has allowed herself to be seduced and abducted by Mellefont. To be sure, this error was committed *before* the play begins. When we see her, she has already recovered her virtuous equilibrium, which then remains static throughout. Here there is an ingenious compromise between the types of tragedy represented by Gottsched's *Cato* (suffering brought on by sin) and Quistorp's *Aurelius* (suffering without sin). In *Miss Sara* we are permitted to enjoy the sweet spectacle of unfaltering virtue and to experience the sorrow of a sad conclusion without jeopardy to the concept of a just and benevolent Providence.

Lessing approached his first complete tragedy on a road leading directly from comedy; [11] consequently *Miss Sara* is altogether different from the earlier *Henzi* in internal structure. Seen from the comic viewpoint, it is a play about a fool, Mellefont, who has an irrational prejudice against marriage, and brings himself and others to grief because he cannot get rid of his mistaken idea. This basically comic plot, similar in structure to Lessing's actual earlier comedies and to *Minna von Barnhelm,* carries along with it the refined sensibility that comedy had been developing in England, France, and Germany in the preceding ten or twenty years. The humble setting of a few rooms in a third-class inn—a setting proper to comedy— was not conducive to the display of bizarrely exaggerated passions and desperate, grandiose actions. The introduction of the *Machtweib* Marwood was necessary to make the play a tragedy; and Marwood, with her outré flamboyance, thrashes about in this tepid setting like a sea monster in a lily pond. Without her, Sara's sufferings could not be taken very seriously, for all their intensity, because in the end she would have led Mellefont to the altar. At most, the play would have been a tearful comedy.

Lessing carefully directed attention away from the fact that Marwood is the only effective tragic component in the play. He supplied Sara with premonitions of doom in the first act, before Marwood even appears on the scene, and he allowed Marwood to escape unpunished after she poisons Sara. It is true that Sara's magnanimity toward her murderess corresponds to the sentimental attitude toward justice already observed in several Alexandrine tragedies. The vague prediction, "Marwood will not escape her fate" (V. x),[12] reminds one of the end of Bernhold's *Irene*. As important as sentimentality, however, was the consideration that punishment of Marwood would have detracted from Sara's all-important death scene and would have drawn too much attention to the element of evil. Furthermore, it is made very clear that Marwood is not acting independently as an evil personage, but as the unwitting instrument of God to carry out His judgment against the guilty Sara. This is revealed in Sara's informative remarks before expiring: "I die and forgive the hand by means of which God is afflicting me" (V, x). Thus Marwood, her bravura and fury notwithstanding, is kept from being an evil rationalist, an incarnate representative of Hell. In this play the principle of evil is neatly secured in its proper subservient place, controlled and administered by God in His mysterious ways. And lest these ways of God seem too mysterious (only to be accepted stoically), and lest poor Sara's punishment seem too harsh, a further explanation is added by her: "God must leave tested virtue a long time as an example to the world, and only weak virtue, which would perhaps succumb to all too frequent tests, does he suddenly remove from the dangerous combat" (V. x). The "punishment," then, turns out to be a benevolent act of Providence to preserve Sara's weak virtue from further sins. The suicide of Mellefont, who realizes painfully that his foolish irrationality has been the indirect cause of Sara's death, requires no such special dialectical explanation. It is the last inevitable error of a life ruined by error, and the question of God's justice is not involved; but even here there is a hope of salvation. Mellefont's last words are a prayer for God's mercy, and Sir William and Waitwell also pray in his behalf.

Lessing's dislike for the "coldness" of neoclassical tragedy is well known, and in *Miss Sara* he overcame coldness, not with the heat of large emotions, but with the warm softness of sentimentality. This

sentimentality consists in the assumption that the spectators will be
touched and pleased by the sight of virtuous actions. It is the same
assumption that was made for the tearful comedy by Gellert, who
spoke of ". . . the wonderful power of virtue . . . At any rate
it is not in our power to choose between approval or disapproval
of what is good, upright, and praiseworthy. We are simply carried
away by the natural beauty and charm of these things; and even
the most worthless person finds pleasure, against his will as it were,
in the contemplation of an excellent character, although he himself
neither possesses one nor makes any effort to possess one." [13] The
same assumption was also made, of course, by the tragedies of the
Deutsche Schaubühne, for all their rationalism. But the rigidity of
their Alexandrines, the superhuman spiritual strength of their personages, and the remoteness of the settings—to say nothing of the
meager ability of the authors—spoke less directly to the hearts of the
spectators than *Miss Sara Sampson*. A white-haired father who,
instead of being angered by the elopement of his daughter, is eager
only to forgive her and to accept both her and her seducer as his
children; an affectionate daughter whose only sin consists in having
been too susceptible to the uncontrollable emotion of love and
who blames herself unsparingly, feeling altogether unworthy of
forgiveness; a faithful servant, grown old in the service of this family,
treated and worthy of being treated as a friend—these are the characters who are supposed to make virtue attractive, irresistible. On
the other side there is Mellefont, the seducer. In him one deplores
the stunting of a virtue that could have grown strong in his
naturally good heart, and one wonders at the changes for the better
which Sara has already worked in him during their short acquaint-
anceship. In all of these, one is made to see that there is much more
good than evil in the world, and that this is the best of all possible
worlds. If there has to be one vicious character—Mellefont's jealous
cast-off mistress Marwood—at least her actions are under Heaven's
control, and besides, she has a little daughter who is a very angel
of virtue. Thus even in the camp of evil a pure blossom is growing.
The play is sentimental not only because it was written in the 1750's,
when the emphasis on feelings was supplanting the emphasis on
reason, but also because the explicitly rationalistic philosophy of
the Enlightenment took a view of the world which was inherently
sentimental, seeing the good and the happy, and hiding or explaining
away the bad.

The emotion which Lessing described as *"Mitleid"* in his correspondence with Mendelssohn and Nicolai (1756–1757) and which
he felt was the only one for tragedy (although he added a species

of "fear" temporarily in his *Hamburgische Dramaturgie*) was perhaps closer than he realized to the "admiration" that he summarily rejected. For what touches and arouses the desire to weep in *Miss Sara Sampson* is not so much the misfortunes that assail the characters to whom one is drawn as it is to the brave and magnanimous way these characters meet and accept their misfortune. And since Sara and Sir William, the father, are not cast in a heroic mold, but are ordinary middle-class people (despite the father's baronetcy), one does not take so much for granted their ability to cope with misfortune, to cling to virtue, and to bow before the will of Providence. Consequently, in addition to laying claim to our pity, they also excite our admiration. Their "widow's pence" of strength makes a much deeper impression than the fabulous resources of an Aurelius, a Banise, or an Octavia. Admiration is not cold, as Lessing believed. Either allied with pity or standing alone, it is able to move the heart. The important thing is to make the admirable persons human.

Miss Sara was soon followed by two fairly well-known bourgeois works, Pfeil's *Lucie Woodvil* and Brawe's *Freygeist;* but the publication of two other virtually unknown dramas shows that the interest stirred up by the English imports resulted almost immediately in a larger number of German middle-class tragedies than is generally supposed. These two dramas were entitled *Cleveland* and *Das Mutter-Söhnchen.*

Cleveland, oder die redliche Untreue was published anonymously at Breslau and Leipzig in 1757; but since its preface is dated September 1, 1755, it must be assumed that the actual composition occurred in the year of *Miss Sara* and *Rhynsolt und Sapphira.* Published together with this tragedy is a *"Schauspiel"* in prose called *Cleveland, oder der irrende Philosoph,* also with the date 1757. Both dramas are bound together with a tragedy by Johann Heinrich Steffens (1711–1784) entitled *Clarissa,* published in Celle in 1765.[14] Hence it is likely that the two *Clevelands* were also written by Steffens, rector of the Latin school at Celle, who had a keen and persevering interest in the drama. The earliest evidence of this was his translation of Plautus' *Aulularia* in 1743, which was followed in 1746 by his revised version of Sophocles' *Oedipus* and an essay, *Von der Moralität der Schauspiele.* In 1749 he came out with an original Alexandrine tragedy, *Placidus, oder Eustach,* and in 1752 he published a drama entitled *Die Christin Gabinie,* which has also been attributed to him as an original,[15] but without recognition of the strong possibility that it was only a translation of a French tragedy written in 1699 by David Augustin de Brueys. In 1755 he published a translation of Moore's *Gamester* under the title *Beverley, oder der Spieler,*[16] and thereafter quite a large number of translations and adaptations, including a Latin version of *Emilia Galotti*. It is disturbing that the two *Clevelands* have the publishing place Breslau and Leipzig, when the rest of Steffens' works appeared in Celle. However, they were published again in 1768 in Celle,[17] which renders matters more regular. The error of assigning the second of the two *Clevelands*, the *"Schauspiel,"* to the year 1765 [18] evidently depends on the circumstance, explained above, that these two works were bound together in that year, for unknown reasons, with the tragedy *Clarissa*.

Cleveland, oder die redliche Untreue is a middle-class tragedy by virtue of its bourgeois personages, but the author made a compromise with "regular" tragedy by retaining a dialogue of rhymed Alexandrines. The Unity of Time is also kept, as in *Rhynsolt und Sapphira* and *Miss Sara*, but not the Unity of Place, for although the first four acts take place in an African seaport, the last one is on an island in the sea. Except for the absence of any personages of high rank (the fact that Cleveland is the son of Oliver Cromwell is not brought out), this play can be very aptly compared with Schönaich's *Zayde*, which in spirit and plot is not too far removed from a middle-class tragedy. Both have a romantic North African locale, both deal with matters of the heart instead of historical events, and both derive from French novels. Steffens' source, which he urges everyone to read, was Antoine François Prévost's *Histoire de M. Cleveland, fils naturel de Cromwell, ou le philosophe anglois* (1732). The English names taken from this novel give Steffens' tragedy a more authentically bourgeois look than *Zayde* had. Schönaich would not have been pleased to think that his tragedy verged on the middle-class genre, while Steffens, translator of Moore's *Gamester* and later author of *Clarissa*, felt no prejudice against it. Moreover, the tone and atmosphere of *Cleveland* are more intimate and domestic than the tone and atmosphere of *Zayde*. It seems quite incongruous that Steffens forced the dialogue into Alexandrine form.

Theoretically it was analogous to the practice of Greek tragic poets to detach one episode from a novel (as they did from an epic or legend) and to dramatize it. The episode here was the one involving the desertion of Cleveland by his wife Fanny out of jealousy of another woman, Lallin. However, to supply these characters and this action with a context required the inclusion of much complicated exposition, and in spite of the author's efforts, one never becomes clear about the background. Then, at the end, there is no proper feeling of finality, and the problem of the play is not resolved. Furthermore, the plot of this episode, with its un-German emphasis on the intricacies of a love triangle, is not well suited to tragedy, because it loses itself in subtleties of the emotions and lacks strong, clear outlines. As a man between two women, Cleveland might be thought comparable to Mellefont in *Miss Sara Sampson,* but here the difference between the German and the Gallic (through Prévost) attitude makes itself plainly felt. Mellefont faced a clear-cut moral dilemma having little to do with the mysterious emotion of love: either he would succumb to his lower instincts by returning to his body's mistress, Marwood, or he would rise to virtuous heights by marrying the mate of his soul, Sara. Cleveland, however, is associated with two women of equal virtue but of contrasting personality, each holding a different attraction for his heart. He loves them both and would like to keep both around him, but the one who is his wife will not tolerate any such arrangement. It is a serious defect in the play that the other woman, Lallin, appears in just one scene, in which she has little to say. Presumably Steffens felt it was beyond his powers to portray her fully in addition to Fanny. He could not reproduce the situation of the novel in all its psychological refinement.

Unlike Mellefont, Cleveland is represented as a completely virtuous individual. The only villainous role in the drama is played by a Frenchman named Gelin, a basically good person and a faithful friend to Cleveland. Love for Fanny sidetracks him, temporarily, into vice. Through him the triangle is expanded into a square. Fanny is jealous of Lallin because Cleveland is fond of her, and Gelin is jealous of Cleveland because Fanny wants to be true to him. Cleveland's only fault is one that a good German *Aufklärer* like Gottsched would have regarded as a laudable evidence of manliness: he spends so much time in serious philosophical study that he has no time for his wife. Yet his regard for her is extremely high, for he tells her, "I worship you, my love,/ Next to God you are and will remain my supreme good on earth" (I. i). Unfortunately his dour personality is not well suited to chase away the melancholy that afflicts Fanny, or so he thinks. He lacks the ability to "jest" (*scherzen*) which, in the vocabulary of the Anacreontic poets of the day, was not merely a frivolous or flippant pastime, but a quite rational means of meeting and overcoming the problems of life. Cleveland believes that Gelin will be able to help Fanny with his "sprightly jests," and thus unwittingly provides Gelin with an opportunity to be around Fanny and to influence her. The real reason for Fanny's sad mood, however, is Cleveland's desire to leave North Africa and return to England. She could have endured her husband's interest in Lallin in a country where it is the custom to have more than one wife, but in England she will feel mortified. In any case, she is profoundly irritated because Lallin seems to supply her husband with intellectual stimulation while she, Fanny, is merely the plaything of his leisure hours: "He shoves me forcibly out of his library room;/ She, that horrid Lallin, may almost always/ Be around my husband" (I. vi).

Gelin finds Fanny's state of mind all that he could ask for, and it is not hard to persuade her that Cleveland is actually being unfaithful to her with Lallin. Together they are the hidden observers of a meeting between Cleveland and Lallin during which Cleveland says innocently but nevertheless sincerely, "I have always honored Lallin with a blameless impulse,/ And if there were no Fanny, then I would even say that I love her" (II. iv). The upshot of their interview is that Lallin is to go along to England, where she is to be the companion of Cleveland's studious hours, while Fanny is to remain his wife in other respects and have Gelin around her to keep her amused. Fanny's reaction to what she has overheard is violent. If Cleveland is so much attracted to Lallin's mind, there is no reason why he should not carry on sexual relations with her as well. Gelin suggests that this is already happening, and tells Fanny that she can see it for herself if she will but spy on one of Cleveland's after-midnight trysts with Lallin in the garden. Although Gelin himself is driven by his passion for Fanny, he does not fail to remind her that she must conduct herself unemotionally in this matter: "Oh, try to diminish your grief through reason;/ You must speak calmly with the traitor" (II. v).

It is never made clear what actually happens in the garden, and the innocence of Cleveland's behavior before and afterwards inclines the reader to judge that no breach of the marriage vows has occurred. Fanny, however, is convinced that she has witnessed an adulterous act, and Gelin is able to take advantage of her consternation to obtain her agreement to run away with him. Fanny's hurt and anger lead her to utter perhaps the most tasteless line in all of German tragedy: "He does not find time to grant his wife a kiss/ Until after his bold mouth foams with the saliva of a whore" (III. iii). Nevertheless, she is not quite sure that she is doing the virtuous thing by running away from him with another man. Informed that Cleveland is sleeping, she decides to stand beside his bed. This maneuver will serve as an oracle: "Suppose that he awakes; then Providence is not willing/ That I should flee" (III. iii). As she gazes on the sleeping Cleveland, she can see the virtue beaming from his countenance, so that her love for him returns. But Gelin comes in and persuades her to go away on the ship that he has engaged. Too late Cleveland wakes up, not only to physical consciousness but to the realization that it is Fanny whom he loves more than his intellectual pursuits: "Oh, if my kiss could free her from her grief,/ Then I would forsake books and friends and everything else/ In order to hold her in my arms without interruption" (III. vi).

Once he is told that Fanny has fled, Cleveland ceases to be a rational person. Apparently philosophy is no cure for real misfortune, for when his brother Bridge talks to Cleveland about reason and reminds him how heretofore not even riches have made him swerve from the path of virtue, Cleveland retorts, "Quite right. But first teach my heart how to be without feelings" (IV. iii). He proceeds from a physical inability to tell one person from another to a mood of blasphemy against God and thence to a resolve to kill not only himself but his two young sons as well—a startling case history of irrationality. And his healing occurs not through an appeal to his reason but through an appeal to his heart, the same heart whose violent grief has overthrown his reason temporarily. Even as he raises his sword to slay his children, his younger son throws himself at his father's feet and begs for his life. Cleveland, deeply touched, drops his sword and allows himself to be persuaded to make his peace with God: "All right, I shall live then for my children's happiness,/ And I submit to the divine will./ Oh, Heaven! if still greater torments await me,/ Then give me strength enough to bear my misery!" (IV. vi). An interesting comparison may be made here with Stranitzky's *Der betrogene Ehemann* at the point where Admetus is left on shore while Alcumene departs in a ship. Admetus, too, loses his mind from grief, but this is looked upon as a meet punishment for his sins.

The fifth act finds Cleveland and his friends ashore on an island to which a wind has blown the ship wherein they were pursuing Fanny and Gelin. To the surprise of Cleveland's brother Bridge and some other comrades, Gelin soon appears on the island, too, but without Fanny. Bridge's demand for the return of Fanny leads to a duel in which Bridge is run through by Gelin. The dying Bridge sentimentally hopes that regret for this act will make a better man of his erstwhile friend Gelin; but Gelin is already remorseful, and he kisses the corpse of Bridge. Then he cries aloud for death, and Drink, another of the Englishmen, obligingly stabs him. These mournful sights are now hidden from the eye by the fall of the middle stage curtain on which are painted the harbor of the island and a ship floating at anchor. The author apologizes in a note for having changed the scene in the midst of an act.[19] In front of the backdrop Cleveland is discovered all alone, and his soliloquy reveals that he has stood the test sent him by Providence and that from now on he will be capable of enduring any further misfortune without murmuring: "Unknowable Arm, You Who guide my destiny,/ I do not know Your purpose in afflicting me;/ But since truth says that You are perfect,/ Therefore I believe that Your chastisement is always profitable to me./ . . . No misfortune shall ever so completely discourage me again./ . . . O erring understanding, you increase the woes of men" (V. v). This strengthening of the hero's character represents the only definitive result of the play's action. Yet even that is ludicrously jeopardized when Cleveland, on being informed that Gelin has reported that Fanny was untrue (a lie, of course), once more draws his sword to commit suicide. He is dissuaded only with difficulty by Bridge, who has been brought back on stage once more, not quite dead yet after all. Then for the second time Bridge affords us an edifying death scene, and the tragedy is over.

Providence and the rationality of the world-order are scarcely put in a good light by the dismal end of this play. No doubt, however, Steffens hoped that everyone would either see or read the untragic sequel, *Cleveland, oder der irrende Philosoph.* In this prose play Fanny returns to a happy reunion with Cleveland in France. Even Gelin, who to all appearances had been killed by Drink in the "tragedy" (surely Steffens intended no pun in this!), comes back on the scene. He has made good his crime by bringing Fanny back to her husband. And to add a special aura of blessing to the reunion, the daughter of Fanny and Cleveland, lost and presumed dead as a little girl, returns a fully grown young woman. In all of this, Steffens' accomplishment was mostly a negative one. He demonstrated that there was great danger to tragedy in drawing its subjects from contemporary sentimental novels.

The second of these long-forgotten plays, *Das Mutter-Söhnchen,* was published anonymously in Liegnitz in 1756.[20] The author's anonymity has remained intact, unfortunately. It would be of interest to know who composed this quaint dramatization of the juvenile delinquency problem in the eighteenth century. The play is in three acts, in prose, and completely bourgeois in character. Like the other middle-class dramas of the 1750's, *Das Mutter-Söhnchen* does not treat the friction between the middle-class and the aristocrats, and it contains no political implications. There is only a concentrated emphasis on a problem existing within the middle class itself; and there is also present the new, rather bold conviction that the wayward son of an ordinary bourgeois family is as worthy a subject of tragedy as the disobedient heir of a historical realm. Whether consciously or not, the author duplicated Lessing's procedure by arriving at bourgeois tragedy through a comic formula, whereas Martini came to it through the *Haupt- und Staatsaktion* and Steffens through the novel. The situation of a household headed by a foolish and indulgent widow and populated by several children, some of whom are virtuous and others wayward, is thoroughly in the province of comedy. In Germany, Madame Gottsched's comedy *Die Haus-französinn* offered virtually the same situation of a mismanaged household, and in the 1770's Lenz was still to feel so strongly the comic background of the comparable household situation in *Der Hofmeister* that he called the play a *"Lustspiel"* instead of the more appropriate *Schauspiel* or even *Trauerspiel*.[21] The names in *Das Mutter-Söhnchen*, such as "Frau Argonte," "Herr Durant," "Richard," and "Samson," are obviously borrowed from contemporary comedy, where it was also not uncommon to have German or Latin descriptive names like others in this play: "Herr Sittlich," "Prudentius," "Raufbold," "Weltson." Furthermore, the total dedication of the play to the illustration of one specific moral issue—the proper rearing of children—is much more akin both to the theory and practice of comedy since the time of Molière than it is to tragedy. For despite Gottsched's early theoretical emphasis on the illustration of a moral principle, the tragedy, as has been shown, dealt with striking events from which moral teachings could be deduced in passing and was not aimed directly against any existing social abuse.

To be sure, the play's comedy has been turned into a tragedy in the journalistic sense of that term. In everyday life, the thoughtless and vicious procedures of tens of thousands of persons are carried on with impunity; yet now and then in isolated cases they may result in a calamity and then this appears in black headlines as a "tragedy." So in this drama the foolish indulgence of an overly fond mother not only produces the inevitable and annoying (yet essentially comic) situation in which a wayward son makes an uproar at home and acquires a bad reputation in the community, but also the exceptional circumstance that this son kills two innocent people and himself as well. Should anyone feel that there was artistic improbability in this, or wonder whether this mother and son were not exaggerated, then there is an answer in the preface to the play that does not rest on artistic judgment but on the statistical facts of life, which are so often different from the general opinions held by people: "Whoever asks thus must as yet have a very limited knowledge of the world." [22] This is less the answer of a dramatist than of a police official.

The tutor in the house of Frau Argonte is a worthy man, as his name, Herr Sittlich, immediately points out. Thanks to him, two of the children, Prudentius and Gertrude, are growing up as paragons of virtue. They are fortunate because their silly mother does not care much for them and leaves them entirely in the tutor's care. She is, however, fond of the youngest child Richard, and her constant interference with Herr Sittlich's Spartan methods (thrashings and homework) are turning the little fellow into a copy of the eldest child Samson. The latter, a fully grown youth, is an unregenerate ruffian who has always been spoiled by his mother. His only pretense to knowledge consists of a few phrases of bad French, and yet he is conceited and thinks he knows more than the earnest Sittlich. He is a drunkard who beats his little brother Richard, and who is in trouble for having assaulted and beaten an old man in the street; but he shows no concern, saying that the old man should have known better than to get in the way of a drunkard—and his mother smiles at this witticism. He is, moreover, a spendthrift and is going through his mother's fortune. Not content with getting her money, he brazenly talks her out of her jewelry, saying, "Such a splendid ornament is not suitable for an old woman like you, anyhow" (I. vi). In addition he attempts to seduce his sister Gertrude, and offers her money not to tell that he has kissed her. Presently we learn that Samson has seduced the younger sister of his ugly but wealthy fiancée, and the girls' brother Raufbold challenges him to a duel. In answer to a query, Samson replies in the words of an evil rationalist: "What do you mean, conscience? Old women are the ones who have a conscience" (I. vii). But instead of being a rationalist he is a human animal practically without a soul—the product of an irrational education. He cannot see the point of fighting a duel merely because a girl has been dishonored: "There are plenty of men who consort with the sisters of their wives just as intimately as with their wives; and yet they live a peaceful life as respectable people" (I. vii). One cannot avoid thinking of the life of Gottfried August Bürger when reading these words.

Not satisfied with his other misdeeds, Samson now tries to seduce Rosimunde, the wife of Herr Ehrlieb. Her virtue has always been proof against him, but at last she is tempted by his mother's jeweled cross. She accepts it and admits him to her room. Next, Samson, who is worried about the impending duel, arranges with his second, the despicable Weltson, that Weltson should stab Raufbold in the back if he seems to be gaining the advantage. Then Samson and Weltson will run away; but first it will be necessary to get money. Samson persuades his mother to lend him her seal, because "that isn't suitable for a woman" (II. ii), and with this authority he can borrow thousands. Far from feeling gratitude toward his mother, Samson threatens her with his sword when she wants to restrain him from going to kill Raufbold. In spite of everything, however, she still wants to raise money to cover his new debts, and gets very angry at Gertrude and Prudentius and the family guardian Herr Dorant when they oppose her plan. The duel takes place, and Raufbold is treacherously murdered. In order to get the money necessary for flight, Samson decides to rob and kill Herr Dorant.

But the trap of his own crimes begins to close around Samson. Rosimunde, now remorseful, comes to return the jewelry that caused her downfall. Despite appearances, she has not actually committed adultery, but she feels terribly guilty nevertheless: "Ah, God! what torment can be caused by a tender conscience. I have not yet committed an overtly shameful act. But even the first step towards vice makes me an object of horror to myself. What if I had really committed adultery—" (III. ii). The severity of her punishment corresponds to the tenderness of her conscience, as was the case with Miss Sara Sampson. When she fights off Samson's drastic advances, she wounds him with a dagger, and he retaliates by shooting her with a pistol. Shortly thereafter the police come in to arrest Samson for the murder of Raufbold. He shoots at them but is soon overpowered. Meanwhile Rosimunde is dying, although she is trying to close her wound by holding her handkerchief against it. Like Miss Sara, she is not bitter about her fate: "I am dying, may God convert my murderer" (III. vi). But Samson does not escape so easily as Marwood did. His only good fortune is that he manages to avoid a trial and execution by seizing Rosimunde's dagger and stabbing himself fatally with it. He dies blaming his mother for everything.

It might well seem an injustice on the part of Providence that the virtually innocent Rosimunde should die, whereas the deeply guilty Frau Argonte is not punished at all. Rosimunde, after all, has committed a far less flagrant sin than Sara Sampson. In the preface, however, an attempt is made to explain and justify the situation: "It does not run counter to virtue that the author has Rosimunde die, since she dies in such a beautiful state of mind. . . . Perhaps some would still say that Frau Argonte deserves death rather than Rosimunde. My answer is, very true! But Rosimunde was to die now in a good state of mind, while Frau Argonte was to be brought to her senses for the sake of her good children." [23] Rosimunde, then, is a sacrifice to the prevailing taste for an edifying death scene, a vogue of long standing now given a special impetus by the beautiful death scene of Miss Sara Sampson. But Frau Argonte, like the fool in a comedy, has just been given a good lesson. She promises not to interfere any more with Herr Sittlich's efforts to educate the children; therefore little Richard will be spared the fate of turning out like his elder brother.

It is evident that *Das Mutter-Söhnchen* borrowed some elements from *Miss Sara Sampson;* but the play recognized immediately as the "sister" of *Sara* was *Lucie Woodvil*, published in 1756 in the 42nd issue of the *Neue Erweiterungen der Erkenntnis und des Vergnügens.*[24] The relationship, however, is hardly more than superficial, for *Lucie Woodvil* fails to adopt the inner structure of its ostensible model. Instead, it adopts the formula originated by Schlegel in *Canut* and carried on by Martini, that is, the horrendous and amazing depiction of evil in a relentless war against the principle of virtue. And it gives this formula a new development: the evil rationalist succeeds in ruining a basically good individual, like Satan in his function of snaring souls away from God.

The author of *Lucie Woodvil* was Johann Gottlob Benjamin Pfeil (1732–1800), although his identity was not established for modern scholarship until 1878 in an article by Karl Goedeke.[25] In his maturity a magistrate in Rammelsburg near Eisleben, Pfeil was embarrassed about his early dramatic work, although, in his youth, he had been avidly interested in middle-class tragedy. He expressed his ideas on the subject in an essay, *Vom bürgerlichen Trauerspiel* (July, 1755),[26] published in the same month in which *Miss Sara Sampson* was originally performed. The essay, whether by coincidence or design, amounted to a defense of Lessing's play, because although Pfeil criticized certain features of middle-class drama (sensational murder cases, executions on the gallows, and characters from the lower classes),[27] these features were referable only to the *London Merchant* and were not to be found in the more genteel *Miss Sara*. His own play was a patent attempt to imitate *Miss Sara*. The title consists of the name of a young Englishwoman; there is a father named "Sir Willhelm Southwell"; there is a maid named "Betty" like Sara's Betty; there is a young man, Karl, between two women, one wicked and the other virtuous; one of the woman wants Karl to marry her because he has seduced her; and he hesitates to do so, although he loves her. But these similarities, striking as they are, do not suffice to make *Lucie* the sister of *Sara*. For the titular heroine of Pfeil's play is a portrait of evil, not of virtue. She and her maid Betty jointly represent the type inaugurated by Rhynsolt.

Lucie is said to have been virtuous once, before the time of the play, but she is already wicked when we first meet her, and her wickedness steadily increases. As the audience is rather naively informed in the very first scene, pride constitutes the evil element in Lucie's nature; it predisposes her to unvirtuous action and eventually gains the upper hand completely. The deplorable state of Lucie's heart, which, besides being proud, has also been weak (her love for Karl has led to seduction and pregnancy), is emphasized several times, as when Sir Willhelm says, "God! protect Lucie's virtue against her own heart" (I. i), or when Lucie says, ". . . it is my own wretched heart which has made me unhappy" (I. iv), or when Robert, the father of the virtuous Amalie, says, ". . . reason and virtue will teach Lucie how to govern her heart" (II. iii). In such remarks the old-fashioned rationalistic view of the heart as the seat of blind emotions is paramount. But other references indicate that the author also held a more sentimental and progressive view of this organ of the soul, as when Robert says, "I have never believed that a father should be permitted to tyrannize over the heart of his child" (II. iii), or when Sir Willhelm says, "It does not matter what your parents were. Your heart alone can either raise you above their position or drag you down below it" (I. iii).

It is bitter news to Lucie that Sir Willhelm, Karl's father, wants him to marry Amalie, and that Karl is willing to do so. Her pride comes to the fore. While she does regret her lost innocence, saying, like Schiller's Robber Moor, "Happy times, when virtue and innocence were my playfellows . . ." (I. iv), she mainly dreads being humiliated before the world at the birth of her child: "The world will find out my shame. It will despise me, not because I am evil, but because I have made my vice known" (I. iv). She finds it hard enough to humble herself before Karl in order to obtain his reluctant consent to marry her. Although relieved, she adds, "But it is a terrible victory. It has cost me my idol, my pride" (II. x). Amalie sweetly renounces her own claims on Karl and demands that he must be honorable in regard to Lucie. Amalie's goodness, however, is another wound to Lucie's pride, so that she begins to hate Amalie insanely. Karl finally does marry Lucie in secret; but when Sir Willhelm hears of this he wants to separate the pair and send Karl off to America. Growing ever more ruthless, Lucie decides to murder Sir Willhelm, and she expresses her intention with the programmatically anti-moral purposiveness of the evil rationalist: "If he dies virtuously, very well, then I will be avenging myself through the death of this virtuous man on this virtue which I hate and on Heaven itself . . ." (IV. x). She conquers the good impulse which reminds her that Sir Willhelm has been kind and has treated her like a daughter. Then, when the poisoning has been accomplished, from Robert comes the annihilating information that in marrying Karl she has married her own half-brother. Sir Willhelm was not only

Karl's father, but Lucie's father as well. In despair, Lucie kills her wicked adviser Betty and then commits suicide. Her dreadful fate underlines the terrible danger that lies in the commission of a single initial unvirtuous act (the theme introduced by the secretary Siegmund in *Rhynsolt und Sapphira*), and Robert's closing speech sums up this moral lesson: "Come, my Amalie, let us tremble in quiet respect before this justice, which does not allow even the least crime to go unpunished. Let us learn from Karl and Lucie's unhappy example that the greatest vice no longer horrifies him who has not first recoiled from the very smallest one" (V. xii). Perhaps an illicit love affair can be called "the very smallest vice" in comparison to the ensuing incest, patricide, murder, and suicide.

Whatever their defects and culpable actions, Lucie and Karl cannot be called the primary cause of the shocking events. That cause is Sir Willhelm himself, who sired Lucie illegitimately and then hid the facts of her birth from everyone. Does this mean that Pfeil has written a fate tragedy, a successor to the *Haupt- und Staatsaktion* about Charles XII,[28] and thus abrogated the optimistic philosophy of Enlightenment? The answer, of course, is that the inevitability of Lucie and Karl's disastrous career is not genuine fate, but, instead, an application of the biblical threat that the sins of the fathers will be visited on the children. A similar case may be seen in the Carlson and Mariane episode in Gellert's novel, *Die schwedische Gräfin von G . . .* Retribution for error is so automatic in a rational universe that Sir Willhelm's whole virtuous life subsequent to that youthful escapade is no atonement. Realizing this, he rebukes himself for uttering a complaint about Karl and Lucie: "But, old scoundrel that I am! Do I, through my lamentations, want to add still another burden of crime on my already weak back? When did the justice of Heaven ever let a crime go unpunished?" (III. ix). Robert tries to throw a softer light on this by reminding Sir Willhelm that even God's punishments are benevolent: "Friend, you forget that trials are the only things which can make virtue great, and that virtue is genuine only when it contemplates its greatest sufferings with the very same serene, indifferent expression with which it was accustomed in its more peaceful days to contemplate its good fortune" (III. ix). But this does not help to explain why Sir Willhelm's punishment has to be wrought by means of the spiritual ruin of Lucie and Karl. Karl concludes that he and Lucie were born expressly to serve God's vengeance, and he audaciously castigates God for this: "Karl is innocent. He suffers without deserving to. You, Heaven! blush that You have compelled him to be vicious" (V. xii). This frightful blasphemy is certainly not meant to be taken as the opinion of the author. Amalie, hearing it, at once begs God to forgive Karl, because he is not in possession of his reason. Still, there is no feeling of sweet submission and comfort in sadness, as at the end of *Miss Sara;* the feeling is, rather, one of horror and fear. In the shambles at the end only Amalie and Robert, who have been perfectly virtuous throughout, remain unharmed.

Truly, Lucie and Karl have acted so abominably that one is disinclined to plead any case for them against Providence. Lucie manages to keep a modicum of our sympathy, because she retains some vestiges of her former decency and her downward progress is accompanied by regrets and self-accusations. Her hatred of virtue is half remorse at having lost her own: "And who is Lucie in comparison to them all? The most despicable creature who has ever lived. A wretched woman full of pride without honor, an ingrate, a hypocrite who has to hide under the mask of virtue . . . a barbarous compulsion! Can I bear it to see others being virtuous around me, without being so myself?" (IV. i). Lucie's tragedy is that of the devil who still remembers heaven with regret. If one is willing to overlook the banality of the concept of virtue, then there is real pathos in Lucie's cry, "Oh, with what great effort we purchase our vices and the punishments for them, when often the strictest virtue would not have cost us half so much effort!" (IV. ii). Karl, on the other hand, is as unsympathetic a figure as Samson, the *"Mutter-Söhnchen,"* for he takes a fiendish delight in being an accomplished seducer. He is an incredibly outspoken cad, egotist, and sadist, who enjoys Lucie's pathetic situation: "Karl sees your tears, hears your curses as a victor hears the tears and curses of his conquered slave" (II. i). He is obviously the fantastic daydream creation of an author who sat down to imagine the gorgeously wicked person he himself could be if he were not, unfortunately, so moral and virtuous. It is the common mistake of a minor author to confuse such a self-indulgent daydream with an actual artistic creation. Karl has the most lordly contempt for sober virtue. When his father and Robert go to visit a dying friend in order, as Robert says, ". . . to devote . . . a few minutes of my life to the most useful art, the art of learning how to die" (II. vi), Karl remarks to his servant, "Let them learn their art of dying, Jakob. Karl, the happy Karl, understands the better art of living, of living happily" (II. vii). Thinking of his conquest over Lucie, Karl preens himself extravagantly, saying, "Yes, of what use are feminine pride and feminine virtue against me? Did not Lucie possess both? Heaven! Behold the greatness of my joy and envy me!" (II. vii). Next to such presumption even the hybris expressed in Greek tragedy pales.

The worst improbability in the plot is that Karl is suddenly persuaded by Lucie's pleading and Amalie's arguments to marry Lucie. But the explanation is given that Karl actually loves Lucie and that all his frightful bravado is due to the fact that he fears unhappiness if he abandons his pose of "rational" coldness and opens his heart to feeling. He is, then, a would-be evil rationalist who does not quite have the stomach for the role. And, as he feared, doing the right thing in regard to Lucie does not bring him repose: "Worthless virtue, I was happy as long as I was vicious; and now, since I have begun to have feeling for you, I am miserable" (III. viii). His blasphemous speech at the end of the play offers little evidence that he is truly on the right path. Presumably, he too will commit suicide.

The most absolutely evil character in this play, however, is Lucie's maid and confidante Betty, whose rather cheerful name has no congruity with her Satanic personality. Her enmity toward virtue is coldly rational and cannot be excused as the aberration of a wilful heart. She is like Martini's Rhynsolt in her logically realistic denial of the whole system of virtue, for which she substitutes her own selfish, unsentimental philosophy. Utterly cynical, she thinks that marriage between Lucie and Karl is surrender to a silly prejudice, which will make their union acceptable "in the eyes of the rabble" (I. iv). This attitude is the direct opposite of Miss Sara's, who was willing to keep marriage with Mellefont a secret from the world at large and desired the ceremony only to put her soul privately at peace with God. Betty considers virtue childish and chides Lucie about it, saying, "You and your everlasting virtue! Will you never forget your old maxims?" (I. iv). Her manner is scornfully superior, as though she belonged to a new race of beings who have made the great discovery that the intellect can and should be put to the service of self: "But we great spirits, who are beyond all these narrow concepts, we know more wisely that all efforts wasted on virtue are useless . . ." (IV. ii). She wants to substitute a new, specious system of ethics for true morality—a Nietzschean ethic beyond good and evil. When Lucie is remorseful for having poisoned Sir Willhelm, Betty seeks to comfort her with thoughts drawn from this new, cold-blooded ethic: "Why do you not forget these childish concepts of vice and virtue? What are vice and virtue? Inventions of self-interest and superstition . . . What have you done that is so dreadful? You have brought rest to an old man who was perhaps just as tired of this world as it was of him . . ." (V. vi). A similar argument is used by Schiller's Franz Moor when he tries to kill his father. Although Betty is not solely responsible for Lucie's wicked actions, she has certainly encouraged her to commit them, and thus plays the role of a devil in the ruination of Lucie's soul. She has nothing material to gain from Lucie's downfall, but is simply the diabolical evangelist of the new amorality. It cannot be said, however, that she wilfully deceives Lucie. Instead, Lucie goes to her voluntarily as to one who is more skilled in an art one wishes to learn: "Come, Betty, teach me to be vicious and to be calm in the midst of vice like you" (IV. x).

This frenzied drama with its whirling passions and dire, unnatural deeds was the strongest tragedy that had yet been written for the German stage. As far as was possible within the framework of the rationalistic-Pietistic philosophy of the day, *Lucie Woodvil* reproduced the pity and fear associated with Greek tragedy, stopping short, however, before the pessimism of Greek tragedy. It is truly a middle-class tragedy, because it is a thoroughgoing restatement in bourgeois terms of the German neoclassical tragedy as developed by Schlegel, whereas *Miss Sara Sampson* and *Das Mutter-Söhnchen* were evolved from comedy. *Lucie Woodvil* presents evil in action and depicts the degeneration of a soul; *Miss Sara* concentrates on virtue and shows the apotheosis of a soul. Thus, in spite of *Miss Sara's* greater fame, it was *Lucie Woodvil* that actually moved along with the current of the development of German tragedy.

Closely related to *Lucie Woodvil* is *Der Freygeist* (1757) by Joachim Wilhelm von Brawe (1738–1758), which was first published by Nicolai in the supplementary volume (*Anhang*) to the first two volumes of the new journal, *Bibliothek der schönen Wissenschaften und freyen Künste*, in 1758. It was one of three tragedies—two of them middle-class, significantly—submitted for the prize contest announced by Nicolai in 1756; but the prize went to a heroic Alexandrine tragedy, Cronegk's *Codrus*. Brawe, whose untimely death prevented him from enjoying the considerable fame and popularity won by *Der Freygeist* in the following two decades, was the friend of Ewald von Kleist and, as one of Kleist's frequent table companions, also became well acquainted with Lessing.[29] Indeed, this young university student has come to be regarded as a pupil of Lessing. It would therefore be logical to assume that Brawe imitated *Miss Sara Sampson* in his own first dramatic attempt—as commentators generally have assumed [30]—but actually there is no special similarity between the two plays except that the setting of *Der Freygeist* is also an English inn. On the other hand, the influence of *Lucie Woodvil* is clear. Brawe, however, has not spread the characteristics of evil rationalism among two or three; he has assigned the only really active role in the play to his one single evil rationalist character. The titular hero lacks a will of his own and is the pitiful dupe of a monstrously wicked counsellor. This is a motif to be found later, in a less exaggerated form, in Goethe's *Clavigo*.

Henley, as this hateful character is named, is a male counterpart to Betty in *Lucie Woodvil*. Like her he preaches an amorality which he deems superior to the gospel of virtue, and he counts himself among the "great spirits" who see true virtue in what the "common horde" weakly and stupidly regards as vice (I. iii).[31] However, there is an explanation for Henley's wickedness, something that was lacking in the characterization of Betty. He is motivated by an inordinate desire for revenge on a young man named Clerdon, whom everyone has always preferred to Henley and who is loved by Amalia, the girl Henley wanted for himself. The similarity of this situation to that in Schiller's *Die Räuber* is self-evident, even though the attractive and unattractive men here are not brothers, but distant relatives whose families live on neighboring estates. The revenge motif was not a new one in German tragedy, as has been shown, but until *Der Freygeist* it had not been made the main subject of a play. Brawe was undoubtedly inspired to do this by his reading of Edward Young's *The Revenge* (1721), whose villain, the Moor Zanga (in turn modeled on Iago), goes about destroying his enemy with the same false friendship used by Henley, but with better justification than Henley's for his actions. Jealousy of another man's virtue and preferment was also a well-established theme in German tragedy; but both this and the revenge motif were brought to previously unheard-of heights in *Der Freygeist*.

Henley's matchless villainy consists in his intention of ruining Clerdon, not only in this life, but beyond: "Vulgar spirits are satisfied if they can only poison the present life of their adversaries. Such narrow boundaries were not made for me. If possible, I intend to pursue my offender past the portals of the grave and to revel in the proud supposition that I have destroyed for him even that happiness which otherwise is raised above all mortal powers" (I. iii). His efforts, of course, will most likely incur his own damnation also, but with appalling *sang-froid* he is able to envision a future in which he may repent of his sins and still be saved: "And am I not safe because of my youth and health? Old age will perhaps tame this violent fire within me, and then when my enemies have long since become the prey of destruction I shall still have time—" (I. iii). This outdoes the devil, for even Satan does not plan to escape punishment for his crimes. It is curious to see an idea, which seems natural and comprehensible in a Hamlet bent on securing damnation for Claudius, give Henley in this play the aspect of a monster of viciousness. But Hamlet is a complete human being with many thoughts, whereas Henley is an incarnation of only this one.

Henley fits the standard pattern for devils very well. Although he preaches amorality and regards himself as above the vulgar moral prejudices of ordinary men, he is still, paradoxically, clearly aware of the error of the freethinking to which he has succeeded in converting Clerdon, and he knows that true religion is the only safeguard for virtue.[32] This knowledge is attested to in his description of how he has misled Clerdon: "My first attempt was to combat his love for religion; I did not dare to make him acquainted with vice before that. . . . I led him into little misdeeds which upset his peace of mind and soon implanted in him a secret irritation with religion, which was punishing him for these misdeeds. . . . He became a freethinker. In this moment my revenge was assured. In vain his thoughts strove to erect the flimsy structure called the religion of the upright man. I praised this endeavor. But soon I dragged him from one crime to another. His strongest armor was no longer there to protect him" (I. i). Like a devil, the consummate evil rationalist can believe the whole truth of God and salvation and yet combat this truth out of hatred for it and its adherents. Henley has no valid reason for revenge, for Clerdon has never intentionally injured or offended him; Clerdon is simply the better man, and has therefore had more good fortune. As is also the case with Franz Moor, Henley's jealous hatred of an individual who has outshone him is—in addition to its value as psychological motivation —a symbol of his boundless enmity toward virtue as a concept. In emulation of Satan, Henley attacks God through the destruction of one of God's favorites, whom he hates just because he is a favorite. As a human being Henley is an absurd caricature; as a mask for the elemental forces of evil he is remarkably impressive.

Clerdon, the "freethinker" of the title, is rendered wholly passive by his dependence on Henley for wicked impulses and on his virtuous friend Granville (and Granville's sister Amalia) for good impulses. His soul is the prize for which these opposing forces, all met in an English inn, contend. His tragic misstep was passive also. It consists in having allowed Henley, a seemingly harmless person, attach himself to him in the first place. Having become a freethinker, Clerdon is on the road to ruin, however good he may be at heart. The "natural religion" in which he now sincerely believes sanctions such vices as extravagance and disobedience to one's father. Granville tries to awaken Clerdon to the falseness of these views by telling him that his old father, whom he has disobeyed, has died in poverty because of Clerdon's extravagance. This appeal to

Clerdon's sentiments is made the more touching by the added information that the father died virtuously, accepting his hard fate with joy and forgiving his wayward son. But Henley counteracts this attack on the heart by addressing himself again to Clerdon's reason. As Franz Moor was to do many years later, Henley robs the death of a father of its pathos: "A worn-out old man has to submit to the universal destiny, and he is at the same time liberated from the burdens of old age" (II. v). Fear of divine punishment is dismissed as irrational: "To think that the prejudice of our animal years [childhood] can so often take us by surprise again, even when we think we have completely suppressed them! Compose yourself, Clerdon. Show yourself to be a man raised above the vulgar rabble in all respects, also in respect to what usually casts them down" (II. v). To be great, then, is to be above the softness of heartfelt emotion. Henley's perverse rationalism allows evil passions full sway, but requires strictest control of good emotions leading toward virtue.

Granville, playing the role of angel to Henley's devil, returns with a still stronger assault on Clerdon's heart. The father has not only died in poverty, but in debtors' prison, where hunger and neglect hastened his end. This terrible news, accompanied by Granville's stern warnings that Clerdon should not test God's patience too far, almost has the desired effect. But then the relentless Henley (like Wurm in Schiller's *Kabale und Liebe*) remembers that Clerdon is "proud, hot-headed, jealous" (III. i), and he concludes that these characteristics (not regarded here as particularly bad in themselves) will insure Clerdon's belief in the authenticity of a letter which he will forge exposing Granville as Clerdon's enemy. The forged letter results in a duel. Clerdon still has some scruples against dueling, but Henley dismisses these as mere prejudice and superstition. In the duel Granville is mortally wounded; he himself has had several opportunities to kill Clerdon, but has refused to hit home. There follows a splendidly virtuous death scene in which Granville forgives his murderer and also convinces Clerdon that he did not write the forged letter. In dying, Granville makes a last attempt to save Clerdon's soul by begging him not to take un-Christian revenge on Henley: ". . . submit yourself again to the gentle laws of religion, and then these themselves will teach you how to forgive him—" (IV. vi). Granville's death is certainly unmerited and would impress us as a poor reward for virtue if its injustice were not overshadowed by the beautiful thought that he has given his life for his friend and is now on his way to heaven. As can be seen from the preface to *Das Mutter-Söhnchen*, the sentimental beauty of a death was considered reason enough for including it. The popular taste for such death scenes, as the success of Little Eva's passing demonstrates in *Uncle Tom's Cabin,* was very enduring and is possibly not extinct even now.

Clerdon, however, is left inconsolable and desperate. With the death of his father and the murder of his best friend on his conscience, he is sure that God cannot forgive him. Amalia generously encourages him, in spite of the fact that he has killed her brother, and his servant Truworth tells him that God wants only repentance and subjection. Truworth, in a paroxysm of virtue, offers to take the blame and punishment for Granville's death on himself, because he is so old and near death anyhow—a curious twist of Henley's earlier evil idea that Clerdon's father was old enough to die. Truworth, who in his dog-like faithfulness suggests the Daniel of Schiller's *Räuber,* ardently kisses Clerdon's hand, exclaiming, ". . . Oh, my master! My dearest master, how fortunate I am that I can die for you!" (V. iv). Obviously, the good as well as the evil characters of this play pass all bounds of credibility. Clerdon is not so ignoble as to accept this sacrifice, for he is no longer a freethinker: "Name of a freethinker of which I was once so proud, how I curse you now! Oh, may woe like mine strike those who first invented it, who first gave it its baleful fame" (V. v). Unfortunately, Clerdon has strayed too far from the path of virtue to retrace his steps, and therefore he falls still farther by determining to punish Henley. The latter taunts him diabolically with a frank admission of his whole procedure. Enraged and horrified, Clerdon stabs Henley and then himself, to Henley's complete delight: "I am dying!—But my enemy is dying at my side—I am avenged—O triumph! O revenge!" (V. vi).

Just as Lessing in his identically named comedy (1749) made the notorious freethinkers the object of his satire, so Brawe aimed his tragedy at this one specific goal. One is not tempted, however, to look for parallels between his work and Lessing's, or to suggest that Brawe arrived at middle-class tragedy by way of comedy. The revenge and evil counselor motifs, to say nothing of the enormity of the offenses against both earthly and heavenly fathers, make Brawe's *Freygeist* unquestionably tragic. Freethinking was a subject that could be regarded as a mere stupid aberration, which was Lessing's cool view, or as a terribly dangerous philosophy weakening the system of virtue, which was Brawe's apparent conviction. One step in its direction enmeshes the foot in a net of evil. It seems altogether indefensible to read the play as an assault on the accepted morality of the time—to interpret Henley as the secret spokesman of the author.[33] Very probably it did thrill Brawe and his audience to have Henley's dynamism unleashed; but it was a thrill of horror, and Henley was meant as an example of the false prophets of free-thinking, with nothing heroic about him. To be sure, he might be a "hero" in the technical sense of main character, as was Ulfo in *Canut*. But whereas Ulfo's reckless bravery might win a certain grudging sympathy from the spectators, Henley's sneaking wickedness could not attract them. The play is a study in the operation of evil, and it seeks primarily, through the medium of horror and shock, to warn those who witness it against a danger surrounding them. This does not mean, naturally, that the author was unaware of the entertainment value of horror and shock. Certainly, his play helped to make these terms synonymous with tragedy during that period and up through Storm and Stress.

In 1759 there appeared the last of this first series of middle-class tragedies, *Der Renegat* by Karl Theodor Breithaupt, a young law student at Helmstedt about whom neither dates nor further biographical data are available. Stirred to action by Nicolai's prize contest, he submitted *Der Renegat* through Lessing; [34] then, apparently undaunted by his first failure, sent in a tragedy entitled *Barbarussa und Zaphire* to the second contest in 1758. This won the prize; but the author's satisfaction must have been spoiled by the editor's public announcement that it was not really a good play, only just the best of a group of poor entries.[35] To justify his choice, the editor (C. F. Weisse, after Nicolai's retirement in January, 1759) published an anonymous entry entitled *Gafforio* directly next to *Barbarussa und Zaphire*. *Gafforio* showed how bad a tragedy could be.

Breithaupt's *Renegat*, an unmistakably middle-class tragedy despite its Alexandrine dialogue and exotic locale, is a much more interesting work than his prize-winning *Barbarussa und Zaphire*. Although *Der Renegat* was originally written at the same time as Brawe's *Freygeist* for the contest announced in 1756, it was, according to Breithaupt's statement in the preface, so extensively revised for its publication (Helmstedt, 1759) that it could be called an entirely new play.[36] In the meantime, *Der Freygeist* had appeared in print, and the similarities between Brawe's play and Breithaupt's suggest strongly a relationship between the two. Yet the central motif of *Der Renegat*, that of the son who forsakes both his religion and his father, which represents the basic similarity between the plays, was already present in the original version. Nicolai had briefly described the plot of *Der Renegat* in his preface to the *Anhang* of the first two volumes of the *Bibliothek* and had remarked about the similarity of the titular hero to that of *Der Freygeist*.[37] Accordingly, the influence cannot be assumed. There is a parallel to this situation in the "prize contest" [38] conducted by Schröder in Hamburg in 1775, when Leisewitz, Klinger, and a third, anonymous author simultaneously sent in tragedies on the subject of a pair of hostile brothers.[39]

The main characters of *Der Renegat*, as is usual in domestic tragedies at this time, are mostly English, even though the setting of the action is Turkey. Like *Der Freygeist*, this is a religious tragedy: a young man deserts Christian principles of virtue for a pseudo-rational code of self-indulgence. This time the evil code is labeled "Mohammedanism," but its tenets are the same as those assigned by Brawe to freethinking and by Martini and Pfeil to an unspecified philosophy. The misguided youth Edward, who has adopted the Turkish name "Zapor," concentrates on a legitimate facet of the Enlightened *Weltanschauung*, cudæmonism, and perverts it, as Rhynsolt, Betty, and Henley perverted the Enlightened emphasis on reason and on freedom from prejudice. Edward-Zapor's credo is that God wants man to be happy; but he defines happiness as the careless indulgence of sinful desires: "He who created us gave us our life here for our welfare,/ And not so that it should be sacrificed in torments./ . . . He created men equal. Oh, if He willed their pain,/ Then why did He give us a heart sensitive to joy?/ My heart follows those impulses which make it happier./ The others are a dream which flees when we awaken./ . . . . Hail to me! You are conquered, you dreams of blind youth./ Denial of one's self is the virtue of a fanatic" (I. i).[40] These conclusions have been reached through an exercise of reason, which as a concept is obviously growing ever more suspect: "But time and reason open our eyes,/ Over which prejudice draws the curtain of error" (I. i).

Edward has run away from home because his father would not forgive him for certain youthful indiscretions. Upon his arrival in far-off Turkey he was at first made a slave, but when his master, Orchan, was able to convince him of the truth of the "Mohammedan" philosophy [41] his fortunes vastly improved. Orchan plays the role of evil counselor in this drama without, however, leaving a horrifying impression of dynamic evil. Presumably one cannot expect any knowledge of true virtue from a "Mohammedan," and Orchan is to be regarded as more unfortunate than evil. At the end, in fact, he desires to be converted to Christianity. Thus religious provincialism blunts the point of evil rationalism in this play. Orchan's task with Edward is made easy because Edward's bond with law and religion has been weakened by his father's unforgiving attitude

—this is an anticipation of Karl Moor's situation in *Die Räuber*. As the play opens, an old family retainer, Welwood, arrives in Turkey to persuade Edward to return to England, inasmuch as the father, Grandlove, has had a change of heart. Here a certain superficial similarity to *Miss Sara Sampson* can be detected. Edward, however, unlike Sara, is not touched. With cold obstinacy he goes through with his determination to adopt Mohammedanism formally. Welwood warns him of the relentless justice of God: "Believe it, that vices are followed by regret, regret by grief,/ And grief by punishment" (I. i). Edward counters with a bitter criticism of Christianity, one evidently not applauded by the author: "And still these people dare to boast of a faith/ Which they call love, while they deride other teachings/ And call persecution grace and hate, religion" (I. ii). Schönaich and Lessing would have had these words spoken in the name of religious tolerance; but for Breithaupt they show that Edward confuses his own father's lack of charity with a lack of charity on the part of Christians in general. Conversely, because one man, Orchan, has shown him kindness, he concludes that Mohammedanism, rather than Christianity, is the true religion. He wants Welwood to tell his father ". . . that here in the midst of wild barbarism/ Is a heart full of nobility, a father-heart,/ That here fathers do not hate innocent sons,/ Are not irreconcilable, do not force their sons to run away" (II. ii). This speech reveals that Edward has not been a reprobate from the start. Indeed, as with Lucie Woodvil, the original fault lies not with the child, but with the father. The highest virtue of an earthly father, and his best procedure, as has been shown in *Miss Sara* and *Der Freygeist*, is that he forgives the sins of his children; but Grandlove does this for Edward too belatedly. Stern punishment is best left to the Heavenly Father, who can judge more precisely whether a sin has been committed or not.

It is no particular surprise when Grandlove and his daughter Therise also show up in Turkey, having been stranded by a shipwreck. The sudden appearance of persons believed to be far away or even dead was one of the most hackneyed devices of French classical tragedy and it was also common in eighteenth-century novels. It must be said, on the other hand, that German tragedy had heretofore made little use of the device, which cannot fail to produce an impression of artificiality. Orchan's treatment of the shipwrecked pair now exposes the falseness of his religion; but at the same time it is clear that Orchan has a native streak of humanitarianism. Thus, he is touched by Grandlove's sorrow and he frees him; nevertheless he wants to force both father and daughter to become Moslems, by torture if necessary. Therise begs him in the name of humanity to have pity on them: "So have a human heart, so let yourself be persuaded,/ So let helpless people find mercy through their tears!" (II. vi). This reference to tears was of great importance in a sentimental epoch. Tears were the evidence of a heart sensitive to virtue and they were thought to be able to move another heart and open it to virtue.[42] When their effect fails and Orchan remains obdurate, Grandlove exclaims in astonishment, "What a barbarian! If tears/ Are in vain, how is one then to appease a furious tyrant!" (II. vii).

Grandlove has become a better father since Edward's flight, and he regrets his earlier harshness, saying, "Alas! My duty was to be merciful,/ For punishments chastise, but they do not effect improvement;/ Yet I grew angry—Oh, my son!" (II. vii). Surely all would have turned out well if Edward could have met Grandlove immediately upon his arrival, but the two are kept apart by devices as artificial as those used by Lessing to keep Sara and Sir William Sampson apart. Edward does meet Therise and, not knowing she is his sister, falls in love with her—an echo of *Lucie Woodvil* which adds to the impression that this play is a pastiche of the preceding middle-class tragedies. When Therise refuses to become a Moslem, Edward suspects Welwood of making her obstinate. He resolves to kill Welwood in revenge and also in order to demonstrate his zeal for Mohammed, who is ignorantly regarded as a deity. The poison of Edward's new beliefs is working fast. At first he talked sophistically of not denying himself pleasures; now he sees no reason for balking at murder to get what he wants. Meanwhile Grandlove has been sitting in a dark prison cell, brooding over the state of the world, "Where bold vice puffs itself up in superfluity of wealth./ While innocence is oppressed and virtue goes in chains" (IV. i). The darkness of the cell is not just a bow in the direction of realism; it has a purpose which may now easily be guessed. Presently Edward enters the cell, dagger drawn in the intention of slaying Welwood, and although doubts still plague him, he casts them off, crying, "Murder is religion, hallowed be revenge!" (IV. v). In the cell's obscure light he now stabs—his own father, Grandlove. This patricide committed by mistake in darkness was a feature probably borrowed by the author from Quistorp's first tragedy, *Alcestes* (1742).

Grandlove has suffered one of those fatal wounds that permit the victim to live until the end of the fifth act. He has time to express the most extraordinary, the most edifying magnanimity. He begs God to forgive his unknown assailant, and this throws Edward into confusion. Therise, seeing her father dying, criticizes God—another familiar touch: "Oh, God! You could look down upon this from Your heaven" (IV. vii). But immediately Grandlove returns the customary virtuous rebuke: "Honor His graciousness, which never altogether forgets us,/ And, even when it kills, still deserves our adoration" (IV. vii). Edward is not so far gone in vice that he is immune to despair when he realizes whom he has killed. Far from cursing him, his dying father embraces and forgives him, earnestly entreating him to come back to Christianity. Grandlove's death is perhaps justified as a punishment for having been too severe a father. But it is scarcely sad, because we almost see him entering heaven as he rapturously cries, "God! what a never felt delight/ Streams through my heart!—Oh, happiness!—How blessed is death!—I hear harmonies—" (V. v). Edward, however, feels the Furies chasing him and kills himself out of remorse, like Mellefont and Clerdon. Then Welwood prays for his soul, and therefore we feel that perhaps there is a chance Edward will not be damned after all. Here the example of Mellefont probably guided the author.

Der Renegat, despite some interesting features, is a dull, poorly plotted, unconvincing play. Since it derives extensively from the earlier plays already discussed, but does not carry forward any development, it makes a fitting conclusion to the first set of middle-class tragedies in Germany. Even its one apparently new theme, that of the son resenting his treatment by the parent, is partially anticipated in *Das Mutter-Söhnchen*, where the mother is basically responsible for her son's actions, and he resents the too-lenient treatment given him. As a depiction of evil in action *Der Renegat* carries little power, because Edward is more unfortunate and confused than wicked, and his evil genius, Orchan, lacks dynamism and turns soft in the end. In 1759, the meaningful development of the tragedy of evil action was already in the hands of an author who strove to give new life to the Alexandrine heroic tragedy and who had little interest in middle-class drama at first. But discussion of Christian Felix Weisse's tragedies must be preceded by an investigation of the state of heroic tragedy during this period that had seen the first heyday of middle-class plays.

VII

FROM ALEXANDRINES TO BLANK VERSE:
HEROIC TRAGEDY IN THE LATE 1750's

WHEN FRIEDRICH NICOLAI wrote his *Abhandlung vom Trauerspiel* for the first issue of the *Bibliothek der schönen Wissenschaften* in 1757, he meant to add a section dealing with the middle-class tragedy; but this intention, which has the earmarks of an afterthought, was never carried out. To him, tragedy still signified above all the heroic, neoclassical tragedy in Alexandrine verse with "regular" form, and with characters drawn from history or legend whose fates involved the future of dynasties or nations. It is in keeping with this neglect of middle-class tragedy in the essay that Nicolai also decided to award the prize in his drama contest to Cronegk's *Codrus* rather than to either of the two middle-class tragedies submitted. To be sure, the official reasons he gave for his choice were manifold: better characterizations, more appropriate sentiments, more proper and better executed expression and style.[1] Since these reasons, however, are preceded by many blunt criticisms of both the characters and the sentiments in *Codrus*, one is tempted to conclude that it was eventually the expression and style (i.e., the Alexandrines and the standard neoclassical form) and the heroic subject matter that won his approval. Coming after the great success of the English middle-class tragedies and of *Miss Sara Sampson*, Nicolai's well-publicized awarding of the contest prize to *Codrus* was the first counterblow struck for heroic tragedy against the invasion of the new style. The steady output of uninspired Alexandrine works had stopped abruptly in 1755.[2] A new period began for heroic tragedy in 1758 with *Codrus*, a period which from the beginning showed greater vigor and the promise of continued development. But Alexandrine verse, that reminder of a stodgy past, could not continue much longer as its obligatory hallmark.

The new vigor discernible in *Codrus* cannot very well be ascribed to any deliberate plan on the author's part to counteract the success of the middle-class tragedy. It was just a coincidence that Johann Friedrich von Cronegk (1731–1758) was gifted with enough talent and temperament to bring more energy and enthusiasm to the composition of heroic tragedy than anyone since Schlegel. Actually, while writing *Codrus* in 1754 and 1755,[3] Cronegk was far away from the latest developments on the German stage and very possibly knew nothing about them. The young Franconian baron, son of a high-ranking general, was at the time on an extended "cavalier's tour" which brought him into contact with the leading dramatists of Italy and France; and he had finished his *Codrus*, except for polishing and revisions, before he returned to his native Anspach in 1756.[4] Although the text was known to Cronegk's friends even before its completion, it was not published by Nicolai until 1758,[5] after the death of the author. Then it began to be performed frequently all over Germany.[6] Its popularity, which exceeded that of any Alexandrine tragedy since *Canut*, is a good indication of the new energy which it contained. There was a certain new verve in its dialogue, a new pathos in its many didactic passages, and somehow a greater attractiveness about its characters. Its qualities were sufficient to regain the attention of a public still excited by the novelty of middle-class tragedy.

Yet *Codrus* is seriously marred by some glaring weaknesses which the author himself modestly and frankly admitted and which contemporary critics, always severe, pointed out in detail. The play was inspired by the story of the fabled last king of Athens, a genuinely dramatic material involving the self-sacrifice of Codrus, who, knowing from an oracle that his death will save Athens, provokes a quarrel with the besieging Dorian soldiers and is killed. But the simple pathos of this legend was not enough for Cronegk.[7] For the climax of his play he invented (or borrowed) a ticklish situation in which a young man, Medon, is given a terrible choice: he is permitted to save the life of only one of three persons all equally dear to him: his king, his mother, and his sweetheart. Such a brain-teasing situation is better suited to treatment in an Italian novella, because its effect lies more in its challenge to come up with a clever solution than in any insight into human emotions which it may provide; it is an intellectual novelty. After the excitement of Medon's choice, Codrus' self-sacrifice degenerates into an anti-climax. This, and the emphasis throughout on Medon, rather than on the titular hero, are the principal weaknesses of the tragedy.

Codrus is an old-fashioned play insofar as it gives a portrait of a perfectly virtuous and sorely tried man—the king—without transferring the central interest to the forces of evil. It is true that the king is a somewhat passive figure; but the more active personage, Medon, is also virtuous. The wicked character Artander is present merely to bring about the necessary trying circumstances. Various facets and degrees of virtue are shown in the various characters in order that the purest form of virtue, represented by Codrus himself, may be clearly highlighted. He is a benevolent, paternal ruler, the dearest political ideal of the Enlightenment. He is in love with Philaide, a weakness of character that Cronegk would scarcely have permitted him had it not been for the influence of French tragedy. Philaide does not love Codrus in return, since her heart still belongs to Medon, a young hero presumed to be dead. Before long—again as in the French tragedies with which Cronegk was thoroughly familiar—Medon turns up alive, and the first conflict shown is the one between love and duty. Elisinde, the mother of Medon, has a very severe notion of virtue, like Cato, and like Adelheid in *Vitichab und Dankwart*. She wants Philaide to put duty before inclination, by marrying Codrus and giving up Medon. But Medon belongs to a rebellious younger generation and he retorts, "No king and no God rules over our love" (II. i). Elisinde returns the old, rigidly rationalistic answer, "Reason and wisdom quiet the battle of passions,/ And the pain of virtue helps to embellish its victory." She will not even allow him to grieve over his loss: "But true virtue must resist melancholy./ Be courageous! Only the faint-hearted bow to grief" (II. i). This is not the last word, however. Medon gives in without being convinced, for he feels that something must be wrong if virtue produces sadness. More vehement than he, Philaide criticizes the gods and wants to die: "Is your anger finally exhausted, tyrannical fate!" (II. ii). Codrus takes a humane view of the problem and mildly rebukes Elisinde, saying, "Virtue often goes too far in great hearts;/ It intends to be sublime and instead becomes harsh" (III. iii). He generously renounces his claims on Philaide; but, oddly enough, he conquers his own desires by precisely the means which Elisinde had recommended to the young lovers: "Reason often conquers the impulses of great hearts" (III. v). The contradiction here illustrates the philosophical difficulties of the period, when the emotions were rapidly regaining recognition as a valid factor in human behavior, and yet few men were ready to attack the supremacy of reason. Perhaps one is meant to infer from this case that reason is useful in subduing unrequited love, but it should not be applied to stifle the mutual love of two good persons.

The second and more important conflict concerns Codrus' wish to save Athens from the Dorians as opposed to his instinct for self-preservation. The oracle has told him that the city will be saved by the blood of a king, and he fears that this means his own. Codrus combats the nagging uncertainty with reason and virtue, not seeking, like Schiller's Wallenstein, to control fate: "A wise man remains calm,/ Tolerates a favorable fortune, can keep his composure in misfortune,/ Is never too secure, but never without hope" (I. iii). Nevertheless, a bad dream about the destruction of Athens makes him realize that "Human beings are the plaything of an unknown power!" (I. iii). At another time he says: "We err like blind men with an uncertain tread,/ And an unknown power governs every step./ . . . Only virtue alone can lead us/ Through the obscurity on safe paths to immortality" (II. v). His conflict is sharpened when Artander, leader of the Dorians, offers peace if the Athenians will merely provide a human sacrifice. Artander holds the lives of his subjects in contempt, and his view of the gods is deistically tinged, with evil results: "[Zeus] rests upon Olympus and is not so close to us./ Men of low degree are there for my sake;/ I am Zeus to them" (III. vi). Codrus, who feels that Heaven has called upon him to protect his subjects rather than to sacrifice them, rejects the plan of Artander. Through treachery Artander thereupon takes Codrus captive in his own palace. Instead of feeling foolish, as well he might, Codrus takes this opportunity to make comparisons between apparent victory and true victory, apparent freedom and true freedom, the false joys of vice and the true joys of virtue, etc., and to point out that temporal misfortunes do not disprove the doctrine of Providence's benevolence, for justice must inevitably, albeit tardily, come to the fore: "I do not feel the chains;/ It is enough that my heart remains free—I am not vanquished./ My arm in enchained, but my spirit is not tied./ . . . Heaven is just and rewards virtue./ It often lies in the dust, to be sure, while vice often wears a crown./ But eventually His avenging court will come./ It often delays, it rests, but it does not sleep forever./ . . . Do you think that he [Artander] is happy and I am unhappy?/ He trembles on his throne, but I am free in my bonds./ His heart is full of unrest, in mine dwells peace" (III. viii). This purely reflective and didactic speech exemplifies Cronegk's attitude toward his play—an attitude shared to a greater or lesser degree by the other German dramatists, including Lessing. Not a word in it advances the action or characterizes the speaker as an individual. Still, this kind of speech is the most important thing in the play. The action is carried forward in brief, interspersed speeches; indeed, it seems to be there only to provide openings for the long moralistic disquisitions. The poet regarded his play to a great extent as a vehicle for moral teaching. If the French tragedy excelled in action, and the English tragedy in characters, as Gottsched and Schlegel said,[8] then the German tragedy of the time excelled in moralizing—which is not to say that the audiences always approved of this. An illustrative anecdote can be found in Möser's *Harlequin,* where we read of a butcher who, while watching a performance of *Canut,* broke into Estrithe's long speech about the inadequacy of dueling as a way of deciding any questions (while Ulfo and Godewin are fighting off-stage), with the outcry, "Devil take all that chatter. In the meantime they are going to stab each other dead fifty times!" [9]

With Artander in power, Codrus, Philaide, and Elisinde are sentenced to death. Then Artander recognizes Medon as a man who spared his life in the latest battle between the Dorians and the Athenians, and he grants him the boon that one of the three prisoners may be saved at his request. Medon feels that the choice is impossible: "Any one of the choices offends nature and duty./ You gods! is this how you protect virtue?" (IV. v). Inevitably this is followed by Codrus' virtuous rejoinder, "Stop, O Medon, do what tenderness and duty/ And your heart command, and do not revile Heaven!/ . . . Who are you, to call fate to account?/ Despair is just as disgraceful as low faintheartedness./ Be steadfast!" (IV. v). Each of the three slated to die now comes to Medon generously urging him to save one of the two others. Medon again questions the actions of Providence, but this time he manages to preserve his faith: "Did You give us free, sublime souls only in order/ To torment our softened hearts the more keenly?/ But no, You are too great to take Your pleasure in this,/ And You created us only that we might be happy here" (IV. vii). Medon finally solves his problem cleverly, but not in a way that insures happiness for himself or Philaide on earth. He will choose Codrus, and exchange Elisinde's life for his own; then he and Philaide will die together and find happiness in the afterlife: "Death itself is conquered by your might, O love!" (IV. viii). This passage is noteworthy as the first instance in German tragedy since Stranitzky of a pair of lovers who look forward to heaven for the married bliss denied them on earth.

Artander expects Medon to choose Philaide, for he knows love only as a destructive passion: "Where love prevails, every other emotion must be silent!/ Duty, virtue, and reason lose their power" (V. i). Like Pharnaces in *Cato,* he believes that virtue is merely a matter of appearances: "That person passes for virtuous, who knows how to dissemble./ The one who does not know this is called vicious" (V. i). Naturally he is unpleasantly surprised when he hears Medon's decision. But when Medon is being led off to execution, Elisinde suddenly forgets her stoical passivity and attacks Artander with a dagger. Showing again that he represents the ultimate in virtue, Codrus holds her back and saves Artander's life. The author could not have made it more obvious that his plot is not controlled by dramatic principles, but by a moral philosophy. Here was a golden opportunity for solving all the troubles of his friends and of Athens, but Codrus refuses it, because virtue forbids murder and revenge. The relation of this action to the action of Odoardo in *Emilia Galotti* is striking. Odoardo, too, has an opportunity to solve his problems by stabbing the prince, but refuses it on rational and virtuous grounds. What recourse is then left to him? He must kill his own daughter, which is the same as killing himself. And what does Codrus do? Having given up the chance of killing his adversary, he goes off secretly to pick a fight with Artander's guards and is killed by them—a sophistical way of both avoiding and achieving suicide. Strict virtue demands this procedure, and the gods have commanded it through their oracle, which said that Athens would be saved by the blood of a king. Lessing (in 1772) used Odoardo's actions as a *reductio ad absurdum* of the principle of passivity applied too categorically. Cronegk, on the other hand, is sincere in his admiration of Codrus' action.

Nevertheless, he found it difficult to connect the king's death with the rescue of Athens. The only way was to resort to supernatural occurrences. Thunder crashes, lightning flashes, and an army of Thebans appears from nowhere to rout the Dorians. This prompts Artander, in the manner of frustrated villains before him, to defy the gods: "Through my greater fury/ I still defy their wrath. If I could only live/ To deserve their vengeance through still greater crimes!" (V. x). In contrast to this disgusting spectacle of a wicked man driven mad by his helpless rage, a beautiful death scene ensues as the mortally wounded Codrus is carried back on stage. There is no bitterness whatever about the fate of this virtuous man. His death has saved Athens, has saved Elisinde, and has saved Medon and Philaide, who may now enjoy their marriage on earth after all. Codrus sighs patriotically, "How beautiful is death, death for the fatherland!" (V. xiii); and he enters into eternal bliss. To forestall any misplaced emotion of sadness, Elisinde closes the play with the instruction, "His death is not to be wept over, but to be admired" (V. xiii). This perfectly exemplifies the kind of coldness which Lessing criticized in tragedies whose main goal was admiration of the hero.

Cronegk's second tragedy, *Olint und Sophronia*,[10] was left incomplete when the author suddenly died of smallpox in the very first hour of the year 1758—it was as if Nicolai's contest exerted a baneful influence over both him and his close competitor Brawe, who died of smallpox approximately three months later. It is a tribute to Cronegk's reputation that his *Olint und Sophronia* was chosen to be the opening presentation of the new National Theater in Hamburg in 1767. On account of this honor, the play was subjected to an extended and rather annihilating criticism by Lessing in the first articles of his *Hamburgische Dramaturgie;* but thereby *Olint und Sophronia* and its author have maintained an enduring, even if mournful, fame. It does not seem quite fair to have attacked the play on the basis of its "Christianity," as Lessing did. It is a Christian play only insofar as its sympathetic characters profess this faith; their ideas, on the other hand, are "Enlightened" rather than Christian. One of them says, for example, "Virtue and reason first brought my heart to faith" (I. ii).[11] Lessing's objections to the Christian character on the tragic stage were as follows: "Is not the character of the true Christian, one might say, completely untheatrical? Do not the quiet passivity and the constant gentleness which are its most essential traits conflict with the whole business of tragedy, which is to cleanse passions through passions? Does not its expectation of a blissful reward after this life contradict the unselfishness with which we wish to see all great and good actions undertaken and carried out on stage?" [12] Persuasive and reasonable as these remarks are, surely they can be applied with equal justice to the ideal Enlightened character. These are the very characteristics observed time and time again in the tragedies of the period—Lessing's own not excluded—whether the persons be classical, Oriental, or English. Sara Sampson surely possesses "quiet passivity and constant gentleness," and she expects a blissful existence in heaven. Much the same is true also of Emilia Galotti with her "This life is all that the wicked have." [13] Lessing's objections are actually a criticism of all the tragedies based on the philosophy of Enlightenment. By putting the label "Christian" on what he instinctively most disliked in contemporary tragedy, the passive acceptance of misfortune, he was able to deceive his readers—and perhaps himself as well—into thinking that a really vital, powerful tragic style, like that of the Greeks and of Shakespeare, could be achieved by exiling Christianity from the stage, without departing from the philosophy of Enlightenment. It is noteworthy that when Weisse produced a more powerful kind of tragedy by neglecting the principles of this philosophy, Lessing took him to task sharply (*Hamburgische Dramaturgie*, St. 79).

As a matter of fact, Cronegk's hero Olint is passively calm only when it comes to exposing his life to danger for the sake of duty, or what he considers a duty. He says to his father Evander, "My God has taught me how to defy death calmly./ Know your son, who as a true Christian/ Is ready to die for God and fatherland"

(I. ii). He is not at all calm when it is a question of rescuing a crucifix from its place of degradation in a mosque in Jerusalem: "Eternal God! who can be calm,/ And behold the tyrants desecrating a divine image?" (I. ii). With delightful sarcasm Lessing described the readiness to die professed by Olint and other personages in the drama: "Anyone that is a Christian in *Olint und Sophronia* thinks no more of being tortured and of dying than of drinking a glass of water." [14] But Lessing particularly disliked what he considered Olint's useless reason for risking death, the mere rescue of a crucifix: "Now we live in a time in which the voice of sound reason rings so loudly that no madman who rushes headlong to his death, without any need, scorning all his responsibilities as a citizen, may appropriate for himself the title of martyr." [15] What Lessing failed to mention is that in the play Evander expresses similar sentiments: "O son! your youthful courage pushes you too far:/ Your life is now of more use to God than your shed blood./. . . . He who desires the martyr's crown simply out of impatience/ Is not worthy of this ornament. The pain of death is easy;/ God prefers to be glorified through long suffering and patience./ . . . Melancholy often likes to disguise itself as virtue" (I. ii). As in *Codrus*, so here also Cronegk was interested in contrasting various shades of virtuous action in order to bring to light that which is purest. One cannot assume that Olint's rashness has the author's complete approval. If he had lived to conclude the tragedy himself, this point would probably have been made more definitely.

Olint's recovery of the crucifix has a result that more than justifies Evander's fears and warnings: Aladin, the Moslem ruler of Jerusalem, gives orders that all Christians in the city are to be killed if the guilty one is not found by nightfall. To prevent such a catastrophe, Sophronia, whom Olint loves very spiritually ("I love her, but with the same pure impulse/ With which unfettered souls love each other in a better world" [I. ii]), accuses herself falsely of the deed. Her attitude toward death is like Olint's: "To die calmly is the greatest duty of Christians" (II. i); but her confidante Serena, like Olint's father, warns against this: "Duty commands that we endure death calmly:/ But no duty demands that we seek death out./ . . . But false courage/ Is defiant and rash, and runs wildly toward it" (II. i). Moreover, Sophronia's self-sacrifice involves deception, which cannot be good even though she tries to excuse it by saying, "Providence will pardon that a feminine ruse/ Is the only means of achieving this great goal" (II. i). The kind of "Christianity" to which Sophronia subscribes is plainly shown in her advice to Serena about the way to get to heaven. She and her friends will be united there, ". . . if you love virtue" (II. i). It is doubtful that Cronegk viewed Sophronia's well-meant plan as anything but an honorable mistake, for it is certainly not entirely virtuous. As soon as Olint hears of it, he naturally gives himself up to Aladin. In spite of the desperate appearance of things, the closing choric song of the second act (Cronegk departed slightly from Gottsched's norm in this tragedy by concluding each act with a short cantata sung by a chorus of Christian virgins) is resolutely optimistic: "Justice and the right must conquer:/ He whose hope is in God and Providence/ Will never be defeated."

The imprisonment of both lovers leads to a tantalizing situation similar to the one in *Codrus*, but it is not quite so novel, for it had already been used in the dramas involving Orestes and Pylades: which one of the two shall die, when both claim to be guilty? The ruler of Jerusalem (like Thoas before him) is confused: "Each one chooses death and boasts of his crime" (III. i). The lovers argue, trying to convince each other that one and not the other should die, but to no avail. As Sophronia says, it is an "Unhappy noble strife!" (III. ii). We may guess, to judge from what happens in *Codrus*, that Olint would have finally figured out a way for them to die together, but that at the last minute Providence would have arranged the military overthrow of the Moslems by Godfrey of Bouillon who has an army nearby, and they would have been saved. Possibly Clorinde, a Persian warrior princess also in love with Olint, would have died to provide the ending with an element of sadness. In Cronegk's source, Tasso's *Gerusalemme liberata*, the lovers are saved from death by Clorinde's intervention.

It seems certain that Cronegk intended Clorinde to play an important part in the unraveling of the plot, for he took much care to make her an interesting character. She is a strange, flamboyant creature with pronounced Amazon behavior, and she also has nobility of soul in large quantities. It was thus that Cronegk found her in Tasso's epic. But by making her into a rejected lover, Cronegk fashioned her also into an early prototype of Schiller's Lady Milford in *Kabale und Liebe*. She possesses Milford's scorn of subterfuge and of princes. Thus she tells her confidante frankly about her love for the brave soldier Olint: "To conceal keen-mindedly what one feels in one's heart/ Is a mark of cleverness and a merit; but only for low souls./ A sublime heart cannot stoop to such artfulness." Olint may not be of royal blood, but Clorinde has more respect for honors that are won than for those that are inherited: "Who are those mortals who live in palaces,/ Before whom the world bows and whom one calls princes?/ Often slaves, whom the people envy because they do not know them,/ Mere mortals, proud only of vain privileges/ Bestowed on them by birth, but servitors at heart./ . . . If fortune were true and not a false illusion,/ Then (doubt not) Olint would be a king./ Fortune may refuse him the splendor which adorns the crown:/ But it is better to be worthy of a crown than to wear one" (I. iv). Like Milford, she has "a great heart," and she is too proud not to fear the humiliation that would be her lot if Olint should refuse her love. At some length she expresses her envy of simple folk who do not have to worry about their reputation in the eyes of the world and are permitted to live virtuously according to their hearts. She is the first personage in German tragedy of the time to sound this chord so emphatically and sentimentally: "O happy man, who, remote/ From the splendor of proud crowns, learns to live for himself!/ O happy, happy folk, satisfied to be in lowly huts,/ With unenfeebled courage, with natural customs,/ Loyal to virtue, nature, and noble simplicity,/ Unknown to the prince, poor, lowly, but free!/ Your heart, free from vice, gives itself to its quiet impulses;/ Your fame is peace, you fortune is loving and being loved:/ A life without compulsion, and the sight of loved ones/ Are all that can make this world beautiful and existence happy" (I. iv). Such a speech reminds one that Rousseau's *Discours sur l'origine de l'inégalité* (1754) was the talk of Paris during Cronegk's sojourn there; and its sincere pathos is clear evidence of the new talent that Cronegk brought to the heroic tragedy.

When Olint politely declines Clorinde's offer of marriage and (like Schiller's Ferdinand von Walter) candidly admits that he loves Sophronia, Clorinde is naturally enraged and determines to kill Sophronia. Her immoderate speeches now have a tone of Baroque frenzy equal to that of Lessing's Marwood: "She shall perish by my hand, by my hand./ In desperation, untamed, with horrid pleasure/ I shall tear her false heart out of her riven breast:/ Then shall Olint see her stiffened at my feet;/ Then her black blood shall flow upon the traitor./ . . . No lion, roaring for blood in desolate wastelands,/ No tiger, filling the forest with terror and death,/ Equals me in his anger and rage—" (III. iv).[16] Clorinde's bitter disappointment causes her to utter reckless words in favor of revenge: "Also in revenge dwells a divine pleasure./ Also in revenge a heart shows how great it is,/ And remains admirable, even in madness" (IV. iii). Obviously, her emotions have made Clorinde wicked; but like Lady Milford's, her fearsomeness and evil are only temporary. Just as Lady Milford's change of heart is effected through an interview with her rival, Luise; so Clorinde is improved through an interview with

Sophronia. The latter, to be sure, is not pert and desperate like Luise. Sophronia meets Clorinde's murderous threats with so much angelic composure and charity that the Amazon begins to weep. Clorinde says, "Yes, your virtue conquers. Away, cursed steel!" (IV. iv), and decides to become a Christian. The implication here is that a heathen may have a good and noble heart, but in order to attain perfection has to become a Christian—an idea that scarcely could appeal to Lessing. Cronegk's manuscript breaks off shortly after this point, but since Clorinde has resolved to rescue Olint and Sophronia it is evident that the author intended to bring their romance to a happy conclusion.

Very little room is given to the depiction of evil action in the tragedy. The character of the wicked Moslem priest Ismenor is not deeply explored, nor is it exploited. Aladin, the sultan, is presented as a despot with a low opinion of his subjects: "With torture and punishment must the citizen of this earth/ Be held back from rage and crime./ They are, when one punishes them with stern torment,/ Only pious out of fear of punishment, virtuous out of timorousness" (III. i). But this was also Wolff's opinion of the mass of mankind who had not as yet learned to act as reasonable beings.[17] Aladin is neither vicious nor unjust, so that it is possible that Cronegk might have shown him at the end impressed by the virtue of Olint and Sophronia, and perhaps the intervention of Godfrey of Bouillon was not going to be necessary.

If there is relatively little evil in the play, there is on the other hand a great deal of emphasis on the idea that this world is a vale of tears (not the desirable kind!) and a place to be exchanged for heaven at the earliest opportunity. It was a commonplace in the tragedies written before *Olint und Sophronia* for the threatened hero or heroine to look forward to a perfect afterlife. Here, however, there are overtones of a genuine world-weariness not typical of the Enlightenment. Sophronia's confidante Serena expresses a completely hopeless view about the rulers of this earth: "At the courts of proud princes, in the splendid palace,/ Quiet virtue always goes unrecognized, or else is hated:/ Innocence retreats faintheartedly and in the proud rooms/ Lets vice shine victoriously in its uneasy gold" (II. i). Enlightened trust in Providence is transformed into frightened helplessness in Evander's speech about the futility of trying to reckon with the future: "The outcome of future times is concealed by the power of Providence/ From curious mortals with impenetrable night./ For Its final purpose It knows how to combine all things;/ It laughs at our hopes and is often angry when we weep" (II. iv). Though this is meant to be comforting, it is so drastic that

Providence seems less like a benevolent father than a capricious tyrant. The most melancholy passage in the play is in the choric song at the end of Act Three. This hymn in praise of death could not but sound weak and morbid to a sturdy, healthy rationalist. It is lent poignancy by the fact that its author himself was standing at the brink of the grave at the age of 26; but unlike the tubercular Ludwig Hölty, who also sang of death, he was not aware of his imminent demise. The Christian virgins desire death as a refuge: "Happy death! Longed-for quiet!/ Nothing disturbs your sacred peace./ How softly your deep slumber buries/ Mankind's ever active grief!/ Gently the rigid limbs sink/ Down in the dust./ The liberated soul flies/To better worlds rejoicing" (III. iv). It is difficult to say which aspect of death—bodily disintegration or spiritual release— is considered most attractive in this song. But the words "peace," "slumber," "rigid limbs," and "dust" indicate an attachment to the physical grave which is new in German tragedy; and it is not religious (despite Bach's "Come, sweet death," which tries to take the natural sting away) or philosophical, or even tragic. It is romantically lyrical, and perhaps pathological. As a man of the Enlightenment, Lessing should not have attacked the "Christianity" in Cronegk's tragedy, but its incipient romanticism.

Again, if Cronegk had finished his work, its melancholy would probably have been alleviated and discredited at the end. Political despair would have been changed into rejoicing and satisfaction; the uncertainty of the future would have proved to be only the prelude to general relief and good fortune; and the lovers would have recovered from their preoccupation with death. The ending tacked on in 1764 by Cassian Anton von Roschmann-Hörburg (1739–1806) cannot possibly be regarded as a fulfillment of Cronegk's intentions.[18] The question uppermost in Roschmann's mind was one that never occurred to Cronegk at all, namely, whether Olint will prove loyal to Aladin, as general of his army, or whether as a loyal Christian he will go over to the side of Godfrey of Bouillon. With the utmost absurdity Sophronia and Evander are shown to be very eager for Olint to remain faithful to Aladin, as if treason to an infidel tyrant who has sentenced him to death were a greater sin than refusing to fight for the victory of the Christian forces. It seems perfectly ridiculous for Sophronia to fear the victory of Godfrey of Bouillon and to speak as though it were a Christian's duty to oppose him: "Is it possible, can Olint betray the state and us?—/ God! can he be capable of such black crimes?—/ Oh, no! No Christian has ever yet broken faith so badly,/ Has never so neglected the duty of a subject" (V. iv). At last Roschmann has Sophronia die of poison administered by Ismenor and lets Olint die of battle wounds received while fighting against the Christians; but neither of these deaths has anything to do with the original problem of the play. It is really astonishing that *Olint und Sophronia* could ever have been selected for performance in Hamburg with this preposterous fifth act. It was no auspicious beginning for the National Theater.

No doubt influenced by the success of Cronegk's *Codrus* in the first of Nicolai's prize contests, Karl Theodor Breithaupt, the author of *Der Renegat,* entered the second prize contest of 1758 with a regular heroic Alexandrine tragedy, *Barbarussa und Zaphire.*[19] This time, without the competition of Cronegk and Brawe, he was rather grudgingly awarded the prize. The judges' lack of enthusiasm about *Barbarussa und Zaphire* is easily understood, for the play is tedious, poorly organized, and often ludicrous. Moreover, its morality is very doubtful. The plot is based loosely on the history of the early Barbary pirate Arouj (nicknamed Barbarossa by the Spaniards) and his brother Khair-ed-Din, who terrorized the western Mediterranean area in the first half of the sixteenth century. Breithaupt, however, is not interested in Barbarossa's piratical exploits. It is enough for him that Barbarossa is a tyrant over Algiers and that he has become such through the murder of the rightful ruler Selim. Beyond this Breithaupt lets his imagination, or perhaps some fanciful historical account, take over. The action of the play, then, deals with Barbarossa's vain efforts to marry Zaphire, the virtuous widow of the murdered Selim. Since neither of the two alters his attitude—constant desire on the one hand, constant refusal on the other—the plot is very static throughout the play, and the five acts drag on under the burden of abortive and inconclusive doings.

Suggestive of French influence and less in accord with Gottsched and his followers is Barbarossa's total domination by the passion of love. In earlier tragedy, the only main personage shown to be hopelessly and helplessly in love was a woman, Dido, whereas Flavius in *Herrmann* and Araspes in *Panthea* were figures of the second rank and, besides, were thoroughly castigated for their unmanly weakness. In the 1750's the love motif had grown stronger, as *Araxane* and Schönaich's dramas (particularly *Zarine und Stryangäus*) indicate, and in the middle-class tragedies it was very important. Barbarossa, however, is a new phenomenon in that his love has enslaved him to the point where he can no longer act according to his normal instincts as a wicked and ruthless tyrant. He is, for all his power and threats, abjectly at the mercy of the unyielding Zaphire. In one sense love has improved and softened his character; in another it has unmanned him and robbed him of his initiative, as one of his advisers says reproachfully, "A woman conquers you! And you have conquered the world!" (I. iii). It was fear of such a humiliating subjection that had made many a tragic hero reluctant to fall in love. Zaphire's rejection of Barbarossa's advances has nothing to do with loving him or not loving him; she cannot marry the man who has murdered her husband, and that is all that matters. The murderer of one's husband is to be hated and, if possible, punished; one's personal feelings toward him do not count.[20] Zaphire coldly sees through Barbarossa's desperate attempts to pin the guilt for Selim's death first on a slave, and then on one of his own advisers, both of whom are promptly executed. Zaphire's son, who was presumed to be dead but (as in French tragedy) has suddenly turned up alive, is equally unshakable in his defiance of Barbarossa. Further proof that love is having a marvelous effect on Barbarossa's character is that he cannot hate young Selim: "Surely he is a hero! I am taken with admiration for him./ And—what? could I possibly be capable of pity?" (III. ii).

It is a reminder of Breithaupt's interest in the middle-class tragedy that one of the characters, Hamet, is a faithful servant—as Zaphire says, "A servant, but more like a friend" (I. i). Although he seems to have forsaken her to serve Barbarossa, actually this is a pretense camouflaging his plans for a revolt against the tyrant. It is a sign of the doubtful morality of the play that this double-dealing is not condemned, but is approved of by Zaphire's confidante as "a clever dissimulation" (I. i). When the revolt fails (almost before one realizes what it is all about, so poor is the exposition), and young Selim is in Barbarossa's hands, the tyrant realizes that the life of the son could be used as the price for Zaphire's acquiescence. At first he overcomes his weakness and feels happy when he orders Selim's execution: "So now again I am the unconquered hero,/ Whose arm can dethrone or preserve kings,/ The immovable one, whom no woman's tears/ Persuade to dishonorable clemency, when he should take revenge,/ Even if Zaphire should plead at my very feet" (III. iii). Shortly thereafter Zaphire does come in and Barbarossa gives in to her entreaties: "Clemency and compassion conquer me against my will./ . . . Alas! she has my whole heart, my whole love again" (III. v). Even when she still refuses to marry him, he cannot stop loving her. In his distress he ludicrously keeps ordering and canceling the execution of young Selim.

In the meantime Selim escapes his guards and is bent on killing Barbarossa. But this action is stopped before it gets started by Hamet's arrangement that mother and son should flee, while he himself will stay behind to ward off their pursuers. Like a properly sentimental servant, Hamet feels it is a privilege to die for his masters, but the opportunity for a beautiful death scene is bypassed: Hamet is killed off-stage. The flight of Zaphire and Selim is interrupted by Barbarossa's general Chereddin (the historical Khair-ed-Din), and thus another promising action leads nowhere. The only result is that Barbarossa now is not only torn between executing and not executing Selim, but Zaphire as well. He expresses his tormented state of mind in an impassioned and remarkably unstilted speech: "I want to be her conqueror, love her, hate her,/ Want to enjoy her, want to be completely happy through her,/ Want to calm her, kill her, liberate her./ May she rule over me and the conquered earth,/ I want to become her master, tyrant, her slave, her murderer./ No, I want to be happy. Inexpressible feeling,/ Leave my heart!— I want—I do not know what I want!" (IV. xiii).

Zaphire's decision to kill herself in order to escape Barbarossa is a morally questionable step. But before she commits suicide, she breaks sufficiently with the rule of passivity to attempt to kill Barbarossa with her dagger. Indeed, none of the virtuous characters in this play has any compunction about vigorous action in self-defense, and this is not so much an indication that Breithaupt was progressive in his thought as an indication that he was careless about approved morality. True, he lets Zaphire wonder momentarily about the justice of this killing, but she soon convinces herself that it is all right: "—Is it not a crime, though?/ Can it be a crime to avenge the disgrace of the world?/. . . . May everything that might soften me flee out of my breast!" (V. iv). Unfortunately, she is able only to wound Barbarossa. Then by a subterfuge she obtains a private interview with Selim, and both stab themselves to death. Zaphire's view of the world at this juncture is shockingly pessimistic. She asks her son ironically whether he can "Leave a world/ In which Heaven itself drives us to desperation/ And where you have nothing but torment, I nothing but shame?" (V. viii). The author's lack of philosophical depth is apparent in such an irresponsible speech. Yet it is to be assumed, as Barbarossa does, that the two desperate suicides are safely in heaven. Their situation is comparable with the ending of Lessing's *Emilia Galotti*—up to a point. Like Zaphire, Emilia is ready to commit suicide to escape the unwelcome love of her sovereign. But Lessing carefully, even if only technically, prevents her from becoming a suicide by having her father slay her.

Barbarossa's concluding monologue expresses frustration and rage to such a degree of violence that one is reminded of the final outburst of Admetus in the *Haupt- und Staatsaktion, Der betrogene Ehemann*. The disappointed lover is unwilling to recognize the unbridgeable barrier between earth and heaven, and imagines that he can overcome it by very excess of fury and ruthlessness: "I shall pile corpse on corpse, skeleton on skeleton,/ And conquer and kill my way into heaven./ Then I shall enter up there on high with tumultuous rejoicing,/ Tear you away from your spouse, tear you away from heaven,/ And ruin my enemy—" (V. viii). Nevertheless, the unblessed love of Barbarossa must capitulate in the end before the virtuous love of Zaphire and her husband, which shows the spirituality of its nature by its continuance in the afterlife: "In front of me I see you going into his arms./ There, there she embraces him and feels what to her is complete rapture!/ . . . I am sinking!—Corpses, world, plunge, fall back on me,/ Cover, save me from her terrible glance!" (V. viii). All this frenzied pathos at the end cannot disguise the fact that Breithaupt's second tragedy is sadly lacking in both plot and moral viewpoint. The author has nothing definite to say; at most he wishes to present the portrait of what might have been in more expert hands an interesting character—a tyrant who is partially improved by love. Although Barbarossa is not virtuous, he is by no means altogether evil. Too wicked for the concept of tragic guilt to have any meaning, he is too good to be considered an outright villain. Zaphire is stiffly virtuous, and the injustice of her death, which is morally compromised by her suicide, is mitigated only by the vision of her happiness in heaven. Unlike Cronegk's tragedies, Breithaupt's *Barbarussa und Zaphire* does not impress one as a renewal of the Alexandrine tragedy, but as a late survival of the receded wave of Gottsched's influence, possessing not even moral certitude. Uncertainty of moral goal, however, as will be seen from the discussion of Weisse's tragedies, may be considered as one of the trends of the late 1750's.

Cronegk's renewal of the Alexandrine tragedy was itself only the belated flare-up of a dying fire, although Weisse carried on Cronegk's endeavor for a few more years with great success. The real future of the heroic tragedy in verse was predicated on a disassociation from the standard French model which became more and more identified with the dead and buried past in the minds of forward-looking young critics and authors. Paradoxically, the still older model of Shakespeare acquired an aura of timeliness and freshness; and the works of more recent English authors, Addison, Rowe, Thomson, and Young, appeared to be an excellent compromise between the unbridled "wildness" of Shakespeare and the stiffness of the French classicists. The heroic verse tragedy in Germany found in English drama one particular stylistic feature that seemed to epitomize and symbolize the new liberty for which it sought. This was the unrhymed iambic meter, the blank verse of English drama. Simultaneously and without knowledge of each other's action, two young poets, Joachim Wilhelm von Brawe and Christoph Martin Wieland, took the bold step of writing a German tragedy in blank verse.

Brawe was led to this far-sighted decision by his noted mentor Lessing, whose fragment *Kleonnis* was written in blank verse.[21] Thus Lessing, who himself never brought a heroic tragedy to completion although he sketched plans for many of them, was instrumental in opening a new path for the genre through his young admirer. To be sure, it was necessary for Lessing to produce his *Nathan* more than twenty years later (1779) before the new meter actually made a great impression on the public and became the standard for German classical drama. Nevertheless, the beginnings made by Brawe, Wieland, and a little later by Weisse not only helped to prepare for this result, but also subtly provided a freer, less stylized, more natural dialogue for heroic drama.

Brawe began writing his *Brutus* in 1757, early in the year, and was able to finish it before his death in April, 1758.[22] It was not published, however, until Ramler and Lessing's brother Karl took over that task and presented it to the public, together with *Der Freygeist*, in 1768. Thus whatever influence the play might have exerted was delayed by ten years. It is discussed here not because of its influence but to demonstrate the direction that heroic tragedy was taking in 1757 and 1758. The meter, of course, was very new; but there were also old and traditional features in *Brutus*. It was traditional to choose a subject from Roman history; the figure of Brutus, on the other hand, had acquired some new glamor for having been treated by Shakespeare in *Julius Caesar*. This was as yet the only play by Shakespeare in German translation.[23] Strictly traditional were Brawe's observance of the Unities; the solemn, dance-like alternation of his characters upon the scene; and his indifference to realism. Accordingly, the play makes an impression totally different from his *Freygeist*, even though the revenge motif which is so strikingly utilized in the latter also plays an integral role in the plot of *Brutus*. In spite of the historical background, the plot of *Brutus* is as fictional as the plot of the *Freygeist*.

Brutus is not merely the titular, but also the actual hero of the drama. In one sense, this represents a step backward to the time before the evil genius began to take over the chief action; but Brutus is a virtuous hero of a kind the earlier dramatists had not been able to create. That is to say, he is both human and virile, and the combination lends him a plasticity hitherto unknown in German tragedy. From the beginning, Brawe makes us conscious of the inevitable doom hanging over the head of Brutus; and this doom is not rooted in the external situation but in the past actions of Brutus, so that we feel he has already subconsciously passed judgment on himself. With all his might he will consciously strive to preserve the freedom of Rome and to defeat the forces of Antony and Octavianus, just as if there were really a good chance of success. Inwardly, however, he knows that he must fail because he is guilty of the assassination of Caesar, a noble and idealistic crime, certainly; but a crime nevertheless. Brutus represents the most satisfactory type of tragic hero, the one who finds himself isolated against the universe and who yet maintains his dignity as a man. Lessing had also presented a heroine, Sara Sampson, whose tragic guilt was incurred before the action of the play begins. But whereas Sara is a passive, repentant sinner remorseful because of a private, shameful misstep, Brutus is basically unrepentant, although not defiant, because his guilt is the result of an action based on a noble, suprapersonal motivation. Like Behrmann's Timoleon, he has sacrificed his own peace of mind for an ideal, for the fatherland. Consequently his situation is not merely pitiful, but truly tragic; and because of Brawe's skill, it becomes tragic in the grand manner.[24]

For once, the Unity of Time, which enforces concentration on only the last hours of an extended action, adds to the dramatic effect instead of seeming unnatural and forced or simply unimportant—the latter being the case in most of the tragedies examined heretofore. To have the drama open on the morning of the day of a critical battle, and to have the scene laid in the tent of the commanding general, who is discovered all alone with his thoughts about a dream that has troubled him through the night—this is an impressive beginning. Brutus is faced with more than the usual uncertainty about the outcome of the battle, for his dream vision has actually prophesied his defeat, death, and the end of the Roman republic: "The wrath of the gods,—/ This is all that I fear!—too fiercely enkindled/ Against Rome because of crimes, wars against us. And what/ Can a hero do, if in the combat there moves against him/ The omnipotence of this anger?" (I. ii).[25] The narration of a prophetic dream is a feature that this drama has in common with *Miss Sara* and *Codrus;* but it was still something fairly new in German tragedy of the eighteenth century.[26] Brawe makes the dream of Brutus psychologically convincing by connecting it with Brutus' guilt feelings regarding Caesar, who appears in the dream calling for revenge. Suspense and curiosity are aroused by the vengeful specter's fateful threat and prediction that Rome's downfall will be wreaked by Brutus' blood, i.e., by Brutus' son; and yet Brutus' only son was lost to him in infancy. The audience of the day, being familiar with translations of French tragedies, would not doubt that Brutus' son would soon appear, but it would take a while before they could guess how, under what guise.

Brutus' favored lieutenant is young Marcius, the son of his worst enemy, Publius, a very wicked man. Publius is not a complete villain, however, because his desire for revenge against Brutus is not purely diabolical. He is the last survivor of a family of Samnites wiped out by Brutus while they were trying to defend the liberty of their homeland. While Publius surely offends against virtue in his desire for revenge and in the deception he practices to carry it out, his patriotic motivation is an excuse that saves him from being considered the enemy of virtue. Here there is only a human conflict between individuals, one of whom is nobler and more sympathetic than the other. Love is not given even a minor role in this tragedy. Like Baumgarten's *Der sterbende Socrates* (1741) and the woman-less fragment *Henzi*, it anticipates Lessing's *Philotas* with the innovation of an all-male cast. Perhaps this is the reason why *Brutus*, as well as *Philotas*, had no success on the stage.[27] Marcius, the youth who is torn between his loyalty to his father, Publius, and his admiration for the character and ideals of Brutus, is fortunate in not having his life still further complicated by the demands of a sweetheart. In this simplicity of plot line there may be observed, not improbably, the guiding hand of Brawe's friend Lessing. The figure of Marcius may well owe something to Flavius in Schlegel's *Herrmann*, who was also distressed by divided loyalties, but Flavius' difficulties were compounded by the "weakening" passion of love. Publius makes use of Marcius as no father should. He forces him to pretend to be Brutus' ally and to win his complete trust; then, at the crucial point in that battle, Marcius is to turn the troops under his command against Brutus. Marcius, who not only likes Brutus very much personally, but also considers Rome (not Samnium) as his fatherland, asks Publius in despair, ". . . what did I do, my father, that/ You have condemned me to the/ Blackest of crimes which the world has seen?" (III. i). But when Publius insists, Marcius reluctantly gives in, for Publius has promised Antony that Marcius will obey, giving his own life in pledge. Although Marcius bitterly curses his father, he ends by putting filial piety above loyalty and patriotism. In a similar situation, Brutus shows himself to be one degree nobler than this. Publius tells him that his supposedly dead son actually has grown to maturity and is now a prisoner in the camp of Antony and Octavianus; that this son will be executed unless Brutus makes peace with them. Brutus is overjoyed to hear

that his beloved son still lives, but he will not compromise the welfare of Rome to save him from death: "To the gods I leave/ The fate
of my son. No way permitted/ By duty offers itself to me, that I
might/ Save him: must not his death be/ The earnest resolve of
the gods?" (II. v). Again quite possibly in compliance with Lessing's
prompting, this apparent stoicism is warmed by Brutus' free expression of the pain which this decision costs him: "I feel/ Entirely
how great a sacrifice I intend to/ Bring to the fatherland. I feel it,
as grief,/ Which words cannot exhaust, overflows me/ . . . Forgive me, son! only duty, only fatherland/ Do I prefer to you!" (II.
v). In fairness to Marcius, of course, it must be recalled that in
previous tragedies the filial duty of a child has been regarded as
far more binding than the duty of parents to children.

Through a letter—that indispensable property in eighteenth-
century tragedies—Brutus is warned of Marcius' treachery, and a
most effective scene ensues when Brutus, unwilling to believe evil
of Marcius, confronts him with this letter. Brutus' kindness is a
torment to Marcius, who almost admits the truth, but stops himself.
In a desperate effort to steel himself for the crime he hates, Marcius
tries to cast off all his feelings of humanity: "The human part is
gone, and all Hell is/ In me. Divinities whom the night created, I
feel, I feel it, you are inspiring me" (III. vii). Here there is a truly
gripping, truly pitiful situation, and the language with which Marcius
expresses his raging emotions, though extravagant, does not seem
to be mere theatrical bombast. The beginning of the fourth act
brings the news of defeat. Soon the disillusioned Brutus returns to his
tent, blaming himself for having trusted the treacherous Marcius:
"More than the safety/ Of Rome I loved that guilty man. O thought!/
Lethal thought: It is gone on account of me,/ Through my fault,
my fatherland! Torment/ Never yet felt rises up furiously in me"
(IV. iv). Still greater sorrow awaits Brutus, however, when the
wounded Publius is brought in, for before he dies he enjoys the final
triumph of telling Brutus that Marcius is not actually his, but Brutus'
own lost son. The author does not allow this exquisite revenge to
build up the importance of Publius' role, as it might well have done.
Instead, it properly magnifies the character and suffering of Brutus,
who weeps bitter tears of shame. He is not a practiced sentimentalist
who knows the joy of tears shed for virtue: "Behold me in my
degradation,/. . . . behold the first tears which/ These eyes have
wept" (IV. viii). It is a moment of poignancy comparable to that in
Schiller's *Don Carlos*, when Philip weeps because of Marquis Posa.

The shifting tides of battle next bring Marcius back to Brutus'
camp. He reports that he has now killed Brutus in battle, at least

indirectly. He had fought his way toward Brutus with the intention of killing him, but Brutus, seeing him, plunged the sword in his own breast, crying, "One crime I shall/ Spare you" (V. ii). The mortally wounded Brutus, in the traditional way of Alexandrine tragedy, is carried back on to stage, where he utters a long lament for Rome which has more references to "virtue" than are to be found in the rest of the play. He looks forward to a better existence in heaven, "Where no Antony threatens the virtuous man/ With disgrace and slavery. . . ." (V. iii). In spite of the new blank verse, this speech is full of old clichés and sententiousness. A more genuine tone returns when Marcius again comes into Brutus' presence. It is a critical and tragic scene, for Marcius must learn to his horror that he is the son of Brutus, a parricide as well as a traitor, and that there was no necessity for his crime. Brutus is not all soft sentiment, like Sir William Sampson. He rebukes Marcius with profound anger for having been the downfall of Rome. But he remains a father nevertheless, and when Marcius pleads broken-heartedly for pity, if not forgiveness, Brutus cannot withhold this and says, movingly, "Forgive, you gods of my nation! you Zeus!/ You holy justice! forgive,/ If Brutus now, softened, conquered, weak,/ Does not act like a Roman.—Rise, unhappy one!—/ In a moment of horror I/ See you as my son. The gods will it.—/ Embrace me. You have my compassion. Ah!/ They tell you, my tears tell you/ How much I am your father" (V. iv). Through this noble and natural forgiveness Brutus retains his position as the central figure, and our main sympathy, which might easily have been transferred to Marcius, remains with him.

In the last scene Antony enters the tent, thinking to enjoy his victory over Brutus, whom he calls a "stoic." Brutus points out in a long death speech that his virtuous way of life has been better than Antony's. Like Gottsched's Cato, Brutus asks the gods to forgive his suicide: "Forgive/ That I hastened the death which I/ Should have awaited from you" (V. v). Should he then have allowed his son to become guilty of actual parricide? This ticklish question is begged by the author, who now regrettably was less interested in the basic moral issues raised by the play than in ending the tragedy with a beautiful death scene. Brutus suddenly becomes a more sentimental father than before: "My misery, my death/ I pardon for you. I do not feel them any more./ I only feel tenderness, fatherhood." He even refuses to curse the wicked Antony, and thus, having fulfilled all the requirements for beautiful dying, he breathes his last in a rapture: "It comes, the blessed—the moment.—" (V. v). This conventional, sweetly virtuous death fits awkwardly indeed on the rugged masculinity of Brutus' characterization otherwise. For the sake of this kind of death Brawe forfeited the opportunity of stating the significance of Brutus' tragic fault in its relationship to the catastrophe. He dies forgiving instead of understanding or being resigned. A few lines about the unsearchable justice of the gods, who impose duties on the one hand and punishments on the other without asking whether it is possible to perform the duties and remain innocent, might have underlined the poignancy of the situation more than Brutus' conventional piety—but, of course, would have demonstrated too distinctly that this tragedy (like Behrmann's *Timoleon*) really does not meet very well the requirements of the popular optimistic philosophy. As the ending stands, Brutus becomes a kind of saint whose death will have to be avenged on Antony by the gods, as Marcius predicts. Marcius himself, like his counterpart Clerdon in *Der Freygeist*, is unable to accept the forgiveness extended him and commits suicide with utter hopelessness: "Away, struggling life! take/ Me, abyss! Earth! be freed of me!" (V. v). Since we know and can sympathize with Marcius' mental torment earlier in the play, the manner of his death and seemingly inevitable damnation do not appear justified. Rather, one suspects that the author liked the lurid effect of such a frenzied death scene and that he considered it an artistically appropriate contrast to the blessed death of Brutus. In sum, the conclusion of *Brutus* disappoints the expectations so skillfully aroused in the body of the play, and the promise of a great tragedy is not fulfilled. Whatever the drama's shortcomings, however, the reader can be grateful for its genuine characterizations, its gripping plot, and its universal emotions, which are neither watered down with tiresome saintliness (for the most part) nor exaggerated beyond all credibility into demonic passions. *Brutus*, to a much greater extent than *Codrus* and *Olint und Sophronia*, anticipated the new direction to be taken by German heroic tragedy toward the end of the century. But at the time of its composition the near future still lay with plays either of middle-class sentiment or of unnatural ferocity. There was no audience for a play that featured simple manliness and depth rather than effusiveness of emotion.

In the summer of 1757, when Brawe had already begun writing *Brutus*, the young Christoph Martin Wieland (at that time residing in Zürich) became sufficiently enthusiastic about an English drama, *Lady Jane Grey* (1715) by Nicholas Rowe, to undertake an adaptation of it in German. The play was then presented as *Lady Johanna Gray* in Winterthur, in July, 1758, by the Ackermann troupe.[28] It was published in Zürich in the same month without mention of

Rowe, a circumstance that called down upon its author's head a merciless exposure by Lessing in the 63rd and 64th *Literaturbriefe*. Despite Lessing's scornful and satirical comments, the reader of both tragedies will plainly see that Wieland's is sufficiently different to deserve the title of an original work, even though Wieland was so unethical as to appropriate and translate several speeches practically verbatim from Rowe. Lessing, otherwise an admirer of simple plots, jeered at Wieland for not using all the complications of the English play, saying that the last three acts of Rowe had now been stretched into five acts of little action. He ignored that Wieland had said in his preface: "I proposed to use the customary simplicity of Euripides . . . as my model." [29] In another mood, as in the 32nd article of the *Hamburgische Dramaturgie* for example,[30] Lessing might well have praised Wieland for his effort. At any rate Lessing could not and did not object to the meter in which *Lady Johanna Gray* (like its English counterpart) was written, that is to say, unrhymed iambic pentameter. This was the first play in blank verse to be performed on a German language stage, and the unfamiliar meter was no hindrance to its success or understanding in Switzerland. Wieland's blank verse was different from Brawe's in that many of his lines ended in unaccented syllables.

In doing away with the figure of Pembroke, who in Rowe's tragedy claims a large share of attention as a rejected suitor of Lady Jane's, Wieland succeeded in focusing the whole dramatic interest of his play upon the titular heroine. Passive endurance is the keynote of *Lady Johanna Gray*, as it was of *Aurelius* and *Banise* in Gottsched's *Schaubühne*. Lady Jane, to be sure, is not rescued in the end. As is the case with Camerer's Octavia and Bernhold's Joan of Arc, virtue does not preserve her from physical extinction. She is a martyr, however, whose death is technically justified by the guilt she has incurred, ever so innocently, by accepting a crown she had no right to wear. But the point that the author wishes to emphasize is by no means divine punishment or the weakness of virtue. Once Providence and the rational world-order have been duly taken care of, Wieland can devote his main efforts to the loving depiction of his edifying heroine, and he does not have to cancel the sweetly sad emotions he has aroused by the necessity of saving her from death. This procedure was closely akin to that followed by Lessing in *Miss Sara Sampson*, to which *Lady Johanna Gray* is more of a sister (though historical and aristocratic) than are the other actual middle-class tragedies of the 1750's. It was Wieland's frank purpose, as he states in his preface of 1758, to win his audience for virtue not through reason but through an example irresistible to their hearts—a thoroughly sentimental approach: "The tragedy is dedicated to the noble purpose of presenting the great, the beautiful, and the heroic qualities of virtue in the most moving manner, to awaken and to entertain in the most lively way the feelings of humanity and of sympathetic participation in everything pertaining to human beings, and generally to depict virtue in actions and to depict it true to life, and to compel people to admire and love it . . . It would not be a bad thing if poets and actors were looked upon as persons whose task in life it is to amuse the public in the most rational way and to improve it in the most pleasurable way." [31] In this play Wieland has tried to give sentimentality a genuinely tragic stature by failing to reward his heroine with earthly happiness at last; but the prospect of heavenly happiness (as in *Miss Sara Sampson* also) keeps the feeling at least bittersweet.

That virtue should be considered "great" or "heroic" is evidence of a sentimental enthusiasm about the concept foreign to the attitudes of Thomasius and Wolff. The heroic greatness of Wieland's Jane Grey is not achieved through a rationalistic suppression of all feelings. There is a restful harmony between her reason and her emotions which suggests the author's predilection for the philosophy of Shaftesbury; but it was probably this gentle harmony that aroused Lessing's scorn, so that he called her a "dear pious" girl surrounded by a flock of "dear pious" relatives and friends.[32] Lady Jane makes a definite point of her rejection of stoicism which ought to have pleased Lessing, because this anticipates his well-known remarks in the first chapter of *Laokoon*.[33] Jane says, as she weeps for the death of her cousin and friend, King Edward VI, "Heaven is not angered by pious tears,/ The tax paid by humanity; it does not demand/ That we smile at its blows unfeelingly" (I. i). Neither Lessing nor anyone else with an optimistic, energetic outlook could be very much pleased, however, with Jane's innate melancholy. Before her troubles even get off to a good start we find her expecting no happiness in earthly life and longing for death: "Oh! come, surround me, you worthy images/ Of death and sweet repose in the quiet grave,/ And of the triumph of the unfettered soul/ Which soars away from the dust!" (I. iii). Such otherworldliness exceeds even that found in *Olint und Sophronia*, for in Cronegk's drama as well as in earlier German tragedies, whether "Christian" or not, the heroes and heroines have thought of death as a release and a relief only after their trials and troubles have brought them to the brink of it. Lady Jane is ready to leave before the struggle begins.

One can sympathize with Jane's desire to escape the problems of life. She is of very tender years to have to begin coping with the destinies of a kingdom. She cannot harbor any ambition for the throne of England, for she knows that Edward's surviving sisters, Mary and Elizabeth, have a better right than she. More punctilious than the older persons surrounding her, she resists the argument that her acceptance of the queenship would prevent Mary Tudor from bringing Catholicism and civil war to England. Her reply is that God rules the world, not man's wisdom; He demands of us not foresight and final accomplishment, but the pure virtue of each succeeding action. With this point of view it is obvious that Jane, though professing only to be a Christian, could also qualify as a disciple of Kant, and surely as a heroine of Schiller. Virtue forbids Jane from helping her country, for the end does not justify the means. If tyranny and persecution follow upon her refusal to ascend the English throne, then these must be borne by the people as a just punishment for their sins. Reforms and good government are blessings sent to people who have reformed themselves inwardly; but they are not to be won through revolutions or tricky, opportunistic dealings. What Jane has to say on this subject might almost be a paraphrase of Luther: [34] "If Providence wants to punish us/ Through wicked princes, through oppression, through tyrants,/ Then it only does what we have long deserved,/ It chastises us through our own vices./ The princes are bad only because we are!/ The flatterers, the degenerate courtiers,/ The slavish souls are the ones who make tyrants!" (II. ii). Just one course of action is left open to a nation as a whole: it may reform *itself*. But an individual who suffers misfortune may already be reformed; for him only passive acceptance is possible. The connection between this passivity and Luther's teachings cannot be overlooked. Rationalism is less passive, although it adopted in secular form various Lutheran attitudes. Pietism is more passive, on the other hand, in that it concentrates on God rather than on man and rejects worldliness. It is a return to early Lutheranism. Thus Gellert and the young Wieland emphasize passivity, whereas Lessing recognizes situations in which passivity may be relinquished for action.

Yet, before the second act of the tragedy is over, Lady Jane accepts the English crown. She does so with a bad conscience and many misgivings; actually she is forced into it by her elders, who take advantage of her youth and the submissiveness of her sex.[35] If her acceptance is a sin or tragic guilt, then this is a "guiltless guilt" that may be compared with Emilia Galotti's "guilty" obedience to her mother in not telling Count Appiani of her encounter with the Prince of Guastalla—an obedience that indirectly brings about the Count's death. Jane Grey's feelings of guilt only enhance the per-

fection of her moral sense, as do Sara Sampson's. But in comparison
to Jane, Sara is a grievous sinner, for whereas Sara's misstep involved
a personal pleasure, Jane acts only in behalf of her people. The
wearing of England's crown does not afford Jane a single moment
of pleasure. With a distaste for courtly life which includes a strong
note of pessimism about city culture in general (an ever recurrent
theme in Wieland's writings), she exclaims to her husband, Guilford, "Oh! if we lived/ Far from the inconstant joys of the court,/
In solitude and known by none! If our happiness/ Were hidden by
a simple thatched roof from the envy/ Of the great world! Oh,
would that I lived there with you/ In the lap of unartificial nature"
(III. ii). She imagines herself, to be sure, in a sentimentally idealized
nature, where she would be a pink and white shepherdess and en-
twine her curls "with fresh roses." One gains the impression that if
she could live thus she would be able to overcome her melancholy
otherworldliness. But alas, nature is less accessible to her than the
joys of heaven. Her longings, of course, do not affect her virtuous
passivity. Her fate is in God's hands: "In quiet humility/ I surrender myself to His will!" (III. ii).

The greatness of Jane's virtue shines forth when the good fortune
which has briefly put her on the throne abruptly changes to bad
fortune. Mary Tudor's forces conquer the supporters of Lady Jane,
whose army turns out to be made up of traitors. Guilford, although
a "dear pious husband," in Lessing's phrase, becomes too enraged to
accept this blow passively. He does not blame Providence for the
defeat, however, but the infamousness of men. Jane, on the other
hand, recognizes the will of God in this and restrains Guilford
when he wants to go out and rally virtuous men to her cause: "Oh!
Guilford, stay! Show your greatness/ Through manly patience!
To resist fate/ Is false heroism!" His less than perfect answer is,
"Virtue, Queen,/ Does not recoil from every obstacle" (III. iii).
Lady Jane's extreme passivity here is more comprehensible if one
remembers that she is conscious of the fact that she has, in a sense,
usurped the throne. Later, when it comes to light that Northumber-
land basely forced the dying King Edward to change his will in
Jane's favor and that this ambitious man hopes to be the real ruler
of England through her, we understand that Jane was right to have
misgivings. The greatness of the heroine is found in her absolute,
unswerving submission to the will of God, a submission wiser and
more correct than any rational human wisdom. She achieves sublimity, not by act of reason or will, but through submissiveness. In
this she is different from Schiller's Mary Stuart, who by a conscious
act of will grasps a death which otherwise would merely have been

forced upon her. Lady Jane's attitude is Pietistic sentimentality in full flower: her conscience is so tender that she fantastically exaggerates her own guilt. Such innocence and unwarranted self-depreciation could not but bring tears to the eyes of the most hardened sinner. In his preface of 1770 Wieland reported that the spectators did indeed weep copiously.[36]

A further severe trial awaits Lady Jane in the proposal made to her by Bishop Gardiner. If she will return to Catholicism, Mary Tudor will grant her not only her life, but the lives of her father and husband as well. Jane has no trouble refusing this offer for herself, but the involvement of her loved ones makes her decision more difficult. Once again she lets God's will carry the day over her natural inclinations. Death is, after all, the portal to heaven: "What better thing can a virtuous person/ Wish for himself and for those whom he loves/ Than a beautiful death?" (IV. iv). The whole fifth act is then devoted to Jane's own beautiful death, or at least the preparations for it on the morning of execution. One is strongly reminded here of the last act of Schiller's *Maria Stuart*. As in Schiller's play, the heroine is not seen at first; instead, her mother and her lady-in-waiting discuss her marvelous calm. Then the curtain to the rear stage is lifted to reveal the Lady Jane herself. Like Schiller's Mary, Jane praises the freedom that death will bring from prison life, regarded as being especially galling to royal personages: "Oh! my enemies!/ You love me when you intend to hate me!/ You intend to punish me, and you make me happy!/ Indeed you are only opening the prison in which/ My royal spirit perhaps still for a long time/ Would have had to long for/ The freedom to which it was born" (V. ii). But there is no stoicism about her attitude. It pains her "tender heart" (V. ii) to have to leave her mother. Calm reason comes to her aid by proving that all fear of death is unfounded. Death would, of course, be terrible indeed if it were not for immortality. She encourages Guilford with very reasonable words when he shrinks from the idea of witnessing her execution: "Are you shocked/ By the manner of my death? Would I be the less dead/ If, after long torment, a disease/ Were to kill me?" (V. iii). This same astonishingly rational composure supports her when Guilford is the one to be executed first and his corpse is brought into her cell. Instead of giving way to grief and horror, she rejoices in the thought that this dead body will one day be resurrected—a consideration that is orthodox Christian rather than Enlightened. Like the last person to get on an excursion train, she cries out to the spirits of her departed loved ones, "I follow, I follow! Come, welcome death!/ Oh, come! and restore me to their arms!" (V. vi).

Through the course of the play the heroine has grown steadily in spiritual stature. Although already perfectly virtuous at the beginning, emotional weakness did persuade her to make a false step. But from that time onward she is made greater through trials, and the fifth act, which is practically barren of external plot action, carries the "action" within Jane's soul to an unprecedented peak, so that she can find a great measure of happiness and satisfaction in what ought to be a most depressing situation. This spiritual development, despite the passivity of the heroine, saves the play from being a monotonous display of unchanging virtue, of unassailable and smug perfection. Without actually "doing" anything, the heroine remains interesting and engaging. Moreover, although she is fearless and admirable, she deserves and wins our compassion—much more so than the Lady Jane of Rowe's play, who is seen less often and undergoes no particular development. In this concentration on virtue Wieland was following a trend set for heroic tragedy by the *Deutsche Schaubühne* and perpetuated by Cronegk. *Lady Johanna Gray* forms a connecting link between these earlier works and Goethe's *Iphigenie* and *Egmont*, and Schiller's *Maria Stuart* and *Die Jungfrau von Orleans*. Like the earlier tragedies, Wieland's play makes the assumption that the tragic emotions are aroused and satisfied by the spectacle of a good hero standing steadfast under the buffeting of great misfortune. Like the later ones, his play makes the further assumption that the tragic emotions will be infinitely heightened if the good hero grows in moral stature throughout the play and if the climax consists of a particularly difficult moral decision made in the face of a strong temptation to follow the natural desires of the heart (i.e., Jane's refusal to become a Catholic). Once the decision is triumphantly made, the hero (or the heroine, as is more often the case) seems to have wrenched himself free from ordinary human existence and floats like an angel above the heads of the rest of mankind. This kind of tragedy is altogether idealistic; and pity and fear, which soften the heart of the spectator, resolve themselves into thrilled admiration and a desire to emulate. Wieland was the first German author who really succeeded in creating a positive function for tragedy in the world of Enlightenment. Gottsched and his followers and successors had only managed to *reconcile* the stark facts of tragedy with their optimistic philosophy; Wieland is able to turn tragedy into a glorification of individual virtue and of human potentialities. No longer is his main concern an unconvincing justification of the temporal world, for he has moved on to a less Philistine employment of Enlightened ideas: he applies them to the ennobling of the individual human spirit. This, as is well known, was to be the accomplishment of German Classicism in the last part of the century. Wieland's contribution to this accomplishment in *Lady Johanna Gray* should not be overlooked.

As Wieland was bringing the trend of virtue to new heights, the opposite trend—that of depicting unnatural evil—was also gaining materially in strength. *Lady Johanna Gray* had some striking new features: blank verse, free handling of the Unities of Place and Time, and a more intimate portrayal of historical personages; but it lacked a fascinating villain. And this lack jeopardized the play's critical recognition and popular success outside of Switzerland. Lessing's *Miss Sara Sampson*, which stood so close, spiritually, to *Lady Johanna Gray*, was redeemed in regard to the opposite trend by the presence of Marwood. Wieland, living in quiet Zürich and having as yet hardly emerged from his early "seraphic" stage, was not fully equipped to satisfy the tastes of German audiences. In worldly Leipzig, however, a tragic poet was just then rising to prominence who knew better than anyone else how to revive the heroic tragedy by making use of dynamic evil. This was Christian Felix Weisse; and from his camp [37] came the anonymous review of *Lady Johanna Gray* in 1759 which set forth the main shortcoming of Wieland's play as follows, "The critics who advise poets to present nothing but perfectly virtuous personages on stage may learn from the example of this tragedy how harmful their advice is for tragic poets. The character of the disgraceful Gardiner is the only one which enlivens the action at all." [38] Weisse was careful that the same could not be said of his works.

VIII

CHRISTIAN FELIX WEISSE
AND THE ATTRACTION OF EVIL

THE MOST PROLIFIC and popular writer of tragedies in Germany before 1770 was a man whose name is now remembered chiefly because Lessing subjected his most successful tragedy, *Richard III*, to an annihilating criticism in *Stücke* 73, 74, and 79 of the *Hamburgische Dramaturgie*. In his own time, however, Weisse (1726–1804) was not merely, as he is now, a shadowy figure often confused with Christian Weise, the playwriting rector of the Gymnasium at Zittau in the latter part of the seventeenth century. He was a prominent dramatist in Leipzig, author of many comedies and *Singspiele* in addition to tragedies, and from 1759 until the 1780's [1] he edited the *Bibliothek der schönen Wissenschaften und der freyen Künste* and its successor, the *Neue Bibliothek*. It was Weisse who assumed without delay the task abandoned by Cronegk and Brawe on the occasion of their premature deaths and realized their goal of infusing genuine life and verve into the heroic tragedy. Like Brawe and Wieland, although seven years later, he made the transition to blank verse; like Cronegk, he started out by giving the Alexandrine tragedy a surprisingly strong—but limited—renewed lease on life. The favorable contemporary opinion of Weisse is to be seen in the words of Christian Heinrich Schmid in 1775: "He was the first who beat a kind of midway path between French coldness and British enthusiasm, between British lack of restraint and French delicacy. We have him to thank for being the first to put heart-rending situations and high tragic expression into the heroic tragedy. In respect to the latter he avoided he sententious declamations of his predecessors and substituted feeling and images which sometimes inspire him to lyrical tirades." [2] Whether Weisse actually struck a medium between French and English taste is a point not only open to question but also one very difficult to define. On the other hand, it is plainly discernible that he brought unusual talent to the writing of tragedies. His zealous effort is shown by the fact that he completed ten of them between 1758 and 1774,[3] and six of these within the first six years of this period. The motif that he carried to its highest point of development was that of the dynamic, diabolically evil rationalist. Weisse went farther than any predecessor in making the evil personality frankly the hero and in reducing the good and morally mixed characters to distinctly minor positions. This was an incongruous feat for a man who, despite the aggressive nature of his civil office (he became a district tax collector in Leipzig in 1762 and remained in this well-paid post until his old age),[4] was himself mild, indecisive, and rather timid.[5] But perhaps his interest in portraying the uninhibited actions of powerful, evil persons betrays an inner dissatisfaction with the gentleness and meekness of his own nature.

Eduard III, written in 1758 [6] and published in the first volume of Weisse's *Beytrag zum deutschen Theater* (Leipzig, 1759), a series containing only his own works,[7] was the first completed tragedy from Weisse's pen; but it already shows quite clearly the direction the author would take. The play's titular hero, young King Edward III, is still a virtuous personage, but the central figure of the drama and by far the most arresting is the thoroughly wicked Mortimer. Having consciously rejected virtue in order to live by a realistic and immoral code, Mortimer is hindered by no scruples on his way to a throne which he thinks he deserves simply because he is ruthless and ambitious: "Conscience—virtue—trifles! for the sake of a crown/ One can easily fill the world with blood and murder—" (I. iii). No explanation is given for Mortimer's corruptness of heart, nor is it intimated that he has ever been different. He uses his reason in the service of his wicked passion and with it stifles any glimmerings of good feelings his heart may still put forth. With his wickedness he combines a tremendous energy and vitality, so that the good people around him seem supine and indecisive in comparison. By his side there is a somewhat less evil satellite, Queen Isabella, wife of the deposed king, Edward II. Although not wholly bad, she is so completely the slave of her illicit passion for Mortimer that she does her best to act according to his code. She exemplifies the Enlightened principle that feelings are blind and lead one away from the path of virtue unless controlled by calm reason. This unholy couple has removed Edward II from his throne and imprisoned him, and now seeks to rule through the young Edward III. The latter has ideas of kingship diametrically opposed to those of Mortimer: "I shall now exert myself to be worthy of the throne—/ . . . I do not want to be feared, but to be loved./ Only up to this point have I struck blows; from now on I want to forgive" (I. iv). But unlike Wieland, Weisse is not stirred by a young ruler's virtue. Edward III does not rise independently to heights of moral greatness, but remains dependent throughout on what he is told by other people, and these others are either caught up in the vortex of evil or have just recently withdrawn themselves therefrom.

To the latter category belong Edmund and Lancaster, two nobles who now regret having had a hand in bringing Isabella and Mortimer to power. They have used questionable means to achieve what they consider a worthy goal—that is, a change of regime—and their attitude toward the rebellious people is generous: "It is a question of using benevolence to make friends of the citizens" (I. ii). When they see that the new regime promises to be worse than the old, and that Edward II is presently a prisoner in the castle dungeon, they want to restore their former king to the throne and they enlist the aid of Edward III in this endeavor. Edmund cautions Edward III against false advisers like Mortimer and counsels him to trust only himself, to find out things for himself—even though there is always the danger of error. Apparently Weisse does not have absolute confidence in the power of reason and therefore he concludes, through Edmund, that it is sufficient to have had good, honest intentions: "—to base the throne quite firmly,/ You must erect it on the foundation of truth itself,/ Doing with your own hands, seeing with your own eyes./ . . . suppose that you should fail,/ Still you will have enough consolation if your heart declares to you/ That virtue itself dictated the error to you—" (III. ii). A generation earlier, Pitschel had underlined in his *Darius* the inexcusability of an error of judgment; but Weisse, the spokesman of a more sentimental age, prefers the reality of a good heart to the unattainable ideal of perfect judgment. Nevertheless, Weisse emphasizes, as the rest of the plot demonstrates, that a heart that disregards reason will very certainly plunge its possessor into error and trouble.

Mortimer's plan is devilishly fine: he wants the imprisoned Edward II to be executed by the command of his unsuspecting son. The old king is to be represented as an impostor to Edward III, and consequently the two must not meet face to face. If the young king had followed Edmund's advice about doing and seeing things for himself, all would have been well. Instead, he cooperates with the efforts of Mortimer and Isabella to keep him away from the so-called "impostor." The wiles they use are clever. Isabella accuses Edmund and Lancaster of lies and treachery and underscores her arguments with appeals to Edward's sense of filial piety. She produces the inevitable forged letter in proof that Edmund and Lancaster are traitors. Young Edward is convinced, but is not angry. Like Schiller's Don Carlos, Edward can remain loyal to friends he believes are false, and though sick at heart, he refuses to fight them: "I do not desire a throne which has to be acquired through blood,/

Through blood which has even put itself in danger for me and you" (IV. v). Then, however, Mortimer brings news that Norfolk is approaching with an army to assist the traitors Edmund and Lancaster, and Isabella passionately threatens to cast herself before the swords of this army. At this Edward III gives in and signs the death warrant both for the "impostor" and for the "traitors." Thus he becomes the murderer of his father and of his truest friends, and Mortimer has succeeded.

But his success is short-lived. Almost immediately the forces of Norfolk take over the castle and Mortimer is their prisoner. The enormity of her crimes suddenly overwhelms Isabella, whose despair is as boundless as that of the damned on Judgment Day: "You walls of this castle, fall upon me, cover,/ Cover the courtesan! Despair, death, and revenge!/ . . . Heaven is hostile to me: I am a burden to the earth,/ My own heart damns me, and the daylight is hateful to me" (V. iii). Mortimer, like a genuine demon, remains hard of heart to the end. In what is practically a parody of the customary reproach of the virtuous against Providence for not having protected them as they expected, Mortimer bitterly censures destiny for having so badly rewarded his rationality: "Damned fate! Ha! you reward cleverness thus?/ You give me the rope and the ax, when you promised me crowns!" (V. iv). It is interesting to note that Mortimer refers to his rational intelligence as "*Klugheit*," and not as "*Vernunft*." Edward III, however, uses the latter word when lamenting that he allowed himself to be misled: "O sad reason, too late you enlighten me" (V. v). Evidently the author wishes to make a distinction between intelligence employed rightly and intelligence employed wrongly, for in supporting the importance of the heart in the attainment of virtue he does not wish to denigrate the rational faculty wholly. Therefore the word *Vernunft* keeps the connotation of the reason used as a judge over the desires of the heart, while the word *Klugheit* connotes the intelligence used unscrupulously in the service of an overriding passion.[8]

Justice is meted out to the various characters strictly in accord with the nature of their crimes. Mortimer, the worst one by far, never realizes the condition of his soul, feels no regret, and is delivered through his execution straight to Hell. Isabella, whose state of uneasy conscience at last develops into terrible remorse, suffers the pangs of Hell while yet alive. Since the bishop says he is going to pray for her, one feels that her soul is not without hope. Edward III, who has committed evil inadvertently, is prevented from committing suicide by his friend Norfolk, and we assume that he will live to reign over England as a sadder and wiser king. We may agree with Norfolk, who complains that God has been unjust in permitting the unmerited deaths of Edward II, Edmund, and Lancaster. The bishop's answer to Norfolk is, "O Norfolk! let us not criticize the ways of Providence:/ The revenge of God can and will not sleep forever!" (V. ii). It must not be forgotten than Lancaster and Edmund were guilty of a crime in their rebellion against the old king, even though they subsequently repented of this. And as for Edward II, it has been related by Edmund that he was an unwise king who trusted the word of venal courtiers instead of investigating matters for himself, and thus brought on his own difficulties—like father, like son. When these things are considered, it will be seen that this drama carefully preserves the philosophical attitude of the day intact. Nor does it lack for pronounced expression of the contemporary exaggerated sentimentality. Edward III weeps when he hears about the poor prisoner in the dungeon, and Edmund heartily approves: "You are weeping? ah, do not conceal the noble tears!/ They are a better adornment for a manly face than defiance is/ When they flow because of humane love and noble pity" (IV. iii). Unfortunately this very softness, being unaccompanied by moral greatness or wisdom, robs Edward of all heroic stature, and Mortimer and Isabella are allowed to run away with the drama.

Weisse's second tragedy, *Richard III* (1759), carries this development of the evil, rationalistic character much farther—indeed, to its pinnacle. For the first time since Bernhold's *Irene* (which was the only previous instance) a thoroughly vicious person becomes the sole titular hero of a historical tragedy. There is little in Weisse's writings to indicate that he held detailed theoretical views about tragedy or that he carefully analyzed the tragic emotions. His works indicate that he desired first of all to shock and startle, and that he diligently sought out for his subjects the most striking and lurid events in history, particularly those in which one outstandingly wicked individual was the cause of the trouble. Probably he felt justified in naming his tragedy after the wicked individual in this case because Richard was an actual king, and not just a power behind the throne like Mortimer. Shakespeare did not serve as his model, if we are to believe Weisse's own declaration,[9] and truly there is nothing in the play to suggest a Shakespearian influence. But, like Shakespeare, he was fascinated by the evil magnitude of his hero. Because of this he neglected the requirements of the rational philosophy which he had carefully observed in *Eduard II*, with the result that the drama leaves one in critical doubt about Providence and the neatly ordered universe.

Weisse's *Richard*, composed in the latter days of the Alexandrine tragedy, became the most popular for all Alexandrine tragedies ever written in Germany, with the possible exception of Gottsched's *Cato*.[10] Doubtless, the skillful handling of the verse contributed to this popularity—even Lessing was ready to admit that this drama had many "beauties": "Poetry of expression; images; tirades; brave sentiments; a fiery, overpowering dialogue; felicitous occasions for the actor to run through the whole range of his voice with the most manifold variations. . . ."[11] But surely the secret of the play's success lay in the fact that its hero, or rather, its heroic villain, was a classic case of evil rationality. Richard's one ruling passion, ambition, has completely sealed his heart, and his high intelligence is perversely employed to turn all virtuous scruples to ridicule. He has a definite set of amoral principles which are a travesty of the principles of virtue and true reason. Like the virtuous rationalist he sincerely tries to keep his emotions in check, and he considers the dictates of his rational faculty (*Klugheit*, not *Vernunft*) as absolute duties. Thus, when callously relating that he has poisoned his wife, he explains how he overcame his natural inclinations: "Perhaps I mourned her; I know she loved me;/ However my pride commanded, and this I also obeyed" (I. i). At another place he declares, ". . . I did not kill my wife in vain,/ Intelligence gave me this command, and therefore it was a duty" (I. ii). Such ordinary human emotions as remorse are unknown to him. In a bad dream related in the opening scene (like the bad dream of Brawe's *Brutus*) he has been haunted by the ghosts of the men he has killed in his career, but they do not trouble his conscience. He is only afraid that their revenge may overtake him and frustrate his ambition. The threat of damnation does not worry his "great spirit"; the joys of heaven, as his accomplice Catesby says, knowing what Richard believes, are merely "the property of cowardice" (I. ii). Richard operates according to a philosophy totally different from that of the eighteenth century in its goals, but disturbingly similar to it in its methods. In this he resembles his literary forebears Ulfo, Rhynsolt, Henley, and Betty (in *Lucie Woodvil*). Richard is morally more evil than his hypocritical associate Catesby, who flatters him for the sake of personal gain and does not really share his convictions. But in comparison Catesby seems despicable, whereas Richard has the dark splendor of the amoral "great spirit." However much both author and audience may have deplored this evil genius, they must have been strongly attracted to his superhuman freedom of action untrammeled by the scruples and feelings of virtuous men. He has the freedom for which Elizabeth pines in Schiller's *Maria*

Stuart and which enforced virtuousness prevents her from achieving. Perhaps there is a bit of Elizabeth in everyone.

The virtuous persons whom Richard opposes gain great sympathy because of their terrible enemy, just as sympathy is easily won for the cowering victims of a lion let loose in an arena. Their little group is composed altogether of women and children: the widowed queen (wife of Edward IV), her daughter Princess Elizabeth, and the two infant princes, Edward and York. Richard plans to murder the boys and then to marry their sister, in order to lend his throne an aura of legitimacy. Completely helpless, these pitiable creatures have only their virtue and the promised protection of Providence to rely on. They are aware that virtue is subjected to tests, and that it becomes great through these tests if they are steadfastly withstood. The princess says to her mother, "To be great in misfortune, this you taught me also" (II. i); and she fully expects to be protected: "Perhaps we shall soon be thanking Providence for our rescue" (II. i). The elder prince, Edward, is quite passive—and philosophical far beyond his years!—in his readiness to let Richard keep the throne: "But Queen, he may wear the crown in peace,/ A trivial loss which I shall never lament!" (II. ii). Perhaps he has imbibed these views with mother's milk, for the widowed queen also expresses willingness to abandon the deceptive delights of majesty for a life of idyllic retirement (like Wieland's Lady Jane Grey and other tragic figures of the 1750's): "Yes, would a lowly vale provide us a refuge,/ We would be less great, but far happier" (II. ii). Passivity, however, stops short at cowardice, an emotion that never, never afflicts the truly virtuous in tragedies of this period. Catesby says menacingly to Edward, "You are in my power, know it, and fear me!" But Edward answers (like Condé in Gottsched's *Die parisische Bluthochzeit*) in a manner foreshadowing the Schillerian ideal of spiritual freedom, "I am, but not my heart, for it despises you" (II. iii).

Princess Elizabeth is in a still worse situation, if possible, than her young brothers. They must only wait passively for death or liberation, while she is faced with a bewildering problem. Richard, in urging her to marry him, has made it clear that the life of her brothers depends on her consent. But Elizabeth is not only in love with the Duke of Richmond; she also finds Richard unspeakably repulsive. Moreover, aside from the fact that he is her blood uncle, marriage with him would not be virtuous because he is a self-made widower. The struggle to arrive at a decision shakes Elizabeth out of her passivity, but it also induces her to adopt a plan of action which cannot be called strictly virtuous: "Is it a crime to slay the murderer,/ The robber and the foe of the days of our life,/ Whom shame, rapine, and murder have long since branded an outlaw?/ No, it is a worthy deed, a merit! So let it be! on the first night/ I shall avenge the cherished blood of my friends—" (III. i). Fortunately for Elizabeth's character, this plan never proceeds beyond mere words spoken in a state of irrational excitement.

Meanwhile, Providence seems to be coming to the rescue in the person of the Duke of Richmond, who is advancing against Richard with an army. No coward, Richard is determined to defeat his foe and take his head as a prize. And before the battle is joined, he intends to murder the young princes. When a natural sympathy for his nephews, plus fear of retaliation, rises in his breast at the contemplation of this cruel deed, he quickly fights down these unwelcome feelings and enters the prison door to perform the deed with his own hands. In the interest of stage decorum the frightful murder of the children is committed behind the scenes. Nevertheless, the screams of one of the boys are heard, and Richard emerges holding a bloody dagger. Then the tides of fortune begin to turn against Richard. Catesby brings the bad news that their army has been defeated by Richmond. Realizing his ambitions have been thwarted after all, Richard rages madly, but without a sign of repentance for his wickedness. While he still lives, he intends to cause as much destruction as possible. Berserk, he lashes about himself with total lack of regard for what he is doing, and the diabolical grandeur of his accompanying words is impressive in spite of the fact that modern taste recoils from such lack of restraint in the speech of a stage villain: "Once more I shall arm myself with every terror,/ Where I can bring desolation, there I will make desolate,/ Let my dagger still murder wherever it can,/ As long as my arm moves, whether friend, enemy, or subject:/ I shall sow the long way with corpses,/ And thus in streams of blood go to the grave—to Hell" (IV. vi). To prove that this is no empty threat he stabs Catesby to death without provocation and then dashes out to fight Richmond's army. Catesby, being a less hardened criminal than Richard, repents his actions before breathing his last and acknowledges the justice of his unexpected punishment: "God could no longer see me, wretch that I am, go unpunished" (IV. vii).

The last act, which is rather anticlimactic, is devoted to the lamentations of the survivors of Richard's cruelties. The horrible but touching details of the murder of the princes are narrated by a sympathetic eyewitness, the jailer Tyrel, who also describes the despair and attempted suicide of their mother. Stanley, a friend of the queen, thereupon utters a statement evidently intended by the author to give reassurance that Providence has not been unjust in permitting Richard's deeds: "How terrible, Eternal One, is Your secret counsel!/ Even on children You avenge the misdeed of the fathers;/ But You do not allow the criminals to escape/ Who themselves perform Your vengeance, although unwittingly!" (V. ii). No more information is given concerning the paternal guilt that God is supposedly punishing here. If this is meant to serve as a justification for the princes' death, then surely a great deal more should have been made known about it earlier, as was the case in *Lucie Woodvil*, where the paternal guilt motif (seen also in Brawe's *Brutus*) made its first appearance in German tragedy of this period. At best, Stanley's words offer an Old Testament justification, whereas the Enlightened philosophy with its benevolent Providence made no provision for such delayed punishment visited upon children, particularly not if they themselves were personally innocent of any crime. The widowed queen has great difficulty in reconciling herself to a passive acceptance of God's will in this matter. She tells Stanley, "Count all their wounds, weigh every drop of blood,/ Then teach me, if you can, contentment and courage" (V. iii). When she hears that Richmond has been victorious, she says "A consolation, but God, how weak a one!" (V. iii). Even when she is told that Richard has died in battle, cursing God (and therefore going straight to Hell), her resentment is appeased very little: "You, revenge of God, have tolerated him long enough!/ And why did Your thunder-car not start up long ago/ And swoop in wrath down upon the head of the criminal,/ Before he robbed us of a throne and me of my children!" (V. iii). Nevertheless, her desire is not to rebel against God, for she declares she is going to spend the rest of her life in a convent. A measure of happiness is left only for Princess Elizabeth, since she may now marry the Duke of Richmond and ascend the throne of England with him. In 1765, following the advice of the great actor Ekhof, Weisse published a new version of *Richard III* which contained no important changes in the plot but had some additional scenes, which made it possible to postpone the death of Catesby and Richard's departure until the beginning of the fifth act. In order to give the fifth act still more interest, the Duke of Richmond is introduced on stage before the end, and it is he who relates the death of Richard.

The outstanding popularity of *Richard III* gives its tragic attitude special importance. In this drama, to a degree not seen before in the work of an Enlightened German playwright, a thoroughly evil and unsympathetic character who is an outspoken opponent of the rational-virtuous philosophy becomes the tragic hero. The death of the princes, touching as it is, is viewed by the author not from the perspective of these victims and their mother (as it would have been if Wieland had treated this subject), but from the perspective of the villain-hero. That is to say, one's attention is not called primarily to the attitude of the victims toward their impending fate ("Will this happen to us and how shall we meet it?") but to the attitude of the perpetrator ("Shall I be able to carry out my plan and realize my ambition?"). In this regard, Weisse did with Richard what Schlegel had done with his Ulfo, and the relationship between the two figures is very clear, except that Ulfo pales beside Richard in intensity and repulsiveness. But the fact that no author after Weisse continued his innovation of creating an out-and-out hero of evil— and Weisse himself did it no more after the completion of his *Rosemunde* (1761)—suggests that the culmination of this development had been reached. Although the dynamically evil character was to play an important role in tragedies during the rest of the century, he was obliged always to cede his dominating position to the good, or mostly good, hero who gained interest by abandoning passivity for action.

Lessing's criticism of *Richard III* concentrated on the problem of the evil hero, although by the time Lessing set down his thoughts on this in the *Hamburgische Dramaturgie* (1769), Weisse had already abandoned the portrayal of such figures. Once Lessing had made it clear that, artistically speaking, Weisse's drama shriveled into nothing in comparison with Shakespeare's *Richard III*, the rest of his remarks were motivated entirely by his philosophical views. Despite all his references to Aristotle and the artistic unsuitability of an evil hero in tragedy, Lessing was principally annoyed by Weisse's unphilosophical assumption that a human being can actually attain to the degree of heartless wickedness depicted in Richard, and by Weisse's careless handling of the duty imposed on all authors to uphold the rationality of the world-order. To Lessing, the possibility of depravity like Richard's is a "horrible idea," [12] because he believes in the essential goodness of the human heart: how can it become Enlightened and perfected otherwise? A human may well have many failings and commit errors which not only merit but also receive just punishment: this does not contradict the rational world order and it arouses pity as well. Richard's crimes, however, are not those of a human being: "But he is such a horrid fellow, such a devil incarnate, in whom we find absolutely not a single trait similar to ours, that I believe we could see him delivered over before our eyes to the torments of Hell without the slightest feeling for him, and without the slightest fear that such punishment may be

awaiting us too, knowing that it results only from crimes like his." [13]
Thus Richard cannot arouse pity and fear of the particular kind
that Lessing deems fit for tragedy. Still worse, the punishment actually received by Richard is as good as none at all, for to die in
battle is honorable and more like a reward than a penalty. Here
Lessing, to be sure, ignores the circumstance that Richard does not
take a patriotic, self-sacrificing attitude toward death on the battle
field, but regards it with hatred as the frustration of his ambition,
and the beginning of an eternity in Hell. Nevertheless, Lessing's dissatisfaction with Richard's relatively heroic demise is understandable. Its similarity (aside from the eternity in Hell) with the fate
of many a brave good warrior casts grave doubt on the honesty and
rationality of Providence and weakens the foundation of eighteenth-
century optimism. Tragedy, supposed to be an organ of instruction
in the philosophy of Enlightenment, here seems to be working at
cross purposes with that philosophy. Besides letting Richard off
lightly, the author makes innocent persons suffer in a way Providence ought not to allow. The feeling of misery caused by the murder of the princes is accompanied, Lessing says, by a "murmuring
against Providence." [14] He overlooks the one statement in the play
which implies an inherited guilt; but he would probably have rejected
this idea anyway. He admits that dreadful and inexplicable events
occur in real life. These, however, need not disturb our optimistic
theory, because we can say to ourselves that if we knew all the facts,
as God does, we could see the justice that was operative: ". . . thus
it will have its good reasons in the eternal infinite connection of all
things." [15] The dramatist, on the other hand, does not possess full
divine cognizance of all the facts, and therefore he must be careful
to construct a dramatic world without disturbing and inexplicable features. His drama should be "a whole . . . , which is fully
rounded, where one thing is fully explained by another, where no
difficulty arises . . . the whole of this mortal creator should be a
silhouette of the Whole of the eternal Creator; should accustom us
to the thought, how in it everything turns out for the best. . . ." [16]
So strong is Lessing's feeling about the responsibility of an author
that he would like to see all stories detrimental to one's trust in the
rational world-order banned: "Away with them from the stage!
Away, if it were possible, with them from all books!" [17] From this
outburst one may see that Lessing, famed for his religious tolerance,
was capable of a certain amount of Inquisitorial thought where his
own beliefs were concerned. His whole argument, moreover, is a
most noteworthy indication of the seriousness with which the morality of the tragedy was regarded by educated men of the time.

Lessing, to be sure, is well aware that the popularity of *Richard III* rested on the spectators' delight in the hero's freedom of action: "Even enormity in crimes derives advantage from the feelings which greatness and bravery arouse in us." [18] He believes, as Schiller would later believe (and express in his essay *Über den Grund des Vergnügens an tragischen Gegenständen,* 1791), that the purposiveness of a character was sufficient in itself to sustain the interest of the spectators: ". . . whatever has purpose is loved by us so much that it affords us pleasure, even independently of the morality of the purpose." [19] To this statement one might add that Richard's purposiveness is interesting precisely because it *is* evil and immoral and in defiance of all conventions. He is an evil Prometheus rebelling against good gods, instead of the other way round. The probability that the audience secretly delighted in Richard's cavalier treatment of the accepted code is side-stepped by Lessing and made over into a harmless interest in the carrying out of a purpose, any purpose. This interpretation left him free to explain away the popularity of the drama without casting doubt on the natural goodness of the audience; and it also provided a way to belittle the value of the drama, for, as he said, the mere arousing of interest in some character's purposiveness is not enough to justify the trouble and expense involved in putting on something as grand as a tragedy.[20] It was thus that Lessing disposed of the most famous work of a man who had been a close friend and associate of his youth, because he, Lessing, could not endure the thought that tragedy should be equated with the frightful behavior of a wicked hero.

Weisse's third tragedy, *Krispus,* was actually one of his first attempts in the genre, and he conceived the plan for it in the early 1750's. But it was completed only in 1760 and then not published until 1764, after having been revised.[21] The plot of *Krispus* bears an obvious resemblance to that of Racine's *Phèdre* and Euripides' *Hippolytus,* but it is based on an actual occurrence in Roman history of the fourth century A.D. which in its broad outlines repeated the old Greek legend in real life. The author of *Krispus* had different aims in mind than either Euripides or Racine, for, instead of delineating the passion of love (something ordinarily beneath the dignity of an Enlightened tragic poet), he wanted to study the transition of the character Fausta from a state of relative humanity to one of absolute inhumanity through the adoption of an amoral code. It is hard to imagine how Weisse could have conceived her character in the way he does until after he had created Mortimer and Richard. On the other hand, his Crispus is a conventional model of virtue, a typical tragic figure of the 1740's and early 1750's. Unlike Sara Sampson and

Jane Grey, Crispus has no great warmth of moral greatness. His motivation at a crucial juncture, as will be seen, is so obscure that Crispus puzzles us far more than he inspires us.

Crispus is the son of Emperor Constantine the Great; as a moral person, however, he is the creation of his tutor Lactantius. A preceptor reminiscent of Christian Fürchtegott Gellert (a good friend of Weisse's),[22] Lactantius lays as much emphasis on heart as on reason. Crispus is said to have a ". . . kind, loving heart and gentle, quiet virtue," and besides, his heart is "great," "noble," and "governed by humane graciousness" (I. i). He worships the Christian God with pure piety and, lastly, has courage and understanding. Lactantius, however, is concerned by Crispus' love for Helena, a captive heathen princess who is about to accept baptism. True, Crispus is irresistibly attracted to this girl for reasons approved by rationalists and sentimentalists alike: "Her virtuous heart more than the glow of beauty,/ Her always even temper, her courage in danger—/ Can a feeling heart resist so much charm?" (I. i). Nevertheless, Lactantius views this love as a desire (*Begierde*) that is blinding Crispus' reason to his duty, which is to join his father Constantine in his campaign against heathen enemies: "The enemies in the field are not half so fearful,/ Prince, as untamed desires which war against us./ The greatest victory is to conquer one's heart, one's self" (I. i). Crispus is not yet old and wise enough—i.e., his reason is not yet mature enough—to recognize the traps set by error. He admits this himself when Helena tries to dissuade him from leaving her to join Constantine: "Princess, alas! how often youth deceives us!/ How steep is the path of virtue and duty!" (I. iii). Errors of judgment attributable to insufficient maturity constitute the only tragic guilt that can be assigned to Crispus, but we have already seen from the cases of Gottsched's Agis and Wieland's Jane Grey that such errors were thought to justify the most severe punishment. Crispus' decision to remain at home with Helena proves to be his undoing.

The virtuous young man arouses mixed emotions in the less admirable characters at the court. The author's attitude is too sentimental to allow virtue to inspire pure hatred in another person (as in Brawe's *Freygeist*); but it is not quite sentimental enough to make virtue exert an all-powerful converting influence. Licinius, another heathen captive who is jealous of Crispus' success with Helena, says, "Cruel Crispus! alas! how cordially I hate you!/ But you do not deserve it:—and this tortures me!" (I. v). Yet he is determined to have his revenge. Still more complicated is the attitude of Empress Fausta, Crispus' stepmother. Once she hated him because he stood in the way of her own son's advancement. But when Crispus proved that he wanted no advantage that the son of Fausta could not share, her heart was won by this generosity—in fact, she fell passionately in love with him. The oddness of this situation demonstrates to what an extent the drama of this period based the motivations of its characters on the tenets, or the clichés, of the current philosophy rather than on the genuine emotions of human beings. Fausta, although not a personage of outstanding virtue, understands love only in a rationalistic, idealistic sense, without the admixture of animal-sensual feelings. Yet love is an emotion, and emotions lead to vice and trouble. Whereas Fausta's love is rational in one sense, it is irrational in another, because a stepmother is not supposed to fall in love with her stepson. Before long the emotion grows too strong for reason to control, and it leads Fausta into criminality and eventually into complete amorality. All this would have been much more comprehensible if the author had condescended to depict a woman low enough to feel love in terms of plain desire. It is difficult to understand how Fausta can speak of a love based on another person's virtuous conduct in the following way: "O glow which consumes me, which reason cannot quell,/ Which burns the more strongly, the more I combat it!" (II. ii). It was, to be sure, not only Weisse who combined rational love with expressions of great passion. Lessing also let the passionately determined Minna von Barnhelm fall in love with Tellheim *before she saw him*, on account of his generosity. And the love of Schiller's Ferdinand and Luise, in *Kabale und Liebe*, for all its heatedness, is as pure as the love of the seraphs.

From thoughts of love Fausta soon turns to thoughts of murder. She can hardly hope for Crispus' favor, and it seems as if that hope pales before the delight she feels in the very audacity of her unvirtuous determination: "I must have one or the other! his heart, or else his life!/ . . . Yes! it is a crime; but what a beautiful crime!/ I would venture it, even if God should avenge it with all His thunderbolts" (II. iii). One can no longer speak of error or weakness when a character clearly recognizes the viciousness of a decision and still grasps it defiantly. Inasmuch as Fausta could be touched by Crispus' virtue, one can say that she begins the play as a not altogether hopeless character. Through her adherence to an evil determination, however, she becomes another Richard III, and thereby she attains a diabolical freedom of action that makes everyone else in the play look pale and lifeless.

After she has declared her love and is repulsed by Crispus, Fausta does not waste a moment in feeling ashamed or disappointed. She thinks only of the danger she will be in if Crispus tells this to Constantine, and of course she also wants to punish Crispus. But the vulgar hatred of the woman scorned does not adequately explain her subsequent actions. Like the love that briefly preceded it, it is simply a means to unleash the dynamic evil heretofore just barely held at bay in the depths of her personality, and from now on she rushes to ever-increasing heights of magnificently vicious action. Fausta's ambition, as befits a woman, is not so overwhelming as Richard's. She merely wants to preserve her position as Empress and her life. At first she resorts to lies and claims that Crispus has assaulted her—the classic strategem of Potiphar's wife. Here it shows, however, that the wicked character has full freedom to use any and all means available to defend itself. Poor virtuous Crispus, on the other hand, is robbed by *his* code of any active means of defense. As Helena "correctly" instructs him, he should bend all efforts inwards to acquire perfect self-control: "This is the greatest struggle: to wrestle with silent sorrows;/ And this the greatest victory: to control them through noble-mindedness" (III. ii). When Crispus attempts the only way of action open to him as a passive personality, that is to say, flight, he is quickly taken prisoner. Helena bravely tells Fausta that Fausta's love for Crispus was a sin; but Fausta is beyond reproof, inasmuch as her new code does not recognize the basis for such reproof. To her, the concept of nature—and "nature" appears to mean getting what one wants—is all-important, while concepts like virtue and law are mere prejudices: "Virtue! Law! Nonsense! Who has prescribed them?/ Nature itself commands us to love what comes our way;/ The impulse, the inner feeling is her only law,/ Otherwise an animal in the forest would be happier than we" (III. iv). It need hardly be stated that these sentiments are a startling abnegation of the ideas dearest to the period. According to Fausta, virtue does not raise us to the level of angels, but makes us lower than the animals. And this is not the only iconoclastic idea she utters. Still more remarkable is her reaction when she hears that Constantine has returned, which means that her struggle for survival will now begin in earnest. She reflects for a moment on what she has lost through her wicked behavior, which has incurred the anger of the gods. She asks herself, "Now—What have I left?—" Then, after a pause indicated by a stage direction, comes the answer, one short, defiant monosyllable: "Me!" (III. viii). This constitutes the most impressive act ending so far seen in German tragedy. In this one word the adherent of the amoral code sums up the perverse strength and attraction of her position.

Fausta's self-reliance, consciously felt and expressed, marks a noteworthy advance in the development of characterization in German tragedy. Admirable characters had always relied strongly on a combination of reason, heart, virtue, and Providence, and they never stood for themselves, but for a suprapersonal ideal. Vicious characters, to be sure, could not rely on the same combination of factors; but they set up another, a vicious suprapersonal ideal, by which they fashioned and at the same time excused their actions. Thus Schlegel's Ulfo did what was "right" according to his lights, and Nicolai acknowledged this fact in his *Abhandlung vom Trauerspiel*, saying that ". . . the false system of honor, the appearance of heroism . . ." makes Ulfo just sympathetic enough to be tragic.[23] Even Henley in *Der Freygeist* and Betty in *Lucie Woodvil* found "excuses" for their behavior in a perverse philosophy, the idea of the "great spirit," and not in themselves as individuals. Weisse's own Mortimer and Richard depend on a faculty called "intelligence" (*Klugheit*), which, though an ingredient of the psyche, is still somehow not identical with their innermost selves. Fausta herself flaunts a false philosophy; but eventually it is no longer this amoral code which determines her behavior or provides promise of success. Instead, she uses and relies only on her own self, her innermost being, which is completely individual and not suprapersonal. She stands for nothing except for herself. In this respect she is different from any other character, good or evil, who had appeared in German tragedy up to that time. And thus she gives German tragedy an element that great tragedy has always had in rich measure: the element of the individual, the great human being thrown back completely on his own resources and engaged in splendid but hopeless struggle with a hostile universe. Because of the overwhelming prestige of the Enlightened philosophy this development of the tragic character could come at first only through the evil personage. To have allowed the virtuous character to express self-reliance would have seemed a denial of all that the century professed to believe.

Fausta's self-reliance gains in interest and in a kind of sympathy because she is struggling to save her own life and is not devoted to a cold, relentless ambition. Our secret regard for her is not so severely complicated by our pity for her innocent victim as was the case in *Richard III*, for Crispus is a much worthier adversary than were the two small princes and their helpless mother and sister. Consequently Fausta does not outdo Richard in sheer impressiveness of wickedness—he remains the unchallenged champion of the evil rationalists and the culmination of their development. But Fausta's characterization shows a way to pass beyond the evil rationalist, the devil incarnate, to the active human being who is not a mere passive, virtuous puppet but a figure of genuinely tragic proportions. One cannot help feeling in sympathy with Fausta's courage and cunning. As the danger grows, her daring increases in proportion. She has no trouble convincing Constantine that Crispus is guilty of assaulting her. Although the Emperor must be admired for his impartiality in matters of justice ("But he who can tolerate crimes committed by his own relatives/ Which he punishes in ordinary citizens is nothing but a tyrant" [IV. iv]), one also scorns him because Fausta manages him so easily. There is a rigidity about Constantine's virtue which not only renders it rather unappealing but also points up the insufficiency of virtue as an absolute guide—another evidence of Weisse's equivocal attitude toward the accepted philosophy. Crispus reminds his father of the battles they have fought side by side and of the many proofs he has given of his worthiness, but Constantine answers, as though he were God Himself: "The deeds which your reputation has gathered/ Are expunged from the Book of Time by the single misdeed,/ Expunged from my breast" (IV. v). There is no recognition of possible human error here, no patience with defects, no room for natural affection. Constantine has the uncompromising view of breaches of the moral law which was stated by Gellert in one of his *Moralische Charaktere* entitled "The Man with one Vice and many Virtues": "According to the language of the world he has only one defect and many virtues; according to the language of truth he really has no virtue. . . ." [24] Crispus in his way is equally unbending. He knows that God sometimes sends unmerited trials to purify the human soul, and so he accepts his troubles doggedly, without further attempt to clear his name. Like Quistorp's Aurelius in a similar situation, he is overcome by the feeling that all earthly honor and joy are vanity, gives up life, and supinely longs for death: "What is the world to me?—Nothing!/ Death proclaims peace, delight, and blessing to me:/ I approach it now, enraptured, with open arms" (V. i). Against two such wooden natures Fausta cannot fail to show to advantage.

The unbridgeable difference between Crispus and Fausta comes to light dramatically in the prison scene where the two face each other for the last time. Fausta, feeling less secure about her deception of Constantine, tries to persuade Crispus to flee, for his flight will be mute evidence of his guilt and then her position will be unassailable. But Crispus refuses her offer of help, the motives of which he perceives. He lives for principle and is more than willing to die for it, whereas Fausta cares nothing for that. He tells her, "You fear the punishment, but not the shame" (V. ii). Fausta simply interprets his steadfastness as defiance, and indeed there is a strong note of defiance in Crispus' speeches, as one regularly finds in dramas of this time when virtue faces vice in a showdown.[25] Crispus is defiant because God will with absolute certainty reward virtue in heaven even though vice is not always punished on earth: "If I, as a martyr, am to atone for your shame:/ Then there is a judge yonder for whom innocence has value/ . . . Who not only rewards virtue only here, but eternally there,/ And punishes the more severely, the longer he delays" (V. ii). Hereupon Fausta presents Crispus with a cup of poison. If he persists in refusing to flee, then he must drink this and die. At this crucial point, Crispus reacts in an unexpected and puzzling manner. He seizes the cup with alacrity and drains it. Although there is a dramatic shock in this action which demonstrates Weisse's ability to bring an audience to the edge of its seats, the motivation behind it is not altogether unambiguous. To grasp death so eagerly, when his innocence ought to have encouraged him to resist until execution was actually forced on him, smacks of bitterness and pique rather than of virtuous heroism. It is as much a suicide as the death of Gottsched's Cato, and yet Crispus does not imitate Cato's repentance for his rashness. Apparently the death of Crispus is supposed to be as admirable as that of Wieland's Jane Grey, but that is not the effect that is gained.

The poison works very slowly on Crispus, so that two long scenes can be filled with his beautiful demise and the lamentations of his friends. Lactantius utters words of praise which leave no doubt that the author regarded Crispus and his final act with approval: "How great you are, my prince! You are made far greater/ By this last victory than by the splendor of all your victories" (V. iv). Nevertheless, Lactantius stops Helena when she also wants to drink poison: "A Christian never takes what does not belong to him./ Your life is not yours" (V. v). This makes matters more confusing than edifying, for what real difference exists between Helena's desire to die and Crispus'? It would have been clearer, perhaps, if Weisse had forfeited the methods of execution usual among persons high up in Roman society (the poison cup or some other form of suicide) and had substituted a means of death in which no voluntary or semi-voluntary action of the condemned was possible. Then Crispus would have seemed less foolishly obstinate and self-destructive. In her sorrow, Helena cries out the conventional accusations against God: "Why did He give me such a heart,/ Much too sensitive to happiness and grief?" and "God of gods!/ Alas! all too long You withhold Your thunderbolts!/ Why does Your avenging sword delay and not/ Slay the criminal before he cuts down the pious?" (V. v). Lactantius returns the approved answer to this question: "Boldness asks, why? The Creator's wise will/ Is customarily veiled from us by a dark night;/ Yonder the curtain will rise, yonder all will be light./ Innocence suffers here, but it does not ask why" (V. v). The answer to the *why* is implicit in Crispus' decision to dally at home with Helena instead of joining his father in battle as he should have done; but this matter is forgotten as Crispus expires in the midst of heavenly visions like a true martyr.

The scene that follows this, although devoted to a depiction of evil self-reliance, leaves a much more positive impression. The truth about Crispus' innocence soon comes out and Constantine realizes his mistake. He falls into a state of feeble mourning and self-accusation, while Helena laments and rages. Lactantius is kept busy uttering rational reproaches to deter him from suicide. Fausta stalks into this scene "with a great steadfastness," as the stage direction commands. She boldly and proudly admits her guilt. So great is her disdain for weak feelings of shame that she regrets that Crispus cannot see how he is getting his revenge: "What? Crispus is not alive anymore?/ And cannot see himself avenged?—I came hither too late" (V. vii). When Constantine starts talking of punishment she interrupts him scornfully: "I laugh at you! and will spare you the trouble!/ My arm is strong enough!" (V. vii). After she stabs herself, she refuses to give them the satisfaction of hearing her repent of her deed: "That mighty triumph she will not grant you!" (V. vii). This powerfully self-willed death, if meant as a horrifying contrast to the sweet demise of Crispus, goes wide of the mark. Fausta has retained her independence and her individuality, and though her plans are thwarted, she herself never suffers defeat. Her passing, unmarred either by laments or by furious curses, is a triumph of the personality. Her evil deeds can be deplored, but her strength of personality is moving. In this respect, she is closer to Schlegel's Ulfo than to any of the intervening evil personages of dynamic power; but she also makes a step forward in anticipation of the human greatness and self-determination of Classical heroes and heroines.

The next tragedy after *Krispus* was *Mustapha und Zeangir*, which was written in 1761 and published in 1763 in the second volume of the *Beytrag zum Theater*. The original inspiration for this work, however, may well go back, like that of *Krispus,* to Weisse's first years in Leipzig, for in 1748 Lessing had in mind a tragedy on the same subject, with the title *Giangir,* of which he wrote a few scenes. While Weisse possibly did not see Lessing's manuscript, there can scarcely be a doubt that Lessing discussed the historical material with him.[26] The author's reliance on an early first sketch of *Mustapha und Zeangir,* if such a thing could be posited, would do much to explain the character and role of the chief personage Mustapha, who is a virtuous hero of the type popular in the 1740's and early 1750's. Certainly he does not fit well in the series comprising Mortimer, Richard, Fausta—and Rosamund, who was soon to follow. On the other hand, he is much like Crispus, who also belongs to a previous era. Indeed, the whole play seems to belong to a previous era, because not even the evil characters rise to spectacularly dynamic action. It is easier to believe that Weisse in this drama revamped the versification and some other details of a manuscript belonging to his youth than it is to believe that he suddenly and temporarily changed into a Cronegk or a Wieland, only to change back again for his next work, *Rosemunde*. But the lack of any documentary proof forbids any serious speculation about such a manuscript.

Mustapha und Zeangir [27] marks Weisse's one excursion into the exotic world of the Near East, an environment for which he evidences little or no real feeling or understanding. The material for the plot was taken from an episode in the reign of Sultan Suleiman the Magnificent (1494–1566). With the aid of the grand vizier Rustan, the sultan's wife Roxane (historically Roxelane) is trying to influence Suleiman against his son Mustapha—the offspring of an earlier marriage—in order that Mustapha may be executed and her own young son Zeangir be named heir to the throne. The similarity of this situation to the plot of *Krispus* is immediately apparent and again points to a close connection, conceivably also one of time, between the two plays. There is, however, no passion on the part of Roxane (as with Fausta) to complicate matters and offer an opportunity for the special development of her character. She admits that Mustapha would make a good ruler: "Yes, Nature has never seen anything more excellent:/ If I did not want to be the mother of a sultan,/ I would grant him the throne before all other men" (I. i).[28] But ambition remains the keynote of her character, and she trusts so much in the powers of intelligence that she even defies the divinity, that is, "the Prophet": "And him I do not fear,/ So long as might and cunning promise us the triumph" (I. i). Despite this fiery attitude, Roxane is a very pale copy of Weisse's other evil rationalists and fails to dominate the action. Her son Zeangir is as good as she is evil. As yet too young to be rational, this boy lives by his emotions. But since he has grown up under the virtuous influence of his elder brother Mustapha, his heart has retained its childish purity. He revels in weeping, ever the sign of the person whose virtue is more dependent on heart than on reason: "—excuse these tears!/ They are too rich in delight for me to resist them!" (I. ii).

Roxane, a rationalist, reprimands him for his emotionalism: "Prince! You are still lacking in experience,/ You judge according to feeling, and trust your eyesight" (I. ii). Zeangir's high estimate of Mustapha is based on the excellence of Mustapha's *heart*. Lack of rational calm in Zeangir is shown by his rash desire to slay anyone who wants to hurt Mustapha. Finally, Zeangir is of the opinion that Mustapha should not have obeyed Suleiman's command to return to court. Emotional impulsiveness here makes Zeangir insufficiently subservient to the majestic law of filial piety. Obviously he traces his lineage as a tragic personage back a few years to Medon in Cronegk's *Codrus,* who was the first of a series of gallant, warm-hearted young heroes with too little regard, sometimes, for the stricter rules of virtue; and Lessing's Philotas may also be considered a dramatic relative of Zeangir.[29] It cannot be said what Lessing intended to make of his young hero in the *Giangir* of 1748, for the fragment contains no scene in which he either appears or is spoken of.

Suleiman himself is evil without being an evil rationalist—he is, in other words, an old-fashioned tyrant like the Nero in Camerer's *Octavia* or the Timophanes in Behrmann's *Timoleon.* He is a character of almost ludicrous irrationality, whose desires are so set on the illusions (*Scheingüter,* in Christian Wolff's vocabulary) of sovereignty and wealth that the constant fear of losing these things has made him a prey to eternal suspiciousness. Only the power over life and death which he wields lends him a certain dignity. Suleiman is not heartless. His trouble is that his reason is so weak and confused that he consistently mistakes the bad for the good, and a lifetime of such erroneous action has hardened him into a regular tyrant. Whereas Zeangir's emotionality usurps reason's proper place in his actions (he is, after all, immature), Suleiman's faulty reason is forever sidetracking his good emotions. As Lessing shows in *Nathan der Weise* in the character of the Friar, if one's head is weak, then it is better to trust one's feelings and avoid excessive reasoning. Suleiman is too easily deceived by the unscrupulous Roxane and Rustan when they suggest that Mustapha is working to deprive him of his realm. Exactly opposite to Suleiman, Zeangir lets his heart correctly tell him that Mustapha's virtuous friendship is a dearer possession than succession to the throne, and he exclaims, "This young heart swells with a higher ambition,/ And friendship is worth more to me than throne and scepter" (I. iv). This is laudable, of course. But a greater use of reason might well have prevented Zeangir from believing in the friendship of the crafty Rustan.

In contrast to all these personages—good, bad, and worst—Mustapha is a man who combines a superior reasoning faculty with perfection of heart. He does not share Zeangir's view that Suleiman's wickedness has deprived him of his rights as a father: "In the battle of virtue,/ My friend, rash youth has conquered over your duty;/ But our heart does not release us from our duties,/ Even if the whole world did so—" (II. ii). Mustapha also does not share Zeangir's enthusiasm for action against the forces of evil, or his careless attitude toward death. He counsels, "Now quietly subject/ Yourself in the dust with me to the wise will of Providence!/ Whatever storms threaten the just man,/ He should neither take his own life nor fear death./ Heaven alone knows what things are profitable for us,/ I surrender myself to it, and it will protect me" (II. ii). Furthermore, his reason keeps him from being easily deceived. In spite of Zeangir's recommendation, Mustapha refuses to trust Rustan.

An interesting scene occurs when Mustapha and Suleiman discuss Mustapha's administration of an outlying province of the Turkish empire, from which position he has just been recalled to court. If, as Weisse's biographer has pointed out, Mustapha and Zeangir foreshadow the relationship between Schiller's Marquis Posa and Don Carlos,[30] then one can with equal justice say that Mustapha and Suleiman in this scene foreshadow the great interview in Schiller's play between Posa and King Philip of Spain. The question under discussion is the proper method of making good citizens out of people. Mustapha declares that he has ruled his province with charity and justice (i.e., rationally, or as God rules the earth): "I succored the poor, and I did not tolerate injustice;/ I always defended your rights and the law;/ Punished wickedness and supported innocence,/ Practiced justice with a hand free of bribes—" (II. iii). To the weakminded Suleiman such governing looks like treason, because it has not produced the illusory blessing of gold which came flowing in as long as his pashas controlled the province. Mustapha patiently points out that it is better to uphold the law than to acquire gold through accepting the bribes of wealthy miscreants. Suleiman, vainly trying to understand, supposes that his son's virtuous scruples were merely a hypocritical cover for his fear that harsh methods of raising money would get him in trouble. Mustapha need not have been afraid: "So, if they had accused you, I would have pretended to/ Punish you and would have secretly protected you:" (II. iii). This statement is a more pointed satire on corrupt royal practices than one customarily finds in Alexandrine tragedies of this period.[31] Unsentimentally, but in line with numerous other earlier tragedies, the blame for bad government is not put on dishonest ministers (as in Martini's *Rhynsolt und Sapphire*) but is laid squarely on the shoulders of the monarch himself. The specific nature of the bad government described—acceptance of bribes, preferential justice, confiscatory taxation, secret protection of dishonest officials—suggests that the author was not broaching the question academically, but was making references to conditions in contemporary Europe. To be sure, it is the misuse of absolutism, not the institution itself, which comes under fire; and the abuses mentioned are just as common in republics as in kingdoms. Mustapha goes on to state that his just rule produced tangible good effects of more lasting value than immediate revenue: "Tired of everlasting turmoil, discord fell asleep,/ Calm reigned within, and outside there was proud peace,/ The Persians feared you, who otherwise planned on unrest,/ And your subjects carried out your commands with pleasure" (II. iii). No monarch has to be jealous of his deputies when they win the affection of their subjects, for the virtue of the deputies only redounds to the fame of the monarch. To illustrate this point, the author uses a comparison that also underlies Barthold Brockes' collection of poetry, *Irdisches Vergnügen in Gott* (first volume, 1721), and has Mustapha say, "Thus one praises in the creature which is adorned with charm and beauty/ The Creator, who imprinted therein His divine image—" (II. iii). It is a thought that was used again by Lessing in *Emilia Galotti* (I. iv) and by Schiller in *Kabale und Liebe* (I. iii). It is a somewhat jarring note, however, that the fine sentiments expressed by Mustapha on the subject of government do not include a high opinion of common people. When Suleiman suspiciously asks why the populace cheered Mustapha so exuberantly on his entry into the capital, Mustapha replies contemptuously: "You know the silly people: they choose without virtue/ On the basis of delusion and caprice, and often love youth,/ Change, novelty!" (II. iii). This is, of course, only the Enlightened philosopher's usual condescending, schoolmasterish attitude toward the irrational, as yet unperfected mob. But Mustapha's words sound harsh to those familiar with the idealistic view of humanity expressed by Schiller's Marquis Posa.

Even though Mustapha cannot bring his father to make an open confession that a just method of governing is better than a tyrannical one, still he does succeed (like Marquis Posa with King Philip) in awakening the old ruffian to a more kindly paternal feeling toward himself. The sultan is puzzled by his new feelings; then, thanks to Roxane, his deficient reasoning power comes to the conclusion that kindliness is only weakness: "Will I in eternity wrestle with this weakness?/ No, no, the sultan shall still conquer the father in me" (II. vi). Zeangir now advises Mustapha to flee with his wife and child. Flight is, he says "What reason commands" (III. ii). It will be

remembered that Grimm's Banise resorted to flight as the last virtuous means left to her, and she considered it necessary so that her
final submission to execution would not have the earmarks of suicide. But Weisse is disposed to regard Zeangir's advice as emotional.
Therefore he lets Mustapha counter with the argument that Suleiman's wrath cannot be evaded through flight. This is a case where
mortal man is powerless and must, in a wholly passive manner, entrust his fate altogether to the benevolence of Providence. Virtue
here results in complete immobility. Zeangir still feels that Providence is obligated to protect the well-being of good persons: "Alas!
can Heaven indeed, can it hate innocence,/ And abandon it to be a
prey for evil?" (III. ii). This, of course, is a crucial question and
one that Weisse was not always able to answer convincingly in
his earlier tragedies. But here Mustapha begs the question by professing a faith in God which is not dependent on temporal happiness and reward: "Friend, what He does is always done right,/ The
pious man worships Him also when suffering./ . . . and if fate's
fury casts me/ To the ground: oh, then believe He means it well
with us—/ Nothing will be lacking for my happiness, and nothing
for yours!" (III. ii). Thereupon he relates at length a splendid
dream he has had about Paradise, where he finds his wife and child,
and also his friend Zeangir, in indescribable bliss. This dream represents the most determined effort in any German tragedy of the
period to give a tangible quality to the intangibility of virtue's reward after death. Through it one is meant to understand that
Mustapha's passivity is not a matter of emotional fanaticism; it only
stands to reason that he should be calm and patient about what may
happen to him on earth if death means entry into such a marvelously
furnished heaven. After this we would be ready to let him die without guilt, and still we would feel no bitterness against Providence.
But Weisse now arranges for a tragic guilt that leads directly to
the catastrophe. It was what Gottsched had also done in his *Cato*.

Mustapha, fearless for himself, does feel the conventional concern for those near and dear to him. His love for his wife Fatime, it
is made clear, is of the spiritual Klopstockian variety that super-
seded the earlier "rational love" and was to become the prevailing
love ideal of the Storm and Stress. Fatime says that her death will
be unimportant, because the world ". . . has women enough to fill
your harem—"; and Mustapha answers, "But not my heart!—enough!
to still the thirst of lust,/ But no Fatimes—" (III. iii). He weeps
when bidding farewell to wife and child, but does not want his
tears misconstrued as a sign of cowardice. They are at once the
sign of a feeling heart and also a heaven-sent refreshment to such a

heart: "Nature! when your feeling speaks in our soul,/ Then we struggle in vain, and tears become a duty!/ Heaven's highest favor! In this life of misery/ It has given us unfortunate ones this one happiness!" (III. v). These lines indicate that Mustapha, although a rationalist, is not an extremist who ruthlessly exterminates all emotion. Nevertheless, it is through his feeling for Fatime that Mustapha is induced to commit the one nonvirtuous act that directly results in his downfall.

A diabolical plot hatched by Roxane and Rustan arranges that Fatime shall be condemned to execution in place of Mustapha. Rustan counts on this to have a devastating effect on Zeangir, who will then easily be duped into persuading Mustapha to write a compromising letter to the hostile king of Persia, in which Mustapha will state that he does not love Fatime, but wants to marry the Persian princess. Rustan convinces Zeangir that when Suleiman sees this, he will conclude that the execution of Fatime will mean nothing to Mustapha, and therefore cancel it. But Rustan fails to add that Suleiman will also accuse Mustapha of having entered into treasonable negotiations with Persia. Zeangir, in the foolish belief that Rustan is sincerely trying to help, goes to Mustapha with the proposed letter. Mustapha at once disapproves of the deceit involved: "Duty advises me against it!" and Zeangir replies: "Duty? Innocence beseeches with outstretched arms:/ Is it not a duty to take pity on innocence?" Mustapha still demurs: "But not to trick my father deceitfully—" Finally, with much reluctance, Mustapha agrees to copy the letter for Fatime's sake: "What an effort it costs to commit a vice!" The similarity of his situation to that of Luise in Schiller's *Kabale und Liebe* is unmistakable. But Mustapha is plagued by a greater sense of guilt: "Wretched lines—Woe! do not be on my grave/ The monument of the disgrace which I have earned!" (IV. vii). Thus Mustapha acts against reason and virtue, and a tragic guilt is established for him, although it scarcely detracts from his perfection of character that he follows his heart in this matter. Before long he realizes that the letter, while it may save Fatime, will surely cause his own death. But he accepts this fact joyfully: "Misfortune—is the good fortune of the wise and the good!/ They may bleed undeservedly from its blows,/ But it cleanses and purifies them here for immortality:/ . . . Let it become night around me; within me everything is light:—/ Let them fell the tree now, then tomorrow it will not waver" (IV. ix). At this juncture Mustapha has nearly attained the sublimity of Wieland's Lady Jane, whose role as a tragic character is in all respects parallel to his. The phrase, "within me everything is light," is by far the most affecting one in the whole play; it recalls to mind the words of Faust when at the end of his life he has been blinded by Care: "The night seems to penetrate ever more deeply,/ but within there gleams bright light:".[32]

As soon as Suleiman's slaves have mortally wounded Mustapha, Suleiman discovers another letter in which Mustapha assures Fatime that he loves her and admits that it was a shameful thing to deceive Suleiman, as Rustan suggested he do. Belatedly, Suleiman recognizes what he has lost in Mustapha and he feels desperate remorse for his stupidity and wickedness. Rustan must suffer death for his treachery, but Roxane is still clever enough to join in the accusation of her accomplice and thus save herself from Suleiman's anger. Oddly enough, she attributes this maneuver to the aid of Providence: "Heaven inspired me with this fortunate decision!" (V. vi). Her just punishment, however, comes from another quarter. Zeangir foils her ambition to be the mother of a sultan by committing suicide before her eyes: "To take vengeance/ On my own life for your crime, which I may not punish" (V. vii). This suicide fits in logically enough with Zeangir's impulsive, emotional nature. His mentor Mustapha would never have approved of it. There is, on the other hand, some doubt about the author's moral attitude toward it. Although he triumphantly upholds the strict principles of reason and virtue, he also seems prone to excuse and glorify those of his characters who impulsively take their own lives. One cannot therefore call Weisse a consistent and dependable tragic moralist.

Also written in 1761, in the latter part of the year, was *Rosemunde*, which was published together with *Mustapha und Zeangir* in the second volume of the *Beytrag zum deutschen Theater* (1763). *Rosemunde* was Weisse's last Alexandrine tragedy. It is a strange work, badly constructed and confusing, yet full of compelling passion. It uses far too much the exasperating device of having the characters pledge one another to silence on certain matters, so that the action depends to a great extent on needless misunderstandings. Still, the characters themselves, especially the two women, are powerfully drawn, and they express themselves so vehemently that it is impossible not to be impressed. In his search for striking subject matter Weisse went fairly far afield this time, to the history of the Lombard kingdom in northern Italy in the sixth century A.D. The event he seized upon was grim and unnatural, and provided an opportunity to portray not just one, but two *Machtweiber*. The tragedy is unique for its time in that it has only four characters in spite of its full length of five acts.[33] This small cast—a feature that accounts for the term "simplicity" used by Schmid in connection with *Rosemunde*—and the horror of its plot inhibited the success of the play on the stage, although it was given at various times and places.[34] Actually the play is not simple, but quite complicated. The relationships between the four characters are involved enough for twice as great a number.

Most vicious of all is the titular heroine Rosamund, who, with the help of her present husband Hellmich, killed her first husband, the Lombard king Alboin. This was an act of revenge on the part of Rosamund, for Alboin had previously slain her father and stolen his kingdom. Now the chain of revenge lengthens itself, for Rosamund's daughter Albissvinth wishes to slay Hellmich. Albissvinth also suspects that her mother is not innocent, and that she put Hellmich up to the murder of Alboin. A further complication arises from the fact that Rosamund is no longer in love with Hellmich, being madly attracted to Longinus, the Exarch of Ravenna. Longinus, however, is in love with Albissvinth, and she with him. Only for her sake has Longinus given Rosamund and Hellmich refuge in Ravenna after the murder of Alboin has roused the Lombards against them. Albissvinth urges Longinus to slay Hellmich, but Longinus is bound by the pledge of protection which he gave to all three fugitives. This already hopeless entanglement is made worse because everyone concerned is withholding something from someone else. First, Rosamund forbids her daughter, on pain of death, to love Longinus, but she does not explain that she, Rosamund, is in love with him. Then Albissvinth makes Longinus swear not to tell Rosamund that he wants to marry Albissvinth, but she does not explain why. Next, Rosamund, to test Longinus, makes Hellmich offer Albissvinth to Longinus in marriage. Longinus refuses the offer, without explaining why. But Hellmich suspects that Longinus loves Rosamund instead, and is foolish enough to tell this to Rosamund. Thereupon Rosamund has an interview with Longinus and misunderstands his evasive speeches to mean that he loves her as she does him. Now she plans to do away with Hellmich. By pretending that she now feels remorse for the murder of Alboin and wants to take vengeance for it, she persuades Albissvinth to attack Hellmich. But before she has time to act, Albissvinth is told by Longinus that Rosamund loves him, and that is the reason she wants to get rid of Hellmich. Finally Albissvinth is convinced that her mother is betraying her, and she goes to Rosamund to dissuade her from wanting to kill Hellmich. Albissvinth, however, does not explain why her mind is changed. Furious, Rosamund chases her daughter away with a dagger. When Hellmich comes to Rosamund, she hypocritically tells him that she has just foiled a plan of Albissvinth to kill him. While Hellmich is thanking Rosamund, she gives him a poisoned drink. Before he dies he has time enough to compel Rosamund to drink also, at dagger point. With her last strength Rosamund tries to kill Albissvinth, but the attempt fails, and Longinus and Albissvinth are left to live together in peace. Certainly this plot offers the ultimate in complications, lies, and deceptions, and the four players change their positions like the last few pieces on a chessboard.

Nevertheless, the author's basic intention comes through clearly. He wished to examine the problem of revenge, and to condemn revenge in good Enlightened fashion. Thereby he created what is in many respects the first character in German tragedy who undergoes a genuine soul struggle and emerges at the end of the play a better and wiser person, after having come very near to moral shipwreck—this is Albissvinth. It might be said that Kiosem in Krüger's *Mahommed IV* also ends the play as a better and wiser woman, but she undergoes no struggle. From a coldly wicked criminal she is turned into a repentant sinner by the power of sentiment. Albissvinth is not saved by such a sudden conversion coming from the outside. Like Schiller's Lady Milford, her virtue is a developing flower that finally bursts a confining and restraining layer of vice. Albissvinth breaks with tradition in being neither a wholly virtuous nor a wholly vicious person, nor a sweet Miss Sara with one blot on her escutcheon. Perhaps her closest predecessor would be the Clorinde in Cronegk's *Olint und Sophronia*, whose rough virtue, thanks to the influence of Sophronia's "Christianity," finally shines through her formidable exterior.[35] Albissvinth is a confused person who does not know how to deal with the circumstances in which she is placed. Without abandoning herself to an amoral code she is determined to satisfy her natural desire to avenge the death of her father. Her nature is too active to accept the properly quiet attitude of passivity toward the misfortunes and injustices of the world. She says to herself, "Bewildered and full of terrors,/ Not knowing what I should do and what I should fear!—/ Does destiny always beset untested youth,/ And has it no consolation for me beyond my virtue?" (I. ii).[36] Toward her mother she evinces painfully mixed feelings of anger and affection which express themselves in tones of hurt and outrage: "—Oh, that duty commands/ Me to be obedient to you!" (I. i). Like any normal tragic heroine she can claim that she hates a man (Longinus, because he does not avenge her father) while she actually loves him. But she has progressive, nonrationalistic ideas about love. When Rosamund tells her to forget Longinus, she cries, "Am I ordered what to feel? Is coldness my duty?" (I. i).

In contrast to Albissvinth, Longinus is a man of proved and settled virtue, whose emotions are ruled by reason. Furthermore, he is the dullest of the four characters. As a ruler he would have a legitimate right to punish Hellmich for the murder of Alboin, and he mentions no scruples against such punishment. But he has given his word to protect Hellmich and Rosamund, and it would be altogether against virtue to go back on this promise. If the more legitimate way of taking revenge on Hellmich through Longinus is closed, still Albissvinth is by no means ready to submit and endure the situation passively. When Heaven remains deaf to the pleas of outraged justice it is time, she feels, for the individual to act on his own: "I will no longer burden Heaven with my complaints:/ I myself will equip my weak arm with revenge!/. . . . I must avenge myself, I, if Heaven will not avenge me" (I. iii). It can be seen here that Weisse has made a further step in the development of the self-reliant character. Fausta in *Krispus* relied on herself but had strictly evil intentions. Now Albissvinth relies on herself, having an intent with which one can sympathize. To be sure, it is evil to usurp the prerogatives of God and of legal authorities. Accordingly Albissvinth is not technically virtuous; she is on the threshold of a great sin. But she remains basically a good character. Unlike the older days of German tragedy when Behrmann's Timoleon and Quistorp's Aurelius and Grimm's Balacin (in *Banise*) had been permitted to take virtuous actions of a very drastic kind, tragic characters had become passive. As a result, when Weisse brings back action to virtuous (or sympathetic) characters, such action has to be viewed as unvirtuous and erroneous. Lessing's Odoardo Galotti still has to struggle hopelessly with the problem of action versus inaction, and even Schiller was unable to depict a case of really virtuous, self-reliant action until the last act of *Die Jungfrau von Orleans* and in *Wilhelm Tell*.

Weisse unmistakably has strong sympathy for the nonpassive feelings of Albissvinth. He is always too rationalistic, however, to condone such feelings. Like the typical Storm and Stress playwright, he delights in giving vent to his innermost feelings, but always comes round and judges them in the end. Through Longinus the coolheaded arguments of reason are brought to bear on the matter. First Longinus points out how revenge only begets more revenge: if Albissvinth killed Hellmich, then Rosamund would kill Albissvinth, and then Longinus would kill Rosamund. Although properly horrified, Albissvinth insists that if Heaven will not act, she must. But Longinus argues that Heaven will eventually move: "It will do it, it will remember your rights!/ What it lent crime, it will give innocence" (I. iii). Albissvinth no longer trusts Providence to that extent. Time grows long, and Providence forgets. Longinus reminds her that God has a different view of time: "He, who measures/ Eternities with a nod, from the beginning of time/ Weighed out punishment and reward faithfully for all deeds,/ And never yet cheated a rascal out of his deserts,/ He will not overlook it:—" (I. iii). Unable to refute these statements, Albissvinth still grumbles, "All right! then I must be silent,/ And, crawling, bend myself to the yoke of my father's murderer" (I. iii).

It is not surprising that Albissvinth cannot resist the temptation when Rosamund unexpectedly enlists her aid in a plan to slay Hellmich. Rosamund falsely expresses remorse and declares she will weep for forgiveness. Touchingly ready to love her mother again, if possible, Albissvinth answers, "Do this! and then I will find my mother in you again" (IV. ii). As Rosamund unfolds her strategy for murdering Hellmich, Albissvinth has to struggle with repugnance and with the humane feelings natural to her heart. In this respect she resembles Richard III, and yet the effect made by her conflict with herself is not that of a diabolical mind which stifles all good feelings, but of a misguided personality, which for the sake of what it considers to be a duty assumes a task altogether unsuited to itself. We feel sorry for Albissvinth—and frightened by Richard. Albissvinth sighs, "Ah! my too tender heart is repelled by blood and death!/ But the loud command of revenge lifts this arm:/ It drowns out in me the gentle voice of humanity/ And arms weakness itself with not ignoble wrath" (IV. ii). Pathos is gained in this situation because one knows that this high-spirited, honest girl is being shamefully deceived by her unspeakable mother. When she sees Longinus again, Albissvinth defends her intention fanatically: "No, whoever does not blaze with revenge is a barbarian" (IV. iv). When Longinus reveals how she is being deceived and used by Rosamund, Albissvinth is stunned and deeply shaken. But at least her heart is now opened and no longer resists the voice of reason that tells her to leave revenge to Heaven. Longinus even succeeds in persuading her to try to prevent Rosamund from killing Hellmich. Thus, when Rosamund comes back, full of enthusiasm about the murder and all prepared with a dagger in one hand and a cup of poison in the other, she finds a changed Albissvinth.[37] The daughter accuses the mother of having inveigled Hellmich into killing Alboin; then she hints that Rosamund is in love with Longinus. This is too much for Rosamund, who grows furious and chases Albissvinth from the stage with a dagger. The deaths of Hellmich and Rosamund take place, as related above, without the cooperation of

Albissvinth. The daughter gains much sympathy when, on returning to find her mother in the throes of death, she manifests loving concern instead of indulging in self-righteous vituperation. Rosamund's unmaternal reaction is to try to stab Albissvinth, but the blow glances off the girl's clothing. Albissvinth shows that she now understands the role of Providence in her life: "This garment, no, God has still protected me" (V. iv). The tragedy has a thoroughly satisfactory conclusion, exceptional for Weisse. The wicked are punished, the good live happily ever after, and Providence is vindicated.

Inasmuch as the character of Albissvinth is the one that is most carefully portrayed, one might say that she, rather than the titular heroine Rosamund, is the chief protagonist in the drama. Weisse's preoccupation with the evil hero has passed its zenith and evil begins to be relegated to a somewhat inferior position. Rosamund, for all her blazing dynamism, does not possess the sovereign freedom of action which made Richard III and Fausta perversely attractive. She does not challenge God with a rebellious amoral code, nor does she glory in self-reliance. At one point she refers to her dagger and her poison as means of liberation from oppressive chains, and these weapons fill her with a reckless sense of power: "—Oh, how often have I laughed at mortals!—/ Few of them yet know their entire power!/ How many could raise themselves out of the dust,/ But they continue to creep in the dust, they creep because they live,/ And live because, like insects, they are forgotten,/ In death one cannot use them, and, living, one never misses them" (V. i). The exclamations are in the vein of Richard and Fausta, but with a difference: Rosamund emphasizes the physical means of getting one's own way, whereas the other two emphasized the free spirit of the individual which makes him able to use the means. In her dying, Rosamund is definitely not free. She drinks poison only because Hellmich forces her to do it, and then she suffers tormenting visions that make her cry out for pity and help. Though violently horrific, her death lacks the splendid defiance of Richard's and Fausta's, and she is thoroughly beaten at the end. All in all, Rosamund is less an evil rationalist (not once does she refer to "intelligence") than a woman ruled entirely by blind impulses. Longinus attributes her wickedness to her heart, not to any false ideas she has nurtured: "The heart of a human being, O God! what misery it can cause!" (V. iv). Instead of being diabolical she is merely depraved and disgusting, and entirely without dignity. The passions of revenge and of love have ruined her.

Rosemunde does not suffer much from the smallness of its cast, since up until this time Weisse had really been able to create only five character types of significance, and all but one (the stern but stupid father, e.g., Constantine in *Krispus* and Suleiman in *Mustapha und Zeangir*) are represented in this play. The titular heroine is a relative of Mortimer, Richard, Fausta, and Roxane, while Albissvinth descends from Elizabeth, Helena, and Zeangir, with the admixture of some lively genes from Fausta. Hellmich is the weak accomplice type who rues his crimes, and his predecessors are Isabella in *Eduard III* and Catesby in *Richard III*. Longinus, the rather inactive man of perfect virtue, is a reflection of Edward III, Crispus, and Mustapha. Weisse was as yet unable to portray a *good* but nevertheless dynamically interesting male character. He had brought remarkable brilliance to the last period of the Alexandrine tragedy, and he had relieved this style of stiltedness as no other German dramatist had succeeded in doing. But as long as he wrote Alexandrine tragedies he was unable to stop repeating the same situations and using the same set of characters. Perhaps in realization of this, he paused for a few years before returning to the production of tragedies.[38]

Die Befreiung von Theben, which was published in 1764 in the third volume of the *Beytrag zum deutschen Theater,* is so startlingly different from Weisse's earlier tragedies that one might believe at first it had been written by another author living in another epoch. The most obvious innovation is the use of blank verse, the lines all ending in strong, masculine syllables. Since Brawe's *Brutus* had not yet been published, *Die Befreiung von Theben* was only the second tragedy in blank verse to be presented to the German public, fully six years after Wieland's pioneering *Lady Johanna Gray*. German troupe principals, however, must have feared the new meter, for there is no record that Weisse's play was produced. The blank verse is, as it were, only an external symbol of the wholly new quality of *Die Befreiung von Theben*. Suddenly Weisse seems to have discovered what the English dramatists had always known about the stage: that it is not a place in itself, where actors come to impersonate various characters and speak lines to an audience, but a magic window on the world through which the audience may see apparently real people of any time and place reliving an action in a natural, convincing manner. Not since Gottsched's *Parisische Bluthochzeit* has one so successfully been made aware of the environment beyond the visible scene as in this play. Weisse has also unexpectedly, and temporarily, lost his fascination with the depiction of evil. The play breathes a new mood that one would be at a loss to account for, except that Weisse had already expressed it earlier, not in drama, but in lyric poetry, in his very popular *Amazonenlieder*

(1760–1763). These were full of ecstatic, heroic patriotism engendered by the tumult and excitement of the Seven Years War, and were an imitation of Gleim's better-known *Preußische Kriegslieder von einem Grenadier* (1758–1759). Weisse's "Amazon" experienced war mainly through the adventures and exploits of her heroic lover; and although she gave voice to the feelings of her author's own times, Weisse carefully refrained from identifying her with any particular country or particular war.[39] Similarly, his generalized enthusiasm for heroic patriotism could find an outlet in this drama drawn from ancient Greek history (and supplied with many fictional additions). *Die Befreiung von Theben* recounts the story of the patriotic conspirators in Thebes who masqueraded as female entertainers to gain entry into the banquet hall where the tyrannical Spartan rulers of the town were carousing, and then threw off their disguises to murder the surprised revelers. Instead of Weisse's usual evil monster, weak accomplice, passively virtuous youth, and defiant maiden, this play presents some new characters: a rational, mature patriot, a young, irrational enthusiast, a timid matron who puts family before country, and a young "Amazon." All of these have their counterparts, it is true, in older Alexandrine tragedy, but not in Weisse's works; and he succeeds in giving them an individuality that makes them appear the opposite of hackneyed. The element of evil is kept impersonal until near the end, when it is embodied in the character of the chief Spartan, Archias. He has little chance to do anything, however: the whole emphasis is on the actions of the sympathetic personages. The tensions that arise are not between virtue and vice but, as Fritz Brüggemann points out,[40] between various attitudes among the good characters toward the common problem of overthrowing the tyranny. Furthermore, the tensions are most pronounced within the bosom of the family of Charon, the leader of the conspiracy, so that the play takes on some of the aspects of a middle-class drama.

Die Befreiung von Theben shunts to one side the old, constantly reiterated question of German eighteenth-century tragedy: will Providence protect and reward the virtuous? Instead it gives the stage a new question, a timely one with regard to the period of Storm and Stress soon to dawn: is the old, rational generation right or is the young, emotional generation right about the best method of bringing virtue and justice into the world? More strongly than in any earlier tragedy the dichotomy between heart and reason, viewed as a critical difference in orientation between two generations, comes to expression in this play. For the first time the author effects no compromise between heart and reason. In the end it would seem that the young, thoughtless but enthusiastic generation has the advantage over, and even the plaudits of its elders. Weisse's new tragedy also makes the nonpassive assumption that rebellion against tyrannical usurpers is unquestionably virtuous. This is not particularly surprising, however, because in both *Eduard III* and in *Richard III* the use of force against the usurpers was approved as a matter of course. Passivity, wherever it has been lauded in Weisse's tragedies or in others, has always been demonstrated in regard to legitimate (although wicked) rulers or in regard to the actions of an individual, not those of a duly constituted group. Consequently the willingness of the conspirators in this play, whether young or mature, to take positive action cannot well be construed as a break with the law of passivity (*Gelassenheit*). It had never been considered virtuous for able-bodied men to assume a foreign yoke without murmur or resistance.

It was, accordingly, unnecessary to do more than to state briefly at the beginning that Thebes has lost its freedom as a result of trickery on the part of Sparta. There was no point in devoting a great deal of time to the explanation of the conspirators' motives, as Lessing did in *Henzi,* where the conspiracy was against a legitimate and longstanding government. The only dissenting voice that is heard, as far as the conspiracy is concerned, is that of Charon's wife Arete, whose objection is not idealistic but unheroically practical. The conjugal altercation is carried on with little regard for the dignity of tragic diction. Charon speaks to his wife rudely, using everyday phraseology: "As if you were wiser than I!—Do you know/ That your chatter will soon offend me?" (I. ii).[41] Arete is perhaps the first wholly unphilosophical personage to appear in German tragedy of the eighteenth century. She is neither a rationalist nor a sentimentalist, nor a fool, nor an amoral villain. She acts altogether from natural wifely and maternal instincts. Fear for her loved ones, not passivity as a principle, dictates her aversion to rebellion. She has little understanding of the gods, and little confidence in them—not because her theory of life is hostile to the gods, but because in her naive perspective the world outside her own home is generally a puzzle and an unknown peril. Though common in real life, the presence of such a naive character in a tragedy is a genuine innovation, and an important indication of Weisse's efforts toward greater realism. Her fears about the conspiracy may well have been suggested by those of Portia in Shakespeare's *Julius Caesar,* as Minor pointed out,[42] but her personality seems to have been drawn from observation of real life. Hedwig, Tell's wife in Schiller's drama, has much in common with Arete.

Charon puts idealistic patriotism far above natural family emotions. He conceives of liberty and fatherland as a heightened form of the family emotions: "O freedom, you,/ And you! my fatherland! who encompass/ All love and tenderness for citizen, friend,/ And wife and child!" (I. iii). This is not a sentimental outburst, for it takes reason to comprehend such a thought, and Charon is an eminently rational man. In fact, his rationality is greater than that of his co-conspirators. One of these, the historically famous Pelopidas, reflects too little on the dangers of the enterprise; another, the famous Epaminondas, reflects too much. His concern for the danger, and his concern for the preservation of a humane behavior toward the enemy (*Menschlichkeit*) as well, make Epaminondas appear fretful and unfit for action. A more responsible author than Weisse would surely have avoided this impression, for the principle of humane action was one of the very most important and progressive tenets of the Enlightenment. Weisse, however, lets Epaminondas phrase the concept of humanity in such a way that it sounds more like a feeble reminder than a vigorous purpose: "But friend, let/ Humanity still ever weep a gentle tear/ Into the blood of the tyrants: this/ Will wash our hands clean before posterity/ That neither pride, nor greed, nor private revenge/ Directed our swords: that freedom alone/ Was the soul of this deed and the armor/ Of our sacred city and our noble-mindedness" (I. iv). This speech is entirely in the spirit of Lessing's *Henzi* and of Behrmann's *Timoleon*; however, the answer of Pelopidas assigns humanity only an honorary role in matters concerning liberty and fatherland: "Humanity . . . / . . . Will lend sobriety to our rage,/ If revenge and anger intoxicate it too much" (I. iv). The actions of a third conspirator, Phillidas, offer an affront to absolute morality and reduce this play to the level of the early *Ulysses* of Ludwig.[43] Phillidas has been posing as the friend and comrade of the Spartan rulers, and is at present holding a prolonged feast for them at which they are becoming so carelessly drunken that they will be an easy prey. Wilful deception, hateful to rationalist and sentimentalist alike, and distasteful even to wicked personages, is here accepted without question. That Phillidas has sacrificed his reputation (the Thebans hate him as a quisling) is of no consequence, for the Enlightenment taught that one's own conscience, not the opinion of outsiders, is the deciding factor. But that he poses as a friend, when he is actually an enemy, can scarcely be condoned. In addition to this, all the conspirators, Charon not excepted, agree to Phillidas' plan that they should disguise themselves as women and gain entry to the banquet hall on the pretext of willingness to submit to the lusts of the Spartan revelers. Only one moral value is too sacred to be sacrificed at the altar of patriotism, and that is feminine sexual virtue: the other conspirators are outraged as long as they misunderstand Phillidas to be demanding genuine Theban virgins for the entertainment of the Spartans. In comparison, it is noteworthy that in Schiller's *Kabale und Liebe* Luise Miller consents to fraud in order to save her father, but will not go so far as to sacrifice her virginity to the lusts of the duke.

The cunning plans of the conspirators are based on cool-headed "intelligence" (*Klugheit*), that faculty which in Weisse's earlier dramas only the evil characters had boasted of. On the other hand, Callicrates, the ephebic son of Charon, is altogether directed by his heart. On his way past the palace where the Spartans are feasting he has overheard their scornful references to Theban impotence. Without a moment's reflection Callicrates dashed inside and offered to challenge the Spartans on the spot. Obviously this could only have resulted in his annihilation; but fortunately the guards chased him away contemptuously. Since he judges by appearances alone, Callicrates despises Phillidas, the supposed quisling. Charon treats him like a child, for in the Enlightened sense he is still childish, that is to say, a person without matured rational faculties. His mother Arete points out the great might of Sparta, the improbability of its overthrow by an enslaved people. His answer to this is not reasoned, like the plan of the conspirators, but enthusiastic and irrational: "A free arm is worth a hundred arms/ Which draw their swords for tyranny,/ So long as courage and fatherland inspire it" (II. ii). He believes that the gods are on his side because he is virtuous. If he must die nevertheless, "Oh, then one dies for one's fatherland!/ Is there anywhere a more beautiful death?" (II. ii). Callicrates was doubtless modeled on Lessing's Philotas; but unlike Lessing, Weisse was unable to keep himself from being swept away in admiration for his own young hero.

The "Amazon" beloved by this brave youth is the beautiful and courageous Aspasia. Although not entirely unrelated to the character type represented in Weisse's earlier dramas by Elizabeth, Helena, and Albissvinth, she differs from them in occupying a wholly auxiliary position to the man she loves. All her fire and inspiration is taken from the stronger Callicrates. If she does eventually rise to great heights of independent action, it is only in emulation of her lover, with whose life her own life is intricately interwoven. Indeed, she remarkably adumbrates Thekla in Schiller's *Wallenstein* and, to a less striking extent, Klärchen in Goethe's *Egmont*. When Arete uses every argument at her command in order to persuade her son to leave Thebes and take refuge in Athens, inasmuch as his father has forbidden him to take any part in the conspiracy, Callicrates is much troubled in his mind. Like Schiller's Max Piccolomini, he turns to his sweetheart for her support and advice. Like Schiller's Thekla, Aspasia is torn between the wish to retain her lover and the knowledge that patriotic duty has a higher claim on him than she, and she exclaims, "Your life?—but is it without fame/ Still worthy of our concern?—You live for me: . . . / But only for me? —Ah! why do you make me/ Your judge!—My heart commands you to flee:/ But your fame, duty, and your choice . . . / Callicrates!—Alas! why do you ask me?—" (II. iv). As Thekla's decision in favor of duty strengthens Max Piccolomini, so Aspasia's integrity breathes renewed resolution into Callicrates: "Yes, love, now you are worthy of love!/ You expand my heart, you enflame my arm/ To do great deeds. Now I feel what I am!" (II. iv). Although grave rationalists might shake their heads, Weisse presents here a young hero unashamedly in love.[44] Love, however, does not weaken him for battle—quite the contrary. And his bravery and self-sacrifice are reflected equally in Aspasia, who determines that she will follow him to the grave, if need be: "So shall your grave, the grave of freedom, also/ Be my monument!" (II. iv). Thus Thekla, in Schiller's play, resolves to follow her lover into death. It is to be taken for granted that the devotion of this idealistic pair exists on an exaltedly spiritual plane.

In an interview between father and son, the naive enthusiasm of youth comes in for some stern rebukes. Charon says that Callicrates' rash entry of the palace may have endangered their whole conspiracy and adds, "Fortunate for you/ That desire for fame is your only defect!/ A defect nonetheless: it is mere rashness/ When our courage is not directed by intelligent foresight" (II. v). Though humbled by his father's remonstrances, Callicrates still has faith in his own procedures: "I wonder if my father spoke thus when he/ Was still a youth?—Ulysses was very intelligent,/ But Hector fell at the hand of Achilles" (II. v). But Charon's fears are borne out when Archias, the Spartan chief, becomes suspicious and summons Charon to appear before him. The bad news provokes a discussion about the role played by the gods in these events. Epaminondas says, "And the danger which surrounds us is great:/ But so is hope, if there are still gods/ Who avenge injustice, look graciously upon Thebes,/ And lend sufferers the protection they have pleaded for!" Arete takes little comfort from this, saying, "The gods are often deaf to our pleading!" Epaminondas reaffirms his faith in the proposition that virtue is protected and rewarded: "They are not deaf, if our pleading is just!/ Neither pride nor greed has formed our resolve./ We want only to liberate the fatherland,/ Pull violence and cruelty down from the throne,/ And raise justice upon it." Still skeptical, Arete asks, "And why did the gods not leave us/ Our freedom right away?" Like many a naively forthright query, this one is somewhat embarrassing. Epaminondas replies in the manner of an old-fashioned rationalist: "For punishment,/ Because we entrusted ourselves entirely to traitors." In other words, an error of judgment (as in Pitschel's *Darius*) merits severe chastisement. Pelopidas offers a more affirmative explanation: "For the testing of our courage!" (III. v).

Callicrates has no patience with his elders who are willing to wait for Charon's return from the palace. He rants, "Those wise men indeed!—an everlasting counseling/ How one is to act very shrewdly and intelligently,/ And nothing accomplished! . . . Ha! does one remove mountains,/ If one reflects for a long time, with which hand/ One is to begin, and moves neither one?" (IV. i). Ignoring his father's wishes, Callicrates decides to set himself at the head of the youths of Thebes. With them he will join a host of exiles waiting outside the city gates and storm the Spartan garrison. Aspasia, mindful of filial piety, at first tries to dissuade him, but then his enthusiasm carries her along and she agrees not to disclose his plan or his whereabouts. Her love is transfigured by his great bravery. She envisions him as an Olympic champion, the single-handed conqueror of the Spartan tyrants, and mere earthly domestic happiness fades to nothing in comparison to the glory of being associated with such magnificent heroics: "Aspasia! enviable,/ Blissful maiden! You! Oh, what fame!/ You are loved by Callicrates. . . ." (IV. iii). Spiritual love in this play does not enter heaven, but Valhalla.

Charon does return from the palace, bringing back with him, now that it is too late, a task for his son to perform. Archias has demanded Callicrates for a hostage; otherwise he will not believe the Thebans are not plotting against him. Finding Callicrates gone, Charon is outraged: "His disobedience is worthy of death!" (IV. iv). As in Heinrich von Kleist's *Prinz von Homburg* (1810), the issue raised here is that between obedience and initiative. Luckily, however, Aspasia is ready to step into the breach by offering herself as the hostage. Charon asks her, "Ah! what kind of god inspires you with this courage?" Her answer shows that her actions are quite emotional in origin: "The god of love, your son, my own heart!" (IV. iv). Aspasia is, however, more controlled than her lover. She states that Callicrates would not have been suited to the role of hostage, for he could not have refrained from defying the Spartans: "His first greeting at this feast would/ Certainly be a curse and his answer would be revilement!" (IV. iv).

The fifth act involves the change of scene to the festival hall of the Spartans which has been referred to so often beforehand. This is the boldest break with the Unities yet made by Weisse. In *Krispus*, when it was necessary to show the prison in the last act, he merely directed that the inner curtain should be raised—a frequent device in Alexandrine tragedies. There is no doubt that the complete change of scene is a great advantage to *Die Befreiung von Theben*, for after four acts of tense preparation in the room of a private house (strange setting for a heroic tragedy, but at least it is a house in ancient Greece), we would feel intolerably cheated not to witness the outcome, which takes place in a large and splendid hall. At last the evil adversary is revealed to our eyes—Archias, the chief Spartan. He is glad to accept Aspasia as a hostage when he sees her beauty, and he soon arranges to be alone with her. For this scene Weisse was well prepared by the scene in *Richard III* where Richard makes love to Elizabeth. Archias approaches Aspasia with tender, seductive words which she answers with proud, hard reproaches. He tells her, "The beauty which adorns you/ Excuses you: but do not forget/ That you are a hostage here, that now your person/ And life stand wholly in my hands." Aspasia's answer is that of the young prince in *Richard III:* "But not my soul: Wretch!—/ Oh! it despises you!" (V. iii). Yet she is cool enough to profit from Archias' increasing desire. As he embraces her she slyly draws a dagger and stabs him to death before he really gets his arms around her. What the passive Elizabeth in *Richard III* only half dared to plan, the intrepid Aspasia unreflectingly carries out. Immediately from outside there rises the cry that the other Spartan leaders have been done to death by Charon and the bogus "maidens" who came along with him and Aspasia to the banquet. Aspasia's deed stimulates the conspirators to high admiration; she becomes to them a divine symbol of the concept of freedom—the mood of 1789 is upon them.

Meanwhile it is discovered that outside the banquet hall there is little work left to do, for the Spartan garrison has already been defeated by Callicrates and his young men. Even the Theban women were caught up in the enthusiasm and fought beside them. Unfortunately the heroic Callicrates has received a mortal wound in the melee and is now brought on stage dying. Charon, forgetting his anger at his son's disobedience, and throwing all rationalistic considerations to the winds, could not possibly be prouder of Callicrates' accomplishments. Arete, as restricted and unpatriotic as ever, makes bitter reproaches to Charon; but he declares that if he had ten thousand sons he would gladly sacrifice them all to a death as glorious as this one. With Callicrates dead, it is Aspasia's turn to die. The inspiration of her lover's glorious self-sacrifice opens a heavenly vision to her: she sees Callicrates already in the company of deified heroes—he beckons toward her—and with rapture she plunges the knife into her breast, so that she may join him forever. Charon, as a reward for his maturity and rationality, is left on earth to mourn his loss and to take comfort in the liberty of Thebes; but the enthusiastic youthful generation wings its way from earth to the infinite joys of heaven. To speak of a tragic guilt in Callicrates (disobedience) which justifies his death would be wholly pedantic. The author evidently regards him as guiltless and admirable. But Weisse did have certain doubts, once the exhilaration of portraying the deed was over, about the propriety of Aspasia's suicide. He excused it lamely on historical grounds, saying that it did not contradict what might be expected of a heart nurtured on the Greek religion.[45]

It is hard to draw a moral conclusion from this drama. Who is right in the end, the rational people or the irrational ones? Both are virtuous, and both are successful; it is only their methods that differ. Perhaps Weisse meant to imply that there is after all no *one* best way, and that God uses both the maturely rational people and the enthusiastic young people, both men and women, as He also uses evil people (against their will) to further His benevolent but mysterious ends. Odd as it may seem, this play presents irrationality in a more favorable light than the most famous plays of the Storm and Stress. The final scene contains no wise indictment of the excesses of the heart. This is not a tragedy of error punished, or of tested virtue triumphant, or of gentle renunciation. It is an apotheosis of patriotism in action—an emotion that obviously thrilled the rather shallow thinking and philosophically unsteady Weisse—and one that the sober Lessing regarded with distrust because he feared its excesses.

The second and last of Weisse's tragedies in blank verse, before he turned to the middle-class prose tragedy, was *Atreus und Thyest*, published in 1766 in the fourth volume of the *Beytrag zum deutschen Theater*. Its première performance in Leipzig on January 28, 1767, marks the first opportunity given to an audience in Germany (as exclusive of Switzerland, where Wieland's *Lady Johanna Gray* had been performed some nine years earlier) to witness a play in blank verse.[46] The new metrical form was then introduced to Austria with the performance of Brawe's *Brutus* in Vienna on August 20, 1770. All of these attempts, however, proved abortive, and it was not blank verse but prose which finally drove the Alexandrine off

German stages. Nevertheless, *Atreus und Thyest* did not fail as a result of its new meter; performances of the drama were few because of the grimness of the theme.[47]

In this, the last in his series of heroic tragedies, Weisse returns to his old technique of featuring a dynamically evil character, as though the attraction exerted on him by such a figure were again too strong to resist. Atreus, the king of Mycenae, is another Richard III in that he cruelly murders two royal children. This inhuman deed, made unspeakably worse by the fact that the children's flesh and blood are served to their father Thyestes at a banquet, is nevertheless only a part of the exposition of the drama. Although Thyestes relates the occurrence with dramatic vividness and sentimentality (after the banquet he finds the remains of the children: "Here lay their heads: there their pairs of hands,/ Still folded, as if they pleaded for help" [II. iii][48]), it still belongs to the past, and we neither become acquainted with the children nor observe Atreus in action. The really strong and engaging action in the plot involves Thyestes, a good man with one serious moral transgression in his life history (like the father in Pfeil's *Lucie Woodvil*), and Aegisthus, Atreus' son, a virtuous youth torn between the demands of filial duty and the promptings of his own good heart (like Marcius in Brawe's *Brutus*). The role of Atreus, being well supplied with horrendous speeches, threats, and roars, adds much excitement and color to the tragedy, but the tragic outcome of the plot is only indirectly connected with the villainy of Atreus. The ancient Greek legend which Weisse treats in this tragedy has conditioned him to realize that the fate of a good man, a fate that he "deserves" because of a crime committed long ago, can be as impressive as the machinations of an evil man, or even more so. As a result, he has successfully combined the two main streams of prior tragic development: he has portrayed a forceful hero of virtue without sacrificing a forceful hero of evil—Atreus *and* Thyestes. These hostile brothers, equals in dynamic strength but opposites in personality, strikingly anticipate the famous hostile brothers of the Storm and Stress, those of Leisewitz' *Julius von Tarent*, of Klinger's *Die Zwillinge*, and, most of all, of Schiller's *Die Räuber*.

Weisse invests the well-known mythological history of the Pelopidae, a choice that betrays his inveterate taste for gruesomeness, with modern philosophical meaning. King Atreus is not only a cruel murderer and tyrant, but also something quite alien to the world of mythology: a scoffer at religion. He speaks contemptuously of the "superstition" that makes the people hold the high priest, his enemy, in respect; he considers the oracle at Delphi a venal fraud; and he regards the gods as cold-hearted: "But fortune is false. What else would/ The gods have for a plaything if it were not for man?" (II. v). He doubts that the anger of the gods is very effective. When Aegisthus reminds him that the world trembles at the gods' beckoning, Atreus answers defiantly and skeptically, "Let it tremble! did you see it fall in pieces/ When their wrath blew itself up into a storm?/ Did not the sea become calm again by itself after the tempest?" (I. iv). As with every evil rationalist, Atreus' intelligence is pressed into service to further the demands of his passions (hatred and revenge), and to stifle the warnings and misgivings that arise in his heart. When his passions grow so violent that they threaten to frustrate their own ends, he uses reason to get them under control: ". . . now the storm/ Of passion still rages all too much/ In my breast, so that I cannot come to a certain/ Conclusion:" (I. iv). Despite his monumental rages, he is rationally cool enough to put over deceptions: "Virtue shall lend me its mask" (III. iii). Like Mortimer in *Eduard III*, Atreus has made an accomplice of the woman he loves—his queen, Pelopia. She, like Isabella in that first play, conscientiously but vainly attempts to smother the promptings of her naturally good heart by applying her "intelligence" (*Klugheit*) and also, quite unequivocally stated, her "reason" (*Vernunft*). Aegisthus and Thyestes, on the other hand, listen to their hearts.

As in *Oedipus Rex*, the play's opening situation presents a city suffering from a pestilence whose cause is to be found in the guilt of its king. Atreus has deprived his brother Thyestes of his rightful share of the throne and exiled him. But that is not all. Taking inhuman vengeance for Thyestes' seduction of his first wife Aërope (who was Thyestes' love before she was forced to marry Atreus), Atreus is also guilty of having slain the two young sons of Thyestes and having fed them to their father at a banquet, as stated above. Nevertheless, the pestilence does not fill Atreus with religious awe, nor does he pity the citizens. When the priest tells him that even the sheep and cattle are dying, Atreus has a cynical rejoinder ready: "Then the people can/ Be much less afraid of death: now corpses/ Can batten on corpses!" (I. ii). Atreus only feels anger that he ever permitted his hated brother Thyestes to escape his clutches alive. If he could find Thyestes and slay him, then his troubles would be over. Aegisthus, the virtuous son of this misbegotten tyrant, now unknowingly fulfills Atreus' wicked wish. Having gone to Delphi, where he has received an oracle to the effect that the curse will be lifted from Mycenae as soon as the two brothers are reconciled with blood, Aegisthus has met Thyestes there. In obedience to what he believes the oracle to mean, Aegisthus has brought his uncle back to Mycenae.

Cunning as well as force was required to accomplish this, but Aegisthus (apparently with the author's approval) feels no pangs of conscience: "No, he was abducted through force and cunning!/ The divine word seemed too clear/ For me to let him escape/ To our downfall" (I. iii).

In spite of this act of violence, Aegisthus feels strangely drawn to Thyestes, and he is dismayed when he learns that Atreus intends to destroy him. Aegisthus' heart has been strongly affected by the "good old man" image projected by Thyestes: "My heart floats deep in sorrow, tears/ Rise to my eyes, even against my will!—/ His trembling head! his silvery hair,/ His wretchedness, his prayer, his pleading!—he called/ Me son!—Why did the name seem/ So sweet to me in his mouth?" (I. v). Yet duty, the obligation owed to the commands of a father, persuades Aegisthus to fight down his good feelings: "A labyrinth! my father—yes, duty/ Towards him teaches me obedience: away, nature!/ Your womanish pity . . ." (I. v). Of course, the man for whom the youth feels affection turns out to be his real father, eventually. Aegisthus' heart-inspired virtue is endangered because of a mental confusion for which he cannot really be blamed, and it is doubtful whether even cool reason could help him very much in such a situation. Certainly his mother's counsel does not aid him. She chides him for harboring womanish feelings and charges him to obey Atreus: "And do not believe that you can choose/ When duty teaches you blind obedience" (II. i). In a similar situation, Schiller's Max Piccolomini refuses to let authority override his personal (and categorical) idealism; but Aegisthus accepts his mother's advice and lets responsibility rest with his king and father.

It soon develops, however, that Queen Pelopia is not so unfeeling as she would pretend to be. She speaks of a recent dream, one that modern psychology might term extremely apt: "My father lay in my arms like a lover/ And wept aloud; the thunder rumbled/ Round about, and before I knew what was happening, a dagger/ Entered my heart" (II. ii). At first sight of Thyestes, she is astonished to see that he has the face of the "father" in her dream. Then she is unable to withhold her tears when Thyestes relates the horrid murder of his infant sons. She says in an aside: "You poor old man! how much I pity you!" (II. iii). As Aegisthus was drawn to Thyestes, so is Pelopia. It is the *"cri du sang"* motif of French eighteenth-century literature, and there is nothing rationalistic about it. Weisse's adoption of it is a further indication of his growing interest in the cult of the heart, with its emphasis on mysteriously intuitive "dark feelings." The intuitions of Pelopia and Aegisthus prepare for the eventual revelation of their all-too-close relationship to Thyestes, but the secret itself is kept until near the end. Lessing spoke out strongly in his *Dramaturgie* against the practice of leaving identities unknown to the audience for the purpose of a surprise ending.[49] German authors, in all fairness, seldom did this; and Lessing's criticism was directed toward French tragedies, in particular Voltaire's *Mérope*. Weisse could have taken it as a criticism directed against this play of his also. It is not to be denied, however, that the delayed revelation causes a strong dramatic effect.

The first high point of the drama comes when Atreus and Thyestes confront each other after many years of inimical separation. Atreus has himself under rational control, not with the purpose of overcoming his rage, but of using it with maximum effectiveness. Thyestes, on the other hand, gives vent to his outraged feelings without restraint. His spiritual freedom makes him master of the situation in spite of his physical helplessness. Moral strength triumphant over bodily confinement was, as has been amply demonstrated, a favorite motif in the tragedy of the time and would continue to be so throughout the century. The theme of the hostile brothers, which had been used before with less brilliance in Behrmann's *Timoleon*, gains dramatic intensity here because neither one of the antagonists is in any degree passive. The rational one, being evil, uses reason to *impose*, not to *bear*; whereas the virtuous one, being irrational, makes no attempt to subdue his feelings. The result is perhaps the loudest, bitterest, most hate-filled scene yet to have come upon the German tragic stage.

The priest of Apollo, whom Atreus hates almost as much as he does Thyestes, corrects the baleful parental influence on Aegisthus by clarifying the principle of filial piety. A son is obligated to obey his father only ". . . when he orders what is demanded/ By right, law, and propriety" (III. ii). The priest praises the "noble heart" of Aegisthus, whereas Pelopia had censured her son for being womanish. It was not a sin to bring Thyestes to Mycenae, despite the bad result, for Aegisthus meant well: "The gods judge us according to our purpose,/ Not according to the outcome; that rests entirely/ In their hands" (III. ii). This mild and sensible view of the gods, which plainly makes them equivalent to eighteenth-century Providence, is exchanged for a somewhat harsher doctrine (still, of course, not out of harmony with Enlightenment opinion) when the priest argues the desperate Thyestes out of his emotional doubts about the existence of the gods: "Do not enrage the already wrathful gods/ Through a curse which desperation, which Hell/ Has breathed into your mind! The gods are/ In the weal and woe which their hands send us/ Equally good and wise: think, you have also/ Incited them to anger through many a wicked deed!—/ Through hatred of your brother, through adultery, through murder . . . / . . . Suffer patiently! Beseech them humbly!/ Quietly await the end of your distress!" (III. vi). Thyestes' lack of faith, in contrast to that of Atreus, stems from his misfortunes. Would gods, if they existed, permit such things to occur? But the priest's answer removes the potential danger from this question. Thyestes' own sins justify his severe punishment. But the spectators still might wonder whether the murdered sons deserved *their* fate.

A new and irresistible storm of evil influence descends on Aegisthus in the fourth act. Atreus persuades Pelopia to believe that Thyestes and the priest are plotting to seize the throne of Mycenae and to kill Aegisthus, as years before Atreus killed the sons of Thyestes. The only way to avoid this peril, he says, is to have Aegisthus slay Thyestes secretly and then to pretend to the populace, who prefer Thyestes to Atreus, that their favorite has committed suicide. Again swallowing her kindly feelings, Pelopia replies that she will do "What reason commands" (IV. ii) and will persuade Aegisthus to do the deed. It is interesting to note that the author now makes reason itself (*Vernunft*) the nonvirtuous factor instead of settling for the less controversial "intelligence" (*Klugheit*). The struggle with her humane feelings, however, is far from easy. In order to be "rational" she finds it necessary to go into a kind of emotional frenzy—another sensational episode in this sensational play. She calls on the Furies for aid, and then describes their frightful appearance. She shouts ecstatically, "It seems to me I am now one of the Maenads" (IV. iv). Her subsequent interview with Aegisthus is the second high point of the drama. Both participants reach heights of emotion previously unknown on the German stage, and the hectic effect is the most absolute opposite imaginable to the saccharine, seraphic atmosphere of Wieland's *Lady Johanna Gray* or to the cool stoicism of many other earlier tragedies. Pelopia is strained far past the breaking point of any normal human being because she has to convince not only her unwilling son, but also her own unwilling heart, of the necessity of killing Thyestes. Finally she makes the startling revelation to Aegisthus that he is not the son of Atreus, but the result of her encounter with an unknown rapist who violated her two months before her marriage. If Aegisthus does not obey, she will reveal the secret to Atreus, who will certainly destroy her. Fear for his mother's life proves to be a stronger emotion than his affection for Thyestes, and Aegisthus agrees to go through with the murder. The suspicion already aroused within the spectator that the unknown rapist must be Thyestes himself adds much tension, fear, and pity to the bravura scene between mother and son.

The highest pitch of excitement is attained in the last act, which brings a change of scene from the palace of Atreus to Thyestes' prison cell. Aegisthus stands at the entrance, still struggling with his feelings, while Pelopia accuses him of cowardice and disobedience. Aegisthus, trembling on the brink of unvirtuous action, speaks up once more in defense of his heart in words that reflect the sentimental opinion of the mid-eighteenth century: ". . . the judge here [pointing to his breast]/ Which gives no evil advice. . . ." (V. i). Finally, in complete confusion, he prays for something the gods will surely never grant: "Turn my heart to stone!" (V. i). But the sight of the good old man sleeping, unaware of any danger, proves too much for Aegisthus to bear, and he lets his sword fall to the ground. In the nick of time his heart has saved him from a wicked deed. A good old man—that powerful sentimental symbol in the eighteenth century—has by his mere presence, without saying a word, been able to counteract the cleverest and most desperate machinations of rational evil. It makes no difference that this old man is guilty of some dark crimes. To Aegisthus he represents only the good.

The tragedy, however, is far from over. Thyestes recognizes the sword of Aegisthus as his own, lost many years previously on the night he violated an unknown priestess at the temple in Sicyon. That can only mean that Aegisthus is his son, rather than the son of Atreus, and a sentimental scene of reunion ensues. Unfortunately this is soon interrupted by the terrible revelation that Pelopia, the former priestess, was not just any girl, but Thyestes' own daughter, whom he had given into the care of the priest of Apollo. A rape, bad enough in itself, has now become a horrible act of incest. In the welter of this unspeakable calamity the flaming candle of optimistic Enlightened philosophy gutters and almost goes out entirely. Pelopia, seized by the Furies again, tries to kill Aegisthus with the sword and, failing, turns it on herself instead. She dies in utter despair, like the Jocasta of Sophocles. One might say she is being punished for hearkening to her "reason" and the promptings of Atreus; but the guilt that is the real cause of her suicide is not connected with this error, but with a crime committed unwillingly and unavoidably in the past. Weisse has made her death dramatically effective but not philosophically acceptable. In a Greek or in a modern play this might be no defect whatever; under the circumstances in which the play was written, however, it is an indication that Weisse did not work out his plot as perfectly as he should have done.

The death of Atreus at the hands of Aegisthus now has an anti-climactic effect, for the revelation of the incest demonstrates that the theme of fraternal hostility was not principal but only auxiliary to the theme of the good brother's downfall—as is also the case in Schiller's *Die Räuber*. It is a foreshadowing of the death of Franz Moor in the latter play that before his demise Atreus must admit that the gods are powerful and vengeful after all, and he gasps in terror that "Minos the judge" is coming for him. The priest of Apollo, full of optimism, would fain see in the overthrow of Atreus an obvious proof that the gods are benevolent and just. But Thyestes stops him short by telling him of the incest. Accordingly the priest substitutes a moral more suitable to the play's main theme, to wit, that one sin is enough to ruin a man for life and eternity: "Unhappy Thyestes! this is the fruit/ When one becomes the slave of a sin!/ A second vice is always joined to the first:/ The chain becomes so long and heavy/ That no force can free our hearts from it,/ Until its weight pulls us into the abyss" (V. vi). Evidently the incest is not to be blamed on fate, as in the Greek legend, but on Thyestes' libidinous conduct, which is regarded in Christian-Enlightened fashion as a moral defect. Weisse's last heroic tragedy closes on this sternly warning note of divine retribution for breaches of virtue. The general moral message is not different from that of Gottsched's *Cato*, but the atmosphere in which it is given is infinitely more passionate and terrifying.

The history of the little renascence of verse tragedy brought about by Cronegk and Weisse comes to an end, practically speaking, with *Atreus und Thyest*. It is a coincidence, but not one without significance, that the year in which *Atreus und Thyest* was first performed, 1767, was also the year in which Lessing began his *Hamburgische Dramaturgie*. This work is characterized by its onslaughts against French classical tragedy; but Lessing was no less devastating in respect to the efforts of Cronegk and Weisse. The reputation of French tragedy could withstand Lessing's criticisms. German verse tragedy, on the other hand, faltered and ceased its development for twenty years until 1787, when its glorious period began with Schiller's *Don Carlos* and Goethe's *Iphigenie*. In the meantime, prose held sway and performed the great service of bringing a concern for realism of characterization and setting to the German tragedy. This concern would not be forgotten when verse again came into its own.

IX

THE LITTLE TRAGEDIES

SINCE 1748, when the first three cantos of the *Messias* were presented to the readers of the *"Bremer Beiträge,"* the name of Friedrich Gottlieb Klopstock (1724–1803) had been associated exclusively, and in most cases very enthusiastically, with epic and lyric poetry. But in 1757 Klopstock surprised his large circle of admirers by publishing a drama, a tragedy entitled *Der Tod Adams.* The play was written in Copenhagen,[1] where Klopstock had been living for six years. The foreign origin was quite appropriate to a play that was so completely foreign to the rest of German tragedy as *Der Tod Adams.* Not only did Klopstock ignore the plentiful examples of Alexandrine tragedy; he likewise took no notice of the new fashion of middle-class tragedy, although he must have known *Miss Sara Sampson.*[2] When the "sublime" poet decided to enter the dramatic lists, it had to be in his own highly individualistic way. Not everyone was convinced that this first attempt was successful. Moses Mendelssohn, who reviewed the play anonymously upon its appearance, tactfully suggested that drama was not Klopstock's forte: "It would be desirable if this great spirit would not concern himself with the stage until he has completed his heroic epic."[3] The apparent naïveté of the work was plain for all to see. Mendelssohn wanted to deny it the name of tragedy because it did not obey the "universal rules and laws which are based on nature."[4] Klopstock's fame, as great as it was, was not enough to persuade any theatrical troupe to risk a performance of this strange play.[5]

Certainly *Der Tod Adams* must have seemed odd even to that portion of the public that had accepted the bourgeois tragedy in prose as a legitimate form. Here was a prose "tragedy" neither heroic nor bourgeois, composed of only three acts, and those extremely short. The prose dialogue entirely lacked the contemporary conversational tone of that in *Miss Sara Sampson,* and it was equally remote from the stylized, elegant diction of the Alexandrine tragedies. It was solemn, elevated, severely simple, and semi-biblical. The play had really no plot at all, and the subject matter was unfamiliar, antediluvian, weirdly outside the sphere of ordinary interest. Adam and Eve in the Garden of Eden would have been another question, to be sure; this piquant subject had been treated many years earlier in a popular and ludicrous *Haupt- und Staatsaktion*.[6] But the death of Adam at the age of some nine hundred years, at a dim period of time over which the Bible itself draws a grey and misty veil, was unlikely to be an attractive spectacle for the average playgoer. Klopstock himself realized that the play had little or no chance of being produced and he declared, "I have not composed it with this goal in mind." [7] Yet it would be unwise to bypass *Der Tod Adams* as if it had no more significance than Bodmer's "tragedies" (which are nothing more than historical events related in dialogue). For *Der Tod Adams* inaugurated a quite significant series of "little tragedies" that grew up and flourished alongside the main road of development. These small works were a means of tragic expression for writers who thought more in terms of an ideal theater than of the real theater and who wished to portray a poetic mood or a philosophical thought rather than to present an action. They also made it possible to dramatize actions which, though compelling, were of an anecdotal nature and unfit for a complete treatment in five acts. The little tragedy widened the scope of possibilities and gave the tragic genre a freedom and elasticity that it particularly needed directly after its escape from the total dominion of Gottsched's classical rules.

Klopstock's invention of the little tragedy was a remarkable achievement. There was no model for such a form unless it was the French *tragédie lyrique* which usually had three acts also and sometimes a biblical subject, as for example the Abbé Aunillon's *Isaac ou le sacrifice d'Abraham*, which was presented in 1734 at a French *collège*.[8] Perhaps because of their familiarity with the *tragédie lyrique*, the French received Klopstock's tragedy with an enthusiasm that the modern reader of *Der Tod Adams* finds difficult to comprehend. They had paid no attention to any earlier German drama except, mildly, to *Miss Sara Sampson*. *Der Tod Adams*, which had appeared in a Danish version at the same time it was published in German, was now translated into French in 1761 and then translated or closely imitated seven other times in the 1770's and 1780's, as compared to only once in Italian, English, and Dutch, respectively.[9] The story is told that Napoleon had the version of *Der Tod Adams* by Madame de Genlis (1779) read to him before the battle of Acre in 1799.[10] What Klopstock had created, almost out of nowhere, was the static lyrical drama, the kind of play written a century and a half later by Hofmannsthal and by Maeterlinck. Not all of the subsequent little tragedies were static. But *Der Tod Adams* was not without its influence even on the full-length tragedy of its own generation; for its static construction clearly anticipates Gerstenberg's *Ugolino*.[11]

At a loss for a category in which to fit this new play of Klopstock's, Mendelssohn offered an appropriate new suggestion: it should be called a "pastoral tragedy" (*Schäfertrauerspiel*).[12] The opening of the play would naturally make Mendelssohn think of the conventional pastoral play. The setting is a rustic "hut," and the children and grandchildren of Adam are shown to be leading a simple pastoral existence remote from any kind of "artificial" civilization. They cluster about Adam as the young shepherds and shepherdesses cluster about the old father-shepherd in a typical pastorale. The first thing one hears about is a forthcoming marriage. The bride Selima (a granddaughter) speaks at some length about the fruits, branches, and leaves she has gathered for her bridal bower. All this is just a setting, however. Shortly after it has been established, one's attention is turned to the central and serious figure of Adam, and the resemblance of the drama to the typical pastorale ends. It will be recalled that Schiller, too, began his tragedy, *Die Jungfrau von Orleans*, in a pastoral setting of shepherds, shepherdesses, and marriages, only to turn quickly from that to a concentration on the heroine.

The tragedy of Adam is that he, the first of mankind to be created, must now at last confront the death sentence passed on him ages ago by God. The importance of this event is diminished to an extent by the fact that this is not the first death in the experience of mankind. Not only Abel, but another young man of the family has died, and thus Adam's death struggle loses its uniqueness. Klopstock seeks to make up for this by having the Angel of Death ominously tell Adam that he is to die a particular, unique kind of death: "Some of your progeny will slumber away, others will die; but you are to *die the death!*" (I. vii). The exact implications of this threat are never revealed, and as it turns out, the death of Adam is relatively gentle. To be sure, he is burdened by the thought that his original guilt has introduced death into the world: "But now I must die, and all my children must die! It lies on me like a mountain! It is a horrifying thought!" (I. vii). The supremacy of God is emphasized rather than His benevolence, as in less religious plays: "But He who pronounced the death sentence over me merits worship!" (I. iii). Furthermore, there is none of the customary heroic or optimistic minimizing of death's importance. Adam is not reduced to a fear of death, but he does dwell on its horrors and fails to sweeten them by painting pictures of a bright hereafter: "You will see my torment! I do not fear it, the death for which I have prepared myself for centuries; but I will feel it!" (I. iii). Even the physical facts of death are alluded to. Although it occurs only in passing, still this is unusual in the tragedy of the time (unlike Baroque tragedy): "Now I am still standing on top of the dust! In a few hours I will be decaying beneath it!" (I. iv). On the other hand, the patriarch speaks unapologetically about life's delights, which he gives up only with reluctance: "You lovely fields! You high mountains rich in springs! You cool shading valleys, and you children of the mountains and the valleys, you who bend under the foot of the wanderer or raise your tips over the high clouds! You beneficient fields where I have wandered, where I breathed in life and joy, where I so long and so often was blissful, where I have seen all my children, so many living ones around me!" (II. i). No doubt the emphasis placed on the beauty of life and the ugliness of death is due to the particular subject of this play; but it still was a noteworthy innovation and it anticipated a similar, but much more drastic emphasis in Gerstenberg's *Ugolino*.[13]

Short as the play is, it would not only have been static but intolerably stagnant as well except for the introduction of two episodes providing a semblance of action—but only a semblance, for they lead nowhere. There is the mildly diverting disappearance of a young son, Sunim, who is found unharmed after having wandered away into the wilderness. This matter helps to fill out the third act. In the second act there is the more gripping return of Cain, who visits his dying father in order to aggravate his death throes with a curse. That this may be a part of "*the death*" that Adam has to undergo is indicated when Adam says, "His judge and mine has sent him here" (II. v). Cain starts to pronounce his curse, but a sudden feeling of filial piety overcomes him, and he flees. The sternness of the scene melts away into sentiment as Adam sends his son Seth after Cain with words of forgiveness. When Seth returns he brings assurances that Cain's heart has been touched. The potentially tense encounter between the father and the disowned son is transformed by the magic of virtue into a sentimental deathbed reconciliation. Probably Klopstock would have liked to show Cain as completely rehabilitated, to have saved him as he saved the repentant devil Abbadona in the *Messias*, but this would have meant too bold a departure from biblical tradition. Therefore, the most that Seth can report is that "It seemed, as if he wanted to weep, but he could not" (II. viii).

Eve does not appear until the beginning of the third act. Her entrance achieves a certain dramatic effect, for she is in a state of delight because her youngest son Sunim has just been found, and one awaits with suspense the reaction that will occur as soon as she discovers that Adam is dying. The concern of Adam and Eve for each other adds another sentimental note to the proceedings. In the last scene the stage is filled with the various members of the family, in order that a grand sentimental tableau may be formed. The entrance of young Sunim brings an unexpected joy to the dying father, and, after some hesitation fraught with fearful visions of the murder of Abel, Adam suddenly rises to a level of calmness and serenity and pronounces a blessing over his assembled progeny. At this point something very strange occurs. The Angel of Death had foretold that at the moment of Adam's death the rocks in the hills would come crashing down. And so it is. Just before the final curtain one hears "a hollow noise in the distance," and a moment later a rock does indeed come rolling on to the stage as Adam cries, "O Death! it is you! I die!" (III. iv). In Klopstock's poetic imagination, which took no heed of the realities of the theater, this happening doubtless seemed like something sublime and overpoweringly effective. But when one tries to visualize it even on the best equipped modern stage, one is inclined to agree with Mendelssohn that ". . . all these machines . . . cannot possibly have a good effect." [14]

Klopstock evidently had more in mind here than simply a sentimental spectacle. With his usual deeply religious earnestness he was trying to drive home a universal message. In Adam's blessing the poet reveals the true intention of his drama. This blessing contains the first reference to a happier life beyond the grave and to the relative insignificance of earthly life: "—may He, the great Adored One, give you—much grief—and much joy! and may He thus remind you often, that you must die, in order to become immortal again. What only the earth gives and only the mortal body receives, take that like the wanderer who does not seat himself by the spring, but hurries on" (III. iv). Adam, the first man and the symbol of all mankind, has heretofore faced death with feelings of horror and revulsion. It is a death that he deserves because he has committed the Original Sin, although otherwise he is and has been a perfectly virtuous man (like Miss Sara Sampson and like old Southwell in *Lucie Woodvil* he has the tormenting knowledge of one guilty action in the past). In the process of dying he has suffered, if not physical pangs, at least spiritual ones. Nevertheless, at the last moment death has unmasked itself as nothing really terrible, but as the passageway to a blissful immortality provided by a loving God.

Thus, for the receptive reader this externally actionless play contains a significant and moving inner action which is carried out with much subtlety and beauty. Again, a comparison with *Ugolino* presents itself: the hero of that tragedy also, after horrendous suffering and near-despair, finally achieves serenity in the face of death and affirms the goodness of God. *Der Tod Adams* is, however, a religious play, whereas *Ugolino* is philosophical. In line with his religious attitude, Klopstock was far more concerned with explaining the concept of death in general than with justifying the ways of God in respect to any individual man. He wanted to say that death, while it may be regarded as a dire punishment for sin, has been transformed for Christians into the portal of heaven.

A second famous lyric poet who turned his hand unexpectedly [15] to tragedy at this time was Ewald Christian von Kleist (1715–1759), author of the long descriptive poem *Der Frühling*. Since Kleist was Lessing's dearest friend and therefore undoubtedly familiar with Lessing's views on drama, it is somewhat surprising to find that Kleist's own attempt at a tragedy, *Seneka*, reflects not the influence of *Miss Sara Sampson*, but of Klopstock's *Adam*. *Seneka* is also a little tragedy of three very short acts with simple, dignified prose dialogue and practically no plot at all. Its almost completely static situation deals with Seneca's death and nothing more. Kleist's own explanation for the striking brevity of his *Seneka* is given in his foreword. Here he describes his work as "the first draft of a tragedy" that he had intended to develop into a verse tragedy. Circumstances prevented this, but on the advice of his friends he had this first draft printed.[16] These remarks explain the choice of prose dialogue, but not the other features of *Seneka* which mark it so plainly a "little tragedy." Since *Seneka* was published in 1758, just a year after *Der Tod Adams*, it is likely that Klopstock's example gave Kleist as much encouragement to present his unfinished prose draft to the public as did the advice of his friends. But more important, *Der Tod Adams* also furnished Kleist with the model of a new kind of tragedy suitable for the gentle talents of an elegiac poet. If Kleist did not use this model, then it must be assumed that he somehow duplicated Klopstock's procedure, just a year later, unconsciously and independently.

The first act of Kleist's tragedy finds Seneca retired to his country estate, where he hopes to live a quiet life with his wife Pompeia. He makes the customary slighting remarks about existence at court as compared to the delights of obscurity: "Now we will live to ourselves and no longer deign to remember the vile pride and nonsense of the court" (I. i). Pompeia assures him that he is not running away from responsibility, for he has already done all in his power to prevent the enslavement of Rome. Continuance in Rome would only have meant his death at the hands of an enraged Nero. Moreover, the fate of Rome is in the control of Providence: "Forget what is not in your power and leave the punishment of the tyrant and the rescue of your fatherland to the Being who watches over everything, who, as you have often taught me, arranges everything for the happiness of the world, and avenges the tears of the virtuous and the wise man on his enemies" (I. i). Seneca and his wife differ only on one point: he believes in castigating vices like Nero's in the boldest and most uncompromising way, while Pompeia believes that he would have achieved more positive results with pleas and gentleness. Soon a friend named Polybius brings the couple the sad news that Nero has executed his virtuous wife Octavia. Seneca receives the tidings with stoic calm, reflecting that everyone must die some day and that Octavia is now enjoying the fruits of her virtue in heaven. Pompeia, on the other hand, is inconsolable and more strongly convinced than ever that it would mean death to Seneca to return to Rome, as Polybius urges. Seneca is swayed by Polybius in spite of Pompeia, for he would like to reform Nero, his previously virtuous pupil.

In the second act Seneca's new resolve is shown to be useless, for Nero's soldiers have surrounded his estate. Polybius utters the customary challenge to God to protect Seneca: "If You are just, O Divinity! if You are just, then do not permit this misfortune. Spare the greatest human virtue! Spare him who is most like You on earth!" (II. i). When a captain of Nero's soldiers comes in announcing a death sentence for Seneca, Polybius pretends that he is Seneca and boldly denounces the tyrant. But Seneca himself enters soon after and clears up the question of identity. He rebukes Polybius for being so eager to die: "It is ignoble to despise life as long as one can be of use to the world, and can be happy" (II. iii). When one is old and unfortunate, however, like Seneca, then one can welcome death.

In the third act Seneca appears with bandages on his severed veins, about to die from loss of blood. He confesses that he has led a well-nigh perfect life: "I have followed reason, which You have given me as my guide. Evil has never dishonored me, only weakness has misled me to errors" (III. i). Amid the laments of those standing around, Seneca faints, and Pompeia, mad with sorrow, stabs herself to death. Seeing this, Polybius is sure that vice has conquered over virtue: "The honor of Rome and the honor of the human race are gone, and Nero and her shame remain alive!" (III. i).

Then Seneca awakes from his faint, but is so distressed to find
Pompeia dead that he wants his bandages removed, so that he may
die faster. A messenger enters with news of natural calamities, which
are signs of God's displeasure at the execution of Seneca. In the next
moment Seneca breathes his last and the tragedy is over.

As this quite complete résumé of the drama shows, there is no
true action in the play. Kleist's "first draft" is no tightly knit nucleus
from which a full five-act tragedy could have grown. The one
promising initial development, Seneca's decision to return to Rome,
is frustrated before it has an opportunity to get started. The author
is obviously more interested in projecting a mood than he is depicting a dramatic action. In this respect, Kleist and Klopstock are
entirely alike. There is a difference between them, however, if one
considers their ability to instill a meaning into their little tragedies.
Klopstock was able to put a religious message into *Der Tod Adams*
which gives this small work a well-defined reason for its existence.
Kleist was able to express nothing more than his admiration for
Seneca's virtuous character, together with his own melancholy view
of the world. Seneca is represented as a perfect character whose
death is altogether guiltless. His wife despairingly commits the
crime of suicide. Their friend Octavia has also been put to death
although she is innocent. Is this the reward promised to virtue?
Kleist included the clichés about Providence in his scanty dialogue,
but he did not go to the trouble of justifying the death of his hero.
His interest lay in the beautiful death of Seneca, beautiful because,
although unmerited, it is accepted by him without complaint or
bitterness. Seneca becomes, as it were, a type of Christ on the cross.
Against the serenity and sweetness of such a demise all questions
about justice and reward become superfluous, at least as far as
Kleist was concerned. Accordingly, this little tragedy seems to have
no specific meaning, and is nothing more than an extended sentimental tableau. The stoic philosophy, which figured prominently
in Camerer's *Octavia* (1753) and Creutz's *Seneca* (1754), has left
only the barest perceptible imprint on Kleist's drama. The gentle
poet (who was also a brave officer and died of wounds received
in battle during the Seven Years War) changed Seneca's stoicism
into a soft, elegiac melancholy and world-weariness.

Though it may only have been chance that arranged the resemblance between *Der Tod Adams* and *Seneka*, there can be no
doubt whatever that Margareta Klopstock (1728–1758) wrote her
one tragedy, *Der Tod Abels*, in direct imitation of her husband's
work. The year of composition was 1757,[17] but the work was not
published until 1759, when the bereaved Klopstock included it

among the other works of his deceased wife, which he had printed under the title *Hinterlassene Werke von Margareta Klopstock*. *Der Tod Abels* closely resembles its model. There is the same extreme brevity, the same unadorned but elevated prose dialogue, the same pastoral setting, the same devoutly religious sentiment, and even to a great extent the same cast of characters. There is one striking difference, however. This little play has a complete plot: an action which, although wholly uncomplicated, is suitably equipped with a beginning, middle, and end. Several characters are clearly developed and they stand in a significant dramatic relationship to one another. It might be said that a certain tension is aroused by this plot. Every reader knows that Abel is to be killed, and the suspense engendered by waiting for this catastrophe is skillfully although quietly aroused. As drama, Margareta Klopstock's little tragedy is superior to *Der Tod Adams*. But it lacks the quality of soaring pathos which gave all her husband's creations their unique power. If anyone had been minded to produce these plays, Margareta's could have served as a prologue to *Der Tod Adams*.

Der Tod Abels has only five speaking roles; but a considerable number of mute characters—Adam's many children and their children—are supposed to appear on stage. The authoress planned a step in the direction of lyrical tragedy when she indicated that the ninth scene of the second act was to be sung by all these otherwise mute personages. Her intention, however, was not carried out, for the scene remained unwritten. The play's opening scene establishes the happy existence of Abel and his wife Zilla. This pair has accepted God's covenant with fallen man and therefore they find delight and contentment in life even though Paradise is closed to them. Adam and Eve still weep when they are reminded of their loss, but Abel and Zilla have no such haunting memories. Zilla, her words reflecting the authoress' own warm desire for children,[18] rejoices in the thought of motherhood, forgetting the pain and danger that God had spoken of in his curse on Eve: "Never, Abel, is a lamb born to your sheep that I do not share the joy of its mother. How happily it leaps in its young beauty! How maternally the mother cares for it!" (I. i).[19] She also considers the curse of work as a blessing, for it refreshes mankind. Abel points out that the worst curse of all, death, is also really a blessing, for it leads to a still happier life in eternity. God is truly love, and He has promised to send a Savior. Perhaps this Savior may be born to Zilla. But a portentous shadow is cast across their bliss when the older brother Cain enters, in his customary ill humor. Cain is jealous of Abel's happiness, but his own lack of satisfaction is based on a pessimistic and unreconciled

attitude toward life, rather than on actual misfortune. He despises
his hard work as a farmer and derives no blessing from it. He feels
a bitter resentment against Adam for having sinned and forfeited
Paradise. Zilla decides that Cain has a bad heart, for only a bad heart
could fail to love Abel, who is the epitome of joy and virtue. The
dramatic conflict of the hostile brothers—only one of whom is actually hostile—is thus simply and effectively begun in the first act.

Adam and Eve appear on stage in the second act. Their happiness
in their lot is akin to that of Abel and Zilla, but in the midst of
rejoicing they cannot forget the sickening thought that they have
brought sin upon all their flourishing children. As yet they do not
know the meaning of death, but they fear its first occurrence. Eve
asks, "Death! Fearful one! Who are you? We do not yet know
who you are; but we feel your terrors in all our bones!—Ah, will
Eve die before Adam? or Adam before Eve? Or will Adam have to
bury his sons? Will Eve see Zilla die?—" (II. iii). This speech adds
to the audience's anticipation of what is soon coming. For the moment, however, the mood projected on the scene is one of rejoicing
and thanksgiving. The back part of the stage is opened to reveal
the two altars in the distance, Abel's and Cain's, the one covered
with flowers and the other with the fruits of the field. Only Cain is
unable to lift his heart to join in the festivities.

In the third act the sacrifices are over, and Cain alone comes
back to Adam and Eve. He tells them that God did not accept his
offering. Then he admits that he has slain Abel out of jealousy, but
he does not accept the blame for his act. He tells his parents, "You
have brought sin on us! Know your sin completely! Know its
punishment! Abel is dead! I have killed him! Yonder by the altar,
there he lies" (III. ii). This shocking confession is well prepared
for and has a strong effect. The lamentations of the parents over the
body and their horrified comprehension of the first death in the
history of man are expressed with simplicity and restraint. The
situation is made more poignant by the fact that they do not wrathfully reprimand Cain but pray to God to forgive this murderer who
is nevertheless their son. As parents they are cast wholly in the
sentimental mold; but of course knowledge of their own Original
Sin would have prevented them from becoming vindictive even if
sentiment did not enter into consideration. Cain himself becomes
sentimental in his remorse for the deed he has committed. He has
not acted as an evil rationalist but as a person of overpowering and
misguided passions. He wanted virtue and approval, but not being
able to acquire them, he jealously murdered the person who did
possess them. Now he does not diabolically revel in his victory, but

piteously asks for mercy, although he despairs of being forgiven by God. The brief final scene is a little drama in itself. Zilla comes back from leading the daughters of Adam and Eve to their huts, and she does not suspect the calamity. Then she asks for Abel, and they indicate that he is lying dead. She sinks down quietly beside the body, saying only, "Oh, you judge of the world!—Abel!—" (III. v). The pathos of this little scene is superior to that of most concluding scenes in the full-length tragedies of the time. In this brief work Margareta Klopstock showed herself to be a writer of taste and restraint, two qualities in which most of her male contemporaries were remarkably deficient. *Der Tod Abels* contains many religious sentiments, but it does not have a specific religious message like *Der Tod Adams*. Nor does the authoress make any attempt to justify the death of innocent Abel on philosophical grounds. To her pious nature it was enough that God willed his death, and that He took Abel to a better life in heaven. As her personal letters show, she faced her own untimely death with the same trustful calmness.

In 1759 the little tragedy won its most distinguished adherent, Lessing himself. His one-act drama *Philotas*, which appeared in Berlin in that year, was not, however, a direct outgrowth of the lyrical three-act form created by Klopstock. There was another little tragedy type in existence to which *Philotas* has a more obvious relationship. This type had been inaugurated by the first bourgeois tragedy in France, Landois' *Silvie* (performed 1741, published 1742), which, besides being in prose, had only one act. The first German representative of this type slightly antedated the appearance of *Der Tod Adams*. This was the one-act bourgeois tragedy *Die Lissaboner* by Christian Gottlieb Lieberkühn, which was performed in Breslau in January, 1757, although it was not published until 1758 (after *Der Tod Adams*). Possibly a second representative was *Aurelius*, a one-act tragedy in prose published anonymously at Kiel and Altona in 1757.[20] The one-act length of *Philotas* is its prominent feature, but also the only one of significance which it has in common with the *Silvie* type. Otherwise, *Philotas* is not middle-class or realistic; it has often been discussed in the light of Lessing's Sophoclean studies. Its elevated prose dialogue, its remote subject matter, its simplicity and extreme concentration move it into the orbit of Klopstock's and Kleist's little tragedies. Unlike these two authors, however, Lessing was not motivated by the desire to give expression to a poetic mood. For him, brevity meant an effective distillation of dramatic energy. *Philotas* demonstrates that a little tragedy need not always be the work of a poetic nature ill at ease in the world of the theater. But, like *Der Tod Adams* and *Seneka*, *Philotas* neglects to consider the tastes and requirements of an ordinary audience. It was a *tour de force* and has always occupied a somewhat anomalous position among Lessing's dramas.

Not only the form but also the interpretation of *Philotas* has been rather puzzling to Lessing's admirers. It has been difficult to reconcile Lessing's *Minna* and *Nathan,* as well as his rational, cosmopolitan viewpoint in general, with this apparent glorification of a young super-patriot. Only rarely has anyone ventured to contradict the opinion of Wilhelmian critics that *Philotas* reflects the upsurge of nationalistic feeling aroused in Lessing by the Seven Years War, and that it is therefore related to such patriotic effusions as Gleim's *Grenadierlieder* and Weisse's *Amazonenlieder.*[21] However, it should have been clear from the first that Lessing was as interested in pointing out the defects in Philotas' character as he was in winning sympathy for his hero. Lessing's little tragedy, unlike Kleist's, does not venerate a sage. For, as was also the case with *Miss Sara Sampson,* the basis on which *Philotas* is constructed is essentially comic, rather than tragic. The young "hero" is actually a transmogrified comic fool (like Mellefont), a monomaniac deluded by a chimerical concept of heroism which puts him out of contact with reality and eventually results in his death.

A comparison with Callicrates, the youthful hero of Weisse's *Die Befreiung von Theben,* helps to illustrate this point. Both Philotas and Callicrates are immature adolescents burning to fight for their countries, in spite of the reluctance of their fathers to allow them to do so. To this extent, indeed, Callicrates is very probably a copy of Philotas. Callicrates, however, faces an evil tyranny that must unconditionally be overthrown. His eagerness is ethically inspired, whereas Philotas wants only to prove his manhood in a war against a rival kingdom, for which there is no definite justification and surely no crying need. Thus he says to the rival king, his captor, "All I know is that you and my father are involved in a war; and the right—the right, I believe, is on my father's side. That is what I believe, King, and I intend to believe it for once and all—even if you demonstrate the opposite to me incontrovertibly" (I. vii).[22] These are not the words of a young Callicrates, who follows his heart because he thinks it is a better guide than cool reason. They are the words of a fool without heart or head who is dazzled by the dream of becoming a hero. Philotas, a child in man's armor, presents the ridiculous picture of a would-be warrior who is wounded and captured in his very first skirmish, because his pretensions far exceed his capabilities. Callicrates is misunderstood by his father, badgered by his mother, and treated with scorn by the Spartans, so that his lonely endeavors achieve tragic poignancy; but Philotas is indulged by his father, spoiled by the adulation of the troops, and treated very kindly by his humane captors, so that his persistent desire for heroism seems like stubborn childishness. He is not set apart in the right, which would be a tragic situation, but on the contrary he sets himself apart *in the wrong*, as does every comic fool. Any tragic hero may make disastrous mistakes; may even, like King Lear, live for a while under a foolish delusion. But it is the province of the comic fool to seize and be consumed by a monomania that runs counter to all accepted norms for rational behavior.

To return once more to Callicrates, this young hero's actions are dictated by necessity, and are crowned with success. Lessing, however, carefully arranged the plot of his play to expose the actions of Philotas as totally unnecessary, and their success is a deplorable one. It is nowhere stated that Philotas' father needed his son's help. Though bedded by wounds, the old king has a dependable general to act for him. The capture of Philotas by the rival king Aridäus temporarily puts the father into an unfavorable position, since Aridäus can use Philotas as a hostage and perhaps force a disadvantageous peace. If Philotas had been cognizant of the folly that led to his capture, and had he calmly resolved to make up for his mistake by committing suicide, one might have considered the outcome to be tragic. And indeed, Lessing *might* have written his tragedy thus. But instead he carefully preserved the inherent foolishness of Philotas by rendering such a sacrifice needless. Benevolent Providence plainly takes a hand in the matter by arranging for the capture of Aridäus' son by Philotas' father. With a captive prince in either camp an exchange might have been made without loss of advantage. Accordingly, when Philotas nevertheless persists in his determination to sacrifice his life on the altar of heroism, one's conviction grows that he is a stubborn fool and no hero. It is characteristic of all Lessing's foolish personages that they resist the good offices of Providence in their behalf.

The rationalist among the four personages of this play is King Aridäus. If he had been portrayed as evil, the character of Philotas might have gained stature. But Aridäus is the soul of virtue and humanity. He regrets the loss of his former friendship with the father of Philotas, and he sincerely hopes that the mutual capture of the princes will end a war for which he has little enthusiasm: "Amiable children have often been mediators between disunified fathers" (I. vii). He does not allow the inevitable brutalities of war to blunt his essential humaneness, for he is rational enough not to confuse issues and personalities: "Wars, which kings are compelled to conduct against one another, are not personal enmities" (I. iii). He has full confidence in Providence, feeling certain that Providence demands neither suicide nor compromise with one's strict moral sense: "The gods—I am convinced of this—watch over our virtue as they watch over our life. To preserve both of these as long as possible is their secret and eternal occupation" (I. iii). Although Aridäus is a rationalist, he is not stoical and unemotional, for he declares, "I am a human being, and gladly weep and laugh" (I. vii); and again, "Yes, Prince; what is a king but a father! What is a hero without love for mankind!" (I. vii). These are thoughts that were to be developed at greater length in the first chapter of Lessing's *Laokoon.*

Philotas is the opposite of Aridäus, not because he is evil or because he holds to some amoral code, but because his monomania prevents him from thinking or feeling clearly. He repulses Aridäus' friendship, since his patriotism will not let him discern the *man* within the foe. He does not honor life as a divine gift; instead, he supposes that life is something one gives in exchange for glory. He compromises his virtue with deceitfulness employed against worthy persons, all in the name of patriotism. First, he tricks an honest fellow captive, Parmenio, who is to be used as a messenger, into agreeing to persuade his father to delay the exchange of prisoners for a little while. He knows how to excite and agitate the simple Parmenio to the point where Parmenio loses all sense of proportion and cries, "Now I will do anything for you! Even—say the word, and I will commit a crime, a dastardly deed for you!" (I. v). Anyone familiar with *Nathan der Weise* will realize that Lessing was warning here against an enthusiasm that lends spurious justification to immoral acts. Moreover, Parmenio here illustrates Thomasius' "prejudice of authority," that is, the desire to take action not because it is intrinsically good, but because it is recommended by a person whom one admires.[23] Secondly, Philotas tricks Aridäus into giving him a sword, and with this he commits suicide. The dying Philotas says, ". . . soon the quieted countries will enjoy the fruits of my death" (I. viii). But one knows that a better peace, based on mutual agreement, would have come without this death. Philotas really dies for the phantom of victory. He has placed patriotism above his humanity. At this point Aridäus exemplifies the behavior of a true human being. His first reaction is highly emotional, as is to be expected. For a moment he is tempted to nullify the advantage Philotas has gained through suicide by abandoning his own son to Philotas' father. But he promptly recovers his senses and decides that his son is more important to him than any military victory. He will end the war, get his son back, and then abdicate his throne. The nonsense of war is too much for him to bear any longer: "Do you people think that a person never gets enough of it?" (I. viii).

In view of all this, one may wonder why this tragedy was ever interpreted as a paean to war and super-patriotism. The evident reason is that there are various passages in the text which at first sight seem to support such a conclusion. Aridäus himself at the end calls Philotas "the greater victor" (I. viii). These speeches and remarks, however, ought not to be taken at face value, for then they give rise to inexplicable contradictions. Their purpose is actually in full agreement with the rest of the play, for they illustrate the dangerous attraction of the intemperate enthusiasm radiating from Philotas. He himself is scarcely more than a child; yet such is the power of patriotic fervor that it gains him the admiration of mature and rational men who know better. Strato, the general of Aridäus, says to Philotas, "I am angry; you should not have moved me so.—I am becoming a child along with you—" (I. ii). Aridäus praises Philotas for his "early, manly speech" and hopes that his own son may speak as worthily (I. iii). Parmenio is so swayed that he asserts, "Your father is good; but you will be better than he" (I. v). Patriotism, with its attendant attributes of bravery, resolution, and self-sacrifice, exerts great magnetism, especially when it is made incarnate in a noble youth who has not yet been hardened by life. Lessing wishes to give patriotism and heroism every beauty and advantage possible because his case against these concepts rests upon the proposition that in spite of all excellences, patriotism and heroism are false and foolish *when placed above essential humanity*. Reason, virtue, and humanity are the only true guides to action, and any idea that transgresses against them, no matter how beautiful and admirable in appearance, is a snare and a delusion. *Philotas* is no exception in the line of Lessing's other dramas, but a very genuine product of the same mind that fashioned *Nathan der Weise*, a mind which in its turn was fashioned by the ideals of the Enlightenment. Like the earlier little tragedies, *Philotas* was not put on stage.[24] Probably its small cast of characters, all of them masculine, and the unusual one-act form were enough to make the theatrical producers doubtful, while the extremely simple plot and the odd hero discouraged them completely. Although its text was doubtless read widely, *Philotas* did not succeed in turning the writers of tragedy toward an interest in the self-imposed tribulations of monomaniac fools. Such portrayals remained generally in the province of comedy.

The next little tragedy to appear was likewise a one-acter: *Der Einsiedler*, by the Alsatian, Gottlieb Konrad Pfeffel (1736–1809).

In spite of blindness, Pfeffel was, from 1773 on, a prominent educator with a school of his own in Colmar; and was an extraordinarily active author who wrote many fables, essays, and verse tales, and was also greatly interested in the theater. *Der Einsiedler,* published in Karlsruhe in 1761, was one of Pfeffel's two earliest attempts at drama,[25] and it was the first of the little tragedies (except for the one-act bourgeois play, *Die Lissaboner*) to reach the stage. The author did not aim at writing a tragedy that would stand by itself. His modest intention, imitating directly neither Klopstock nor Lessing, was to furnish a new kind of tragic *Nachspiel* [26] which would be a more suitable conclusion to a theatrical evening featuring a full-length tragedy than the customary comic *Nachspiel.*[27] The fact that *Nachspiele* were regularly just one act in length would give some precedent for the diminutive size of this drama even if there had been no series of little tragedies preceding it. Size, however, is not the only factor that determines whether a work is to be characterized as a little tragedy. The style is also a factor, and the style of *Der Einsiedler,* like that of *Der Tod Adams,* is lyrical, dreamy, and detached. Its setting is pastoral, and it is practically without plot. But it differs from the others and is an important landmark in that it is written in verse, in rhymed Alexandrines. (Verse would be used again in some later little tragedies.) Like *Philotas,* this play's one act has eight scenes, but its over-all length is not equal to Lessing's play. No particular philosophical or religious purpose is evident in the little play, although it is not lacking in pious phrases about Providence and virtue. The author's whole intent, it would seem, was to stimulate a sentimentally happy mood in the spectators by showing them the long-awaited ending to a hermit's exile. It is the most untragic tragedy imaginable.

The opening scene presents Theodor, the Hermit, in anxious wonderment about the fate of his friend Fromhold, who has been absent for a long time. Theodor has been a hermit for fifteen years, ever since he was driven out of his homeland, where he had held a position of power. His wife died early in this exile, and her flower-covered grave is in plain view on the stage. Their daughter Seraphina has grown up in this faraway place thinking that Theodor is only her foster-father, and she is ignorant of her true high heritage. But she is quite content with the beauties of nature, which bring her close to God, and she does not wish to return to civilization: "Should I exchange all this for a world/ Where virtue is offended and only vice is loved,/ Where there are conquerors and people who deny God?" (I. ii).[28] Theodor wants to send her to his friend Adelskron who will take care of her. In any case, Seraphina seems to be well off, and Theodor's Heaven-directed lament scarcely seems warranted: "Will You do no miracle to preserve this child?" (I. ii).

Before long a stranger appears and Seraphina flees. But the stranger is only Theodor's friend Fromhold, who has finally returned. Fromhold thanks Providence for guidance: "But have I not always then noticed/ That a higher, hidden hand strengthened me?/ You do it, Eternal One, for the benefit of the righteous man!" (I. iv). He has a letter for Theodor which states that his enemies have been found out and punished, so that the years of exile are over. To this news Theodor replies, "Providence be praised, which has done everything well!" (I. v). Indeed, Providence has been thoughtful enough to send along a young man for Seraphina. It is the son of Adelskron, and he is waiting now in the valley. As Fromhold says, ". . . the hand of Providence created him for Seraphina" (I. v). The old men fear, however, that Seraphina may be afraid of young Adelskron. Therefore they decide to deceive her into believing at first that he is her brother. This is not a wicked deception, for, as Theodor says, it is "A little trick, it cannot be culpable" (I. v). Thereupon Theodor proceeds to inform Seraphina that she is his real daughter, that she is a countess, and that Fromhold has brought his son and daughter to see them. When Fromhold greets Seraphina as "countess" she cries, "Oh, not that, this word has no charm for me" (I. viii). In the proper sentimental fashion, she regards him as a friend rather than a servant. Her sweetness almost kills the two old men. Fromhold exclaims, "And—Heaven! I am perishing—O bliss! O grief!" and Theodor says, "Come, my friend, otherwise she will break my heart" (I. viii). They both leave, weeping, and Seraphina is left alone with young Adelskron. In a very short time he reveals his true identity, for he could not resist: "A flood of bliss— It would have killed me" (I. viii). Seraphina accepts the young man's hand, and this pleases Theodor so much that he resolves to return home with them, even though his wife is dead and must remain in this place of exile: "My heart does not permit me to forsake you, children,/ Otherwise I would perish here alone upon this grave" (I. viii). It is obvious that this play is really about nothing at all, and that it is sentimental to an absurd degree. The dangers inherent in the little tragedy are plentifully demonstrated in *Der Einsiedler*, which is pointless and maudlin. Lessing's terse judgment in the *Hamburgische Dramaturgie*, Stück XIV, is thoroughly justified: ". . . his [Pfeffel's] *Hermit* . . . is supposed to be a little tragedy, which could be used to follow moving plays instead of the all too merry *Nachspiele*. The purpose is fine; but we would still prefer to turn from weeping to laughing, rather than to yawning." [29]

After *Der Einsiedler* the production of little tragedies paused.[30] Then, after three years another was published, of all places, in Vienna, which was ordinarily out of contact with the latest developments in German drama. This was the *Alzimire* of Christian Gottlieb Klemm (1736–1810?), printed in 1764 in Klemm's journal, *Der österreichische Patriot*.[31] The same author acquired a little more than local fame through his satirical comedy, *Der auf den Parnaß versetzte grüne Hut* (1767). *Alzimire* was described in a contemporary review as a ridiculously bloody *Haupt- und Staatsaktion*.[32] This is not true; it is not particularly bloody, and instead of being a *Haupt- und Staatsaktion* it is an Alexandrine tragedy in miniature. Not a proper successor either to *Der Tod Adams*, *Philotas*, or *Der Einsiedler*, Klemm's little tragedy is a potentially full-size work arbitrarily shrunken to the point where all that remains is the incongruously massive bone structure of a complex plot, while characterization and details are dispensed with. The events take place in the twinkling of an eye. Exposition is scattered unskillfully through the first nine scenes, so that during most of the play one is left wondering what all the commotion is really about. Fortunately, a knowledge of other Alexandrine tragedies can help the reader to a fairly reliable orientation from the beginning.

Neither locale nor time of the drama is indicated, and some of the personages have Greek names, others presumably Turkish ones. The titular heroine Alzimire is an evil *Machtweib* devoid of gentle feelings. Alone on stage in the opening scene, she wrathfully declares her hatred for the king, Philon, and his minister Philomet, both of whom she wants to kill. She plans to ascend the throne herself with the aid of a general named Gofin, who will also be done away with: "The rabble is dazzled by gold, and Gofin by the dream of honor./ Puffed up by arrogance, he is already hurrying to serve me./ Let him serve me and die" (I. i). Of all the personages named, only Alzimire has any sort of "role," and this consists mainly of various violent posturings. Her emotions express no individuality and do not awaken interest. Philomet, the minister, is as pallidly virtuous as Alzimire is tiresomely vicious. Through his words one begins to recognize dimly that Alzimire's position at court has been that of the king's mistress, and that she is now being dismissed because she has brought nothing but trouble to the land. Although Philomet has spurned her, she is in love with him, not the king: "I offered you treasures, and the crown, and splendor./ Honor beckoned you, my heart was devoted to you./ Ah, God! and it still is" (I. ii). The failure of her renewed appeal rouses her to fury, and she rejoices when the general, Gofin, tells her that Philomet and the king are to be assassinated that night: "O night, O rapture!/ With what delight my eye shall look upon it" (I. iii).

Toward the king she makes a false show of affection, and then becomes menacing when he remains unmoved. He regrets that Alzimire's baleful influence has led him to become a tyrant. He has gone so far as to put his own virtuous queen to death in order to enjoy his illicit love (perhaps a motif borrowed from the Nepomuck material). Alzimire accepts no responsibility; she blames *him* for having taken away her innocence by seducing her. This is an interesting facet of the situation which the author fails to develop. In a soliloquy the king admits that Alzimire still has power over his heart, but he is trying to gain rational control over his emotions: "O Philon! be master of yourself, avoid low pleasure!/ Be great, conquer yourself, tear her from your breast" (I. vi). A predictable twist is given to the intrigue when Gofin leads the king to suspect that the instigator of unrest in the royal army is Philomet. But before long—for nothing is of long duration in this extremely brief play—Philomet wins back the king's confidence and turns him completely against Alzimire. The king waxes ecstatic: "What do I feel? You are returning me to the state and to myself./ May my people be then forever my brothers./ May Heaven's vengeance pour curses, death, trouble on me,/ If I ever again forget to be the solace of the country./ I feel a holy fire glowing mightily in me;/ A beam of virtue! Yes. She shall flee this very day,/ The courtesan—" (I. ix). A few moments later Philomet announces that the rebellion has been put down and that Gofin has been killed. Alzimire, however, is not quite vanquished. In a rage she lifts her dagger against Philomet, who is saved only because King Philon steps between them and receives the wound himself. The king states that his death is justified on account of his past wickedness; but Philomet logically regrets that Philon was killed just when he was about to bring blessings to the country. Alzimire is thereupon led away to execution. She gnashes her teeth unrepentantly: "Instead of a throne, death!" (I. xii).

In its miniature form this tragedy verges on the absurd. Yet the plot offers the opportunity for interesting characterizations. There is a degree of novelty in the situation of a king who has been forced into tyranny by his mistress and who wants to reform. It is too bad that Klemm saw fit to condense his rich material so ruthlessly; he only succeeded in pointing up the woeful condition of serious German drama in Vienna.

Whereas *Alzimire* gives the impression of a long tragedy that
has been condensed, Klopstock's second drama, *Salomo*, also published in 1764, seems to be a little tragedy in spite of its length. The
five acts and numerous speaking roles of *Salomo* mark it as a normal
tragedy; but its curiously remote atmosphere, its static external
plot, and its lyrical dialogue betray its close relationship to *Der
Tod Adams*. Therefore it is more suitable to include it among the
little tragedies than elsewhere. *Salomo* failed to create a great stir,
was not produced,[33] and has since been almost completely forgotten.
This is unfortunate, because *Salomo* is a very original drama with
a remarkably fluid dialogue in verse, mainly unrhymed iambic pentameter. Klopstock described the unique verse form in his preface:
"Verses of five feet alternate with ones of six feet, but in such a way
that the former remain dominant. The iambic verses are interrupted
occasionally by a trochaic verse of the kind that the ancients called
a hendecasyllable. The anapaest takes the place of the iambus where
this seems to be required for necessary alternation or by the contents. And for these same reasons the verse is sometimes concluded
by an ionic, a third paeon, or even a pyrrhic." [34] The description
is highly technical, but the verse itself is limpid and quietly melodi-
ous, infinitely superior to the heavy, rumbling Alexandrine verse and
more malleable and gentle than strict blank verse.[35] The vocabulary
is of great simplicity and goes together with the meter to make a
charming and elegant dramatic dialogue. Perhaps, however, this
dialogue would not lend itself so well to a less lyrical play.

This tragedy is most deficient in external action. The hero has no
war to fight, no rebellion to put down, no love to struggle for or
against. Instead of these ordinary conflicts, Solomon's friends attempt to bring him back from religious error, and finally succeed.
That is the whole drama. Klopstock was able to fill out five acts
from this meager subject matter without recourse to subplots and
actions introduced for action's sake alone. He did bring in more
speaking personages (thirteen) than was usual in tragedies of the
time, but each one has his own necessary relationship to the development of the main character. The successive arrival on the scene of
each of these characters constitutes whatever minimal external action the play contains. Most of the personages are only partially characterized, but this deficiency only serves to fix the fascinating characterization of Solomon in the center of attention. This tragedy does
not dramatize a historical event; it illuminates the state of a man's
soul. The author naturally had a didactic purpose, a religious purpose. The didacticism, however, is contemplative and thoughtful,
and it is not driven home in an obvious, sententious manner. As in

Der Tod Adams, Klopstock was not inspired by an actual event related in Scripture, but chose to depict an unrecorded struggle in the life of a man who had been specially blessed by God and who then had sinned against Him most grievously.

At the beginning two of Solomon's friends, Chalkol and Darda, express their horror at Solomon's devotion to the god Moloch. Darda feels that Solomon is now very much in need of their friendship, which is a concept transcending earthly existence (a favorite Klopstockian theme): "For friendship is/ Eternal, is only in its infancy here" (I. i). But Chalkol cannot tolerate Solomon's sacrifice of children at the rites of Moloch. At this, one wonders what kind of a monster Solomon will be shown to be. When he appears, however, instead of a fire-breathing tyrant one sees an inwardly tortured human being afflicted with a subtle spiritual malaise. One begins to wait impatiently for insight into Solomon's mysterious soul—this is suspense of a vastly different sort from that in other tragedies of the time, and Solomon is very different from the usual hero, or villain. The other characters hover about him like well-intentioned physicians to whose ministrations the sick man scarcely responds. It is true that Klopstock assigns a specific cause for Solomon's malaise, that is, his erroneous ideas on religion. But the representation of Solomon's condition goes beyond cut-and-dried rationality into the romantic and inexplicable. He is an angel fallen from grace because he has had the temerity to exercise his reason in a realm where only simple faith can be properly operative. Therefore he cannot be restored through reason, but only through the grace of God—a situation quite contrary to that of Lessing's *Nathan.* Its delicacy was misunderstood by a contemporary rationalistic reviewer, who judged Solomon to be stubbornly (i.e., unrationally) resistant to the arguments of his friends and then suddenly and illogically converted to the truth by an event with no rational meaning: "Chalkol tells the king about the people's behavior at the sacrifice of the boys, and at Nathan's prayer in the temple. This narration seems to make a greater impression on him than all the previous events and admonitions together." [36] Since this reviewer conceived only of rational errors corrected by rational means, it is natural that he was dissatisfied with Solomon's detachment and inertia and sudden, unmerited improvement: "His obstinate delusion makes us indifferent to his conversion, and his strange cruelty arouses more horror than terror in us." [37] Actually Solomon is not stubborn. He is under a spell of evil which can be broken only by the touch of God upon his heart.

One of his first utterances establishes the hopeless state of his soul: "To live is/ Much more bitter than death" (I. ii). He does not trust the shallow optimism of those who claim that justice rules on earth: "So you know that the Sublime One punishes?/ What if it were the spirits below him who do it?/ Do you know whether they are just? But who/ Under this sun can know it,/ This sun which lets it become night, as in the soul/ There is now night, and now day?" (I. ii). Like other dramas of the time, this one warns against the use of the reason to the detriment of the heart, but here the warning is specifically religious rather than philosophical. Solomon's choice of Moloch as his god was a rational choice, because Moloch is said to be the chief of all the lower gods who administer the earth as deputies of the Supreme Deity, who is unconcerned about the earth. It was therefore wise to win the favor of this chief deputy. Solomon can even rationalistically condone the horrible sacrifice of children to Moloch: "And as to that, what of the blood of the boys?/ Can he, who is not immortal, die too soon?/ We miserable dust, often we die too late,/ Too late, and never too soon" (I. ii). Thus Solomon gives consent to crimes more monstrous than those of Richard III, and yet we sympathize with him, because he acts out of spiritual despair, and not with an evil will. Solomon has received the high gift of wisdom from God, but he has used it only to arrive at the false conclusion that God does not stoop to concern Himself with the world, and that there is no rational world-order: "After long nights of reflection/ I could discover nothing else, when I saw/ That the good man had to suffer, and that the evil man was happy!" (I. vi). The author indicates hereby that reason is a shaky basis for an optimistic viewpoint, while heart and faith are a better one.

Heman, whose sorrow over Solomon's apostasy has brought him literally to the point of death, wants to make one last attempt to save the king. Darda reminds him that any conversion must take place directly in Solomon's heart, and God alone can accomplish that. Heman therefore resolves to plead with God, after his death, to take pity on the king. In this instance Klopstock comes close to the Roman Catholic doctrine of the intercession of the saints. Another friend, Sarja, who returns to Jerusalem after years in foreign lands, brings the unwelcome news that Jeroboam is now living at the palace of the king of Egypt, where he is getting ready to wage war on Solomon in order to take away ten tribes from Israel. Solomon is not very much disturbed, for he would not mind dying in war: "I do not cry for revenge! but I am/ Tired of living!" (II. ii). This talk of war is interrupted by the entrance of one of Solomon's many queens, Semira, who ushers in the latest sacrificial victims. The stage takes on an operatic appearance, for a chorus of female singers has also entered and now begins to intone a solemn and impressive song about the sacrifice. The mother of one of the victims begs piteously for her son's life, while the other mother refuses to demean herself before the merciless king. Solomon, more remote than ever, has little to say, and one cannot fathom the thoughts passing through his mind.

When, in the third act, Chalkol asks whether the boys who are to be sacrificed can yet be saved, Solomon answers, "Leave the fate of the boys/ To the gods. They are not my concern or yours" (III. i). His mind is at present occupied with his own resolve to die. Like Faust, he is curious about forbidden secrets: "I go beyond/ To see what is truth" (III. ii). Yet he looks upon death as "the fearsome step" (III. ii), whereas Heman, in Darda's description, has died happily: "If angels died,/ They would die thus!" (III. ii). Solomon's mood deepens, and he wishes more blood than that of just two boys were being shed, so that his despair might be increased: "Oh, that there were more! Then their blood would frighten me!/ Then you, despair, would finally/ Grasp me and violently cast me down!/ For I want to go down into the valley of death!/ Down into its depths" (III. v). This is dialogue of an effete morbidness not met with earlier in German tragedy. Solomon cannot be interpreted in terms of the customary types found in the tragedies of the time. Changeable, not out of caprice like a Baroque tyrant, but because of deep-seated dissatisfaction with himself, he soon assures Darda that he will not continue to shed blood. As though from a long distance, Chalkol's dreadful description of the sacrifice penetrates the benumbed consciousness of the king, and he says musingly, "As long as I offered sacrifices, never yet has/ The blood of the boys terrified me. Now it seems to me that I hear/ Their lamenting around me" (III. vi). As though this dim feeling were only a disturbance to his melancholy and self-centered reflections, he calls for singers to restore his soul. More and more preoccupied with his own death, Solomon appears to be irretrievably lost. When the mother of one of the sacrificed boys bitterly upbraids Solomon, he says very little. Even such lamentations are not enough to break the spell on his heart.

The fourth act brings an unexpected fantastic element into the play. Klopstock, unconcerned about the actual theatrical fashions of the time, here stipulates the presentation of a heathen ritual on stage (which had been done before only in Grimm's *Banise* and von Trenck's *Araxane*) and even allows a pair of devils to cavort before the audience. Only Lessing had heretofore ventured to include actual devils in a serious play, in the unfinished *Faust* of which just one scene was made known to the public in the seventeenth *Literatur-*

brief. Solomon has decided, in his perverse way, to ask Moloch, rather than Jehovah as Chalkol has suggested, the question: will there be a war in which he can die, so that suicide will be unnecessary? The heathen priest sets up an altar in the darkened palace hall, and he is set to summon up a spirit from the dead to answer Solomon's query. Two personages, supposedly hermits of Moloch, enter to assist the priest. These are actually devils in disguise. For a while everyone leaves the hall, and the devils have an opportunity to speak forth in their true characters. One of them turns out to be Moloch himself, and the other is a god named Chamos. They quarrel over the soul of Solomon, but their ultimate concern is that he may elude them both, for, as Chamos says, "Do you not see, how deeply/ He honors God? and only does not dare to approach Him?" (IV. viii). Their fears are borne out when, during the ritual, Solomon refuses to kneel before the altar of Moloch. He has always regarded this god as merely a poor substitute given to men because Jehovah is too sublime for them. Thus one sees that his idolatry is not of a common sort, but is a strange type of deism. The ritual is then suddenly transformed into a triumph for Jehovah, and the first sign is given that God has not abandoned Solomon after all. The heathen priest, instead of receiving an answer to his question, is struck down before the altar by an invisible force, and the disguised devils take to their heels.

The disastrous end of this ceremony makes Solomon feel that God is interested in earthly affairs after all, but now this becomes a fearful instead of a comforting thought. At first (in the fifth act) he stubbornly refuses to admit that the force that struck down the priest came from God; but his resistance breaks when Chalkol relates to him how the populace has reacted to the events of the day, and how they have followed the prophet Nathan to the temple. All at once Solomon feels abandoned to a severe court of justice: "The judge here, my people! and yonder, the Lord!—/ So it seems to me now" (V. iv). This surrender to fear is the first step toward Solomon's salvation. As a Protestant theologian would put it, he now stands condemned before the Law and recognizes his errors; next it will be the Gospel's turn to find its way into his repentant heart. Solomon's explanation for his return to the truth is of surprising simplicity. He has merely reflected on what God did in his father David's life and what He has done in Solomon's own life—that is enough to convince him that God indeed takes a vital role in the lives of men. But why did wise Solomon not realize this simple truth earlier? Klopstock deliberately makes a mockery of reason by pointing out that Solomon's reason carried him far afield and into profound mazes of thought, yet all its vaunted power was unable to grasp one obvious truth. Only when it is wedded to God's grace can reason be of service, and grace had departed from Solomon as a result of sin: "Just that was the night which/ Surrounded me! This was the judgment which lay upon me/ And which was the punishment for my sensuality,/ This, that radiance became dimness for me" (V. vi). From a more secular viewpoint one could say that this very spiritual author wanted to show that sensual passion clouds the reason and should therefore be avoided. But this is not a drama about Enlightened philosophy. It is about sin, punishment, grace, and forgiveness. It is deeply religious, like the author's great epic.

The last part of the play shows, at too great length, Solomon's hesitancy about asking God for information about his future and the future of Israel. Through three lengthy, static scenes Solomon worries, now with Chalkol, now with Darda, about the possible result of Nathan's intercession with God, and finally he receives the disappointing news that God has failed to answer at all. Things seem to be back where they started. But Nathan manages to give the situation a happy conclusion by recalling an old prophecy: Solomon, if he sinned, would be punished in a human way, but that he would never be rejected by God as Saul was. On hearing this, Solomon is filled with joy and gratitude, and he makes plans to sacrifice again in the temple of the true God. He has been sorely beset throughout the play by the punishments inflicted for sin (loss of grace and proper reason); but he has come out victorious at last, the beneficiary of God's love. He does not have to suffer downfall like the unregenerate tyrants of other tragedies, nor are his many heinous crimes punished as severely as the one small infraction committed by Lessing's Miss Sara. This religious play does not stress virtue, but the extreme lenience shown by God to those whom He loves. Accordingly, it stands in great contrast to the other tragedies of the eighteenth century. Klopstock's *Salomo* was a noble attempt to create a moving drama about man's relationship to God; but the profundity of its thought and the originality of its characterization are not a sufficient recompense for the tediousness of a drawn-out static situation.

The next little tragedy of this period was *Hermes und Nestan, oder das Orakel* by Johann Friedrich Löwen (1729–1771), originally published in the fourth volume of his *Schriften* (Hamburg, 1765–1766). Löwen is remembered particularly in connection with his directorship of the short-lived Hamburg National Theater enterprise (1767–1768), to which Lessing, as the theater's official critic, brought an unmerited fame with his *Hamburgische Dramaturgie*. Married to an actress, and himself an actor, Löwen wrote a history of the German theater which not unnaturally dealt more with the actors of the past than with the writers. As the first such history in existence, it is still of interest. His one tragedy, *Hermes und Nestan*, is the work of an actor with a memory full of other plays and an eye open to the latest novelties and developments in taste. Probably he was attracted to the little tragedy because the latest play by the famous Lessing was a little tragedy. At any rate, *Hermes und Nestan*, with its elevated prose dialogue, its ancient Greek (Lydian) setting, its pseudo-historical events, its hyperbolic idealism, and its relatively concentrated plot is the closest and only true successor to *Philotas* among German tragedies.[38] Löwen's plot, which he is supposed to have taken from a Greek anecdote in a French journal,[39] is still by no means a match for that of *Philotas* in simplicity and directness. It was necessary for Löwen to write two acts instead of just one, and the action is by turns flaccid and contrived. *Hermes und Nestan* possesses neither the lyric quality of the Klopstockian "little tragedy" nor the stripped-down athleticism of *Philotas*. Löwen had hardly any conception of the inner necessity of the form he chose, and for him brevity was not much more than a crutch for his failing imagination.

The situation of *Hermes und Nestan* is dramatic enough: two young and deeply devoted friends find themselves in love with the same young woman. But Löwen worked out the plot so unsubtly and crammed it full of so many hackneyed motifs that the play became a preposterous hodgepodge. Without knowledge of the original source one cannot say how many of the motifs belonged to it and how many were drawn from the actor-author's memory of other dramas. A more original and able dramatist would have eliminated some of them in the interest of realism and clarity. Löwen, however, seems to fear that excitement will flag if he omits any one of these sure-fire features: oracle, mistaken identity, scheming minister, revelatory letter, human sacrifice, armed revolt. Matters of this kind, which might be digestible in a full-length Alexandrine tragedy of the older fashion, fairly choke this little tragedy.

The titular heroes have been raised together remote from human society and have recently been recalled to the court of King Dorus of Lydia. One of the youths, Nestan, is the prince of Lydia, and Dorus had exiled him with his companion Hermes because of an oracle which threatened that a monster would kill him. Now that Nestan has attained manhood he may come back. Certainly this is a very contrived way to bring about a confusion in the identity of these two youths—which is revealed at the end in a surprise—but Löwen may well have found the story thus in his anecdote. Nestan, whose heart and emotions are his guides, expresses the customary dislike for court life and politics: "What a terrible teacher for this heart, which is filled with nothing but feelings of humanity!" (I. i).[40] The teacher to whom he refers is the prime minister Orxus, whose beautiful daughter Osmire makes quite a different impression on him, one that he cannot understand: "Fifteen years went by for me in happy ignorance. I felt nothing of the force with which an irresistible impulse pulls us along. Friendship was known to me— but not love" (I. i). Yet his conception of love is more progressive than that of the other two young people in the play. When Osmire reminds Nestan that she is still under the jurisdiction of her father, he counters by saying, "Love listens only to the commands of the heart" (I. ii). When Hermes advises him to let reason conquer his love, Nestan replies, "Reason?—Ah, what can it do against the feelings which surge up here?" (I. iii). The rational advice of Osmire and Hermes is based to a great extent on the fact that they are secretly in love with each other, so that Nestan without realizing it is a mere interloper. But Hermes is idealistic and self-sacrificing enough to put the claims of friendship above those of love; that is to say, with the aid of reason he tries to follow duty instead of inclination. Less idealistically, Osmire looks upon this attitude as a betrayal. The situation here is much the same as in Derschau's *Orest und Pylades*, where Pylades puts friendship for Orestes above his love for Tomire; but at least Orestes was not in love with Tomire, and Pylades did not have to contemplate ceding his sweetheart to his friend. Hermes himself wonders whether his friendship ideal is not passing beyond the bounds of reason and becoming "enthusiasm." Osmire, it develops, has ideas about love that are as progressive as those of Nestan, to whom she had pretended that she felt herself subject to her father. When the ambitious Orxus, wanting his daughter to become a queen, urges her to accept the hand of Nestan, Osmire courageously declares her views: "A lover who has any other rights over us than those given by love soon becomes a hateful tyrant. Perhaps I am wrong in the eyes of the world; but nature, which has given me this feeling and which does not usually lead us astray, means more to me than rank, dignity, and crowns" (I. vii). This speech shows that the author was well aware of the new trend of thought which was soon to result in the Storm and Stress. Nature, or the mysterious, irrational forces in the world, are a better guide to virtuous action than reason, which too often becomes mere cleverness and promotes materialism.

To be sure, the love of which Osmire speaks is predominantly spiritual in its make-up. Therefore, while she refuses to marry Nestan, she does not insist on marrying Hermes, and offers to go to live in solitude. Orxus decides that the only thing to do is to get rid of Hermes, and he quickly concocts an absurd plan. He will make it appear that Hermes is the leader of a band of assassins, and then convince King Dorus that Hermes is the "monster" spoken of in the oracle. Dorus will then execute Hermes. The villainy of Orxus rests on the premise that emotion can becloud reason and result in vice (as was usually the case with villains before the evil rationalist came into prominence). Orxus admits this to himself, saying, "Where intelligence can accomplish nothing, then fury must step into its place" (I. ix). Orxus' surrender to emotion, however, does not imply by any means that emotion is bad in itself. Nestan, who is altogether ruled by emotion, is a far better man than Orxus, who had at first been rational. Nestan's firm belief in the rights of love especially preserve him from allowing Osmire to be forced into marrying him, once he discovers that she does not care for him. Nestan tells the tyrannical father, "No, Orxus! paternal authority takes no precedence over the feelings which love begets—" (I. vii). This youthful cry of independence, anticipating the spirit of Storm and Stress, typifies the revolt of the younger generation often depicted in the tragedies of the 1760's.

The play builds up a little suspense in the second act, for Hermes is arrested and sentenced to die at the sacrificial altar. Now it is Nestan's turn to show how good a friend he is, and he passionately defends Hermes before the king. Here another blow is dealt to rationalism. Dorus concludes that emotion is obscuring Nestan's reason and making him condone Hermes' wickedness. Actually, of course, Nestan and his emotions are in the right, while Dorus with his reason is quite wrong about Hermes. Only Hermes seems able to keep reason and emotion in the proper harmony, and evidently the author intended Hermes to be the most perfect of all the characters in the play. In many a Storm and Stress drama also the extremes of emotion and reason would be criticized, while the harmonious personality would at last be shown as the best. In a farewell scene, Osmire sacrifices filial duty to love by telling Hermes that Orxus is his murderer, but Hermes does not encourage her rebelliousness: "But consider that this cruel man nevertheless remains your father" (II. vii). Nestan unexpectedly witnesses the parting embrace of Hermes and Osmire and for the first time understands that these two are in love. Calm as always, Hermes succeeds in justifying himself to Nestan, and he shows great, saintly composure in the face of impending death. He passively refuses to exert himself in his own defense and counsels the desperate Nestan not to use violence either.

At this point the influence of Weisse's *Mustapha und Zeangir*, with its wise, passive older brother and headstrong younger brother, is strongly suggested, for Nestan does not heed Hermes' advice. Instead, his emotional belief in action impells him to gather a group of warriors (which is always done in tragedies of the time without the slightest difficulty) and to invade the temple so that Hermes may be rescued by force. Since Nestan and his men are wearing masks (an awkward device!), King Dorus has no compunction about ordering his soldiers to resist, and Nestan is killed. His wild emotionalism has led directly to his death, and nothing has been contributed to Hermes' release. Hermes, on the other hand, lives to see his passive composure rewarded with undreamed-of happiness (he is therefore a counterpart to Quistorp's Aurelius). Just before the sacrifice is to begin, the high priest produces a letter from Dorus' dead queen which, on her orders, he has been keeping hidden for years. This letter—a most wretched *deus ex machina*—reveals that Hermes, not Nestan, is the real prince of Lydia. At this disclosure Orxus' villainy also comes to light, and he commits suicide. Both of the exaggerated personalities, Nestan and Orxus, have come to grief, while the balanced Hermes receives life, bride, and throne. The perfect and admirable hero reaps the blessings that Providence owes him, and the play ends in an atmosphere of optimism.

Hermes und Nestan was the last little tragedy of any significance which appeared within the period covered in this study. Two more one-act tragedies were included, however, in an anonymous volume called *Dramatische und andere Gedichte von . . .* published in Zürich in 1768. One of them, entitled *Damon und Pythias*, was in rhymed verses, according to a review in Klotz's *Deutsche Bibliothek*,[41] and presumably the other, entitled *Nomares*, had the same form. The reviewer considered both playlets to be beneath criticism. Indeed, after Klopstock and Lessing, no dramatist of stature chose to compose a little tragedy. But the little genre continued to attract very minor authors throughout the rest of the century. Most of these later productions were in prose with bourgeois subject matter of various kinds. Such plays would have more connection with Lieberkühn's *Die Lissaboner* and Landois' *Silvie* than with the little tragedy as described in this chapter.

X

PROSE TRAGEDIES 1760–1768

PROSE HAD WON its first entry into German tragedy through the new bourgeois tragedy, but soon thereafter the little tragedy demonstrated that prose was admissible even when the author was not trying to approximate the speech of middle-class personages. Klopstock and Lessing demonstrated that prose dialogue was equally capable of bearing poetic thought and of being molded to the elegant periods appropriate to the highborn. In the decade beginning in 1760 prose was to become the medium in which all types of tragedy could be written; and before the decade was over prose had become virtually the *only* medium for tragedy. Its triumph was sure when in 1767 Weisse, the champion successively of Alexandrine tragedy and then of blank verse tragedy, suddenly abandoned all verse and brought out his sensationally successful *Romeo and Julie* in prose. From that time on until 1787, the year of *Iphigenie auf Tauris* and *Don Carlos,* tragedies in verse were scarce in German literature, and most authors, including all those of any consequence, wrote their tragedies in prose. It was not just the difficulty of translating Shakespeare's verse which influenced Wieland and Eschenburg to render almost all his dramas into prose for their epoch-making Shakespeare edition (1762–1766 and 1775–1777).[1] Wieland's decision was wholly in line with the emerging dramatic fashion of the 1760's. The marvelous freedom of prose, a much more important matter than freedom in respect to the Unities of Place and Time, was something in which dramatists could profitably revel. Lessing soon carried prose dialogue to an apex of clarity and distinction in *Emilia Galotti;* Goethe made it into a rousing reproduction of sixteenth-century conversation in *Götz von Berlichingen;* and the best of the Storm and Stress dramatists, Lenz and Wagner, endowed it with an astonishingly naturalistic tone. It is most doubtful whether the shift from Alexandrines to blank verse, which would have occurred more swiftly without the existence of this extended era of prose, would also have been so fruitful without it. For the

era of prose banished forever the overly conventional, stiff, and un-
real atmosphere of earlier German tragedy.

The first prose tragedy of the 1760's was, not surprisingly, a
middle-class work—Wieland's *Clementina von Porretta*, published
in Zürich in 1760. *Clementina* belongs to that not inconsiderable
series of German eighteenth-century plays that are direct dramati-
zations of novels. It is a faithful rendering of the central episode in
Richardson's novel *Sir Charles Grandison* (1753–1754), to which
it owes, along with everything else, the motif of love thwarted by
a confessional difference (Catholic-Protestant) in the lovers, a
motif not typical of bourgeois drama in Germany. (It is true
that religious difference was also a hindrance—but not the only
one—to the love of Don Sancho and the Tunisian princess in
Schönaich's *Zayde* [1754], an Alexandrine tragedy taken from a
novel.) *Clementina von Porretta* follows none of the patterns established by the first wave of bourgeois tragedies, especially not the
leading one, which featured the ruination of a good person by a
diabolical evil rationalist. The middle-class tragedies of the sixties
were to follow no dominant trend. Each of them depicted, rather,
some different aspect of middle-class life. In *Clementina*, to be sure,
middle-class life is to be understood in the very broadest sense possible—for all the main characters are nobles of one degree or
another. However, neither historical facts, legend, nor persons of
royal blood or sovereign position are involved. The play is "tragic"
only insofar as the sufferings of the lovers are real and perilous. The
ending is catastrophic in regard to the happiness of these lovers,
but no deaths occur.

In a play that follows a novel so closely, the dramatist's main
function is to condense the material before him to a practicable
brevity. Situation, action, conflicts, big scenes, and characterization are all already there, waiting to be used.[2] When the novel is
as long, detailed, and leisurely as *Sir Charles Grandison*, however,
the dramatist's work of condensation is a considerable one. Wieland
in this case managed quite skillfully to create a true drama out of
the extended epistolary narrative that was his inspiration. He kept
the exposition, which might easily have become highly complicated
and impossibly long-winded, down to the barest minimum. This
circumstance, although one is grateful for it, does lend the play a
curious quality of suspension. The personages and their situation do
not grow organically and do not have their whole existence within
the framework of Wieland's five-act drama. Rather, the drama is
like a section cut from a larger organism, the communications there-
with being severed but still transmitting faint and vague impressions

of the greater body. An ordinary play with the same small amount of action would not need so many characters; they are here, nevertheless, because the long novel needed them all. Persons familiar with the novel would presumably derive a richer enjoyment from the play because they would know all of these characters much better. Yet it cannot be denied that Wieland made his play sufficiently independent to be adequately understood by anyone.

The first few scenes quickly sketch out what is actually a very complicated situation involving a great deal of anterior action. The author does not care to do more than to set the scene upon which the single action of his drama, which is relatively simple, may be developed. A noble family of Bologna, the Porrettas, are awaiting the arrival of an English friend, Sir Charles Grandison, whom they have entreated to visit them because their daughter Clementina is mentally ill as a result of her hopeless love for him. She refuses to consider Count Belvedere, the admirer favored by her family, because Grandison, on a previous visit to Bologna, has captured her heart. The proud Porrettas dislike having had to beg Grandison to return, but Clementina's life seems to depend on him. Both Clementina and Grandison are immaculately virtuous. Not the slightest blemish mars their conduct, not even an innocent error such as that which the author attributed to Lady Jane Grey in his first tragedy. The only hindrance to their union—since Grandison also tenderly loves Clementina—is religion, for Grandison is a loyal Protestant, while Clementina is an equally loyal Roman Catholic. Neither religion is represented as being detrimental to an individual's virtue, and nothing in the play suggests the hostile or fearful attitude toward Catholicism evinced in *Lady Johanna Gray*. On the other hand, it is regarded as a part of virtue not to sacrifice one's religious convictions for the sake of some desired benefit such as marriage. Wieland's (and Richardson's) sense of tolerance does not permit a careless or superior attitude toward creed. The problem, however, is one of loyalty rather than of dogma and theological arguments. The love of Grandison and Clementina is on the purest, highest spiritual plane, and by almost all standards they are made for each other. When two such persons are kept apart by a scruple as delicate as that of religion, then the finest, most delicate emotions are brought into play. This struggle between virtue and virtue was made to order for devotees of the sentimental.[3] As is fitting in a sentimental work, the heart is regarded as being at least as important as the reason, if not more so, in the preservation of virtue. The Porretta family's father-confessor, Pater Marescotti, particularly advocates the heart. It sounds oddly paradoxical when, in discussing

Clementina's mental illness, he says, ". . . her reason had to become the victim of her virtue" (I. i).⁴ Can virtue, the product of reason, become the destroyer of reason? Pater Marescotti fires another shaft at rationalism when he attempts to calm the angry emotions of Count Belvedere: "Come, Sir Count! I will accompany you into the park. The sight of nature and the gentle quiet of a lonely grove are often more suited to mollify our passions than the most valid reasonings" (I. ii). This confidence in the beneficial effect of out-door nature is an aspect of the coming period of irrationalism.

The play's action revolves around the efforts of Clementina, her parents, and her youngest brother Jeronymo to persuade Grandison to become a Catholic, and around the resistance shown by Clementina's suitor Belvedere and her oldest brother, the General. Grandison's progress through these tangled affairs is that of an angel—but scarcely that of an impassioned lover. With pain but without weakness he answers to his sweetheart's plea, "Ah, Clementina, beloved Clementina, dearer than my life, dearer than anything which this world can give or take away, but not dearer than my conscience and my soul!" (II. xiv). In despair, the Porrettas at last agree to a mixed marriage in which both participants would keep their respective religions, and Grandison agrees to this, for he is no proselytizer: "The very attitude of mind which prohibits me from acting against my convictions prohibits me from upsetting others in theirs" (III. x). Unfortunately, Clementina is too scrupulous to accept the compromise; she continues to insist that her husband must be a Catholic. Since this is obviously impossible as far as Grandison is concerned, Clementina conceives the idea that Heaven wants her to renounce him. She, whose virtue has been dictated chiefly by her heart, now finds that this heart nurtures a desire which, though apparently pure, is not pleasing to God. Nothing is left to do except to call upon reason. Through force of reason she must conquer herself, thus rising to a saintly sublimity, and the pattern of the heroine's development in *Lady Johanna Gray* here repeats itself. Submission to divine command and renunciation of Grandison calls for a grandeur of soul which is beyond ordinary human beings; it is the "moral grandeur" (*moralische Größe*) that Wieland, anticipating Schiller, thought tragedy should aim at depicting. Clementina exclaims, "Yes! I want to act grandly, I want to act like an immortal!" (V. iv). Reason as used in connection with this action is not regarded as an indicator of truth, but as a laudable control over one's natural instincts and desires. That is to say, it takes over the attributes of will power, as it very frequently does in eighteenth-century parlance. Accordingly, Grandison can say, "I admire her principles, although I am not convinced of their truth" (V. x). Clementina explains to her mother the exact process she has just undergone: "The decision was to the disadvantage of my heart. I doubted, my heart revolted against the declarations of my reason, I could not trust myself" (V. xi). But the young woman's step to sublimity was not made altogether on her own. Religion, in the person of the Virgin Mary (to whose potency the Protestant Wieland raises not the slightest objection), has strengthened her resolve. People with ordinary cold practical reason like Clementina's father and elder brothers may consider her ideas mere enthusiasm (*Schwärmerei*). Her mother, however, is more perceptive, saying, "I admire you and honor the secret guidance of Providence" (V. xi).

Clementina climbs to lonelier heights of virtue than Grandison, but she does not match her peerless lover in the ability to demonstrate the attractive force of virtue. Even his rival Belvedere says, "I hate this Grandison for being my rival, yet I must admire his virtues!" Before long, all his enmity disappears and he says, "I succumb to the superior power of your virtue" (I. vii). So tamed is Belvedere that he not only gives up his claims on Clementina but also strives to reconcile her brother, the General, with Grandison. The General hates Grandison for having put the Porretta family in the humiliating position of having to beg him to marry their daughter. With cold fury he tells Grandison that he is not deceived by fine talk of noble-mindedness, but insults cannot destroy Grandison's composure. He uses the occasion to make a little sermon against irrational passions (as opposed, of course, to sentimental feelings): "How despicable a blind passion makes even the noblest persons!" (IV. v). When the General challenges him to a duel, Grandison accepts. He has already refused one duel with Belvedere, and perhaps a second refusal would have made him appear a coward. Nevertheless, no duel ensues, for the General also becomes the friend of the irresistibly good Grandison. In the bourgeois tragedies of the 1750's, virtue often aroused envy, hatred, and persecution, whereas in Wieland's play it exercises a gentle humane influence over its environment, much as in Goethe's later *Iphigenie*. The mother of Clementina sums the matter up, saying, "It is impossible to resist the merits of this man" (IV. xiv).

Still, Wieland's optimism about the effects of humane virtue does not include a belief in earthly happiness for those who practice it. No better man than Grandison could exist, but his happiness does not extend beyond a sense of freedom from guilt and remorse. He wonders about this state of affairs: ". . . I exert myself to make others happy, and am not happy myself!—O virtue! How powerful is your charm, how irresistible is your beauty! Since you become the dearer to us, the more we suffer for your sake!" (I. viii). Sometimes, it is true, misfortunes resolve themselves into temporal happiness. When Clementina's mother asks, ". . . I believe, I hope, we are all upright. Why, why must we then be so very unhappy?"— Pater Marescotti answers, "But the chastisements of Heaven are always vindicated by their results" (II. vi). Grandison is less sanguine than this, saying, "Ah, Clementina! our happiness is reserved for another world!" (III. xiv), and again, "O bliss!—Lovely word! You do not dwell beneath the moon. With excited desire we pursue you: we think we are touching you, and we embrace only a shadow" (IV. iv). Such pessimism about the world logically leads to a somewhat morbid desire for death (also observed in Wieland's *Lady Johanna Gray*). Clementina cries, "Oh, that I were already with those who slumber in the grave! Oh, that my soul were already unfettered and rescued for that world beyond, where virtue no longer has to struggle, and bliss does not border on eternal misery! . . . My days are coming to an end—Comforting hope!" (V. iv). Grandison totally negates the idea of worldly happiness by saying, "Oh, Clementina, if a better life were not waiting for us, what a misfortune it would be to be born!" (V. x). In the novel these disappointed lovers do indeed find happiness at last, with other partners, but in the play Wieland allows their pessimistic statements to stand unchallenged by the course of events. His intention, doubtless, was to emphasize that there is no other motivation for Grandison's noble deeds except the love of virtue itself. For this sentimentally exalted personage the tangible benefits held out to virtuous behavior by rationalism in its earlier period are no longer necessary. Clementina says of him, "His virtue elevates him above every reward; by itself it makes him great and happy" (V. xi). The only comfort left to the lovers is that in heaven their confessional differences will no longer matter. Like social classes and nationalities, the various confessions seem to be mundane arrangements only, although they may not be lightly disregarded because of that. Wieland's tragic viewpoint, like Schiller's, did not concern itself with the vindication of the world as it is but with the glorification of individual virtue and of human potentialities. To his contemporaries who, like Lessing, were still trying to think of the world as a reasonably enjoyable place to live, a place that was gradually growing better thanks to the efforts of Enlightened people, Wieland's oversensitive, overspiritualized characters seemed to be "enthusiasts" (*Schwärmer*) and sick with melancholy. Lessing made the last great statement of his ideal in *Nathan der Weise*, the hero of which is also perfectly virtuous, but nevertheless practical and dedicated to the principle that life is happy and valuable and that the rewards of good deeds are not reserved for heaven alone. *Clementina von Porretta* found slight appreciation outside of Switzerland, where it was published and performed; [5] and it marked the end of his Pietistic, "seraphic" phase. In his subsequent and most characteristic works he did not remain true to the ideal of superhuman moral sublimity, but instead skeptically depicted the frailty of virtue when it is confronted with strong temptation.

The heavy production of various kinds of tragedy during the years 1755–1760 was followed by a barren period of two years during which the genre was represented only by Pfeffel's anemic little *Einsiedler* (1761) and Johann Gotthelf Lindner's school drama *Abdolonymus und Alexander* (published 1762, written 1758), which was not even explicitly designated as a tragedy. Whether or not this sudden cessation in the appearance of new tragedies reflects the increasing weariness of the Seven Years War, the resumption of production coincides, at any rate, with the coming of peace in 1763 (Peace of Hubertusburg, February 15, 1763). In this year Weisse contributed two more Alexandrine tragedies, *Mustapha* and *Rosemunde*, and there appeared the first original prose tragedy since *Clementina*. The interrupted stream had begun to flow strongly again. The prose tragedy was a middle-class piece by Johann Jakob Dusch (1725–1787) entitled *Der Bankerot*.[6] Dusch was not a man of the theater but a professor at the Gymnasium in Altona, whose numerous literary works included many didactic poems but no other drama except a one-act pastoral play.[7] Nevertheless, *Der Bankerot* is a reasonably competent piece of work, and one wonders why it failed to attract attention in its own time.[8] The play's most noteworthy feature is its choice of subject matter, which is drawn from the world of commerce, a new milieu. The bourgeois dramas of the 1750's had all shown a preoccupation with purely personal human relationships, and the personages in them seemed to have nothing but leisure hours. This was also true of Wieland's *Clementine;* their setting was always in an inn or a private dwelling. Dusch's inspiration apparently passed over these German dramas in order to draw directly on the famous English middle-class tragedy, *The London Merchant,* which had many scenes set in an everyday business environment and contained some dialogue of a technically commercial nature. But whereas *The London Merchant* primarily treated the subject of a youth's moral downfall (to which the commercial setting was more or less incidental), *Der Bankerot* has a plot grounded entirely in the special circumstances surrounding a businessman.

One may therefore look for still another and stronger influence. This is to be found most probably in Diderot, whose dramatic theories had lately been translated into German by Lessing.⁹ Diderot's doctrine (as set forth in his *Entretiens sur le Fils naturel*) that the manifold "conditions" of life should be represented in drama, i.e., that a comprehensive picture should be given of a particular profession or way of life, could hardly be more perfectly put into practice than it is in *Der Bankerot*. Although Lessing's comedy, *Minna von Barnhelm*, can be said to show the "condition" of a soldier, Dusch's tragedy shows the "condition" of a businessman much more completely and single-mindedly. To be sure, one would call *Der Bankerot* serious rather than tragic, since it has a happy ending, with even the chief villain kindly provided for. Yet there is no comic element in the play, and it is by no means the only contemporary tragedy without a catastrophe. The two heroes are to be pitied and admired rather than scorned, and they are exposed to genuine dangers that are averted just in the nick of time.

The same type of situation used frequently in heroic tragedies is here translated into bourgeois terms. Instead of a kingdom, a large business house is at stake. The "royal" family is composed of a virtuous financier, his wife, their marriageable daughter, and their younger son. The "prime minister" or perhaps "general" is the head clerk of the firm, who, though suspected of treachery, is in reality loyal. The villainous usurper who wants to take over the "kingdom" is an unscrupulous partner by the name of Gerrards, a relative of the financier's wife. The scene of action is an office connected with the dwelling of Erast, the financier; and the Unity of Time is strictly observed, since all the action is supposed to happen within the time required to put on the play. As might be expected, these are extraordinarily full hours. One soon discovers that the firm of Erast, evidently a kind of wholesale agency, is facing a crisis. One of its two guarantors in Holland is rumored to have gone bankrupt, while at the same time Erast's partner Gerrards is demanding the immediate return of the money he has invested in the firm. Erast is therefore confronted with complete ruin. Ordinarily, if the Dutch bank were failing, Gerrards, as partner with Erast, would have to suffer a share of the loss. But he has safeguarded himself by insisting that he be paid out with drafts on "Harlem," the bank he believes to be sound. Thus he will get all of his money, and Erast, with only the failing bank "Dalem" to depend on, will lose all of his. To be sure, lest Erast see through this selfish maneuver, Gerrards has started a false rumor that "Harlem" rather than "Dalem" is the weak bank. Moreover, Gerrards is trying to buy some ships belonging to the firm. The ships are overdue, and Erast considers them lost at sea; but Gerrards has knowledge that they are not lost, and he plans to acquire them at a low price before Erast finds out about their safety. Gerrards is negotiating this deal under the cover of a third party, and he is impatient because the honest Erast is loath to sell property that may well not exist. The chief clerk Ehrhart says, "He is very conscientious; selling things which are given up for lost he calls cheating." But Gerrards laughs at such naïveté: "The honest fool! How was he ever able to get so rich!" He himself is not so punctilious: "Conscience must peep through its fingers a bit" (I. i).[10]

Erast is virtuous and passive, whereas Gerrards is evil and active; but Gerrards is not a diabolical evil rationalist. He is, indeed, a villain of the older type, a person whose reason is not sharp enough to distinguish between genuine values and ephemeral ones like money. He does not categorically deny the validity of virtue, but his understanding cannot cope with the blind emotions of his heart which have persuaded him that the possession of money is more worthwhile than such intangibles as loyalty, gratitude, and honesty. Since he errs in rational judgment and his evil is not rooted in Satanism, the good characters can agree at the end that he is not beyond hope: "We have humbled him; this chastisement was beneficial to him. . . . Vice is punished; let us preserve the human being!" (V. viii). Ehrhart, who is the play's second hero, is as virtuous as his employer Erast, but he is not passive. Employing good common sense and eschewing sentimentality and exaggerated *Gelassenheit,* the author permits Ehrhart to come to the aid of Providence with his own initiative, even though Ehrhart's plan involves a wilful deception. Specifically, Ehrhart pretends to be Gerrards' accomplice, so that he may gain exact knowledge of his machinations and then foil them. Upon opening a letter meant for Gerrards, Ehrhart asks, "Is it not allowed to take preventive measures against trickery?" (II. iv). Naturally Ehrhart's imposture arouses the suspicion of the Erast family and increases their sorrows. Ehrhart himself is grieved by having to bear the reproaches of persons in whose interest he is working and whose daughter he loves. He represents the figure of virtue wrongfully accused, as did Quistorp's Aurelius. At times his grief causes his speeches to rise bombastically above the sober level of the dialogue as a whole: "The Ehrhart who a short time ago was so honest, so beloved, so happy is now as despicable and hated as the creeping poisonous worm, whom I scarcely deign to crush underfoot: is a curse, a monster which pollutes the air and poisons the rays of the sun—Oh! what pains are raging here, where happy peace ought to dwell next to my quiet conscience" (III. vii). A speech like this begins, faintly, to call to mind Schiller's prose dialogue; and Ehrhart's intrigue in a good cause, his mysterious moves which are not clarified until the end, and his pleas for continuation of trust despite appearances are features that anticipate Schiller's portrayal of Marquis Posa in *Don Carlos*. Unlike the pure idealist Schiller, however, the unsentimental rationalist Dusch fully approves of his hero's secretive maneuvers and rewards him with complete success.

The somewhat Philistine character of practical Enlightened thought in Germany comes to the fore in the delineation of Erast's character. His actions are confined to giving examples through word and deed of model behavior in a businessman and father. As a Wolffian moralist he refuses to pin his hopes on the whims of fortune and he believes that ill fortune serves a rational purpose: "Foolish person, who depends alone on the beckoning of fortune! His heart alternates between rapture and despair according to the obstinacy of chance.—My son, become better acquainted with life: joy is unfaithful, and grief has its good side!" (III. iv). Nevertheless, he does not despise material wealth in itself. He finds its possession defensible not only on practical but on moral grounds: "To what sins poverty can force a man: mighty poverty, which peoples the prisons with criminals and delivers rascals over to the sword of justice! This terrible poverty, which takes every prerogative, what is it not able to do with the resolutions of thoughtless youth when against the civil laws and the weak strength of a dying virtue it summons up all the impulses of nature, hunger, shame, and ambition: when need and despair become the judges over propriety and human love, over life and death!" (IV. i). It is admirable that Erast never gives way to despair. Even when his creditors put their seal on everything movable in his house, and he is very suddenly reduced to a diet of bread and water, he maintains full confidence in Heaven: "He has His wise purposes; and the wicked are tools through which He conducts His destinies: as worms and predatory animals promote the great cycle of nature" (IV. ii). Still more admirable is his refusal to collect debts from people in poor circumstances, although he is himself in dire straits for cash: "Deceivers can be constrained to make good their wrongs; but poverty must be a sacred refuge which protects the unfortunate man from violence" (I. iii). He declines to invest a widow's money, in spite of the help this might give him in his predicament, because he no longer feels that he can do so properly. He angrily rejects the proposal of a smooth-dealing broker who advises him to make the most of his impending bankruptcy by borrowing all the money he can and then not repaying it: "Poverty with my honorable name is far more valuable to me than riches combined with disgrace" (IV. iii). He instructs his rather immature son on the vanity of ill-gotten gains: "The ones who are plundered are always happier, despite their poverty, than their enriched plunderers" (IV. iv). In all business matters, his ideal is charitable helpfulness rather than cold profit: "Services which we render our fellowmen, even if we suffer loss thereby, still repay the loss with a secret and heartfelt pleasure" (I. iv). Finally, it is to be noted that Erast agrees with the general Enlightened view that people are not basically evil: "I consider all to be human beings; none completely good, none completely bad" (I. iv). Truly, *Der Bankerot* is a treasure trove of eighteenth-century didactic sententiousness— a German substitute for the *Vicar of Wakefield*.

The author's rationalism did not cause him to ignore the fact, however, that he was writing for, among others, a new generation of sentimental young people. In the old-fashioned way Erast has forbidden his daughter Julchen to go on considering marriage with the "disloyal" Ehrhart. In deference to parental omnipotence Julchen asks her lover, "May my will come into the question, when my parents give a command?" But Ehrhart, who is unsentimental when it somes to offering active resistance to evil, is altogether sentimental in regard to the rights of emotional young people: "It is an unjust command which prescribes laws to love!" (I. ii). Julchen herself considers love to be one emotion that reason cannot control. She will obediently try to forget Ehrhart, but is not at all sure of success: "Yes, my father, your will shall control all my inclinations—if it is possible for a human virtue to prescribe inclinations to nature and the heart" (IV. v). On the other hand, Erast will not force his daughter to marry a wealthy suitor who could save the family from bankruptcy: "Your heart shall always retain its voice" (IV. v). In Pietistic fashion, young Ehrhart listens for the voice of God in his heart when his reason is no longer capable of answering all questions. Irrational feeling as well as rational conclusions keep him optimistic about the benevolence of Providence: "Heaven predicts the good success of affairs to the honest man beforehand through an obscure instinct, through a certain joyful confidence" (II. iv). Yet the author wants to make it quite clear that Ehrhart is not motivated to good actions by love (like a French hero), and therefore a distinction is made between the *heart* and the emotion that has its origin there, *love*. He says to Erast's son, "But do not think that it is only because of love for her and because of hope of getting her that I observe laws which must constantly be held sacred by every honorable man, without any ulterior purposes. No, Erast, my honor does not base itself on such low principles. I act according to the command of my heart and of my conscience" (V. i).

To return to the question of reason, however, one need but look at the nature of Gerrards' villainy. His lack of first-rate reasoning power is perfectly apparent, and his only cleverness consists in the awkward attempts he makes to get the things his blind desires represent as valuable. His most absurd error is to have misplaced his confidence in Ehrhart, who only pretends to be his accomplice. Gerrards is unable to distinguish real from false friendship, because he does not understand that a relationship based merely on common self-interest, which he has tried to establish between himself and Ehrhart, is as variable and untrustworthy as fortune's wheel. He is unintelligent enough to give Ehrhart a letter stating that the ships (believed to be lost) are definitely safe. In Ehrhart's hands this letter will be a sure means of helping Erast, and how could Gerrards be so careless? Ehrhart says, "The pursuit of profit . . . often makes even the crafty man blind" (II. iv). It is a plain case of emotion overcoming clear reason. The author's purpose is to teach that evil, being in essence an error of reason, is no match for virtue with its higher rationality. Furthermore, Gerrards is quite mistaken about which of the Dutch guarantor-banks is bankrupt. He thinks it is "Dalem," but Ehrhart is sure it is "Harlem," the one from which Gerrards expects to receive his funds. About Gerrards' unsuccessful maneuver Ehrhart has this to say: "I do not want to determine whether it was a trick, or whether it was stupidity, with which Heaven sometimes strikes the finest deceivers when they plan to injure its darlings. It is enough for me that I am certain he believed in Dalem's bankruptcy and he fully intended to be paid out with drafts on Harlem" (III. i). Events prove that it was indeed stupidity that made Gerrards believe the wrong bank was ruined. In the end he must stand the full loss, and Erast has not been bilked of a penny. Ehrhart is able to put a stop to the sale of the ships and he is revealed as Erast's truest friend. Virtue both active and passive has won out over wickedness. But virtue is not vindictive in victory, for Erast and Ehrhart are willing to provide for the destitute Gerrards, now that he has been taught his lesson. Thus ends this bourgeois "tragedy" which seeks to give a dignified status in the theater to the problems of a businessman. Unfortunately, however, Dusch did not succeed in making a business house and its threatened collapse as

awe-inspiring a subject as the downfall of a kingdom. The bourgeois
tragedy, if it was to remain tragedy, could not follow the example
of *Der Bankerot.*

The next prose tragedy did not make its appearance until 1765,
while in the intervening year Weisse published *Krispus* and his first
blank verse tragedy, *Die Befreiung von Theben.* The new prose
work was a bourgeois tragedy fashioned, like Wieland's *Clementina,*
from a novel by Richardson; and the author was Johann Heinrich
Steffens, who had already dramatized a novel by Abbé Prévost in
his *Cleveland.* Steffens' *Clarissa,*[11] written approximately a decade
after *Cleveland,* does not show much improvement in the powers of
the good rector of the Gymnasium at Celle. Indeed, he seems less
able to cope with the intricate complexities of the social novel
Clarissa than with the varied events of Prévost's adventure novel.
In *Cleveland* he was able to select one single rather tragic episode; in
Clarissa he chose to depict the long-drawn-out and edifying death
of the heroine, and this necessitated acquainting the audience in detail with the young lady's previous history and the complicated circumstances leading to her demise. In other words, it was impossible
to dramatize the climax of this novel without narrating practically
all the rest of it. Richardson had not written a series of adventures,
but had created and constantly heightened a single situation. Rector
Steffens might have been wiser to depict the whole history of
Clarissa Harlowe in five carefully chosen acts corresponding to the
various turning points in the heroine's life. Perhaps influenced by
the French custom of depicting only the final part of a history, or
perhaps influenced by Lessing's *Miss Sara* which does the same thing,
he instead put only Clarissa's last hours on stage, and divided these
into three long tiresome acts. They are tiresome for two reasons:
because so much time is devoted to the baldest kind of exposition,
and because there is really no plot. Clarissa is dying at the beginning
and dead at the end, while those around her comment, lament, or
repent. In dialogue, length, characters, setting, and moral atmosphere, this is surely a middle-class tragedy; but its static situation is
quite reminiscent of Klopstock's little tragedy, *Der Tod Adams.*
Adam's death, however, came with the accompaniment of a certain
moral development. In Clarissa's death one watches nothing more
than the progressive weakening caused by a mortal illness. Her
soul remains the same at the end as it was in the beginning—perfect.
The question of a tragic guilt or of a justification of Providence's
action in regard to Clarissa is of little or no importance. In this
tragedy one is simply privileged to be a spectator at the deathbed
of a blessed saint, so that one may learn the art of dying.

Measured by any standard, Clarissa's plight is unjust in the extreme. She has been spitefully treated by her jealous brother and sister, and even now her hard-hearted family refuses to become reconciled with her. It was their cruelty that persuaded her to take refuge with Lovelace, and it is Lovelace's fault entirely that instead of finding refuge she discovered herself to be in a house of ill repute whose wicked mistress had her sent to jail and then tried to make a prostitute of her. In the novel, Lovelace went so far as actually to seduce Clarissa while she was under the effects of a drug; but the German dramatist preferred to omit this most ugly incident and stated only that a drug was administered by the evil procuress. Clarissa's death comes as a result of the drug's effect on her. Innocent as she is, Clarissa feels that she has sinned by leaving home against her family's orders, and that death is punishment for this sin. In contrast to Lessing's Sara Sampson, who really has sinned by leaving her kindly father and running off with her lover, Clarissa is guilty only in her oversensitive imagination. Her fastidious conscience does not convince one of the justice of her punishment, but instead makes one still more impressed with her saintliness.

Clarissa's abductor Lovelace (Steffens renders the name grotesquely as "Löwelace") is as wicked as Clarissa is good, but it is evident that her virtue and her suffering have at least made some changes for the better in him. His friend Belford has been completely won over to virtue by Clarissa, whom he now so solicitously attends. Belford puts the blame for Lovelace's actions on a lack of religion: "He however acted according to principles which fashion has introduced among the freethinkers—" (I. i). Lovelace is still too depraved to agree to marry Clarissa. He thinks that, after all, the story of her dying might be just a trick to ensnare him into matrimony. She steadfastly refuses to see Lovelace, not out of spite, but because she does not want him to disturb her preparations for death. She hopes that her death will finally convert him, and she admits, "Once I could have loved him—" (I. ix).

The author's faithfulness to his source causes him to introduce many characters on stage whom he is unable to explain or to characterize properly. In this regard he transgresses even more egregiously than Wieland in *Clementina*. Much use is made of the rear stage. Its curtain is raised repeatedly in order to reveal Clarissa's inner apartment, the death chamber. The dreadfully long and undramatic speeches that are constantly being uttered by the various characters point all too plainly to their source in the lengthy letters of the original novel. Steffens' originality has surely not been strained. Everything that is interesting in the play is to be found in the novel, and everything that is dull and awkward is due to his inability to handle his voluminous material with dexterity. He found it quite impossible to have all the action conducted in Clarissa's apartments, and therefore in the second act the scene is transferred to a coffee house. There a lively exchange takes place between Clarissa's cousin Morden, who has come to look after her interests, and the eccentric, fiery Lovelace, who resents any interference. The dialogue in this act is quicker and more dramatic than anywhere else in the play; but this is because it has been taken almost verbatim from an excellent dialogue in the original novel, reported by Lovelace in his letter of August 29 written to Belford.[12] Steffens' German version of this dialogue, in fairness to his ability as a playwright, is considerably terser and more exciting than the English original; and Steffens has succeeded in making Lovelace a still more extravagant and whimsical personage than he is in the novel, whether or not this is to be considered a laudable accomplishment. But the effect of the act is marred by the appearance of a new character, Mowbray, whose part in the proceedings is completely puzzling unless one is familiar with the novel. The brief involvement of Brand, a busybody who has been sending reports on Clarissa to the Harlowe family, is likewise unnecessary and troublesome.

In the third act the scene is set again in Clarissa's apartments. All the most affecting incidents preceding the heroine's death in the novel, most of them occurring several days before this melancholy event, are lumped together in these scenes, which cannot take more than three-quarters of an hour to elapse. The most striking incident is the delivery of Clarissa's coffin into her room by her own order. She reads and writes on it, using it as a desk. Having observed that Richardson includes several poetic biblical meditations of Clarissa's in his text, Steffens now causes his Clarissa (though but minutes away from a natural death) to write, or rather to dictate, a "death ode." In view of her debilitated state, it seems ridiculous when one of her female attendants asks her to sing this ode for the assembled friends. She tries to comply, but can only recite it. In keeping with the novel's frequent emphasis on the vital difference between the religious way of life and that of the wicked "libertines," Steffens has Belford express his admiration for the courage with which this frail young woman endures all hardships, whereas a freethinker in her position would have committed suicide long ago: "But here is a woman who acts according to nobler, firmer principles, who has not merited the evils against which she struggles, who regards this life as a transitory period of testing . . ." (III. v). From Scene Six onwards, all of Clarissa's speeches (most of them are quite lengthy) are interspersed profusely with dashes, to indicate her halting, moribund delivery. Richardson had used this device sparingly, and mostly in the heroine's last moments, but Steffens has employed it immoderately. The actual dying is accomplished in the eleventh scene. There is no bitterness, nothing but peace, serenity, and moral uplift in her beautiful death. It is dramatically poignant, however, when her dear friend Anna Howe arrives just moments too late to see her alive for a last time. The various long-drawn-out developments in the novel after Clarissa's death are hastily and drastically telescoped in the concluding scene. Lovelace enters Clarissa's apartments, wounded mortally, and is followed by Morden, who has won the duel that Lovelace started. After Lovelace breathes his miserable last, Morden ends the play with a statement that reiterates the moral lesson of the whole: "One sees in the death of a Clarissa and in the end of a Lovelace the handwriting on the wall either for himself or against himself" (III. xvii). In contrast to Wieland, Steffens has by no means been able to turn his source novel into a genuine, independent play. Like a modern cinema writer, he has done little more than adapt it, higgledy-piggledy, for presentation by actors. In his dramatization of Prévost's *Cleveland*, on the other hand, Steffens had worked with great independence to create a drama with altogether original dialogue from a simply and swiftly narrated episode.

A valiant attempt to find a new and original direction for the bourgeois tragedy was made at approximately this same time by the prolific author and professional actor Johann Christian Brandes (1735–1799), who during his lifetime of travel and trouble furnished the German stage with upwards of twenty-five new and passably expert comedies, tragedies, *Schauspiele*, and monodramas. The work in question here is entitled *Miss Fanny, oder der Schiffbruch*, which was written in 1765 and published in 1766.[13] According to a review in Klotz's *Deutsche Bibliothek der schönen Wissenschaften*, the plot was not original with Brandes: "The invention is said to stem from a novel, but I cannot remember which one. . . . Perhaps even from one of the many [imitations of] Robinson Crusoe!"[14] A notation in Jördens' *Lexikon*, which is repeated in Goedeke's *Grundriß*, states that Brandes' plot was dependent on Prévost's *Manon Lescaut*.[15] If this is the case, Brandes must be credited with almost complete originality, for the only correspondence between Prévost's novel and Brandes' drama is that Fanny, like Manon, has to fight off the advances of a young man in a governmental position upon her arrival in the New World, and this young man is killed (in *Manon Lescaut* only apparently killed) by the faithful lover who has accompanied her from Europe. Otherwise the circumstances and characters in the drama are totally different. But Brandes' originality, in any case, consisted mostly in his ability to assemble a congeries of motifs and situations already often used in earlier plays. The verdict of the *Deutsche Bibliothek* that the professional actor Brandes was exceedingly familiar with the extant body of contemporary drama, seems to be justified: ". . . but the multitude of plays, many a one of which he so often helps to perform or sees performed, makes him so familiar with the economy, situation, and even the individual touches of other authors that often his plays look as though they were put together out of hundreds." [16] However correct, this opinion is also a bit unfair, inasmuch as the plays of greater German dramatists, notably Schiller, were often heavily dependent on situations and motifs already in existence in German drama.

At any rate, there is no one play that *Miss Fanny* even remotely duplicates. Indeed, the exotic American setting of the play was something quite new for bourgeois tragedy; [17] and the idea of combining some features of the heroic tragedy with the middle-class elements was definitely an innovation. Moreover, the circumstance of the shipwreck, and the scenes played at night in a "wild, rocky region" or at midnight in a garden with a gravestone, give the drama an excitingly romantic atmosphere different from the usual indoor stuffiness of bourgeois tragedies. Unfortunately, Brandes was more capable of serving up to his audience things with a fairly reliable appeal than he was of expressing anything from within himself. He was also somewhat careless and ambiguous about the moral lessons taught in his drama. But he had good reason to be pleased with the first reception accorded *Miss Fanny*, which was performed in Munich, Berlin, and elsewhere.[18] He himself reported, however, that his pleasure was diminished when Lessing, to whom he had submitted the play for criticism, returned an unfavorable opinion of it.[19] The play's popularity was evidently short-lived, because the *Deutsche Bibliothek* in 1768 speaks of it as having failed on account of its bombastic dialogue and its repulsive villain.[20] To be sure, Weisse's Richard III was still very popular, and fifteen years later the repulsive Franz Moor in Schiller's *Räuber* was to be a smashing success.

An indication that the taste for such villains may have been already on the wane (cf. the unpopularity of Weisse's *Rosemunde* and *Atreus und Thyest*) is the fact that *Miss Fanny* was almost the only prose tragedy of the 1760's to carry on the tradition of the evil rationalist character. William Siward, in the play, is the totalitarian ruler of an island "in America" (presumably in the West Indies). It can be seen at once that a typical condition of the heroic tragedy is being fulfilled—this plot is going to deal with a tyrant. Furthermore, a rebellion of oppressed citizens is vaguely under way, and this feature is of course heroic rather than bourgeois. A fair damsel and her lover are washed up on the island's shore, and the tyrant is inflamed with passion for her. She must marry him, or dire punishment will follow. This also fits in neatly with the heroic. On the other hand, this fire-breathing evil rationalist of a tyrant is of middle-class origin, and his father, John Siward, is a virtuous, kindly, bourgeois greybeard like all the fathers so far seen in family tragedies. There are also two dignified, virtuous servants who are treated as friends—a favorite bourgeois touch. The unhappy young lovers are likewise of the middle class. This curious combination of heroic and bourgeois produces neither a realistic nor a historic atmosphere, but adds to the romantic one induced by the settings. In *Der Bankerot* the typical situation of a heroic tragedy had been completely restated in terms of a middle-class business establishment. In *Miss Fanny*, however, the transformation is only imperfectly achieved, and the resultant hybrid is somewhat monstrous. None of the action can make a serious claim to credibility, and its constant extravagance amazes and titillates but fails to move one. There is a strong suggestion of the coming Storm and Stress in *Miss Fanny*, a foretaste of such extravagant plays as Klinger's *Sturm und Drang* and Schiller's *Räuber*. These also combine the heroic and the bourgeois; but thanks to the greater talent of their authors they are more impressive than *Miss Fanny*.

The heroine is a girl of perfect virtue who combines passivity with a certain practicality. Being washed up on a foreign shore, utterly penniless, does not depress her. To her lover Nelton she says, "Our love is our happiness; we will earn our sustenance with the work of our hands . . ." (I. i).[21] She distinguishes rationally between higher and lower goods: "The world may well fail to love us for our riches, if only our virtue and love earn us esteem, if only our own conscience does not reproach us" (I. i). With all her demureness, Fanny has no compunctions about having followed her heart to the New World. She has not been afraid, like Miss Sara Sampson, to entrust her life to the frail planks of a seagoing ship while still unmarried to her lover. To be sure, we are to assume that they have lived like brother and sister! Nelton is more audacious in the Storm and Stress manner than any sympathetic hero yet seen. He has defied the command of his father and has left family, friends, and country for Fanny's sake (here possibly a certain slight resemblance to the Chevalier Des Grieux in *Manon Lescaut* may be noted). Neither he nor Fanny feels any guilt. Actually, Nelton's father has less rationality than his son, for he saw in Fanny only a poor maid servant without connections, although ". . . with the best heart in the world, with understanding, virtue, and beauty" (II. iv). This is a motif characteristic of the Storm and Stress, the rights of love versus class distinctions. Here, as in other matters of reform, the younger generation was trying to put into effect what their elders had been theorizing about since the days of Thomasius and Wolff. Nelton's love for Fanny is a rational one, based on true values rather than material ones, and his father's objection is based on the most arrant prejudice. The question of parental authority, usually of most serious importance to children even when the father is in the wrong, is not broached by Brandes at all. The whole emphasis is placed upon the false use of reason by the older generation, reason used primarily to stifle the natural and good feelings of the heart.

William Siward, the villain, is a young man, but he is a prime example of the false use of reason. His father, John Siward, is at a loss to understand this, because he has given the boy a proper rational education: "Can I reproach myself in regard to his education? Certainly not!" (I. vii). What, then, is the cause of William's depravity? John Siward's answer to this question implies that there is a diabolical quality in the son's nature which is beyond the reach of education: "His own heart, which has collected evil things and until now kept them hidden in its innermost folds,—yes, this is the only cause!" (I. vii). To the father, William is no rationalist, but "a slave of his passions" (I. iv). Yet evidence is soon forthcoming from William himself that not all glimmers of good feeling have been extinguished in his heart (for was it not one of the dearest beliefs of the Enlightenment that all human beings are born with an essential propensity for goodness?). When he sees Fanny, he is attracted *by her virtue* (as Weisse's Fausta was attracted to Crispus): ". . . a secret impulse, an impulse which is not based on sensuality alone, forced me to [love you] on first sight" (II. viii). But when he is repulsed by Fanny, he tries to use his reason to defeat the good feelings of his heart, as he has already defeated his feelings toward his father and his tutor, Well: "Heart! weak heart! you make me senseless! Why can I not make you unfeeling? To everything!" (II. ix). The evil rationalist, in league with the devil, uses reason to stifle the *wrong* emotions. Fanny, from the standpoint of true reason, warns William about the sure punishment that follows the pursuit of wicked passions. He regards such admonitions, however, as prejudices; and when his father reminds him of the duties of filial piety and gratitude, William's evil rationalism dismisses these virtues as prejudices also: "What kind of thanks do I owe you?—My existence was not brought about by any personal interest in me; your pleasure only was the sensual cause of it, and since you allowed your pleasure too much leeway, a coincidence became the cause of my existence" (III. iv).

Awkwardly phrased as this is, it clearly anticipates a more skillful presentation of the same thought by Schiller's Franz Moor: "I have heard a great deal of chatter about a so-called family love . . . it is your father! he has given you life, you are his flesh, his blood —so he shall be sacred to you. . . . I should like to ask, however, why he made me? . . . Where is the sacred part? Perhaps in the act itself, by which I was conceived? As if this was anything more than an animal procedure for the quieting of animal desires?" (*Die Räuber*, I. i). William Siward also says, ". . . a traditional prejudice puts a higher value on the lives of our relatives than on the lives of other people" (III. vi), and with this he bolsters up his wicked, "rationalistic" plan for parricide: "What does the world care about the fate of an old used-up man? His life is of slight use to it; he is scarcely noticed" (III. v). Here again, Franz Moor's words offer a striking parallel: "A light blown out, which in any case is just taking advantage of the last drops of oil—it is nothing more" (*Die Räuber*, II. i). William Siward is enraged when his heart in spite of him entertains the pangs of conscience: "Is this conscience? What? Am I then no longer master of myself?—Patience! I will surely stifle you, effeminate feeling!" (III. vii). This, too, finds a parallel in Franz Moor's speech: "Conscience, that splenetical, gouty moralist, may be able to chase wrinkled old women out of bordellos and torture old usurers on their deathbeds—but I shall never grant him a hearing" (*Die Räuber*, IV. ii). There is a parallel between William Siward and Schiller's Queen Elizabeth in *Maria Stuart* in that William is as impatient of restrictions as Schiller's magnificent villainess, and especially hates having to pretend to be virtuous: "What does my power, my sovereignty profit me, if I may not be master over myself and over my actions? . . . Ah, intolerable dissimulation! For years I had to bend myself to your yoke, until I reached my goal! Now I am master, now I banish you forever!" (I. x). This speech bears comparison with Elizabeth's soliloquy in *Maria Stuart* (IV. x).[22] Finally, there is a certain parallel between William's actions in regard to Fanny and the actions of Prince Hettore toward Emilia in Lessing's *Emilia Galotti*. Like Lessing's prince, William falls in love with a girl betrothed to another man; like the prince, he resorts to legal subterfuges to separate Fanny from her protector and to keep her in his house; again like the prince, he tries to get rid of Fanny's lover without involving himself openly.

All the foregoing comparisons demonstrate that *Miss Fanny* struck on chords that would be used in the great compositions yet to come. But, as has been stated, Brandes very extensively employed motifs already on hand. William Siward's plan to get rid both of his father and of Fanny's lover, Nelton, seems to have been suggested by Breithaupt's *Renegat*. Nelton is to be tricked into killing John Siward in the belief that he is killing William. John will be standing at midnight by the grave monument of his dead wife. Bates, a servant, will tell Nelton that John is William, and in the darkness Nelton will be deceived. This mistaken identity resulting from darkness is reminiscent of the unintentional stabbing of the father by the son in *Der Renegat*. As the situation works out in *Miss Fanny*, the one who is killed by Nelton is not John Siward, but Steely, another survivor of the shipwreck, who has acted as a foster father to Fanny in England. The motif of contrast between good father and bad son might also have come from *Der Renegat*—or from *Lucie Woodvil* or from *Der Freygeist*. The opposite motif—good child, bad parent—is fairly typical of the earlier Alexandrine tragedy. The motif of virtuous revolution, which is of considerable importance in *Miss Fanny*, had been treated before in *Timoleon* and *Henzi*.

As ever, violence is here regarded as the very last alternative. One hears that a rebellion is brewing among the islanders because two of their number have been unjustly executed. Well the tutor approves of their unrest, but John Siward is more passive: "Only rational ideas, petitions, and pleas are to be the weapons which I want to use against him. . . . I want absolutely no violence" (I. viii). Well obediently attempts to reason with William, and includes a phrase not new to German tragedy: "Look, gracious sir: you possess, to be sure, sovereignty over us and our island, but not sovereignty over our hearts" (I. ix). When words prove unavailing, Well sees fit to reprove John Siward's abuse of passivity: "Sir, through your much too great patience you almost deserve a part of your fate" (IV. i). This rebuke anticipates the indictment of passivity which Lessing clearly implied in his characterization of the father in *Emilia Galotti*.[23] Presently Brandes employs an ancient motif in revealing to us that Fanny, thought to be a poor servant girl, is really the long-lost daughter of John Siward and therefore the sister of William. When John learns of this, he thinks that perhaps the news will still soften William's heart and make rebellion unnecessary. Unfortunately, William does not find out Fanny's identity in time. Instead, John Siward is told of his son's plans for parricide, and at last reluctantly gives his consent to revolution: "Cruel duty for a father! Yet I will, I must fulfill it" (V. ii).

John Siward's decision comes too late to save the life of his newly discovered daughter, who is senselessly killed by William as a first retaliation for the rebellion: "This is the first blood lust! These were drops! Soon streams shall follow!" (V. vi). His raving recalls the behavior of Weisse's Richard after he has heard about Richmond's attack. Fanny dies in the approved, unresentful way, desiring (like Miss Sara Sampson) no revenge on her murderer: "No, Nelton! For our love's sake! Heaven must be the avenger! . . . I can no longer avoid death now,—I await it with calmness" (V. vii). The fact that her brother is the murderer removes some of the marvelousness from her virtue, for few sisters (in plays, at any rate) would act differently in her situation. For all of that, Nelton stabs William at his first opportunity. In dying, William suddenly breaks all rules for the behavior of evil rationalists by experiencing a conversion and begging forgiveness for his wrongs. This may be viewed as the answer to Fanny's prayer, "Ah, God!— the monster! Will You not perform a miracle and improve him?" (V. vi). Nevertheless, we are not asked to forego the thrilling horrors of a wicked wretch's death: William shouts and screams and sees terrifying visions of doom.

William's condition is shown to be at least indirectly related to an error on his father's part. It is not anything so crude as adultery, as was the case with Lucie Woodvil's father, and fate plays no part, as it did in *Lucie Woodvil;* nor is it the foolish indulgence of waywardness, as with the mother in *Das Mutter-Söhnchen*. John Siward has simply been too good a father. William does not fail to mention this before he dies: "Your far too great paternal love was a mistake" (V. ix). William is referring to the fact that John turned the island's government over to him after he had pretended for a long time to be a virtuous and deserving youth. The similarity of the situation to *King Lear* was probably not recognized by the author, for Shakespeare's plots were not yet widely known in Germany. John had admitted his error early in the play when he said, "How unwisely parents act, if they cede the sovereignty to their children prematurely!" (I. v.) Consequently the *Deutsche Bibliothek* remarked, "Everyone drew this moral from the play: You fathers, do not be so simple, and do not give your children so much leeway!" [24] Furthermore, although John Siward frequently scolds and remonstrates with his son, he waits too long to use force (the rebellion) against him, and this may be called too great love. It is then evident that the play shows both evil rationalism and sentimental passivity to be at fault. That much would be clear. But the clarity of the author's moral intent becomes obscured when proper education, the hope of the century, has not helped William; and when a quite perfect and harmless heroine is cruelly murdered. Moreover, young Nelton, who has not been at all passive, is shown to have nothing left but despair, although he does at least refrain from suicide, which John Siward describes as being "characteristic of small souls only" (V. ix). It gives one pause when neither Nelton's murder of poor old Steely by mistake nor his retribution against William is especially criticized by anyone. The most confusing thing of all, however, is John Siward's unwillingness to admit his guilt in the whole deplorable situation: "I can reproach myself with nothing, nothing except a too sensitive and tender heart! Is this punishable?—My purpose was virtue. God! Why did I then have to become immeasurably wretched?" (V. ix). Are we to conclude that sentimentality is not wrong after all, and that Providence is to blame for what has happened as much as William? John's words, which as a curtain speech naturally go unanswered and uncorrected, are an unprecedented accusation leveled against Providence and the promise to reward virtue. But it is hard to imagine Brandes, a man who was very much aware of his lack of education and the modesty of his talents, as setting himself purposely against the prevailing Enlightened philosophy. One explanation for the confusion of moral intent in *Miss Fanny* is that Brandes had nothing more definite in mind than the wish to excite and astound his audience. Another, however, is that tragedy and pessimism were becoming more closely allied in the late 1760's.

In the same year with *Miss Fanny* there appeared a most interesting experiment in prose tragedy, in this case not a bourgeois work. It was called *Ludewig der Strenge,* and was published anonymously in Breslau in 1766. In 1767 the text received a wider circulation by being printed again in the fourth volume of *Theater der Deutschen.* According to a notation in Kayser's *Vollständiges Bücher-Lexikon,*[25] the author was one Ludwig Wilhelm von Langenau. This notation lists the date of publication of *Ludewig der Strenge* as 1776, which is either a mistake or a possible second edition.[26] Little is known about the author, except that he was a Silesian nobleman who resigned as Prussian *Oberamstrat* in Breslau in order to retire to his estate in Neumark, where he died after 1766. Besides *Ludewig der Strenge* he published some poems and speeches, mostly concerned with Silesia.[27] The subject of the drama, however, is not Silesian, but is drawn from medieval Bavarian history. It is a noteworthy piece of work, because it is the first *Ritterdrama* to be written for the German theater.[28]

The choice of subject matter is indicative of the awakening interest in the German past during the latter part of the eighteenth century. This was not the sternly moral and patriotic interest that induced Schlegel, Möser, and Schönaich to resurrect Arminius and his fellow heroes as examples of German rectitude. Rather, it was a romantic interest that sought out the colorful, the dashing, and the strange, in order that a contemporary German audience might for a while escape the humdrum present in a medieval dream. *Ludewig der Strenge* antedates by seven years the play which is generally thought of as the first *Ritterstück*—Goethe's *Götz von Berlichingen* (1773). It has by no means so full and complicated a plot as *Götz*, nor does its action spread over a vast canvas with dozens of speaking and non-speaking roles. But if its similarity to *Götz* must be very cautiously put forward, there is, on the other hand, little difficulty in recognizing *Ludewig der Strenge*, with its sensational historical incident and its Bavarian locale, as a forerunner of Törring's *Agnes Bernauerin* (1780) and Babo's *Otto von Wittelsbach* (1782), two classical examples of the *Ritterstück*.

The author of *Ludewig der Strenge* still honored the Gottschedian rules enough to condense his material within the strict boundaries of the Unities, as was quite normal during the 1760's. But condensation, not typical of later *Ritterstücke*, has only added to the impact of this tragedy. The rule of decorum is broken once, when a young woman is brutally killed on stage. The prose dialogue, as far as heaviness and long-windedness are concerned, is not much of an improvement over old-fashioned Alexandrines. Nevertheless, the prose manages to lend the play a somberly realistic atmosphere that is subtly but definitely different from the stagey conventionality of contemporary verse tragedies. Prose, to be sure, was not able to make either *Philotas* or *Hermes und Nestan* realistic. Perhaps it is the combination of prose with a naively earnest tone of expression and with an authentic Bavarian incident which makes *Ludewig der Strenge* the first German historical or heroic tragedy in which one really has the impression that persons long dead have come back to life to play out their pitiful actions before one's eyes. It is a ghostly, spectral life to which they have returned, for the author's talent was not sufficient to give them true flesh and blood; but at least one seldom doubts the truth of what they are doing.

The history of literature ought not to have bypassed this play without a word. It embodies the transition from that sort of historical tragedy that comes into being because the author has rummaged around in his library until he has found an incident startling or morally edifying enough to dramatize, to the sort that arises because the author has truly been touched and inspired by some story, so that he desires to communicate his feelings about it to others through a dramatization. In this change from an intellectual to a subjective approach to historical tragedy, Bernhold's *Johanna, die Heldin von Orleans* may be an early sign of what was to come, but *Ludewig der Strenge* is a noteworthy milestone. In a sentence added to the conventional indication of place and time of the tragedy, the author gives a hint concerning the subjective, emotional inspiration for his work: "The story took place, according to the epitaph of Duchess Marie which is to be found in the Church of the Cross in Donauwörth, on the XV calends of February, that is, on January 18, 1256." [29] One can easily imagine von Langenau on a visit one day to the church in Donauwörth, stopping curiously before the grave of Marie of Brabant and becoming engrossed in her tragic history. Then he must have found out all he could about the ancient crime that laid her in an untimely grave, and he, who presumably had never written a drama before, had no rest until he put all of this into a drama. This is admittedly a romantic reconstruction of the genesis of *Ludewig der Strenge;* but it seems to be borne out by the romantic quality of the drama, a quality not to be found in the tragedies of other and better writers who found their subject matter by flipping through the pages of history books.

Naturally, this play cannot deny its close relationship to the epoch in which its author lived. The heroine, Duchess Marie, is represented as a woman of saintly virtue, and she has an entourage of similarly perfect people. On the other side there is her very imperfect husband, Duke Ludwig of Bavaria, and his evil counsellor, Breithorst, whose unscrupulous machinations cause Ludwig to execute the innocent Marie for infidelity. Like Henley in Brawe's *Freygeist*, Breithorst is motivated by revenge. It is, however, not a monumental but a petty vengefulness, based on his grievance against the Duchess for having helped the son of her governess to get the position of Statthalter of Mannheim, which he had wanted for himself. Despite the pettiness of his motivation, Breithorst might have become a regular evil rationalist if he were not forced to assume a virtuous mask through most of the play. Thus he has little opportunity to display the terrifying depths of his wickedness. Intelligence (*Klugheit*), as one would expect, is his guide in life. He asks, for instance, "Is it possible that my intelligence will suffer shipwreck? . . . Do not forsake me, clever mind!" (III. ii). But only at the end, when his villainy has been exposed, does his actual kinship to the Richards and the Henleys show forth. Since his heart is capable of no feeling except delight in the sufferings of others, he experiences no fear or remorse in the face of death. Ludwig decides that his viciousness must be more than human in origin: "Tell, wretch! whether Satan bodily possesses you, that at the edge of the grave you can still rejoice over your crimes?" (V. vii). It is decided that he shall be turned over to the Statthalter of Mannheim, whose mother, as Marie's governess, has also fallen a victim to Ludwig's fury. The Statthalter, as a bereaved son, will know how to punish exquisitely the man whose deceitfulness set the Duke off on an orgy of slaughter. But Breithorst defiantly retorts, "I scorn the slowness of torture, which, so long as it lasts, will only renew the pleasure of my fulfilled revenge" (V. vii).

The character of Duke Ludwig owes little to previous tragedy, probably because it was not based on literary tradition, but imitated from the well-established historical personality of this Bavarian ruler. Duke Ludwig, although renowned for his ruthlessness and violent rage, was evidently oppressed by doubts and remorse after he had his wife cruelly executed.[30] There was no set figure in German tragedy to match Ludwig's combination of really reprehensible wickedness and essential good-heartedness, although he well exemplifies the Enlightened dictum that there is danger in allowing the emotions to escape the control of reason. Furious and benighted tyrants had been seen before on the German stage, notably Weisse's Constantine and Suleiman; but there had been no one as yet with the explosive, hairtrigger passion of Ludwig. When Ludwig suspects that Marie has been unfaithful, Breithorst has only to withhold the proof of her innocence. Then Ludwig promptly takes the initiative in accusing and punishing her. He does not have to be coaxed and convinced and dexterously led by his evil counsellor, for this is no Othello-Iago situation nor a repetition of Young's *Revenge*, however great the surface similarity may be. The important thing is Ludwig's fearful anger, and not the means by which this anger is unleashed. One might say that Ludwig possesses the demonic quality, the titanism of a Storm and Stress personality; but he lacks the slightest idealism that would gain him sympathy, and the inhumanity of his cruel fury strikes terror and revulsion into one's heart. The terrible force of this anger is effectively suggested in the first two acts of the play, when the helpless women, Marie, her governess Kunigunde, and her young lady-in-waiting Helika, flutter about the castle like trapped doves in dread expectation of Ludwig's arrival. They know that a misinterpreted letter of Marie's has convinced Ludwig of her unfaithfulness and that he has abruptly murdered the messenger who innocently put the letter in his hand. Ludwig's entrance in the third act is suitably terrifying. He stalks in holding the bloody sword with which he has just slaughtered the castellan Trautwert, who tried to help the women escape.

From that time on, the depiction of Ludwig's fury in action does not disappoint the expectations built up in the first two acts. He is certain that he is justified, and regrets only that his impatience prevents him from dealing out more dreadful punishments than mere sudden death by a sword thrust: "The traitor Trautwert was punished too gently. . . . I was too heated, and he was unworthy of an honorable death by my hand! But it shall be seen tomorrow what his vices deserve, when the dogs drag his guts around on the streets" (III. i). Dialogue of such crude intensity had seldom been heard since Gottsched's reform of the theater. Nor had such a scene been written as that in which Ludwig plunges his sword into the breast of Helika, who is brave enough to face him after Marie's execution and call him the murderer of her dear mistress (IV. v). But Ludwig is at the peak of his cruelty in the somewhat earlier scene of Marie's "trial" when, acting both as the accuser and the judge of Marie, he will not listen to her defense and harshly orders her away to be beheaded (IV. iii). Unspeakable tyrant as he is, his remorse is not incredible when he learns that Marie was absolutely innocent. The violence of his anger is transformed into equally unsparing self-accusation. However, the play does not end in Ludwig's despair. His saintly sister Elizabeth reminds him that there is no sin too great to be forgiven. Comforted by this thought, Ludwig sinks to his knees in prayer and vows to found the cloister and church of Fürstenfeld as penance. Only with a strong infusion of orthodox Christian religious feeling can such an ending take place, for like the ending of Klopstock's *Salomo* it certainly does not satisfy the demands of rationalistic justice. The quiet and conciliatory conclusion of the horrifying incident makes this drama into a morality play in which the guilty man is not duly punished, but chastised and forgiven.

The fate of Marie, to be sure, is characteristic of the familiar martyr tragedy, whether Christian or stoic. Although innocent, she does not look upon her approaching death as an injustice. In the first place, her marriage up to this point has provided her with more happiness than most people enjoy in an entire normal lifetime. In the second place, she regards martyrdom as a privilege. Finally, she manages to absolve her husband from guilt in the affair. Thus, she addresses him in her imagination before he returns to the castle, "I can indeed attain the martyr's crown through you without having to call you my tyrant. Not a hair falls from our heads without the will of the Most High. An angel of death, armed by His command, is not a tyrant" (II. iv). Though saintly, Marie also shows practical rationality in reflecting that a quick death by execution is preferable to a painful natural demise; and she will also have an easier departure than those martyrs who were torn to pieces by animals in the Roman arena. The castellan Trautwert, however, does not approve of her passivity: "In conscience I am duty bound to remind you that neglectfulness of life is suicide" (II. v). Marie cannot see how her patient acceptance of the will of Providence can be confused with suicide. Moreover, it never seems to occur to her (or to the author) that her martyrdom is less Christian (i.e., dying for one's faith) than it is stoic (i.e., like the Roman Octavia, dying rather than acting in one's own defense). Only when Kunigunde tells Marie that the lives of her women are also in danger, and when Elizabeth (Ludwig's sister) calls Trautwert's proposal for flight "rational," does she agree to leave the castle. Consequently, any criticism to the effect that her death might be considered a suicide is allayed. But Marie relinquishes her martyr's mood with reluctance: "Perhaps by this I am forfeiting a joyous willingness to die which might fail me in my hour of death" (II. v). And, as it turns out, Marie was right in not wanting to go, for the attempted flight, which is intercepted, only adds to Ludwig's conviction that she is guilty. It must not be supposed that Marie's acceptance of death is depicted as something easy and natural for her, as if she were just waiting for something like this to come along so that she could be a martyr. At first she is frightened and dismayed, and only subsequently conquers herself with reason and religion.

In the "trial" scene, Marie's character shines forth with an irresistible charm and grace. Wisely, the author gives her no bombastic bravura speeches; she always speaks modestly and gently. Her saintliness is tempered by her love for her husband and her realization that under all his fury there is still the faithful lover she has known. Conversely, her love is tempered by her genuine joy at the prospect of heaven. She displays a poise, grace, and sweetness unparalleled in the female personages of German tragedy before this time. In a dignified way, she maintains her innocence, and her desire for martyrdom does not extinguish the natural human wish to clear herself and regain her husband's confidence. The joy of martyrdom is always nicely balanced as an alternative, in case she *must* die; it is not a stubborn and fanatical compulsion, like that of Cronegk's Sophronia, which she displays. When all hope is gone, and she is about to be led off to execution, she makes a long farewell speech which is a masterpiece of restraint and delicacy. In it she speaks of her gladness to die, and at the same time she comforts Ludwig: "Because duty can command no further effort to save my life, therefore my conscience permits me to thank you sincerely for hastening the wished-for goal of my woe. . . . Shall I so happily go out of the world and not at the same time assure you, my sovereign and lord! that I have already had a foretaste of heaven in your arms? How few hours have you been my angry judge? On the other hand, several years, every day of them, have convinced my delighted soul of this, that except for your amiable company all the charms of the world would be nothing but worthless illusions to me. . . . Not a drop of my spurting blood can disturb your peace of mind: for up until the sword stroke each one of them will be enlivened by my gratitude and loyalty to you" (IV. iii). She wishes him every blessing for a long and happy life, and then "bows with a loving expression" (as the stage direction says) just as she is led away. One almost begins to feel pity for Ludwig, because he is losing such a wife. It is noteworthy that her saintliness is shown to go hand in hand with the emotion of love. To describe conjugal love as a foretaste of heaven—this is indeed a daring step and a strong testimony of the importance gained by love in this decade.

One need not seek far to discover the reasons why *Ludewig der Strenge* was neglected and passed over by contemporary critics (and apparently by theatrical directors as well). The time was not yet ripe for a heroic martyr tragedy based on medieval Bavarian history. Only an eccentric, provincial, and non-professional writer would select such subject matter, and the literary world could not spare much attention for his work. Klotz's *Deutsche Bibliothek* dismisses the play with one scornful, superficial statement: "*Ludewig der Strenge*, about whose author one would fain weep." [31] The sincerity of the play's feeling, the delicacy of the heroine, and the crude power of the "hero," are admittedly to be found only by the reader who studies the text with a sympathetic eye, not by the one who requires a smooth, flowing dialogue. But it is ironical that many less expert works enjoyed both production on stage and critical comment (even though unfavorable). Among the readers of the *Theater der Deutschen*, where *Ludewig der Strenge* was reprinted in 1767, there must have been some authors who later on profited from its new historical spirit. The honor of being a pioneer must be accorded its author. In a sense, because it is in prose, has five full acts, and yet is not bourgeois in character, *Ludewig der Strenge* is also a forerunner of *Ugolino*—a play that could not be ignored.

The next prose tragedy that was published, however, was again a middle-class work, and again it was based on a novel, or perhaps two novels. In 1767 Helferich Peter Sturz (1736–1779), a secretary in the Danish diplomatic service and a member of the German literary circle in Copenhagen,[32] brought out a tragedy entitled *Julie*.[33] The author himself declared that the drama's source was a recent novel, *The History of Julia Mandeville* (1763), by Frances Brooke, one of England's minor but once popular female authors. Sturz explained, however, that he had borrowed only the catastrophe, and that the dialogue and the characters were original with him.[34] He said nothing about a possible second indebtedness, which was to Rousseau's novel, *La nouvelle Héloïse* (1761). In *Julie* Sturz returned to the personal relationships and private settings of the bourgeois tragedies of the 1750's. He did not follow Dusch into the depiction of a "condition" nor Brandes into an exotic locale and the addition of heroic elements. But he did greatly enlarge on one feature that both Dusch and Brandes had touched on briefly: the right of a child to love some person other than the fiancé or fiancée selected by the father. Opposition to paternal wishes in the choice of a mate is the whole subject of *Julie*. This motif had already attracted wide attention through Rousseau's *La nouvelle Héloïse*, a part of which Franz von Heufeld, a Viennese playwright, dramatized in a serious comedy (or *drame*) called *Julie, oder Wettstreit der Pflicht und Liebe* (1766). The affair of Rousseau's original lovers had ended in a bittersweet renunciation, but Heufeld let them be united in a happy marriage, as befitted the type of play he meant to write. Sturz's *Julie*, on the other hand, makes its lovers, who, despite their "originality," are close relatives of Rousseau's St. Preux and Julie, unmistakably tragic through the catastrophic ending borrowed from *Julia Mandeville*. Here an important innovation needs to be mentioned: Sturz (for the first time since the days of the *Haupt- und Staatsaktionen*) introduced a comic personage into his tragedy, not unconsciously but intentionally. He ventured to do this because, according to his assertion, he cared nothing for the rules[35]—a bold statement heralding a new epoch in drama. As the *Deutsche Bibliothek* pointed out, Sturz's comical "Captain" owes much to the eccentric role of the "Commander" in Diderot's *Le père de famille* (1758);[36] Diderot's play, however, was not a tragedy even in designation, but an example of the *drame*. The *Deutsche Bibliothek* did not applaud Sturz's combination of the comic with the tragic, and Schmid in his *Chronologie* was equally cool.[37] Still, the play was performed four times in the fall of 1767 at the Hamburg National Theater,[38] unfortunately too late to be included in the discussions of Lessing's *Hamburgische Dramaturgie*.

The love of Sturz's Julie for her suitor Belmont is definitely not a rational one. Like Miss Sara Sampson, Julie falls in love because of her highly sentient heart: "How should I have resisted this love, dearest aunt? It arose with our ability to feel. . . ." (I. i).[39] Julie's aunt underscores this by saying, ". . . one's first love, child, is usually not rational" (I. i). At the same time, Julie insists that Belmont has excellent character and many good qualities, and is lacking only in money. Accordingly, we conclude that her love, emotional though it is, does not run counter to the demands of a rational love. To reject Belmont because he is poor may be a realistic decision, but it does not sound like an ideally rational one. Wealth is an illusion (*Scheingut*) in comparison to virtue. Julie protests that her father, Herr von Wohlau, was cruel to have promised her hand to Woldemar, whom she does not love—although he, too, is a man of fine character, and rich.[40] To make matters worse, Herr von Wohlau made the promise to Woldemar's father as the latter lay dying, thus making the agreement especially binding. Julie's aunt is affected by the girl's tears; but as an old-fashioned person who considers all feeling as a hindrance to clear thinking, she tells her, ". . . I cannot say you are right, child! for you move me more than you convince me" (I. i). Herr von Wohlau is more rigid a rationalist than the aunt. To him, his daughter's tears are mere "puling" and he feels it would be shameful to let them prevail over "all human reason" (I. ii). The usual gentle, loving bourgeois father has disappeared from the scene here. But worse by far is an uncle, the Captain, a military man of boorish manners, in whom the principle of reason has been reduced to an open absurdity. Even Herr von Wohlau strongly disapproves of his brother's drastic methods of bludgeoning "reason" into the young people. The first scenes of the play demonstrate the complete breach that exists between the older generation with its distrust of feeling and the younger generation with its attitude that feeling (particularly love) is the most essential thing in life.

If in Julie one can recognize a spokeswoman of the new era of sentiment, then in Belmont one can already see the typical young men of Storm and Stress drama. On meeting him, one wonders how good a judge of character Julie really is. True, he is full of feeling and warmth. But he gives no ear at all to reason and moderation, so that he is unable to distinguish between good and bad feelings and is an easy prey to criminal impulses. He goes against tradition by refusing to acknowledge the virtuous qualities of his rival Woldemar, although his more moderate confidant Werneck rebukes him for this and tells him to be calmer (*gelassen*). Belmont is enkindled by a new sort of demonism. Formerly, the demonic quality had been reserved for evil rationalists; now it is transferred to a basically attractive personage for whom the cult of the heart has become fanaticism. Nelton in *Miss Fanny* evinced some of this demonism. But Belmont is a much more pronounced case. He rages hyperbolically, "Command the storm winds to whisper—and the flame to loiter; you bid me to be calm? Oh, Werneck—you are cold—you do not know passion—" (I. x). The transition from passive to active virtue in tragedy had scarcely begun, enthusiasm and the heart had just gained some respectability, and already the dangers inherent in following the heart are being indicated, and by the very authors who are supposed to be combatting old-fashioned rationalism. Reason in its best sense would always be regarded as an ideal, both in the Storm and Stress and later. Julie, though more moderate than Belmont, is also led astray by emotion. She admits to her governess, Frau Dalton, that love is interfering with her religion: "Yes, can you believe it? he disturbs even the worshipfulness of my prayers, his picture hovers before me, even when I direct my eyes to heaven" (II. i). This was also to be Luise Miller's problem in Schiller's *Kabale und Liebe* (I. iii). Julie is aristocratic enough to believe that only gentlefolk have feelings like hers: "Oh, why was I not born in a hut, accustomed to work and to suffering; then I would not have such a sensitive soul" (II. i). This is oddly out of keeping with the usual more sentimental reasons expressed for desiring the simple life.

The virtuous rival Woldemar, belonging to the younger generation also, is likewise a man of feeling. He has been unable rationally to master his love for Julie, although he knows it is the cause of her sadness. Knowing his virtue, Julie appeals to his generosity, asking him to stop loving her—a rather unfair demand from someone who herself has so little self-control. Nevertheless, he does force himself to tell Herr von Wohlau that he will never marry Julie: "Never was a passion more violent; but I would have to be a villain—if I did not suppress it as though it were a vicious desire—" (II. vi). The happy balance of heart and reason within Woldemar makes a very attractive contrast to the excessive rationality of von Wohlau and the excessive emotionalism of Belmont. Julie's tears, the strongest weapon in virtue's arsenal, have brought Woldemar to a truly heroic act of renunciation. Herr von Wohlau counters, "But tears, Woldemar, are not rational conclusions" (II. vi). Unfortunately, this "rational" father is not wise enough to prevent a private interview between the Captain and Julie in which the madcap uncle tries to browbeat Julie and finally drags her off to be locked in her room. The counterpoint of comedy and sentimentality in this scene is grotesque but somehow effective.

In the third act the plot becomes quite complicated, mainly because of Belmont's insane jealousy of Woldemar. He will not believe that Julie has spoken to Woldemar only to entreat him to relinquish her. He expresses himself with early Schillerian extravagance: "Oh, Werneck! I am doubly wretched, I have tasted the raptures of a happy love, I was raised to the summit from which I saw the great of this earth far below me! Now I have fallen; I writhe down here in the dust" (III. ii). On a wild impulse he returns to Julie a portrait that she had given him, and Julie thinks this means he loves her no longer. Frau Dalton says the picture may only be Belmont's way of telling her that he has returned to the vicinity. Thereupon Julie asks Woldemar to help her escape her father's house where she is no better than a prisoner. Woldemar offers to take her to his mother. Since this move (reminiscent of the flight of Richardson's Clarissa Harlowe and Lessing's Miss Sara) is necessary for the development of the plot, the author does not let it occur to Woldemar that he has no right to remove a daughter from under the paternal roof. Nor is any tragic fault imputed here to Julie. Indeed, the flight has the effect of improving Herr von Wohlau. He is overcome by remorse for his harshness and rages at the Captain, whom he orders from his house. Woldemar now speaks very generously in favor of the love of Julie and Belmont, and the aunt offers to enrich Belmont from her own estate. Then Herr von Wohlau at last consents to the marriage. Is there to be a happy ending in the middle of the fourth act? The author resorts to a most questionable device to prevent one: a stupid servant (another comedy type) overhears that a marriage is to take place in two days. He supposes that it will unite Julie and Woldemar, and reports this news to Belmont. The latter promptly falls into a paroxysm of rage and despair: "Revenge—revenge—it calls from deep within my soul— what do I care for the world?—what are laws?—I can lose nothing —What is virtue?—virtue be damned—" (IV. xi). When Woldemar meets him, Belmont will not listen to a word of reason, but starts attacking him. Disgustedly remarking that Belmont is not worthy of Julie, Woldemar accepts the challenge to a duel. At this point, two alternatives were open to the author: either Woldemar could have been mortally wounded, thus receiving very poor payment for his unusual virtue, or Belmont could have been killed in just punishment for his lack of rationality. The author chose the second alternative. Although Belmont deserves his fate, a great deal of the blame falls on Herr von Wohlau, who kept the true lovers apart.

Because of Belmont's death, Julie loses her mind. It is intimated that she, too, will soon die; and Herr von Wohlau will not survive her very long.

In this play one has the impression that the Storm and Stress has begun. It appeals to the audience's uncritical sympathy for the two ill-starred lovers, while calm reflections about justice, Providence, and a rational universe are conspicuously absent. As was explained above, the persons who suffer have incurred guilt of one kind or another, and only the perfectly virtuous character, Woldemar, comes off well. But in the last act, when Belmont is killed and Julie mourns, one is not led to reflect on their imperfections but about the pitifulness of their misfortunes. False reason, which spurns and stifles emotion, is obviously castigated. The other side of the picture, however, the mistake of allowing the emotions to blot out reason altogether, is more sympathetically treated. The author does not didactically chisel out a simple answer for the troubles of Julie and Belmont. They are less examples of erroneous behavior than helpless victims of forces far stronger than themselves: their emotions, their fate, and the harshness of their elders. It is not enough to say that Belmont should not have been so headstrong and jealous, or that Julie should not have let love interfere with her devotions. These matters technically exonerate Providence, but they do not erase the impression that society is at fault in its hostility to lovers. In *Julie* we see that human beings can get into situations where they are to be neither admired nor criticized, but only pitied. *Julie* had few predecessors as a German tragedy in which the chief emotion is pity. Perhaps only Schlegel's *Dido* might be mentioned in this category, and with reservations because of the disapproving attitude taken toward the emotion of love in that play. This must sound quite wrong to those who think of *Miss Sara Sampson* as an archetype of the tragedy of pity; but the tears that flowed for Sara were inspired as much by admiration as by pity. Sara, although she is victimized by others, always remains spiritually in control of herself. Julie and Belmont are just poor helpless creatures who arouse no admiration and ask only for compassion.

This obscure tragedy by Sturz may perhaps be added to the rather long list of literary works which had an influence on Schiller's *Kabale und Liebe*. Even if one discounts what both plays evidently owe to the rebellious daughter motif established by *La nouvelle Héloïse*, and overlooks the characteristics that both Belmont and Schiller's Ferdinand may well have derived independently of each other from St. Preux in Rousseau's novel, there are still similarities between *Julie* and *Kabale und Liebe* worthy of mention. The example of Julie's interrupted prayers has been cited. Belmont's un-reasoning jealousy (not a ruling trait in Rousseau's St. Preux) is much like Ferdinand's. Constantly suspicious of unfaithfulness on the part of Julie—as Ferdinand is in regard to Luise—Belmont loses his head completely when he thinks that Woldemar and Julie are to be mar-ried. Then not even Woldemar's plain statement, "I surrender my rights" (IV. xii), can bring him to his senses. This temporary in-sanity brings to mind the refusal or incapability of Schiller's Fer-dinand to hear Marshal von Kalb's frantic asseverations that he has had nothing to do with Luise. Most important, Schiller might have seen in *Julie* an example of a German tragedy in which there were whole scenes of a decidedly comic nature, thanks to a personage as much the caricature of a military officer as Schiller's Marshal von Kalb was the caricature of a courtier. Generally speaking, Sturz created in *Julie* a tragic pattern that would still be valid in the 1780's when *Kabale und Liebe* was written: the tragedy in which hero and heroine are ruled by emotion and are objects of pity rather than admiration, while their sad fate is engineered by outside forces to which they succumb.

If *Julie* had no significant predecessors as a tragedy of pity, it did, however, have a remarkably similar companion in a prose bourgeois tragedy that appeared almost simultaneously with it. This was Christian Felix Weisse's *Romeo und Julie*, published in the fall of 1767 in the fifth volume of Weisse's *Beytrag zum deutschen Theater*.[41] Before its publication, *Romeo und Julie* had enjoyed an extraordinarily successful series of performances in Leipzig begin-ning on April 27, 1767. These performances continued until the end of the year and then the play began winning applause in other German cities.[42] Inspired, of course, by Shakespeare's tragedy, this *Romeo und Julie* had a tragic pattern essentially the same as that of Sturz's *Julie*. But despite all similarities, coincidence and not in-fluence was at work here. There is scarcely a remote possibility that Sturz could have known or used Weisse's drama, for he was living in Copenhagen during the Leipzig performance of the as yet un-printed *Romeo und Julie*. Weisse's drama is clearly the more ex-cellent work, and its great popular success proved that uncritical pity without moral edification was the emotion that the public had been waiting to experience—and furthermore, that love, as a tragic subject, was more attractive than any other. *Romeo und Julie* was received with unprecedented enthusiasm.[43] The *Deutsche Biblio-thek*, usually so caustic in its criticisms, had the most unbounded praise for this work: "I have gladly lingered long over this play, which I would place at the head of our tragedies, if such a decision were not too bold for me." [44] If comparisons with Shakespeare were made, the consensus was that Weisse had improved on him, and this was an opinion with which Weisse modestly agreed, pointing out in his preface that Shakespeare had not worked from the best sources and had filled his play with many trivial matters and infantile humor.[45] Small wonder that Lessing felt called upon to emphasize the true difference in stature between Weisse and Shakespeare in the *Hamburgische Dramaturgie* (St. 73). Weisse established the originality of his work by carefully naming his "better sources," the original novellas of Bandello and Luigi da Porto. If his own generation had not been so unfamiliar with Shakespeare's works,[46] Weisse would not have been obliged to assert his originality so explicitly. Anyone who has read both versions does not need to be convinced that Weisse's is not an adaptation of Shakespeare's text. On the other hand, a few of the speeches contain reminiscences of Shakespearian passages, insofar as prose can reproduce Shakespeare's poetry. The prose dialogue, especially when the lovers speak, is frequently very flowery. Weisse realized this and defended his use of extravagant expressions on the grounds that love makes young people imaginative and fantastic.[47] At any rate, such dialogue showed that prose did not have to be always matter-of-fact and everyday in tone. The use of prose in *Romeo und Julie* by a highly respected author who had previously distinguished himself in verse tragedy marks the victory of prose and the beginning of its twenty-year reign.

No doubt Weisse felt that it was logical to employ prose in a work dealing with a private, domestic situation and involving only middle-class characters. But his work was unlike any other bourgeois tragedy, with the sole exception of Sturz's *Julie*, in its unbourgeois emphasis on the rights and the beauty of young love. It is even unlike *Julie* because of its romanticized Italian setting (altogether different from the contemporary, unromantic Italy depicted in Lessing's *Emilia Galotti* in 1772), and because of the absence of any conventionally good, moderately rational character like Sturz's Woldemar. The voice of emotion is not restrained in Weisse's drama as it is in Sturz's, where only Belmont occasionally flares out with an eccentric, passionate speech. A hot wind of passion blows through *Romeo und Julie* from beginning to end, dispersing all the stodginess of moralizing, rationality, virtuous mincing, and bloodless sentimentality. What was accomplished in older plays by a villain—a Marwood, a Henley—is here accomplished by a sympathetic pair of young people. To be sure, Weisse did not depart so far from conventional morality as to represent his hero and heroine as admirable. Not only are they the victims of cruel parents, but also of their own weakness. Weisse does not fail to point out that they should have acted more rationally, but he does not censure them for their failures. The prevailing atmosphere is one of romantic pessimism: youthful love can find its consummation only in death, and death is not even sweetened by a Klopstockian vision of heavenly bliss. The orthodoxy of the philosophy in his tragedies had, of course, never been Weisse's prime concern.

With his usual skill Weisse was able to condense his rather complex source material into the framework of the Unities. The only change of scene occurs in the fifth act, which of necessity takes place in a tomb. There had been fifth-act scene changes also in *Krispus, Die Befreiung von Theben,* and *Atreus und Thyest.* Condensation required the inclusion of some long expository speeches and the sacrifice of Shakespeare's famous balcony scene, but it promoted a speedier and more intense action. Romeo appears relatively briefly, only in Act One and in Act Five, so that he retains his position as hero mainly because Julie is constantly talking about him. The play is Julie's vehicle, and its immediate success in Leipzig was in great part due to the brilliant acting of Karoline Schulz of the Koch troupe in this role.[48] The character is not decked out with the customary exalted virtue. She is deceitful in pretending to weep for her murdered cousin Tebaldo when she is actually mourning Romeo's departure from Verona. She is far from calm and passive. When her confidante Laura asks what she would do if she lost a bridegroom, she cries, ". . . I would tear the heart out of my body and lay it in his coffin" (I. ii). It is not Romeo's virtue that she speaks about, and her love for him is not especially spiritual: "I saw him, Laura! and my heart followed my eyes . . . then Romeo extended to me his silken, his soft, oh, his dear, warm, welcome hand! With every finger which touched me, he pressed an arrow of love into my heart" (I. ii). Her description of their clandestine meetings is filled with a lyric ardor remarkable for Weisse, though but a pale reflection of Shakespeare's poetry. There are frequent references to the world of nature outside the room shown on the stage, so that we are made conscious of the moon, the night, the flowers, and the birds. This feature, which unfortunately is absent from most of the earlier German tragedies, is certainly a heritage from Shakespeare. Truly, Shakespeare's influence temporarily made a new dramatist of Weisse and encouraged him to break with tradition.

Although Romeo must flee Verona because he has killed Tebaldo (an act which he could not avoid), he comes to take leave of Julie. In her impulsive, active way she wants to dress in men's clothing and accompany him on his exile. Such a masquerade would have been commonplace in eighteenth-century comedy, but it had so far been out of place in tragedy. She sees nothing to hinder her plan because she and Romeo are already secretly married, and she is fearless: "Danger, Romeo? summon up all the arrows of misfortune which can threaten you, and see if I do not catch them all in my breast and smile besides" (I. iii). Such gallant hyperbole brings to mind some dialogue written by the young Schiller—but for his young men, not for his young women.[49] It is easy to see why Weisse felt the necessity of going on the defensive about his flowery language. Romeo's passion does not quite equal Julie's, and he even retains some rationalistic traits. It is told that in the midst of a general street battle between the feuding Montecchio and Capellet clans, Romeo had tried to be a peacemaker; but the raging Tebaldo kept attacking him, and would not desist after being twice disarmed. Finally he had fairly spitted himself on Romeo's sword. In his treatment of Julie, Romeo also tries to be circumspect. It is true that he can be still more hyperbolic than Julie: ". . . a thousand times will I sacrifice my life for yours, and still ask whether I do not have ten thousand more lives to give you—" (I. iii). But he is not dedicated to thoughts of suicide and death like Julie and he rejects her plan to dress in men's clothing and accompany him. Their flight together would mean certain capture and execution for him, and eternal separation for them both. He advises her to endure the time of his exile "With hope and patience, Julie!" (I. iii). He optimistically informs her that the Prince of Verona has said his exile will not be long, and then they will be able to love in peace. Julie cannot share his optimism. He speaks of the short distance that will lie between them: ". . . hardly a day's trip from Verona, and how short that is especially for love!" To this Julie answers, "No, no, you are wrong: for love it is whole worlds apart!" (I. iii). After his departure, Julie weeps copiously, but her tears are mere emotional release and have nothing to do with virtue. They are regarded as an antidote to intolerable sorrow: "Oh! Laura! now tears are coming—now I shall feel a little better" (I. v).

Romeo's optimism has not taken into account the greatest obstacle in their way, the intention of Julie's father that she should marry the Count of Lodrona without delay. The Count is a worthy choice, as Julie's mother says: "But the Count has all the good qualities which our daughter's husband must have: rank, estate, outward dignity, virtue—" (II. i). In her old-fashioned way she presumes that this should be enough to awaken a rational love in her child. But Julie's confidante Laura speaks for the new generation: "What if she nevertheless should have no heart for him?" (II. i). According to this view, love is something more than a recognition of good qualities. If Julie's mother has little understanding of irrational love, her husband has none whatever. To Herr von Capellet rationalism is a cloak for total heartlessness and selfish wilfulness. He considers all emotions nonsense, except for his own anger. Like the father in Sturz's *Julie*, he calls his daughter's weeping "puling"; her grief is "splenetic" and she is a "fool." He is cynical about women: "As long as girls still play with their dolls they are candid . . . but scarcely have they matured to seriousness when we find they have also become hypocrites" (II. iii). A child's duty, according to him —and this had been the attitude of the century—is solely to obey. He belies his own pretensions to rationality, however, when he refuses to give Julie reasons why she should marry the Count: "If one begins to reason too much with children, then it is no wonder if they become obstinate" (II. iii). Much of Herr von Capellet's vehemence may be traced to Shakespeare's explosive father Capulet; but Weisse had portrayed wicked fathers in *Krispus* and *Mustapha und Zeangir* and an unbending one in *Die Befreiung von Theben*, so that he was himself familiar with the type. Shakespeare's Capulet had been only one of the factors in the tragedy of Romeo and Juliet, in which the main culprit was the ancient feud of the two Veronese families. But in Weisse's play Julie's father and his ambition for her become the chief factor in the tragedy, whereas the feud is secondary.

As the action progresses, Julie's melancholy grows more pronounced. The thought of death, connected with moonlight as was the style of the time, exerts a powerful influence over her: ". . . the ghost of Tebaldo beckoned to me in the moonlight that I should come soon! Oh, was that not sweet for me?" (II. v). Julie's violent passion sweeps away the sensible advice offered by her mother, who is not unkind. Not once does Julie show faith in Providence. Laura says that Heaven will send the means of rescue, but Julie spurns this consolation with the words, "The Heaven which hangs down darkly over me? the Heaven pregnant with bolts of lightning?" (II. vi). When Laura advises calmness and patience, Julie calls her "a sorry comforter" (II. vi). Her attitude toward her father is not submissive, as was the attitude of children in the older tragedies. She calls him "cruel father" to his face (although she immediately asks pardon for this), and when his back is turned speaks very rebelliously: "Ah! go then, adamant father!—tyranny does not make a heart more gentle . . . I feel it flying upward instead of bowing down . . ." (III. iii). When Benvoglio, the physician who takes the place of Shakespeare's Friar Lawrence, offers her the perilous way of escape through a sleeping potion, she accepts it valiantly, although she shares with Shakespeare's Juliet the normal aversion to being placed alive amidst moldering corpses. But she neither thanks Providence for this means of escape nor does she ask the aid of Providence. Indeed, it is established later on that this potion does not have divine approval. Her only virtuous reaction is a qualm about the deception she is about to practise on her parents: "Alas, deceit has never entered my soul: it was always pure and immaculate, like man after the first creation: the overly cruel plan of my parents, of inclosing me in hateful bonds, teaches me deceit. Ah! who is the greatest criminal, the one who teaches, or the one who commits?" (III. v). This speech shows that this play belongs to the eighteenth century. The author is satisfied, however, with the mere mention of the desirability of truthfulness, a prime ideal of his time. He does not have his heroine live according to this ideal, and yet she is excused. Julie finds it necessary to tell some elaborate lies to Laura, also. Here, however, a tragic misstep is involved, for the failure to include the faithful Laura in the secret has a direct bearing on the catastrophe. Had Laura known about the potion, she would not have told Romeo's servant that Julie was dead, and Romeo would not have taken poison. But love has robbed Julie of all scruples. She does not enjoy doing unvirtuous acts, but she does them: "—oh, Romeo, I must, I must!—Your name devours all other feelings!" (III. ix). Weisse thus provides Julie with a tragic guilt but does not seriously suggest that she might have or ought to have avoided it. He permits emotionalism to run away with didacticism.

Predictably, Julie's pretended death brings violent remorse to Herr von Capellet. The mother promptly enters on a spectacular series of fainting spells. Benvoglio utters some conventional pious statements: "Providence has wanted this: we must submit to its guidance!" (IV. vi); but our knowledge of his duplicity makes these words ring with unusual hollowness. Shakespeare's Capulet had felt a simple sorrow at Juliet's death, while Weisse's Capellet gets desperate because he realizes he is being punished for a sin—tyrannical fatherhood. Obviously, Weisse has recast the father in a shape more meaningful for his progressive century, which believed in filial obedience, to be sure, but based this principle upon the assumption that fathers would treat their children rationally and fairly. The mother's swoonings are a mute but still conspicuous expression of a heart anguished by remorse as well as grief. The author cannot let this scene go by without moralistic observations, even though the death of Julie is not genuine; therefore Benvoglio is called upon to make them, however poorly they jibe with his own less than idealistic conduct.

The fifth act of Weisse's play presented German audiences with an unconventional stage setting that was still more romantic than the rocky landscapes and moonlit garden of *Miss Fanny*. The eerie grave vault of the Capellets was a worthy forerunner of the ghastly starvation tower in Gerstenberg's *Ugolino*. In the midst of all this dust and dissolution lies the beautiful but motionless form of Julie. Then the despairing and self-accusing Romeo dashes in, bitterly regretting that he did not allow Julie to flee with him, as she had desired. Although his servant Pietro has brought him the news of her death, the messenger of Benvoglio with the true story has not reached him in time. Fate, too (or is it Providence?), has turned away from the lovers. Pietro anxiously tells Romeo, "Suicide is a crime" (V. i). It is now Romeo's turn to practice deceit. He pacifies his faithful servant by surrendering his sword, but he conceals a vial of poison. As soon as Pietro has gone, Romeo addresses Julie's "corpse" at some length, and then drinks the poison. He wants to join Julie in death, although it is not clear what will become of their spirits in the afterlife. Apparently, Romeo's suicide precludes a hope of their reunion in heaven, unless Providence decides to be more kind than just. Pietro, returning, calls his master's act a crime, but Romeo answers, "If it is a crime, then may God in His infinite mercy be merciful to me!" (V. iii). Thus God is urged to take a sentimental view of lovers and to make exceptions in their behalf. The reading of such a scene could easily undermine the strict religious doctrines taught to young people. Schiller showed how this could happen: thanks to her modern reading, Luise Miller in *Kabale und Liebe* believes that she and Ferdinand can commit suicide and yet be forgiven.

Before the poison takes its effect, Julie awakens from her death-like slumber. This was a situation found by Weisse in his Italian sources but not present in the later English version of the story that Shakespeare presumably utilized.[50] It was one well suited to the purposes of the eighteenth-century dramatist, for Julie's awakening not only sharpens the irony of the tragedy, but also gives the opportunity for some moral reflections, which in this play are long overdue. From the beginning, Romeo has been characterized as the more rational of the two lovers. Now he recognizes that his excessive emotionality has caused his ruin: "No, Julie! You must live! I see my crime! Pietro indeed warned me! I should have had more confidence in Providence, then I would have been saved, have been happy—you would have been, too. Let my example frighten you!" (V. iv). At the same time, the moralizing does not gain the upper hand. Romeo's *"mea culpa"* trails off into a pathetic and helpless accusation of "fate" as the real culprit in the affair: "I see—fate—wanted it this way. Nothing but errors—without intent! without guilt—" (V. v). Julie pays no attention to Romeo's admonitions. When he has breathed his last, she looks about desperately for a means of ending her life. Benvoglio, who has entered meanwhile, tries vainly to appeal to her reason. He has belatedly learned that human cleverness—amoral intelligence *(Klugheit)*—offers no reliable way out of difficulties. Accordingly, the clever sleeping potion could not bring happiness to the lovers. In an effort to moralize, however, Benvoglio becomes still gloomier than Romeo by ascribing the disaster not to an impersonal fate but to God, who is generally thought of as more benevolent: "—God wanted it this way—God—consider this—human wisdom was useless: I thought I had attained the highest summit of prescience and intelligence:—but see—everything has failed! Resolve, I beg you, resolve to live!—" (V. v). Perhaps this speech is meant as a plea for trust in Providence, but it has more the sound of a pessimistic injunction to accept the will of God, however cruel that may be, and not to offend Him with further sinning. Benvoglio does not stress the morality or immorality of active effort, but the pointlessness of it. Therefore we are led to pity Romeo and Juliet rather than to remonstrate with them. In any case, Benvoglio's words are lost on Julie, who espies Romeo's sword (dropped by Pietro, who by another unfortunate coincidence brought it back in with him) and pierces herself with it. She dies crying, "God have mercy on me!" (V. v). Like Romeo, she cannot rely on God's justice, for she has been emotional and impetuous instead of rational and virtuous. But at least she can count on the audience's sympathy.

In the stage production it was found advisable to let the tragedy end with the death of Julie.[51] In his second edition of the play (Leipzig, 1769) Weisse saw fit to adopt this slight abbreviation of the text of *Romeo und Julie,* but he could not forbear to attach the original two concluding scenes as a supplement.[52] In these the father of Romeo, old Montecchio, is introduced for the first time as he comes face to face with Capellet over the corpses of their children. Shakespeare had used the meeting of the Montagus and the Capulets before the mayor of Verona to show the punishment of the families for their uncivic feuding which had produced such lamentable results. Weisse uses the meeting of the fathers to cast a very tardy glow of optimism on the pessimistic story he has told. The death of these young people is regarded as a punishment—and a just and logical one—for the sinful hostility of the fathers. Montecchio says, "—while you weep with me over the loss of our two children—so let us lament our hatred, our—irreconcilability!—oh, how happy we could have been!" (V. vii). One is reminded here of the situation in *Lucie Woodvil*, where the sins and deaths of the children are revealed as a divine punishment of the father. Yet the reconciliation of the fathers (and of their families) is a positive good, and make one reflect that the worst of Providence's punishments include an element of benevolence after all. The final speech, which is spoken by Montecchio, almost makes the death of the lovers seem worthwhile: "Oh! thus the death of our dear children has had one good effect!—God bless you!—[He embraces him.] May this grievous death unite our families in tears shed in common for my eternally beloved Romeo and your eternally beloved Julie!" (V. vii). The theatrical directors were correct in omitting this little epilogue, not only because its action was anticlimactic, but especially because its optimistic, conciliatory mood clashed with the fierce passion and pessimism of the rest of the tragedy.

The next year, 1768, opened the great era of prose tragedy with the publication of *Ugolino*, the first of a series in which the titles *Emilia Galotti*, *Die Kindermörderin*, *Die Räuber*, *Kabale und Liebe*, and *Egmont* stand out with particular prominence. But besides *Ugolino*, which is the subject of the concluding chapter of this study, two other prose tragedies of incomparably less importance were published in 1768,[53] both anonymously. One, which is mentioned critically only in the *Deutsche Bibliothek*, was entitled *Die versäumte Erziehung*[54] and was a feeble imitation of *Miss Sara Sampson*. Unwisely, the unknown author followed Lessing in attempting to create a middle-class tragedy on a framework of comedy. Lessing, at least, had been able to imbue his central character with true tragic pathos; but the heroine of *Die versäumte Erziehung* is nothing more than an exaggerated and stupid little prig, while the other personages lack dignity and depth. A preposterous fifth act turns this didactic and stuffy comedy into a tragedy by main force. The first four acts, however, are not completely devoid of interest. They could be described as an imaginary prologue to *Miss Sara Sampson*, showing the process by which the unprincipled seducer steals the virtuous daughter from under the nose of her father.

Leander (a name more appropriate to comedy than to middle-class tragedy) has raised his daughter in seclusion since the death of his wife, whose help as a parent he has sorely missed. Wilhelmine, the daughter, does not seem to be the product of a "neglected education," for it is clear that Leander has spared no effort in making her into the very model of a female philosopher of virtue. She reads the works of Young, and declares that she never reads anything useless. She becomes enthusiastic about a moral passage that she finds in a new weekly magazine. The title must therefore signify that her education was all "in vain" (rather than "neglected") because she does not put its precepts into practice when temptation comes. Temptation appears in the person of a libertine nobleman, the Count of Königsberg, who insinuates himself into the household and through his ingratiating manners wins the confidence of Leander, who is not very perspicacious. The Count speaks the language of virtue with Leander, but takes every opportunity to talk boldly of love with Wilhelmine. Although a hypocrite and a seducer, Königsberg is not altogether evil. Like Lessing's Mellefont, of whom he is obviously a copy, Königsberg has an active conscience that reproaches him for his immorality. It is strange that a person with such a good heart can nevertheless carry out wicked designs with such unswerving purpose. He argues with himself thus: "How the sad circumstances regarding the death of his [Leander's] wife moved me, and the untiring effort which this good old man afterwards expended on the education of his child: as he was relating this I was almost ready to give up my whole plan.—But how long can the young man intoxicated with lusts resist his desires?—Now my views are still good, and my rational conclusions are still correct; but as soon as I see her, I will be what I was before. And what am I then? A deceiver, a shameful seducer, who from this moment on ought to recognize himself to be unworthy of the privilege of higher birth" (I. v). The question of misalliance, which is brought in when Königsberg tries to deceive Wilhelmine with a promise of marriage, gives this play a motif in common with Schiller's later *Kabale und Liebe*. Like Schiller's Luise, Wilhelmine regards such an unequal union as quite impossible: "a thing . . . which contradicts reason and propriety. . . ." (II. i). But Königsberg, without the sincerity of Schiller's Ferdinand, claims to be above all the prejudices of class : "How could I elevate myself and my family more than by a marriage with you! it consists mostly of persons who, like me, admit that in all conditions of life only the wise and rational man is to be esteemed, and that we can assert our rank in the world not only by a procession of ancestors but rather by the inner value of the soul, which we acquire through industry and attentiveness" (II. i).

Wilhelmine gradually becomes affected by Königsberg's advances. Her resistance is weakened by the clever arguments of her friend Laura, who is secretly in Königsberg's pay. In their discussions, Wilhelmine's remarks are mainly a prosy rehash of Wolffian ethical principles, as, for instance, "You call something happiness, Laura, which I indeed do not consider to be. To submit to a passion which, if it does not make us unhappy, yet makes us despicable in the eyes of a rational person, can, to my way of thinking, frustrate our happiness, but not promote it" (II. iii). After hearing a number of such remarks, Laura exclaims, "You and your confounded philosophy! You must be thinking of getting a doctor's degree with it one of these days!" (II. iii). The reader is inclined to concur with this opinion. It is soon revealed that Laura is no more a basically wicked individual than Königsberg himself. The play lacks a genuine villain. When Laura sees that her attacks on Wilhelmine's morality are succeeding, she remonstrates with herself in a soliloquy: "Bitter reproach for you, Laura! since you are the wretched tool for this: but let someone place himself in my circumstances, and then let there be an investigation to see in how far I deserve to be blamed.—Only a few characters are so constituted that they can steadfastly put up with constant poverty. . . . If I had been able through other means to procure bearable days for myself, then I would certainly not have purchased them at the expense of a friend whom I loved with the greatest tenderness and like my own soul" (III. v).

The wisdom of Königsberg's crafty and mendacious procedure is shown by contrast in a comical scene wherein another nobleman, the fatuous Marquis of Bourgogne, makes an honest and open attempt to take Wilhelmine for his mistress. The Marquis is a caricature of a courtier whose brittle manners and affected conversation bring Schiller's Marshal von Kalb to mind: "I am quite tired. I have just now come from the Duke, and not much time is left until I must again be at the assemblée" (III. vi). When the Marquis coolly proposes to pay Wilhelmine twenty thousand *Thaler* and her father ten thousand in addition, and to give her a house on one of his estates which he will have the right to visit at stated intervals, the girl and her father are outraged and fairly throw their aristocratic guest out of the house. The Marquis, as he hustles out, threatens them with revenge. His impudence only makes Königsberg gain value in the eyes of Wilhelmine and Leander. The latter, whose dignified middle-class profession is banking, now decides to venture on a business trip, thus leaving the door open to Königsberg's plan of seduction. Königsberg soon convinces Wilhelmine that she must leave with him in order to get married. She knows this is wrong, but her resistance to evil is as weak as her lover's: "But where shall I get the strength to support my good intention? And how could I defend myself, when the Count has put the whole household under obligation to himself" (IV. xiii).

Although the Unity of Place is observed in this play, the Unity of Time is transgressed with surprising freedom. The process of seduction evidently continues through a number of days (not exactly numbered), and there is a definite statement in the dialogue that between Acts Four and Five one night has elapsed.[55] At the beginning of Act Five both Laura and a servant, Servatius, bewail their part in the Count's plot, now that it is too late. Leander returns from his trip and, on hearing the bad news, falls into a faint. Then suddenly the most unexpected and anticlimactic action begins: the Marquis of Bourgogne returns to Leander's house, leading in no one but Wilhelmine herself, whose virginity is still presumably intact. According to the story told, the Count and Wilhelmine were set upon by robbers and only the Marquis' bravery (he was conveniently at hand) saved the girl from death. The Count, on the other hand, was murdered. One feels that this is a happy ending, and that the curtain must now fall. But no! Wilhelmine in a soliloquy develops some perversely conscientious thoughts about her unworthiness (thoughts apparently based on Sara Sampson's hesitation to accept the forgiveness offered by her father), and before her long speech is over she takes out a dagger and stabs herself mortally. The move is so uncalled for that one's reaction is laughter rather than shock. Leander comes in to find his daughter in her blood, and they take a rather sententious farewell of one another. A physician who is a spectator to this says, aside, "Truly, a moving scene!" (V. x). It is, however, only pointless and ridiculous. But the play is still not finished. Now the Count is brought back to Leander's house, wounded but not yet dead. He reveals that the robbers who attacked him were actually in the pay of the Marquis, who was seeking revenge— an indirect but striking parallel to the plot of Lessing's *Emilia Galotti*. Once the Count breathes his last, after uttering many expressions of repentance for having abducted Wilhelmine, Leander stands over him (as Sir William Sampson did over Mellefont) and judges that he has a good chance for divine forgiveness: "His life was a chain of vices; but his end all the richer in beauty. Here virtue was seen to revive on all sides" (V. xi). In his closing words Leander comes to the realization that the tragedy was the result of his foolish confidence in the Count and of his daughter's "disregarded education."

The other prose work, which is as weak or still weaker than the first, was *Inckle und Yaricko* (Frankfurt & Leipzig, 1768), a tragedy in three acts.[56] The author is presumed to be [57] Johann Heinrich Faber (died 1791), a university professor at Mainz and later the secretary of the imperial envoy at Frankfort. Faber also published in 1768 an *Inkle und Yariko* in verse with a plot nearly identical to that of the prose tragedy—hence the supposition that he was author of both versions. Faber's principal literary activity was not original authorship but the translation of French comedies and musical plays into German. He published more than two dozen such translations within the following eight years.[58] The subject matter of *Inckle und Yaricko* was derived from a famous anecdote contributed by Richard Steele to *The Spectator* in 1711. This material had inspired Gellert to compose a moral verse tale (1746) and Gessner to invent a sequel (1756), while Pfeffel sketched out the plot of a tragedy that was a continuation rather than a dramatization of the original (1766).[59] Except for the virtually unnoticed attempt of an obscure Englishman in 1742,[60] Faber's prose work was the first drama actually to be written on this very popular subject, although the story had already had considerable influence on Chamfort's comedy, *La jeune Indienne* (1764).[61]

Faber, imitating the procedure of "regular" tragedies, begins his drama with the last phase of the total action. Unlike Gessner and Pfeffel, he does not continue the plot beyond its original ending, but he fits it out generously with additional characters and situations and alters the ending to meet the demands of poetic justice. When we meet him, the young English merchant Inkle has already had his idyll in the American wilderness with the beautiful Indian girl Yarico and he has returned to civilization with her in tow. The author betrays a somewhat vague knowledge of geography and of population in the western hemisphere. He lets Inkle, who has left England in order to make a quick fortune in America, speak of reaching the shores of "India," where he collected a hoard of gold and jewels. One cannot tell whether the real India is meant, or whether this is a poetic name for America, or whether the reference is to the West Indies.[62] Then Inkle relates that his ship was wrecked, and his treasures lost (these were quite uncharacteristic of what was to be found in North America), and his comrades were massacred by savage "blacks." Nevertheless, Yarico, who nurtured and loved Inkle in the forest after this disaster, is clearly designated as an Indian. We learn that not all of Inkle's white companions perished: his servant Jacob also survived, after having dragged Inkle from the waves. One does not know exactly what Jacob was doing while Yarico was caring for Inkle. All that seems to have mattered to the author is that a gentleman, at any rate in a drama, must have his servant about under any and all circumstances. Eventually a ship passed by and delivered all three, Inkle, Yarico, and Jacob, safely to Barbados. As the play begins, they have evidently taken up residence on the island at an inn.

Inkle is no longer grateful that he was saved from shipwreck and tended by a faithful Indian girl. He says to Jacob in a ranting tone, "Oh, why was I not buried under a deep wave! Oh, why was I not slain by a savage hand, like my comrades? . . . Why did you not plunge me into the sea? Jacob, why did you not kill me?" (I. i). Like one of Lessing's "fools," Inkle has lost his confidence in Providence: "Have You given us our reason, cruel Providence, only that we may envy each other's good fortune? Or that we should creep around on earth poorer than cattle? How unjustly You rule" (I. ii). The reason for all these perfervid exclamations is that Inkle's English fiancée, Elisabethe, her confidante Clementine, and Inkle's brother Steyley have also come to Barbados to meet him, although it is not disclosed how they knew he would be there. Inkle's great shame and fear is to appear before Elisabethe as a pauper and an unfaithful lover. Obviously, the author has invented these new personages in order to give stronger motivation for Inkle's subsequent action, the selling of Yarico, than was given in the original story, where he is moved by a cold-hearted desire to turn a profit.[63] But even the presence of a fiancée and the loss of wealth through shipwreck did not satisfy the author's wish to explain Inkle's villainy. The young man must also receive a letter notifying him that his warehouse in England has been plundered by thieves. Thus his financial situation appears completely hopeless, and Inkle would commit suicide except that his friend Belvedere (another newly invented personage and unexpected arrival in Barbados) prevents him. Belvedere possesses sympathetic qualities as a loyal and understanding friend, but he urges Inkle to "defy" Providence by preaching to him that Providence is malevolent.

The existence of Yarico is made known to Elisabethe in a quite roundabout way. First, Yarico is shown in a sentimental mood and setting as she walks in a garden and talks to herself aloud about Inkle's sudden, disquieting indifference. She is overheard by Clementine, Elisabethe's confidante, who soon cajoles the heartsick Indian into relating her whole story, including Yarico's account of her idyllic childhood and the abduction of her father by some European slave traders. Putting two and two together, Clementine figures out that Inkle has been unfaithful to Elisabethe, while Yarico begins to suspect that Elisabethe has prior rights on Inkle's love. Clementine now hurries off to apprise Elisabethe of what she has learned. In the meantime, Belvedere suggests to Inkle that the best way to rid himself both of financial and social embarrassment is to sell Yarico into slavery. Inkle, a complete cad and moral coward, eagerly grasps this solution: "Oh, divine advice!—Already my love for Yarico is extinguished—already I am angry at myself for not having brought along more such savages. Come, let us fly to the slave trader— Come, let us win our fortune by means of this creature" (II. iv). No sooner do they leave when Elisabethe appears in the garden to express her wrath at Inkle. Then she leaves, and Inkle and Belvedere come back, followed by the slave trader, who finds nothing strange about carrying on business in this very same garden. Yarico, as she is turned over to this brutal man, reveals that she is pregnant, but this news only prompts Inkle to demand a higher price for her.

In Richard Steele's anecdote the Indian girl remained a slave. But the German author was loath to see such virtue go unrewarded. The apparent misfortune turns out to be a disguised piece of good luck, for Yarico unexpectedly discovers her long-lost father among the other slaves. They confirm their identities by means of pictures they carry "engraved in reed" (III. i). It is determined that it was Belvedere who had captured Yarico's father and sold him into slavery. Hearing this, Inkle's virtuous brother Steyley reflects sadly about the perversity of Inkle and Belvedere, ". . . such are the fruits of a friendship—based on selfishness and frivolity" (III. ii). Steyley promptly purchases freedom for both Yarico and her father, who are to accompany him and Elisabethe back to England where they will learn "revelation," i.e., Christianity. Inkle, on the other hand, is punished without delay for his vices. Elisabethe spurns him on sight, and Steyley disowns him. Even the money received for Yarico's sale is withheld from Inkle and given to the Indian girl instead. Thereupon Inkle and Belvedere degenerate completely, and their ragings are accompanied by thunder and lightning. They want to follow Steyley's departing ship and murder him and the others; but then Inkle is suddenly struck by lightning. Somehow this is not enough to kill him. Belvedere, however, obligingly finishes the job with a dagger and then stabs himself. This "tragic" conclusion is as forced and ridiculous as the one in *Die versäumte Erziehung*.

Richard Steele's original anecdote had been peculiarly effective because it had managed, with simple candor, to symbolize perfectly the rape of the New World by European mercantile opportunism. The fate of Yarico had touched the hearts of those who read *The Spectator*—perhaps because it also touched their consciences. But the uncomprehending German author submerged the poignancy of his material in a morass of conventional sentimentality and lost the broader meaning of Inkle's villainy in an awkward attempt to establish a psychology for the character that he himself, in his limited sphere of experience, could understand. Having tacked together what appeared to him a more dramatic plot out of preposterous or insipid complications, he tried to give it a tragic dignity by pumping its dialogue full of false and windy pathos. Such shallowness and banality could only arouse scorn in the Germany of 1768. There was no longer much room in the world of German drama for the efforts of well-meaning, untalented amateurs. The amateurs, nevertheless, continued to write. A field they claimed for themselves was the now abandoned one of verse tragedy.

XI

THE TWILIGHT OF VERSE TRAGEDY

IT HAS BEEN SHOWN in the preceding chapter that the tragedies written in prose during the 1760's, although perhaps not of genuine excellence, were usually at least interesting because of the freshness of their plots and settings, and because of new ideas and styles of dialogue. On the other hand, a tragedy of the 1760's written in verse, unless by Weisse or Klopstock, is certain to be of mediocre quality. Those authors who insisted on writing verse tragedies were men of little talent, either provincials unaware of the new vogue for prose or reactionaries still under the influence of Gottsched and his outmoded reform. Thus, when one comes upon an obscure Alexandrine tragedy entitled *Montezum* published in Königsberg in 1763,[1] it is hardly astonishing to discover that its author was Schönaich, Gottsched's foremost disciple, here emitting his feeble swan song as a poet. In 1766, Cornelius Hermann von Ayrenhoff (1733–1819) opened his not very illustrious literary career with an Alexandrine tragedy entitled *Aurelius*.[2] Ayrenhoff was an Austrian, and Austria at the time was "provincial" in respect to its theatrical development, which had not kept pace with that of central and northern Germany. Vienna in the early 1760's was like Saxony in the early 1730's, as Nicolai remarked on a visit to the Austrian capital.[3] Vienna's Gottsched was Josef von Sonnenfels, and thanks to his influence, a taste for the "regular" tragedy was being belatedly encouraged. In this special situation an Alexandrine tragedy could still be regarded as something progressive. Ayrenhoff wrote a second Alexandrine tragedy in 1768, *Hermann und Thusnelde*,[4] a needless addition to the Hermann tragedies written by Schlegel, Möser, and Schönaich. It was soon to be totally eclipsed by Klopstock's prose *Bardieten*, the first of which, *Hermanns Schlacht*, was published in 1769. In 1770 Ayrenhoff himself turned to prose in his second Hermann tragedy, *Tumelicus;* but in 1772 he went back to Alexandrines in his four-act tragedy *Antiope*, which he dedicated to Lessing. So local was his fame that Lessing had to ask his fiancée, then in Vienna, for information about this unknown author of a tragedy which struck him as being very mediocre.⁵ Yet *Der Postzug* (1769), a comedy by Ayrenhoff, pleased Berlin audiences in 1771, and this was reported to Lessing by his brother Karl without mention of the author's name,⁶ which Karl perhaps did not know.

The classic provincial and reactionary was one Ludwig Friedrich Hudemann (1703–1770), a man of Gottsched's own generation, of whose substantial number of Alexandrine tragedies only the *Schicksal der Tochter Jephthah* (Büzow und Wismar, 1767) can be discussed here. Although Hudemann received his education at several good universities and lived for a while in Hamburg, his chief domicile was Henstedt in Norderditmarschen, where he served as an official of the Duke of Schleswig-Holstein. It was from this provincial nest that he viewed the world and sent out his dramas upon it. As a youth in Hamburg he had had a taste for opera which he had been bold enough to proclaim in an essay published in 1732.⁷ Gottsched, however, soon converted him to the Alexandrine tragedy. Some years later he began to write "regular" tragedies himself, and kept this indefatigable (and unprogressive) activity up until his death. Evidently a deeply religious man, Hudemann chose his subjects mostly from Bible history, and he liked to publish his own pious plays along with translations of tragedies by Racine. His first tragedy, *Diocletianus* (1751), was published together with his translation of *Phèdre;* his second, *Jesabel* (1753), appeared together with *Athalie.* In his third, *Der Brudermord des Kains* (1765), he surprisingly turned to prose, probably, as the subject matter suggests, under the influence of Klopstock's *Tod Adams* and Margareta Klopstock's *Tod Abels.*⁸ Then in 1767 he went back to his former practice and joined his Alexandrine tragedy *Schicksal der Tochter Jephthah* with a translation of Racine's *Iphigénie.* The reason for this juxtaposition was that he wished to contrast two instances of daughter-sacrifice, a heathen one and a biblical one, ". . . to place in their most charming light the advantages of Christian morality over heathen ethics."⁹ It did not occur to Hudemann that the companion pieces he chose for his own hapless tragedies showed up the artistic weaknesses of the latter in the most pitiless way. Racine and Hudemann—one can hardly imagine a less likely team. But in the case of *Das Schicksal der Tochter Jephthah* and *Iphigénie* the smug provincial author rested securely in his conviction that a Christian would certainly be more edified by his tragedy than by Racine's, which, for all its "wit," depicted such damnable vices as ambition, anger, bitterness, and fleshly love. He evidently had no concern about the literary vice of boring people.

The story of Jephthah and his daughter (Judges, 11) had been a

great favorite with ecclesiastical authors for centuries.[10] An anonymous Jesuit wrote a *Jephte* in the German language in 1755 at Düsseldorf which had been performed but left in manuscript,[11] and there
were numerous Latin dramas on the subject. It is very doubtful that
Hudemann had any knowledge of the Düsseldorf play which, like
his own, featured arias and choral parts. Hudemann's early predilection for the opera, or the choruses in Racine's *Esther* and *Athalie*,
to say nothing of the example of Greek tragedy, could well account
for the choral parts that he included not only in this work but also
in his previous verse tragedies. Semah, as the daughter of Jephthah is
called by Hudemann, has her own chorus of maidens, and in the
fifth act a special chorus of Levites is also introduced. These choruses
are supposed to be accompanied by an orchestra, of which a prominent feature, according to the author's directions, must be "muted
violins." The choral songs and arias are in stanzas of varying lengths
in which the lines of iambic meter are uneven, but generally shorter
than six feet. In his elaborate use of choruses Hudemann goes far
beyond Cronegk in *Olint und Sophronia*, or beyond himself, for
that matter, in his first tragedy, *Diocletianus*. His employment of the
speaking voice against a musical background (as in IV. vi) suggests
the technique of the monodrama, a genre which was to become popular in the 1770's. Truly, in such matters this tragedy appears to belong to another tradition than that of the sober, intellectual tragedy
of the Gottsched school. The spectacular sacrifice scene in the fifth
act, however, has a direct ancestor in the sacrifice scene of Grimm's
Banise. And when the chorus is silent (its activity centers mainly
around the beginning or end of an act) the regular dialogue is in
conventional rhymed Alexandrines that draw on an old-fashioned
and conventional tragic vocabulary. The technique of construction,
the handling of scenes, and the delineation of characters show no
advance beyond the tragedies of Gottsched's *Schaubühne;* indeed,
in all of these particulars Hudemann's tragedy is distinctly inferior
to those older works.

The simple and scanty facts of the biblical account did not provide enough material to fill more than two acts of a tragedy, and
Hudemann's own imagination was not lively enough to supply any
real substance for the three other acts which he felt compelled to
place between those two. He disdained to invent a petty intrigue
that might at least have given the illusion of action in the middle of
the play. It is possible that Klopstock's religious dramas influenced
him to avoid complications of plot. But he wholly lacked Klopstock's profundity and enthusiasm, so that he had recourse only to
sterile repetition, and his central three acts are made up of nothing

more than vapid reflections on what has already happened and idle speculations on what is yet to happen. An intrigue, however meaningless, would be preferable to this. Hudemann's decision, apparently, in spite of the fine phrases in his preface about religious edification, was to exploit the biblical account for all possible suspense. After an opening scene consisting of a choral song, led by Semah, the action begins in the second scene with Jephthah's return from a victory over the Ammonites, accompanied by his officers and guard. Semah comes up gleefully to congratulate him and is brusquely rebuffed by her father, who then leaves. All attention is drawn now to the possible reason for Jephthah's unfatherly behavior, which is regarded with the utmost seriousness and vague foreboding. Semah, an obedient daughter and passive heroine of the older school, disagrees with the advice of her confidante to find out what is wrong with Jephthah. Passive virtue will be her only defense: "In quiet modesty I shall await his grace,/ And soften his heart only with silence and patience" (I. iii). With rational calm she explains to her mother Chavah that even the most innocent emotion, filial affection, can be blind: "To vindicate him I will gladly condemn myself,/ Boldly and without permission I stepped before his face./ Thus love can err in its stirring,/ If it is lacking in intelligence! I interrupted his thinking./ At the wrong time I tried to enfold him in my arms" (I. iv). She rebukes her fiancé Hezron for criticizing her father's rudeness and tells him not to be too impatient about marrying her: "Always avoid, Hezron, violence of inclination" (I. v). Docilely, Hezron wishes to comply with Semah's good advice. But he realizes that his own reason is not strong enough to control his emotions: "My weak mind will never protect me against myself" (I. vi). Therefore he will call on God to help him. One need only compare these insipid rationalistic speeches with the passionate outbursts in Weisse's *Romeo und Julie* to understand how reactionary was the outlook of the dramatist Hudemann.

The second act introduces a possible reason for Jephthah's melancholy mood, his troubles with the rebellious forces of Ephraim, who is threatening Jephthah's judgeship over Israel. General Gael urges the use of force against Ephraim, but Jephthah passively waits for God to act in his behalf, and is loath to take offense against his "brother." Thus we see that Jephthah is a sentimentalist in virtue, and no tyrant. But we are still in suspense in regard to his mood and his treatment of Semah, and the bulk of this act is taken up with futile hand-wringing on the part of Semah's mother, confidante, and fiancé. In the third act Semah comes before Jephthah and apologizes for angering him, excusing herself on the basis that her reason

is still youthful and her emotions still strong. All he will say, however, is that she shall stand beside him as he sacrifices and that his
actions then will show what is troubling him. Semah then confesses
to her mother that she has had a disturbing dream about a sacrifice
in which she was somehow drawn toward heaven. The mother
ordinarily (as a good rationalist) discounts dreams, but in this case
she is inclined to believe the Lord wishes to predict Semah's death.
This hinting increases the suspense to a certain degree, but its effect
is mostly spoiled by the lengthy, boring speeches and the lack of
both action and conflict. A little excitement is promised when Hezron misconstrues Semah's reluctance to see him and wonders if she
is untrue. But his certainty about her virtue soon conquers his doubts
and the situation is ended before it really begins. In the fourth act
there is another reference to Ephraim and more worrying by Hezron
and Semah's mother, but there is no development of plot until at
last Jephthah reveals the rash oath he made to God that in gratitude
for the defeat of the Ammonites he would make a sacrifice of the
first living being that greeted him on his return home. The first to
greet him was his daughter Semah, and now he has to sacrifice her.
His horror at seeing her explains his rude acceptance of her greeting.
Semah, of course, receives this news with complete equanimity: "It is
enough that you love me: this cheers my death,/ Although my body
is threatened soon with dissolution" (IV. v). Jephthah, on the other
hand, berates himself for having made the oath, and declares that
he will not be able to live up to it without God's help.

   With this revelation, suspense of the unknown is exchanged for
dread of the inevitable. But the first four scenes of the fifth act are
wasted on more pointless worrying by the still uninformed mother
and fiancé, and then at last the gates of the temple open upon a
changed and spectacular scene. We see the sacrificial altar, a chorus
of Levites, the gathered populace, and Semah, crowned with fresh
flowers, accompanied by her maidens. The solemnity of the moment
is jarred when Hezron, finally awake to what is happening, grasps
the arm of the Levite wielding the sacrificial knife. He wants to
stop the sacrifice, or die himself. But Semah is against suicide: "Oh,
no! your death then becomes a game of blind impulses;/ Mine is
ordered by love consecrated to God" (V. v). He then subsides, as
does Semah's mother, and Semah tells the Levite to remove her
head, "Which too long a time has robbed my spirit of the most
beautiful life!" (V. v). In the religious ecstasy of this moment all
question of right and wrong and of justice and reward of virtue,
which the author had never brought up anyway, is forgotten. The
perfect heroine is about to become the perfect martyr, and all around

her are properly edified. But Hudemann, for all of this, had not forgotten that he was a man of the Enlightenment. The rational God in whom he believed could not, would not, ask for human sacrifice. Such bloodthirstiness was not imputed even to the classical deities in Enlightened tragedies. Therefore Hudemann suddenly equated the biblical story of Jephthah's daughter with the biblical story of Abraham and Isaac, and the sacrifice for which all are mentally prepared is stopped.[12] A prophet enters and calls a halt to the proceedings, giving a more progressive opinion of God's desires: "His eye does not appreciate the blood,/ Which reposes in the fat bodies of sacrificial animals;/ Still less does He command the slaughter of valuable human beings./ He will only heed the service of pure souls,/ Which, living, devote their whole being to His praise" (V. vi). Thus religion and Enlightened philosophy are joined together to the satisfaction of the author, although probably not to less rationalistic theologians who recognize a difference between the God-to-man relationship in the Old and New Testaments. The play ends in what Hudemann stipulates is to be a symphony, while Semah—having quickly recovered from her urgent desire for the other life—sings a victory song together with the chorus. The sudden happy turn of events is not dramatically necessary, for we do not emotionally require the rescue of Semah (as we did require the rescue of Banise from an unjust heathen sacrifices in Grimm's *Schaubühne* tragedy);[13] but Hudemann drowns out any misgivings about the anticlimax in a blast of music.

This play was the only one of his efforts which reached the attention of Germany as a whole, but, unfortunately for poor Hudemann, this was achieved by means of an annihilating review in Klotz's *Deutsche Bibliothek der schönen Wissenschaften*. The irreverent critic of this often savagely mordant journal chose to regard the reactionary author as a hypocrite trying to hide his ineptness with a show of piety. He said in closing, "But a man who speaks with such a holy expression ought also to reflect that it is one of the unrecognized sins to spoil so much paper, to spend one's time so badly, and instead of putting one's hands to some good work to write down such miserable verses."[14] It was only in vilifying terms like these that the work of an old *"Gottschedianer"* could be publicly discussed in the 1760's. Nevertheless Hudemann, either blissfully unaware of this review or smugly indifferent to the opinions of the literary world, published one further tragedy, *Der Tod Johannes des Täufers*, in the year of his death (1770).

Besides the *Schicksal der Tochter Jephthah* another verse tragedy appeared in 1767. This was *Osmann*, published anonymously in Berlin. The unnamed author was assumed to be Johann Wilhelm Casparson (1729–1802),[15] whose father had been Swedish but had settled in Giessen as a postal official. By profession a teacher at the Collegium in Cassel, Casparson also dabbled in literature. In his youth he was a loyal follower of Gottsched and was active in founding and nurturing a branch of Gottsched's society, *Die Gesellschaft der freien Künste* (1752), in Cassel.[16] But his relations with Gottsched cooled because of Casparson's too open admiration of Klopstock and Haller,[17] and after Gottsched's death he published a satire in which he indicated that both Gottsched and Bodmer had failed to keep pace with the progress of German literature.[18] The half-bourgeois, half-romantic, and altogether exotic subject chosen for his first tragedy shows a good deal of independence and progressiveness on the author's part. His use of blank verse rather than Alexandrines is another evidence of his desire to move with the times. He was the first German author to go to the newly popular French author Marmontel for material from which to construct a new drama.[19] Evidently, however, Casparson only *thought* that his source was a moral tale by Marmontel. Save for a fleeting resemblance to Marmontel's *Soliman II* in the opening situation of *Osmann* (i.e., a European slave girl resists the advances of her Turkish master with spirit and violence), not one of the *Contes moraux* (1761) has any relationship to the complicated plot of Casparson's tragedy.[20] For all of this, Casparson's early training in Gottschedian "regularity" was still very much a part of him. The fact that he used verse, even blank verse, in a drama whose contemporary, non-heroic subject obviously called for prose shows little awareness of the latest taste. But he was still more old-fashioned in treating his essentially bourgeois material as though it were a tale of Oriental palace intrigue, like Krüger's *Mahommed IV* in Gottsched's *Schaubühne*. He apparently felt that a tragedy had to have an air of sovereignty about it, and that it had to be stiff and unrealistic. *Osmann* can be most closely compared with Breithaupt's *Renegat* (1759), which is also a bourgeois tragedy in verse (Alexandrines) with a Turkish setting.[21] But *Der Renegat*, although eight years older, is much less stiff and conventional in its plot construction and characterizations than *Osmann*.

The titular hero of Casparson's tragedy is a paragon of virtue, and his good qualities are all the more interesting because he is a Turk, a wealthy man with many slaves. His seraglio is different from most: "I always thought it ignoble/ To imprison a number of women and/ To sacrifice them to voluptuousness. It was only/ The refuge of persecuted virtue, which/ Here could dwell securely" (I. i).[22] He is in love with a new slave, a French woman whom he calls Fatime, but she repulses him unwaveringly. Osmann's French friend, Brosse, advises him to conquer his desire and to free this young woman. With the aid of reason, Osmann proceeds to suppress his love: "Must/ Not reason be at the helm and/ Flee the rocks on which love suffers shipwreck?/ How hard this struggle is!—how the heart/ Traitorously resists the reason!" (I. iii). Not only does Osmann bring himself to free his fair slave, but he also agrees to help find her husband, who was caught by pirates just as she was, but sold to another master. Her real name is Mme de Rouille. All would be well now except for Brosse, the Frenchman, who un-masks himself in the second act as a scoundrel. He is attracted to Mme de Rouille, not only physically, but spiritually, too: "Oh, Heaven, what/ Charms! what virtue You gave her!" (II. i). He concocts a diabolical plan to possess her and rid himself of his rivals. When M. de Rouille is found, Brosse will kill him, but manage to put the blame on Osmann. Brosse's attempts to carry out this plot, which is more complicated and adventurous than is suitable for a bourgeois tragedy, fill out the middle three acts. But the author's awkwardness and stiltedness in bringing these actions about indicate both a lack of talent and a very old-fashioned technique.

Brosse's first move is to shake Mme de Rouille's confidence in Osmann. She rejects his suggestions, but when she is alone, she gives voice to awakening suspicion. As happens only in the poorest trag-edies, Brosse overhears this soliloquy. Then Osmann has to lose a letter saying that de Rouille has been freed and will soon arrive, and of course Brosse has to find this. Moreover, in order to surprise Mme de Rouille, Osmann has to pretend that he still does not know where her husband is. He takes the occasion to give her a moral precept: "Patience/ And reason must moderate/ Too violent desire. Any emotion,/ If it is too strong, becomes vice—" (III. ii). Ac-cordingly, when Brosse shows her the letter, she becomes furious at Osmann's deception and thinks of killing him and herself. She does not think of the obvious thing, which is that Osmann is pre-paring to surprise her. Even Brosse finds it necessary to tell her to curb her rage and use reason. Suddenly altering his original plan (but without explanation to the spectators), Brosse tells Mme de Rouille the preposterous lie that Osmann had sent a servant to kill her husband, but that he, Brosse, had been able to dissuade this servant from the deed. De Rouille is now in another town, and Mme de Rouille should flee with Brosse to meet him there. After some hesitation, Mme de Rouille decides to disguise herself as a Turkish man and go with Brosse. Happily unaware of what is afoot, Osmann is busy having furniture moved into a chamber for the couple which will soon be reunited thanks to his efforts. He fairly chortles with delight over his own virtue: "No! never yet has my heart felt the joy/ Which comes from magnanimity so purely as now,/ . . . Oh, what a happiness is virtue! Already in spirit/ I see the tender lovers! united/ Through me, gently embracing, and rapturously/ Thanking me" (IV. ii). Then comes the sad news of Brosse's treachery, and Osmann makes some wry comments which anticipate those of Sittah in Lessing's *Nathan:* "God, what kind of people these Christians are! Proud/ Of their religion, through their actions/ They make a mockery of the teachings which/ It gives. They boast of a virtue which/ They have never known" (IV. iii). One wonders about Osmann's own ethical code, however, when he abruptly slays a slave who was cooperating in Brosse's plot and says to the wretch, "Feel now/ Forever the punishment of the damned!" (IV. v). Soon after this the runaways are caught—one does not know how—and brought back. For some unaccountable reason Osmann does not seek to take revenge on Brosse, but simply orders him out of the room, and Brosse sneaks into a corner to listen to what is said to the others. M. and Mme de Rouille are now happily reunited at last, while Osmann modestly declines their thanks for his good offices: "I did nothing, except what duty commanded,/ Any virtuous person would have/ Acted as I did" (IV. viii). Like a sentimental king he refuses to punish Brosse: "Now the deceiver is/ Punished enough by himself. We will/ Forgive him and intercede with Heaven for him" (IV. viii). Brosse overhears but is not mellowed. Rushing forth from hiding with a dagger in hand, he tries to kill Mme de Rouille and himself. When stopped, he swears death to them all if they do not kill him now. But Osmann lets him go again, hoping that magnanimity will convert him.

One would think that the play was over now, but the fifth act is still to come, and it is a harrowing one indeed. It starts out pleasantly enough with M. and Mme de Rouille in their conjugal chamber— the third change of scene and an evidence of the author's attempt to be modern and progressive. Unfortunately, his attempts affected only a few external matters. Mme de Rouille now has a better opinion of Turks: "Now/ I blush at my prejudice/ Which never let me seek virtue/ Under a turban" (V. i). But two things still mar their happiness. Mme de Rouille has not found her brother, who was stolen from the family by pirates many years before. Indeed, it was to seek him that she and her husband had come to the Orient. Furthermore, she is worried about the threats of Brosse. Her husband is confident that Providence, which has done so much for them, will go on protecting them. Unfortunately, his confidence is misplaced. Osmann enters with the news that Brosse has suddenly turned Mohammedan. In compliance with the rules of this religion against images, he has divested himself of a picture which the Mufti has given to Osmann. Mme de Rouille identifies the picture: it is her father, and Brosse must be her brother! At this both M. and Mme de Rouille, as the stage direction has it, fall fainting on a sofa. But there is worse to come. Brosse has denounced Osmann to the Grand Vizier as an enemy of the country. It so happens that the Grand Vizier is hostile to Osmann and therefore takes this as an excuse to ruin him. Mme de Rouille is to be turned over to Brosse and her husband is to be put in chains. In a moment Osmann's house is surrounded by soldiers, but his own servants offer to fight for him —this again makes Osmann seem more like a potentate of some sort than a private person. Then Brosse and the Grand Vizier enter the room. M. de Rouille is chained and dragged off, while Mme de Rouille shouts to Brosse that he is her brother. He is immediately convinced, as is the Grand Vizier, who thereupon decides to take Mme de Rouille for his own harem. Mme de Rouille, at this point oddly anticipating Lessing's Emilia Galotti, asks Osmann to kill her in order to save her virtue, and this he does with his dagger. She thanks him before dying. The soldiers drag off Osmann, who, rational to the end, says, "Come and learn from me,/ How beautifully virtue dies, and how courageously/ It faces the cruelest death!" (V. vii). Brosse, however is now subject to the pangs of remorse. Asking God to send him straight to Hell, he kills himself, and the play, thoroughly depleted of its characters now, is over. The only conclusion to be drawn from this tragedy is that virtue must be its own reward, for Providence, though seeming to bring about a happy solution to difficulties, lets vicious persons destroy all the good work in the most incredible and precipitate way. Osmann is a perfect hero. Neither his innocently meant deception of Mme de Rouille nor his murder of the slave is supposed to be regarded as a tragic fault, yet he meets a dreadful fate. Brosse, on the other hand, is an originally virtuous person who lets his reason be overcome by his passion. His fate offers a conventional moral object lesson. Presumably Osmann and the de Rouilles are expected to charm us so much with their virtue and steadfastness that we will be saddened but not shocked at their misfortune. The author may have remembered that Gottsched came to the conclusion that virtue did not always have to be victorious in a tragedy.[23]

Casparson's second tragedy, *Thafnhilde* (Cassel, 1768), was also published anonymously,[24] but no doubt has ever been raised concerning the identity of the author. The plot of this tragedy is taken from early medieval Scandinavian history, a subject to which Casparson was drawn probably because of his own family background. There are no bourgeois elements in the story, and the Unity of Place as well as that of Time are strictly observed. Consequently, the tragedy seems even more old-fashioned and stilted than *Osmann*. The blank verse dialogue is crabbed, awkward, and frequently unclear, and the speeches are sometimes unmercifully long. If both *Osmann* and *Thafnhilde* are indeed the works of Casparson as reported, then one is strongly tempted to speculate that *Thafnhilde* may actually be the earlier of the two tragedies, even though published subsequently to *Osmann*. Except for its lack of rhyming Alexandrines, it would fit neatly among the tragedies in Gottsched's *Schaubühne*, or among those often inexpert tragedies published between 1746 and 1755. One can easily see the same hand at work both in *Osmann* and *Thafnhilde*, for the latter, like the former, is tortuously and clumsily plotted, and all the significant action is reserved for the fifth act. *Thafnhilde* was reviewed in the *Allgemeine deutsche Bibliothek* with all possible consideration for the feelings of the author; but the reviewer, who thought it would have been better if the play had begun with the action in the fifth act, could not resist exclaiming in some exasperation, "For why the tedious first acts, the everlasting prattle about the sacrifice, the death and resurrection of Siegrith, the concealment of Christlif, and all the lengthy explanations?" [25]

The setting of the tragedy is a northern island ruled by a heathen king named Ramund. Thafnhilde, his wife, is a Christian who refuses to perform the required human sacrifices at a very important festival that occurs only once in nine years. If she continues to refuse, the chieftains will demand that she be sacrificed herself so that Ramund can marry the daughter of an ally, a princess named Siegrith whose father is seeking every means of making her Ramund's queen. The situation is rendered less tense when the news is brought that Siegrith has been shipwrecked and drowned. Ramund thinks that perhaps Thafnhilde can be excused from doing sacrifice, now that this other woman is dead. The High Priest, however, insists that Thafnhilde must take part. His concept of the gods is one full of dread, whereas Ramund, more rational than he, believes that the gods reward virtue and therefore cannot be angry with Thafnhilde. But when Ramund's mother Hildegun adds her threats and entreaties to those of the priest, Ramund gives in and assures them that Thafnhilde will perform the sacrifice. Then, in a private conference, the High Priest reveals to Hildegun that Siegrith was not drowned after all. She is but hiding in a grove, waiting to take over as queen as soon as

Thafnhilde is dead. For the priests will kill Thafnhilde even though she does decide to do sacrifice, because she is a Christian. The exposition grows so dense and complicated in this scene that the situation becomes very obscure. It grows still worse when the High Priest adds that Thafnhilde's father is concealing a Christian youth in the castle, and that this will make Ramund jealous. As in *Osmann*, the author here irritates the reader (and no doubt hopelessly confuses the spectator) by issuing some complicated information and then retracting it soon after in favor of different information.

The heroine herself appears for the first time in the second act, and makes her entrance "with glances directed toward heaven" (II. ii).[26] She is the pure martyr type, the logic of whose actions runs counter to all ordinary logic, and whose religious constancy verges on obstinacy. Ramund tries hard to make her see that her refusal to sacrifice may bring war to the island and death to her father Theodolf and himself. Being informed of the secret conference concerning Siegrith's rescue and hiding place, he also warns that his mother and the High Priest are planning to murder Thafnhilde before she sacrifices, but it is not clear in what way this information is meant to be an inducement. In any case, Thafnhilde does not accede to his demands, and Ramund, very sentimental for a supposedly rude Northman, cannot become angry. He cries, "How strongly—how strongly—does my heart speak for you" (II. iii). He is half won over to Thafnhilde's religion, for he tells the High Priest that anyone would objectively prefer Thafnhilde's God to the gods of the priest, and adds, "Your word is not the will of just gods;/ Your hatred alone recasts them into executioners" (II. iv). Whereas in *Osmann* the author had criticized some Christians and idealized a Mohammedan, in this drama it is the heathen who are criticized. In his effort to persuade Thafnhilde, Ramund suggests a broad compromise: Princess Siegrith may do the actual sacrificing, and Thafnhilde need only stand beside her, strewing incense. Then Ramund will reciprocate by sacrificing to the Christian God. But the father, Theodolf, rejects this proposal, too. They can take no part in a heathen, to say nothing of a human, sacrifice. In a soliloquy Theodolf now offers the information that Thafnhilde is not really his daughter, but the daughter of Ramund's dead uncle. Moreover, she has a brother named Christlif, who has been educated in Germany and has now returned and is being kept concealed by Theodolf. The purpose served by introducing these complications is far from obvious, except that the author has to do something in order to fill in five acts. One excuse is that now Theodolf can plan to save Thafnhilde at the last moment by proclaiming her a blood member of the royal family, and thus a sacred descendant of Odin. Another is that now a distinction can be drawn between true and fanatical Christianity, between mature wisdom and youthful rashness. Christlif is eager to dash out and overturn the heathen altars that very minute; but Theodolf warns him, "You would be dying out of pride, and would not have/ Lived for your God—" (III. i). This scene was perhaps inspired by the argument between father and son in the first act of Cronegk's *Olint und Sophronia*,[27] a tragedy with a similar theme. When Christlif resolves to join the king's guard, many of whom are Christians, in order to halt the sacrifice with force, Theodolf is horrified: "Whither, my son, is the fire of youth taking you?/ Alas, fury is not religion! . . . And ought the Christian's sword be stained with blood,/ When he can conquer through intelligence?" (III. ii). And again he warns, "Never follow your blood—always reason,/ And better yet—religion" (III. ii). He has no fault to find, however, with Thafnhilde's sweet submission and readiness to accept death. He prefers complete passivity to Christlif's active virtue.

The complications of the rest of the third act and of the fourth act are too tedious and abortive to be related in detail. Suffice it to say that the arguments between Ramund and Thafnhilde, Ramund and Hildegun, Ramund and the priest continue, and at one point Christlif accuses Thafnhilde of giving in to Ramund and reveals to her that Theodolf is not her real father. Two little daughters of Thafnhilde, who talk as stiltedly as the adult characters, are briefly and pointlessly introduced. The inevitable letter comes into play with as much or more awkwardness than in *Osmann*. The High Priest has captured one Olof, a friend of Christlif's, who bears a letter addressed to Thafnhilde telling all about the revolt planned by Christlif. The letter makes Ramund angry and he shouts for revenge. The priest and Hildegun are happy. In the first scene of the fifth act, Ramund gives violent expression to his grief and weeps so much that one would think Casparson had read Lessing's *Laokoon*, Chapter One, and had decided to turn his cold Northern hero into a demonstrative Greek. When, for some reason, Thafnhilde and Christlif appear together, Ramund has Thafnhilde dragged off to be sacrificed, while Christlif is put in chains, and soon Theodolf, too. But then comes a surprise: the High Priest is also brought in as a prisoner! Unaccountably, he had decided to start an armed revolt of his own and was captured by loyal Christians in Ramund's guard just as he was about to attack the castle. Theodolf suddenly produces papers proving that Thafnhilde and Christlif are cousins of Ramund, but it is still not apparent what bearing this fact has on the plot. In any case, it is too late to save Thafnhilde, who has been sacrificed and burnt on the altar. Ramund furiously kills the exulting High Priest, and then stabs himself. He dies hoping that God will have mercy on him. Christlif blames his rashness for having precipitated the catastrophe. Instead of punishment, however, he receives the kingship, and henceforth Christianity will be the island's religion. Theodolf can think of nothing else to say but "How inconceivable, Lord! are Thy ways,/ How incomprehensible Thy judgment!" It seems manifestly unfair to give Providence any share of the blame for the incomprehensibility of the action. To read this work is to be confirmed in the opinion that verse tragedy was now in the hands of the most mediocre talents. In 1771 Casparson did at last turn to prose, the poetic prose used by Klopstock in his *Bardieten*. Unfortunately *Theutomal*, as this third and last tragedy was entitled, was as bad as the first two.[28]

It will be remembered from the preceding chapter that Johann Heinrich Faber's prose *Inckle und Yaricko* (1768) was joined in the same year by what Faber undoubtedly considered to be a finished and superior product, his five-act *Inkle und Yariko* in rhymed Alexandrines. In contrast to the murky blank verse of *Thafnhilde*, the Alexandrine couplets of *Inkle und Yariko* are as simple and clear as could be desired. They are free of the high-flown, pathetic terms and phrases heretofore characteristic of tragic verse. This dialogue is as close to the prose of a bourgeois tragedy as lines with meter and rhyme can possibly be; it is actually much less bombastic than the dialogue of the prose version. The plot of this other version is followed in the main. Certain additions and amplifications have been made necessary, of course, by the expansion to five acts. Thus the first act is made up entirely of conversations between Inkle's fiancée Elizabeth, her confidante Betty (Clementine in the prose version), and Inkle's virtuous brother Steyley. Inkle himself does not appear until the second act, Yarico until the third. The sensational death of Inkle by lightning plus stabbing has been reduced to plain stabbing.

The characters are practically the same as in the prose version. Inkle is motivated again by complete impoverishment to sell Yarico into slavery, and Yarico is again all love, magnanimity, and sentiment, until she breaks out in lamentations and accusations when she realizes what is happening to her. More emphasis is put on the relationship between Elizabeth and Steyley, with the result that these subordinate roles gain slightly in interest. Since she has known Steyley, Elizabeth is no longer sure that she feels the same toward Inkle. She recalls her opposition to Inkle's trade expedition in the first place. His excuse for leaving, which was to earn a fortune for her, humiliated her: "As if self-interest had taught me to think so low/ That I desired only Inkle's gold and not his heart" (I. i).[29] Steyley, whatever he may feel for her, has acted impeccably and is so honorable that he tries all persuasion to make her keep loving Inkle. The theme of the rival brothers is not pursued, for the perfection of Steyley's virtue removes all jealousy and suspicion from Inkle's heart. Perhaps the play would have been more interesting if the fraternal conflict had been added, but Faber already had more to handle than he was able.

Inkle expresses his woe in a long soliloquy (a technique Gottsched had ruled against) which is overheard by his friend Borston (Belvedere in the prose version), who comes from nowhere to greet Inkle. Entrances and exits in this play are handled with a disregard for realism that would be offensive even in the earliest Alexandrine tragedies. Borston, as in the other version, is a curious mixture of sincere friendship and sinful defiance: "What is Heaven's anger? An illusion which deceives us,/ Which calls for our revenge, to be sure, but not for timorousness./ What is Providence? It plays with blind men;/ Show it a courageous heart: then its anger disappears" (II. viii). This speech is more stupid than evil. Both Borston and Inkle are rather pitiful villains, small in thought and in actions.

Yarico introduces herself with a soliloquy of nearly eighty lines, in which she reviews her kind treatment of Inkle in the wilderness and wonders why she has not seen him in the three days since they have come to Barbados. Betty now encounters her and at once Yarico grows suspicious: the fiancé of Elizabeth described by Betty must be Inkle. Thereupon Yarico tells Betty the story of their meeting and love, and this long narration is a recasting, by the author's admission, of the Gellert verse tale. Yarico, however, adds details about her earlier life which neither Gellert nor the *Spectator* had supplied. She describes the death of her mother, and how her father tenderly raised her in the forest, and how he was captured by sailors and taken away. Not in the slightest degree does she sound like an Indian girl. Her every word and every sentiment are those of a cultivated European. Whereas Gellert had spoken only of Yarico's primary attraction to Inkle's fair skin and curly hair, Faber lets the Indian maiden say, "I saw the charm of virtue in all his features" (III. ii). But soon Yarico is faced with the discovery that Inkle is not virtuous after all. Borston has talked him into restoring his fortunes by selling Yarico into slavery, so that he will not have to face Elizabeth as a pauper. In the original story one could understand the logic of Inkle's action, even while condemning it and him. His loveless heart let him think of the Indian girl simply as merchandise to be sold. But here so much has been made of Inkle's total impoverishment and his need of appearing successful in Elizabeth's eyes that Yarico would have to be made out of pure gold in order that her sale might accomplish its purpose. In strengthening the motivation for the sale the author has rendered the sale itself hopelessly inadequate and, consequently, absurd. The ten pounds sterling offered by the slave dealer, even the extra three pounds tacked on when he learns that Yarico is pregnant, are hardly enough to put Inkle back on his feet financially and certainly do not compensate for the shame and heartache that the author makes him feel. The scenes with the slave dealer, however, are the most dramatic in the play (III. ix & x).

Providence holds a guiding hand over Yarico in her misfortune, for in a fellow slave she rediscovers her lost father, whom the author, displaying further his lamentable ignorance of American aboriginal culture, has given the Moslem name Ibrim. The old Indian, like Yarico, is conversant in modern European ethical ideals (which were at that time thought to be universal), and only lacks tutoring in Christianity to be perfect. Before he recognizes his daughter, he sees that "In her features there shine innocence and virtue," and when he thinks of her plight he exclaims, "Ah! let my old eyes weep tears of pity!" (IV. i). Yarico, a very bourgeois-minded Indian, is ashamed to appear pregnant and without a husband: "If this is my father: then he will now learn,/ That his hopes were so poorly based,/ That through your [Inkle's] vice I have dishonored my father himself,/ Who beforehand always taught me the path of virtue./ How the daughter will blush now before his gaze!/ Ah! my crime will kill the best of fathers!" (IV. i). To have Steyley speak of this blushing, weeping, delicately spoken girl as "the savage" (IV. ii) puts the final touch of unconscious hilarity to these supposedly moving scenes.

Happiness soon comes to Yarico and Ibrim when Steyley purchases their freedom. But Inkle's punishment begins at the same time. When he feels remorse for what he has done, his bad counsellor Borston suggests that suicide is the only way out for both of them. The motivation for this self-inflicted punishment seems extremely weak, and it can be said with justice that they die of the fifth act. Borston, it is reported, has died shouting curses at Providence like an evil rationalist; but Inkle is brought on stage, moribund, to ask forgiveness of Yarico and to join the hands of Elizabeth and Steyley. Therefore this play, unlike the prose version, ends on a note of optimism and reconciliation. The contemporary review in Klotz's *Deutsche Bibliothek* proves that it is not only from the vantage point of two centuries later that Faber's *Inkle und Yariko* appears ridiculous.[30]

The publication of two more verse tragedies in 1768 was recorded also in the *Deutsche Bibliothek* in a fairly extended review.[31] These were published together, anonymously, in a volume entitled *Proben dramatischer Gedichte* (Nürnberg, 1768), and were called individually *Rhynsolt und Lucia* and *Naemi und Seba*. Nürnberg in the 1760's was, in theatrical matters, a provincial town, and the anonymous author confessed that he had no access to a good German stage.[32] Little wonder, then, that he still essayed to write tragedies in verse. He evinced some idea of progress, however, in writing the first work, *Rhynsolt und Lucia*, in blank verse. The reviewer points out that some dactyls are mixed in with the iambic meter, and occasional six-foot verses appear. The plot, like that of Martini's prose tragedy, *Rhynsolt und Sapphira* (1755), is taken from Gellert's verse tale, which in turn, like "Inkle und Yariko," was adapted from a narrative in the *Spectator*. The Nürnberg author's plot, like Martini's, differs from Gellert's narrative in that the heroine does not commit adultery with Rhynsolt in an effort to save her husband's life. This bow in the direction of decorum is denounced by the reviewer, who cites Sara Sampson and Pelopia (in Weisse's *Atreus und Thyest*) as examples of unchaste women who have not offended the sensibilities of German audiences. But in this regard the anonymous author, for all his provincialism, was a better judge of contemporary taste than the unknown worldly reviewer, who should have been pleased with the outspoken Storm and Stress plays of the next decade. Sara had become unchaste through momentary weakness and Pelopia against her will, while Lucia (in Gellert's verse tale) gave in to Rhynsolt after due reflection and consultation with her husband Danfeld, who made the sacrificial decision in order to save his skin. The German audiences could accept Sara and Pelopia, but not a Lucia who went counter to all the idealism of German tragedy by regarding temporal existence as a more valuable thing than honor.[33] What could pass in a historical verse tale would not necessarily succeed in a drama. The modern reader, to be sure, can agree with the reviewer that the plot becomes more poignant (if less edifying) when Lucia sacrifices her virtue and still, through Rhynsolt's treachery, loses her husband's life. But the reviewer who signs himself only as "Thst," had broader tastes than one generally finds recorded at the time.[34]

This breadth of taste is demonstrated further in his rejection of the character of Rhynsolt, whom the author, again very possibly in imitation of Martini, seems to have made into a dynamic evil rationalist. It will be remembered that the *Deutsche Bibliothek* had also voiced disapproval of such a character in the review of Brandes'

Miss Fanny,[35] and that review was also signed "Thst." The reviewer does not regard diabolical characters as artistic, but as creations of dramatic beginners—a blow at Weisse's earlier villains which may or may not have been intended. He would have preferred a Rhynsolt of ordinary human mold, but with one dominating weakness, the love of women (animal love, to be sure!), which leads him into crime. One can see that this would have been satisfactory to the rationalistic mind, and it would also coincide with the general psychology of some of Shakespeare's heroes. Says the reviewer, "The botchers of tragedy make all their villains as black as the devil, and cause them to boast of their wickedness." [36] This statement is certainly less philosophical than Lessing's statement of objection to the evil rationalist character in the *Hamburgische Dramaturgie* (Stücke 74 & 79); but its mood and meaning are generally the same, and the views of both Lessing and this reviewer reflect the actual practice of the better dramatists in the late 1760's and beyond. The best days of the evil rationalist were over. True, Schiller revived this figure in Franz Moor and gave it greater power and impressiveness than it had ever enjoyed before. This phenomenon does not alter the fact, however, that the trend was away from monsters and toward more sympathetic villains. The vogue for saints or near-saints, especially feminine ones, was more persistent. Evidently, the Lucia of this tragedy was one of this company, and to reward her virtue the author, more soft-hearted than either Gellert or Martini, lets her husband remain alive.

The second of the tragedies, *Naemi und Seba,* was another treatment of the theme of Jephthah's daughter, but the reviewer's account of the plot indicates no dependence on Hudemann's drama of the previous year. No comment is offered concerning the type of verse used, and one assumes therefore that it was not different from the verse of *Rhynsolt und Lucia,* although choral passages are also introduced, presumably in imitation of Racine's *Athalie.* As in a French tragedy, most of the action revolves around a love triangle, and the father-daughter relationship becomes a secondary consideration.[37] Naemi, as Jephthah's daughter is called here, is in love with Seba, and rejects the love of Pinehas, a priest. When Jephthah asks the priest for an opinion on his unfortunate oath, Pinehas, full of vengefulness, insists that it must be carried out literally. Thus the fate of Jephthah's daughter is removed from the realm of the religious and sublime, and is brought down to emotional terms comprehensible to the ordinary theater-goer, the most ordinary one. Less squeamish than Hudemann (whereas in *Rhynsolt und Lucia* he had been a little more squeamish than Martini), the author lets the heroine actually be sacrificed in the fifth act. In deference to decorum this takes place behind the scenes and is only narrated. But, in the old fashioned way of plays like Gottsched's *Cato* (1732), Schlegel's *Dido* (1744), Creutz's *Seneka* (1754), Cronegk's *Codrus* (1757), and Faber's *Inkle und Yariko* (1768), Naemi is carried on stage to die. The absurdity of treating a sacrificial victim in this conventional way is so great that the reviewer was inspired to deliver a comic account of the scene, and this can be regarded as a devastating comment on the whole outmoded technique: "The poet did not want to have the sacrifice take place on stage, but, in order that the spectators might be convinced of her death, Naemi is not butchered forthwith, but, like one of those hens who have already felt the fatal knife, yet often still escape from the murderous hand and tumble around in the farmyard, thus Naemi is brought in procession on to the stage and has to bleed to death there. This seems so strange even to her that she exclaims, 'Why have I been brought back here?' She dies, and now the old man raves so that one's hair stands on end." [38]

Such were the feeble works that marked the twilight of verse tragedy. Only in Vienna could it continue to flourish for a few more years, thanks to that city's retarded dramatic development and to the prolific industry of its untalented authors. One of them, Paul Weidmann (1746–1810), published no less than ten Alexandrine tragedies in 1771 and 1772. In Germany proper, the only important use of Alexandrines was by Friedrich Wilhelm Gotter (1746–1797) in his *Orest und Elektra* (published 1774 in Gotha), which was not an original work, but adapted from Voltaire and Crébillon. Otherwise there were only a few Alexandrine tragedies of negligible value. A Saxon officer, Hans Karl von Trautzschen (1730–1812), included two of them in his ambitious two-part *Deutsches Theater* (Leipzig, 1772–1773). It is possible that these two dramas, called *Temusin* and *Wittekind*, were written at some considerably earlier date, when they would still have been in fashion. About the second one, the *Allgemeine deutsche Bibliothek* had this to say: "A tragedy *Wittekind* appearing here [in the second volume of the *Deutsches Theater*] is, in addition to everything else, in tedious Alexandrines, which have been dismissed from the German stage for some time. Mr. v. T. will surely not salvage their honor." [39] In 1774 an anonymous tragedy in rhymed Alexandrines entitled *Der sächsische Prinzenraub* was published in Gera and Leipzig, supposedly translated from Latin by one P. F. J., and in the same year there appeared in Göttingen, also anonymously, *Die Chineser*, which was in Alexandrines but contained some shorter lines as well. In 1776 Ayrenhoff's last Alexandrine tragedy, *Kleopatra und Antonius*, still made its original appearance in Vienna, and in 1783, Gotter's Alexandrine tragedy *Alzire* (adapted from Voltaire and first published in 1787) was performed there; nevertheless, it may be said with certainty that after 1774 twilight had passed into night for the Alexandrine tragedy.

Tragedy in blank verse scarcely fared better, in spite of its later bright destiny. Klopstock's *David* (1772) was the only tragedy in blank verse by a major author in the 1770's. Two others, the *Merope* (1774) of Gotter, adapted from Voltaire, and the *Batilde* (1778) of August Friedrich von Goué (1743–1789), boasted authors of recognized, if only minor, stature. Beyond these tragedies there were only Trautzschen's *Belisar* (1772), based on the novel by Marmontel, which looked in print as though it were prose, but actually scanned like blank verse; and the one-act *Darius* (München, 1775) of Joseph von Speckner, who also had written a prose tragedy.[40] There is a remarkable contrast in numbers between these few verse tragedies and the many tragedies in prose which were published after 1768. Between 1775 and 1787, practically speaking, all tragedy, whether bourgeois or historical in subject matter, was in prose. First in the procession of great prose tragedies was Gerstenberg's *Ugolino*.

XII

UGOLINO—A CULMINATION
AND A BEGINNING

HEINRICH WILHELM VON GERSTENBERG (1737–1823) was born in Tondern, a town in northern Schleswig which at various times in its history has been (and is now) a part of Denmark. Gerstenberg, whose father was in Danish military service, himself served in the Danish army from 1760 until 1771 and lived for some years in Copenhagen. But the young man's German family heritage was carefully maintained through his education in Altona and Jena, and his keen interest in German literature demonstrated itself from 1759 onwards in his publication of both original poems and literary criticism. His *Kriegslieder eines königlich dänischen Grenadiers* (1762) and his *Gedicht eines Skalden* (1766) made him famous as a poet. The latter work was the first to make use of Nordic legend, and therefore it attracted much attention and imitation. As a critic Gerstenberg published a journal, *Briefe über Merkwürdigkeiten der Litteratur* (1766–1767), in which he made a name for himself as an enthusiastic admirer and intelligent interpreter of Shakespeare. Then from his home in Copenhagen, where he was a member of Klopstock's intimate circle, he in 1768 gave the Germans their first great tragedy, *Ugolino*.[1] The peculiarly beneficial role played by Denmark in German literature of the eighteenth century may be noted here again.

It is true that *Ugolino* can hardly stand comparison with the well-known classic works of German tragedy, and it is not the artistic equal of the second great German tragedy, Lessing's *Emilia Galotti* (1772). But it certainly deserves to be called "great" in contrast to the many mediocre works that preceded it, and it is superior even to the best of these earlier works, Lessing's *Miss Sara Sampson*. While reading *Ugolino* one forgets the often stilted and flowery language and minimizes the imperfections in characterization and structure. These defects do not prevent the play from exerting its mood and transmitting its feelings, and at the end one is profoundly moved. Neither special training nor special historical interests are required for the enjoyment of *Ugolino;* a taste for trag-

edy is all that is necessary. The force of the work has not decreased
through the years, and, indeed, few other German tragedies produce
such a singularly powerful and sustained effect. Thus *Ugolino* may
be called a beginning—the beginning of the great period of German tragedy. But it was also a culmination—the culmination of the
development of tragedy in the period of Enlightenment. *Ugolino*
may have come to the German public as a surprise,[2] but it was nevertheless an entirely natural outgrowth of the many minor and obscure works that had gone before. Any drama at that time which
was particularly passionate and realistic was apt to be called "Shakespearian," and any drama with just a few characters and an uncomplicated plot was called "Greek"; *Ugolino* received both these ap-
pellations. It was, however, as German as any tragedy might be.

Klotz's *Bibliothek der schönen Wissenschaften*[3] and Nicolai's
Allgemeine deutsche Bibliothek[4] both devoted long articles to a
discussion of the new work. The author of the review in the *Allgemeine deutsche Bibliothek* was none other than Herder. Unfortunately, neither reviewer understood that when a great drama finally
makes its appearance after decades of unsuccessful attempts, one
ought to spend more time in pointing out its beauties than in looking for and exposing its faults. The reviewer in Klotz's *Bibliothek*,
a journal notable for its scornful treatment of new dramas, adopted
a lofty and disdainful attitude toward the dialogue and characters
which succeeded only in revealing his own lack of comprehension
and feeling. Herder, although he recognized the power of *Ugolino*
by saying that the author was ". . . a poet of the first magnitude,
of savage and tender imagination, of deep human feeling, and of an
ineffable inner sense . . . ,"[5] nevertheless devoted most of his remarks to adverse criticism. Later commentators, although they have
not been blind to the defects in *Ugolino*, have more appropriately
worked to establish the importance and excellence of this first enduring German tragedy.[6]

The text of *Ugolino* has an oddly modern appearance because
the author alone among his contemporaries has dispensed with the
customary scene divisions within the acts. It is true that the nature
of the subject matter and the setting—a father and his three sons
confined to a prison tower, where they are condemned to starve
—did not encourage the usual entrances and exits that produced
the scene divisions in other plays. A few entrances and exits were
introduced, however: namely, the eldest son's return from examin-
ing a hole in the tower's roof; Ugolino's exit and re-entry for a
similar examination; the eldest son's entry in a coffin in Act Three;
the departure of the silent coffin bearers; and Ugolino's retirement

now and again to parts of the tower not visible on stage. Evidently Gerstenberg did not regard these slight alterations of the situation on stage as significant enough to be noted. In any case, his decision to ignore the scene divisions underlines the peculiar construction of his tragedy. It is not composed of a chain of scenes, that is, of a series of encounters between various characters by means of which a linear plot is unfolded. It is based, rather, on the constant heightening of one scene with a practically stable component of characters. Although unusual, this kind of structure was not without precedent in German tragedy. Klopstock, Gerstenberg's good friend, had taken long preliminary strides to such a tragedy in his *Tod Adams* and *Salomo*. Herder's casual mention of the similarity of *Ugolino* to *Der Tod Adams* fails to take this significant factor into account, for in the same breath Herder added that Lessing's *Philotas* was also similar to *Ugolino*.[7] Obviously, his only basis of comparison was "Greek simplicity," that vague term implying a small cast of characters and a stripped-down singleness of dramatic purpose, since the tightly plotted and action-filled *Philotas* is otherwise quite different from the static tragedy of Gerstenberg.

Like *Der Tod Adams*, *Ugolino* is virtually without a plot, and it dramatizes only the mental state of a dying patriarch. On account of its brevity, *Der Tod Adams* was not a conspicuously hazardous or taxing undertaking for Klopstock. But the five full acts of *Ugolino*, even though Gerstenberg had the characters and fate of the three sons to deal with besides the father, were a test of ingenuity and dramatic skill which most authors would have shied away from. It would have been possible, of course, to dramatize the whole story of Ugolino's strife with Bishop Ruggieri for the rule of Pisa. Not only the famous account in the "Inferno" of the *Divine Comedy* but the official history of Pisa would have offered abundant material from which Gerstenberg could have fashioned a conventional tragedy of action and intrigue. The fact that he chose to depict only the starvation tower suggests strongly that he worked from a different sort of inspiration than that of the writers of conventional heroic tragedy. Like the author of *Ludewig der Strenge*[8] he wrote because a unique occurrence had emotionally stirred him, and not because he was intellectually delighted to have discovered material for a sensational plot. Something of the same emotion may have inspired Klopstock to treat the death of Adam dramatically, but in Klopstock emotion was always thoroughly tempered by religious intention. If the singular death of the Roman heroine Virginia, which was the basis of *Emilia Galotti*, had been able to stir Lessing more profoundly, then perhaps *Emilia Galotti* might have been a more emotionally satisfying tragedy.

The stage directions at the beginning of the play, though very brief, are a definite break with the story as told by Dante, and are made in the interest of producing the greatest possible dramatic effect. Instead of being made conscious of a dim daylight stealing through a crack in the tower's roof, we are told, "The time of representation a stormy night." [9] The Unities of Time and Place are very strictly observed, as might be imagined in view of the subject matter, but we are made very conscious of the world and the elements outside of the tower, as well as of the mood-creating value of the visible stage setting itself. In both respects *Ugolino* shows a relationship to Brandes' *Miss Fanny* and Weisse's *Romeo und Julie,* in which visible settings and references to conditions outside add greatly to the total dramatic effect. It is, however, a striking innovation when toward the end of the fifth act orchestral music is introduced as an obbligato to Ugolino's great final speech, imitating with its tonalities the varying emotions expressed in the words. This might be compared with the use of music in the sacrificial scene of Grimm's *Banise* [10] or throughout in Hudemann's *Schicksal der Tochter Jephthah,*[11] where an influence of the opera is to be sought. Gerstenberg's use of music was criticized as lacking in verisimilitude by the reviewer in the *Deutsche Bibliothek.*[12] Goethe let music sound forth magically, however, at the end of *Egmont*—and was criticized by Schiller for doing so. But Schiller himself employed a musical obbligato to Joan of Arc's soliloquy in the fourth act of his *Jungfrau von Orleans.*

These theatrical effects help to create an atmosphere from which the spectators will draw feelings of pity and horror. This was the author's evident and very successful intention. Yet Gerstenberg was too steeped in the traditions of German tragedy to make pity and horror the sole or even the main purpose of his tragic plan. Transcending both emotions was admiration for a virtuous hero. Ugolino, the wretchedly suffering father, unable to do anything to help either himself or his innocent children, has been described as a "non-hero." [13] Still, efforts are made from the outset to impress his heroic qualities on us, lest, encountering him only in prison, we might be inclined to doubt these. In the eyes of his second son Anselmo, who is admittedly given to the exaggerated sentiments of Lessing's Philotas, Ugolino is too great to inspire compassion: "You? And it would have to be a god alone who would pity you. Such a great man as you does not need to be pitied by the world. My mother has often told me that you are a very great man; everyone says so" (I). Anselmo's words might be discounted as a childish attempt to reassure himself and his father, but they are reinforced by the more measured sentiments of the oldest son, Francesco, who praises his father for his virtue: "Oh, it is a great, a marvelously great spirit which dwells in this man, our father! He depreciates his merits, in order to justify his fate" (I). It is on the theme of admiration that the inner, intense action of the externally static play is built. This is as true of Gerstenberg's *Ugolino* as it was of Quistorp's *Aurelius*,[14] Camerer's *Octavia*,[15] or any other of the many past tragedies in which an admirable character was the central interest. A character does not have to be stoical and unfeeling in order to arouse admiration. This truth had been demonstrated in Lessing's *Miss Sara* and in Wieland's *Jane Grey*. A comparison with Jane Grey appears to be very natural. Jane Grey, together with her loved ones, is also condemned to death by a cruel and vindictive opponent in politics. The question is not whether she will escape or Providence will reward her virtue, but whether she will have the fortitude to accept the judgment of Providence without losing her confidence in its promises. This, with much greater pathos and strain, is also the central question of *Ugolino:* will Ugolino be able to maintain his dignity as a virtuous, Providence-trusting hero, or will he fail under the test? The emphasis is no longer on the promises of God and the proofs of the rationalism of the world order, but on the ability of a man to cling to his faith in these promises in the absence of proofs. What Gottsched's Cato had failed to do because of a defect in reason, Ugolino will succeed in doing through strength of character. Ugolino's struggle with temptation, a struggle akin to Job's, provides the suspense in the drama. Never before in German tragedy had this struggle been depicted with so much intensity.

In the first act, there is still some hope of rescue. Although the prisoners in the tower are hungry, they tell themselves that perhaps the guard who brings their food has merely been delayed by illness or accident. Moreover, Francesco has discovered a way to escape through a hole in the tower roof, and he intends to rally some friends in Pisa to their aid. As we first see him, Ugolino is calm and sufficiently passive to oppose Francesco's plan for escape on the grounds that flight is unworthy of any of them: "A Gherardesca ought not to flee as though he were a bandit" (I). But his anger against Bishop Ruggieri is meanwhile raging at white heat: "Oh, Ruggieri! Wretch! If I could only have you in my hand like this!— to kick your hellish soul out of your body like this!" (I). Despite this passion, it is clear that Ugolino, in contrast to young Francesco, represents the mature rationalist who regards passivity (*Gelassenheit*) as the wisest approach to life's problems. Providence, after all, has not put him into this position without a cause. He recognizes that he himself has been guilty of overweening ambition in allowing himself to be named Prince of Pisa just after the town, through his efforts, had been freed of its latest tyrant. Schiller had his Fiesco punished for the same misguided act in Genoa. Ugolino's tragic fault had to be definitely stated, as always in the tragedy of that time, to exonerate Providence from the suspicion of injustice, and also—here a matter of greater significance—to provide Ugolino with a foundation for his ultimate acceptance of God's will.[16] A tragedy was still possible without a guilt, of course, but only a martyr tragedy. Ugolino would have had to become very saintly or very stoical, and somehow the gloomy horror of the prison cell would have had to be transfigured with visions of heavenly bliss. Such measures would have been necessary, as in Weisse's *Mustapha und Zeangir*,[17] to prevent the play from spreading an intolerable and blasphemously un Enlightened pessimism over the spectators. But Gerstenberg did not intend to make his starvation tower merely a poorly lit and incommodious vestibule to heaven; he wished it to be an arena in which a human soul fights its way to greatness. To this end the introduction of a tragic guilt was necessary.

If Ugolino represents reason, Francesco represents the younger generation of emotionalists who do not hesitate to put virtue into action against vice. Even the sacred paternal command cannot deter him. Ugolino, after inspection of the hole in the roof, forbids Francesco to make the dangerous leap. To the youth this is "A voice of thunder" (I), but he nevertheless disobeys it, saying to his father (who is not present), "Call him disobedient, rash, as you will; Francesco shall save you!" (I). Gerstenberg, however, was not sentimental about youthful enthusiasm, like Weisse, who in *Die Befreiung von Theben* allowed Callicrates' disobedience to result in the liberation of his city.[18] Francesco's well-meant but irrational effort results only in his quick capture and return to the tower. Still worse, Francesco brings back the dispiriting news that Ugolino's wife has been murdered and that Ruggieri has decided to throw the key to the tower into the Arno. Without Francesco's desperate step, Ugolino might at least have been spared the certainty of doom and have been comforted by the thought that his wife was safe. On account of Francesco's disobedience, the last frail support to Ugolino's spirit is ripped away in the third act, and the hero must face the great struggle from that point on in utter spiritual nakedness.

The second act, lying between the important developmental

points of the acts preceding and following it, might well have presented an embarrassingly barren stretch to a less original author than
Gerstenberg. To him, however, it was an opportunity to luxuriate
in the emotions that the situation of the starvation tower had originally stirred in him. This second act is almost wholly devoted to
description—description through actions, in the sense of Lessing's
Laokoon—and there was no precedent for such an act even in the
plays of Shakespeare, which supposedly influenced Gerstenberg.
The most prominent feature is a remarkable dialogue between the
two younger sons, Anselmo and Gaddo. Thirteen years and six
years old respectively, Anselmo and Gaddo call to mind the young
princes in Weisse's *Richard III*, the first reasonably genuine children in German tragedy. But the sons of Ugolino far outstrip
Weisse's princes in naturalness. When Anselmo is trying to be
grown-up, as in Act One, he makes an unnatural impression; but in
his dialogue with Gaddo he manages almost perfectly to represent
the elder brother who is himself still a child. In little Gaddo's speeches
there is hardly ever a false note. He is one of the truest and most
poignantly characterized children in all of German drama. The two
boys, half delirious with hunger and half sustained by the strong
imagination of childhood, indulge in fantasies about food and about
their playgrounds at home. Quite naturalistically, they even fall into
an angry argument about a forest that shall belong to Anselmo and
into which Gaddo shall not be allowed to step foot. It is disappointing to find that Herder was starchily unmoved by the charm of this
dialogue:

. . . to be sure, children are like that; but must not the spectator sympathize too childishly with such children, and too long childishly, just
in order to be able to bear their characteristic chatter at all? And if such
word play often does not even have enough dignity and circumspection
in words, in certain expressions, is it theatrical? And if it goes so far as
to verge on the ridiculous, is it tragic? . . . It is thus in the ridiculous,
childish scene where Gaddo has dreamed of eating, and is still dream-
ing, and Anselmo on his part has something else in mind, which Gaddo
does not understand: and for pages they harry each other with words.
. . . I know that Gerstenberg, this great expert on the British [poet]
. . . explains [Shakespeare's] word plays excellently in terms of his own
time; but Shakespeare for our time? [19]

What Herder's cold judgment has missed entirely is that Gerstenberg was not interested here in any imitation of Shakespearian or
euphuistic play with words. There is nothing remotely "witty"
about the boys' dialogue. Gerstenberg, plainly, had been struck to
the heart by the idea of two children condemned to starvation, and

he wanted to communicate the horror and pity of this situation by honestly depicting the probable mental state of such children. This was of more concern to him than whether the dialogue would be "theatrical" or "tragic" as those terms were then understood. Although the scene with the two children is a static one, it serves the function of informing the spectators about the advance of the process of starvation, the spectral shadow that looms larger and larger until it threatens to engulf the hero's soul as well as his body.

We are also made aware of a development of Ugolino's psychology in the second act. His calm rationality has been seriously disturbed by Francesco's disobedient escape from the tower. Against his better judgment he is thrilled and becomes hopeful. At first he says that Francesco had no right to expect the assistance of Providence, "After the manner of all thoughtless people, who first defy Providence, and then demand its support" (II). Then he is carried away by a surge of enthusiasm: "A great step! What a youth! . . . if the sneaking dogs only do not capture this all too bold young man, then there is some hope, Gherardesca!" (II). After this, a gentler emotion comes over him. Anselmo sings a hymn whose theme is passive trust in Providence: "With a quiet spirit I will beseech You! / Wisdom, look down from Your heights, / Look down gently on me!" (II). At this Ugolino begins to weep. His tears denote the transition from a rational to an emotional attitude toward the situation. Active hope has released the tight control that reason had exerted over his heart, and his feeling is now ". . . a midway condition between inexpressible joy, and—inexpressible seriousness" (II). The tears are not born of sadness, but are the outward sign that his heart has asserted itself.

The storm of passion which breaks in the third act is prepared for by Ugolino's turn to emotionalism in the second, and it is an illustration of the perils involved in releasing the heart from rational control. When two coffins are carried into the tower room, one of them is found to contain Francesco, whose mission has been unsuccessful. Although still alive, he has been given a slow poison by Ruggieri. Now Ugolino becomes grievously enraged and treats poor Francesco with the utmost severity. The dashing of an irrational hope causes the unleashing of an irrational anger. The discovery of his wife's corpse in the second coffin makes Ugolino lay hands violently on Francesco and curse him. This was another scene displeasing to Herder: ". . . but I still detest the father who lets himself be so overcome, no matter by what feeling, that he rages such a long time against his innocent, good-hearted, sympathizing child." [20] Aside from the fact that Francesco is not altogether "in-

nocent," Herder fails to see that Gerstenberg does not intend us
to approve of Ugolino at this point. He is showing what happens
when the heart is uncontrolled. The father is purposely exhibited
here on the same level with his younger children who, with their
immature reason, also speak bitter reproaches against Francesco.
One's pity need not be stifled by the humiliating spectacle of a
father behaving like a child, unless pity is to be understood as mere
gentle *Empfindsamkeit,* reveling tearfully in virtuous tableaux. Herder appears, indeed, to prefer *Empfindsamkeit* to more violent emotions, for he says, in regard to some examples of quietly sentimental
dialogue in this play, "Scenes of this kind, gently moving scenes of
children and their father, many gentle traits of a sweet and settled
soul, which with its calm lifts us above ourselves; such are frequent,
and they are the most beautiful for our feeling." [21] But Gerstenberg
did not want his whole tragedy played on muted strings. Perhaps
a virtuously mild-mannered Ugolino (an Italian Sir William Sampson) would have been more edifying at this point; but he would
certainly have been less effective.

In the development of Ugolino's psychology, reason has been
displaced by hope, which has brought heart to the fore. Now heart
has lost the support of hope, and the passions it breeds are not virtuous. Consequently, Ugolino's position is extremely vulnerable. As
he begins to reflect on the refined savagery of the punishment Ruggieri has planned, Ugolino nearly gives in to despair. It appears to
be only a matter of time before he actually does so: "But why did
I have to fall on account of this great envier? Why was it not he?
Why did Providence lend to him, of all the most wretched men in
creation only to him—only to him—only to him—oh, it wounds
every thought of my soul!—why only to him its scourge?" (III).
Francesco, who through the approach of death has become calm
and passive, answers, "In order to fill to the brim his measure of
damnation" (III). This answer scarcely satisfies Ugolino, who cannot erase this case of triumphant evil from his inner vision. Bitterly,
but still struggling to maintain his trust, he cries out, "Is it then true,
heavenly Father! But no! no! I will not murmur! You [Francesco],
justify the ways of Providence" (III). In this moment of greatest
peril Francesco actually does come to the aid of Ugolino. First, with
the story of the key's being thrown into the Arno, he underlines the
inevitability of their physical doom. Then with his own unselfish
calm and courage he gives Ugolino an example of how to face this
doom. The poison in his blood has already removed him from the
mortal sphere, although he is still alive, and has bestowed on this
youth of twenty years a quite angelic maturity of spirit. His nobility

dissolves the father's unworthy rage and transforms it into the warmest admiration: "How much I have misunderstood you! Your heart is a sublime heart, Francesco! I admire you. I contemplate you with rapture" (III). It is the blessed power of virtue which emanates from Francesco, and this is able to purify Ugolino's heart.

The state of his reason is still not clear. In a gripping monologue at the beginning of Act Four, Ugolino reflects that he himself, because of his ambition, has been the cause of his family's downfall. But this idea is not conceived in a coolly rational manner and, as can be imagined, it brings him closer to despair than consolation. The worsening physical condition of little Gaddo, and his piteous misunderstanding of the circumstances—he thinks his parents do not love him anymore because they do not feed him—incite Ugolino to cry out to Heaven for punishment upon himself. Then one hears from off-stage the hollow slamming and locking of the tower door. This was an effect borrowed from Dante; but Gerstenberg made it his own by introducing it at just the right moment in his drama. As the dreadful sound dies away Anselmo, who has been duly characterized from the outset as the most unstable of the sons, begins to lose his mind. Whereas poison has made Francesco all spirit, hunger eventually makes Anselmo all body. Now begins the series of gruesome actions that illustrate the bestiality of which human beings are capable when physical demands blot out the spirit. Anselmo's attack on Gaddo is somewhat palliated by his delusion that Gaddo is a marten that has been stealing eggs from his hens; still, there is malice in what he does, for Francesco says in dismay, "How can viciousness enter the eye, when the heart is so good, so brotherly?" (IV). The sign of his emergence from the evil fit, as might be expected, is a tear, the visible symbol of a virtuous heart. Francesco says, "His cheeks glow. He is melting, really melting . . . His eye weeps. God be praised! there falls the tear!" (IV). Shielded from knowledge of Anselmo's behavior by one of his occasional retirements to hidden recesses of the tower, Ugolino returns to his sons in a calmly rational state of mind. He recalls the happy days of the past without bitterness and, prompted by Francesco, reflects on the greater happiness of the world to come: "Human life is to be sure very happy; but the higher life after death is much happier still: it has no vicissitudes, it is a higher life. Ah! the heart of our Creator overflowed with paternal grace when He created human beings. He placed them in an earthly garden and prepared them for the transition into a garden of heaven" (IV). Ugolino's optimism, as stated here, is more religious than the philosophy of Wolff on which it is presumably based. Wolff had empha-

sized that immutable happiness could be achieved on earth by the
exercise of reason and virtue; but Ugolino weighs up the good things
in life against the bad ones, finds the former preponderant, and
waits for a perfect life only in heaven. In the last analysis, Wolff's
"happiness" was little more than stoicism, and to counteract this impression he spoke as much about the tangible rewards of virtue as
about the intangible ones that are not subject to removal. Ugolino's concept of earthly happiness, a compromise with the facts of
life, indicates what had become of Wolffian optimism in practice.

After the above speech, Ugolino turns to himself in an aside,
saying, "Down, my heart! So far you have done well, Ugolino!"
(IV). This is a clear indication that his calmness has been the
product of a conscious rational exertion, and that his emotions are
not yet virtuously transfigured, but only chained. The crux of the
problem is concisely stated by Francesco when, feeling death near,
he entrusts Anselmo with the duty of lending moral support to
Ugolino: "I fear our father's silence. He is poor in words, heavily
laden with grief, more heavily than any human being before him
has been. If he can assert his soul to the end, then he will be the
greatest mortal on earth, as he was the greatest in Pisa" (V). This is
the ethical content of the drama which develops naturally and im-
pressively from the original emotional inspiration. Ugolino's spirit
must arise, triumphantly virtuous and noble in its resistance to despair, from the most severe temptation ever invented by the forces
of evil and permitted by God. In order that the triumph may be
all the greater, Ugolino has to come very close to defeat, and cannot show the bloodless impassivity of an Aurelius, or the sweet
seraphic renunciation of a Jane Grey. Gerstenberg here leads us
into the spiritual world of the classical Schiller, and perhaps outdoes even Schiller in intensity.[22] Francesco realizes something that
Ugolino himself does not yet fully understand: Ruggieri has designs not just on Ugolino's life, but on his soul as well. In this respect Ruggieri traces his ancestry back to the evil rationalist Henley
in Brawe's *Freygeist;* [23] but whereas Henley was successful and reduced Clerdon to despair, Ruggieri will be unsuccessful and suffer
damnation alone. Francesco says, "Ruggieri shall not triumph over
the soul of a Gherardesca! . . . Let Ruggieri be the only one who
rages, but also the only one whose teeth will chatter! Let him, who
now rejoices, be the one who whimpers and creeps like an insect!"
(V). All this is expressed, to be sure, in religious terms—Soul, Hell,
Heaven. But the ideas are essentially the ones Schiller expressed a
generation later in terms of free will, necessity, and sublimity. The
same principle is operative, the demonstration of individual human

magnificence in the face of overwhelming physical forces. Before *Ugolino*, the tragic hero's virtue most often had the aspect of a rigid suit of armor covering hidden human weakness. One chink in the armor, or one moment of nakedness, and the forces of evil could overcome the helpless hero. His strength was in the armor, not in himself. But Ugolino's strength *is* in himself, so that he emerges finally as a great individual rather than as a great example of virtue. Despite the fact that what he is struggling for is a state of passive acceptance, our interest is directed not to the static maintenance of that state (as in Quistorp's *Aurelius*), but to the dynamic effort expended in achieving it. This is not the blustering titanism so often associated with the figures of Storm and Stress, but the human greatness displayed by the dramatic heroes of German Classicism.

Despair is not the only specter haunting the starvation tower. Another is the impure passion of revenge. Francesco, who in Schillerian terminology would now be called a "beautiful soul," has the proper attitude toward this sin. When Anselmo cries out for revenge against Ruggieri, his elder brother corrects him: "There is only One [i.e., divine revenge]. Forgive him." Anselmo should pray for Ruggieri, for "Thus those who are offended take revenge in heaven" (V). Francesco had believed in taking action, even to the extent of going contrary to his father's command, so long as some positive benefit might be won. But revenge rescues nothing, and is a negative action. It carries with it too much animal desire and animal satisfaction to be consonant with the highest development of the human spirit. It could possibly be a part of that development, in the sense that its absence would indicate cowardice or submission, but in the end the spirit must rise above it.[24]

The death of Francesco and the failure of Anselmo to support his father were necessary events if Ugolino was to win his struggle by his own power—and this, of course, was the author's intention. Far from being a help, Anselmo swiftly falls prey again to hunger madness. In the play's most dreadful scene he bends over his mother's corpse like a werewolf to consume her flesh. This time it is no delusion. He knows this is his mother and prefers her body to that of his late brother because the latter may be poisonous. Repulsive as this spectacle is, it must not be mistaken for mere Grand-Guignol. It is evidence of Gerstenberg's overwhelming desire to make the situation of the tower entirely vivid. What other German dramatist since the Baroque period had dared to jar the nerves and sensibilities of his audience so drastically? But Gerstenberg was motivated by compassion, and, unlike the Baroque dramatists, did not revel in cruelties and horrors. As far as the plot is concerned, the terrible scene is necessary because it gives Ugolino the most severe shock of all. When he comes upon Anselmo, who is about to perform the abominable act, he thinks the sight is more than he can bear: "The human being is only human; nothing more. Lord in heaven! Your burdens are too heavy!" (V). Then comes his discovery of Francesco's death, followed by the last pitiable whimperings of Gaddo for ". . . half of half a morsel" (V). Anselmo feels remorse for his bestiality and rises to a kind of insane nobility by offering himself as food to his father. But now madness strikes Ugolino himself. He mistakes Anselmo for Ruggieri and bloodily wounds the poor wretch with his hand. This is the nadir. Seeing what he has done, Ugolino cries out, "Cursed be the woman who bore me!" (V). It is only one half-step more before he will curse God, too. He throws himself on the ground, saying, "Here consecrate yourself to the earth for ever!" (V).

At this point, to judge from the remarks in his letter to Lessing,[25] Gerstenberg originally intended to end his tragedy. In the opinion of Albert Malte Wagner, this would have made for ". . . a much stronger conclusion . . . a truly sublime ending." [26] It would have been a better ending, however, only if Gerstenberg had planned to show his hero *beaten* by the forces of evil to which he is exposed. Although he has technically been saved from ultimate despair by the omission of any explicit curse uttered against Providence itself, he is still to all appearances a despairing and vanquished man. Lessing read the tragedy with this original ending as sent to him in manuscript by Gerstenberg, and it had a devastating effect on him.[27] He recognized the fact that Ugolino was being represented as a virtuous person who trusts in Providence to the end. Yet even Lessing, who consistently advocated optimism and trust in Providence in his own dramas, came to the conclusion that it would be better for Ugolino to commit suicide than to await starvation: "Reason commands me to submit patiently to Providence in all cases; it forbids me to put an end to my misery through destruction of myself. Why? Because I may hope at all times that I will see my misery ended without this violent means. Providence can end it, and will end it, as soon as is best for me. In this hope Ugolino walked his fearful path until the end. He did well, that he would rather starve than lay a hand on himself. . . . Ugolino must hold out, because he does not know what could happen to him at any moment: and we, who know that nothing can come to pass to help him, we—are indignant that he holds out." [28] When Gerstenberg read these words he saw that the ending of the play did not do justice to the character of Ugolino as he had depicted and developed it, and in answer to Lessing he wrote, "The course and the goal of my drama was a starvation; whether Providence will save the unfortunate man, or whether he will endure to the end in accord with his character, that is the problem: what could be easier than to cut through this problem with a suicide? But that is not your meaning.[29] You only want, if I have understood you correctly, to have the spectator more satisfied regarding this point; and therefore I have you to thank for a situation without which, as I now realize, Ugolino's character would not be worked out completely enough."[30] A. M. Wagner declares that the new ending is totally unsuited to the meaning of the drama, and that "Gerstenberg here becomes a man of the Enlightenment."[31] Actually, as Gerstenberg himself explained in his letter, the new ending is necessary to complete the proper understanding of the drama. It is an eminently suitable ending, and Gerstenberg was a man of the Enlightenment not only there, but from the beginning in *Ugolino*. What sets him apart from most of the other Enlightened tragic poets is his poetic nature and emotional inspiration.

The new ending, which was readied for the first printing of the drama, consists of additional dialogue, during the course of which Ugolino is gradually brought back from the brink of despair. In his letter, Gerstenberg tells us that reason is responsible for Ugolino's improved attitude, but the tears that are shed indicate that heart and feeling are operative, too, at least in the preliminary stages of the change: ". . . gradually, as seems natural to me in such a case, the emotion cools, he reasons about his resolve, as a Catholic might reason, and partly according to the concepts of the audience, tears relieve him, and the play closes now with an acquiescence which leaves the spectator . . . a much more cheerful prospect than before."[32] In a paroxysm of emotion Ugolino rises from the ground beside Anselmo and swears to dash out his own brains against the prison wall. But he stops short of this, and reason returns. Suicide would mean damnation, and the total victory of Ruggieri: "And how the Pisan, my companion in damnation, would bare his teeth!" (V). The scene described in Dante's "Inferno" (Canto 32) will not come to pass for this Ugolino. He will take his wife and sons for his example, he, whose tragic guilt justifies his punishment: "They did not murmur! Thus, heads bowed down, into dissolution! Thus they! No complaint in their souls! Ah! how would it be if the criminal rebelled!" (V). Thereupon Ugolino weeps; but this is the last expression of sentiment, and pure reason (as in a Schillerian tragedy) takes the ascendancy. He stops weeping and says, "An unmanly tear!" (V). Standing in what is described as a "noble attitude," he quotes some passages from the Lord's great speech at the end of the Book of Job which declare how impossible it is for man to understand the ways of God and yet how worthy God is of human trust. Ugolino's final, deeply stirring words are those of a conqueror who faces his God with confidence and who has overcome his rancor toward his adversaries: "I will gird my loins, like a man. I lift up my eye to God. My torn soul is mended. . . . And then be praised by me, you who cast this body away to dissolution! Very near am I to the goal!" (V). Thus concludes the first tragedy in German literature which magnifies the power of the individual human spirit in its independence of the physical world.

Gerstenberg's inadequate first ending was not Lessing's only objection to *Ugolino*. The starvation tower offended him even more acutely than the Tower in which Richard III slew his two nephews. In his letter he speaks of ". . . a feeling . . . which I do not remember having experienced in any tragedy except *Ugolino.*—My pity became a burden to me: or rather, my pity stopped being pity and became a completely painful feeling." [33] The sufferings of Ugolino and his sons were out of harmony with Lessing's notions of a rational universe and a benevolent Providence, and these philosophical shortcomings made him doubt the esthetic validity of the work. In reading it he ceased feeling pity, because to him pity was a "sweet torment," [34] and a sensation he wished to prolong. Certain decorous limits had to be set to the sufferings endured by the dramatic characters, even if they had incurred some guilt. Otherwise Lessing's esthetic pity would be routed by the wholly painful and unesthetic idea that God is cruel and heartless. Lessing's feeling in this matter is like that expressed by Herder in his review. But Gerstenberg held to a more rigorous concept of pity, and he defended his views stoutly in his answer to Lessing: "Furthermore it seems to me that it may sometimes be good to let the spectator suffer a little more intensely at the misfortune of his fellow man than just to the point of amusement." [35]

Without giving up the maintenance of the good reputation of Providence, Gerstenberg rebels against the shallow, sentimentally tinged didacticism that conceals from view the bitter realities of life. He lets pity be augmented to a degree almost unbearable, because he is not afraid to shake the human heart to its depths. He has confidence that the spectator will still be able to comprehend the greatness of Ugolino's spirit and to learn a deeper lesson about the relationship of man to God. With this conviction about his drama, Gerstenberg could preserve his original inspiration—the desire to re-create a uniquely impressive situation—and harmonize it with a moral theme and the tradition of German tragedy. His *Ugolino* conforms to the philosophical requirements of the Enlightenment in that it launches no frontal attack against the concept of a rational universe and a benevolent Providence; but at the same time it shows the way out of the restrictions of Enlightened tragedy into the true grandeur of the genre. In this sense *Ugolino* is both a culmination and a beginning. After it, the history of German tragedy is no longer to be told in terms of obscure works by forgotten dramatists, but in terms of masterpieces.

CHRONOLOGICAL LIST

OF PUBLISHED TRAGEDIES, 1729–1768

ONLY PLAYS BELIEVED to be originals or free adaptations (not mere translations) of foreign works are listed. Plays which were not printed, whether surviving in manuscript or not, have not been included. The date given in the left-hand column designates, as far as possible, the year of composition, i.e., the year in which composition, excluding later revisions, was completed. Where this is entirely unknown, the date of publication is given instead, in parentheses. The right-hand column lists the dates of publication for all the plays, and these dates, of course, do not show chronological order. Those works which are not discussed in the main text of this book are marked with an asterisk.

Composed		*Published*
1729 or 1730	*Ulysses, oder der für todt gehaltene aber endlich glücklich wieder gefundene Ehegemahl,* by Christian Gottlieb Ludwig. 5 acts, Alexandrines.	1752
1730	*Der sterbende Cato,* by Johann Christoph Gottsched. 5 acts, Alexandrines.	1732
1733	**Die Horazier,* by Friedrich Georg Behrmann. 5 acts, Alexandrines.	1752
1735	*Timoleon, der Bürgerfreund,* by Behrmann. 5 acts, Alexandrines.	1741
1736	*Die Trojanerinnen* (orig. *Hekuba*), by Johann Elias Schlegel. 5 acts, Alexandrines.	1747
1737	*Orest und Pylades* (orig. *Die Geschwister in Taurien*), by Schlegel. 5 acts, Alexandrines.	1761
1738	*Darius,* by Theodor Leberecht Pitschel. 5 acts, Alexandrines.	1741
1739	*Dido,* by Schlegel. 5 acts, Alexandrines.	1744
1740	*Lucretia,* by Schlegel. 5 acts, prose (brief sketch not intended by the author for publication).	1762

(1740) *Telemachs Begebenheiten auf der Insel der* 1740
        Göttin Calypso, by J. G. Heubel (?). 5 acts,
        Alexandrines.

1740   *Der sterbende Socrates*, by Nathanael Baum- 1741
        garten. 5 acts, Alexandrines.

1741   *Alcestes, oder die ungleiche Vaterliebe*, by 1742
        Theodor Johann Quistorp. 5 acts, Alexan-
        drines.

1741   *Herrmann*, by Schlegel. 5 acts, Alexandrines. 1743

1741   *Banise*, by Friedrich Melchior Grimm. 5 acts, 1743
        Alexandrines.

1742   *Aurelius, oder Denkmaal der Zärtlichkeit*, 1743
        by Quistorp. 5 acts, Alexandrines.

1744   *Mahommed IV*, by Ephraim Benjamin Krü- 1744
        ger. 5 acts, Alexandrines.

1744   *Panthea*, by Luise Adelgunde Victorie Gott- 1744
        sched. 5 acts, Alexandrines.

1744   *Die parisische Bluthochzeit König Heinrichs* 1745
        von Navarra, by J. C. Gottsched. 5 acts,
        Alexandrines.

(1745) *Agis, König zu Sparta*, by J. C. Gottsched. 1745
        5 acts, Alexandrines.

(1746) *Vitichab und Dankwart, die Allemanischen* 1746
        Brüder, by Krüger. 5 acts, Alexandrines.

1746   *Canut*, by Schlegel. 5 acts, Alexandrines. 1746

(1747) *Orest und Pylades, oder das Denkmaal der* 1747
        Freundschaft, by Christoph Friedrich von
        Derschau. 5 acts, Alexandrines.

(1748) *Octavia*, by Johann Friedrich Camerer. 5 1748
        acts, Alexandrines.

1748   *Arminius*, by Justus Möser. 5 acts, Alexan- 1749
        drines.

(1749) *Placidus, oder Eustach*, by Johann Heinrich 1749
        Steffens. 5 acts, Alexandrines.

1749   *Henzi*, by Gotthold Ephraim Lessing. Frag- 1753
        ment, Alexandrines.

(1751) *Diocletianus der Christenverfolger*, by Lud- 1751
        wig Friedrich Hudemann. 5 acts, Alexan-
        drines.

(1752) *Irene oder die von der Herrschsucht erstickte* 1752
        Mutter-Liebe, by Johann Gottfried Bernhold.
        5 acts, Alexandrines.

(1752) *Johanna die Heldin von Orleans*, by Bernhold. 1752
        5 acts, Alexandrines.

(1753)	*Jesabel*, by Hudemann. 5 acts, Alexandrines.	1753
(1754)	*Seneca*, by Friedrich Casimir von Creutz. 5 acts, Alexandrines.	1754
(1754)	*Araxane*, by Friedrich von Trenck. 3 acts, Alexandrines.	1754
(1754)	*Zayde, oder die Afrikanerin*, by Christoph Otto von Schönaich. 5 acts, Alexandrines.	1754
(1754)	*Mariamne und Herodes*, by Schönaich. 5 acts, Alexandrines.	1754
(1754)	*Thusnelde und Hermann*, by Schönaich. 5 acts, Alexandrines.	1754
(1754)	*Zarine und Stryangäus*, by Schönaich. 5 acts, Alexandrines.	1754
(1754)	*Urlogese, Prinzessin der Parthier*, author unknown, form unknown.	1754
(1755)	*Virginia*, by Johann Samuel Patzke. 5 acts, Alexandrines.	1755
(1755)	*Das Groß-Müthig und Befreyte Solothurn*, by Franz Jacob Hermann. 5 acts, Alexandrines.	1755
1755	*Rhynsolt und Sapphira*, by Christian Leberecht Martini. 3 acts, prose.	1755
1755	*Miss Sara Sampson*, by Lessing. 5 acts, prose.	1755
1755	*Cleveland, oder die redliche Untreue*, by Steffens. 5 acts, Alexandrines.	1757
1755	*Codrus*, by Johann Friedrich von Cronegk. 5 acts, Alexandrines.	1758
(1756)	*Das Mutter-Söhnchen*, author unknown. 3 acts, prose.	1756
(1756)	*Glycine*, author unknown. 1 act, prose (?).	1756
1756	*Lucie Woodvil*, by Johann Gottlob Benjamin Pfeil. 5 acts, prose.	1756
1756	*Die Lissaboner*, by Christian Gottlieb Lieberkühn. 1 act, prose.	1758
1756	*Der Tod Adams*, by Friedrich Gottlieb Klopstock. 3 acts, prose.	1757
(1757)	*Constantine, oder die triumphirende Liebe zur Tugend, über die besiegten Laster*, by Johann Christian Schwarz. 5 acts, Alexandrines.	1757
(1757)	*Brigitta, oder der Sieg des Christenthums*, by Schwarz. 5 acts, Alexandrines.	1757
(1757)	*Aurelius*, author unknown. 1 act, prose.	1757
1757	*Der Freygeist*, by Joachim Wilhelm von Brawe. 5 acts, prose.	1758

1757	*Der Renegat*, by Karl Theodor Breithaupt. 5 acts, Alexandrines.	1759
1757	*Der Tod Abels*, by Margareta Moller Klopstock. 3 acts, prose.	1759
1757	*Olint und Sophronia*, by Cronegk. Fragment, Alexandrines.	1760
(1758)	**Candaules*, by Georg Wilhelm Schmidt. 5 acts, Alexandrines.	1758
1758	*Seneka*, by Ewald Christian von Kleist. 3 acts, prose.	1758
1758	*Lady Johanna Gray*, by Christoph Martin Wieland. 5 acts, blank verse.	1758
1758	*Philotas*, by Lessing. 1 act, prose.	1759
1758	*Eduard III*, by Christian Felix Weisse. 5 acts, Alexandrines.	1759
1758	*Brutus*, by Brawe. 5 acts, blank verse.	1768
1758	**Abdolonymus und Alexander*, by Johann Gotthelf Lindner. 5 acts (?), Alexandrines. (tragedy?)	1762
1758 or 1759	*Barbarussa und Zaphire*, by Breithaupt. 5 acts, Alexandrines.	1760
1758 or 1759	**Gafforio*, author unknown. 5 acts, Alexandrines.	1760
1759	*Richard III*, by Weisse. 5 acts, Alexandrines.	1759
1759 or 1760	*Clementina von Porretta*, by Wieland. 5 acts, prose.	1760
(1760)	**Polydor, oder die unglücklichen Geschwister*, author unknown. 5 acts, Alexandrines (?).	1760
1760	*Krispus*, by Weisse. 5 acts, Alexandrines.	1764
(1761)	**Junius Brutus*, by Salomon Hirzel. 5 acts, prose.	1761
(1761)	*Der Einsiedler*, by Gottlieb Konrad Pfeffel. 1 act, Alexandrines.	1761
1761	*Mustapha und Zeangir*, by Weisse. 5 acts, Alexandrines.	1763
1761	*Rosemunde*, by Weisse. 5 acts, Alexandrines.	1763
(1763)	**Montezum*, by Schönaich. 5 acts, Alexandrines.	1763
(1763)	*Der Bankerot*, by Johann Jakob Dusch. 5 acts, prose.	1763
1763	*Salomo*, by F. G. Klopstock. 5 acts, irregular blank verse.	1764
(1764)	*Alzimire*, by Christian Gottlieb Klemm. 1 act, Alexandrines.	1764

(1764)   *Die Befreiung von Theben,* by Weisse. 5   1764
acts, blank verse.

(1765)   **Der Brudermord des Kains,* by Hudemann.   1765
5 acts (?), prose.

(1765)   **Karl von Drontheim,* by Otto Nathanael   1765
Baumgarten. 5 acts, prose (?).

(1765)   *Clarissa,* by Steffens. 3 acts, prose.   1765

1765   *Miss Fanny, oder der Schiffbruch,* by Johann   1766
Christian Brandes. 5 acts, prose.

(1766)   *Hermes und Nestan, oder das Orakel,* by Jo-   1766
hann Friedrich Löwen. 2 acts, prose.

(1766)   *Aurelius, oder Wettstreit der Großmuth,* by   1766
Cornelius Hermann von Ayrenhoff. 5 acts,
Alexandrines.

(1766)   *Ludewig der Strenge,* by Ludwig Wilhelm   1766
von Langenau. 5 acts, prose.

1766   *Atreus und Thyest,* by Weisse. 5 acts, blank   1766
verse.

(1767)   *Das Schicksal der Tochter Jephthah,* by   1767
Hudemann. 5 acts, Alexandrines.

(1767)   *Osmann,* by Johann Wilhelm Casparson (?).   1767
5 acts, Alexandrines.

(1767)   *Julie,* by Helferich Peter Sturz. 5 acts, prose.   1767

1767   *Romeo und Julie,* by Weisse. 5 acts, prose.   1767

1767   *Ugolino,* by Heinrich Wilhelm von Gersten-   1768
berg. 5 acts, prose.

(1768)   *Rhynsolt und Lucia,* by J. W. Rose. 5 acts,   1768
blank verse. (Discussed on basis of contem-
porary review only.)

(1768)   *Naemi und Seba,* by Rose. 5 acts, blank verse   1768
(?). (Discussed on basis of contemporary
review only.)

(1768)   *Thafnhilde,* by Casparson. 5 acts, blank verse.   1768

(1768)   **Herrmann und Thusnelde,* by Ayrenhoff. 5   1768
acts, Alexandrines.

(1768)   **Damon und Pythias,* author unknown. 1 act,   1768
verse.

(1768)   **Nomares,* author unknown. 1 act, verse (?).   1768

(1768)   *Inckle und Yaricko,* by Johann Heinrich   1768
Faber. 3 acts, prose.

(1768)   *Inkle und Yariko,* by Faber. 5 acts, Alexan-   1768
drines.

(1768)   *Die versäumte Erziehung,* author unknown.   1768
5 acts, prose.

Appendix B

BRIEF COMMENTS ON PLAYS

NOT INCLUDED IN THE MAIN TEXT

Der sterbende Socrates. By Nathanael Baumgarten (Berlin, 1741). 5 acts, Alexandrines.

Except in its title, this work shows no influence of Gottsched's *Der sterbende Cato.* In regard to subject matter, a superficial comparison with Klopstock's *Der Tod Adams* might be made; but there is little reason to suppose that this eccentric, stilted play has any connection with Klopstock's lyrical drama or with the development of German tragedy in any respect. Altogether a closet drama, *Socrates* was published, according to the preface, without Baumgarten's intent or knowledge. There is no plot, simply an awkward depiction of Socrates' last hours in prison, as he talks with several friends. The clergyman-author takes an objective view of his hero, and, while Socrates' philosophy is aired in numerous speeches, the play itself offers no distinct philosophical message. Socrates is not shown as a complete martyr, inasmuch as there is some question whether his death is not, at least in part, an act of suicide. Respect for decorum impels Socrates to drink his hemlock off-stage, come back to say his farewells, and then go off stage again to die. On the other hand, a humorous note is brought in when Xantippe comes to the prison and Socrates refuses to see her; and one role, that of a prison guard, has plain earmarks of the old Hanswurst. The Alexandrine dialogue is liberally and whimsically interspersed with sets of lines in iambic and anapaestic tetrameter, and the work is little more than half as long as most Alexandrine tragedies.

Alcestes, oder die ungleiche Vaterliebe. By Theodor Johann Quistorp (Rostock, 1742). 5 acts, Alexandrines.

When this was written (1741), Quistorp, also the author of *Aurelius,* was not yet able to draw a moral, manage a plot, or even to keep his five acts approximately to the same length. The always poorly motivated action of the play involves a royal father and his two sons, brothers who are rivals for the same throne and for the hand of the same girl, who pretends to be in love with both. Love plays a great part in the proceedings, although the author professes to disapprove of the emotion. Twice a kiss between the lovers is directly indicated, something to be found in no other German tragedy of the time. The royal father's favoritism for the younger son results in his own death in a curious way: the jealous older son, mistakenly believing, in the dark, that he is attacking his brother, actually stabs old King Alcestes to the heart. This murder in the dark anticipates the one in Breithaupt's *Renegat*. All the main personages have severe character flaws—indeed, not one is truly sympathetic—and they deserve their fates. A gruesome feature, harking back to the *Haupt- und Staatsaktionen,* is the scene in which the heroine's head is brought in on a platter. Her execution, however, was the just reward for her duplicity in love. The only virtuous person is the heroine's confidante, who is represented as Jewish, presumably because it would have been an anachronism to introduce a Christian into ancient Corinth. This rather short work makes the general impression of being sketchy and unfinished.

Placidus, oder Eustach. By Johann Heinrich Steffens (Celle, 1749). 5 acts, Alexandrines.

In this period only two tragedies, remarkably enough, dealt, probably in imitation of the French *Gabinie*, with the Roman persecutions of early Christians. *Placidus* was the first of these. Steffens wrote it expressly for performance by his pupils at the Lyceum of Celle. His later dramas are also weak, but not quite so wooden and preposterous as this original attempt at playwriting. The first three acts show how Placidus, a Roman general under the emperor Hadrian, is suddenly reunited with his long-lost and widely dispersed family at a military camp. In an absurdly unrealistic way, whereby the *cri du sang* comes into its own, Placidus discovers in succession his two sons and his wife, and the play seems about to come to a happy ending with the blessings of the humane and friendly Hadrian. But no! the fourth and fifth acts depict the downfall of Placidus, who refuses to sacrifice to the Roman gods, because he and his wife are Christians. In a few minutes he has also made Christians of his sons, and their drastic reaction to conversion is a wild attempt to destroy the heathen altar under Hadrian's very eyes. Not unnaturally such behavior results in their being thrown to the lions, who by a miracle leave them unharmed. In defiance of the rebellious attitude of the troops who are faithful to their general, Hadrian eventually gives orders that Placidus and his whole family should be burnt at the stake. No miracle prevents this, but the joy and steadfastness of Placidus, his wife, and sons make their death a triumph and several other Romans around Hadrian are converted to Christianity. This play reveals an exceedingly naive concept of Christian faith and ethics, and its philosophical content is unusually low. The title should have been simply *Placidus,* for the "oder Eustach" is involved only when the wife, on first recognizing Placidus, calls him "Eustach." Her use of this name is not further explained. The plot is supposed to have a historical basis, but the treatment has rendered it completely incredible.

Diocletianus der Christenverfolger. By Ludwig Friedrich Hudemann (Wismar & Leipzig, 1751). 5 acts, Alexandrines.

This, the second of the Roman persecution tragedies, uses material closely related to that of De Bruey's *Gabinie.* The main emphasis, if one can speak of emphasis in such a weak, unsure production, is as much upon the imperial persecutor as upon his victims. Diocletian is not a villain, but almost a tragic hero, because his sympathetic qualities counterbalance his flaws of character and errors of judgment. He loves a Christian girl, and has the highest regard for a Christian general of the Theban legions. He orders their execution most reluctantly and regrets his decision immediately, but too late. Then his despair is more pitiable than the fate of the Christians, who welcome death with unalloyed enthusiasm. Utter lack of skill in characterization and faltering arrangement of plot rob this play of its potential interest. Yet one can scarcely say that Hudemann's later play *Jephthah* is a significant improvement over this first attempt. Each act concludes with a choral section, an innovation introduced by Hudemann and based on his interest in the opera. A few years later, Cronegk also used choruses in *Olint und Sophronia.* Both authors, however, may well have been influenced by the use of choruses in Racine's *Athalie.*

Virginia. By Johann Samuel Patzke (Frankfurt & Leipzig, 1755). 5 acts, Alexandrines.

Although this is an interesting and comparatively well written tragedy (Lessing accorded it some faint praise in a review in the *Berlinische privilegirte Zeitung*), it serves mainly to point up the superiority of Lessing's treatment of the same plot material in *Emilia Galotti* (1772). Like Lessing, Patzke makes the fate of a daughter who dies at the hand of her father the chief feature of the drama and does not complete the action with the overthrow of the guilty tyrant who has caused this tragic infanticide. Patzke, however, was at a loss to provide fascinating characterizations and enough action in the first four acts. Virginius does not appear until the fifth act, while Virginia herself appears only occasionally and briefly before that. Most of the dialogue is devoted to boring conventional arguments between Virginia's fiancé Icilius, an emotionalist who wants to use force to save Virginia, and Numitorius, her uncle, who counsels patience and reason; and with equally tedious arguments between the lustful tyrant Appius and his pandering advisor Claudius about whether Appius should go through with his plans or not. The last act is much the best: briefly and clearly Virginius establishes that there is no help either from Icilius and the populace, or from Numitorius and the senate, which will save his daughter from Appius and his dishonest "legal" maneuvers. Then with sorrow, and after a simple, affecting speech, he kills Virginia, who would "rapturously give a thousand lives" to preserve her virtue. The final act is by no means so exciting and intricate as Lessing's in *Emilia Galotti;* but it is perhaps, in spite of the stiff Alexandrines, more moving and satisfying. Patzke admits in the preface that his play will arouse only terror and horror because its innocent heroine dies and vice goes unpunished—a really daring neglect of the philosophical proprieties. But he tries to stave off criticism by drawing a comparison with *Oedipus.* While Patzke also refers in the preface to his admiration for Schlegel's *Canut,* there does not seem to be the slightest influence of Ulfo on Appius, who is a dull tyrant, the helpless victim of his emotions, and not an evil rationalist.

Das Groß-Müthig und Befreyte Solothurn. By Franz Jacob Hermann (Solothurn, 1755). 5 acts, Alexandrines.

This drama, which was performed in 1755 by leading citizens of Solothurn, owes its existence solely to a spirit of local patriotism and thus it stands aside from the main stream of German tragedy. Yet its ecclesiastical author understood the rules of Alexandrine tragedy, and he handled the plot, characterization, and dialogue with considerable skill. The play is over-long, however, because of his predilection for very lengthy and detailed speeches in the more static scenes. As in Lessing's *Henzi,* all the roles are masculine, and untitled citizens take part in the action without lending the play a bourgeois atmosphere. The medieval setting makes this a forerunner of the *Ritterdrama,* although the author is not concerned with romantic coloring and historical flavor; he is a rationalist and a patriot, and his only goal is to commemorate the unusual virtue and magnanimity shown by the citizens of Solothurn during the siege of the town in 1318 by Duke Leopold of Austria. Even though they believe that one of their citizens, young Buchegg, has been cruelly executed by the Austrians, the men of Solothurn coolly conquer prejudice and emotion to go to the rescue of Austrian soldiers drowning in the River Aar after a bridge has collapsed; and they return the captured leader of these men in compliance with "international law." Duke Leopold, who is pictured as a gentle and Enlightened ruler, thereupon grants Solothurn its freedom and returns young Buchegg, who has not been executed after all. Although a rationalist, the author is too pious to exclude a supernatural element of the story as told in the chronicle: Leopold has an off-stage vision of St. Ursus and others standing guard on the walls of Solothurn. Threats of death and slaughter are heard throughout the play, but the ending is happy for all participants on both sides. Even the two Austrian villains are not punished for their harshness and underhanded methods. One very interesting feature of this play is a long discussion between young Buchegg and Count Homburg, an Austrian sympathizer, about the relative merits of monarchy and democracy. Buchegg defends democracy more eloquently and philosophically than any figure in German tragedy before Marquis Posa (III. iv).

Candaules. By Georg Wilhelm Schmidt (Karlsruhe, 1758). 5 acts, Alexandrines.

The rather smooth dialogue of this play contrasts sharply with the awkwardly handled plot and total lack of characterization. The material is that used also by Hebbel for his *Gyges* (1854), but Schmidt follows Herodotus exclusively and leaves out the magic ring of the Platonic version. Unwisely, the story's one distinctive feature, i.e., the introduction of Gyges into the queen's chamber by King Candaules, who is so delighted with his wife's beauty that he must share the sight with another, has been placed before the beginning of the drama and thus loses its strong effect. Action is supplied (contrary to Herodotus' account) by the efforts of the crown prince, Zophyrus, to marry Olympia. She has been promised to Gyges, but he is in love with Queen Thamyris. This typically French love complication develops alongside the original plot, which deals with Thamyris' endeavors to take revenge on Candaules for having displayed her to Gyges. She makes Gyges believe she is in love with him, and persuades him to prove his love to her by rebelling against Candaules and killing him. Thus love has a hand in every action in the play. Even the various confidants are in love, and at the end there are three marriages. Gyges and Thamyris are considered to be morally at fault and are punished with death, while Candaules, who has been "dead" since the beginning of Act Four, returns alive at the end of Act Five to bless the union of Zophyrus and Olympia.

This ending, as well as the complexity and frequent irregularities of construction, strongly suggest that the author was influenced by Viennese taste in drama. Schmidt is quite unable to cope with the *liaison des scènes* and fails to keep within the limits of any of the three Unities. Changes of scene occur several times without being mentioned except obliquely in the dialogue, and at least two nights elapse, to judge from remarks made at random. But these are errors or inadequacies in construction rather than boldness or freedom, and one gathers that Schmidt hopes they will go unnoticed by the critics. What little ethical thought there is in the play is both superficial and illogical.

Junius Brutus. By Salomon Hirzel (Zürich, 1761). 5 acts, prose.

This work is closely akin to the "tragedies" of Bodmer, i.e., history undramatically related in dialogue form. It is devoid of interesting features and would not have been included in the main discussions in any case.

Montezum. By Christoph Otto von Schönaich, published anonymously (Königsberg, 1763). 5 acts, Alexandrines.

Schönaich's last tragedy is at least as weak as any of his four earlier attempts. Its theme, used before in his *Zayde,* is the un-Christian actions of Christians in a land reputedly heathen, but actually the home of virtue and humanity. The author's ethical message is carried in many long, undramatic speeches, while the action itself is concentrated on a conventional French love triangle. Cortez and his Spaniards have abused the friendship of kindly old (!) Montezuma, whose realm of noble savages is at last beginning to rouse itself against the cruel invaders. For all their exotic garb, the Aztecs have the delicacy and fine manners of cultivated Europeans. Their ritual of human sacrifice is passed off as a relatively harmless method of disposing of captive enemies. The Aztecs are not to blame if God has not enlightened them about the way He truly prefers to be worshipped. To be sure, the scene is laid in the temple of sacrifice, and the smoking altar is exploited for its theatrical effect (as in Grimm's *Banise*); but the one sacrifice scheduled during the play is arranged for in as humane a way as possible, and then is not performed—much to the delight of Montezuma and his priests. The intended victim is Marina, Cortez' Aztec wife, who has been captured incognito and sentenced to die. Her real name, however, is Zares, and she was formerly the wife of an Aztec hero, Gatimozin (historically Guatemotzin), who is thought to be dead. But Gatimozin suddenly reappears from the provinces at the head of a doughty band of warriors who have had some surprising success against the Spaniards. Zares is saved when he recognizes her at the altar; nevertheless, she faces a dilemma, because she is torn between her old and her new husbands. The bulk of the action on stage (while battles surge to and fro behind the scenes) is taken up with Zares' problems of the heart. At the end, after Montezuma has been fatally wounded by a stray arrow and Gatimozin has left to found a new Aztec kingdom in the provinces, Zares still has not made up her mind. Montezuma has little to do with this central love plot. He dies as a martyr halfway believing in an afterlife as a reward for his virtue. Cortez is seen only briefly. There is no villain except the unfortunate Spanish penchant for gold.

NOTES

1. Reihe Aufklärung, Vols. 3, 6, 8, 11, 12. It is worthy of note that *Canut* has recently been reprinted in the anthology *Deutsche Dichtung im 18. Jahrhundert*, ed. Adalbert Elschenbroich (München, 1960).
2. Vols. 42 (ed. Johannes Crüger) and 72 (ed. Jacob Minor).
3. Vols. X, XIII (ed. Rudolf Payer von Thurn).
4. See particularly Eugen Wolff, *Johann Elias Schlegel* (Berlin, 1889); Johannes Rentsch, *Johann Elias Schlegel als Trauerspieldichter* (Leipzig, 1890); Herman Büncmann, *Elias Schlegel und Wieland als Bearbeiter antiker Tragödien* (Leipzig, 1928); J. Minor, *Christian Felix Weiße und seine Beziehungen zur deutschen Literatur des achtzehnten Jahrhunderts* (Innsbruck, 1880); August Sauer, *Joachim Wilhelm von Brawe, der Schüler Lessings* (Straßburg & London, 1878); W. Gensel, *J. F. von Cronegk, sein Leben und seine Schriften* (diss. Leipzig, 1894).
5. See principally his biographers, Gustav Waniek, *Gottsched und die deutsche Litteratur seiner Zeit* (Leipzig, 1897), pp. 184–192, 401–402, and Eugen Reichel, *Gottsched* (Berlin, 1908–1912), I, 627–646, II, 339–340, note 147. See also the introduction to *Cato* by Johannes Crüger in *Deutsche National-Litteratur* (Berlin & Stuttgart, n.d.), XLII, 31–40, and, for a recent discussion of this play, Karl Otto Conrady's essay in *Das deutsche Drama vom Barock bis zur Gegenwart*, ed. Benno von Wiese (Düsseldorf, 1958), I, 61–78.
6. Alexander Schum, *Studien zur deutschen Alexandrinertragödie* (diss. Würzburg, 1919); Erich Kriessbach, *Die Trauerspiele in Gottscheds "Deutscher Schaubühne"* (diss. Halle/Saale, 1927).
7. Charlotte von Wymetal, *The Hero and his Opponent in the Heroic Tragedy from Gottsched to Lessing* (unpub. diss. Yale, 1955).
8. The following texts were finally located, but not in time to be included in the discussions. For a brief comment on each one, see Appendix B.
   Der sterbende Socrates, by Nathanael Baumgarten (Berlin, 1741), 5 A., Alex. Universitätsbibliothek, Göttingen.
   Alcestes, oder die ungleiche Vaterliebe, by Theodor Johann Quistorp (Rostock, 1742), 5 A., Alex. Universitätsbibliothek, Göttingen.
   Placidus, oder Eustach, by Johann Heinrich Steffens (Celle, 1749), 5 A., Alex. Herzog August Bibliothek, Wolfenbüttel.
   Diocletianus der Christenverfolger, by Ludwig Friedrich Hudemann (Wismar & Leipzig, 1751), 5 A., Alex. Universitätsbibliothek, Göttingen.
   Virginia, by Johann Samuel Patzke (Frankfurt & Leipzig, 1755), 5 A., Alex. Preußische Staatsbibliothek, Marburg.

Das Groß-Müthig und Befreyte Solothurn, by Franz Jacob Hermann (Solothurn, 1755), 5 A., Alex. Bayerische Staatsbibliothek, Munich.
Candaules, by Georg Wilhelm Schmidt (Karlsruhe, 1758), 5 A., Alex. Bayerische Staatsbibliothek, Munich.
Junius Brutus, by Salomon Hirzel (Zürich, 1761), 5 A., prose. Österreichische Nationalbibliothek, Vienna.
Montezum, anon. (Königsberg, 1763), 5 A., Alex. [Written by Christoph Otto von Schönaich.] Preußische Staatsbibliothek, Marburg.

Not yet located were the following:

Die Horazier, by Georg Behrmann (Hamburg, 1752), presented on stage in 1733, 5 A., Alex. [Reputed to be a free adaptation of Corneille's *Horace.*]
Telemachs Begebenheiten auf der Insel der Göttin Calypso, anon. (Liegnitz, 1740), 5 A., Alex. [Written by J. G. Heubel.]
Jesabel, by Ludwig Friedrich Hudemann (Rostock & Wismar, 1753), 5 A., Alex.
Urlogese, Prinzessin der Parthier, anon., in *Sammlung dramatischer Gedichte* (Leipzig & Rostock, 1754) [5 A., Alex.?]
Glycine, anon., in *Neue Erweiterungen der Erkenntnis und des Witzes,* VII (Frankfurt & Leipzig, 1756), 1 A. [prose?]
Constantine, oder die triumphirende Liebe zur Tugend, über die besiegten Laster, by Johann Christian Schwarz, in his *Sammlung einiger seiner Gedichte* (Regensburg, 1757), 5 A., Alex.
Brigitta, oder der Sieg des Christenthums, by Schwarz, in *Sammlung einiger seiner Gedichte* (Regensburg, 1757), 5 A., Alex.
Aurelius, anon. (Kiel & Altona, 1757), 1 A., prose.
Die Lissaboner, by Christian Gottlieb Lieberkühn (Breslau, 1758), 1 A., prose.
Polydor, oder die unglücklichen Geschwister, anon. (Wismar, 1760), 5 A. [Alex.?]
Abdolonymus und Alexander, by Johann Gotthelf Lindner, in *Beytrag zu Schulhandlungen* (Königsberg, 1762), [5 A.?], Alexandrines. [Entitled "tragedy"?].
Der Brudermord des Kains, by Hudemann (Büzow & Wismar, 1765), [5 A.?], prose.
Karl von Drontheim, anon. (Berlin, 1765), 5 A. [prose?] [Written by Otto Nathanael Baumgarten, who is not identical with the author of *Der sterbende Socrates,* despite the similarity of names.]
Rhynsolt und Lucia, anon., in *Proben dramatischer Gedichte* (Nürnberg, 1768), 5 A., blank verse. [Written by J. W. Rose]
Naemi und Seba, anon., in *Proben dramatischer Gedichte* (Nürnberg, 1768), 5 A., [blank verse?] [Written by J. W. Rose]

9. For a full acount of most of Bodmer's "tragedies," see Anthony Scenna, *The Treatment of Ancient Legend and History in Bodmer,* Columbia University Germanic Studies, new series, no. 5 (New York, 1937). This author admits, pp. 148–149, "One of the first general

observations which strike the reader of these plays is that their action is anecdotal, their style narrative and descriptive rather than dramatic or dynamic. . . . To say that Bodmer's plays have an anecdotal quality means that he does not use a plot involving dramatic action . . ."

10. *Bibliothek der schönen Wissenschaften und der freyen Künste*, Anhang zu dem dritten und vierten Bande (Leipzig, 1760).

11. *Hamburgische Dramaturgie*, St. 78. In *Lessings Werke*, ed. Julius Petersen & Waldemar von Olshausen (Berlin, Leipzig, Wien, Stuttgart, n.d.), V, 327.

12. *Die deutsche Schaubühne zu Wienn nach alten und neuen Mustern*, 8 vols. (Wien, 1749–1760). Volume V was published in 1754. Its preface is without pagination.

13. *Theater der Deutschen*, 18 vols. (Breslau & Leipzig, 1766–1776). The first volume, or "Erster Theil," examined by me bears the date "1768" and the notice "Zweyte Auflage." It contains the preface, without pagination.

14. From *Abhandlung von der Nachahmung*, in *Johann Elias Schlegels Aesthetische und Dramaturgische Schriften*, ed. J. von Antoniewicz, Deutsche Litteratur-Denkmale des 18. und 19. Jahrhunderts, no. 26 (Heilbronn, 1887), p. 135.

15. See the reprinting of the *Abhandlung vom Trauerspiel* in *Deutsche National-Litteratur*, LXXII, 336 & 337.

CHAPTER I

1. See Fritz Homeyer, *Stranitzkys Drama vom "Heiligen Nepomuck,"* Palaestra LXII (Berlin, 1907), pp. 9, 12–41.

2. Carl Heine, *Das Schauspiel der deutschen Wanderbühne vor Gottsched* (Halle/Saale, 1889), p. 4.

3. These texts are printed in *Wiener Haupt- und Staatsaktionen*, ed. Rudolf Payer von Thurn, Schriften des literarischen Vereins in Wien, X & XIII, 2 vols. (Wien, 1908 & 1910).

4. Christian Heinrich Schmid, *Chronologie des deutschen Theaters*, ed. Paul Legband (Berlin, 1902), p. 30.

5. R. E. Prutz, *Vorlesungen über die Geschichte des deutschen Theaters* (Berlin, 1847), pp. 178, 182. Also Carl Heine, *op. cit.*, p. 28. Heine, however, sees a gradually increasing independence and separation of the Hanswurst-scenes from the serious part of the drama.

6. Fritz Homeyer, *op. cit.*, found definite sources for five of the plays, and made the assumption that the other nine were also adaptations of operas (p. 77). An operatic source for a sixth one, *Cosroes*, was found by Hans Trutter, "Neue Forschungen über Stranitzky und seine Werke," *Euphorion*, XXIV (1922), 324.

7. Even Homeyer (*op. cit.*, p. 73) can find little or no evidence to sup-

port an assumption that the political part of *Die Enthaubtung Ciceronis* was based on an opera. In regard to *Der betrogene Ehemann,* it is perhaps worth mentioning that this play was considered the best of Stranitzky's works by Hans Trutter, in his review of Payer von Thurn's *Wiener Haupt- und Staatsaktionen, Euphorion,* XXI (1914), 834.

8. For a brief synopsis of the plots of Stranitzky's plays, see Fritz Homeyer, *op. cit.,* pp. 13–77, and (less reliably) Karl Weiss, *Die Wiener Haupt- und Staatsactionen* (Wien, 1854), pp. 59–107.

9. R. E. Prutz, *Vorlesungen,* p. 179.

10. Auguste Ehrhard, *Les comédies de Molière en Allemagne* (Paris, 1888), pp. 14, 23.

11. G. Belouin, *De Gottsched à Lessing* (Paris, 1909), p. 23. See also a detailed account of the Hanswurst, his origin, his development, and his personality, in Moriz Enzinger, *Die Entwicklung des Wiener Theaters vom 16. zum 19. Jahrhundert (Stoffe und Motive).* Schriften der Gesellschaft für Theatergeschichte, Vols. 28 & 29 (Berlin, 1918–1919), I, 298–412.

12. Fritz Homeyer, *op. cit.,* pp. 7–8, and R. E. Prutz, *op. cit.,* p. 181.

13. The attempt of Fritz Homeyer, *op. cit.,* to attribute the play to Stranitzky is not only unconvincing in itself but has also been definitively rejected by Hans Trutter, "Neue Forschungen über Stranitzky," 287–309.

14. Homeyer, *op. cit.,* p. 201, note *a.* Also Payer von Thurn's introduction to *Wiener Haupt- und Staatsaktionen,* I, vii.

15. All quotations from *Die glorreiche Marter des Heyligen Joannes von Nepomukh* are taken from the text as printed in the *Anhang* to Fritz Homeyer's monograph.

16. Homeyer, *op. cit.,* p. 122, has pointed out that the model for this character, at least in part, was Ann Boleyn in Hallmann's tragedy *Catharina* (written before 1680). The figure of Ahalibama is significantly changed in the Alexandrine version of *Nepomuck* (1766); in conformity with the sentimental ideals of the mid-eighteenth century she is depicted as far less earthy and sensuous, and she even virtuously rejects the advances of Wenzel. Homeyer, *op. cit.,* p. 102 ff., chooses to regard this Alexandrine adaptation as a late printing of a drama actually antedating the *Haupt- und Staatsaktion,* and claims that the latter was adopted from the Alexandrine tragedy. His arguments in support of this very forced assumption are quite unconvincing. There can hardly be a reasonable doubt that the Alexandrine *Nepomuck* is in fact an adaptation of the *Haupt- und Staatsaktion.*

17. It is characteristic of *Haupt- und Staatsaktionen* to be divided into three rather than into five acts.

18. See the *Einleitung* to Carl Heine's edition of *Der unglückseelige Todes-Fall Caroli XII* (Halle/Saale, 1888), p. xiv. Quotations from the drama subsequently made in this chapter are taken from this edition.

19. See Moritz Fürstenau, *Zur Geschichte der Musik und des Theaters am Hofe zu Dresden* (Dresden, 1861–1862), II, 304–305. The notice mentions the presentation of this drama, with the remark, ". . . wo Harlekin ein lustiger Kuiraßreucher nebst einer geschwätzigen Marketenderin die Seriosität dieser Action adoucirte."

20. Cf. Job 5:19.

CHAPTER II

1. See *Lessings Werke*, ed. Julius Petersen, Waldemar von Olshausen, *et al.* (Berlin, Leipzig, Wien, Stuttgart, n.d.), IV, 56.

2. It was played in 1740 in the small town of Camenz (Saxony), as Gottsched reports in the preface to *Die deutsche Schaubühne*, 4. Theil (Leipzig, 1743), 20–21. Camenz was Lessing's birthplace, and it is, at any rate, at least possible that the eleven-year-old future derider of Gottsched made his first contact with living theater at this performance. Herder also, as he himself tells us in his memorial *Ueber Thomas Abbts Schriften*, received an early impression of the theater from an amateur performance (by a cast of young ladies!) of a Gottschedian Alexandrine tragedy, Creutz's *Seneca*. See *Herders sämmtliche Werke*, ed. Bernhard Suphan (Berlin, 1877–1913), II, 312.

3. See Theodor W. Danzel, *Gottsched und seine Zeit, Auszüge aus seinem Briefwechsel* (Leipzig, 1848), pp. 132–133. Also Friedrich Johann von Reden-Esbeck, *Caroline Neuber und ihre Zeitgenossen* (Leipzig, 1881), p. 190.

4. T. W. Danzel, *op. cit.*, p. 132.

5. See the preface (unpaginated) to the first edition of *Timoleon* (Hamburg, 1741).

6. In the *Critische Beyträge*, VII (1741), 668, Gottsched speaks of *Ulysses* as having been written and played more than ten years before, i.e., in 1730 or earlier. The passage is quoted by Alexander Schum, *op. cit.*, p. 5.

7. See Gustav Waniek, *Gottsched und die deutsche Litteratur seiner Zeit*, p. 199. All quotations here from *Ulysses* are taken from the text as printed in *Die deutsche Schaubühne zu Wienn*, III.

8. *Allgemeine Deutsche Biographie*, XIX (Leipzig, 1884), 600.

9. Waniek, *op. cit.*, p. 198.

10. See *Hamburgische Dramaturgie*, St. 48, in *Lessings Werke*, ed. Petersen-Olshausen, V, 207.

11. The most recent discussion of the play is Karl Otto Conrady's essay, "Gottsched. Sterbender Cato," in *Das deutsche Drama vom Barock bis zur Gegenwart*, ed. Benno von Wiese (Düsseldorf, 1958), I, 61–78. This author considers *Cato* to be intrinsically unworthy of "eine geschlossene Werkinterpretation" (62), and accordingly devotes most

of his essay to a discussion of Gottsched's dramatic theory and its historical position and importance.

12. Waniek, *op. cit.*, p. 187.
13. All quotations here from *Der sterbende Cato* are taken from the text as printed in *Deutsche National-Litteratur*, Vol. XLII.
14. See the *Vorrede* as printed in *Deutsche National-Litteratur*, XLII, 53.
15. In *Deutsche Literatur*, Reihe Aufklärung, II, 160.
16. *Ibid.*, 161.
17. *Deutsche National-Litteratur*, XLII, 53.
18. *Deutsche National-Litteratur*, XLII, 54.
19. Waniek, *op. cit.*, p. 193; Eduard Davrient, *Geschichte der deutschen Schauspielkunst*, 2nd ed. Hans Devrient (Berlin, 1905), II, 272–273. Another work by Koch included in the earliest repertory was *Sancio und Sinilde*, a "*Schauspiel*," adapted from an opera by König (Waniek, p. 193). *Cajus Fabritius*, by Johann Samuel Müller, was also adapted from an opera (Waniek, p. 210) or was, as Gottsched noted in his *Nöthiger Vorrath zur Geschichte der deutschen dramatischen Dichtkunst* (Leipzig, 1757–1765), I, 308, "ein aus dem Italienischen übersetztes Stück."
20. Waniek, *op. cit.*, p. 193, note 1.
21. This tragedy, written by Mlle Barbier (with Abbé Pellegrin) and presented in Paris in 1709, was published in Paris in 1710 and again in Leyden in 1723. See François & Claude Parfaict, *Histoire du Théâtre François depuis son origine jusqu'à présent* (Paris, 1734–1749), XV, 486.
22. Franz Ferdinand Heitmüller, *Hamburgische Dramatiker zur Zeit Gottscheds* (diss. Jena publ. at Wandsbeck, 1890), pp. 12–13.
23. *Timoleon, der Bürgerfreund*, ein Trauerspiel des Herrn Georg Behrmann (Hamburg, 1741). All subsequent quotations are taken from this, the original edition of the drama. There were several others within the following decade (see Heitmüller, *op. cit.*, p. 21).
24. See Gottsched's *Vorrede* to *Cato*, ed. cit., p. 54.
25. *Emilia Galotti* (V. vi).
26. Demaristia's next line, however, softens this: "Er sterbe—Nein, er leb. Ich kann mich nicht entschliessen."

CHAPTER III

1. Except *Der sterbende Cato*, discussed in Chapter II, and Schlegel's *Dido* and *Herrmann*, which will be discussed in Chapter IV.
2. It was originally supposed to contain a translation by Gottsched of Aristotle's *Poetics*, and translations by Schlegel of Sophocles' *Oedipus* and *Electra*. Of these, only the *Oedipus* materialized, and that too late. See Waniek, *op. cit.*, p. 397.

3. Cf. Danzel, *op. cit.*, p. 158.

4. The most vehement denunciation was, of course, by Lessing in his seventeenth *Literaturbrief* (1759).

5. The second edition was published 1746–1750 under the title, *Die deutsche Schaubühne nach den Regeln der alten Griechen und Römern eingerichtet.* Other drama collections were the "Schönemannsche Schaubühne" (all translations), published in four volumes 1748–1749; *Die deutsche Schaubühne zu Wienn nach alten und neuen Mustern* (Wien, 1749–1760), 8 vols.; *Neue Schaubühne oder ausgesuchte Lustspiele der Ausländer* (Frankfurt & Leipzig, 1750), 1 vol.; *Deutsche Schauspiele welche in Wien auf dem k. k. Hoftheater aufgeführet worden* (Wien, 1750), 1 vol.

6. These dates, which are unavailable in the usual biographical reference works, are deduced from remarks in Waniek, *op. cit.*, pp. 383 & 480.

7. *Ibid.*, p. 382, where it is stated that Pitschel did not become a "Dozent" until 1740.

8. *Die deutsche Schaubühne*, 3. Theil (Leipzig, 1741), p. vii (*Vorrede*).

9. The famous lines beginning, "Der Poet wählet sich einen moralischen Lehrsatz . . ." give the novice author instructions about plot formulation and where to obtain the *names* of the characters. When he speaks of characterization, Gottsched clearly implies that the characters are to be made to fit into the plot-actions which are already determined: "Es muß also der Poet seinen Hauptpersonen eine solche Gemütsbeschaffenheit geben, daraus man ihre künftige Handlungen wahrscheinlich vermuten, und wenn sie geschehen, leicht begreifen kann." See the excerpt from the *Versuch einer critischen Dichtkunst* in *Deutsche Literatur*, Reihe Aufklärung, III, 41 & 46.

10. See excerpt from *Versuch einer critischen Dichtkunst, ed. cit.*, 38.

11. See Gottsched's *Vorrede* to the first edition of *Cato* (1732); Schlegel's *Auszug eines Briefes*, in *Johann Elias Schlegels Aesthetische und Dramaturgische Schriften*, pp. 6, 8; Nicolai's *Abhandlung vom Trauerspiel;* Gellert's *De comoedia commovente.*

12. (Leipzig, 1794), 4. Theil, 555.

13. *G. E. Lessings sämtliche Schriften*, ed. Karl Lachmann, 3rd ed. revised by Franz Muncker (Stuttgart, Berlin, Leipzig, 1886–1924), XVII, 133 (letter to Nicolai, 21 January, 1758).

14. Waniek, *op. cit.*, p. 399.

15. This was Quistorp's second published tragedy. His first was entitled *Alcestes, oder die ungleiche Vaterliebe* (Rostock, 1742).

16. *Ed. cit.*, p. 207.

17. It is, however, only an assumption that there was a source-material for this play. The plot has no historical basis, but it is not impossible that Quistorp read the story somewhere and accepted it as historical. On the other hand, he may simply have invented a "fable" and then given the personages historical names. This would have been in accord with Gottsched's prescription for tragedy in the *Versuch einer critischen Dichtkunst.*

18. The defects are well pointed out by Alexander Schum, *op. cit.*, p. 47. The scene, which is Aurelius' dwelling, is appropriate enough for his murder of Valerius, but it hardly lends itself to such later actions as the imprisonment of Aurelius and the functioning of Trajan's court. Trajan behaves there, with his retinue, exactly as if he were in his own palace.

19. In *Vernünftige Gedanken von der Menschen Tun und Lassen, ed. cit.*, p. 159.

20. The text from which quotations are taken is to be found in the series *Theater der Deutschen*, 9. Theil (Königsberg & Leipzig, 1770), 179–268.

21. *Laokoon*, chapter 4, in *Lessings Werke*, ed. Petersen-Olshausen, IV, 311.

22. Grimm was the friend of Rousseau and Diderot and, along with the latter, composed the famous *Correspondance littéraire, philosophique, critique adressée à un souverain d'Allemagne*, which was carried on between 1753 and 1792, and later published (Paris, 1812–1813). Grimm kept up relations with Gottsched, however, until 1754. See the article on Grimm in *Allgemeine Deutsche Biographie*.

23. Waniek, *op. cit.*, p. 399.

24. "Ich bin mein Tage kein Liebhaber von Romanen, am wenigsten aber von der asiatischen Banise gewesen." *Schaubühne*, IV, 17.

25. *Ibid.*

26. *Ibid.*, 16.

27. *Ibid.*, 17–18.

28. Ziegler used, with great freedom, an account of Peguan history in a work by Erasmus Francisci, *Ost-und West-Indischer, wie auch Sinesischer Lust- und Staatsgarten* (Nürnberg, 1668), which used as one of its sources Gasparo Balbi's *Viaggio dell' Indie orientali* (Venetia, 1590). (See Felix Bobertag's introduction to the *Asiatische Banise*, in *Deutsche National-Litteratur*, XXXVII, vii.) The personal names used by Ziegler are not to be found in the more modern *History of Burma* by G. E. Harvey (London, 1925), wherein the mid-sixteenth-century conqueror of Pegu is called Bayinnaung rather than Chaumigrem, and is treated more as a hero than as a tyrant (see pp. 162–179).

29. According to H. K. Kettler, *Baroque Tradition in the Literature of the Enlightenment 1700–1750* (Cambridge, n.d.), pp. 100, 114–117, the *Asiatische Banise* was one of the most widely read books in the eighteenth century, and it was frequently dramatized for the popular stage.

30. Waniek, *op. cit.*, p. 306: ". . . konnte Gottsched i. J. 1741 das völlige Verschwinden der deutschen [Oper] mit Triumph verkünden."

31. Joseph Pinatel, *Le drame bourgeois en Allemagne au XVIIIe siècle* (Lyon, 1938), p. 171.

32. Heinz Kindermann, *Theatergeschichte der Goethezeit* (Wien, 1948), p. 175.

33. See Hermann Anders Krüger, *Deutsches Literatur-Lexikon* (München, 1914), p. 247.
34. Waniek, *op. cit.*, p. 384; Danzel, *op. cit.*, pp. 166–169.
35. Quoted in the introduction to Bodmer's *Parodierter Cato*, in *Deutsche National-Litteratur*, XLII, ed. Johannes Crüger, 129.
36. *Deutsche Schaubühne*, V, 18. Probably Krüger's source work was Jacques Auguste de Thou, *Historia sui temporis* (1604–1608).
37. *Deutsche Schaubühne*, V, 18.
38. In the eighteenth century Madame Gottsched's example was followed only by Margareta Klopstock, whose *Der Tod Abels* was published posthumously in 1759, and by Christiane Caroline Lucius, who in 1778 published a tragedy entitled *Düval und Charmille* (see S. Etta Schreiber, *The German Woman in the Age of Enlightenment*, Columbia University Germanic Studies No. 19, New Series [New York, 1948], p. 123, note 36).
39. In the introduction to *Panthea, Deutsche Schaubühne*, V.
40. *Ibid.*, 6–7.
41. She invented the whole intrigue which connects the death of Abradates with the lust of Araspes for Panthea. She presents Hystaspes in a most unfavorable light, whereas in the *Cyropaedia* he is a man of excellent character. Indeed, except for the character of Cyrus, the captivity of Panthea, the manner of her death, and the battle against Croesus, almost everything in the play is quite different from the *Cyropaedia*.
42. *Deutsche Schaubühne*, V, 10.
43. *Ed. cit.*, p. 204.
44. From *Akademische Vorlesung über die Frage: Ob man in theatralischen Gedichten allezeit die Tugend als belohnt, und das Laster als bestraft vorstellen müsse?* in *Gesammelte Schriften von Johann Christoph Gottsched*, ed. Eugen Reichel (Berlin, n.d.), VI, 281.
45. *Ibid.*, 283.
46. *Historia sui temporis.*
47. Introduction to the *Bluthochzeit* in *Deutsche Schaubühne*, 2nd ed., VI (Leipzig, 1750)—without pagination.
48. *Ibid.*
49. *Ibid.*
50. "Erstlich ist es kein Fehler, wenn ein Trauerspiel Schrecken und Mitleiden bey den Zuschauern erweckt; sondern der eigentliche Zweck desselben. . . . Es wird also ein besondres Zeichen von der Güte dieses Schauspiels seyn, wenn es die Zuschauer mit Grausen und Abscheu erfüllen wird. Die Größe der Laster und Schandthaten fällt an den größten Leuten, destomehr in die Augen, und wirkt einen desto größern Schauer, je unerhörter sie ist: und eben dadurch wird ein Gedicht erbaulich." *Ibid.*
51. Eugen Reichel, *Gottsched* (Berlin, 1908–1912), I, 626.
52. Waniek, *op. cit.*, p. 399.

53. *Op. cit.*, II, 339, note 147.
54. *Don Carlos* (III. x), ll. 3171–3180.
55. *Versuch einer critischen Dichtkunst, ed. cit.*, p. 47.
56. That is, the Catholic ruling family. See Reichel, *op. cit.*, II, 339–340, note 147.
57. See Fritz Brüggemann's brief introduction to his edition of the play in *Deutsche Literatur*, Reihe Aufklärung, III, 85.
58. See Reichel, *op. cit.*, II, 339, note 147.
59. *Deutsche Schaubühne*, 2nd ed., VI (no pagination in the *Vorrede*).
60. *Ibid.*
61. Erich Kriessbach, *op. cit.*, p. 97.

CHAPTER IV

1. See Danzel, *op. cit.*, p. 145; Eugen Wolff, *Johann Elias Schlegel*, p. 6.
2. Wolff, *op. cit.*, p. 6.
3. See Johann Heinrich Schlegel's *Vorbericht* to *Die Trojanerinnen* in *Joh. Elias Schlegels Werke*, ed. Johann Heinrich Schlegel (Kopenhagen & Leipzig, 1761–1770), I, 140–141.
4. In Johann Elias Schlegel's volume, *Theatralische Werke* (Kopenhagen, 1747). Quotations here, however, are taken from the text as printed in J. H. Schlegel's edition of his brother's works, volume I.
5. See *Versuch einer critischen Dichtkunst, ed. cit.*, p. 48.
6. G. Belouin dubs Agamemnon "le contemplatif" and says that he initiates a type which then became traditional in German literature, in fact, one of the two favorite types, the other being "l'homme d'action," like Ulfo in *Canut*. See *De Gottsched à Lessing*, p. 138. "Contemplative," however, would seem to be a less accurate descriptive term for Agamemnon than "well-intentioned but weak."
7. In J. H. Schlegel's edition of his brother's works. See this edition, I, 3–4 (*Vorbericht* to *Orest und Pylades*). Quotations here are taken from the text of the tragedy as printed in this volume.
8. Observed by Alexander Schum, *op. cit.*, p. 13.
9. *Vorrede* to the first edition of *Cato* (1732), as printed in *Deutsche National-Litteratur*, XLII, 53. "Was waget nämlich ein Verliebter nicht, um seinen Gegenstand zu sprechen!"
10. This speech recalls to mind Joan of Arc's famous lament in Schiller's *Jungfrau von Orleans*: "Konnt' ich dieses Herz verhärten,/ Das der Himmel fühlend schuf! etc." (IV. i), ll. 2596 ff.
11. See *Versuch einer critischen Dichtkunst, ed. cit.*, pp. 50–51.
12. See the *Vorbericht* to *Dido* in J. H. Schlegel's edition of his brother's works, I, 71 ff.
13. He said, concerning love in the French tragedy, "Hierüber wird der Charakter ganz vergessen, und die Helden haben fast keinen anderen,

als diesen, daß sie verliebt sind. . . . Aber wir thun den Deutschen
einen schlechten Dienst, wenn wir sie zu Weibern machen, und
ihnen Leute als Muster der Helden vorstellen wollen, deren Leben
an dem Blicke ihrer Geliebten als an einem Faden hängt" (*Auszug
eines Briefes*, in *Schlegels Aesthetische und Dramaturgische Schriften*,
p. 6).

14. *Deutsche Schaubühne*, V, 15.

15. *Ibid.*, 13.

16. All quotations from *Dido* here are taken from the text as printed in
the fifth volume of the *Deutsche Schaubühne*.

17. See *Vorbericht* in *Werke*, I, 71.

18. J. H. Schlegel's *Vorbericht* to *Herrmann* in *Werke*, I, 285.

19. Eugen Wolff, *op. cit.*, p. 40.

20. *Vorbericht* to *Herrmann*, *Werke*, I, 285.

21. See Gottsched's introduction to *Dido*, *Schaubühne*, V, 15.

22. *Vergleichung Shakespears und Andreas Gryphs*, in *Schlegels Aesthetische und Dramaturgische Schriften*, p. 92.

23. The *Arminius* of Campistron was not written to glorify the German
past. Its locale was the camp of Varus, and its main subject was love.
(See Johannes Rentsch, *Johann Elias Schlegel als Trauerspieldichter*
p. 60.)

24. All quotations from *Herrmann* are taken from the text of the drama
as printed in the fourth volume of the *Deutsche Schaubühne*.

25. Rentsch, *op. cit.*, p. 59.

26. *Canut's* many performances and relatively long endurance on the
stage (at least until 1768) are noted by Eugen Wolff, *op. cit.*, p. 137
and Johannes Rentsch, *op. cit.*, p. 71.

27. His third attempt, *Gothrika*, was begun in 1749 and not completed.
(See Eugen Wolff, *op. cit.*, p. 88.)

28. Letter to Nicolai of November, 1756, in *G. E. Lessings Sämtliche
Schriften*, ed. Lachmann-Muncker, XVII, 86.

29. Nicolai, *Abhandlung vom Trauerspiel*, in *Deutsche National-Litteratur*, LXXII, 355.

30. Letter to Mendelssohn, 18 Dec., 1756, in *Sämtliche Schriften*, ed.
Lachmann-Muncker, XVII, 86.

31. In *Schlegels Aesthetische und Dramaturgische Schriften*, p. 135.

32. *Abhandlung vom Trauerspiel*, ed. cit., p. 353.

33. The author said of Ulfo, "Er war bey seiner großen Tapferkeit von
sehr wildem Gemüthe, ein Charakter, von welchem ich mich zu sagen
getraue, daß er vormals bey den deutschen und nordischen Völkern
sehr gemein war, und daß die meisten unter ihnen die Tapferkeit
für die einzige Tugend hielten" (quoted by J. H. Schlegel in his
Vorbericht to *Canut* in *Werke*, I, 215–216).

34. *Abhandlung vom Trauerspiel*, ed. cit., pp. 351–352. Modern critics,
to be sure, go farther than Nicolai in their appreciation of Ulfo's
qualities. Fritz Brüggemann regards his activity as "Reaktion auf
diese [bürgerliche] Gemeinschaft, sie ist nicht vor-, sondern nachbür-

gerlich." To him, Ulfo is "der erste subjektivistische Charakter auf der deutschen Bühne . . ." *almost,* but not quite! In the final analysis, the play is still not Storm and Stress, but "seinem innersten Sinn nach ein ausgesprochenes Dokument der vierziger Jahre . . ." (*Die bürgerliche Gemeinschaftskultur der vierziger Jahre,* Zweiter Teil: Drama, *Deutsche Literatur,* Reihe Aufklärung, VI, 13–15). On the other hand, Kurt May, basing his contention on an analysis of the language and syntax of Ulfo's speeches, roundly declares that Ulfo *is* the hero of the tragedy and that *Canut* definitely is the first Storm and Stress drama: "Wie weit bewusst oder nicht, Johann Elias Schlegel hat also keinen *Canut,* sondern doch eine Tragödie *Ulfo* gedichtet, die erste sturm- und drangartige Konzeption überhaupt hat er 1746 in eine Gestalt gedichtet, die in den entscheidenden Partien unter den Resten einer Alexandrinertragödie vom Gottsche-dischen Typus wie unter einer stehengebliebenen Verschalung sturm- und dranghafte Züge trägt" ("Johann Elias Schlegels 'Canut' im Wettstreit der geistesgeschichtlichen und formgeschichtlichen For-schung," *Trivium,* VII, No. 4 (1949), p. 281).

35. Quotations are taken from the text of *Canut* as printed in the first volume of J. H. Schlegel's edition of his brother's works.
36. *Sämtliche Schriften,* ed. Lachmann-Muncker, IX, 9.

CHAPTER V

1. See *Alt-Wiener Theater* (*Schilderungen von Zeitgenossen*), ed. Paul Wertheimer (Wien, n.d.), p. 45.
2. This prefatory letter has no pagination in the edition used for this study, published in Frankfurt and Leipzig in 1748. All quotations from the text of the play are taken from this edition.
3. See Krüger's *Nöthige Ablehnung des Scherzes über die Allemanischen Brüder welchen ein paar lose Freunde aus Leipzig in dem Ham-burgischen Correspondenten einrücken lassen* (Frankfurt & Leipzig, 1748), p. 13. This essay is together with the play in the same volume.
4. According to Waniek, *op. cit.,* p. 526, it was J. A. Schlegel and Gärtner who criticized the *Allemanische Brüder.* Nevertheless, not they, but Mylius and Kästner are the ones mentioned repeatedly in the text of the *Nöthige Ablehnung,* which was Krüger's defense of his play.
5. See *Nöthige Ablehnung,* p. 48.
6. The history of the Alemannic tribes written by Ammianus Marcell-linus, a Roman living in Cologne in the latter part of the fourth century. See Julius Cramer, *Die Geschichte der Allemanne als Gauge-schichte* (Breslau, 1899), p. 44.
7. Julius Cramer, *op. cit.,* pp. 59, 145, 149.
8. This second line recalls to mind the outcry of Schiller's Joan of Arc:

"Konnt' ich dieses Herz verhärten,
Das der Himmel fühlend schuf!"
(*Jungfrau von Orleans*, IV. i).

9. Purposely omitted here is a play published at Cölln am Rhein (Cologne) in 1746 with the fanciful title *Der traurige Ritter, in schwarzer Gestalt, in den Gebirgen Schottlands* (prose). The author, who facetiously claims to have translated the play from the French, is identified only as "K. P. L." Waniek, *op. cit.*, p. 495, lists this play as a tragedy and erroneously cites the place of publication as Celle. Actually the work is only a bitter political pasquill on the English Pretender Charles Stuart, and a grotesque comedy, not a tragedy at all. Nor did the author claim that he was translating from the French in order to avoid criticism for deviation from Gottschedian rules, as Waniek deduces. This pretense, as the preface of the work makes clear, is merely a part of the elaborate framework of jesting on which the play rests.

10. The text used for this study, however, is to be found in the forty-ninth volume of a collection preserved in the Österreichische Nationalbibliothek called simply *Deutsche Schaubühne*, without indication either of place or date. The numerous volumes of this collection are not made up of reprints but of unbound copies of actual individual editions of the plays. The title page of the edition of *Orest und Pylades* in this volume bears the date 1756 and states that the tragedy was performed in Vienna at the birthday festival of Maria Theresa, presumably also in 1756 (May 13). Concerning the year of the festival see Harald Kunz, "Höfisches Theater in Wien zur Zeit der Maria Theresia," *Jahrbuch der Gesellschaft für Wiener Theaterforschung*, 1953/1954 (Wien, 1958), 98. That a "regular" tragedy was performed for this festival is evidence that the Gottschedian reform must have had the approval of the Austrian court.

11. See Waniek, *op. cit.*, p. 493.

12. *Ibid.*, p. 660.

13. *Auszug eines Schreibens von dem Herrn Verfasser an einen Freund*, p. 84 (paginated in succession to the edition of the play itself): ". . . [Lagrange's tragedy] welches mir anfänglich unbekannt gewesen, und dessen Einrichtung von der meinigen gänzlich unterschieden ist."

14. *Ibid.*, 85.

15. In the text used, the name Thoas alternates frequently with the misprinted form *Troas*.

16. Original place of publication was Wolfenbüttel. The text for this study, however, is to be found in *Die deutsche Schaubühne zu Wienn*, IV (1753).

17. See George Christoph Hamberger, *Das gelehrte Teutschland*, neue durchgehends vermehrte und verbesserte Auflage (Lemgo, 1772), p. 95.

18. See Waniek, *op. cit.*, p. 493.

19. Seneca: Es wird dir nie am Glück, an wahrem Glücke fehlen.
    Dein Geist vergehet nicht.
    Octavia: Mein Vater, ist das wahr?
    Seneca: So sagt uns die Vernunft.
20. His *Schrifften*, II. Theil.
21. See Waldemar Oehlke's introduction in *Lessings Werke*, ed. Petersen-Olshausen, X, 58. This volume is also the source for all quotations from the drama used here.
22. Christian Thomasius, *Ausübung der Sittenlehre* (1696), in *Aus der Frühzeit der deutschen Aufklärung*, ed. F. Brüggemann, *Deutsche Literatur*, Reihe Aufklärung, I (Weimar, Wien, Leipzig, 1928). Here Thomasius lists *Tapferkeit* among the virtues belonging to a man's conduct in rational self-love, and (on page 44) he adds that lack of rationality destroys true bravery: ". . . und anstatt einer Tapferkeit sind wir entweder tollkühne oder furchtsam."
23. Pharnaces: ". . . Was schont man um ein Reich!
    Ein glücklich Bubenstück sieht oft der Tugend gleich."
                                        (*Der sterbende Cato*, I. vii)
24. Gräfin Terzky: "Entworfen bloß, ist's ein gemeiner Frevel,
    Vollführt, ist's ein unsterblich Unternehmen;
    Und wenn es glückt, so ist es auch verziehn,
    Denn aller Ausgang ist ein Gottesurteil."
                                        (*Wallensteins Tod*, I. vii)
25. Hannover & Göttingen, 1749. All quotations here, however, are taken from the text as printed in *Die deutsche Schaubühne zu Wienn*, II (Wien, 1752).
26. Nürnberg, bey Stein und Raspe, 1752. The two plays were published separately, but in the same year and by the same publisher. All quotations here are taken from these two original (and only) editions.
27. See the *Allgemeine Deutsche Biographie*, II, 466. The title pages of both his plays describe him as "der Alumnorum und der Oekonomie auf der Altdorfischen hohen Schule Inspektor."
28. This passage is in the second scene to be numbered "fifth" in the fifth act. There are also two "sixth" scenes.
29. This honor was accorded her because she restored image-worship in the churches. Irene died on Lesbos in 803 A.D. after being deposed by Nicephorus in 802.
30. "Es hat die Pucelle d'Orleans zu ihren Zeiten ein ganz ungemeines Aufsehn in der Welt gemachet; wie dann auch ihre herrliche Thaten unstrittig verdient haben. Wann dies fürtreffliche Jungfer ein Mann gewesen wäre, so würde sie ohne Zweifel unter die grössten Helden und tapfersten Heerfürer Franckreichs von jederman gezählet worden seyn." (The *Vorrede* is unpaginated.)
31. See Wilhelm Grenzmann, *Die Jungfrau von Orleans*, Stoff- und Motivgeschichte der deutschen Literatur 1 (Berlin und Leipzig, 1929), pp. 4–14.

32. In this connection, however, Bernhold was speaking specifically of Joan's unfeminine manner of dress. Nevertheless, a person who uses cunning in one instance may be logically expected to use it in another.

33. See my article, "A Neglected Model for *Kabale und Liebe*," *The Journal of English and Germanic Philology*, Vol. LVII, no. 1 (January, 1958).

34. Frankfurt am Main, bei Franz Varrentrapp, 1754. The edition is anonymous, but no doubt exists as to the identity of the author. All quotations are taken from the original edition.

35. This *Vorbericht* is unpaginated.

36. P. 83.

37. P. 84.

38. *Nathan der Weise* (IV. vii).

39. Ed. Constant von Würzbach, Theil 47 (Wien, 1883), 148.

40. Opinions, however, can differ. Alexander Schum, *op. cit.*, p. 41, speaks of the play's "reiche und auch spannende Handlung" and says further (p. 46), "Als Anfangsarbeit ist dieses Werk trotz erheblicher Mängel im Aufbau . . . recht beachtenswert, und es hätte sicher mehr Aufsehen gemacht, wenn es bühnengerechter gewesen wäre."

41. See Harald Kunz, *op. cit.*, 85.

42. *Ibid.*, 87.

43. See the introduction to Joseph Kurz's *Prinzessin Pumphia* in *Wiener Neudrucke*, No. 2 (Wien, 1883), p. iv, and Harald Kunz, *op. cit.*, 19.

44. Breslau, 1754. All quotations here are taken from this edition. Schönaich was one of the first eighteenth-century German authors to publish his own plays in collected form. He was preceded in this by Gellert, whose collected comedies were published in 1747, and by Johann Elias Schlegel, whose *Theatralische Werke* (incomplete) also appeared in 1747; he was followed by C. F. Weisse with his *Beytrag zum Theater* (5 vols., 1759–1768). Schönaich's volume, of course, could not include his later tragedy *Montezum*, published at Königsberg, 1763.

45. *Gesammelte Schriften von Johann Christoph Gottsched*, ed. Eugen Reichel, VI, 248.

46. See Waniek, *op. cit.*, p. 570.

47. According to Karl Heinrich Jördens, *Lexikon deutscher Dichter und Prosaisten* (Leipzig, 1806–1811), IV, 610, *Zarine und Stryangäus* was published separately, *before* the collection, in the fourth volume of *Neue Erweiterungen der Erkenntniß und des Vergnügens*. This journal, however, appeared between 1753 and 1762 in twelve volumes comprising seventy-two issues (see Carl Diesch, *Bibliographie der germanistischen Zeitschriften* [Leipzig, 1927], p. 48). Accordingly it is more likely that the play was printed in the fourth *issue* than in the fourth *volume*.

48. This review is dated February 22, 1755. See *G. E. Lessings Sämtliche Schriften*, Lachmann-Muncker, VII, 10.

49. *Versuch,* p. 5.
50. *Versuch,* p. 7.
51. From *Auszug eines Briefes,* in *Johann Elias Schlegels Aesthetische und Dramaturgische Schriften,* p. 4.
52. *Sämtliche Schriften,* ed. Lachmann-Muncker, VII, 10.
53. From *Die Schaubühne als eine moralische Anstalt betrachtet,* in *Schillers sämtliche Werke,* Säkular-Ausgabe (Stuttgart & Berlin, n.d.), XI, 95.
54. "Man wird mirs übel nehmen, daß ich mich unterstanden habe, einen so ernsthaften Herrn, als Germanicus ist, verliebt vorzustellen. Ich will es gerade heraus sagen. Erstlich, lieben die ernsthaften Herren nicht auch?" *Versuch,* p. 12.
55. I have been unable to discover Schönaich's source.
56. Schönaich's incorrect version of the admittedly confusing title of this novel is *Herkules und Herkuladiska,* which indicates that he may have been thinking of Buchholtz' first work, *Herkules und Valiska.*
57. *Versuch,* p. 16.

CHAPTER VI

1. Lawrence M. Price, *English Literature in Germany* (Berkeley & Los Angeles, 1953), p. 150. The date of the translation, by H. A. Bassewitz, was 1752. In a much altered form, *The London Merchant* was also presented in Vienna in 1754. See Harald Kunz, *op. cit.,* 93, and L. M. Price, "George Barnwell on the German Stage," *Monatshefte für deutschen Unterricht,* Vol. 35, Nos. 3 & 4 (1943), 207.
2. G. Belouin, *De Gottsched à Lessing,* p. 254.
3. Price, *English Literature in Germany,* p. 152.
4. Altona & Leipzig, 1755.
5. This assumption is based on the fact that everyone, from eighteenth-century commentators onward, has regarded it as a follower, not a predecessor of *Miss Sara Sampson,* which became known to the public on July 10, 1755, the date of its first performance. I have been unable to ascertain the month in which *Rhynsolt und Sapphira* first appeared.
6. Christian Heinrich Schmid, *Chronologie des deutschen Theaters, ed. cit.,* p. 116.
7. Karl Goedeke, *Grundriß zur Geschichte der deutschen Dichtung,* 2nd ed., IV. 1, 74.
8. The historical incident was already widely known to the German public through Gellert's verse tale, "Rhynsolt und Lucia," in the collection, *Lehrgedichte und Erzählungen* (1754). See further F. Brüggemann's short introduction to his edition of *Rhynsolt und Sapphira* in *Die Anfänge des bürgerlichen Trauerspiels in den fünfziger Jahren, Deutsche Literatur,* Reihe Aufklärung, VIII (Leipzig,

1934), 90. This edition is the source of all quotations used here.

9. In the initial stage directions there is the time phrase characteristically a part of the Alexandrine tragedy, "Die Handlung fängt des Abends an und dauert bis nach Mitternacht." Prose bourgeois tragedies generally omitted the time phrase (but Brandes' *Fanny*, 1766, is an exception).

10. *Sämtliche Schriften*, ed. Lachmann-Muncker, XVII, 67.

11. See my article, "Lessing's Manipulation of a Single Comic Theme," *Modern Language Quarterly*, Vol. 18, No. 3 (September, 1957), pp. 183–198.

12. All quotations from *Miss Sara Sampson* are taken from the text as printed in *Lessings Werke*, ed. Petersen-Olshausen, I.

13. *De comoedia commovente* (1751) in Lessing's translation, *Lessings sämtliche Schriften*, ed. Lachmann-Muncker, VI, 45.

14. Also combined in the same volume are two comedies, *Der Augenarzt* and *Die Gespenster*, both anonymous. These and the two *Clevelands* are included in the part called *Neue Theatralische Versuche* (Breslau & Leipzig, 1757), while *Clarissa* is at the front with the date 1765 and the place "Zelle, bey George Conrad Gsellius." The comedies are nowhere attributed to Steffens.

15. By Waniek, *op. cit.*, p. 494 and Goedeke, *Grundriß*, 2nd ed., III, 372. The play, with publication place indicated as Celle, date 1752, and author as Joh. Hein. Steffens, is listed in J. C. Gottsched, *Nöthiger Vorrath zur Geschichte der deutschen dramatischen Dichtkunst* II, 278. However, the *Nöthiger Vorrath*, I, 308, also lists a *Gabinie* published in Frankfurt & Leipzig in 1733 under the initials "P. B." Furthermore an anonymous *Gabinie* was reprinted in the second volume of *Die deutsche Schaubühne zu Wienn* in 1752. Examination of this last-mentioned *Gabinie* reveals that it is a literal translation of the French *Gabinie* (1699) by David Augustin de Brueys. Was the *Gabinie* of 1733 by "P. B." the same translation of the same French play? Comparison of the long titles of the 1752 *Gabinie* and the 1733 *Gabinie* strongly suggests that two printings of the very same text are here in question: (1752) "Die standhafte Christinn Gabinie, welche unter der letztern zehenden schwersten Haupt-Verfolgung Kaisers Diocletiani enthauptet worden"—(1733) "Gabinie Tragedie chretienne. Oder die unter der letzteren zehenten schweren Haupt-Verfolgung Kaysers Diocletiani standhaffte Christin Gabinie." It seems highly likely that the *Gabinie* attributed to Steffens was neither a new play on the subject nor even a new translation of the French *Gabinie*, but simply still another printing of the original translation of 1733.

16. See *Meta Klopstock geborene Moller Briefwechsel mit Klopstock*, ed. Hermann Tiemann (Maximilian-Gesellschaft, 1956), III, 892.

17. See J. G. Meusel, *Erster Nachtrag zu dem gelehrten Teutschland* (Lemgo, 1774), p. 279, where the "Schauspiel" is mentioned, and

Goedeke, *op. cit.*, 2nd ed., III, 372, where the "Trauerspiel" is mentioned. (In both cases the plays are attributed to Steffens.)

18. In Heinsius, *Allgemeines Bücher-Lexikon*, IV, 265, and Kayser, *Bücher-Lexicon*, VI, 96.

19. It will be remembered that Lessing also regarded a change of scenery within an act as inadvisable. See *Hamburgische Dramaturgie*, St. 44.

20. The copy of the original text examined by me, and the source of all quotations used here, is bound without its covers in the twenty-sixth volume of the collection entitled *Deutsche Schaubühne* (no place or date), to be found in the Nationalbibliothek in Vienna, Austria.

21. A still closer parallel is offered in Goldoni's comedy *Il Tutore* (1751), in which a virtuous tutor tries to restrain a foolish widowed mother from setting her daughter a bad example.

22. Preface to *Das Mutter-Söhnchen*, p. 3.

23. *Ibid.*, p. 4.

24. See the introduction to *Lucie Woodvil* in Brüggemann, *Anfänge des bürgerlichen Trauerspiels*, *Deutsche Literatur*, Reihe Aufklärung, VIII, 191.

25. Karl Goedeke, "Pfeil," *Archiv für Litteraturgeschichte*, VII (Leipzig, 1878), 527–528.

26. In the 31st number of the *Neue Erweiterungen der Erkenntnis und des Vergnügens*. See *Allgemeine Deutsche Biographie*, XXV (Leipzig, 1887), 656.

27. *Ibid.*

28. See Chapter I, pp. 15–19.

29. See August Sauer, *Joachim Wilhelm von Brawe*, Quellen und Forschungen zur Sprach- und Culturgeschichte der germanischen Völker no. 30 (Strassburg, 1878), p. 6.

30. See Belouin, *op. cit.*, p. 287, where it is stated that *Der Freygeist* is an imitation of *Miss Sara*. Also Sauer, *op. cit.*, pp. 11 & 45–49, and John Louis Kind, *Edward Young in Germany*, Columbia University Germanic Studies, vol. II, no. 3 (New York & London, 1906), p. 127.

31. All quotations here are from the original text as printed in the *Anhang* to the first and second volumes of Nicolai's *Bibliothek*.

32. Obviously the author did not concur with Wolff's argument in the *Sittenlehre der Sineser* (1721) that human reason can attain to moral truth by its own power. On this point Brawe is more orthodox than "Enlightened." To be sure, Brawe probably also felt the influence of Lessing's views as brought out in the comedy, *Der Freigeist* (1749). Lessing showed religion aligned with virtue and decried free-thinking as irresponsible and an excuse for vice. Nevertheless, as is well known, Lessing's ideas on religion were themselves far from orthodox.

33. F. Brüggemann does this (*Anfänge des bürgerlichen Schauspiels*, p. 17): "Die Unbedingtheit der seelischen Haltung bleibt das entscheidend Charakteristische an dieser Gestalt; und da der Dichter selbst ihr im Grunde seines Herzens recht gibt, geht daraus hervor, daß er

Henley ungebrochen sterben läßt. Die bürgerliche Moral siegt keinesweges über ihn, sondern er über sie . . ."

34. See Lessing's letter to Mendelssohn (October 22, 1757) in *Sämtliche Schriften*, ed. Lachmann-Muncker, XVII, 126, and also footnote 1 on that page. It is of interest that Bodmer was also stirred by announcement of the prize contest and that he sent in his *Friedrich von Tockenburg* (written 1756–1757, published 1761) under a "Nordic" pseudonym through an intermediary named Feddersen. But he apparently never learned whether Feddersen followed his instructions, and the work was not mentioned by Nicolai. See Jakob Baechtold, *Geschichte der deutschen Literatur in der Schweiz* (Frauenfeld, 1892), p. 640.

35. *Vorrede* to *Anhang zu dem dritten und vierten Bande der Bibliothek der schönen Wissenschaften und der freyen Künste* (Leipzig, 1760), pp. 1–2.

36. See August Sauer, *op. cit.*, p. 84.

37. P. xxi.

38. Heinz Kindermann, *Theatergeschichte der Goethezeit*, p. 332 ff., points out that this was no regular prize contest, like those of Nicolai, but "Hier ging es um den großzügigen Versuch eines Privattheaters, von sich aus . . . ein Abkommen zu treffen, das den Dramatikern das bis dahin nur von den Wiener Hoftheatern gewährte Recht auf ein bestimmtes Honorar einräumte" (p. 333). Since only one of the dramas submitted was accepted and granted the honorarium (100 thalers), however, it is hard to see why a line must be drawn between Schröder's offer and Nicolai's prize contests.

39. L. M. Price, *English Literature in Germany*, p. 192, suggests that both Leisewitz and Klinger (as Schiller, some years late) were influenced by C. F. D. Schubart's story in the *Schwäbisches Magazin*, *Zur Geschichte des menschlichen Herzens* (1775). A similar common source to explain the similarity of theme between *Der Renegat* and *Der Freygeist* cannot be so conveniently indicated.

40. All quotations here are taken from the text as printed in *Theater der Deutschen*, II (Berlin & Leipzig, 1768), where it is designated as "ein bürgerliches Trauerspiel."

41. Another example of ignorance of the Moslem religion. Cf. discussion of von Trenck's *Araxane* in Chapter V, p. 149.

42. In *De la comoedia commovente*, Gellert spoke of tears as "Zeugen der Rührung" accompanying the "Empfindung der Menschlichkeit," and he compared them to "dem sanften Regen . . . welcher die Saaten nicht allein erquickt, sondern auch fruchtbar macht." See *ed. cit.*, pp. 48–49.

CHAPTER VII

1. "Aber in dem Codrus sind vergleichunsweise [*sic*] die Charaktere besser beobachtet, die Sentimens angemessener, und der Ausdruck und Schreibart anständiger und ausgearbeiteter; dieses hat uns bewogen, dem Codrus den Vorzug vor dem Freygeiste zu geben." *Vorrede* to *Anhang zu dem ersten und zweiten Bande der Bibliothek der schönen Wissenschaften*, p. xxi.

2. Patzke's *Virginia*, which Lessing complimented slightly in the *Berlinische privilegirte Zeitung*, ended the series. Hermann's *Das Groß-Müthig und Befreyte Solothurn*, also published in 1755 (in Switzerland), was a marginal work inspired by local patriotism, and can scarcely be reckoned together with the German series. In 1756 no original Alexandrine tragedy was published, and 1757 was almost as barren. Schwarz's *Constantine* and *Brigitta* appeared in 1757 in his *Sammlung einiger seiner Gedichte*, but only Gottsched seems to have noticed this fact, mentioning it in his *Nöthiger Vorrath*, II, 292.

3. According to Schmid, *Chronologie des deutschen Theaters*, p. 217, Cronegk began work on *Codrus* when he was twenty, that is to say, as early as 1751.

4. Henriette Feuerbach, *Uz und Cronegk* (Leipzig, 1866), pp. 104–109.

5. It was first published by Nicolai in the *Anhang zu dem ersten und zweiten Bande der Bibliothek der schönen Wissenschaften und der freyen Künste* (Leipzig, 1758). All quotations here are taken from this original edition.

6. Schmid, *op. cit.*, p. 127.

7. Cf. Lessing's sketch of a simplified plot for *Codrus* in his letter to Mendelssohn, Feb. 18, 1758, in *Schriften*, ed. Lachmann-Muncker, XVII, 138–139. Cronegk himself realized, however, that he had erred: "Ich schätze nichts höher, als die edle Einfalt der alten tragischen Dichter. Ein ganz einfacher und ungekünstelter Plan hat Vortheile vor andern, und die neuern französischen Tragödienschreiber haben mich verführt, als ich den Plan zum Codrus verfertigte. Die Wahl des Medons im vierten Aufzuge blendete mich; ich glaubte, diese Situation . . . wäre rührend genug, und noch niemals auf der Bühne erschienen." See *Gedanken über das Trauerspiel Codrus in einem Briefe an H . . .* , in the *Anhang*, pp. 89–90.

8. Gottsched in his *Vorrede* to *Der sterbende Cato* (1732), *Deutsche National-Litteratur*, XLII, 50; Schlegel in his *Vergleichung Shakespears und Andreas Gryphs, Aesthetische und dramaturgische Schriften*, ed. cit., p. 78.

9. *Justus Mösers sämmtliche Werke* (Berlin, 1843–1858), IX, 83.

10. Published in Cronegk's *Schriften*, ed. Johann Peter Uz (Anspach, 1760), I.

11. All quotations here are from the text as edited by J. Minor in *Deutsche National-Litteratur*, LXXII.
12. *Lessings Werke*, ed. Petersen-Olshausen, V, 31–32.
13. *Emilia Galotti*, V. vii.
14. *Lessings Werke*, V, 29.
15. *Ibid.*, 30
16. The last lines are oddly similar to Claudia's speech in *Emilia Galotti*, III. viii: "Was kümmert es die Löwin, der man die Jungen geraubt, in wessen Walde sie brüllet?"
17. See *Vernünftige Gedanken von der Menschen Tun und Lassen*, Chapter 1, in *Deutsche Literatur*, Reihe Aufklärung, II, 153.
18. This was also the opinion of Lessing, who said, "Der Ergänzer hat, allem Ansehen nach, die Geschichte ganz anders geendet, als sie Cronegk zu enden willens gewesen." See *Hamburgische Dramaturgie*, St. 2, *Lessings Werke*, V, 32.
19. Published by Nicolai in the *Anhang zu dem dritten und vierten Bande der Bibliothek der schönen Wissenschaften und der freyen Künste* (Leipzig, 1760). All quotations here are taken from this source.
20. The situation here may be compared with that of von Trenck's Araxane, who is supposed to hate the murderer of her brother, but cannot.
21. See J. Minor's introduction to *Brutus, Deutsche National-Litteratur*, LXXII, 209, and A. Sauer, *Brawe*, pp. 138–144.
22. Sauer, *op. cit.*, p. 52.
23. Translated in Alexandrines by von Borcke and published in 1741. In 1758, the year in which *Brutus* was completed, a second translation from Shakespeare, his *Romeo and Juliet*, appeared in a collection entitled *Neue Probestücke der Englischen Schaubühne*, published in Basel (3 vols.). The anonymous translator rendered the Shakespearian tragedy in rather inexpert German blank verse.
24. Sauer, *op. cit.*, pp. 61–62.
25. All quotations here are from the text as printed in *Deutsche National-Litteratur*, LXII.
26. The narration of a dream is, to be sure, a very old feature of tragedies in general.
27. It was produced only once, but with an excellent cast. This was in 1770 in Vienna. See introduction by J. Minor, 209. In a contemporary account Josef von Sonnenfels attributed its lack of success to the unfamiliar meter, which he described as being most difficult for the spectators to understand. See Sauer, *op. cit.*, pp. 77–78. Perhaps the actors tried to read the lines with the same cadence used for Alexandrines, a cadence suited to a line which is not only longer, but also has a definite caesura, and a rhyme at the end. It is conceivable that such a cadence might make the blank verse, which when read correctly has the effect of rhythmic prose, sound slurred and indistinct.
28. Victor Michel, *C.-M. Wieland* (Paris, 1938), pp. 181–182. In Karl

Goedeke, *Grundriß*, 2nd ed., IV. 1, 199, the date of the performance is stated erroneously as July 20, 1756. The reason for this error is an incorrect dateline on a letter of Wieland's wherein the performance is mentioned; and the matter is explained in Gruber's biography of Wieland, in *C. M. Wielands sämmtliche Werke*, ed. J. G. Gruber Leipzig, 1824–1828), L, 251. Friedrich Sengle, *C. M. Wieland* (Stuttgart, 1949), p. 103, gives the date in passing and without documentation as 1757. Michel's and Gruber's documentation leaves no doubt that the correct date is July 20, 1758.

29. *Wielands gesammelte Schriften*, ed. Deutsche Kommission der Königlich Preußischen Akademie der Wissenschaften (Berlin, 1909–1939), Erste Abteilung, III, 147. The text of *Lady Johanna Gray* printed in this volume is the source of all quotations here.

30. "Und schlägt der Dichter diesen Weg ein [that of interpreting historical events rather than that of complicating them with invented intrigues and sub-plots], sagt ihm sein Genie, daß er darauf nicht schimpflich ermatten werde: so ist mit eins auch jene magere Kürze seiner Fabel verschwunden; es bekümmert ihn nun nicht mehr, wie er mit so wenigen Vorfällen fünf Akte füllen wolle; ihm ist nur bange, daß fünf Akte alle den Stoff nicht fassen werden, der sich unter seiner Bearbeitung aus sich selbst immer mehr und mehr vergrößert, etc." *Lessings Werke*, ed. Petersen-Olshausen, V, 146.

31. *Wielands Schriften*, Erste Abteilung, III, 147–148.

32. See the 63rd *Literaturbrief*, *Lessings Werke*, IV, 169.

33. "Soweit auch Homer sonst seine Helden über die menschliche Natur erhebt, so treu bleiben sie ihr doch stets, wenn es auf das Gefühl der Schmerzen und Beleidigungen, wenn es auf die Äußerung dieses Gefühls durch Schreien, oder durch Tränen, oder durch Scheltworte ankömmt. Nach ihren Taten sind es Geschöpfe höherer Art; nach ihren Empfindungen wahre Menschen." *Lessings Werke*, IV, 295.

34. Cf. Martin Luther, *Eine treue Vermahnung zu allen Christen sich zu hüten vor Aufruhr und Empörung* (1522).

35. Jane's guilt is given a romantic, modern interpretation by Emilie Marx, *Wieland und das Drama* (Strassburg, 1914), pp. 57–58, who regards Jane's capitulation as an effect of her love for her husband: "Es ist die Schwäche des Weibs dem geliebten Manne gegenüber" (p. 57). This is an interesting idea, but I do not believe the text supports it. Guilford's plea is the last of a series which has already shaken Jane's resistance.

36. *Wielands Schriften*, Erste Abteilung, III, 217.

37. Jakob Minor, *Christian Felix Weisse und seine Beziehungen zur deutschen Literatur* (Innsbruck, 1880), p. 202, surmises that the review was written by Weisse himself, or by someone who "doch seine Art zu tragieren charakteristisch ausspricht." But the review was reprinted in Mendelssohn's *Gesammelte Schriften* (Leipzig, 1843–1845), IV, 1, 484 ff., as one of the author's contributions to the *Bibliothek*.

Accordingly one must assume that Mendelssohn shared Weisse's views on tragedy.

38. *Bibliothek der schönen Wissenschaften und der freyen Künste*, Bd. IV, St. 2 (Leipzig, 1759), 801–802.

CHAPTER VIII

1. See J. Minor, *C. F. Weiße*, p. 300. The exact year of the end of Weisse's editorship is not determined.
2. *Chronologie des deutschen Theaters, ed. cit.*, p. 130. Schmid's reference to the path between French and English styles is an obvious paraphrase of Weisse's own description of his procedure as described in the preface to the first volume of his *Beytrag zum deutschen Theater* in 1759.
3. See J. Minor, p. 200. The last two tragedies, *Die Flucht* (1770) and *Jean Calas* (1774), fall outside the scope of this study. *Romeo und Julie* (1767) will be discussed in Chapter X.
4. J. Minor, p. 42.
5. *Ibid.*, p. 366 ff.
6. *Ibid.*, p. 25.
7. All quotations here, however, are taken from the text as printed in *Das Theater der Deutschen*, I (Berlin & Leipzig, 1768).
8. The use of *klug* and *Klugheit* to denote a selfish, shrewd employment of the rational faculty is characteristic of the second half of the eighteenth century. See, for one famous example, the exchange between Nathan and Saladin over the words *weise* and *klug* in Lessing's *Nathan der Weise* (III. v), ll. 1799–1811.
9. Weisse stated in his brief preface, "Shakespeare . . . hat auch aus dem Leben Richard des Dritten ein historisches Trauerspiel verfertiget. Der Verfasser des gegenwärtigen würde es niemals gewagt haben, diesem großen Meister nachzuarbeiten, und den schrecklichsten Zug aus dieses Königs Geschichte zum Inhalte eines neuen Trauerspiels zu machen, wenn er sich nicht zu spät daran erinnert hätte." See J. Minor's edition of *Richard III* in *Deutsche National-Litteratur*, LXXII, 3. All quotations from the text here are taken from this edition.
10. See Schmid's *Chronologie, ed. cit.*, p. 130, where (in 1775) the play is called "eines der berühmtesten Tyrannenstücke, welches alle Theater aufführen." J. Minor relates interesting matters about its good reception in his biography of Weisse, pp. 209–210. The play held the stage until the end of the century, after having been recast in prose in 1788 by Johann Perchtold.
11. *Hamburgische Dramaturgie*, St. 79, in *Lessings Werke*, ed. Petersen-Olshausen, V, 330.
12. *Ibid.* (St. 74), 310.

13. *Ibid.* (St. 79), 328.
14. *Ibid.*, 329.
15. *Ibid.*, 329.
16. *Ibid.*, 329–330.
17. *Ibid.*, 330.
18. *Ibid.*, 330.
19. *Ibid.*, 331.
20. *Ibid.*, 331.
21. J. Minor, *C. F. Weiße*, p. 213. *Krispus* was first published in the third volume of Weisse's *Beytrag zum deutschen Theater*. All passages quoted here, however, are drawn from the text as printed in *Deutsche Literatur*, Reihe Aufklärung, XII (F. Brüggemann, *Das Drama des Gegeneinander in den sechziger Jahren* [Leipzig, 1938]).
22. J. Minor, *C. F. Weiße*, pp. 15–16.
23. *Ed. cit., Deutsche National-Litteratur*, LXXII, 352.
24. *Gellert's Sämmtliche Schriften* (Berlin und Leipzig, 1856), VII, 197.
25. F. Brüggemann is inaccurate when he describes the defiance of Weisse's virtuous characters as something new. He says, for example, in regard to the defiance of the queen in *Richard III*, "Wo in der ganzen Literatur des 18. Jahrhunderts, in der sich seit der Insel Felsenburg die Guten und die Bösen gegenüber gestanden haben, ist von den Tugendhaften, die Kampf und Angriff aus Grundsatz verwarfen, der Tyrannei gegenüber je eine solche Sprache gewagt worden? Ihr Geist war bishin der Geist des Zueinander und nicht der Geist des Gegeneinander, der jetzt aber alle inneren Bindungen zerbricht, die Haltung der Menschen ganz verändert und neu bestimmt und damit für die Literatur die seelischen Voraussetzungen schafft für die besondere Dichtungsgattung, die auf kämpferische Lebenshaltung angewiesen ist: das Drama" (from the introduction to *Das Drama des Gegeneinander*, p. 28). Professor Brüggemann might have found similarly expressed defiance to evil in numerous earlier Alexandrine tragedies, e.g., Behrmann's *Timoleon*, Grimm's *Banise*, Bernhold's *Johanna*. The division between *"Gegeneinander"* and *"Zueinander"* is artificial and not truly descriptive.
26. See Waldemar Oehlke's introduction to *Giangir* in *Lessings Werke*, ed. Petersen-Olshausen, X, 32.
27. Weisse uses the form "Zeangir" in imitation of one of his historical sources for the events of the plot, de Thou's *Historia sui temporis*. His other source, Busbecq's *Turkish Letters*, has the form "Giangir" used by Lessing. See Waldemar Oehlke in *Lessings Werke*, X, 31.
28. All quotations here are taken from the text as printed in *Theater der Deutschen*, VI (Berlin & Leipzig, 1768).
29. This relationship has been pointed out by J. Minor, *Weiße*, p. 219.
30. *Ibid.*, p. 221.
31. I cannot agree with Brüggemann, however, in his introduction to *Das Drama des Gegeneinander*, p. 35, where he states that ". . . in Weißes Trauerspiel der Absolutismus aber bereits 1761 in der unerhörtesten

Weise an den Pranger gestellt war . . ." A play like Behrmann's
Timoleon was, after all, still stronger because of its indictment of
absolutism as a form of government. The same could be said of
Gottsched's *Cato*. It was nothing unusual in the early plays, those of
the 1740's as well as those of the 1750's, for characters to be outspoken in their criticism of the misuse of royal power. Wherever a
tyrant was portrayed there was criticism of his actions. Moreover,
good rulers were praised by the detailing of their wise and benevolent
actions. In this practice there was an implied criticism of those rulers
who were lacking in such wisdom and benevolence.

32. *Faust*, Part Two, Act V, *Mitternacht*, ll. 11499–11500.
33. Lessing's *Philotas* (1759) also has only four characters, but the play
    is in one short act.
34. See Schmid, *Chronologie, ed. cit.*, pp. 144 & 182, and J. Minor,
    Weiße, p. 222 and note 3 on that page.
35. Weisse had made steps in the direction of Albissvinth in the char-
    acters of Princess Elizabeth in *Richard III* and of Helena in *Krispus*.
    Both of these princesses possessed enough courage to defy and de-
    nounce evil, but both were also too passive to usurp the prerogative
    of Providence. Elizabeth, however, came close to losing passivity in
    her plan to kill Richard on their wedding night. In the revised version
    of *Richard III*, prepared after *Rosemunde*, she mentions this plan a
    second time (V. ii) and seems to mean to go through with it. Albiss-
    vinth goes much farther than either Elizabeth or Helena, having taken
    over some of the traits of Fausta.
36. All quotations here are from the text as printed in F. Brüggemann,
    Das Drama des Gegeneinander.
37. J. Minor, whose interpretation of Weisse's tragedies seems condi-
    tioned by the fear that someone might accuse him of having the poor
    taste to like such inferior works, is particularly unfair to this play
    when he asserts that the author was afraid of the theme of revenge,
    and that the reason Albissvinth does not carry out her plan to murder
    Hellmich is that she is a braggart who loses courage when faced with
    the actual deed. (See Minor, *Weiße*, p. 224.) Minor's error here,
    which suggests that he did not read the play carefully, has already
    been pointed out by Brüggemann in *Das Drama des Gegeneinander*,
    p. 37. But Brüggemann also errs in maintaining (pp. 36–38) that the
    play promotes the concept of active personal revenge.
38. J. Minor, *Weiße*, p. 225, reports that no date for the actual writing
    of *Die Befreiung von Theben* is known. But there is no reason to sup-
    pose that Weisse composed it much before its publication year of
    1764. Indeed, its changed style would indicate that a significant pause
    had occurred.
39. See J. Minor, *Weiße*, pp. 64–65.
40. *Das Drama des Gegeneinander*, p. 41.
41. All quotations here from *Die Befreiung von Theben* are taken from
    the text as printed in *Das Drama des Gegeneinander*.

42. *Weiße,* pp. 226–227.
43. See Chapter II, pp. 23–26.
44. Callicrates differs markedly from Philotas in this respect. Philotas emphasizes his complete ignorance of women. He is truly just a child.
45. In his preface in the third volume of the *Beytrag.* See J. Minor, *Weiße,* p. 229.
46. See J. Minor, *Weiße,* p. 230 and Schmid, *Chronologie,* pp. 161–162.
47. J. Minor, *Weiße,* pp. 230–231.
48. All quotations here are taken from the text as printed in F. Brüggemann, *Das Drama des Gegeneinander.*
49. St. 48, in *Lessings Werke,* ed. Petersen-Olshausen, V, 207.

CHAPTER IX

1. The first sketch was made in 1753. Then the work was put away until 1755, and finally finished in 1756. See Franz Muncker, *Friedrich Gottlieb Klopstock* (Stuttgart, 1888), p. 299. The play was published simultaneously in Copenhagen and Leipzig.
2. Margareta Klopstock wrote to her sister Elisabeth concerning *Miss Sara* and Moore's *Gamester,* "Ich halte dich für eine Heydinn bis du diese beyden Stücke gelesen hast" (letter of Nov. 7, 1755, in *Meta Klopstock geborene Moller Briefwechsel,* II, 481). One can scarcely imagine that Klopstock himself would be ignorant of these bourgeois tragedies if his wife took this lively interest in them.
3. *Bibliothek der schönen Wissenschaften und der freyen Künste,* II, St. 1 (Leipzig, 1757), 225. It is intriguing to note here that Mendelssohn two years earlier uses almost the same words to criticize Klopstock that Lessing would use in the 17th *Literaturbrief* to annihilate Gottsched: "Es wäre zu wünschen, daß sich Herr Gottsched niemals mit dem Theater vermengt hätte" (*Lessings Werke,* ed. Petersen-Olshausen, IV, 56).
4. *Bibliothek,* II, St. 1, 215.
5. Except for an undoubtedly amateur performance in Halberstadt arranged by Gleim (see F. Muncker, *Klopstock,* p. 305), there is no record of a contemporary stage production of the play in Germany, to the best of my knowledge. On the other hand, translated and adapted versions of the play were performed in France and Italy.
6. See Johannes Bolte, *Von Wanderkomödianten und Handwerkerspielen des 17. und 18. Jahrhunderts,* Sonderausgabe aus den Sitzungsberichte der Preussischen Akademie der Wissenschaften, Phil.-Hist. Klasse, 1934. XIX (Berlin, 1934), p. 14.
7. *Klopstocks gesammelte Werke in vier Bänden.* Mit Einleitung von Franz Muncker (Stuttgart & Berlin, n.d.), IV, 10. All quotations here

from *Der Tod Adams* are taken from the text as printed in the fourth volume of this edition.

8. See Clarence D. Brenner, *A Bibliographical List of Plays in the French Language 1700–1789* (Berkeley, 1947), item 3116.

9. See C. D. Brenner, *op. cit.*, pp. 196–197 and Goedeke, *Grundriß*, 2nd ed., IV. 1, 96.

10. Goedeke, IV. 1, 96.

11. The similarity of construction has been studied in a monograph by Hermann Dollinger, *Die dramatische Handlung in Klopstocks "Der Tod Adams" und Gerstenbergs "Ugolino,"* Bausteine zur Geschichte der deutschen Literatur, XXIX (Halle/Saale, 1930).

12. *Bibliothek der schönen Wissenschaften*, II, St. 1, 213.

13. Compare the happy reminiscences of Ugolino's sons and the unsparing depiction of their death pangs. See Chapter XII, pp. 384, 389–390.

14. *Bibliothek*, II, St. 1, 219. Not all of this critic's objections are just, however. For example, he does not like the kneeling position which Klopstock decrees for the personages receiving Adam's blessing.

15. Evidently Nicolai's prize contest had something to do with his decision to write a tragedy. See August Sauer, *Brawe*, pp. 19–20. Lessing also encouraged Kleist to write *Seneka* in an unfinished ode (1757). See *Lessings Werke*, ed. Petersen-Olshausen, I, 110, ll. 16–30.

16. The quotation from the foreword is not taken from the original printing of the play in *Neue Gedichte von dem Verfasser des Frühlings* (Berlin, 1758) but from *Des Herrn Christian Ewald von Kleist sämtliche Werke* (Berlin, 1766), II, 77. All quotations from the text of *Seneka* used here are also from this latter volume.

17. See letter of 23 August 1757 in *Meta Klopstock Briefwechsel*, II, 644. The date of this would indicate that her play did not owe its inspiration to Gessner's idyll, *Der Tod Abels* (1758). These two works do, however, have certain thoughts in common, not too strange a coincidence in view of the fact that both deal with the same subject in a similarly sentimental way. I have not investigated whether Margareta's little tragedy owes anything to Metastasio's tragic operetta in two acts, *La Morte d'Abel* (1732). At any rate, her work shows no dependence whatever on Christian Heinrich Postel's Hamburg opera, *Cain und Abel* (1689).

18. Even on her deathbed, to which she was brought by the difficult delivery of a dead infant, Margareta declared that in spite of all her pain she still wanted to bear children. See letter of Elisabeth Schmidt, 11 Dec. 1758, in *Klopstocks sämmtliche Werke* (Leipzig, 1823–1826), XI, 64.

19. All quotations here are taken from the work as printed in volume eleven of *Klopstocks sämmtliche Werke* (Leipzig, 1823–1826).

20. For a plot summary of *Die Lissaboner*, see A. Sauer, *Brawe*, p. 83. A summary is also given by Elise Meyer, *Der Einakter in der deutschen Dichtung des achtzehnten Jahrhunderts* (unpub. diss. Leipzig, 1920),

pp. 46–47. The plot is very complicated, with some motifs evidently borrowed from *Miss Sara Sampson* (e.g., an Englishman of questionable morals tries to obtain the virtuous daughter of a Portuguese gentleman as his mistress). One might call it a "short" rather than a "little" tragedy and include it in the chapter on the first middle-class tragedies. The play relied for most of its effect on the topical interest lent by its setting in Lisbon during the aftermath of the famous earthquake (November, 1755). My knowledge of *Aurelius* is derived from Gottsched's *Nöthiger Vorrath zur Geschichte der deutschen dramatischen Dichtkunst*, II, 293, which is the only place I have seen it mentioned. Very likely this *Aurelius* had no connection with Quistorp's *Aurelius*, for, according to its subtitle, it was composed "Nach dem Gesange in dem ersten Stücke der Hamburgischen Beyträge."

21. Two studies which have contradicted the usual interpretation are J. Clivio, *Lessing und das Problem der Tragödie* (Horgen-Zürich, 1928) and K. R. Bergethon, *Some Aspects of G. E. Lessing's Attitude toward Society* (unpub. diss. Cornell, 1945).

22. Quotations from *Philotas* here are taken from the text as printed in volume one of *Lessings Werke*, ed. Petersen-Olshausen. This particular quotation is remarkably close to Christian Thomasius' illustration of the "prejudice of authority," when Thomasius declares that one often hears people say, "Ich werde mich dieses nicht bereden lassen, wenn auch gleich meine Augen mich eines andern versicherten." See Thomasius, *Einleitung zur Vernunftlehre*, in *Deutsche Literatur*, Reihe Aufklärung, I, 38.

23. Thomasius says that people often assert, "Ich will mit diesem vornehmen Mann lieber irren, als mit einem andern Menschen der Wahrheit beipflichten." *Loc. cit.*, 38.

24. According to an article in the *Beytrag zum Reichs-Postreuter* (Altona, 1772), there still had been no performance of *Philotas* as of that year. See Julius W. Braun, *Lessing im Urtheile seiner Zeitgenossen* (Berlin, 1884–1897), I, 411. The play, however, was performed in the 1760's by pupils of the Gymnasium at Halle. See Waldemar Kawerau, *Aus Halles Litteraturleben* (Halle, 1888), p. 13.

25. The place of publication of *Der Einsiedler*, omitted in Goedeke, 2. ed., IV. 1, 247, is supplied in the 3rd edition. IV. 1, 654. The other early work was *Der Schatz*, a pastoral play (Frankfurt, 1761). Later Pfeffel wrote *Dramatische Kinderspiele* (1769) and translated many French plays for his collection called *Theatralische Belustigungen nach französischen Mustern* (1765–1774).

26. Such a "*tragisches Nachspiel*" with the title *Glycine* had already been published in 1756 in *Neue Erweiterungen der Erkenntnis und des Vergnügens*, Vol. VII. I have seen no reference to any production of this *Nachspiel*, and have not succeeded in securing a text of it; but according to Belouin, *De Gottsched à Lessing*, p. 287, it was a bourgeois work

and an imitation of *Miss Sara Sampson*. This statement is vague and calls for possible further investigation.

27. See Schmid, *Chronologie, ed. cit.*, p. 137.

28. All quotations here are from the text of *Der Einsiedler* as printed in *Theater der Deutschen*, XIII (Königsberg & Leipzig, 1773).

29. *Lessings Werke*, ed. Petersen-Olshausen, V, 79–80.

30. Nevertheless, a work which bears close comparison with little tragedy is Salomon Gessner's *Erast* (1762), a one-act play in prose. *Erast* is a sentimental, semi-pastoral idyll with idealized characters: a son who is living in dire poverty with his wife, children, and one faithful servant because his father did not approve of his marriage is reunited, by a lucky chance, with his now repentant father. This play had as much right to the title "tragedy" as did *Der Einsiedler* (that is to say, no right at all); but Gessner did not call it a tragedy. The vagueness with which the title "tragedy" could be used at that time, particularly in reference to little plays like this, is illustrated by the fact that Diderot called his *Les pères malheureux*, which is a close adaptation of *Erast*, "une petite tragédie," while Marmontel called his freer adaptation, *Sylvain*, "comédie mêlée d'ariettes."

31. Vol. I, 145–159. All quotations here are taken from this original source. The playlet was printed again in *Christian Gottlob Klemms Beyträge zum deutschen Theater*, I (Wien, 1767).

32. *Allgemeine deutsche Bibliothek*, XI, 2. Stück (Berlin and Stettin, 1770), 255.

33. According to Schmid, *Chronologie, ed. cit.*, p. 150, this tragedy was written "nicht für Zuschauer, sondern für Leser." Furthermore, only one translation into French is noted in C. D. Brenner, *Bibliographical List of Plays in the French Language*.

34. From the unpaginated preface to the original edition of *Salomo* (Magdeburg, 1764), from which also all the text quotations used here are taken.

35. For a detailed description of the verse in this play see A. Sauer, "Ueber den fünffüssigen Iambus vor Lessing's Nathan," in *Sitzungsberichte der kaiserlichen Akademie der Wissenschaften*, Philosophisch-historische Classe, XC, 3. Heft (Wien, 1878), 653–656. Sauer, however, was not particularly pleased with Klopstock's verse in this drama.

36. *Bibliothek der schönen Wissenschaften*, XII, 2. Stück (Leipzig, 1765), 279.

37. *Ibid.*, 282.

38. Pinatel's description of *Hermes und Nestan* as a "tragédie domestique" showing the influence of Diderot is altogether inept, unless one is to divorce the word "domestic" from all bourgeois connotations. In that case, almost any tragedy could be labeled "domestic" because most of them deal with family matters to the same extent as *Hermes und Nestan*. See Pinatel, *Le drame bourgeois en Allemagne*, p. 53.

39. This incomplete information is offered in K. H. Jördens, *Lexikon deutscher Dichter und Prosaisten*, III, 422.
40. All quotations here are taken from the text of *Hermes und Nestan* as printed in *Theater der Deutschen*, VI (Berlin und Leipzig, 1768).
41. *Deutsche Bibliothek der schönen Wissenschaften*, II, 8. Stück (Halle, 1768), 707.

CHAPTER X

1. Only *Midsummer Night's Dream* (Wieland) and *Richard III* (Eschenburg) were in verse. See Price, *English Literature in Germany*, p. 237. Price points out that Wieland chose prose deliberately, feeling that Shakespeare's verse form was a pure accident, and not integral to the dramas (p. 239). According to Friedrich Sengle, *Wieland*, p. 162, Wieland was simply too busy to bother with verse. But Wieland was a very facile and impassioned versifier, as Sengle also states. Perhaps the truth lies in a combination of these ideas: Wieland recognized that prose was to be the new fashion in tragedy, and it was convenient for him, because of the pressure of time, to translate into prose.
2. The dramatist, however, generally operates more creatively than the modern motion picture writer who adapts a novel for the screen. The latter merely trims down a text for retelling in a visual form. The dramatist, although he, too, uses the materials furnished by the novelist, fashions a new literary entity which exists for itself. The motion picture writer tries to "bring the novel to life," while the dramatist transforms it into another work.
3. Sengle, *Wieland*, p. 114, strongly suggests that Wieland did not take the play seriously: "Aber der Dichter selbst ist im Stillen schon näher daran zu lachen als darüber zu weinen." This may be true, but none of Wieland's cynicism is evident anywhere in the text.
4. All quotations here are taken from the text of *Clementina von Porretta* as printed in *Wielands gesammelte Schriften*, ed. Königlich Preußische Akademie der Wissenschaften, Erste Abteilung, III.
5. It is reported that *Clementina* had a still greater success than *Lady Johanna Gray*. See Sengle, *Wieland*, p. 113.
6. Hamburg & Berlin, bey Johann Heinrich Rüdigern, 1763. The date 1764 given by G. C. Hamberger, *Das gelehrte Teutschland*, p. 147, and by K. H. Jordens, *Lexikon*, I, 417, may refer to a second printing.
7. Lessing perpetuated Dusch's name, after a fashion, by criticizing his abilities harshly and at length in the 41st and 77th *Literaturbriefe*.
8. The play is not mentioned at all in Schmid's *Chronologie*, and the *Bibliothek der schönen Wissenschaften* (Weisse) takes no notice of it. It was, however, performed by the Koch theatrical troupe (according to the author's preface), and it was reprinted in *Theater der*

Deutschen, XIII (1773). Pinatel, *op. cit.*, p. 79, thinks that it had influence on Brandes' *Der geadelte Kaufmann* (1769).

9. *Das Theater des Herrn Diderot*, 1760.
10. All quotations here are taken from the original edition of 1763.
11. Published in Celle, 1765. All quotations here are taken from the original edition.
12. See Samuel Richardson, *Clarissa Harlowe*, with introduction by William Lyon Phelps (New York, n.d.), VII, 299–313.
13. The date of writing is furnished by Jördens, *Lexikon*, I, 190, and this is vaguely corroborated by Schmid, *Chronologie*, p. 161, where it is stated that Brandes published *Miss Fanny* in 1766, but had it ready before that. There was a second printing in 1767, with place designated as Berlin. It was printed again (in revised form, with the title *Der Schiffbruch*) in volume VIII of Brandes' *Sämmtliche dramatische Schriften* (Leipzig, 1790–1791).
14. *Deutsche Bibliothek der schönen Wissenschaften*, II, 8, Stück (Halle, 1768), 642.
15. See Jördens, *Lexikon*, I, 190, and Goedeke, *Grundriß*, 2nd ed., IV. 1, 77.
16. *Deutsche Bibliothek*, II, 8. Stück, 640.
17. One might think that the setting had been suggested to Brandes by the popular French sentimental comedy by Chamfort, *La jeune Indienne* (1764). This was played in French in Vienna in 1765, then in German in Berlin in 1766, at which performance Mme Brandes herself was assigned the leading role. See Lawrence Marsden Price, *Inkle and Yarico Album* (Berkeley, 1937), pp. 93–94. But since Brandes had already written *Miss Fanny* in 1765, it is not likely that the French play could have influenced him.
18. See J. C. Brandes, *Meine Lebensgeschichte*, ed. Willibald Franke (München, 1923), pp. 208 and 211, and Schmid, *Chronologie*, p. 161.
19. *Meine Lebensgeschichte*, p. 212.
20. *Deutsche Bibliothek*, II, 8. Stück, 641. This opinion is echoed by Pinatel, *op. cit.*, p. 62.
21. All quotations are drawn from the original text of 1766.
22. "O Sklaverei des Volksdiensts! Schmähliche
Knechtschaft—Wie bin ich's müde, diesem Götzen
Zu schmeicheln, den mein Innerstes verachtet!
Wann soll ich frei auf diesem Throne stehn!
O, der ist noch nicht König, der der Welt
Gefallen muß! . . .
Doch war's denn meine eigne freie Wahl,
Gerecht zu sein? Die allgewaltige
Notwendigkeit, die auch das freie Wollen
Der Könige zwingt, gebot mir diese Tugend."
(Oh, what slavery it is to serve
the people! Disgraceful

Servitude—How tired I am of
  flattering
This idol which my innermost soul
  despises!
When shall I be free upon this throne?
      . . . . . .
Oh, he is not really a king, who must
Please the world! . . .
But was it then my own free choice
To be upright? All-powerful
Necessity, which rules even over
The free will of kings, forced
  this virtue on me.)

23. See my article, *"Emilia Galotti:* An Indictment of Bourgeois Passivity," *The Journal of English and Germanic Philology,* LII, No. 4 (October, 1953), 480–490.

24. *Deutsche Bibliothek,* II, 8. Stück, 642.

25. See Vol. VI (Leipzig, 1836), section "Schauspiele," 60.

26. Heinsius, *Allgemeines Bücher-Lexikon,* IV (Leipzig, 1813), section "Schauspiele," 311, has the correct date, 1766, but names no author.

27. See *Jöchers Gelehrten-Lexikon,* Ergänzungsband III (Delmenhorst, 1810), 1245.

28. A still earlier example may be *Karl von Drontheim,* a tragedy published anonymously at Berlin in 1765. I have not been able to locate a copy of this work, and no review discloses its contents; but the title would be appropriate for a *Ritterdrama.*

29. All quotations from *Ludewig der Strenge* are taken from the text as printed in *Theater der Deutschen,* IV (1767).

30. See *Allgemeine Deutsche Biographie,* XIX, 498.

31. *Deutsche Bibliothek,* I, 2. Stück, 165.

32. Sturz is now remembered chiefly as the author of some excellent travel letters composed on a trip to England in 1768.

33. *Julie,* ein Trauerspiel in fünf Aufzügen. Mit einem Brief über das deutsche Theater, an die Freunde und Beschützer desselben in Hamburg (Kopenhagen & Leipzig, 1767). *Julie* was printed again in Vol. VI of *Theater der Deutschen* (1768), and in Vol. II of Sturz's *Schriften* (Leipzig, 1779–1782). The editor of *Theater der Deutschen* misspelled the author's name as "Stortz."

34. The truth of this assertion is borne out in the review in Klotz's *Deutsche Bibliothek,* I, 1. Stück, 117–124, where the reviewer deplores the fact that Sturz did not follow his source more exactly. See also Max Koch, *H. S. Sturz nebst einer Abhandlung über die schleswigischen Literaturbriefe* (München, 1879), pp. 149–150.

35. See the discussion of his "Brief über das deutsche Theater" in the *Deutsche Bibliothek,* I, 1. Stück, 119: "Da der Verfasser von dem Wesen des Trauerspiels und den Regeln der grösten Meister nichts wissen will. . . ."

36. *Deutsche Bibliothek*, I, 1. Stück, 119.
37. *Chronologie*, p. 170.
38. *Ibid.*, p. 289 (note to p. 170, 6). According to the list of plays given at the Hamburg Theater printed in *Lessings Werke*, ed. Petersen-Olshausen, V, 427–431, the play was performed only three times.
39. All quotations here are from the text of *Julie* as printed in *Theater der Deutschen*, VI (1768).
40. Woldemar seems to be a compound of two characters in *La nouvelle Héloïse*, Count Wolmar and Lord Edward Bomston.
41. This volume, printed at Leipzig, bore the date 1768, however. See J. Minor, *Weiße*, p. 233.
42. A "successful run" in those days did not mean continuous, day after day performances. A very popular play might be repeated by the same troupe several times in the same month. See the particulars in J. Minor, *Weiße*, pp. 234–236.
43. See J. Minor, *Weiße*, pp. 234–237.
44. *Deutsche Bibliothek*, I, 4. Stück (Halle, 1768), 6.
45. See the *Vorbericht* as printed in Fritz Brüggemann, *Die Aufnahme Shakespeares auf der Bühne der Aufklärung in den sechziger und siebziger Jahren. Deutsche Literatur*, Reihe Aufklärung XI (Leipzig, 1937), 235–236. The text of *Romeo und Julie* as printed in this volume is the source of all quotations used by me here.
46. This was true in spite of the fact that the play had been translated into German in the collection, *Neue Probestücke der Englischen Schaubühne* (Basel, 1758) and by Wieland (1766).
47. *Vorbericht*, ed. cit., p. 236.
48. J. Minor, *Weiße*, pp. 234–235.
49. J. Minor, *Weiße*, pp. 243–244, refers to this similarity: "Es wäre zu untersuchen, ob das überspannt Schwärmerische in spätern bürgerlichen Trauerspielen, wie in Schillers Kabale und Liebe, nicht ebenso sehr auf Einfluß der Weiße'schen Julie und ihrer Nachfolger im bürgerlichen Rührstück, als auf Einfluß Klopstock's zurückzuführen ist." We have observed the same kind of dialogue in Sturz's *Julie*. Weisse's dialogue might be attributed to an effort to emulate Shakespeare, but this could not have been the case with Sturz. Evidently the hyperbolical, rhapsodical style was a spontaneous outgrowth of the new emotional spirit of the times, to which both Sturz and Weisse were sensitive.
50. Arthur Brooke's poem *Romeus and Juliet* (1562). See introduction to *Shakespeare's Tragedy of Romeo and Juliet*, ed. William J. Rolfe (New York, Cincinnati, Chicago, n.d.), p. 14.
51. See *Theater der Deutschen*, VII (Berlin & Leipzig, 1768), note to p. 103. *Romeo und Julie* was reprinted in this volume not long after its initial appearance in the *Beytrag*, Vol. V.
52. See Brüggemann, *Die Aufnahme Shakespeares*, pp. 302–306, and note to p. 302.
53. Bodmer also published in 1768 the prose "tragedy" *Der vierte Hein-*

rich (Lindau, 1768) and the five pieces in the first volume of his *Politische Schauspiele* (Zürich, 1768): *Marcius Brutus, Tarquinius Superbus, Italus, Timoleon, Pelopides.* To call these dialogues "dramas," to say nothing of "tragedies," is an absurdity.

54. Published at Berlin, Königsberg & Leipzig, 1768. There is a copy of this original and only edition at the University of Chicago Library, and all quotations here are taken from this text. The following brief judgment of the play is given in the *Deutsche Bibliothek*, II, 8. Stück, 713: "Ein trauriges Exempel der versäumten Erziehung ist der Verfasser selbst." Other journals ignored the work.

55. Before this, the Unity of Time had been kept with great piety in German tragedy. In both Wieland's *Lady Johanna Gray* and his *Clementina* reference is made, in the first scene of the fifth act, to the passage of a night; but this does not constitute in itself a breach of the Unity of Time, for the action of the first four acts may still be thought to fall within a preceding twenty-four hour period, or less. But in *Die versäumte Erziehung* the definite night is in addition to an indeterminate number of days, so that the limits of the Unity of Time are distinctly overstepped.

56. A copy of this original edition is available at the University of Chicago Library, and all quotations here are taken from this text. The plot of the play is summarized, with many inaccuracies, in Jördens, *Lexikon*, VI, 144–145 (article on Gellert). It is also summarized in a review in the *Deutsche Bibliothek*, III, 9. Stück, 155–161. Here there is only one error, namely that Inkle suffers a second shipwreck before arriving at Barbados. A careful reading of the dialogue reveals that this is not the case.

57. This identification is made in the review in the *Deutsche Bibliothek*, III, 9. Stück, 161. According to Jördens, *Lexikon*, VI, 144, however, the drama was attributed to a Professor Nüscheler in Zürich.

58. See Goedeke, *Grundriß*, 2nd ed., V. 2, 250–251.

59. See L. M. Price, *Inkle and Yarico Album*, p. 75 ff.

60. *Ibid.*, p. 35 ff.

61. *Ibid.*, p. 57 ff.

62. One hesitates to draw the conclusion that this author did not know the difference between India and America. Yet in the Alexandrine version of the play he bestows the Moslem-sounding name of Ibrim on an Indian character (Yarico's father), which suggests that he may have had a confused notion that Indians were Asians.

63. The play's sole contemporary reviewer, however, objected that the invention of a fiancée put Inkle's relationship to Yarico in a bad light from the beginning. Not only had he been disloyal to Elisabethe, but there was also the strong implication that his love for the Indian had been only animal in nature. Thus the beauty of the idyll was destroyed. (See *Deutsche Bibliothek*, III, 9. Stück, 157.) This reviewer has been identified as Christian Heinrich Schmid (see L. M. Price, *Inkle and Yarico Album*, p. 102).

CHAPTER XI

1. A text of this drama has finally been discovered in the Preußische Staatsbibliothek, but too late to be included in the discussion here. Please see Appendix B.
2. Already discussed in Chapter III in connection with Quistorp's *Aurelius*.
3. See Rudolph Lothar, *Das Wiener Burgtheater* (Wien, 1934), p. 26: "Als Nicolai 1761 Wien besuchte, konnte er mit Recht schreiben: 'Die Kultur stände jetzt in Wien wie anno 1731 in Sachsen.'" An example of the state of tragedy in Vienna is furnished by the translation of Pierre Antoine de La Place's *Adèle, comtesse de Ponthieu* (Paris, 1758) which was made anonymously for the birthday celebration of Emperor Francis in 1760. This originally very poor Alexandrine tragedy was rendered still worse by conversion into a German prose so stiff and stilted that it can best be compared to the prose of the old *Haupt- und Staatsaktionen;* then opulent processions and several totally unnecessary elaborate changes of scenery were added to cater to the Viennese love of stage spectacle. No Hanswurst or Harlequin, however, was permitted to take part. Nevertheless, if such awkward dialogue and gratuitous ornament could be presented to the highest-ranking audience, i.e., that of the court, then surely Viennese tragedy in 1760 was not on the same level of development with that of Germany proper, in spite of the fact that a few "regular" German plays had been presented annually since 1747. The interest in Alexandrines in the 1760's may, under such circumstances, be definitely regarded as a sign of progress. The translation was included in the eighth volume of *Die deutsche Schaubühne zu Wienn,* without the name of the French author, under the cumbersome title, *Adelheid in der Sclaverey, oder Tugend und Unschuld bietet aller Verleumdung Trotz.* To my knowledge it has not been pointed out heretofore that this apparent "original" is actually a translation of La Place's *Adèle.* (See, on the other hand, *Bibliographie deutscher Übersetzungen aus dem Französischen 1700–1948,* ed. Hans Fromm [Baden-Baden, 1950–1953], IV, 75, where it is stated that another so-called "original," *Das gerettete Venedig* [Königsberg, 1755], is a translation of La Place's adaptation of Otway's *Venice Preserved.*)
4. This was published again in 1772 under the title *Hermanns Tod.* The confusion of the second title with *Tumelicus* which exists in Schmid, *Chronologie,* p. 297, note to p. 192, should be observed. *Tumelicus* (1770) was a new tragedy; *Hermanns Tod* (1772) was the old *Hermann und Thusnelde.*
5. See Lessing's letter to Eva König, 10 April 1772, in *Lessings sämtliche Schriften,* ed. Lachmann-Muncker, XVIII, 31, and Eva König's reply, 15 June 1772, XX, 185.

6. See letter to Lessing, 10 August 1771, in *Schriften*, ed. Lachmann-Muncker, XX, 64. *Der Postzug* (1769), a two-act comedy, was the one German language play spoken of, and with cordial approval, by Frederick the Great in his essay *De la littérature allemande:* "Les Amants de Thalie ont été plus fortunés; ils nous ont fourni du moins une vraie Comédie originale; c'est le Postzug dont je parle: Ce sont nos moeurs, ce sont nos ridicules, que le Poëte expose sur le Théâtre; la pièce est bien faite. Si Molière avoit travaillé sur le même sujet, il n'auroit pas mieux réussi." See edition by Ludwig Geiger, Deutsche Litteraturdenkmale des 18. und 19. Jahrhunderts, No. 16 (Berlin, 1902), p. 7.

7. *Ludw. Fr. Hudemann's Proben einiger Gedichte und poetischer Übersetzungen. Denen ein Bericht beygefüget worden, welcher von den Vorzügen der Oper von den Tragischen und Comischen Spielen handelt* (Hamburg, 1732). See Waniek, *Gottsched*, pp. 298–300.

8. *Der Brudermord des Kains* seems, however, to have been a full-length drama.

9. From the preface to the original edition, p. 4. This edition, from which all quotations here have been drawn, is available in the collection entitled *Theatralische Sammlung*, CCXXIII (Wien, 1797).

10. See Wilbur Owen Sypherd, *Jephthah and his Daughter* (Univ. of Delaware, 1948).

11. *Ibid.*, pp. 56–57.

12. In the Düsseldorf Jesuit drama the daughter is sacrificed, as is clearly stated in the biblical account. But in the opera *Jephté* (1732) by S. J. Pellegrin there is a happy ending in which the daughter is saved by a priest who enters declaring that God rejects human sacrifice (see W. O. Sypherd, *op. cit.*, p. 120). It is likely that Hudemann was indebted to the French opera for this feature, and also for the daughter's dream, which Pellegrin had assigned to the mother.

13. See Chapter III, p. 54.

14. *Deutsche Bibliothek der schönen Wissenschaften*, I, 3. Stück (Halle, 1768), 185. The play was also mentioned briefly and sarcastically in the *Allgemeine deutsche Bibliothek*, XII, 1. Stück (Berlin und Stettin, 1770), 287.

15. His authorship is revealed in Schmid, *Chronologie*, p. 170, where it is also noted that the play was performed by Döbbelin. Hamberger, *Das gelehrte Teutschland* (Lemgo, 1772), p. 101, also attributed *Osmann* to Casparson. Doubt is thrown on the identification, however, by the laconic statement in Meusel, *Erster Nachtrag zu dem gelehrten Teutschland* (Lemgo, 1774), p. 38, that *Osmann* was *not* written by Casparson.

16. Waniek, *Gottsched*, p. 615.

17. Jördens, *Lexikon*, V, 821.

18. *Sendschreiben J. C. Gottscheds an J. J. Bodmer aus den elisaischen Feldern* (1770). See Waniek, *Gottsched*, p. 677, and Jördens, *Lexikon*, V, 821.

19. He states in his preface that the story of his play comes from Marmontel's "Versuche in moralischen Erzählungen." In 1767 J. J. Eschenburg also published an operetta entitled *Hannchen und Lukas*, whose plot was taken from *Annette et Lubin*, one of Marmontel's *Contes moraux*. This operetta, however, was not an independent work, but a translation or adaptation of a comedy, *Annette et Lubin*, written by Mme Favart on the basis of Marmontel's story. See L. M. Price, *The Vogue of Marmontel on the German Stage*, Univ. of California Publications in Modern Philology, Vol. 27, No. 2 (Berkeley and Los Angeles, 1944), p. 53, and Minor, *Weiße*, p. 164.

20. The collection by Friedrich Valentin Molter, *Marmontels moralische Erzählungen*, 5 vols., 1762–1770, contains some spurious tales, according to L. M. Price, *The Vogue of Marmontel*, p. 98. The author of *Osmann* may have taken one of these for his source.

21. See Chapter VI, pp. 198–199.

22. All quotations here are drawn from the original edition (Berlin, 1767), which is bound in Vol. 18 of a collection in the Österreichische Nationalbibliothek called *Deutsche Schaubühne* (without place or date).

23. See Chapter III, pp. 69–70.

24. This conclusion is drawn from the copy bound in Vol. 18 of the collection *Deutsche Schaubühne* in the Österreichische Nationalbibliothek, where the play's title page bears place, date, and publisher's name, but not the name of the author. Hamberger, Jördens, and Goedeke attribute the play to Casparson without comment; but Kayser puts Casparson's name in parentheses to indicate that the publication was anonymous. Schmid, *Chronologie*, attributes the play to Casparson. The review in the *Allgemeine deutsche Bibliothek*, Anhang zum 1–12. Bande (1771), 631–636, mentions no author.

25. *Allgemeine deutsche Bibliothek*, Anhang zum 1–12. Bande, 633.

26. All quotations here are drawn from the original and only edition.

27. See Chapter VII, p. 210.

28. Schmid, *Chronologie*, p. 202.

29. All quotations here are drawn from the original and only edition, Frankfurt & Leipzig, 1768.

30. *Deutsche Bibliothek der schönen Wissenschaften*, III, 9. Stück, 161–162.

31. *Deutsche Bibliothek der schönen Wissenschaften*, II, 8. Stück, 575–589. The two plays under discussion are also mentioned briefly in the *Allgemeine deutsche Bibliothek*, XII, 1. Stück, 284, and the volume in which they appeared is listed in Heinsius and Kayser. Kayser identifies the author as one J. W. Rose, and Goedeke, 2d ed., Vol. 2, 357, corroborates this, giving the name as Johann Wilhelm Rose (1742–1801). It has not been possible to secure a copy of this volume.

32. *Deutsche Bibliothek der schönen Wissenschaften*, II, 8. Stück, 584.

33. Compare Schiller's Luise in *Kabale und Liebe*, who will deceive in order to rescue her father, but will not become the Duke's mistress;

also Emilia Galotti, whose father kills her before her chastity can be jeopardized.

34. Although the names of Klotz's closest associates are known (e.g., J. C. Jacobi, Riedel, Meusel, Schirach, Harles, Bahrt, Mangelsdorf), the identities of the reviewers in the *Deutsche Bibliothek,* who signed their articles only with initials, have for the most part remained a secret. To judge from a remark of Lessing's, anonymity was the policy of Klotz's circle: "Ich frage nicht, wer die Freunde des Hrn. Klotz sind. Sie wollen unbekannt sein, und ich denke, sie werden es bleiben" (*Briefe antiquarischen Inhalts,* 56. Brief, in *Lessings Werke,* ed. Petersen-Olshausen, XVII, 258). It is also noteworthy that Klotz in the advertisement for his proposed new journal, *Magazin der deutschen Critik* (which never came into being), made a point of assuring all prospective contributors that he would preserve their anonymity (see *Deutsche Bibliothek,* VI, 24. Stück [1771], 752). Very possibly, however, "Thst" was the signature of Christian Heinrich Schmid, author of the *Chronologie des deutschen Theaters:* L. M. Price, *Inkle and Yarico Album,* p. 102, makes the assumption (based on his extensive study of Schmid's literary style) that Schmid was the author of the review in the *Deutsche Bibliothek* of Faber's *Inkle und Yariko.* This review was also signed "Thst."

35. See Chapter X, p. 324.

36. *Deutsche Bibliothek der schönen Wissenschaften,* II. 8. Stück, 584.

37. The actual French version of this story, however, Pellegrin's opera *Jephté* (1732), did not have such a worldly plot. See Sypherd, *op. cit.,* p. 120.

38. *Deutsche Bibliothek der schönen Wissenschaften,* II, 8. Stück, 588.

39. *Allgemeine deutsche Bibliothek,* Anhang zum 13–24. Bande, I (1777), 446.

40. *William Buttler, Baronet von Yorkshire* (München, 1772).

CHAPTER XII

1. The actual places of publication were Hamburg and Bremen. In 1758, stimulated by Nicolai's second prize contest, Gerstenberg had written an Alexandrine tragedy, *Turnus,* which was never printed and has been lost. Presumably it was not even entered in the contest, but it was sent to C. F. Weisse for a critical judgment. (See Albert Malte Wagner, *Heinrich Wilhelm von Gerstenberg und der Sturm und Drang* [Heidelberg, 1920–1924], I, 40.) In 1785, long after the period of his main literary activity, Gerstenberg published *Minona,* a "tragic melodrama" in four acts.

2. See Schmid, *Chronologie,* p. 175.

3. II, 8. Stück (1768), 600–621.

4. XI, 1. Stück (1770), 8–22.

5. *Ibid.*, 9.
6. See Richard Hamel, "Einleitung" to *Ugolino* in Kürschner, *Deutsche National-Literatur*, XLVIII, 207–216; A. M. Wagner, *op. cit.*, II, 286–346; Hermann Dollinger, *Die dramatische Handlung in Klopstocks "Der Tod Adams" und Gerstenbergs "Ugolino," passim;* Hermann Hettner, *Geschichte der deutschen Literatur im achtzehnten Jahrhundert*, 7. ed. E. A. Boucke (Braunschweig, 1926), III, 1. Teil, 89–91; Ferdinand Josef Schneider, *Die deutsche Dichtung vom Ausgang des Barocks bis zum Beginn des Klassizismus 1700–1785* (Stuttgart, 1924), p. 283; Helmut de Boor and Richard Newald, *Geschichte der deutschen Literatur* (München, 1951–1957), VI. 1, 158–159.
7. *Allgemeine deutsche Bibliothek*, XI, 1. Stück, 11.
8. See Chapter X, p. 332.
9. All quotations here are drawn from the text as printed in *Sturm und Drang. Dichtungen aus der Geniezeit*, ed. Karl Freye (Berlin, Leipzig, Wien, Stuttgart, n.d.), I. As is customary, the editor, Freye, regards *Ugolino* as a forerunner of the Storm and Stress dramas, that is, as the earliest of these dramas. He recognizes, however, that the goal of the drama is the preservation of human dignity under the most trying of circumstances and that this is not the goal of the typical Storm and Stress drama. See I, xx.
10. See Chapter III, p. 57.
11. See Chapter XI, p. 360.
12. *Deutsche Bibliothek der schönen Wissenschaften*, II, 8. Stück, 620.
13. See A. M. Wagner, *op. cit.*, II, 319.
14. See Chapter III, pp. 44–49.
15. See Chapter V, pp. 119–122.
16. I cannot agree with A. M. Wagner, *op. cit.*, II, 329, who states that this tragic guilt adds nothing to the tragedy in a moral sense, and that it merely gave Gerstenberg the opportunity to develop his hero's character more gradually: ". . . das Bewußtsein der Schuld gab die Möglichkeit, die Entwicklung des Helden *allmählicher* zu gestalten, durch sie war Variation and Gliederung zu erreichen." Schiller's Mary Stuart had a similar foundation for her acceptance of death in the guilty remembrance of her role in the murder of her husband, Lord Darnley.
17. See Chapter VIII, p. 255.
18. See Chapter VIII, pp. 270–271.
19. *Allgemeine deutsche Bibliothek*, XI, 1. Stück, 17–18.
20. *Ibid.*, 15.
21. *Ibid.*, 21.
22. Schiller's letter to Goethe, 13 March 1801, gives strong testimony of his admiration for *Ugolino*, and his conviction that this drama treated "the highest questions" shows his feeling of kinship to it: ". . . diese Tragödie, welche Sie vielleicht nicht kennen, hat sehr schöne Motive, viel wahres Pathos und wirklich genialisches, obgleich sie kein Werk des guten Geschmacks ist. Man könnte versucht seyn, sich derselben zu

bedienen, um die Idee der Tragödie aufzuklären, weil wirklich die höchsten Fragen darinn zur Sprache kommen" (*Schillers Briefe*, ed. Fritz Jonas [Stuttgart, Leipzig, Berlin, Wien, 1892–1896], VI, 252). Some years earlier (1793) he is reported to have said that he regretted that Gerstenberg had not written more tragedies like *Ugolino*. See *Schillers Gespräche*, ed. Julius Petersen (Leipzig, 1911), p. 226.

23. See Chapter VI, p. 194.

24. Compare Mary Stuart's enjoyment of revenge in her meeting with Elizabeth in Schiller's *Maria Stuart* (III. iv) and her subsequent rejection of this emotion (V. vii).

25. May or June, 1768, in *Lessings sämtliche Schriften*, ed. Lachmann-Muncker, XIX, 254.

26. *Op. cit.*, II, 338.

27. See his letter to Gerstenberg, 25 February 1768, in *Schriften*, ed. Lachmann-Muncker, XVII, 244–249. Lessing had already read the manuscript in July or early August, 1767, and may have been re-reading it for his correspondence with Gerstenberg when he exclaimed in the *Hamburgische Dramaturgie*, St. 79 (dated 2 February 1768), ". . . wenn die Lehre der Vernunft in uns bekleiben soll, wenn wir, bei unserer Unterwerfung, noch Vertrauen und fröhlichen Mut behalten sollen: so ist es höchst nötig, daß wir an die verwirrenden Beispiele solcher unverdienten schrecklichen Verhängnisse so wenig als möglich erinnert werden. Weg mit ihnen von der Bühne! Weg, wenn es sein könnte, aus allen Büchern mit ihnen!" (*Lessings Werke*, ed. Petersen-Olshausen, V, 330). Lessing's primary reference here was to the fate of the young princes in Weisse's *Richard III*, but it seems quite probable that he also had Ugolino's sons in mind.

28. Lachmann-Muncker, XVII, 247–248.

29. Late in his life Gerstenberg republished *Ugolino* in the first volume of his *Vermischte Schriften* (Altona, 1815). In the foreword (written in 1812) he referred again to Lessing's letter and to the desirability of Ugolino's suicide, saying, "Ich werde nun überlegen müssen, wie ich mir diese gute Bemerkung noch itzt zu Nutze machen könne" (p. 30). But the forty-four years which had passed seem to have taken away Gerstenberg's good judgment in artistic matters. He changed the ending so that Ugolino picks up a dagger and stabs himself as the curtain descends, while his final speech intimates that this act has God's approval!

30. Lachmann-Muncker, XIX, 254.

31. *Op. cit.*, II, 339.

32. Lachmann-Muncker, XIX, 254–255.

33. Lachmann-Muncker, XVII, 246.

34. See *Hamburgische Dramaturgie*, St. 79, in *Lessings Werke*, ed. Petersen-Olshausen, V, 329.

35. Lachmann-Muncker, XIX, 254.

BIBLIOGRAPHY

I. *Individual and collected texts*

Anonymous. *Das Mutter-Söhnchen*. Ein prosaisch Bürgerlich Trauerspiel in Drey Aufzügen. Liegnitz, 1756.

——. *Der traurige Ritter, in schwarzer Gestalt, in den Gebirgen Schottlands*. Cölln am Rhein, 1746.

——. *Die deutsche Schaubühne zu Wienn nach alten und neuen Mustern*. Wienn, 1749–1760. [8 vols.] Vols. 2, 3, 4, 5, 7, 8.

——. *Die versäumte Erziehung*, ein Trauerspiel in Prose und fünf Aufzügen. Berlin, Königsberg und Leipzig, 1768.

——. *Neue Theatralische Versuche*. Breslau und Leipzig, 1757.

——. *Theater der Deutschen*. Breslau und Leipzig, 1766–1776. [18 vols.] Vols. 1, 2, 4, 6, 7, 9, 13.

Baumgarten, Nathanael. *Der sterbende Socrates*. Ein Trauerspiel . . . With preface by George Gottfr. Würfel. Berlin, 1741.

Behrmann, Friedrich Georg. *Timoleon, der Bürgerfreund*. Ein Trauerspiel . . . With preface by Johann Matthias Dreyer. Hamburg, 1741.

Bernhold, Johann Gottfried. *Irene oder die von Herrschsucht erstickte Mutter-Liebe*. Ein Trauerspiel . . . Nürnberg, 1752.

——. *la Pucelle d'Orleans oder Johanna die Heldin von Orleans*. Ein Trauerspiel . . . Nürnberg, 1752.

Brandes, Johann Christian. *Miss Fanny oder: Der Schiffbruch*, ein Trauerspiel in fünf Aufzügen. N.p., 1766.

Brüggemann, Fritz, ed. [General editor, Heinz Kindermann]. *Deutsche Literatur. Sammlung literarischer Kunst- und Kulturdenkmäler in Entwicklungsreihen*. Reihe Aufklärung. Leipzig, 1928–1941. [15 vols.] Vols. 1, 2, 3, 6, 8, 11, 12.

Brueys, David Augustin de. *Les œuvres de théâtre de Monsieur de Brueys*. Paris, 1735. [3 vols.] Vol. 1.

[Casparson, Johann Wilhelm ?]. *Osmann*, ein Trauerspiel in fünf Aufzügen. Berlin, 1767.

[——]. *Thafnhilde*, ein Trauerspiel in fünf Aufzügen. Cassel, 1768.

[Creutz, Friedrich Casimir von]. *Seneca*. Ein Trauerspiel. Frankfurt am Main, 1754.

Derschau, Christoph Friedrich von. *Orest und Pylades, oder das Denkmaal der Freundschaft*. Ein Trauerspiel in Versen. N.p., 1756.

Dusch, Johann Jakob. *Der Bankerot*, ein bürgerliches Trauerspiel. Hamburg und Berlin, 1763.

[Faber, Johann Heinrich]. *Inckle und Yaricko*. Ein prosaisches Trauerspiel in Drey Handlungen. Frankfurt und Leipzig, 1768.

————. *Inkle und Yariko,* ein Trauerspiel in Versen und fünf Aufzügen. Frankfurt und Leipzig, 1768.

Freye, Karl, ed. *Sturm und Drang. Dichtungen aus der Geniezeit.* Berlin, Leipzig, Wien, Stuttgart, n.d. [4 vols.] Vol. 1.

Friedrich II, der Große, King of Prussia. *De la littérature allemande,* ed. Ludwig Geiger. Deutsche Litteraturdenkmale des 18. und 19. Jahrhunderts, no. 16. Berlin, 1902.

Gottsched, Johann Christoph, ed. *Die deutsche Schaubühne nach den Regeln und Exempeln der Alten* [last part of the title varies from volume to volume]. Leipzig, 1740–1745. Also 2nd ed., Leipzig, 1746–1750. [6 vols.] Vols. 3, 4, 5, 6.

Hermann, Franz Jacob. *Das Groß-Müthig und Befreyte Solothurn.* Ein Traur-Spiel in fünf Abhandlungen. Solothurn, 1755.

Hirzel, Salomon. *Junius Brutus,* ein Trauerspiel in 5 Akten. Zürich, 1761.

Hudemann, Ludwig Friedrich. *Diocletianus der Christenverfolger und Phädra.* Zwey Trauerspiele. Wismar und Leipzig, 1751.

————. *Zwey Trauerspiele.* I. *Uebersetzung der Iphigenie des Herrn Racine,* II. *Das Schicksal der Tochter Jephthah.* Bützow und Wismar, 1767.

Klemm, Christian Gottlob. *Alzimire.* Trauerspiel in einem Aufzug in Versen. In *Der Oesterreichische Patriot,* vol. 1 (1764), 145–159.

Klopstock, Friedrich Gottlieb. *Salomo,* ein Trauerspiel. Magdeburg, 1764.

[Kohlhard, Johann Joseph ?]. *Der unglückseelige Todes-Fall Caroli XII,* ed. Carl Heine, with introduction. Halle/Saale, 1888.

Krüger, Ephraim Benjamin. *Nöthige Ablehnung des Scherzes über die Allemanischen Brüder welchen ein paar lose Freunde aus Leipzig in dem Hamburgischen Correspondenten einrücken lassen.* Frankfurt und Leipzig, 1748.

————. *Vitichab und Dankwart, die Allemanischen Brüder,* ein Trauerspiel. Frankfurt und Leipzig, 1748.

Kürschner, Joseph, ed. *Deutsche National-Litteratur.* Berlin and Stuttgart, n.d. [164 vols.] Vols. 37, ed. Felix Bobertag; 41, ed. Adolf Frey; 42, ed. Johannes Crüger; 48, ed. R. Hamel; 72, ed. J. Minor.

Lagrange-Chancel, François Joseph de. *Théâtre de Monsieur de la Grange-Chancel.* Amsterdam, 1746. [2 vols.] Vol. 1.

Patzke, Johann Samuel. *Virginia,* ein Trauerspiel. Frankfurt und Leipzig, 1755.

Payer von Thurn, Rudolf, ed. *Wiener Haupt- und Staatsaktionen.* Schriften des literarischen Vereins in Wien, nos. 10 and 13. Wien, 1908 and 1910. [2 vols.]

Quistorp, Theodor Johann. *Alcestes, oder die ungleiche Vaterliebe,* ein Trauerspiel. Rostock, 1742.

Richardson, Samuel. *The History of Clarissa Harlowe.* With introduction by William Lyon Phelps. New York, n.d. [8 vols.]

[Sauer, August, and Werner, Richard M.], eds. *Wiener Neudrucke.* Wien, 1883–1886. [11 vols.] Vol. 2.

Schmidt, Georg Wilhelm. *Candaules.* Ein Trauerspiel. Frankfurt und Leipzig, 1758.

Schönaich, Christoph Otto von. *Montezum.* Ein Trauerspiel in fünf Aufzügen. Königsberg, 1763.

———. *Versuch in der tragischen Dichtkunst.* Breslau, 1754.

Steffens, Johann Heinrich. *Clarissa, ein bürgerliches Trauerspiel, in drei Aufzügen, nach Anleitung der bekanten Geschichte.* Zelle, 1765.

———. *Placidus, oder Eustach, ein Trauerspiel in fünf Aufzügen.* Celle, 1749.

II. *Historical source materials*

Brandes, Johann Christian. *Meine Lebensgeschichte,* ed. Willibald Franke. München, 1923.

Braun, Julius W., ed. *Lessing im Urtheile seiner Zeitgenossen.* Berlin, 1884–1897. [3 vols.] Vol. 1.

Danzel, Theodor W., ed. *Gottsched und seine Zeit. Auszüge aus seinem Briefwechsel.* Leipzig, 1848.

Gottsched, Johann Christoph. *Nöthiger Vorrath zur Geschichte der deutschen dramatischen Dichtkunst.* Leipzig, 1757–1765. [2 vols. and "Kleine Nachlese"—by Gottfried Christian Freiesleben.]

Jonas, Fritz, ed. *Schillers Briefe.* Stuttgart, Leipzig, Berlin, Wien, 1892–1896. [7 vols.] Vol. 6.

Parfaict, François and Claude. *Histoire du Théâtre François depuis son origine jusqu'à présent.* Paris, 1734–1749. [15 vols.]. Vol. 15.

Petersen, Julius, ed. *Schillers Gespräche.* Leipzig, 1911.

Schmid, Christian Heinrich. *Chronologie des deutschen Theaters,* ed. Paul Legband. Schriften der Gesellschaft für Theatergeschichte, no. 1. Leipzig, 1902.

Schütze, Johann Friedrich. *Hamburgische Theater-Geschichte.* Hamburg, 1794.

Tiemann, Hermann, ed. *Meta Klopstock geborene Moller Briefwechsel mit Klopstock.* Maximilian-Gesellschaft, 1956. [3 vols.]

Wertheimer, Paul, ed. *Alt-Wiener Theater (Schilderungen von Zeitgenossen).* Wien, n.d.

III. *Collected works*

Cronegk, Johann Friedrich von. *Schriften,* ed. Johann Peter Uz. Anspach, 1760. [2 vols.] Vol. 2.

Gellert, Christian Fürchtegott. *C. F. Gellert's sämmtliche Schriften,* ed. J. L. Klee. Berlin and Leipzig, 1856. [10 vols.] Vol. 7.

Gerstenberg, Heinrich Wilhelm von. *Gerstenbergs vermischte Schriften.* Altona, 1815. [3 vols.] Vol. 1.

Gottsched, Johann Christoph. *Gesammelte Schriften von Johann Chris-toph Gottsched*, ed. Eugen Reichel. Berlin, n.d. [6 vols.] Vol. 6.

Kleist, Ewald Christian von. *Des Herrn Christian Ewald von Kleist sämtliche Werke*. Berlin, 1766. [2 vols.] Vol. 2.

Klopstock, Friedrich Gottlieb. *Klopstocks gesammelte Werke in vier Bänden*. With introduction by Franz Muncker. Stuttgart and Berlin, n.d. Vol. 4.

———. *Klopstocks sämmtliche Werke*. Leipzig, 1823–1826. [12 vols.] Vol. 11.

Lessing, Gotthold Ephraim. *G. E. Lessings sämtliche Schriften*, ed. Karl Lachmann, 3rd ed. revised by Franz Muncker. Stuttgart, Berlin, Leipzig, 1886–1924. [23 vols.] Vols. 6, 7, 17, 18, 19, 20.

———. *Lessings Werke*, ed. Julius Petersen and Waldemar von Olshausen. Berlin, Leipzig, Wien, Stuttgart, n.d. [25 vols.] Vols. 1, 4, 5, 10, 17.

Möser, Justus. *Justus Mösers sämmtliche Werke*. Berlin, 1843–1858. [10 vols.] Vol. 9.

Schiller, Johann Christoph Friedrich von. *Schillers sämtliche Werke*. Säkular-Ausgabe. Stuttgart und Berlin, n.d. [16 vols.] Vol. 11.

Schlegel, Johann Elias. *Joh. Elias Schlegels Werke*, ed. Johann Heinrich Schlegel. Kopenhagen und Leipzig, 1761–1770. [5 vols.] Vols. 1, 2.

———. *Johann Elias Schlegels Aesthetische und Dramaturgische Schriften*, ed. J. von Antoniewicz. Deutsche Litteraturdenkmale des 18. und 19. Jahrhunderts, no. 26. Heilbronn, 1887.

Wieland, Christoph Martin. *C. M. Wielands sämmtliche Werke*, ed. J. G. Gruber. Leipzig, 1824–1828. [53 vols.] Vol. 50.

———. *Wielands gesammelte Schriften*, ed. Deutsche Kommission der Königlich Preußischen Akademie der Wissenschaften. Berlin, 1909–1939. [25 vols.] 1st section, vol. 3.

IV. *Frequently consulted reference works*

Brenner, Clarence D. *A Bibliographical List of Plays in the French Language 1700–1789*. Berkeley, 1947.

Diesch, Carl. *Bibliographie der germanistischen Zeitschriften*. Leipzig, 1927.

Fromm, Hans, ed. *Bibliographie deutscher Übersetzungen aus dem Französischen 1700–1948*. Baden-Baden, 1950–1953. [6 vols.]

Goedeke, Karl. *Grundriß zur Geschichte der deutschen Dichtung*, 2nd ed. Dresden-Berlin, 1884–1959. [14 vols.] Vols. 3, 4 [pt. 1], 5 [pt. 2]. Also 3rd ed. Dresden-Berlin, 1910–1957. [1 vol.] Vol. 4 [pt. 1], 2nd printing, 1955.

Hamberger, Georg Christoph. *Das gelehrte Teutschland*, 2nd ed. Lemgo, 1772.

Heinsius, Wilhelm. *Allgemeines Bücher-Lexikon*, 2nd ed. Leipzig, 1812–1894. [19 vols.] Vols. 1, 2, 3, 4.

Historische Commission bei der König. Akademie der Wissenschaften (Bavaria), ed. *Allgemeine Deutsche Biographie.* Leipzig, 1875–1912. [56 vols.]
Jöcher, Christian Gottlieb. *Allgemeines Gelehrten-Lexicon.* Leipzig, 1750–1751. Ergänzungsband 1, ed. J. C. Adelung. Leipzig, 1784; Ergänzungsband 3, ed. H. W. Rotermund. Delmenhorst, 1810; Ergänzungsband 4, H. W. Rotermund. Bremen, 1813.
Jördens, Karl Heinrich. *Lexikon deutscher Dichter und Prosaisten.* Leipzig, 1806–1811. [6 vols.]
Kayser, Christian Gottlob. *Vollständiges Bücher-Lexicon.* Leipzig, 1834–1912. [42 vols.] Vols. 1, 2, 3, 4, 5, 6.
Krüger, Hermann Anders. *Deutsches Literatur-Lexikon.* München, 1914.
Meusel, Johann Georg. *Erster Nachtrag zu dem gelehrten Teutschland.* Lemgo, 1774.
Wurzbach, Constant von, ed. *Biographisches Lexikon des Kaiserthums Oesterreich.* Wien, 1856–1891. [60 vols.]

V. *Eighteenth-century journals used*

Allgemeine deutsche Bibliothek, ed. F. Nicolai. Berlin and Stuttgart, 1765–1796. [118 vols.] Vols. 11 (1770); 12 (1770); Anhang zum 1-12. Band. (1771); Anhang zum 13-24. Band (1777).
Bibliothek der schönen Wissenschaften und der freyen Künste, ed. F. Nicolai, M. Mendelssohn, C. F. Weisse. Leipzig, 1757–1765. [12 vols.] Vols. 2 (1757); 4 (1759); 12 (1765); Anhang zu dem 1-2. Band (1758); Anhang zu dem 3-4. Band (1760).
Deutsche Bibliothek der schönen Wissenschaften, ed. C. A. Klotz. Halle, 1767–1771. [6 vols.]. Vols. 1 (1767–1768); 2 (1768); 3 (1769); 6 (1771).

VI. *Histories and commentaries*

Baechtold, Jakob. *Geschichte der deutschen Literatur in der Schweiz.* Frauenfeld, 1892.
Belouin, G. *De Gottsched à Lessing.* Paris, 1909.
Bergethon, K. R. *Some Aspects of G. E. Lessing's Attitude toward Society.* Unpub. diss. Cornell, 1945.
Bolte, Johannes. *Von Wanderkomödianten und Handwerkerspielen des 17. und 18. Jahrhunderts.* Sonderausgabe aus den Sitzungsberichten der Preussischen Akademie der Wissenschaften, Phil.-Hist. Klasse, 1934, no. 19. Berlin, 1934.
Boor, Helmut de, and Newald, Richard. *Geschichte der deutschen Literatur von den Anfängen bis zur Gegenwart.* München, 1949–1957. [6 vols.] Vol. 6, pt. 1.

Bünemann, Hermann. *Elias Schlegel und Wieland als Bearbeiter antiker Tragödien.* Leipzig, 1928.

Clivio, J. *Lessing und das Problem der Tragödie.* Horgen-Zürich, 1928.

Cramer, Julius. *Die Geschichte der Allemanne als Gaugeschichte.* Breslau, 1899.

Devrient, Eduard. *Geschichte der deutschen Schauspielkunst,* 2nd ed. Hans Devrient. Berlin, 1905. [2 vols.] Vol. 1.

Dollinger, Hermann. *Die dramatische Handlung in Klopstocks "Der Tod Adams" und Gerstenbergs "Ugolino."* Bausteine zur Geschichte der deutschen Literatur, no. 29. Halle/Saale, 1930.

Ehrhard, Auguste. *Les comédies de Molière en Allemagne.* Paris, 1888.

Enzinger, Moriz. *Die Entwicklung des Wiener Theaters vom 16. zum 19. Jahrhundert (Stoffe und Motive).* Schriften der Gesellschaft für Theatergeschichte, nos. 28 and 29. Berlin, 1918–1919. [2 vols.]

Feuerbach, Henriette. *Uz und Cronegk.* Leipzig, 1866.

Fürstenau, Moritz. *Zur Geschichte der Musik und des Theaters am Hofe zu Dresden.* Dresden, 1861–1862. [2 vols.] Vol. 2.

Gensel, W. *J. F. von Cronegk, sein Leben und seine Schriften.* Diss. Leipzig, 1894.

Grenzmann, Wilhelm. *Die Jungfrau von Orleans.* Stoff- und Motivgeschichte der deutschen Literatur, no. 1. Berlin und Leipzig, 1929.

Harvey, G. E. *History of Burma.* London, 1925.

Heine, Carl. *Das Schauspiel der deutschen Wanderbühne vor Gottsched.* Halle/Saale, 1889.

Heitmüller, Franz Ferdinand. *Hamburgische Dramatiker zur Zeit Gottscheds.* Diss. Jena, publ. at Wandsbeck, 1890.

Hettner, Hermann. *Geschichte der deutschen Literatur im achtzehnten Jahrhundert.* 7th ed., E. A. Boucke. Braunschweig, 1926.

Homeyer, Fritz. *Stranitzkys Drama vom "Heiligen Nepomuck."* Palaestra, no. 62. Berlin, 1907.

Kawerau, Waldemar. *Aus Halles Litteraturleben.* Culturbilder aus dem Zeitalter der Aufklärung, II. Halle, 1888.

Kettler, H. K. *Baroque Tradition in the Literature of the Enlightenment.* Cambridge, n.d.

Kind, John Louis. *Edward Young in Germany.* Columbia University Germanic Studies, vol. 2, no. 3. New York and London, 1906.

Kindermann, Heinz. *Theatergeschichte der Goethezeit.* Wien, 1948.

Koch, Max. *Helferich Peter Sturz nebst einer Abhandlung über die schleswigischen Literaturbriefe.* München, 1879.

Kriessbach, Erich. *Die Trauerspiele in Gottscheds "Deutsche Schaubühne."* Diss. Halle/Saale, 1927.

Lothar, Rudolph. *Das Wiener Burgtheater.* Wien, 1934.

Marx, Emilie. *Wieland und das Drama.* Freie Forschungen zur deutschen Literaturgeschichte, no. 3. Straßburg, 1914.

Meyer, Elise. *Der Einakter in der deutschen Dichtung des achtzehnten Jahrhunderts.* Unpub. Diss. Leipzig, 1920.

Michel, Victor. *C.-M. Wieland.* Paris, 1938.

Minor, J. *Christian Felix Weiße und seine Beziehungen zur deutschen Literatur des achtzehnten Jahrhunderts.* Innsbruck, 1880.

Muncker, Franz. *Friedrich Gottlieb Klopstock. Geschichte seines Lebens und seiner Schriften.* Stuttgart, 1888.

Pinatel, Joseph. *Le drame bourgeois en Allemagne au XVIIIe siècle.* Lyon, 1938.

Price, Lawrence M. *English Literature in Germany.* University of California Publications in Modern Philology, vol. 37. Berkeley and Los Angeles, 1953.

——. *Inkle and Yarico Album.* Berkeley, 1937.

——. *The Vogue of Marmontel on the German Stage.* University of California Publications in Modern Philology, vol. 27, no. 2. Berkeley and Los Angeles, 1944.

Prutz, R. E. *Vorlesungen über die Geschichte des deutschen Theaters.* Berlin, 1847.

Reden-Esbeck, Friedrich Johann von. *Caroline Neuber und ihre Zeitgenossen.* Leipzig, 1881.

Reichel, Eugen. *Gottsched.* Berlin, 1908–1912. [2 vols.]

Rentsch, Johannes. *Johann Elias Schlegel als Trauerspieldichter.* Leipzig, 1890.

Robinson, Vern W. *The History of the German Play in One Act in the Eighteenth Century.* Unpub. Diss. University of Illinois, 1936.

Sauer, August. *Joachim Wilhelm von Brawe, der Schüler Lessings.* Quellen und Forschungen zur Sprach- und Culturgeschichte der germanischen Völker, no. 30. Strassburg and London, 1878.

Scenna, Anthony. *The Treatment of Ancient Legend and History in Bodmer.* Columbia University Germanic Studies, new series, no. 5. New York, 1937.

Schneider, Ferdinand Josef. *Die deutsche Dichtung vom Ausgang des Barocks bis zum Beginn des Klassizismus 1700–1785.* Epochen der deutschen Literatur, vol. 3. Stuttgart, 1924.

Schreiber, S. Etta. *The German Woman in the Age of Enlightenment.* Columbia University Germanic Studies, new series, no. 19. New York, 1948.

Schum, Alexander. *Studien zur deutschen Alexandrinertragödie.* Diss. Würzburg, 1919.

Sengle, Friedrich. *C. M. Wieland.* Stuttgart, 1949.

——. *Das deutsche Geschichtsdrama.* Stuttgart, 1952.

Sypherd, Wilbur Owen. *Jephthah and his Daughter.* University of Delaware, 1948.

Wagner, Albert Malte. *Heinrich Wilhelm von Gerstenberg und der Sturm und Drang.* Heidelberg, 1920–1924. [2 vols.]

Waniek, Gustav. *Gottsched und die deutsche Litteratur seiner Zeit.* Leipzig, 1897.

[Weilen, Alexander von]. *Geschichte des Wiener Theaterwesens von den ältesten Zeiten bis zu den Anfängen der Hoftheater.* Die Theater Wiens, no. 1. Wien, 1899.

[——] *Zur Wiener Theatergeschichte. Die vom Jahre 1629 bis zum Jahre 1740 am Wiener Hof zur Aufführung gelangten Werke theatralischen Charakters und Oratorien.* Schriften des Österreichischen Vereins für Bibliothekswesen. Wien, 1901.

Weiss, Karl. *Die Wiener Haupt- und Staatsactionen.* Wien, 1854.

Wolff, Eugen. *Johann Elias Schlegel.* Berlin, 1889.

Wymetal, Charlotte von. *The Hero and his Opponent in the Heroic Tragedy from Gottsched to Lessing.* Unpub. diss. Yale, 1955.

VII. *Articles in books and periodicals*

Conrady, Karl Otto. "Gottsched. Sterbender Cato," in *Das deutsche Drama vom Barock bis zur Gegenwart,* ed. Benno von Wiese. Düsseldorf, 1958. [2 vols.] I, 61–78.

Goedeke, Karl. "Pfeil," in *Archiv für Litteraturgeschichte,* VII (1878), 524–528.

Heitner, Robert R. "A Neglected Model for *Kabale und Liebe,*" in *The Journal of English and Germanic Philology,* LVII, no. 1 (1958), 72–85.

——. "*Emilia Galotti:* An Indictment of Bourgeois Passivity," in *The Journal of English and Germanic Philology,* LII, no. 4 (1953), 480–490.

——. "Lessing's Manipulation of a Single Comic Theme," in *Modern Language Quarterly,* vol. 18, no. 3 (1957), 183–198.

Kunz, Harald. "Höfisches Theater in Wien zur Zeit der Maria Theresia," in *Jahrbuch der Gesellschaft für Wiener Theaterforschung* 1953/1954 (Wien, 1958), 3–113.

May, Kurt. "Johann Elias Schlegels 'Canut' im Wettstreit der geistesgeschichtlichen und formgeschichtlichen Forschung," in *Trivium,* vol. 7, no. 4 (1949), 257–285.

Price, Lawrence M. "George Barnwell on the German Stage," in *Monatshefte für deutschen Unterricht,* vol. 35, nos. 3 and 4 (1943), 205–214.

——. "The Bassewitz Translation of *The London Merchant,*" in *The Journal of English and Germanic Philology,* vol. 43, no. 3 (1944), 354–357.

Rolfe, William J. "Introduction" to *Shakespeare's Tragedy of Romeo and Juliet.* New York, Cincinnati, Chicago, n.d., pp. 9–34.

Sauer, August. "Ueber den fünffüssigen Iambus vor Lessing's Nathan," in *Sitzungsberichte der kaiserlichen Akademie der Wissenschaften,* Philosophisch-historische Classe, vol. 90, no. 3 (1878), 625–717.

Trutter, Hans. "Neue Forschungen über Stranitzky und seine Werke," in *Euphorion,* vol. 24 (1922), 287–331.

INDEX OF NAMES AND TITLES

INDEX OF SUBJECTS AND MOTIFS

Action, advocated instead of passivity, 23–24, 34, 228. *See also* Passivity; Virtue

Alexandrine verse, 7, 21, 23, 95, 96, 152, 154, 178, 180, 198, 203, 237, 271, 294, 298, 308, 331, 358, 360, 364, 371, 376, 399, 400, 401, 402, 403, 404, 427 n. 23

Amazons, 100, 165, 211, 264, 267

Ambition, 60, 237, 251, 296, 387

Barbarians, contrasted with civilized persons, 94, 95–96, 163, 166, 200, 404

Baroque tragedy. *See* Tragedy

Blank verse, 219, 223, 225, 231, 232, 263, 271, 298, 308, 364, 368, 371, 374, 427, n. 27

Blasphemy, 36, 42, 50–51, 55, 116, 146, 160, 173, 183, 190–191, 192, 355. *See also* God; Providence

Child, resentful, 187, 202, 288

Children in tragedy, 178, 185, 186, 187, 238, 239, 240, 370, 381, 384–385, 387

Christianity: contrasted with heathen religions, 48, 356, 359, 369, 373, 400–401; criticized, 156, 158, 200, 366, 404

Christians, unvirtuous, 155, 156

Christian tragedy. *See* Tragedy

Citizens, mature, 33. *See also* Common people

Classicism, German, 389

Comic elements in tragedy, 5, 9, 11, 14–15, 21, 176–177, 184–185, 193, 290–291, 293, 340, 342, 350, 352, 399

Comic personage, 10, 11–12, 23, 337, 340, 352. *See also* Hanswurst

Common people: sentimentally regarded, 72; viewed cynically or condescendingly, 121, 206, 254, 273, 339; as needing harsh government, 213

Conscience, 46, 178, 187, 229, 321, 373

Courtiers, 49

Court life, 228, 284, 305. *See also* Kingship

Cri du sang motif, 274, 400

Death: defiant, 4, 14, 174, 197, 250, 297, 333, 356, 373; accepted joyfully, 14, 54, 142, 202, 223, 229, 401, 402; heroic or patriotic, 29, 267, 271; as portal to knowledge, 57, 301; of remorseful or frightened villains, 202, 239, 262, 278, 329, 353, 373; Christian, 284

Deathbed forgiveness, 9, 113, 141–142, 183, 187, 196, 201–202, 224, 282, 367

Death scene, 9, 184, 187, 196–197, 208, 223, 249, 286, 320, 323

Death wish, 45, 47, 54, 75, 86, 159, 160, 164, 183, 197, 214, 226, 229 248, 300, 313, 335–336, 346, 367; regarded as wrong, 82, 86, 210, 285; inspired by patriotism, 140. *See also* Death

Deception, 3–4, 23–25, 60, 79, 86, 89–90, 98, 103, 116, 129–130, 155, 157, 210, 221, 222, 223, 234, 246, 261, 274, 285, 292, 315–316, 344, 347, 348, 351, 365, 368; condoned, 26, 61, 88, 141, 216, 266, 295, 316, 317; regarded as wrong, 34, 60, 73, 91, 93, 159, 166, 211, 256, 347

Decorum, 20, 26; breached by violent death on stage, 7, 13, 45, 56, 142, 158, 168, 182, 187, 196, 197, 201, 202, 224, 239, 270, 277, 285, 297, 307, 329, 331, 334, 348, 349, 353, 356, 367, 371; maintained by placing violent death off stage, 93, 118, 131, 217, 237, 376, 399; maintained in sexual matters, 374

Deism, 125, 206, 302. *See also* God, gods

Deus ex machina, 9, 49, 89, 118, 307

Devils, 194, 195, 301–302

Disguises, 23, 25, 53, 56, 58, 264, 266, 307, 345, 365